CONTENTS

CURTAIN UP!

y first encounter with the works of William Shakespeare could have been – almost was – disastrous. I went to see the Olivier film version of HAMLET and was very bored! I hasten to add that the fault was purely mine. At the age of nine or ten, young boys – and I was no exception – were more interested in seeing dashing swordsmen rescuing pretty damsels in distress or cowboys shooting it out with the bad guys.

At age eleven I was fortunate to win a scholarship to St. Bartholomew's Grammar School, Newbury, and I again encountered the works of the Bard. The school, founded in 1466 or 1467, was steeped in tradition. Among the relatively modern traditions of the school were productions of classic plays (usually, but not exclusively, Shakespearean) at Christmas and a Gilbert and Sullivan opera in the Spring. Both, I suppose, were the seeds that have blossomed into the appreciation and enjoyment that I get from them to this day. I never did follow in the footsteps of one famous Old Newburian, Robert Newton (he played Tybalt in ROMEO AND JULIET in the School's 1920 production), by acting in any of the Shakespearean productions though I did appear in *H.M.S. Pinafore* by Gilbert and Sullivan!

Along with Virgil, Thucydides and Aristophanes in the classics, I had to contend with Chaucer in "Old English" and Shakespeare for my assault upon the then educational qualification, the General Certificate of Education. HENRY V was the Shakespearean play chosen as part of the English Literature section of the examination. Maybe my suffering of "...the slings and arrows of outrageous fortune" was tempered by the wise showing of the Olivier film by the School Film Society just before the examination. A wise move indeed for I was already addicted to the cinema.

In those days, of course, there were no computer games and videos, television was still very limited in its range, crude and for the selected few, and electric gramophones were for the wealthy. During the years of World War II and the years immediately after, the cinema and the radio were the main forms of entertainment. In those days a trip to the cinema brought a main feature, a B feature, a newsreel and maybe a cartoon. In many cinemas there was a change of programme mid-week and often a different programme of re-runs on Sundays.

So, the influences on my formative years are obvious and they remain with me today. Some fade from time to time but they are revived, none more so than the works of Shakespeare. Today when the cinema relies more upon effects than acting, when a book (or a film) seems doomed unless it is filled with sex and foul language, when my native tongue becomes increasingly debased, I find myself turning more and more to the classic works (not only Shakespeare) to enjoy the beauty of my own language.

So I consider myself fortunate that two of my interests – Shakespeare and the cinema – can complement each other. Subconsciously, I suppose, these are the reasons for this book and, as this year celebrates the centenary of the first Shakespearean work committed to film (as far as is known), there was no better incentive.

Eddie Sammons, Palmera, Valencia, Spain 1999

After the above follows a synopsis of the story if it differs greatly from the original. In some cases, only variations to the original may be noted.

Then follow notes of interest on the film with selected details on festival showings and awards. Such is the proliferation of both festivals and publications which give awards, it would be an impossible task to note them all. The selection should be seen as a guide to world opinion as to the film's quality. Some should be taken seriously, others maybe not so.

Most of the awards will be familiar to those accustomed to the film world. The awards given by the American Academy of Motion Picture Arts and Sciences are, at the risk of stating the obvious, better known as the "Oscars". The British Academy Awards are the result of the founding of The British Film Academy in 1948. In 1959 it merged with the Guild of Television Producers and Directors to become the Society of Film and Television Arts (SFTA). Re-organisation occurred again in 1975 and is now known as the British Academy of Film and Television Arts (BAFTA).

The Venice Film Festival's award for Best Film is the "Lion of St. Mark" and the Cannes Festival equivalent is the "Palme d'Or". The Berlin Festival awards the "Golden Bear" to the Best Film and a "Silver Bear" to other categories. "Golden Globe" awards are given by the Hollywood Foreign Press Association.

After, in some cases, will be found critical comment from a variety of sources. Again, the intent is not of completeness but rather to give an indication of opinion from around the world. Finally, if the film is known by any other title(s), there is a note to this effect signified by "aka". This may include titles in other languages. In the case of proper names and simple titles where the foreign title is an obvious local language equivalent, such translated titles may have been ignored. At the end of each principal play chapter will be found a cross-reference of other films mentioned in other chapters which contain scenes from the play in question.

Notes: In view of their specialist nature, animated short films are listed in a special chapter (**ANIMATED SHAKESPEARE**) though feature-length films of this nature will be found under the individual subject play.

In the notation of film and play titles, if there is reference to a film that appears as part of the filmography, it will be shown thus HAMLET.

If there is reference in the general text to a Shakespearean play, then it will shown in its most commonly known form. So HAMLET appears thus rather than HAMLET, PRINCE OF DENMARK. Other films referred to incidentally or of passing interest are noted in *italics*.

Cross references to chapters in this book are also shown in **BOLD** type.

Book and magazine titles are noted in single inverted commas thus: 'Variety'.

Comment on two matters is needed:

SILENT FILMS

The problem of running times of such films has already received comment above. If that were the only problem, then the troubles for the researcher would be greatly reduced. It is not, and they are not. The silent cinema, therefore, remains a most complex area of study.

Thousands of films were turned out quickly to satisfy the demand at the start of this century. Many of these films have been lost for a number of reasons:
a) destroyed accidentally or deliberately
b) mislaid and never found
c) negatives and prints worn out and no effort made to preserve them
d) nitrate film deterioration.

Certainly the wars in Europe during the silent era must have accounted for a tremendous loss of film in the affected countries. Accidents, such as the fire in 1917 at the Thanhouser warehouse, caused tragic losses to the film world.

So, in the absence of film, the researcher has to look to company records (if they exist), copyright documents, contemporary and subsequent written material, photographs and even individuals' memories for information.

The results and conclusions are often suspect. In the case of Thanhouser mentioned above, the loss of the films is tragic because Thanhouser was a serious producer, devoted to Shakespearean works. Here, later information culled is confusing. Who directed what? One source names one person; another names another person. In such cases, the other possibilities have been named in the notes about the film in question.

Vitagraph, a company whose efforts (whatever the results) in bringing Shakespeare to the screen deserves praise, offers equal confusion. Did that driving force James Stuart Blackton direct all the Shakespeare films or was it William Ranous? Again sources are in conflict. Some say that Ranous directed for a few years until he left to join IMP in 1909, others, such as Frenchman, Jean Mitry, could find no evidence that he was involved in any such film as director. Yet actor Paul Panser said in a more-or-less contemporary interview that Ranous did direct the films. A mystery indeed!

Casts, too, for this company give rise to many problems. Cast members have often been identified through physical recognition in relation to the role played. The end result has been composite cast lists from the players contracted to the company. Some filmographers, incidentally, have often listed two Vitagraph films (or one produced by Vitagraph and one by Blackton himself) of the same title – one crediting Ranous, the other crediting Blackton, as director with a partially common cast list. All of which is quite confusing but would Blackton have really produced privately another version of the same film with a similar cast in the same year? After all, Vitagraph was partly his company (he was the co-founder of it) and it is hardly feasible that he would produce a film in direct competition with his own company.

All films made before the introduction of colour film stock are treated as being made in black and white. In fact, many contained colour scenes or were completely in colour or were tinted. If a film is known to have been issued in any of these forms, this has been noted.

The colour was generally achieved by two methods. In the early days, each individual frame was coloured by hand. Later, in 1905, the French Pathé company adopted a method which was often copied and continued in the same concept even into the 1930s. To achieve the colour, a number of prints were made of a film and from each one (usually up to six) areas were cut out according to the colour required. The stencils were run in turn with a complete print through a staining machine, the colour being applied by rotating brushes. Though a lengthy process, once the stencils had been made, the rest was fairly simple.

Tinting was a comparatively simple process aimed more at creating moods and atmosphere. Certain parts of a film were passed through dyes to effect this. Thus blue would be used for night, red for fire or interior shots etc.

There were also other colour-illusion systems but they fall outside the scope of this book. In brief, if a film of this era is noted as being coloured in part or whole, then one of the above systems would have been used. A film noted as being tinted relates to the other, less complex, system set out above.

TELEVISION FILMS/PROGRAMMES/VIDEOGRAMS

It is not intended to include films or programmes made for television transmission or for the videogram market unless such programmes have been made available (initially on film but latterly on video tape for such is now used in some venues) for public viewing. The interpretation of "public viewing" is extended beyond the confines of the commercial cinema to include film festivals, educational venues, exhibitions, clubs, film societies – in brief, anywhere that permits a mass audience outside of the home. In general, if a film from a television source is known to exist on film as opposed to video tape and is available for rental or purchase (and thus, within copyright laws, permitted to be shown to public gatherings), it has been included even if it cannot be ascertained whether or not it served such a function.

Note: References to films issued on the so-called sub-standard gauges 9.5mm. and 8 mm. throughout will be noted. The absence of any such notation about issues on the technically better 16 mm. gauge for private purchase may well give rise to query. The reason for the omission is really one of legality rather than its relative inconvenience of cost, weight and size. Many prints of out-of-copyright films legally exist in this gauge, of course, but the law concerning films not falling into public domain is complex. Often films, irrespective of the gauge on which they were originally made, have been issued on 16 mm. for use by film libraries, societies and even by cinemas. As such, the same rights protect these prints as protect the original releases. The exclusion is, therefore, apart from the uncertainty of what is available, deliberate in its intention of not offending any laws and of not being misleading. This is particularly so in view of the differences between American and European law. Indeed, the number of legally available films on 16 mm. of any sort in Europe for private ownership is a mere handful compared to the situation in America.

CHAPTER I
ANTONY AND CLEOPATRA

Dramatis Personæ:

Marcus Antoninus – Triumvir of Rome*
Domitius Enobarbus, Ventidius, Eros, Scarus, Dercetas, Demetrius, Philo – Mark Antony's friends
Canidius – lieutenant-general to Mark Antony
Silius – Roman Officer under Ventidius
Euphronius – A schoolmaster ambassador from Mark Antony to Octavius

Octavius Caesar – Triumvir of Rome
Maecenas, Agrippa, Dolabella, Proculeius, Thyreus, Gallus – Octavius' friends
Taurus – lieutenant-general to Octavius

Octavia – Octavius' sister and Mark Antony's wife
M. Aemilius Lepidus – Triumvir of Rome

Sextus Pompeius
Menas, Menecrates, Varrius – Pompeius' friends

Cleopatra – Queen of Egypt
Alexas, Mardian, Seleucus, Diomedes – Cleopatra's attendants
Charmian, Iras – Cleopatra's maids
A Soothsayer, A Clown, various Officers, Soldiers, Messengers and Attendants

* Referred to as Mark Antony

The death of Julius Caesar avenged, the conspirators dead, the Roman Empire is now in the hands of the new, second Triumvirate of Mark Antony, Octavius and Lepidus. Mark Antony is in Egypt with Cleopatra when news comes of the death of his wife Fulvia. He begs Cleopatra's permission to return to Rome to deal with affairs of state and she agrees reluctantly.

In Rome, Octavius and Lepidus discuss Mark Antony and the growing power at sea of Pompeius who is liked by many. When Mark Antony arrives he is met by Octavius who complains of acts against him by Mark Antony's family. He criticizes Mark Antony for not supporting him. To bind the two powerful men together, Mark Antony agrees to marry Octavia, Octavius' sister. He prepares to attack Pompeius and vows to return to Egypt.

News of Mark Anthony's marriage reaches Cleopatra while he, Octavius and Lepidus prepare for battle with Pompeius at Misenum. However, agreement is reached with Pompeius who holds a feast for his former enemies. In Parthia, the Triumvirate is avenged for the death of Crassus (one of the first Triumvirate) by Ventidius who kills the Parthian king's son. While in Alexandria, Cleopatra learns all about Octavia.

Pompeius is murdered and a split in the Triumvirate follows. Octavius is unhappy with Mark Antony's territorial claims for Cleopatra. Mark Antony is at Actium with Cleopatra and, surprised that Octavius is near, decides, against the advice of friends, to fight Octavius' fleet. Though Mark Antony may have the superior army, his fleet is ill-equipped. His cause is not helped when Cleopatra's ships desert the battle and Mark Antony, his friends having submitted to Octavius, follows her to Egypt.

Defeated, Mark Antony dismisses his men and Cleopatra tries to console him. They send messages to Octavius who has arrived in Egypt, seeking permission to live in Egypt or Greece. Octavius declines but offers Cleopatra anything but Mark Antony. She is prepared to submit but Mark Antony has the messenger flogged and sent back to Octavius. Mark Antony says he will fight for his army has stayed with him and his fleet has reformed.

Enobarbus, Mark Antony's friend, deserts and Mark Antony sends his property after him but when Enobarbus hears of Octavius' plan to put deserters in the front line, he declares himself a traitor and leaves to die. Mark Antony's troops are initially victorious and he sends word to Cleopatra that his fleet will attack the next day. Again Egyptian support wanes and Antony is defeated. He sends a message to Cleopatra to escape. She, however, follows the advice of her attendants by hiding and sending out the word that she is dead.

On hearing this, Mark Antony falls on his own sword just as a messenger arrives to tell him the truth about Cleopatra. He is taken to her and dies in her arms. Octavius receives the news. Cleopatra begs him to allow her son to rule Egypt and says she wishes to meet him. Guarded while Octavius' arrival is awaited, she tries to stab herself but is stopped and learns that she will be part of Octavius' triumphal entry into Rome.

When Octavius arrives, Cleopatra is submissive and offers him riches and Octavius expresses desires of friendship but tells her that she and her children have three days before leaving for Rome. Though she prepares all her regal attire, she kills herself with two asps concealed in a basket of figs. Her faithful maid, devoted to her Queen, takes her life also.

Octavius finds them and orders that the lovers be buried together and that the armies attend the funeral.

Note: General opinion places the date of this work around 1607 and the inspiration for it as 'The Lives Of The Noble Grecians And Romans Compared Together' by Plutarch through Thomas North's magnificent English language version in 1579 of Jacques Amyot's French translation from the original.

✠ ✠ ✠ ✠ ✠

ANTONY AND CLEOPATRA, THE LOVE STORY OF THE NOBLEST ROMAN AND THE MOST BEAUTIFUL EGYPTIAN
(U.S.A., 1908)

p.c. *Vitagraph.*
d. *James Stuart Blackton.*
l.p. *Maurice Costello (Mark Antony); Florence Lawrence (Cleopatra); Paul Panzer; William F. Ranous; Earle Williams.*
b.w. 995 ft. (303 m.) Sil.

An early short of the play, it probably featured action highlights of the plot while retaining the theme of the story. Willliam F. Ranous is noted as director by some sources, Charles Kent by others.

"The costumes and scenic effects are of the finest." – 'The New York Dramatic Mirror', November 14, 1908.

ANTOINE ET CLÉOPÂTRE
(France, 1910)

p.c. *Film D'Art.*
d. *Albert Capellani.*
l.p.
b.w. 1171 ft. (357 m.) Sil.
This was one of a number of films made in this series.

ANTOINE ET CLÉOPÂTRE
(France, 1913)

p.c. *Pathé.*
d.
l.p.
b.w. 1073 ft. (327 m.) Sil.

Some mystery surrounds this French version and the previous entry. The similarity in length is suspicious enough to induce the thought that the latter was simply a re-edited version of the former. Such action may have been commercially motivated by the announced release of the Italian Cines production (listed in the second part of this individual filmography).

aka: CLEOPATRA; ANTONY AND CLEOPATRA

MARCANTONIO E CLEOPATRA
(Italy, 1916)

p.c. *Palatino/Cines.*

d. *Enrico Guazzoni.*
l.p. *Lyda Borelli (Cleopatra); Amleto Novelli (Mark Antony); Lea Orlandini; Nino Corradi.*
b.w. (?) mins. Sil.

Some sources note this as being produced in 1917 or 1918. No doubt it followed the usual epic standard prevalent in Italian productions at the time.

ANTONY AND CLEOPATRA
(G.B., 1951)

p.c. *Parthian Productions.*
d.
l.p. *Pauline Letts (Cleopatra); Robert Speaight (Mark Antony).*
b.w. 33 mins.

Listed by the British Film Institute, this may be an educational short. No further details known except that Speaight was a Shakespearean actor and he may well have directed this film.

ANTONY AND CLEOPATRA
(G.B./Switzerland/Spain, 1972)

p.c. *Folio Films/Transac/Izaro.*
d. *Charlton Heston.*
l.p. *Charlton Heston (Anthony); Hildegard Neil (Cleopatra); Eric Porter (Enobarbus); John Castle (Octavius); Fernando Rey (Lepidus); Carmen Sevilla (Octavia); Freddie Jones (Pompey); Juan Luis Galiardo (Alexas); Douglas Wilmer (Agrippa); Alba; Fernando Bilbao; Peter Arne; Warren Clarke; Roger Delgado; Joe Melia; Julian Glover; Sancho García; Garrick Hagan; Jane Lapotaire; Monica Peterson; John Hallam.*
Technicolor. 160 mins. ToddAO 35.

This follows basically the play though with excisions. The venture was something of a dream fulfilment for Heston. He had had a small part in the play in Katherine Cornell's 1947 Broadway production and had played the Antony role in a semi-professional film version of **JULIUS CAESAR** (q.v.). His own version was not quite the dream he had hoped. He had wanted Anne Bancroft for the female lead and Orson Welles to direct. Further problems with finance – a budget of a mere $1,600,000 – forced him to film in Spain using some Spanish players. These had to be subsequently dubbed and this, for the males ones, was apparently done, uncredited, by British actor Richard Johnson.

Shown as part of the Everybody's Shakespeare International Festival, London, England, 1994.

"Well-meaning, well-mounted, but quite uninspired rendering." – Leslie Halliwell, 'Halliwell's Film Guide'.

aka: MARCO ANTONIO Y CLEOPATRA

ANTONY AND CLEOPATRA
(G.B., 1974)

p.c. *Realist Film Unit.*
d. *Peter Seabourne.*
l.p. *Linda Renwick (Cleopatra); Gilbert Derrick (Agrippa); David Fennell (Maecenas); Paul Chapman (Enobarbus); Susan Jameson (Iras); Elizabeth Hall (Charmian); Colin Farrell (Clown).*
c. 11 mins.

Two scenes from the play (Act II, Scene 2 and Act V, Scene 2) are featured in this short.

One in a series of educational films, the intent was to reproduce the acting conditions of Elizabethan times. The absence of scenes including Mark Antony is perhaps a little strange.

As this is the first appearance of Peter Seabourne's name and it will appear a number of times, it is perhaps worth mentioning that he was a director responsible for a number of films aimed at younger audiences (for the Children's Film Foundation, for example). His involvement with educational shorts was, therefore, quite logical.

✚ ✚ ✚ ✚ ✚

CLEOPATRA'S LOVER: OR, A NIGHT OF ENCHANTMENT
(U.S.A., 1908)

p.c. *Vitagraph.*
d.
l.p.
b.w. 860 ft. (262 m.) Sil.

This is listed by a reliable American source as being a Vitagraph production. It is included out of interest for, though no synopsis of the plot has been traced, it may well be Shakespeare influenced bearing in mind the company's preoccupation with classic literature at the time. It may, of course, simply be a re-issue and re-edited version of the previous film noted in the first section of this chapter.

aka: A NIGHT OF ENCHANTMENT

CLÉOPÂTRE
(France, 1909)

p.c. *Pathé.*
d. *Ferdinand Zecca, Henri Andréani.*
l.p. *Madeline Roch(e) (Cleopatra); Stacia Napierkowska (Messenger); Rianza (Dancer).*
b.w. 1165 ft. (355 m.) Sil.

Cleopatra visits Mark Antony by boat watched by Octavius. The two lovers leave by boat and Antony and Octavius later argue in the Roman camp. In Egypt Antony enjoys the entertainment while Octavius arrives and declares war. Antony is defeated and commits suicide as does Cleopatra.

Though not credited, Shakespeare's influence is clearly evident. The cast list was obviously longer than that listed above. The length of the film is that listed by American sources. A hand-coloured version also existed. The 'American Film Institute Catalog' gives the length as 1043 ft. (318 m.).

aka: ANTONY AND CLEOPATRA

MARCANTONIO E CLEOPATRA
(Italy, 1913)

p.c. *Palatino/Cines.*
d. *Enrico Guazzoni.*
l.p. *Amleto Novelli (Mark Antony); Gianna Terrible Gonzalès (Cleopatra); Ignazio Lupi; (Octavius); Elsa Leonard (Octavia); Ida Carloni Talli (Sorceress); Carlo Duse; Mathilde Di Marzio (Hagar); Giuseppe Pienmontese; Bruto Castellani; Ruffo Geri.*
b.w. 6562 ft. (2000 m.) Sil.

Adapted from Shakespeare's play but also drawing upon 'The Lives' by Plutarch and 'Cleopatra' by Pietro Cossa, there are certain differences from the Shakespeare story. Charmian plays quite an active role and is in love with Mark Antony for which she dies. Octavia, too, is more involved and actually goes to Egypt to see what is keeping her husband there. 'Variety' at the time was very cynical about the claims made about the film including the number of extras many of whom probably doubled before the camera to swell the numbers. However, the magazine did compliment the film on its handling of the crowd scenes and found it quite spectacular.

The film seems to have been extended to 11482 ft. (3500 m.) for its Portuguese release in 1915. The source of so much additional material is not known.

"...the acting was of less importance than the spectacle..." – Vernon Jarrett, 'The Italian Cinema'.

aka: ANTONY AND CLEOPATRA; MARC-ANTOINE ET CLÉOPÂTRE (as six parts in seventy scenes); CLÉOPATRA; DIE HERRIN DES NILS – CLEOPATRA; ANTONIO E CLEOPATRA

CLEOPATRA
(U.S.A., 1912)

p.c. *Helen Gardner Picture Players for United States Film Company.*
d. *Charles L. Gaskill.*
l.p. *Helen Gardner (Cleopatra); Mr. Sindelar (Marc Antony); Harley Knoles (Kephren); Mr. Waite (Ventidius); Mr. Howard (Pharon); Miss Winter (Charmion); Mr. Osborne (Diomedes); Miss Sindelar (Iras); Robert Gaillard.*
b.w. 6 reels. Sil.

A Roman soldier, Ventidius, issues an order to Cleopatra to meet Marc Antony in Tarsus to answer charges of conspiracy. Antony is under Cleopatra's spell and stays with her even as his wife, Flavia, dies but, for political reasons, he marries Octavia, the sister of Octavius. When Antony's fleet is under siege at Actium, Cleopatra, despite her anger, rushes to him. The desertion of the Egyptian fleet leaves Antony defeated but he rouses enough forces to defend her in Egypt. Defeat greets Antony again and both he and Cleopatra take their own lives.

Two sources form the basis of this film – the Shakespearean one and the play "Cléopâtre" by Victorien Sardou and Émile Moreau. It was first listed as HELEN GARDNER IN CLEOPATRA and was re-released in America in 1918 by the Cleopatra Film Company. Additions were apparently made to the film in 1917 under Gaskill's supervision though some sources credit the supervision to James Stuart Blackton. This film is also listed by some as five reels.

Helen Gardner was the first star – and probably the first woman – to form her own film company. The venture was, however, short-lived. She is also credited with being the first screen "vamp" by some sources though the shortage of her films makes it difficult to confirm or deny this. Her career was of short duration and by the 1920s she was reduced to very minor parts.

CLEOPATRA
(U.S.A., 1917)

p.c. *Fox Film Co.*
d. *J. Gordon Edwards.*
l.p. *Theda Bara (Cleopatra); Fritz Leiber (Caesar); Thurston Hall (Marc Antony); Albert Roscoe (Pharon); Herschell Mayall (Ventidius); Dorothy Drake (Charmian); Henri de Vries (Octavius Caesar); Dell Duncan (Iras); Art Acord (Kephren); Hector V. Sarno (Messenger); Genevieve Blinn; Alfred W. Freemont; Helen Tracy; Violet Merserean.*
b.w. 11 reels. Sil.

Julius Caesar leads his conquering forces into Egypt only to find his heart conquered by Cleopatra. After the murder of Caesar in Rome, Marc Antony journeys to Egypt to subdue Cleopatra. He, too, falls for her charms but he returns to Rome to marry Octavia, the sister of Octavius, for the security of the Triumvirate. As he still loves Cleopatra, he returns to her in Egypt where their forces are defeated and both take their own lives.

The sources for this are Shakespeare's JULIUS CAESAR and ANTONY AND CLEOPATRA plus "Cléopâtre" by Victorien Sardou and Émile Moreau and diverse other historical sources. The film premièred on October 14, 1917, in New York City, U.S.A., where, doubtless, the interest was focused on Theda Bara and whatever costumes she may have worn. Sadly, for the moment, such details remain unknown for the film has been lost. It is included on the "Ten Most Wanted" list of films by the American Film Institute.

Miss Bara was one of twenty stars featured on a set of stamps issued by Fujeira. Her face and a scene from this film adorned the 85DH value stamp.

ANTONY AND CLEOPATRA
(U.S.A., 1924)

p.c. *Universal.*
d. *Bryan Foy.*
l.p.
b.w. 1 reel. Sil.

This is noted as being an hysterical comedy which was hardly what Shakespeare intended.

CLEOPATRA
(U.S.A., 1934)

p.c. *Paramount.*
d. *Cecil B. DeMille.*
l.p. *Claudette Colbert (Cleopatra); Henry Wilcoxon (Mark Antony); Ian Keith (Octavius); Warren William (Julius Caesar); Gertrude Michael (Calpurnia); Arthur Hohl (Brutus); Joseph Schildkraut (Herod); C. Aubrey Smith (Enobarbus); Leonard Mudie (Pothinus); Irving Pichel (Appollodorus); Ian MacLaren (Cassius); Claudia Dell (Octavia); Eleanor Phelps (Charmian); Edwin Maxwell (Casca); John Rutherford (Drussus); Grace Durkin (Iras); Robert Warwick (Achillas); Charles Morris (Cicero); Harry Beresford (Sooth-sayer).*

b.w. 101 mins.

Typical DeMille extravaganza which covers Julius Caesar's infatuation with Cleopatra, her entry into Rome, Caesar's assassination and Mark Antony's voyage to Egypt to bring back Cleopatra in chains. Here he falls under her spell and is declared a traitor against Rome, he is defeated at the battle of Actium and the two lovers commit suicide.

Not from the Bard, of course, but DeMille was clearly influenced by him and George Bernard Shaw's "Caesar and Cleopatra".

Castle Films, the American home movie arm of Universal, released four extracts from CLEOPATRA (each about seven or eight minutes) on 8 mm. and possibly 16 mm. too.

Academy of Motion Picture Arts and Sciences, U.S.A., 1934: Nominations – Best Picture, Best Score (Alex North), Sound Recording (Franklin Henson), Film Editing (Anne Bouchens), Assistant Director (Cullen Tate); Award – Cinematography (Victor Milner).

"...stands out as one of his more intelligent films, thanks in large part to fine performances by all." – Leonard Maltin, 'Movie and Video Guide'.

"Mr. DeMille has here contrived a film which reflects many of the influences of William Shakespeare and at the same time is filled with modern, easy-going dialogue..." – 'The Motion Picture Herald', August 25, 1934.

It would seem appropriate to include the following here:

THE HOLLYWOOD YOU NEVER SEE
(U.S.A., 1934)

p.c. *Paramount.*
d. *Herbert Moulton.*
l.p. *Cecil B. DeMille.*
b.w. 11 mins.

This promotional film of how this epic was made featured DeMille prominently (as did the 1950 rather long trailer for the re-release of the film).

The short film noted above was available for purchase on 8 mm. by the public from the American company, Famous Films.

LA VIDA INTIMA DE MARCO ANTONIO Y CLEOPATRA
(Mexico, 1946)

p.c. *Filmex.*
d. *Roberto Gavaldón.*
l.p. *Luis Sandrini (Mark Antony); María Antonieta Pons (Cleopatra) ; Víctor Junco; José Baviera; Conchita Carracedo; Rafael Banquells; Fernando Casanova; Carlos Villarías; Julián de Meriche; Jesús Graña; Leopoldo Frances; Eva Calvo; Yrma Bernola; Elisa Christy; Roberto Banquells Jr.*
b.w. 89 mins.

This is noted as a comedy version of the story about the two lovers.

Sandrini was an Argentinian comic with big bulging eyes who specialised in parodies of famous (historical) stories. The film, his Mexican début, is full of intentional anachronisms though it is said to be not very funny. His merry leading lady was Cuban.

aka: MARCO ANTONIO Y CLEOPATRA

SERPENT OF THE NILE
(U.S.A., 1953)

p.c. *Columbia.*
d. *William Castle.*
l.p. *Rhonda Fleming (Cleopatra); William Lundigan (Lucilius); Jean Byron (Charmion); Raymond Burr (Mark Antony); Michael Fox (Octavius); John Crawford (Domitius); Michael Ansara (Florus); Jane Easton (Cytheris).*
Technicolor. 79 mins.

After the death of Julius Caesar the conspirators are defeated at the battle of Philippi by Mark Antony. Lucilius, one of Brutus' officers, poses as Brutus but in vain as Brutus commits suicide. Mark Anthony recognises a true Roman in Lucilius and they become

friends. Intent on settling the score with Cleopatra for aiding the conspirators, Mark Anthony and Lucilius set out for Egypt. Cleopatra uses all her wiles on Mark Antony who falls under her spell. Lucilius does not fall for her charms or ploys or, indeed, her love. When Cleopatra's sister is murdered, Lucilius, who was sent to fetch her, is blamed and put under arrest but Mark Antony engineers his escape though he knows Lucilius will fight against him. Lucilius goes to Rome and rouses Octavius into action. Defeated, Mark Antony and Cleopatra commit suicide.

"O mighty Caesar! Dost thou lie so low?
Are all thy conquests, glories, triumphs, spoils
Shrunk to this little measure?"

So speaks Mark Antony over the slain body of Julius Caesar from JULIUS CAESAR, Act III, Scene 1 at the start of the film. For those hoping for a literate version of the story, hopes were quickly dashed for the rest of the script is pure Hollywood. The essence of the plot does remain since it could hardly do differently but a new factor is introduced in the form of Lucilius, a minor character taken from JULIUS CAESAR, for whom Cleopatra shows some love. In fact, Lucilius is really the fulcrum of the story. His substitution for Brutus, and hence his meeting with Mark Antony, is taken again from JULIUS CAESAR.

This particular venture into the world of peplum was made when it was in fashion. It was made on the set of the same production company's piece of biblical hokum *Salome*. Obviously not made to test the audience's cultural level, it has the curiosity value of Rhonda Fleming as Cleopatra and, if she really looked like her, then the foolishness of her two lovers was understandable!

"A celebrated page of history evoked by occasionally sumptuous images. The charm of Rhonda Fleming has not, however, resulted in an unforgettable film." – 'Ciné Revue', September 7, 1978.

CARRY ON CLEO
(G.B., 1964)

p.c. *Adder.*
d. *Gerald Thomas.*
l.p. *Sidney James (Mark Antony); Amanda Barrie (Cleopatra); Jim Dale (Horsa); Kenneth Williams (Julius Caesar); Kenneth Connor (Hengist); Charles Hawtrey (Seneca); Julie Stevens (Gloria); Joan Sims (Calpurnia); Victor Maddern (Sgt. Major); Sheila Hancock (Senna); Tom Clegg (Sosages); David Davenport (Bilius); Michael Ward (Archimedes); John Pertwee (Soothsayer); Tanya Binning (Virginia); Francis de Wolff (Agrippa); Peter Gilmore (Galley Master); Brian Oulton (Brutus); Warren Mitchell (Spencius); Gertan Klauber (Marcus); Ian*

CHAPTER I – ANTONY AND CLEOPATRA

Wilson (Messenger); Brian Rawlinson (Hessian Driver); Narrator: E. V. H. Emmett. Eastman Color. 92 mins.

In ancient Britain, square wheel maker, Hengist Pod is captured by Mark Antony's troops and sold as a slave in Rome. He and his friend Horsa escape and find initial refuge and more with the Vestal Virgins. Horsa displays great courage fighting their pursuers and escapes but Hengist who is left behind, receives credit for it and is made Caesar's bodyguard. Mark Antony guesses the truth but is sent to Egypt to get rid of Cleopatra and put Ptolemy on the throne. Of course, Antony falls for Cleo and the reverse happens. He invites Caesar to visit Cleo and plans to kill him. All goes wrong and Hengist again gets unmerited credit for saving Caesar. Hengist is allowed to return to Britain to his wife Senna where they have many children.

With a square wheel maker (well, it was designed to stop carts rolling backwards down hill) and lines like: "The eunuchs are on strike. They are complaining about loss of assets", it is obvious that any hope of sophistication can be forgotten. The film is going to run true to form for the series.

The "Carry On" films started in 1958 when producer Peter Rogers and director Gerald Thomas made *Carry On Sergeant* and created unintentionally the embryo of what became a virtual cinema institution in Britain. The films parodied everything including contemporary films. Though the credits to this film state: "From an original idea by William Shakespeare" (and the idea was both JULIUS CAESAR and ANTONY AND CLEOPATRA), the subject for attack was clearly 20th. Century Fox's *Cleopatra* (see below). Indeed, the American giant company did sue the producers for use of a poster and won. However, insurance against such an occurrence had been effected and the resultant publicity did the British film no harm at all. Scenes from it were included in the compilation release *That's Carry On!* released in 1977 and in another compilation from Britain of the same year, **TO SEE SUCH FUN**.

Quite what Shakespeare would have thought of it is open to conjecture. The Bard does not seem to have been adverse to a little bawdy humour and so may have approved and said: "That were a jest indeed!". A number of films in this series found their way to the 8 mm. home movie market and this one was no exception. Walton, U.K., issued two versions – as a slightly edited feature and as an eighteen minute condensation.

aka: CUIDADO CON CLEOPATRA

✛ ✛ ✛ ✛ ✛

One can but wonder how Antony fell into the arms of Cleopatra. He may have felt disappointed not to have been named as the successor to Julius Caesar and that the role fell to the weaker Octavius but he was joint head of the then known world. Into that charge fell the protection of Egypt, a legacy bequeathed by the father of Cleopatra.

Though Mark Anthony may have been a man of stature in history and in Shakespeare's eyes, it is surely Cleopatra that has captured the imagination. Shakespeare himself, through Enobarbus, says of her:

"Age cannot wither her, nor custom stale
Her infinite variety: other women cloy
The appetites they feed, but she makes hungry
Where most she satisfies..." (ANTONY AND CLEOPATRA Act II, Scene 2.)

Strangely, she is not noted in history as being a great beauty (or particularly wanton) but she did have that certain something that could beguile men. Above all, she had a desire to preserve Egypt and her fidelity to that cause and, indeed, to Mark Antony did not waver. Certainly, she knew how to use whatever ingredients her charms held.

Film makers (even as early as 1899 – see **CHAPTER XXXIV TO BE OR NOT TO BE**) have not been slow in recognising the attraction that this Egyptian queen has for the public and Mark Antony has often been reduced to secondary status. Not quite so, however, in 20th. Century Fox's expensive and long 1963 production *Cleopatra* where Richard Burton took the role against Elizabeth Taylor in the title one.

The Italians in 1959, in co-production with Spain and France, also covered the story of Octavius sending Antony's friend to him to make him desert Cleopatra in *Le Legioni Di Cleopatra* with Linda Cristal and Georges Marchal in the leading roles with Marchal giving quite a good performance as a sincere Antony. Five years earlier from Italy also came *Due Notti Con Cleopatra*, a comedy with Alberto Sordi and Sophia Loren, the latter in two roles as the queen and her double. The Antony role is very secondary and the film is probably best remembered for Sophia Loren's nude bathing scene. Also from Italy in 1963 came the comedy *Toto E Cleopatra* directed by Fernando Cerchio with French actress Magali Noël as the alluring Queen.

Apart from the films already mentioned the Cleopatra figure has been played by Vivien Leigh in the British film of George Bernard Shaw's *Caesar And Cleopatra* (1945) and Pascale Petit in the 1962 Franco-Italian *Una Regina Per Cesare*. The amount of Shakespeare's influence on these and probably more films on the same theme is unquantifiable and probably nil in the case of the sex film *The Notorious Cleopatra* (1970)! As an historical person she was played by Virginia Mayo in the 1957 Warner Bros. film *The Story Of Mankind* with Helmut Dantine as Antony.

Another interesting aspect of the lady can be found in a film which follows the same line as the De Mille epic, *Cleopatra, Queen Of Sex*. Interesting, not for its title, but for the fact that it is a full length Japanese cartoon (original title not known) made in 1971 by Mushi and directed by Isa Tomita. Much nudity, of course and sex scenes, but it cannot really be classed as a piece of erotica and certainly not as Shakespeare. In the world of animation, Shakespeare had little to do with the script of *Astérix Et Cléopâtre* (1968), one of the French/Belgian films from René Goscinny and Albert Uderzo based on the comic strip character.

The voice for Cleopatra was provided by Micheline Dax.

For other films with scenes from the play see **CHAPTER XXX ALL THE WORLD'S A STAGE**: LAS TRES COMADRES ALEGRES (1952); SHAKESPEARE WALLAH (1965) and EL ABOMINABLE HOMBRE DE LA COSTA DEL SOL (1969) and **CHAPTER XXXII THE IMMORTAL BARD**: EXPLORATIONS IN SHAKESPEARE (1969).

CHAPTER II

AS YOU LIKE IT

Dramatis Personæ:

Duke Senior – the banished duke
Rosalind – his daughter
Amiens, Jaques – his attendant lords

Duke Frederick – his usurper brother
Celia – Frederick's daughter
Le Beau – a courtier
Charles – a court wrestler

Oliver – eldest son of Sir Rowland de Boys
Jaques, Orlando – his younger sons
Adam – an old servant of Sir Rowland now servant to Oliver

Dennis – a servant to Oliver

Touchstone – a clown
Sir Oliver Martext – a country curate
Corin, Silvius – shepherds
William – a country fellow
Hymen – goddess of marriage
Phoebe – a shepherdess
Audrey – a country wench
Lords, pages, foresters and attendants

In one of the provinces of old France, the rightful Duke is usurped by his younger brother, Frederick and goes to the forest of Arden with friends in self-imposed exile. Often they are joined by court youths in their happy, carefree life finding good in adversity despite cold winters. The Duke's daughter, Rosalind stays at court as companion to Frederick's daughter, Celia, becoming good friends and Celia often consoles Rosalind.

One day they go to a wrestling match. It is not the entertainment they had hoped for since a youth is matched against a merciless brute. Frederick, unhappy with the match, asks the girls to dissuade the youth but their pleas merely inflame his desire to fight to the death. He wins but not without much injury. Frederick, pleased at his spirit, takes him under his protection. His pleasure quickly fades when he learns that the youth is Orlando, youngest son of the late Sir Rowland de Boys, a faithful friend of the Duke. Orlando falls in love with Rosalind and she gives him a chain, a token of affection, to wear. This romance further angers Frederick who banishes Rosalind.

Celia accompanies Rosalind travelling for safety in disguise. Rosalind, adopting a man's clothes and name (Ganymede), travels with Celia as "his" sister, Aliena. Though they enjoy the journey, when they reach the forest of Arden they rest in the open air as there are no inns. Somewhat weary and despondent, they readily accept a shepherd's servant's offer of shelter in his master's humble cottage where they stay for some days enjoying the life though Rosalind's thoughts are of Orlando.

When their father died, Orlando was put in the care of his elder brother, Oliver, who failed in his duties though Orlando still managed to become a well-bred youth. Oliver was filled with anger and hatred. Orlando, with little to live for, had entered the

wrestling match. Hearing of Orlando's present circumstances Oliver plots to kill him but a servant, Adam, faithful to Orlando, overhears the plot and goes to warn Orlando with whom he flees to the forest of Arden. There they meet the Duke and are welcomed with food. When Orlando reveals his identity, the Duke takes him under his protection.

Meanwhile, Rosalind is puzzled to find her name carved on a tree with love poems attached. The girls meet Orlando and Rosalind recognises the chain he wears but he is fooled by their disguises. Rosalind challenges him about the carving and he confesses his love for Rosalind and seeks the counsel of his new friend. "He" suggests that they act out the roles so that he may woo properly while "he" will enter into the full spirit of the venture as Rosalind. All goes well to the delight of Celia who delays reminding Rosalind that they must contact her father.

One day Orlando sees a sleeping man menaced by a snake and a lion. Bravely, Orlando saves the man overcoming his emotion having recognised the man as his brother who has so wronged him. Full of remorse, Oliver repents, seeks forgiveness and is reunited with his brother. Orlando has been badly injured in his fight with the lion and begs Oliver to go to the cottage to his friend. On hearing the news Rosalind swoons.

Oliver returns to Orlando and tells him that the "youth" had swooned at the news. He too had fallen in love with Celia and would thus restore all to Orlando as he wished to live as a shepherd with Celia. Orlando tells of the wedding to his friend the "youth" saying he would like to make it a double one with his Rosalind as his bride. The "youth" says that "he" will conjure some magic and make his wish come true.

The next day, Orlando, Oliver and Celia and the "youth" come before the Duke who wonders just what magic will occur saying that if Rosalind can truly come before him she and Orlando may wed with his blessing. The two disguised girls leave, throw off their disguises and return as properly dressed ladies and the double wedding proceeds. Then news comes that Frederick, angered at Celia's desertion and envious of the Duke's way of life, has set out with an army only to be met by a hermit, a holy man, who has induced him to repent. Thus he restores the Duke to his rightful position and retires to a holy house.

Happily back home, the two couples blissfully married, the Duke rewards his loyal friends with peace and prosperity.

Note: As Francis Meres does not include this in his 1598 listing of the plays of Shakespeare but it is in the Stationers' Register as entered by the Lord Chancellor's Men on August 4, 1600, then the play can safely be placed as having been written in 1599 or early 1600. The influence for it is a prose romance of 1590 called 'Rosalynde, Euphues' Golden Legacy', itself based on a pseudo-Chaucerian piece called 'Tale Of Gamelyn'. The play has many riches among which are the famous speech "All the world's a stage..." and a number of songs including the two of the best known ones of Shakespeare – "It Was A Lover And His Lass" and "Blow, Blow Thou Winter Wind".

✤ ✤ ✤ ✤ ✤

AS YOU LIKE IT
(U.S.A., 1908)

p.c. *Kalem Co.*
d. *Sidney Olcott.*
l.p. *Gene Gaunthier?*
b.w. 915 ft. (279 m.) Sil.

Of this early one-reeler, little is known except that it was performed by "an experienced Shakespearean cast". Keanan Buel may have been the director.

AS YOU LIKE IT
(U.S.A., 1912)

p.c. *Vitagraph.*
d. *Charles Kent and/or James Young.*
l.p. *Rose Coghlan (Rosalind); Maurice Costello (Orlando); Robert Gaillard (Oliver); Charles Kent (Jacques); Tefft Johnson (Duke Senior); Robert McWade Sr. (Touchstone); Rose Tapley (Phoebe); Harry Morey (Duke Senior); Kate Price (Audrey); Frank Mason (Amiens); George Ober (Adam); James Morrison (Silvius); Charles Eldridge (Corin); George C. Randolph (Charles the wrestler); Hugh McGowan (William); Leo Delaney (Jacques de Bois); James Young (Le Beau or Sir Rowland de Bois).*
b.w. 2 reels. Sil.

One of the many short films produced by Vitagraph, this would have been a coherent condensation though heavily reliant upon inter-titles for this. The titles occupied almost half a reel. One source gives the film's length as 3000 ft. (914 m.).

Some note James Stuart Blackton as director; others say he produced and directed another version with the same two leading players. Hardly realistic as noted in **CURTAIN UP!**.

AS YOU LIKE IT
(G.B., 1936)

p.c. *Inter-Allied.*
d. *Paul Czinner.*
l.p. *Elizabeth Bergner (Rosalind); Laurence Olivier (Orlando); Sophie Stewart (Celia); Leon Quartermaine (Jacques); Felix Aylmer (Duke Frederick); Richard Ainley (Sylvius); Mackenzie Ward (Touchstone); Aubrey Mather (Corin); Austin Trevor (le Beau); J. Fisher White (Adam); Peter Bull (William); John Laurie (Oliver); Stuart Robertson (Amiens); Dorice Fordred (Audrey); Joan White (Phebe).*
b.w. 96 mins.

This is notable mainly as Laurence Olivier's first Shakespearean screen role. Incidentally, the music was by William Walton who was later to write for Olivier's Shakespearean films. This time, however, the music was not memorable, having been rushed. It was revived on disc in the early 1990s in a series devoted to Walton's film music. Performed by the Academy of St. Martin-in-the-Fields conducted by Neville Marriner, the narration was by John Gielgud. It was released by the British Chandos company.

Blackhawk Films, whose catalogue embraced items of a more educational and artistic nature, released this on 8 mm. for home viewers.

Shown at the Shakespeare Film Festival, Wiesbaden, W. Germany, 1964.

"Overall, an enjoyable production of this Shakespeare comedy." – Leonard Maltin, 'Movie And Video Guide'.

aka: COMO GUSTÉIS

AS YOU LIKE IT
(India, 1966)

p.c. *Children's Film Society of India.*
d. *S. Shanker.*
l.p.
b.w.? Feature.

No further details of this production are known. This is not surprising as the Society, founded in 1955 by the Indian government, devotes itself to making and distributing copies of its own and imported children's film at nominal fees to educational institutions.

AS YOU LIKE IT: AN INTRODUCTION
(G.B., 1969)

p.c. *BHE/Seabourne Enterprises.*

d. *Peter Seabourne.*
l.p. *Jenny Goosens (Rosalind); Brian Spink (Orlando); Delinda Kidd (Celia); Jack Gwillim (Duke Frederick); Alfred Burke (Jacques); Dudley Jones (Touchstone).*
c. 24 mins.

Number five in this series is basically as the title states concentrating on the main theme.

✢ ✢ ✢ ✢ ✢

THE SEVEN AGES
(U.S.A., 1905)

p.c. *Edison.*
d. *Edwin S. Porter.*
l.p. *Florence Auer; Thomas Ince; Alice Kershaw.*
b.w. 500 ft. (152 m.)? Sil.

Inspired by Shakespeare's play, this presented eight tableaux about life and love, each with its own title – Infancy, Playmates, Schoolmates, Lovers, The Soldier, The Judge, Second Childhood, and What Age?

The tableaux, for the most part, comprised two shots – one, a long shot; the other, a close-up of the same scene. Since most of the scenes featured kissing and embracing, the Shakespeare influence was probably merely nominal. The film may have had sound by means of a sound-on-disc system. It may also have been influenced by a series of lantern slides from the Kleine Optical Company entitled "Shakespeare's Seven Ages". The length of the film is approximate.

THE SEVEN AGES OF MAN
(G.B., 1914)

p.c. *Planet Films.*
d. *Charles Vernon.*
l.p. *Bransby Williams.*
b.w. 1000 ft. (305 m.) Sil.

These character studies from infancy to old age were based on Williams' stage success of the same name.

Inspired by Jaques' "All the world's a stage..." speech from Act II, Scene 7 of the play, the title is a rephrasing of "...His act being seven ages."

LOVE IN A WOOD
(G.B., 1915)

p.c. *London-Diploma.*
d. *Maurice Elvey.*
l.p. *Elizabeth Risdon (Rosalind); Gerald Ames (Orlando); Vera Cunningham (Celia); Frank Stanmore (Touchstone); Kennelm Foss (Oliver); Frederick Groves (Duke Frederick); Edward O'Neill (Duke Senior); Cyril Percival; Dolly Tree.*
b.w. 4189 ft. (1277 m.) Sil.

Squire Duke, having financial difficulties, sells all of his estate except a small wood to his common, but rich, neighbour, Frederick. The Squire is promised that he can live out his life on the estate. The daughters of the two men, Rosalind and Celia, are good friends. Their neighbour, Sir Rowland Boyse, is dying and shows preference for his son, Orlando, over his other, elder son, Oliver who is both angry and jealous...

From that brief introduction the source is clear. It was a modern dress (at the time) version of the play, Elizabeth Risdon suggested in 1958, just before she died, in a letter to Professor Ball that the producers may have been looking for an economic, non-royalty script (Britain was then at war with obvious financial problems). She noted that it was fun making it but neither the press nor the public liked it with resultant failure.

AS YOU LIKE IT
(G.B., 1992)

p.c. *George Reinhart/Sands Films/Aim Prods.*
d. *Christine Edzard.*
l.p. *James Fox (Jacques); Cyril Cusack (Adam); Andrew Tiernan (Orlando/Oliver); Celia Bannerman (Celia); Emma Croft (Rosalind); Griff Rhys Jones (Touchstone); Miriam Margolyes (Audrey); Roger Hammond (Corin/le Beau); Ewen Bremner (Sylvius); Don Henderson (Duke Senior/Duke Frederick); Valerie Gogan (Phebe); Cate Fowler; John Tams; Arthur Kelly; Robin Meredith; Bernard Padden; Tony Armatrading; Murray Melvin; Jonathan Cecil; Michael Mears.*
c. 114 mins.

This version of the play made on a low budget has a modern setting. Reaction to it has been mixed.

"Christine Ezzard substitutes a modern cardboard city for the Forest of Arden in her inventive interpretation..." – 'Film Review Special No. 2', 1993.

"...the film's visual drabness is only topped by its verbal flatness."- James Cameron-Wilson, 'Film Review 1993/4'.

✢ ✢ ✢ ✢ ✢

As a play, this does not perhaps have the strongest of plots. It does rather rely upon the interplay of relationships and attitudes which may account for the shortage of screen versions of it. Yet, dominating all, are love and a sense of merriment. Good nature prevails and even wicked brothers repent. Love does, truly, conquer all – all, it seems, except the hearts (and finances) of film makers.

For other films with scenes from the play see **CHAPTER XXX ALL THE WORLD'S A STAGE**: NINA OF THE THEATRE (1914); PEG OF OLD DRURY (1935) and **CHAPTER XXXII THE IMMORTAL BARD**: BEAUTY AND BRIGHTNESS No.4 (1925?); WILLIAM SHAKESPEARE (1955) and EXPLORATIONS IN SHAKESPEARE (1969).

CHAPTER III
THE COMEDY OF ERRORS

Dramatis Personæ:

Solinus – Duke of Ephesus
Aegeon – a merchant of Syracuse
Aemilia – wife of Aegeon and Abbess at Ephesus
Antipholus of Syracuse, Antipholus of Ephesus – twin brothers unknown to each other and sons of Aegeon and Aemilia
Dromio of Syracuse, Dromio of Ephesus – twin brothers and slaves to the brothers Antipholus
Adriana – wife of Antipholus of Ephesus

Luciana – sister of Adriana
Luce – servant to Adriana
Balthazar – a merchant
Angelo – a goldsmith
Merchant – friend of Antipholus of Syracuse
Second Merchant – Angelo's creditor
Dr. Pinch – schoolmaster and conjurer
Courtesan, Jailer, Officers and Attendants

Such is the hatred between the states of Ephesus and Syracuse that any merchant of Syracuse found in Ephesus is subject to a ransom of one thousand ducats or death if this cannot be paid. So when an old merchant of Syracuse called Aegeon finds himself in this position, the Duke of Ephesus enquires why the old man should knowingly let this occur.

Unafraid of death, Aegeon explains that many years ago he had to leave his happy marriage to go on a business trip to Epidamnum. He was away so long and his wife missed him so, that she went to him. No sooner had she arrived than she gave birth to identical twin boys. At the same time another woman at the inn produced a similar set of sons. This woman, being so poor, willingly sold them to Aegeon as servants.

Soon his wife wished to go home with her sons in whom she had much pride. At sea a storm occurred and the crew deserted the ship. Aegeon divided the two sets of twins and bound one pair with himself to one mast, his wife and the other pair to another mast. The ship was wrecked and Aegeon separated from his wife and her charges. Fortunately, Aegeon and the two boys were saved by a fishermen and taken to Syracuse. Of his wife there was no news.

When his son reached eighteen, he asked permission to take his servant to search for his lost mother and their two brothers. Aegeon reluctantly agreed for he feared that he might lose his son. That was seven years ago and Aegeon had been searching for them for five years. He had come to Ephesus because he did not wish to miss any possible place and this was his last hope.

The Duke is moved by this story but cannot disregard the law. He does, however, grant Aegeon a day in which to raise the money. Though the offer is made with kind intent, as Aegeon knows no-one there, it is futile.

As it happens, though not known to him, both his sons who carry the same name, Antipholus, and the two servants, both called Dromio, are in Ephesus. The younger Antipholus and Dromio (these will be noted A to avoid confusion) both arrive by boat but a friend warns them to be silent about their home and trade. The friend also tells of the problems of the old merchant. The elder son and his servant (signified by B) live in Ephesus and Antipholus B is rich and could easily pay his father's ransom if he only knew the truth.

He and Dromio B had both been saved by a fisherman who took them away from their mother and sold them as slaves to the warrior Duke Menaphon, uncle to the Duke of Ephesus. The warrior liked Antipholus B and made him an army officer when he grew up. He was brave and saved the Duke's life who rewarded him with a marriage to Adriana, a rich lady.

Antipholus A sends Dromio A off to an inn where they will dine while he wanders through the streets. He sits and thinks of his quest. Now his relationship with Dromio A is far closer than that of the normal master and servant so when Dromio returns, in reality Dromio B, he wonders why he has returned so soon. Dromio B says that his mistress has sent for him to return home for dinner. Not realising that it it not his own servant he tells him that he takes the relationship too far in jesting so and beats him saying that he has no wife. Dromio B returns home explaining what his apparent master has said. Adriana is upset and, despite the efforts of her sister, Luciana, to dissuade her, thinks her husband is unfaithful.

Antipholus A now goes to the inn where Dromio A is patiently waiting and receives a strong reprimand. Adriana then appears and pleads with Antipholus A to come home reminding him of their love. He is, naturally, surprised, but unable to convince her of his recent arrival, finally agrees to accompany her and Dromio A finds himself in trouble with her cook-maid, his apparent wife! When the true husband and servant return home they are refused admission and told that Adriana is already dining with her man. He is quite perplexed. In the house Antipholus A and Dromio A make their exit with relief though Antipholus A is attracted to Luciana.

In the street the same case of mistaken identity occurs when Antipholus A is given a gold chain by a goldsmith who insists that he ordered it. The two decide to leave Ephesus as quickly as possible feeling some spell is on them.

Meanwhile the goldsmith is arrested for a debt. By chance Antipholus B comes along and the goldsmith begs payment for the chain. Payment is, understandably denied, and a quarrel ensues resulting in the arrest of the goldsmith and Antipholus B. A chance encounter with Dromio A has him sent, bemused, back to Adriana to get the money which she gives him. Returning he meets with his true master who is also bemused at the friendly greetings and kindnesses he has been receiving. He is even more confused and fears sorcery when Dromio B asks him how he has escaped and tells about the arrest.

Now a lady confronts Antipholus A demanding the gold chain he has promised her and the return of the ring she has given him. The virtuous Antipholus B had actually visited her to teach his jealous wife a lesson after being refused admission to his home. This lady, thinking he is mad, confronts Adriana just as Antipholus B returns accompanied by the jailor to get the money which Adriana had given to Dromio A and which he has given to his proper master.

Adriana, remembering the dinner, believes the lady and ties up her husband and his Dromio who supports his story. When she hears that the two are in the streets she fears that they have broken loose and goes out to see. Confronted by Adriana, the two seek refuge in a convent. The abbess listens to Adriana and quickly senses that it is her jealousy, if anything, that has driven her husband mad and reprimands her for her actions. Though Luciana comes to her sister's defence, Adriana admits that this is true but demands to see her husband. This the abbess refuses.

For poor Aegeon the time of execution arrives. The procession to his place of execution is interrupted by Adriana crying out for justice. So, too, does her husband and servant for being tied up by his wife. Aegeon, thinking the man to be his son for whom he has been searching, asks him to pay the ransom but the man denies all knowledge of him.

Then the abbess brings out her two guests. When the Duke sees the two sets of men, he remembers Aegeon's story. All is brought to a joyful conclusion when the abbess reveals that, having lost her sons at sea, she had entered a convent. The Duke pardons Aegeon, Adriana becomes a better wife and Antipholus B marries Luciana. Aegeon and his wife live on for many years in Ephesus.

Note: Precisely when this was written is open to conjecture. The first recorded performance was on December 28, 1594. Its inspirational source, 'Menaechmi' of Plautus in its English translation by "W.W", may have been available to Shakespeare before its entry into the Stationers' Register in 1594. However, style and topical allusions suggest an earlier date of between 1589 and 1591 with the latter more probable.

✤ ✤ ✤ ✤ ✤

A COMEDY OF ERRORS
(U.S.A., 1908)

p.c. *Vitagraph.*
d. *James Stuart Blackton.*
l.p. *Maurice Costello; Florence Lawrence.*
b.w. 495 ft. (151 m.) Sil.

This early abridgement of the play may have used key scenes linked into a coherent synopis, or more likely, was a comic parody and be thus more correctly placed in the second section.

BHOOL BHULAIYAN
(India, 1933)

p.c. *Ranjit.*
d. *Jayant Desai.*
l.p. *Glory; Dixit; Shanta; Kamla K. Adajama; Thatte.*
b.w. Feature.

Listed as "Comedy of Errors", it is logical to assume that this is a local version (in Hindi) of the play. Such adaptations were beginning to appear on the Indian screens at the time. Dixit was a very popular comic of the time in India.

aka: A COMEDY OF ERRORS

BHOOL BHUYAIYAN
(India, 1949)

p.c. *Ranjit.*
d. *Taimur Behramshah.*
l.p. *Agha; Zeb; Gureshi; Laila Bhudo Advani; Pesi Patel; Rasheed; Maruti; Farosh; Kusum Thakkar; Fordeel.*
b.w. Feature.

Similar comments as to the above apply to this which was also in Hindi.

HANSTE REHNA
(India, 1950)

p.c. *Ranjan Pictures.*
d. *Mohammed Hussain.*
l.p. *Mukri; Mumtaz; Heera Sawant; Arvind Kumar; Habib.*
b.w. Feature.

The title may be different, but Indian sources list it as "Comedy of Errors". It was in the Hindi language.

✤ ✤ ✤ ✤ ✤

LA COMEDIA DEGLI EQUIVOCI
(Italy, 1912)

p.c. *Cines.*
d.
l.p.
b.w.650 ft. (198 m.) Sil.

A comedy – what else? – about two army recruits with the same name, the relationship to the original play is limited.

A longer version of this may have been issued at 666 ft. (203 m.).

TWO LITTLE DROMIOS
(U.S.A., 1914)

p.c. *Thanhouser.*
d.
l.p. *Mignon Anderson.*
b.w. 1 reel. Sil.

Two girls, one from the country and one from the city and of similar appearance, cause confusion when the country girl goes to the city and the city girl goes to the country to masquerade as a country girl.

Hardly pure Shakespeare of course, but an interesting little film where the title borrowing has gone beyond the obvious. Indeed, the film obviously sought a little inspiration, too. It was also an opportunity to explore the field of double exposure photography.

OUR RELATIONS
(U.S.A., 1936)

p.c. *Stan Laurel Productions for Hal Roach-M.G.M.*
d. *Harry Lachman.*
l.p. *Stan Laurel; Oliver Hardy; Alan Hale; Sidney Toler; James Finlayson; Daphne Pollard; Iris Adrian; Noel Madison; Betty Healy; Lona Andre; Ralf Harolde; Arthur Houseman; James C. Morton; Lee Phelps; Baldwin Cook; Ruth Warren; Dell Henderson; Harry Bernard; Jim Pierce; Constantine Romanoff; Tiny Sandford; Bobby Dunn.*

b.w. 65 mins.

Stan and Ollie are sailors and entrusted to deliver a ring on shore. Because of their acknowledged weaknesses, they leave their money for safe keeping with their captain to be returned when they come back on board. They are unaware that in the port live their long-lost twin brothers who are happily married. While Stan and Ollie pick up two girls in a saloon, their brothers entertain their wives in a more respectable bar. The inevitable mix-up occurs with the loss of the ring, involvement with gangsters and our two sailors poised for death. Everything is sorted out (rather hastily) at the end.

Though loosely based on 'The Money Box' by W.W. Jacobs, this film "...also has more than a casual relationship to Shakespeare's COMEDY OF ERRORS..." (William K. Everson – 'The Films Of Laurel And Hardy').

This view is certainly held by many and that it also one of the most durable of the comedies made by the famous pair. The film benefits from excellent photography by Rudolph Maté.

One source gives the running time as seventy four minutes but the above is the more commonly noted and in line with the film length of six reels.

The British company Walton Films issued an 8 mm. version edited to fifty-one minutes for purchase by collectors.

aka: C'EST DONC TON FRÈRE; DOS PARES DE MELLIZOS

THE BOYS FROM SYRACUSE
(U.S.A., 1940)

p.c. *Mayfair.*
d. *A. Edward Sutherland.*
l.p. *Allan Jones (Antipholus – both); Martha Raye (Luce); Joe Penner (Dromio – both); Rosemary Lane (Phyllis); Alan Mowbray (Angelo); Irene Harvey (Adriana); Charles Butterworth (Duke of Ephesus); Samuel S. Hinds (Aegon); Eric Blore.*
b.w. 73 mins.

In ancient Greece, two sets of twins are separated. One later becomes Emperor of Ephesus and orders the death of all those from Syracuse found in his land. Unwittingly, he condemns his own father who has set out to look for his lost son. When the other twin arrives, so does confusion.

Loose adaptation of the play, its main blessing is the Rodgers and Hart score. The songs include "Sing For Your Supper", "Falling In Love With Love", "He And She", "Who Are You" and "This Can't Be Love". The show had been a Broadway hit in 1938.

Shown as part of the Everybody's Shakespeare International Festival, London, England, 1994.

"...eliminated all traces of the original's satire, substituting anachronistic vulgarities in place of true humour." – Clive Hirschhorn, 'The Universal Story'.

"Disappointingly ordinary adaptation of...Broadway musical..." – Leonard Maltin, 'Movie and Video Guide'.

THINKING THE WRONG WAY
(Hong Kong, 1956)

p.c. *Ganglian.*
d. *Fang Liu.*
l.p. *Xian Xie; Junhui Shangguan.*
b.w. Feature.

The original title of this film, which was made in the Cantonese dialect, is not known but the Hong Kong Film Archive Office advise that it is based on the play.

LOS GEMELOS ALBOROTADOS
(Mexico, 1981)

p.c. *Producciones Águila.*
d. *Mario Hernández.*
l.p. *Tony Aguilar; Ernesto Gómez Cruz; Lucila Mariscal; Isabela Corona; Tito Junco; Luis Manuel Pelayo; Jorge Patiño; Delia Casanova; Armando Soto La Marina; María Prado; Raúl Martínez; Rocío Cházaro; Marisol Cervantes; Jorge Reynoso; Roberto Montero; Alfredo Gurrolo.*

b.w. Feature.

Based on the play, it is not known if this is a true version, albeit in Spanish, or a derivative version. It may, therefore, be misplaced in this section.

BIG BUSINESS
(U.S.A., 1988)

p.c. *Touchstone Pictures in association with Silver Screen Partners III.*
d. *Jim Abrahams.*
l.p. *Bette Midler (Sadie Sheldon/Sadie Ratliff); Lily Tomlin (Rose Shelton/Rose Ratliff); Fred Ward (Roone Dimmick); Michele Placido (Fabio Alberici); Edward Herrmann (Graham Sherbourne); Daniel Gerroll (Chuck); Barry Primus (Michael); Michael Gross (Dr. Jay Marshall); Deborah Rush (Binky Shelton); Nicholas Coster (Hunt Shelton); Patricia Gaul (Iona Ratliff); J. C. Quinn (Garth Ratliff); Norman Macmillian (Nanny Lewis); Joe Grifasi (Desk Clerk); John Vickery (Hotel Manager); John Hancock (Older Harlan); Mary Gross (Judy); Seth Green (Jason); Leo Burmester (Bum); Lucy Webb (Wenona); Roy Brocksmith (Dr. Parker); Lewis Arquette (Mr. Stokes); Eddie Cordell (Young Harlan); Ritch Brinkley (Mayor Bill Finker) and others.*

Metrocolor. 98 mins. S

In the 1940s in the southern town of Jupiter Hollow, Hunt Sheldon is forced to buy Hollowmade Furniture so that he can use the company hospital because his wife, Binky, is in labour. She gives birth to twin girls as does Iona, wife of Garth Ratliff, in the same hospital. The careless nurse mixes the children up and when Hunt calls his girls Sadie and Rose so does Garth. Years later, Sadie is the head of Moramax Corporation in New York City, Rose is her slightly zany sister. Rose Ratliff is a union organiser in Jupiter Hollow; her sister Sadie dreams of life in the big city. Sadie Shelton plans to sell off Hollowmade Furniture to Italian Fabio Alberici who plans to strip-mine the area. Leading the fight to save the company, Rose and Sadie go to New York where they are mistaken for the Shelton sisters who also book into the hotel. Naturally, mishaps follow especially when Roone, Rose Ratliff's suitor, arrives and quickly wins the heart of Rose Shelton. Dr. Jay Marshall, occasional boyfriend of Rose Shelton, proposes marriage to Rose

Ratliff. While Sadie Shelton seduces Fabio, Sadie Ratliff makes a good impression on Michael, Sadie Shelton's ex-husband. The sisters eventually confront each other just before the stockholder's meeting. The two Roses lock Sadie Shelton in a closet while Sadie Ratliff addresses the meeting and gets the sale of the company rescinded. All four women are suitably matched romantically.

"...BIG BUSINESS, un comedia inspirada en UNA COMEDIA DE ERRORES de Shakespeare..." – no translation needed, surely – so reads part of the introduction of the review in 'Fotogramas'. Well, at least one magazine – and a Spanish one at that – gave credit where it is due. Of course, "inspired" is about as far as the description could go with so many changes. There are the two sets of twins with similar names but of the opposite sex, the two states are replaced by management and union and some other hints of the original remain in the story. It is really a show case for the two lead stars of whom the director said: "I have never seen anyone with the talent of Bette and Lily. They are actresses who can play anything."

aka: ENSALADA DE GEMELAS

✥ ✥ ✥ ✥ ✥

The theme of identical twins in comic or serious form is not uncommon to literature and the cinema. Two sets of twins, however, is a different matter. The plot complications of this play are obvious. For a film, the requirements of trick photography imposed their own difficulties in the earlier days of the cinema though modern techniques have made this simpler.

Even so, there seems to have been little recourse to the concept with or without the Bard as inspiration. The two sets of twins, wrongly matched after adversity, was taken up in a comedy Western, *I Gemilli del Texas*, an Italian/Spanish co-production from 1964 directed by Steno with Walter Chiari, Raimondo Vianello, Diana Lorys and Marta May. The adversity which put the two lots of separated twins into the hands of an army officer and an outlaw respectively was an Indian attack which the twins survived.

With an earlier historical setting, Bud Yorkin's *Start the Revolution Without Me* (U.S.A., 1969) certainly used the theme of two sets of separated twins (Gene Wilder and Donald Sutherland in the dual roles) but the film had nothing to do with Shakespeare. It was a comedy about the French Revolution.

Filming technology has created miracles on the screen making the seemingly impossible appear commonplace. Is it too much to hope that such techniques could be used for a long overdue version of the play on film?

CHAPTER IV

CORIOLANUS

Dramatis Personæ:

Caius Marcius, later known as Coriolanus
Virgilia – his wife
Volumnia – his mother
Young Marcius – his son
Menenius Agrippa – friend to Coriolanus
Valeria – friend to Virgilia
Gentlewoman – attendant to Virgilia

Sicinius Veletus, Junius Brutus – Tribunes
Nicanor – a Roman
Titus Lartius, Cominius – generals against the
  Volscians

Senators, Officers, Aediles, Heralds, Messengers,
  Soldiers of Rome
Citizens of Rome

Tullus Aufidius – Volscian General
Adrian – a Volscian
Lieutenant to Tullus Aufidius
Conspirators with Tullus Aufidius
Servants to Tullus Aufidius

Citizen of Antium

Senators, Lords, Soldiers of Corioli

The citizens of Rome are disgruntled to the point of violence because of the disparity of wealth and, particularly, the price of corn. Although the heroic Caius Marcius has his supporters, he is the one singled out for criticism. Though Menenius, a man respected by the people, defends him and Marcius himself derides the people, clearly he has enemies in Brutus and Sicinius, the appointed tribunes of the people. He also has another enemy in Tullus Aufidius, a former adversary, of the Volscians who is preparing for rebellion in Corioli.

As news of this reaches Rome, Virgilia, Marcius' wife and his mother, Volumnia, discuss the matter as do the soldiers. A battle with the Roman army divided duly ensues, ending, after initial setbacks, with Marcius rallying the troops and bringing support to the beleaguered soldiers. He himself bravely defeats Aufidius (though not killing him) and other Volscians but is himself wounded. The Roman general, Cominius, is full of praise for this noble deed and, reluctantly, Marcius is greeted as a hero in Rome and given the name Coriolanus. Meanwhile, Aufidius is full of hate for the man who defeated him.

Again jealous Sicinius and Brutus criticise Coriolanus and are reluctantly aware that he will receive praise and power. Coriolanus' wife and family are delighted at this, his triumphant return. His two critics know that he is the delight of the people but are hopeful that his deeds will soon fade from public memory and that his former attitude will let him down. They plan to sow the seeds of malice among the crowds. Then, Coriolanus is summoned to the Capitol. There Cominius tells of Coriolanus' heroic deed and the hero is proclaimed a consul which only fires the mischief in Sicinius and Brutus. To confirm this office, which he does not want, Coriolanus must win the support of the people.

He is initially unable to communicate with the people but eventually, appropriately dressed in a gown of humility, gets support. Sicinius and Brutus are prepared to stir up the people and incite those who gave Coriolanus support now to withdraw it. News comes that Aufidius is in Antium and this stirs bitter hatred in Coriolanus. Now Coriolanus unwisely promotes the subjugation of the people saying that given too much freedom, if too much weakness is shown, the ruler will become the ruled. Sicinius does not fail to miss his opportunity to rouse the people to anger and, calling him "traitor", they turn violent. Menenius and Cominius have to hastily escort Coriolanus home. The crowd, despite the arguments of Menenius, are clearly behind Sicinius and Brutus and have a thirst for blood. Fortunately, Menenius is able to convince them that the matter should be handled according to the law. Sicinius agrees but warns that worse will follow if Coriolanus does not present himself to answer the charges.

At home his mother rebukes Coriolanus for his actions and says he must learn diplomacy in dealing with the people and be more humble. Cominius advises him of the public's anger and that he should present himself in the market place and tells him to be mild and gentle or trouble will follow. Though at first refusing to be other than he is, he eventually agrees to heed this advice.

He goes to the market place where Sicinius and Brutus have planned their strategy. Charged with attempted tyranny and thus treason, Coriolanus' best intentions quickly disappear and he lashes out at the people, deriding them. Sicinius seizes his opportunity to brand him a traitor and banishes him from Rome under pain of death if he returns.

Coriolanus makes his farewells to his family promising to keep them informed of where he will be through Cominius who will be with him for a month. Sicinius is jubilant though Coriolanus' mother chides him and praises her son. Later she hears of insurrection in Rome as the authorities are trying to take power from the people. Such events leave the path open for Rome's enemies such as Aufidius.

As it happens, Coriolanus, in disguise, goes to Antium and there seeks out his former enemy, Aufidius. Relating his tale of banishment, he is welcomed by Aufidius. Though this confuses many, one thing is sure – war will follow.

Together they decide to march on Rome where Sicinius and Brutus discuss Coriolanus. Their discussion is interrupted with news that the Volscians have entered Roman territory creating havoc and destruction. As fear of the invasion grows, Menenius and Cominius accuse the two tribunes of creating the problem. Not that Aufidius is completely happy with his new ally whose power he fears.

As the Volscian army approaches Rome, both Cominius and Menenius go to plead with Coriolanus but he turns them away. By this, he demonstrates his resolve to Aufidius. However Coriolanus' mother, wife, son and some women of Rome go to him dressed as if in mourning. His mother humiliates him by begging him on her knees to seek peace with Rome or she and his family will return there to die with the people. He is moved by her pleas and agrees to make a peace with Rome.

Back in Rome Menenius and Sicinius weigh up the chances of success by the women with the knowledge that Brutus is held by the people and will be killed if they fail. News of the women's success comes and Volumnia is hailed as a heroine and worthy of great honours.

In Corioli, however, there are those who conspire against Coriolanus and persuade Aufidius that he has been cheated not only out of total victory, despite all the spoils and the honourable peace that Coriolanus brings, but also out of revenge for those killed in previous encounters with Coriolanus. Aufidius, himself feeling that his own power has been usurped, turns on Coriolanus saying that he has denied the Volscians victory and that those of his people who died have been cheated by the peace that has been made. The people rise in anger and the conspirators kill Coriolanus, for which Aufidius is criticised by some of his lords for a less than honourable deed. He offers himself for trial and orders a funeral befitting a gallant foe and noble soldier.

Note: This political play probably saw its first performance in 1608 or around that time. Never one of the more popular plays, there are those who see in it allegories of the situation in England at that time. There were disturbances over grain, a new Stuart king demanded more than the previous Tudor monarchs and yet seemed to have less authority and there were strong characters making bids for power.

✤ ✤ ✤ ✤ ✤

No direct film version of the play has been traced. One film inspired by it has come to light:

CORIALANO, EROE SENZA PATRIA
(Italy/France, 1963)

p.c. *Dorica Film/Explorer Film 58/Comptoir Français Du Film.*

d. *Giorgio Ferroni.*

l.p. *Gordon Scott (Caius Martius Coriolanus); Lill Brignone (Volumnia); Philippe Hersent (Cominius); Angela Minervini (Livia); Rosalba Neri (Virgilia); Alberto Lupo (Sicinius); Aldo Bufi Landi (Marcus); Nerio Bernardi; Pierre Cressoy.*

Eastman Color. 101 mins.

The ambitious Sicinius finds that a young hero stands in his way to power. The hero, returning in triumph, is given the name Coriolanus by the Senate and proclaims him consul. He does not like the job and soon falls prey to Sicinius who has him banished from Rome. Bitter, Coriolanus joins forces with the Volski, enemies of Rome. He prepares to lead an attack on Rome but is persuaded to seek peace when Sicinius, his greed revealed, is killed. Coriolanus leaves with his wife and son.

Claimed to be inspired by Livy and Shakespeare, this is nothing more than typical Italian peplum. The only difference from the customary climax seems to be that the battle scenes, and thus the spectacle, opens rather than closes the film which is in accordance with the play. The ending, of course, is different to that in the play. Scott was one of the screen's many Tarzans.

aka: THUNDER OF BATTLE; LA TERREUR DES GLADIATORS; HÉROE SIN PATRIA

✤ ✤ ✤ ✤ ✤

The lack of screen versions of this play is both surprising and yet not surprising. If an epic film is intended, the play has its battles but, in commercial cinema terms, in the wrong place. As an example of political conniving, the basis is surely there for a political drama as relevant today as it was then. To be sure, Coriolanus was swept into office, untrained and, at heart, unwillingly. He was out of his depth and was not a lover of the common people but, then, as Shakespeare said: "Faith, there have been many great men that have flatter'd the people, who ne'er lov'd them."

For other films with scenes from the play see **CHAPTER XXXII THE IMMORTAL BARD**: NATIONAL YOUTH THEATRE (1966) and EXPLORATIONS IN SHAKESPEARE (1969).

CHAPTER V

CYMBELINE

Dramatis Personæ:

Cymbeline, King of Britain
Queen – his wife
Imogen – his daughter by a previous queen
Posthumus Leonatus – her husband
Cloten – the Queen's son by a former husband
Helen – a lady attending on Imogen
Guiderius, Arivagus – sons of the King who bear the names Polydore and Cadwal as sons of Morgan.
Belarius – a banished lord who bears the name Morgan
Pisanio – servant to Posthumus
Philario – friend to Posthumus
Iachimo – friend to Philario

French Gentleman – friend to Philario
Two British Captains
Cornelius – a physician
Two Lords of Cymbeline's court
Two Gentlemen of the court
Two Jailers
Caius Lucius – general of Roman forces
Roman Captain
Lords, Ladies, a Soothsayer, Various Romans, Captains, Soldiers, Gentlemen from Spain and Holland, Musicians, Messengers, Attendants, Apparitions

While Augustus Caesar rules in Rome, Cymbeline rules in Britain. He has, by his late wife, a daughter, Imogen, and two sons who were stolen when they were young. His second wife is a cruel woman who hates Imogen but wants her as bride for her son by a previous marriage, Cloten. Thus she hopes to gain the crown for her son in due course.

Imogen thwarts her plan by secretly marrying Posthumus, a respected and educated man, whom Cymbeline has cared for following the death of Posthumus' parents (his father had died in battle serving Cymbeline). Posthumus and Imogen have grown up together but this does not excuse their action and the Queen is quick to inform Cymbeline who is very angry.

Posthumus is banished by Cymbeline and the Queen, with an ulterior motive, arranges for the couple to make their sad farewells. As tokens of fidelity, Imogen gives Posthumus a ring and he gives her a bracelet. Imogen stays in a dejected state at the court while Posthumus resides in Rome.

Here he falls in with some adventurous young men. One, Iachimo, upset that Posthumus praises British women above Roman ones, challenges him to a wager. He says that he can obtain the bracelet from Imogen as proof of her infidelity with him. If he succeeds he gains the ring that Imogen gave to Posthumus, if he loses, then he forfeits a large sum of money.

Iachimo is welcomed by Imogen at the court in Britain as a friend of her husband. He quickly enlists the help of some of Imogen's attendants and is smuggled into her chamber in a chest. While Imogen sleeps, he comes out from hiding and makes careful notes of the room and of Imogen. Secreted out of the

chamber the next day, he then returns to Rome and confronts Posthumus with the "evidence". The agonised Posthumus has no choice but to hand over the ring.

Jealous and angry, Posthumus writes to an old friend, Pisanio, in Britain urging him to take Imogen to Milford Haven and kill her. He writes to Imogen asking her to accompany Pisanio to that town as he himself plans to meet her there. She complies, of course, but Pisanio feels that the deed entrusted to him exceeds his friendship and tells Imogen of his orders. She refuses to return to court but accepts Pisanio's advice that she dress as a boy for safety and await Posthumus' repentance. She, however, determines to go to her husband in Rome.

Before returning to court he gives her a phial given to him by the Queen as a cure. The evil Queen, hating Pisanio for his friendship with Posthumus, has given what she thinks is a deadly poison. However, the physician, knowing the Queen's malicious nature, has prepared only a strong sleep-inducing drug.

Chance takes Imogen to a cave where lives Bellarius. He had falsely been banished by Cymbeline and, out of revenge, abducted Cymbeline's two sons and has brought them up as his own as he grew to love them as his own. They are now two, well-educated young men, Polydore and Cadwal.

Imogen helps herself to food and drink and is discovered by Bellarius and the two young men. They find the "youth" most handsome and refuse the offer of money for the food. Imogen tells them her name is Fidele and, invited to stay, prepares a fine meal for them. The two youths note their new friend's sadness and affection grows between them.

Being unwell, Fidele cannot go hunting with "his" new friends whose qualities the others praise. When they have gone, Fidele takes the potion and falls into a deep sleep.

When they return, Polydore and Cadwal think their friend is dead and perform a perfunctiory burial. Fidele/Imogen awakes from her deep sleep and shakes off her covering of leaves and flowers. She intends to head for Milford Haven.

Events are happening elsewhere. Augustus invades Britain and the Roman army advances to the same forest in which Imogen is journeying. With this army is Posthumus who joins with Cymbeline. Now Imogen is captured by the Romans and, assumed to be a boy, is made page to the Roman general, Lucius.

Cymbeline's army advances and Bellarius, having long repented his past deeds, joins the army with his two "sons". The Britons are almost defeated and Cymbeline nearly killed but Posthumus, Bellarius, Polydore and Cadwal fight bravely and save him.

Lucius and his page are captured as is Iachimo who fought with the Romans. They appear before Cymbeline as does Posthumus, he to receive his death sentence for disobeying the banishment order, and Bellarius, Polydore and Cadwal to receive their reward. Present, too, is Pisanio.

Imogen recognises Posthumus and Iachimo and the ring he is wearing. She does not know that he is the author of her troubles. She is not recognised because of her male attire. Bellarius and Pisanio both recognise Imogen but, of course, as a different person. Posthumus refrains from speaking of his valour in saving the King. He wants no mercy. It is Lucius who speaks out, craving no mercy for himself but pleads for the life of his page whom, he says, is a Briton.

Cymbeline seems to find the page familiar and grants the request. Imogen says she cannot beg for the life of Lucius but asks a boon of the King. This the King grants and she demands that Iachimo tells how he obtained his ring. He tells all and, on hearing this story, so does Posthumus confess. Imogen cannot hold back any longer and reveals her true identity.

Cymbeline is overjoyed to see his daughter and readily forgives Posthumus, acknowledging him as his son-in-law. Bellarius also owns up, admitting that he had abducted the King's sons and presents them to the King. He duly receives forgiveness. With a pardon for Lucius, granted at the request of Imogen, lasting peace is concluded with Rome.

Even Iachimo is set free, unpunished. Later the Queen dies having seen her son, Cloten, killed in a quarrel.

Note: This play probably dates from about 1608 or 1609 or, maybe, 1610. It is noted that Dr. Samuel Forman saw a performance of it at the Globe shortly before September, 1611. Probably the play was not new at that time and the earlier date quoted is in line with the consensus of scholarly opinion and the then current change of vogue to romantic plays.

CYMBELINE
(U.S.A., 1913)

p.c. *Thanhouser.*
d. *Frederick Sullivan*
l.p. *Florence LaBadie (Imogen); James Cruze (Leonatus); Marguerite Snow; Jean Darnell (Queen); William Garwood (Iachimo); William Russell (Cymbeline?); Alphonse Ethier; Henry Benham.*
b.w. 41 mins. Sil.

An abridgement, this would have followed the formula set by companies at the time of keeping key scenes to form a logical plot synopsis.

✤ ✤ ✤ ✤ ✤

If CYMBELINE has received less praise than other works by the Bard, it is perhaps that it contains a number of situations to be found in the more popular plays (assumed death/suicide in ROMEO AND JULIET and ANTONY AND CLEOPATRA, infidelity/jealousy in OTHELLO). Even the seduction/wager plot was not new in those days. Boccaccio had used a similar theme in one of the stories in his 'Decameron'.

This tragic romance – some would call it a tragicomedy – contains a number of Shakespeare's trademarks such as the lover's ring, long-lost children, ultimate forgiveness etc. Whatever the genre, whatever the trademarks, there is in the play more than a touch of humanity.

Maybe it is this familiarity of some of the themes or the length of the play that have placed it among the least popular in cinema terms. As it is, only the one film noted above can be positively identified as having transposed it to the screen.

CHAPTER VI

FALSTAFF

No index of Shakespeare's works will reveal the above title. A deeper look into the cast of characters, however, will reveal the name in a number of plays (see below).

Falstaff was a comic character created by Shakespeare and was popular, along with his companions, with Elizabethan audiences. The character is featured widely in the two parts of HENRY IV and is killed off without actually appearing in HENRY V. Shakespeare revived him in THE MERRY WIVES OF WINDSOR but with a different personality which many have found disappointing in comparison.

FALSTAFF
(France, 1908)

p.c.
d. *Gaston Roudés.*
l.p.
b.w. (?) mins. Sil.

No further details of this short (1 reel?) have been traced.

FALSTAFF
(France, 1911)

p.c. *Éclipse.*
d. *Henri Desfontaines.*
l.p. *Denis d'Inès; André Bacqué; M. Dégeorge; Coste; Yvonne Barjac; Madeleine Barjac; Louise Willy; Françoise Rosay; Paul Villé.*
b.w. 1066 ft. (325m.) Sil.

Based on the opera by Verdi who took the character from Shakespearean plays, it is notable for an early appearance of Françoise Rosay. 'Moving Picture World' of June 24, 1911, stated that it was well acted. It is noted as being in ten scenes.

FALSTAFF THE TAVERN KNIGHT
(G.B., 1923)
See **CHAPTER XVII THE MERRY WIVES OF WINDSOR**

CAMPANADAS A MEDIANOCHE
(Spain/Switzerland, 1966)

p.c. *Internacional Films Española/Alpine.*
d. *Orson Welles.*
l.p. *Orson Welles (Sir John Falstaff); Keith Baxter (Prince Hal); Jean Moreau (Doll Tearsheet); John Gielgud (King Henry IV); Margaret Rutherford (Mistress Quickly); Alan Webb (Justice Shallow); Norman Rodway (Henry Percy); Marina Vlady (Kate Percy); Tony Beckley (Poins); Fernando Rey (Worcester); Walter Chiari (Silence); José Nieto (Northumberland); Michael Aldridge (Pistol);*
Beatrice Welles (Child); Andrew Faulds (Westmoreland); Jeremy Rowe; Paddy Bedford; Julio Peña; Fernando Hilbert; Andrés Mejuto; Keith Pyott; Charles Farrell. Narrator: Ralph Richardson.
b.w. 119 mins.

Henry IV is King of England but there are those who question his right to the throne and how he obtained it. There are murmurs of rebellion not least from Henry Percy.

The King's son, Prince Henry (Hal), lives the life of a wastrel with his friends Poins and the ageing Sir John Falstaff who exerts some influence over the Prince and is ever in debt particularly to Mistress Quickly, the hostess of the dubious inn where they stay.

More serious is the situation with Henry Percy whose plans of rebellion, which he keeps from his wife, grow stronger, despite warnings. He leaves to raise an army supported by various lords.

Hal and Poins plan a trick on Falstaff. After committing a robbery with Falstaff, the two change their clothes and rob him of his booty. Later he boasts of his dealing with the thieves with ever-increasing exaggeration.

The King, learning of Percy's army, regrets the fact that his own son is not like his opponent in character. Unaware of his father's feelings, Hal and Falstaff are busy mocking the King in play acting. Their fun is interrupted with the arrival of the Sheriff looking for the robbers and giving a good description of Falstaff. Hal assures the Sheriff that there are no robbers at the inn. Then Hal goes to join his father while Falstaff leaves to raise men for the army. This he does from his friend, Shallow.

Hal goes to his father and promises to mend his ways. He says he will prove himself in battle against Percy. Percy, too, is anxious to meet Hal. The opportunity soon arrives as the two armies face each other. The King offers, through Lord Worcester, pardons and single combat but Worcester initially fails to tell Percy of this and a bloody battle ensues.

Falstaff manages to escape any encounters during the battle. Hal and Percy meet and Hal is victorious. Hal finds Falstaff on the ground. He thinks he is dead but the fat man has only fallen over and cannot get up. Victory goes to the King and Falstaff brings in Percy's body claiming that he killed him. The King is unhappy at the continuing relationship between his son and Falstaff.

CHAPTER VI – FALSTAFF

By 1408 all rebellions have been subdued but the price to the King's health has been heavy. He constantly collapses and cannot sleep. Hal's continuing absence also worries him. In fact, Hal and Poins receive a letter saying that Falstaff is in London. They plan a surprise visit to him. They watch him as he tries to woo Doll Tearsheet who loves him. Though glad to see Hal, both he and Poins see a change in the Prince.

Hal goes to his father and, believing him dead, takes up the crown and swears an oath to be a good king. But the King is not dead and chastises his son for being so hasty. Hal humbly apologies and vows to change his life style. Content at these words, the tired King dies.

When Falstaff hears from Pistol that his royal friend is now King, he hurries to the coronation and there foolishly breaks through the throng to address the new King. But King Henry V is not the same person as Prince Hal and he quickly tells Falstaff so. He banishes him so that he may not come any closer than ten miles of his majesty. He does, however, make provision for his old friend.

As war with France looms, King Henry V departs for that foreign shore pardoning, before he leaves, Falstaff for some foolishness. While the King is away, the rejected, broken-hearted old rogue dies.

The story of Sir John Falstaff and his friendship with Prince Hal and how this turns to rejection when the Prince assumes the throne, is seen here adapted from THE TRAGEDY OF KING RICHARD THE SECOND, THE FIRST PART OF KING HENRY THE FOURTH, THE SECOND PART OF KING HENRY THE FOURTH, THE LIFE OF KING HENRY THE FIFTH and THE MERRY WIVES OF WINDSOR:

This, the only film in the context of this book, that cannot be neatly classified by virtue of its diverse sources, is an admirable work. Though the cast is multi-national, it is the English players, apart from Welles himself, who, understandably give perhaps the best performances. Margaret Rutherford, in particular, is excellent and the commentary is taken from Holinshed's "Chronicles". The film was acclaimed in Europe but was savaged by critics in America. Time has seen any adverse views change and it is now acknowledged as a masterpiece.

Overall, the project has many virtues. The tracing of one character's life from a number of plays is in itself interesting and the chosen character no less so. Welles had already played the role (it has been said that he was born to play it) on the stage in CHIMES AT MIDNIGHT, again as an adaptation from Shakespeare and logically the forerunner of this film, at the Grand Opera House, Belfast, Northern Ireland, in 1960. The concept was not new to Welles as it was in his mind as far back as 1939. In the film, we see the old man, confused after years of boisterous friendship with his royal companion, suddenly rejected. So much so that his emotions lead to stupid actions by him and thus to rejection of a more forceful and tangible nature. Eventually, the saddened, weary Sir John, unable to accommodate a changing world, dies and as Mistress Quickly says: "And all was as cold as any stone."

Shown at the 23rd. Festival de Cine, Alcalá de Henares, Spain, 1993, as part of "La Europa Medieval en el Cine" presentation.
Shown at the Festival de Cine IberoAmericano, Huelva, Spain, 1986, as part of "Homage to Fernando Rey".
Shown at the Locarno Film Festival, Switzerland, 1997 being director John Carpenter's choice as part of a homage to the last fifty years of American film and the films that have inspired young cineasts.
Cannes Film Festival, France, 1966: Special Twentieth Anniversary of the Festival Award to Orson Welles for this film.
Círculo de Escritores Cinematográficos, Spain, 1965: Art Direction (José Antonio de la Guerra).

"...the good bits are very good indeed." – Angela and Elkan Allan, 'The Sunday Times Guide To Movies On Television'.

"If I wanted to get to Heaven on the basis of one movie...that's the one I would offer up." – Orson Welles.

aka: FALSTAFF (CHIMES AT MIDNIGHT); FALSTAFF

✢ ✢ ✢ ✢ ✢

This lovable rogue whose "means are very slender" and whose "waste is great" may have wished that his "means were greater" and his "waist slenderer", but such a reversal would have destroyed the character. A popular character indeed was Falstaff for not only did Shakespeare feature him as the comic element in a number of plays but future generations saw him transposed to the world of opera by Verdi. A poster for the opera and a brief scene from it was featured in the recent Italian-Spanish period piece *Casa Ricordi* directed by Mauro Bolognini. The voice for Falstaff is that of Guiseppe Taddei from his Philips recording.

For more films featuring the Falstaff character see: **CHAPTER VIII THE FIRST AND SECOND PARTS OF KING HENRY IV, CHAPTER XIII THE LIFE OF KING HENRY V, CHAPTER XVII THE MERRY WIVES OF WINDSOR** and **CHAPTER XXX ALL THE WORLD'S A STAGE:** FALSTAFF IN WIEN (1940); GIUSEPPE VERDI (1953) and **CHAPTER XXXII THE IMMORTAL BARD:** C.E.M.A (1942); FILMFALSTAFF (1965); EXPLORATIONS IN SHAKESPEARE SERIES (1969).

CHAPTER VII

THE FAMOUS HISTORY OF THE LIFE OF KING HENRY THE EIGHTH

Dramatis Personæ:

King Henry VIII
Queen Katherine – his first wife, later divorced
Anne Bullen – her maid of honour and then second
    wife of the King
Patience – woman to Queen Katherine
Griffith – gentleman usher to Queen Katherine
An Old Lady – friend to Anne Bullen
Dr. Butts – the King's physician
Gardiner – King's secretary and later Bishop of
    Winchester
Garter King-at-Arms
Brandon
Lord Chamberlain
Lord Chancellor

Cardinal Wolsey
Cardinal Campeius
Cromwell – servant to Wolsey
Secretaries to Wolsey

Cranmer – Archbishop of Canterbury
Bishop of Lincoln

Duke of Norfolk
Duke of Suffolk
Duke of Buckingham
Surveyor to the Duke of Buckingham
Earl of Surrey
Lord Abergavenny
Lord Sandys (also known as Sir Walter Sandys)
Sir Henry Guildford
Sir Thomas Lovell
Sir Anthony Denny
Sir Nicholas Vaux

Capuchius – ambassador from the Emperor Charles V
Gentlemen, Sergeant-at-Arms, Porter and his man,
    Page to Gardiner, Crier, Lords, Ladies, Judges,
    Scribes, Spirits, Attendants, Servants, Vergers etc.

Lord Abergavenny, the Duke of Norfolk and the Duke of Buckingham discuss the meeting in France of King Henry VIII with the King of France and, while accepting that it was properly done, question the cost of the peace made. They are disturbed, too, at the impudence and political manœuvrings of Cardinal Wolsey. No sooner is Buckingham cautioned about his outspoken behaviour than an officer arrives to arrest Abergavenny and Buckingham and to take them to the Tower of London.

As the King prepares to hear Buckingham's case, Queen Katherine enters and expresses the concern of the people about Wolsey's new taxes. Despite the Cardinal's protestations that they were properly approved, the King pardons the protestors. As for Buckingham, he is damned by one of his own staff who has acted as a spy. The Queen warns Wolsey and there are others who question the visit to France and are unhappy with Wolsey.

The Cardinal throws a banquet at which Anne Bullen (Boleyn) is present. A group of visitors, apparently French speaking, arrives disguised as shepherds. Wolsey realises that one is certainly noble and this one dances with Anne. He then reveals himself as the King and is obviously attracted to Anne.

Buckingham is condemned to death and goes to his fate nobly, proclaiming his innocence and forgiveness to those who spoke against him. Meanwhile, the King is sad, supposedly troubled that he has married his brother's wife. Of course, the truth is his attraction to Anne which the Cardinal plays upon by bringing over a foreign Cardinal Capeius to sit in unbiased judgement in the matter. This is discreetly conveyed to Queen Katherine.

Now Anne, a Queen's maid of honour, is most upset at the distress her situation is causing the Queen whose qualities she respects. This is made more difficult when the King bestows on her the title of Marchioness of Pembroke. She has no choice but to accept but wonders what such a title entails.

Queen Katherine is brought to trial. Though it is formally arranged, she accuses Wolsey calling him her enemy and refuses to be tried by that court making an appeal directly to the Pope. The King, admiring the Queen's spirit, sends the Cardinals after her. They cunningly ply their words so that she gives up the fight and resigns herself to the King's will.

Now it seems that Wolsey's letter to the Pope asking him to withhold judgement about the King's divorce has fallen into the King's hands and he has called upon Archbishop Cranmer, who is resented by Wolsey, for help. Queen Katherine is to become a dowager princess. The marriage to Anne and her coronation is proclaimed. Wolsey does not want this. While Campeius hastens back to Rome, reports come of Wolsey's scheming and he is challenged by the King.

Realising that his letter has betrayed him, he knows his days could be numbered. He is relieved of office and is held under virtual house arrest.

The messenger of the news to Wolsey, the Earl of Surrey, makes clear the treachery that Wolsey has committed, not least in the execution of Buckingham. The Dukes of Suffolk and Norfolk similarly castigate him. The disgraced Wolsey learns from his servant, Cromwell, that Cranmer is now the Archbishop of Canterbury, Sir Thomas Moore now has Wolsey's office and Anne is openly flaunted as Queen. Wolsey bids Cromwell to look to his own safety. Meanwhile, Katherine is officially divorced and taken to Kimbolton where she remains in ill health.

Anne is duly crowned Queen with due pomp and ceremony. Meanwhile, the sick Katherine learns that the broken and disgraced Wolsey has died peacefully. The ailing Katherine writes to the King begging him to look kindly upon their daughter.

Then, at the time when Anne is about to give birth, rumours spread of trouble with Cromwell, who has advanced himself well, and Archbishop Cranmer. The King, losing at cards and worried about Anne, summons Cranmer. He confronts Cranmer and confines him to the Tower until such time as he will be called upon to answer the charges. Then news comes to the King that Anne has borne him a daughter and she asks that he come to her. On his way out, Cranmer notices the earnest look he is given by the King's physician. But Cranmer is also noticed by the King and the esteem in which he is held by some.

The Lord Chancellor presides over Cranmer's hearing. Cranmer protests that he has always acted for the benefit of the King and Realm and that he is loyal to his King. He asks to confront his accusers. This is denied and he is committed to the Tower and is warned that many have spoken against him, more than he thinks. He is accused of forming a new sect and when Cromwell speaks out for Cranmer, he is denounced for being a loyal member of this sect. The lords assembled send him to the Tower, too.

When a guard is called to escort Cranmer, he protests and shows them the King's ring which he wears. The King enters, obviously displeased, and chastises them doubting their so-called wisdom. The rift between monarch and archbishop is healed and the King asks him to christen the newly born child.

Preparations go ahead for the christening which duly takes place with attendant ceremony with Cranmer officiating. He not only eulogises about the child but fortells the future in store for the baby girl.

Note: The daughter of the union of Henry and Katherine of Aragon was Mary who later became Queen Mary (1553-1558) and from the union of Henry and Anne Bullen came Queen Elizabeth I (1558-1603). As Shakespeare lived partially during her reign he would have been well acquainted with the events of it. Thus his forecast for her via Cranmer was hardly prophetic, but rather retrospective as the play, generally accepted as his last, was first performed in 1613. There is also some question as to Shakespeare's sole authorship of the play with there being some argument in learned circles as to Fletcher's involvement. Though past centuries saw the play often performed, it is now somewhat ignored. Strange, too, that though Anne Bullen is really the main catalyst to the events, her part is remarkably small.

✠ ✠ ✠ ✠ ✠

HENRY VIII
(G.B., 1911)

p.c. *Barker Motion Photography.*
d. *Louis N. Parker.*
l.p. *Herbert Beerbohm Tree (Cardinal Wolsey); Arthur Bourchier (Henry VIII); Violet Vanbrugh (Queen Catherine); Laura Cowie (Anne Boleyn); S.A. Cookson (Cardinal); Edward O'Neill (Duke of Suffolk); Basil Gill (Duke of Buckingham); Gerald Lawrence (Earl of Surrey); Charles Fuller (Cranmer); A.E. George (Duke of Norfolk); Reginald Owen (Cromwell); Gerald Edward Sass (Lord Chamberlain); Clifford Heatherley; Lita Barclay; Edmund Goulding; Mrs. Charles Calvert.*
b.w. 2000 ft. (610 m.) Sil.

Five scenes from the production at His Majesty's Theatre made up this which is listed as the first British 2-reel feature by Dennis Gifford in 'The British Film Catalogue'. This is in conflict with the information given in 'The Movie' where the film is noted as 60 mins. (far longer than the length above). The same tome also notes Will Barker as director who apparently paid Tree £1000 for a day's work shooting the film. Tree then insisted that the prints be destroyed after a few months not wishing a lasting record of a mediocre performance to exist. With the loss of the film, the truth will perhaps not be known. The film did, however, move other actors of the day to commit their roles to film. Barker, incidentally, was an enthusiastic character with big ideas but he did build the first Ealing studio in 1910.

✠ ✠ ✠ ✠ ✠

CARDINAL WOLSEY
(U.S.A., 1912)

p.c. *Vitagraph.*
d. *James Stuart Blackton, Lawrence Trimble.*
l.p. *Tefft Johnson (Henry VIII); Clara Kimball Young (Anne Boleyn); Hal Reid (Cardinal Wolsey); Julia Swayne-Gordon (Catherine of Aragon); Logan Paul (Archbishop of Canterbury); George Ober (Bishop of Essex);*

Harold Wilson (King's Friend); Robert Gaillard (King's Secretary).
b.w. 997 ft. (304 m.) Sil.

This short mainly covers the dispute between Wolsey and the King over the Henry's divorce from Catherine of Aragon.

The relationship to the play is somewhat incidental though Shakespeare's lines are used in one inter-title. Some note Charles Kent, James Young and Lawrence Trimble as the directorial team. The film is noted as being in ten scenes.

The play itself was indirectly responsible for the destruction of the Globe theatre. A performance of the play was given on June 30, 1613. It was customary in those days to announce scenes of pomp with cannon fire. An ember from one such as this from the afternoon performance landed on the thatched roof of the theatre which erupted into flames at night. Fortunately, the costumes and, most importantly, the plays were saved. The theatre was quickly rebuilt.

As for the titular character, the rotund, autocratic British monarch Henry VIII (1509 to 1547) is probably best remembered for his six wives and for his establishment of the Church of England. Such a character is a logical choice for the film studios. He has been served better than many characters in his screen representation. He was obviously featured in two films about, and called, *Anne Boleyn* – the first an American film for Vitagraph of 1912 with Clara Kimball Young as the Queen; the second, a French film from Pathé the year after. The great German actor Emil Jannings portrayed him in the 1919 German film *Anna Boleyn*; Charles Laughton gave an Oscar winning performance in Sir Alexander Korda's 1933 film *The Private Life Of Henry VIII*, a role he repeated in M.G.M.'s 1953 film *Young Bess*. 1936 saw Frank Cellier in the role in the British *Tudor Rose*. In 1952 the Disney company filmed in England *The Sword And The Rose* in which James Robertson Justice played the king.

The portly monarch was featured in the film versions of Mark Twain's *The Prince And The Pauper* – an American 1909 silent version, another silent version from the American company, Famous Players in 1915 and the sound versions – U.S.A., 1937 and G.B., 1962. It was filmed again as *Crossed Swords* (U.S.A., 1977). William Keighley, Don Chaffey and Richard Lester were the respective directors and Montagu Love, Paul Rogers and Charlton Heston respectively played the regal role for the sound versions.

Actor-writer Robert Shaw played him in the much praised *A Man For All Seasons* in 1967. Richard Burton was the King in the British *Anne Of The Thousand Days* in 1969 which was devoted to the relationship of Henry with Anne Bullen (Geneviève Bujold) and therefore contained scenes parallel to the Shakespearean play. This is to be expected as both were based on English history.

Much-loved British comedy actor Sid James played the role strictly for bawdy humour in the British comedy of 1971 *Carry On Henry*. Australian actor, Keith Michell, repeated his B.B.C. television role of Henry VIII in the 1972 *Henry VIII And His Six Wives*. With such a wealth of talent applied to the role, it is sad that no-one has looked to the full Shakespeare play. Greater then is the loss of the only known film performance however mediocre Tree may have thought it.

CHAPTER VIII

THE FIRST AND SECOND PARTS OF KING HENRY THE FOURTH

Dramatis Personæ (Part 1):

King Henry IV
Henry – Prince of Wales (Prince Hal), his son
John of Lancaster – another son

Earl of Westmoreland
Sir Walter Blunt

Thomas Percy – Earl of Worcester
Henry Percy – Earl of Northumberland
Henry Percy – his son, called Hotspur
Lady Percy – Hotspur's wife
Edmund Mortimer – Earl of March
Lady Mortimer
Archibald – Earl of Douglas

Archbishop Scroop of York
Owen Glendower
Sir Michael – friend of the Archbishop of York
Sir Richard Vernon

Sir John Falstaff
Poins
Gadshill
Peto
Bardolph
Mistress Quickly
Lords, Officers, Sheriff, Vintner, Drawers,
*   Chamberlain, Carriers, Travellers and Attendants*

King Henry IV of England is weary; weary over the delay in his plans for the Crusades and over rebellion in England. Good news comes that Henry Percy (Hotspur) has gained a great victory against the Scots and Henry wishes that his own son were more like Hotspur even though the hero of the day wishes to keep his prisoners.

Elsewhere the rakish Prince Hal is planning a prank on his ageing mentor, Falstaff. The plan is later executed when Falstaff and his friends rob some travellers but Hal and Poins, disguised, attack the old man and he runs off leaving the booty behind.

When Henry and Hotspur meet, harsh words are exchanged. When the King leaves, Hotspur himself speaks of rebellion to the Lords Worcester and Northumberland. Later, back in Warkworth Castle, he reflects upon the situation concerning rebellion and the support he has. As he decides to leave, he incurs his wife's anger by not telling her the reason for his departure.

In London, at the Boar's Head Tavern in Eastcheap, an exhausted Falstaff meets with Hal, Poins and Francis. He gives then a progressively exaggerated account of the attack upon him. The meeting is interrupted by the arrival of a nobleman from the King whom Falstaff sends away. The group of revellers stages a mock play about the King which is hastily abandoned when the Sheriff arrives looking for the robbers and a fat man in particular. The others disappear, leaving Peto and the Prince. The Prince confronts the Sheriff and tells him he knows nothing of the affair or the man. When the Sheriff has gone, Falstaff is found asleep and Hal picks his pocket but finds only a bill for his food and drink.

In Bangor, Hotspur, Worcester, Mortimer and Owen Glendower meet to form an agreement over the spoils and land should their rebellion succeed. After this, their ladies join them in peace and song.

At Court, Henry receives his son Hal whom he castigates for his frivolous ways. He tells him of the rebellion and Hal promises that Hotspur shall pay. News arrives that the rebels have formed an army. The King plans to engage it in the Shrewsbury area.

At the Boar's Head Inn, Falstaff is accusing everyone of theft but Mistress Quickly merely chastises him for his unpaid bills. The Prince arrives and confesses to the theft and produces the bill, something far different from the sum of money Falstaff claims has been stolen. Then the Prince gives the old knight his orders for the forthcoming battle.

Hotspur in the rebel camp near Shrewsbury learns that his father is ill and that the King is marching against him. Meanwhile, on a road near Coventry, Hal meets Falstaff and his ragged band of men. They know that a battle is imminent, a battle that Hotspur would readily fight that night.

Such enthusiasm is curtailed by the arrival of Sir William Blunt with a conciliatory message from the King. This only infuriates Hotspur who reminds Blunt of all the good deeds they have done for the King. At least, the battle is delayed.

The dawn of the next day sees Lord Worcester at the King's camp. He and Vernon state their reluctance to rebel but say they are forced to by the King's lack of reward for them. Hal, to save unnecessary bloodshed, extols Hotspur's valour and proposes single combat between them. The fear of battle leads Falstaff to voice his own fearful emotions of death.

Worcester and Vernon withhold the challenge but are forced to admit it as Douglas also knows of it. A messenger arrives with a letter but Hotspur casts it aside as the King advances. The battle lines are drawn up.

Douglas kills Blunt believing him to be the King but Hotspur points out that he has been deceived by his similar appearance. Elsewhere on the battlefield, Hal meets an exhausted Falstaff who is, as ever, full of his usual bravado and jest.

The Prince is slightly wounded but, against the King's advice, does not retire from battle. The King comes face to face with Douglas and in the fight that follows, the King finds himself in danger. Hal arrives and drives off Douglas and thus redeems himself somewhat in the King's eyes.

Douglas then encounters Falstaff who falls as if dead and so Douglas leaves. At last Hal and Hotspur come face to face and engage in a fight that leads to the mortally wounding of Hotspur. Hal comments on his adversary's bravery and, then seeing Falstaff and thinking him dead, leaves. But Falstaff is not dead.

He sees the dying Hotspur and finishes him with his sword. He picks up the body thinking to gain glory for himself. This surprises Lord John of Lancaster and disgusts the Prince.

Trumpets sound the retreat of the rebels. Worcester and Vernon are captured and, after rebuke by the King, are sent to execution. Hal, respecting a worthy opponent, asks to punish Douglas himself and sets him free. The King then despatches Lord John of Lancaster to the north to deal with the Earl of Northumberland while he and Hal plan their march to Wales to meet Glendower and the Earl of March and thus end the rebellion.

Note: This was written shortly after RICHARD II and is closely linked to that play. As that play was written just before 1596, it follows that this one most likely dates from 1597. Despite its title, the play is not chiefly concerned with King Henry IV but, rather, it is the figure of his son, later Henry V, who dominates. This may be due to Samuel Daniel's poem 'The Famous Victories of Henry V' which promoted the Prince's role at the battle at Shrewsbury. As usual, Shakespeare relied upon 'Chronicals of the History of England'.

✣ ✣ ✣ ✣ ✣

HENRY IV PART I: AN INTRODUCTION
(G.B., 1971)

p.c. *Seabourne Enterprises/Anvil Films.*
d. *Peter Seabourne.*
l.p.
c. 17 mins.

An educational short, extracts from Act II, Scene 4 and Act V, Scene 4 are featured.

✣ ✣ ✣ ✣ ✣

Dramatis Personæ (Part 2):

King Henry IV
His sons:
  Henry, Prince of Wales (Prince Hal)
  Thomas – Duke of Clarence
  John of Lancaster
  Humphrey of Gloucester

Loyal to the King:
  Earl of Warwick
  Earl of Westmoreland
  Earl of Surrey
  Gower
  Harcourt
  Blunt

Opposed to the King:
  Earl of Northumberland
  Archbishop Scroop of York
  Lord Mowbray
  Lord Hastings
  Lord Bardolph
  Sir John Coleville
  Lady Northumberland

Lady Percy
Travers and Morton – retainers to Northumberland

Sir John Falstaff
His associates:
  His Page
  Bardolph
  Pistol
  Poins
  Peto
  Mistress Quickly
  Doll Tearsheet

Shallow and Silence – Country Justices
Mouldy, Shadow, Wart, Feeble, Bullcalf – recruits
Fang and Snare – Sheriff's Officers
Lord Chief Justice
His Servant
A Porter, a Dancer, Lords, Attendants, Grooms, Drawers, Officers, Soldiers, Messengers, Beadles etc.
Rumour – the presenter

News of the Shrewsbury defeat and the death of his son is brought to the Earl of Northumberland at Warkworth Castle by Lord Bardolph. This is confirmed by Morton who tells of the flight of the army and the fate of some of the conspirators. In his grief, Northumberland realises the need to make the best of the situation and to make new friendships.

In London, Falstaff meets the Lord Chief Justice who is well aware of Falstaff's part in the robbery (see Part 1). He says that Falstaff's actions at Shrewsbury have done little to enhance his reputation and he chides the old knight for misleading the young Prince about whom they exchange views. Falstaff is reminded that the King has separated him from the Prince by sending him with John of Lancaster to the north while the Prince goes to Wales. Falstaff, aware of his own lack of funds, unsuccessfully tries to borrow from the Lord Chief Justice.

In York, Archbishop Scroop meets with the Lords Bardolph and Hastings and Thomas Mowbray to assess the situation and wonder if they can rely upon Northumberland. They find comfort that the King's forces are divided – part in France, part in the north of England and part in Wales.

Falstaff, too, has his problems in London. He is greatly in debt to Mistress Quickly for his lodgings at the Boar's Head Inn. She has taken out an action against him but the officers charged with serving it are afraid of Falstaff's reactions. He protests loudly, so loudly that the Lord Chief Justice arrives. Mistress Quickly explains her case and of Falstaff's promise to wed her. The Lord Chief Justice dismisses Falstaff's arguments for he knows him too well and tells him to honour his word and his debts. As news comes by Gower that the King and the Prince are not far away, Falstaff uses this diversion to wheedle his way back into Mistress Quickly's favour and her purse.

Indeed, the Prince is not far away and he expresses to Poins his concern which, he finds difficult to show, for his father's health. A letter arrives from Falstaff and the Prince and Poins plan to spy upon their rotund friend.

At Warkworth Castle, the Earl of Northumberland confers with his wife and widowed daughter-in-law. He decides that his wife has given him sound advice and he resolves to go to Scotland until the political climate improves.

Trouble is also brewing at the Boar's Head Inn. Mistress Quickly and Doll Tearsheet assist Falstaff who immediately enters a verbal battle with Doll. To make matters worse, the arrival of Ancient Pistol is announced to the disgust of Mistress Quickly. She despises his character and is worried about the effect his presence will have upon her good name locally. The men scuffle and Pistol is slightly injured by Falstaff who earns Doll's admiration.

Hal and Poins, disguised, hear Falstaff discuss them rather unfavourably with Doll. They reveal themselves and Hal is far from pleased with Falstaff. A messenger arrives for Hal saying that the King is at Westminster and the Prince and Poins leave at once. So, too, does Falstaff since there are those who call for him. In fact, he travels to Gloucester to raise more soldiers.

The King wanders, unable to sleep. He calls for Lords Warwick and Surrey and Sir John Blunt. They arrive and with them news of Glendower's defeat and death. The King wishes that the wars were over and that he could travel to the Holy Land.

Now that Northumberland is in Scotland, the Archbishop of York, Lord Hastings and Mowbray amass their forces. They are told that some thirty thousand soldiers oppose them only a mile away. Westmoreland, as royal envoy, arrives and questions the Archbishop's motives since he is a man of peace. He replies with a letter of grievances which Westmoreland says he will deliver. It is, for them, a matter of awaiting the King's reply.

The grievances are raised again when John of Lancaster meets the rebels between the two forces. They discuss the matter and John feels the King's purposes have been misunderstood. They drink together and John gives his word that redress will be made once the armies are disbanded. However, with the rebel army gone, its leaders are arrested for treason and other rebels are pursued.

Falstaff himself arrests one, Coleville, and hands him over to John who sends all the rebels to York for execution. On hearing that the King is ill, they prepare to return to London, Falstaff going by way of Gloucester.

At Westminster, the King addresses the Lords. He receives news of the events at York and of the defeat of a combined Scottish and English force led by Northumberland and Lord Bardolph. The King is, however, quite weary and faints. He is carried to his chamber where he sleeps.

Prince Hal and his brother Clarence arrive. Hal, thinking his father dead, puts on the crown. The King awakens and, seeing that the crown has gone, calls for his lords and demands to know why they left him. They point out that the Prince was with him. He sends them to find him.

Lord Warwick finds the Prince weeping and takes him to the King who chides his son. The Prince begs forgiveness. This he gives and, having summarised his life, himself begs God's forgiveness. John, too, arrives.

The King enquires the name of the chamber in which he rests. On being told it is the Jerusalem Chamber, he says that this is the place where he will lie and where he will die. When the King dies, the new king, Henry V, assures his brothers that he will care for them and he and the Lord Chief Justice make their peace.

In Gloucester, Falstaff arrives. There, he and his friends enjoy themselves feasting, wining and singing. When news comes of the old King's death, Falstaff and his company hasten to London as Falstaff feels that the new King will need him.

More in need of Falstaff are Mistress Quickly and Doll Tearsheet who have to call upon the beadles to quell a disturbance at the inn. Indeed, the new King has little need of Falstaff. He ignores the old man's calls and rejects him, banishing him ten miles from the royal person upon pain of death.

Still thinking that the new King will come to him, Falstaff waits, lumbered with debts. John arrives with the Lord Chief Justice and Falstaff is arrested and, with his followers, sent to Fleet prison. John tells the Lord Chief Justice that all the King's former followers will be provided for but are banished until their words become more modest and wise.

The King recalls Parliament. John foresees war with France soon.

The epilogue advises of the return of Falstaff and also Queen Katherine of France to make the people happy.

Note: This last part of what be termed a trilogy dealing with the reigns of Richard II and and Henry IV probably dates from the Spring of 1598. It was at a time when Shakespeare was at full literary power. He drew upon one of his favourite sources Raphael Holinshed's 'Chronicals Of The History Of England'. He may well have relied upon other sources of the period.

✤ ✤ ✤ ✤ ✤

KING HENRY IV PART II
(G.B., 1974)

p.c. *Seabourne Enterprises.*
d. *Peter Seabourne.*
l.p. *Michael Pennington; Natasha Pyne; David Suchet.*
c. 6 mins.

This brief extract, the third in the series, is taken from Act II, Scene 2.

✤ ✤ ✤ ✤ ✤

FAUSTÃO
(Brazil, 1971)

p.c. *Difilm.*
d. *Eduardo Coutinho.*

l.p. *Eliezar Gomes; Jorge Gomes; Anecy Rocha; Gracindo Freiré; José Pimental.*
c.? 103 mins.

Faustão is a bandit living in the north-east of Brazil in the last century. He moves from town to town with a group of friends, thieving or just enjoying the pleasures of life.

According to Brazilian sources this is based on THE LIFE OF HENRY THE FIFTH. Those acquainted with the works of Shakespeare will quickly realise that this is not so. It is not altogether false since the story clearly parallels the pre-monarchial days of the future king when he passed his days committing nefarious deeds and carousing with Falstaff and others. These events are chronicled in both parts of HENRY IV and since the placing of films in this book, with a few exceptions, is guided by the source play, this is the logical setting for it.

MY OWN PRIVATE IDAHO
(U.S.A., 1991)

p.c. *Idaho Productions.*
d. *Gus Van Sant.*
l.p. *River Phoenix (Mike Waters); Keanu Reeves (Scott Favor); William Richert (Bob Pigeon); James Russo (Richard Waters); Chiara Caselli (Carmella); Rodney Harvey (Gary); Michael Parker (Digger); Jessie Thomas (Denise); Flea (Budd); Sally Curtice (Jane Lightwork); Udo Kier (Hans); Tom Troupe (Jack Favor); Robert Lee Pitchlynn (Walt); Grace Zabriskie (Alena); Wade Evans (Wade); Matt Evert (Coverboy); Mickey Cottrell (Daddy Carroll); Scott Patrick Green (Coverboy/Cafe Kid); Shaun Jordan (Cafe Kid); Tom Cramer (Coverboy); Vana O'Brien (Sharon Waters); George Conner (Bad George); Shawn Jones (Cafe Kid); Oliver Kirk (Indian Cop); Joshua Halladay (Baby Mike); Stanley Hainesworth (Dirtman); Stephen Clark Pachosa (Hotel Manager); Lannie Swerdlow (Disco Manager); Douglas Tollenen (Little Richard); Wally Gaarsland, Mark Weaver, Bryan Wilson, Conrad Montgomery (Rock Promoters); Pat Patterson, Steve Vernelson, Mike Cascadden (Cops); Eric Hull (Mayor's Aide); Greg Murphy (Carl); James A. Arling (Minister); James Caviezel (Airline Clerk); Melanie Mosely (Lounge Hostess); Ana Cavinato (Stewardess); Tiger Warren (Himself); David Reppinhagen (Yuppie); Massimo DeCataldo, Pao Pei Andreoli, Robert Egon, Paolo Baiocco (Italian Street Boys); Mario Stracciarolo (Mike's Italian Client).*
c. 102 mins. S

Mike Waters, a hustler who suffers from fits, awakens in a rough sleeping house in Seattle being sexually enjoyed by an overweight man. Later, he is picked up and taken to the house of a rich woman where he meets Scott Favor, the irresponsible son of the mayor of Portland. Scott, who is soon due for an inheritance, helps Mike when he has another fit and takes him away to sleep. The next day Mike meets Hans, a rich German, and again falls asleep. The two end up in Portland where they meet up with Scott. Here a group of hustlers is led and influenced by Bob Pigeon. They take over a derelict building which is raided by the police. The police are looking for Bob and they advise Scott to go to his disapproving father. This he does then sets off with Mike to find Mike's mother. This leads them to Idaho where they meet Mike's brother and father. They meet Hans again in Snake River and finally they go to Italy only to find Mike's mother has returned to America. Scott abandons Mike for a farmer's daughter and becomes an upright citizen following the death of his father. Bob follows Scott but he refuses to acknowledge his former mentor and Bob dies of a fever. Mike finds himself on the road again, hustling.

There is no difficulty in recognising the basic theme here for it has been done before and more correctly, in literary terms, in **CAMPANADAS A MEDIANOCHE**. Here the subject matter takes on the form of a road movie, mixing sex and nudity with a curious blend of Shakespearean dialogue and street slang. The characters are readily identifiable – Scott (Prince Hal), Richard, his father (King Henry IV) and Bob Pigeon (Falstaff).

Shown at the New York Film Festival, U.S.A., 1991 (with great success).

National Society of Film Critics Awards, U.S.A., 1992: Best Actor (River Phoenix).

Venice Film Festival, Italy, 1991: Best Actor (River Phoenix).

"A genuine poetic voice is at work...and it fascinates us with its strength and clarity." – '1992 Motion Picture Guide Annual'.

"Pompous and cruel homage by Gus Van Sant to Shakespeare's HENRY IV." – 'TP', No.1508.

aka: MI IDAHO PRIVADO; DAS ENDE DER UNSCHULD

✤ ✤ ✤ ✤ ✤

Much of these two plays is covered in the film **CAMPANADAS A MEDIANOCHE** (see **CHAPTER VI FALSTAFF**). The man himself who reigned 1399 to 1413 was not a good administrator. Though his reign started mildly enough even though he gained the crown by a broken pledge, it was plagued by revolt, war and impecuniosity. His many blunders such as the execution of Archbishop Scrope (Scroop), weighed heavily upon him (he described himself in his will as: "I, Henry, sinful wretch...") and affected his health. As he says in the play: "Uneasy lies the head that wears a crown" (Part 2, Act III, Scene 1). True words, indeed, and words that are forever pertinent to those who hold positions of responsibility and power.

For other films with scenes from the plays see

CHAPTER XXXII THE IMMORTAL BARD: EXPLORATIONS IN SHAKESPEARE (1969).

CHAPTER IX
HAMLET, PRINCE OF DENMARK

Dramatis Personæ:

Hamlet – Prince of Denmark and nephew of King
   Claudius
Horatio – his friend
Ghost of Hamlet's father

Claudius – King of Denmark
Gertrude – Queen of Denmark and Hamlet's mother

Polonius – Lord Chamberlain
Ophelia – his daughter
Laertes – his son
Reynaldo – servant to Polonius
Voltemand, Cornelius, Rosencrantz, Osric,

Guildenstern, A Gentleman – courtiers
Marcellus, Bernardo – officers
Francisco – a soldier

Fortinbras – Prince of Norway
Norwegian captain
English Ambassadors

Players, A priest.
Two clowns (grave-diggers)
Lords, Ladies, Officers, Soldiers, Sailors, Messengers
   and Attendants

When Queen Gertrude of Denmark marries, unlawfully, Claudius, the brother of her husband who has been dead barely two months, there are feelings of suspicion about the death of the late king. More so, since Claudius lacks all the fine qualities of his brother.

Most affected is Hamlet, the young, sensitive Prince who has effectively been usurped from the throne. It is the loss of his father and the shame that he feels at his mother's marriage that sends him into moods of despair. Dressing in black, he forsakes all his normal pursuits and will not listen to his mother's pleas and even wears black to her wedding.

He is worried by the manner of his father's death (supposedly from a snake bite while he slept in the garden) and believes that his uncle may have had a hand in the matter. He is not sure whether or not his mother was party to the supposed crime.

Hamlet hears a rumour, confirmed by his good friend Horatio, that an apparition has been seen in the castle area. The ghost appears at midnight clad in armour similar to that which the late king wore. It seems to want to speak but cannot do so and fades at dawn.

Hamlet reasons that the ghost must be appearing for a purpose and, with Horatio and a guard, Marcellus, waits one night upon the platform where the ghost normally appears. Their wait in the cold is rewarded when the spirit appears. Hamlet is at first frightened and cries out for divine protection but then becomes bolder and speaks to the ghost who signals him to follow him. Despite pleas from his companions, Hamlet does so.

The ghost confirms that it is the spirit of his father and that Claudius was responsible for his death having poured a poison into his ear while he slept in the garden. The spirit decries Gertrude's actions but demands that whatever revenge Hamlet may seek, no harm must become Gertrude. Hamlet agrees and swears his two companions to secrecy about the matter.

Already weak from depression, the impact of the encounter almost drives Hamlet mad. He realises that his present state of mind may reveal his suspicions and so feigns madness. The deception works and the King and Queen believe that this cannot be the result of the death of his father but rather it is love that has induced this state of mind.

Before these events, Hamlet had shown his affections to Ophelia, daughter of the chief counsellor for state affairs, Polonius. Now he treats her rudely and unkindly as part of his deception. She suffers this treatment with understanding and thinks only of Hamlet's finer qualities. Her suffering is rewarded by a letter from Hamlet, who feels guilty for his conduct towards her, expressing love and passion. This she shows to her father who, in turn, tells the King and Queen which seems to confirm to them that Hamlet's problem is one of love.

Hamlet cannot shake off the impression of his father's ghost and becomes more unsettled. He is not sure if the ghost was an evil spirit sent to obsess his mind with revenge. His uncertainty is resolved when some travelling players arrive at the castle. Hamlet, pleased with their past work, particularly their interpretation of the death of Priam of Troy and the mourning of his wife, Hecuba, asks them to act out this piece again and is so moved that his mind is set on one course – to obtain proof of his uncle's guilt.

In his actor friends he sees a way to do this and writes a play which parallels his father's death and his mother's remarriage. He asks them to enact the play and invites the King and Queen to the performance. Unaware of the play's content, they accept. As the play progresses, the King is clearly disturbed and when the murder scene occurs, rushes from the chamber pretending illness.

Convinced of his uncle's guilt, Hamlet is summoned by the Queen before he can plan a course of action. Anxious to know what happens, the King induces Polonius to hide in the Queen's room as his spy. The Queen makes clear her displeasure with Hamlet's actions. Much play is made upon the word "father" and the argument becomes more heated. Hamlet grasps his mother so tightly by the wrist that the hidden Polonius cries out. Thinking it is Claudius, Hamlet runs Polonius through with his sword.

Horrified, the Queen condemns his act but he says her crime is much greater. He begs, bullies and chastises her to make her change her ways. So ferocious is his attack that the ghost of his father appears to remind him of his pledge that he should not harm the Queen. Finally, convincing the Queen that he is not mad, Hamlet obtains her agreement that she will respect the memory of her dead husband, bless her son as her son and not consort with Claudius.

Hamlet now has time to ponder his action in killing the father of the woman he loves. Claudius seizes the opportunity to send Hamlet away. He cannot have him killed for the Prince is popular. Under the pretext of protecting Hamlet, Claudius sends him to England on official business. Two companions are sent with Hamlet carrying a letter which ensures that Hamlet will be executed when he lands in England. However, Hamlet learns of the letter's contents, cleverly erases his own name and substitutes the names of his companions.

At sea, the party is attacked by pirates. Out-numbered his two companions flee to England to meet their unexpected fate and Hamlet, despite a brave fight is captured. The pirates, realising Hamlet's worth and his possible future value as a friend, return him safely to Denmark.

There, Hamlet is greeted by a sad sight – the funeral of Ophelia. This gentle girl, saddened by the death of her father at the hand of the man she loved, had gone out of her mind. Obsessed with flowers, while collecting some, she had fallen into a stream and drowned.

There is much grief at the funeral from the Queen and Ophelia's brother, Laertes. Hamlet, too, is grief stricken and falls upon the grave with Laertes. The angry brother and Hamlet fight but are pulled apart and seem to make their peace.

Claudius cunningly plays upon Laertes' latent wish for revenge and suggests a friendly duel between Laertes and Hamlet, both good swordsmen, as a show of reconciliation. At the match, Laertes has a sharp poisoned weapon while Hamlet, unaware of this, has the customary blunt sword used in such matches.

Cheered on by the King, Hamlet seems, at first, to be superior until Laertes shows his form and delivers a mortal thrust. Incensed, Hamlet gains Laertes' weapon and deals him an equally deadly thrust. At that moment the Queen cries out that she has been poisoned. The King, as a contingency plan should Hamlet win, has prepared a poisoned cup for him. He has failed to tell the Queen and she has unwittingly drunk from it.

Realising that treachery surrounds him, Hamlet orders all doors to be locked. Laertes confesses all and begs forgiveness. Hamlet takes Laertes' venomous sword and, though weakened and near to death, takes his revenge upon Claudius. Horatio, Hamlet's dear friend, asks to join Hamlet in death but the Prince begs him to live and tell the world what has happened.

Note: This play seems to date from 1600 or 1601 or, perhaps, 1602. The source of inspiration is somewhat vague but is probably the fifth volume of 'Histoires Tragiques' by François Belleforest. This itself is a free version of the twelfth-century 'Historia Danica' by Saxo Germanicus. There may be other sources steeped in folklore.

✚ ✚ ✚ ✚ ✚

HAMLET, SCÈNE DE DUEL
(France, 1900)

p.c.   *Phono Cinéma Théâtre.*
d.   *Clément Maurice.*
l.p.   *Sarah Bernhardt (Hamlet); Pierre Magnier (Laertes); Suzanne Seylor.*
b.w. *174 ft. (53 m.)*

This, as might be expected, featured the duel scene from HAMLET and was part of a presentation at the Universal Exposition, Paris, 1900. Famous theatre stars of the day presented short scenes from their repertoires. Featured also in the selection were Réjan and Coquelin but it is the Divine Sarah dressed as a man that provides the interest. The sound, mainly of effects, was by means of a disc electronically synchronised and was said to be reasonably satisfactory.

HAMLET, PRINCE OF DENMARK
(France, 1907)

p.c.   *Star Film.*
d.   *Georges Méliès.*
l.p.   *Georges Méliès (Hamlet).*
b.w. *574 ft. (175 m.) Sil.*

No. 980.987 in the Méliès catalogue of films, sadly, no copies of the film seem to have survived. The film concentrates on the mental troubles of the Prince. It opens with the grave digging scene, moves to Hamlet seeing his father's ghost which demands revenge and also that of Ophelia which he tries to embrace when she throws him flowers from her crown. The final scene is the famous duel sequence and the resultant deaths.

HAMLET
(France, 1908)

p.c. *Société Cinématographique des Auteurs et Gens de Lettres/Pathé.*
d. *Albert Capellani.*
l.p. *Jacques Grétillat; Henri Desfontaines; Benedict; Colonna Romano.*
b.w. 1 reel. Sil.

It has not been possible to find a synopsis of this version. It is of interest that two of the cast – Grétillat and Romano – were in a version made two or three years later. It seems logical to assume that they played the same roles in this as in the later version.

AMLETO
(Italy, 1908)

p.c. *Cines.*
d. *Mario Caserini.*
l.p. *Dante Cappelli (Hamlet); Fernanda Negri Pouget.*
b.w. 853 ft. (260 m.) Sil.

See notes after the 1910 version from the same company. The cast may not be correct and Maria Casperini may be present for she and Pouget (noted in the later film) were among the players whom Caserini used at the time. The American release was slightly longer.

aka: HAMLET

AMLETO
(Italy, 1908)

p.c. *Cines.*
d. *Giuseppe de Liguoro.*
l.p.
b.w. 761 ft. (232 m.) Sil.

Not in Bernardini's listing of the Italian silent cinema, a number of sources note it.

AMLETO
(Italy, 1909)

p.c. *Società Anonima Fabricazione Films Italiana.*
d. *Luca Comerio.*
l.p. *Ruggero Ruggeri (Hamlet).*
b.w. 843 ft. (257 m.) Sil.

An Italian source notes the production year as 1908 and an American source puts the production company as Milano.

HAMLET
(Denmark, 1910)

p.c. *Nordisk.*
d. *August Blom.*
l.p. *Alwin Neuss (Hamlet); Aage Hertel (Claudius); Emilie Sannom (Ophelia); Ella La Cour (Gertrud); Rigmor Jerichau; Einar Zangenberg; Oscar Langkilde; Axel Mattson; Carl Rosenbaum.*
b.w. 1063 ft. (324 m.). Sil.

An early Danish Shakespearean entry, it probably followed the common path of condensing the story into about fifteen minutes. All the text was from Shakespeare. It was apparently filmed at Kronberg Castle.

AMLETO
(Italy, 1910)

p.c. *Cines.*
d. *Mario Caserini.*
l.p. *Amletto Novelli (Hamlet); Fernanda Negri Pouget (Ophelia).*
b.w. 1066 ft. (325 m.) Sil.

The film is known to contain scenes of Hamlet wooing Ophelia, her madness, Hamlet greeting the actors and Hamlet feigning madness as he reads.

Certain confusion surrounds this and the earlier production by the same company particularly in the cast of both versions. Two versions *were* made and some note Dante Capelli as Hamlet and Maria Casperini also in the cast.

HAMLET
(France, 1910)

p.c. *Pathé/Lux.*
d. *Gérard Bourgeois.*
l.p. *Paul Mounet-Sully (Hamlet); Yvonne Barjac.*
b.w. 951 ft. (290 m.) Sil.

Only fragments of this film survive.

HAMLET
(France, 1910)

p.c. *Film D'Art.*
d. *André Calmettes.*
l.p. *Sarah Bernhardt (Hamlet); Edouard de Max; Chameroy; Henri Pouctal.*
b.w. 1 reel. Sil.

Jean Mitry lists this film as having been made but it has not been possible to confirm this. Calmettes did direct a later version of the play but did the great Bernhardt reprise her earlier role in this film? It is a matter of conjecture but the source is surely reliable.

HAMLET
(Russia, 1910)

Reports reveal that J. Jdanov made about twenty "Talking Films" about this time in Russia. The system was not a film miracle – simply actors reciting on or off stage to projected images. Among the items filmed is said to be the monologue from HAMLET.

HAMLET
(France, 1911)

p.c. *Éclipse.*
d. *Henri Desfontaines.*
l.p. *Jacques Grétillat (Hamlet); Colonna Romano (Gertrude).*
b.w. 1 reel. Sil.

The duration is put as ten minutes and as being made a year previous by some sources.

HAMLET
(G.B., 1912)

p.c. *Barker.*
d. *W. G. Barker.*
l.p. *Charles Raymond (Hamlet); Dorothy Foster (Ophelia); Constance Backner (Gertrude).*
b.w. 1525 ft. (465 m.) Sil.

An abbreviated version, this shows how the ghost of Hamlet's father urges him on to vengeance. It is reported that this was made in under six hours on a budget of £180.

HAMLET
(G.B., 1913)

p.c. *Hepworth Manufacturing Company for Gaumont.*
d. *E. Hay Plumb.*
l.p. *Johnstone Forbes-Robertson (Hamlet); Walter Ringham (Claudius); Adeline Bourne (Gertrude); Gertrude Elliott (Ophelia); Alex Scott-Gatty (Laertes); S. A. Cookson (Horatio); Montague Rutherford (Rosencrantz); Percy Rhodes (Ghost); J. H. Barnes (Polonius); Grendon Bentley (Fortinbras); E. A. Ross (Guildenstern); Robert Atkins (Player King/ Marcellus); George Hayes (Osric); Richard Andean (Player/Bernardo); Eric Adeney (Reynaldo/Francisco); J. H. Riley, S. T. Pearce (Grave-diggers).*
b.w. 100 mins. Sil.

Made at a cost of £10,000, a large sum then, at Hepworth's Walton-on-Thames studio with outdoor locations at Hartsbourne Manor, Hertfordshire, and Lulworth Cove, Dorset, it was one of the first productions in Europe or America of such length. It was cut by ten minutes for re-release in the 1920s. Fortunately, a copy of this print was discovered by Forbes-Robertson's son-in-law in 1958. He presented it to Britain's National Film Archive. A specialist audience which included Laurence Olivier and John Gielgud, saw a special screening of it at Britain's National Film Theatre, London, on the night of Monday, April 25, 1960. A number of different length versions appear to exist and one source quotes the original release length as 5800 ft. (1768 m.) which would produce a shorter running time that that quoted above.

Forbes-Robertson retired officially the year the film was made. He was one of the greatest actors of the period and had been trained by Sir Henry Irving at the Lyceum Theatre, London, in the 1880s in the presentation of Shakespeare. His wife, Gertrude Elliott played Ophelia in the film.

The film was generally greeted with considerable acclaim both by the public and critics.

HAMLET
(U.S.A., 1913)

p.c. *Vitagraph.*
d. *James Stuart Blackton.*
l.p. *James Young (Hamlet); Clara Kimball Young (Ophelia); Charles Kent(Polonius); Julia Swayne-Gordon (Gertrude); Harry Morey; Maurice Costello; Arthur Cozing (Laertes).*
b.w. 15 mins. Sil.

This was one of a number of essentially complete versions of Shakespearean plays produced by this company in the early days of the cinema.

HAMLET
(U.S.A., 1913)

p.c. *Various.*
d. *Various.*
l.p. *Various.*
b.w. 11 mins. Sil.

This is listed as being shown. It seems it was a compilation of clips from unidentified films about the subject.

HAMLET
(G.B., 1914)

p.c. *Eric Williams Speaking Pictures.*
d. *Eric Williams.*
l.p. *Eric Williams (Hamlet).*
b.w. (?) mins. Sil. (see text)

While this was being shown, Eric Williams recited from the stage. One of a series following the same format, it was intended to bring famous scenes from literature and the theatre to a wider public. Williams was a former principal of Worthing Collegiate, England, but then turned to being a professional elocutionist. Other films by him appear appropriately elsewhere.

AMLETO
(Italy, 1914)

p.c. *Società Ambrosio.*
d. *Arrigo Frusta.*
l.p. *Arthur Hamilton Revelle (Hamlet).*
b.w. (?) mins. Sil.

Not in the Bernardini listing of the Italian silent films, an American source notes the director as Arturo Ambrosio which may have been the result of confusion with the name of the director with the producer and the actor.

HAMLET
(France, 1914)

p.c. *Film D'Art.*
d. *André Calmettes.*
l.p. *Paul Mounet-Sully (Hamlet).*
b.w. (?) mins. Sil.

This may have been produced in 1913.

AMLETO
(Italy, 1917)

p.c. *Rodolfi Film.*
d. *Eleuterio Rodolfi.*
l.p. *Ruggero Ruggeri (Hamlet); Elena Markowska (Ophelia); A.Martelli (Claudius); Armand Pouget (Ghost); Mercedes Brignone (Gertrude); Gerardo Penia (Laertes).*
b.w. 7448 ft. (2270 m.) Sil.

A more-or-less complete version of the play, this contains some striking scenes and trick effects. Ruggeri was a noted, if somewhat flamboyant and theatrical, actor in his own land at the time. Despite his style, his performance is noted as being impressive.

HAMLET
(Germany, 1920)

p.c. *Art Film.*
d. *Sven Gade, Heinz Schall.*
l.p. *Asta Nielsen (Hamlet); Paul Conraid (Ghost); Mathilde Brandt (Gertrude); Eduard von Winterstein (Claudius); Heinz Stieda (Horatio); Hans Junkermann (Polonius); Anton de Verdie (Laertes); Lilly Jacobsson (Ophelia); Fritz Achterberg (Fortinbras).*
b.w. 136 mins. Sil.

As the King of Denmark lies wounded in battle, his wife, Gertrude, gives birth to a girl but says it is a boy to preserve succession of the crown. Hamlet grows up disguised as a boy and returns from college when her father dies, the consequence of a plot by Gertrude and Claudius, the King's brother. The couple marry with Claudius taking the crown and a voice tells Hamlet to revenge her father. She feigns madness and courts Ophelia to thwart Horatio who loves Ophelia because Hamlet loves Horatio herself. Hamlet enlists a group of players to re-enact her father's death. She fails to kill Claudius but kills Polonius, Ophelia's father, instead. Claudius sends Hamlet to Norway with orders (which she changes) that she is to be killed. She is greeted by Fortinbras, her friend, and the Norwegians invade Denmark. Ophelia drowns and Hamlet sets fire to the castle killing Claudius. Gertrude and Laertes plan Hamlet's death in a duel and she is mortally wounded. While Gertrude accidentally takes poison, Hamlet's true sex is revealed. She dies in Horatio's arms professing her love for him.

Danish actress Asta Nielsen followed Sarah Bernhardt in playing the male lead in this. She was exploring the idea that Hamlet was really a woman whose sex had been disguised so that she could inherit the Danish throne. This theme was attributed to an American scholar, Dr. Edward P. Vining, in a book by him. The story owes much to the original Danish legend.

Art Film was Miss Nielsen's own company and this was the first film made by it. There appears to be some mystery over the original length of the film. The above running time is from a German source but an English source notes the original length as 7764 ft. (2367 m.) and thus about ten minutes shorter. The version currently shown runs about seventy-three minutes.

For the American opening of the film, music was provided by Herman Hand who conducted an augmented orchestra and the film attracted the public. Director Ernst Lubitsch called Miss Nielsen "art itself" although he clearly had a stronger vested interest in the German star Pola Negri who was a bigger attraction commercially though maybe not artistically.

Shown as part of the Everybody's Shakespeare International Festival, London, England, 1994.
Shown at the Shakespeare Film Festival, Wiesbaden, W. Germany, 1964.

"Late-expressionistic interpretation of the Hamlet theme with exquisite décor and elaborate picture composition..." – 'Lexikon Filme Im Fernsehen'.

aka: HAMLET: THE DRAMA OF VENGEANCE

KHUN-E-NAHAK
(India, 1928)

p.c. *Excelsior Film.*
d. *Dada Athavale?*
l.p. *Yakhal; Rampyari; K.C. Roy.*
b.w. Feature. Sil.

This is noted as being an Indian (dialect for the intertitles unknown, but possibly initially Hindi) version of HAMLET. No further details are available of this, the first of a number of versions of the play from this country.

aka: HAMLET

HAMLET
(U.S.A., 1933)

p.c. *R.K.O./Pioneer.*
d. *Robert E. Jones, Margaret Carrington.*
l.p. *John Barrymore (Hamlet); Irving Pinchel; Reginald Denny; Donald Crisp.*
Technicolor. 5 mins.

Though, for obvious reasons, never commercially shown, it is worth including this screen test for a proposed production of the play which was never completed. The featured extracts are from Act I, Scene 2, and Act II, Scene 2. Some sources give a running time of ten minutes.

KHOON KA KHOON
(India, 1935)

p.c.	*Stage Films/Minerva Movietone.*
d.	*Sohrab Merwanji Modi.*
l.p.	*Sohrad Merwanji Modi (Hamlet); Naseem Banu (Ophelia); Shamshadbai (Gertrude); Fazal Karim; Ghulam Hussein; Obali Mai; Shamshad; Gauhar; Ghulam Mohiyuddin; Rampiary; Eruch Tarapore.*
b.w. 122 mins.

This Indian version, in Urdu, won much acclaim for its dialogue at the time of its release.

Reported as being a film version of the stage performance which was noted for the performance by Modi, he dominated even the performances of his two female co-stars whom he used from his previous stage production. He was a leading director of the era in India specialising in screen versions of his own performances and epic films which were Muslim orientated.

HAMLET
(G.B., 1948)

p.c.	*Two Cities.*
d.	*Laurence Olivier.*
l.p.	*Laurence Olivier (Hamlet); Eileen Herlie (Gertrude); Basil Sydney (Claudius); Norman Wooland (Horatio); Jean Simmons (Ophelia); Felix Aylmer (Polonius); Terence Morgan (Laertes); Stanley Holloway (Grave-digger); John Laurie (Francisco); Esmond Knight (Bernardo); Anthony Quayle (Marcellus); Niall McGinnis (Captain); Harcourt Williams (Player); Peter Cushing (Osric); Russell Thorndyke (Priest); Tony Tarver (Player);Christopher Lee; Anthony Bushell; John Gielgud (Voice of Ghost).*
b.w. 155 mins.

One of the most important screen adaptations of Shakespeare, this was filmed in black and white as Olivier saw Hamlet as "an engraving rather than a painting". Olivier trimmed the text, excising some of the sub-plots (Rosencrantz and Guildenstern do not appear, for example). Even so, the cost still ran to double the budget. Some American sources state that the film was not successful as a major release, yet the magazine 'Variety' reported its box-office takings for America in 1948 as $3,250,000, sharing seventeenth position for the year with *Key Largo*. Olivier once again teamed with English composer William Walton for the incidental music some of which may have been available on the old 78 r.p.m. records (RCA notes releases of the music) and Walton made a recording of it conducting the Philharmonia Orchestra along with other works he did for **HENRY V** and **RICHARD III** (Issued on British H.M.V. Concert Classics). The same company also issued "Walton: Music for Shakespearean Films" which featured the "Funeral March" and "Hamlet and Ophelia (a poem for orchestra)". Sir Charles Groves was the conductor of the Royal Liverpool Philharmonic Orchestra for this recording. A more modern recording was released by the British Chandos company in the early 1990s with Neville Marriner conducting the Academy of St. Martin-in-the-Fields with John Gielgud as narrator.

A book, 'The Film Hamlet', was published at the time. Well illustrated, it was a series of essays on various aspects of the film's production. Olivier wrote the Preface to it.

Subsequent to the death of Olivier, both San Marino and Sierra Leone issued commemorative stamps. The San Marino set was called "I Grandi dello Spettacolo" and the L600 value stamp featured the actor in a scene from the film. The much larger set from Sierra Leone presented a miniature sheet (value Le250) of Olivier in the film. It bore the apt quotation "Goodnight sweet Prince".

Shown as part of the Everybody's Shakespeare International Festival, London, England, 1994.

Shown at the Shakespeare Film Festival, Wiesbaden, W. Germany, 1964.

Academy of Motion Picture Arts and Sciences, U.S.A., 1948: Nominations – Best Director (Laurence Olivier), Best Supporting Actress (Jean Simmons), Best Score of a Dramatic or Comedy Picture (William Walton); Awards – Best Picture; Best Actor (Laurence Olivier), Best Art Direction/Set Direction (Roger K. Furse, Carmen Dillon), Best Costume Design (black and white film) (Roger K. Furse).

British Film Academy, G.B., 1948: Best Film.

Círculo de Escritores Cinematigráficos, Spain, 1949: Best Foreign Film.

Hollywood Foreign Press Association Golden Globe Awards, U.S.A., 1948: Best Motion Picture-Foreign; Best Actor (Laurence Olivier).

Kinema Jumpo Annual Best Ten Films, Japan, 1949: Listed fourth.

National Board of Review Awards, U.S.A., 1948: Listed in Ten Best Films.

New York Film Critics Awards, U.S.A., 1948: Best Actor (Laurence Olivier).

'New York Times' Annual Ten Best List, U.S.A., 1948: Listed sixth.

'Picturegoer' magazine annual award, G.B., 1949.

Union of Danish Film Critics, Denmark, 1949: Foreign Film award.

Venice Film Festival, Italy, 1948: Best Film, International Grand Prize, Best Actress (Jean Simmons), Best Photography (Desmond Dickison).

"...impressive and provocative film." – Roger Manvell, 'Penguin Film Review No.8'.

"Unsurpassable adaptation of the Shakespeare classic." – 'Guía De Espectador' (Club Express), Spain.

The première of the film was attended by the Queen of England (now the Queen Mother) and members of the British Government. This event was covered – and it seems appropriate to include it here – by:

BRITISH MOVIETONE NEWS Vol. 20 No. 988 (G.B., 1948)

About one minute of this black and white newsreel was devoted to the arrival and, later, presentation of the cast to the dignitaries mentioned above.

It is also logical to include the following two short films...

GREAT MOMENTS FROM "HAMLET" (G.B., 1950)

Laurence Olivier presented this release which was intended for the home movie market (8 mm. and, logically, 16 mm.). Produced by the Rank Organisation, Jean Simmons, Felix Aylmer and Terence Morgan were also featured along with Olivier. The film lasts nine minutes.

SETS AND COSTUMES FOR "HAMLET" (G.B., 1948)

A documentary about the making of the sets and costumes for the film, Laurence Olivier is noted as the director. Scenes from the six-minute film in black and white are featured. Another short which appears to date from 1950 about Elsinore covers the same ground and may be a re-compilation or reissue.

...and the longer

HAMLET
(credits as for the feature film) – 51 mins.

This release, probably for study purposes, contains the ghost scene, the closet scene, the grave-diggers' scene and the final duel.

HAMLET AT ELSINORE (Eire, 1951)

p.c.
d. *Hilton Edwards.*
l.p. *Micheál MacLiammóir and the Gate Theatre Company.*
c. *Feature.*

In 1951, the full company went to Elsinore Castle in Denmark to make a film of the stage production of HAMLET. The scenery was simply a platform erected in the castle grounds.

KHOON-E-NAHAG (India, 1954)

p.c. *Hindustan Ehitra.*
d. *Kishore Sahu.*
l.p. *Kishore Sahu (Hamlet); Mala Sinha (Ophelia); Venus Bannerjee (Gertrude); Kamal Jit (Laertes); Hiralal (Claudius); S. Nazir (Polonius).*
b.w. 127 mins.

This Urdu version of the play received a unanimous critical and public verdict in its country of origin upon release – it was a gigantic flop!

aka: HAMLET

RÉPÉTITION CHEZ JEAN LOUIS BARRAULT (France, 196?)

p.c.
d. *Robert Hessens.*
l.p. *Jean Louis Barrault; Mme. Daste Gilabert.*
b.w. 19 mins.

A rehearsal (well, part of it) of HAMLET is seen on the stage of the Théâtre de France.

HAMLET (W. Germany, 1962)

p.c. *Bavaria Atelier.*
d. *Franz Peter Wirth.*
l.p. *Maximillian Schell (Hamlet); Wanda Roth (Gertrude); Dunja Movar (Ophelia); HansCaninberg (Claudius); Franz Schafheitlin (Polonius); Dieter Kirchlechner (Laertes);Karl Michael Vogel (Horatio); Herbert Bottcher (Guildenstern); Karl Lieffen (Osric);Eckard Dux (Rosencrantz); Rolf Boysen (Bernardo); Michael Paryla (Francisco); Paul Verhoeven (Grave-digger); Alexander Engel (Ghost); Adolf Gerstung (Player).*
b.w. 130 mins.

Based on A. W. von Schlegel's translation of the Shakespeare play, this was originally made for television. It was shown theatrically in America where it was dubbed back into English!

Shown at the San Francisco Film Festival, U.S.A., 1962.
Shown at the Shakespeare Film Festival, Wiesbaden, W. Germany, 1964.

GAMLET (U.S.S.R., 1964)

p.c. *Lenfilm.*
d. *Grigori Kozintsev.*
l.p. *Innokenti Smoktunovsky (Hamlet); Anastasia Vertinskaya (Ophelia); Michale Nazwanov (Claudius); Elza Radzin-Szolkonis (Gertrude); Yuri Tolbeyev (Polonius); V. Erenberg (Horatio); A.Krevald (Fortinbras); S. Oleksenko (Laertes); I. Dmitriev (Guildenstern); V. Medvedev (Rosencrantz); V. Chekoerski, V. Kolpakor (Grave-diggers); A. Lauter (Priest); R. Aren, A. Chekaerskii, Y. Berkun (Actors); B. Ilyasov; P. Kilgas; Andrei Popov; N. Kuzmin; B. Moreno; F. Fedorovsky; V. Shchennikov.*
b.w. 150 mins. Sovscope.

This Russian version, made in celebration of the four hundredth anniversary of the birth of Shakespeare, is based on Boris Pasternak's translation and has the benefit of an excellent score by Dmitri Shostakovich which was performed by the Leningrad State Orchestra. It is both effective and authentic, often inspired by early Elizabethan music. The film itself may not offer anything new in the character of the subject though the director said that he had tried to rescue the character from the Freudian complexes imposed upon him by twentieth century actors and given back to the tragedy its essential conflict of reason and sentiment. There are some splendid, imaginative moments in the film with photography which is often sombre and atmospheric.

Shostakovich's score gave form to a suite of the incidental music which was recorded by the National Philharmonic Orchestra conducted by Bernard Hermann, the first recording of it in the west. It is to be found on the English Decca release "Music From Great Shakespearean Films". The music was combined with that for a stage production by the same composer to form the basis of a colour ballet film made by Ekran for Russian television in 1969. S. Evlachishvili directed the film with Maris Liepa as Hamlet and Irina Kholina as Ophelia.

The film's director set out his views on his work in the book 'Shakespeare: Time and Conscience' and in an interview with Kira Kulikova in 1963. He said: "One of the hardest knots in writing the script was the question of what cuts to make in the text. The screen cannot vie with the stage in carrying over the entire text. It has to be abridged.".

A 1966 set of two stamps to commemorate the Soviet cinema featured a scene from this film on the 10K value stamp.

Shown as part of the Everybody's Shakespeare International Festival, London, England, 1994.
Shown at the London Film Festival, England, 1964.
Shown at the New York Film Festival, U.S.A., 1964.
British Film Institute Council Annual Film Award, G.B., 1964.
Lenin Prizes, U.S.S.R., 1965: Best Director (Grigori Kozintsev), Best Actor (Innokenti Smoktunovsky).
National Board of Review Awards, U.S.A., 1966: Listed in Best Foreign Films section.
Soviet Film Festival, Leningrad, U.S.S.R., 1964: Special Jury Prize, Best Film Score (Dmitri Shostakovich), Soviet Guild of Artists Diploma for Art Direction (E. Ene, G. Kropachev).
Shakespeare Film Festival, Weisbaden, W. Germany, 1964: Gold Medal.
Sovyetski Ekran Poll, U.S.S.R., 1964: Best Film; Best Actor (Innokenti Smoktunovsky).
Venice Film Festival, Italy, 1964: Special Jury Prize.

"...possibly the finest Shakespearean film yet..." – Roger Manvell writing in 1966 in his book, 'New Cinema In Europe'.

HAMLET
(U.S.A., 1964)

p.c. *Electronovision.*
d. *Bill Colleran (supervisory).*
l.p. *Richard Burton (Hamlet); Eileen Herlie (Gertrude); Alfred Drake (Claudius); William Redfield (Guildenstern); Hume Cronyn (Polonius); George Rose (Grave-digger); George Voskovec (Player); Philip Coolidge (Voltimand); John Cullem (Laertes); Michael Ebert (Francisco); Dillon Evans (Osric/ Reynaldo); Clement Fowler (Rosencrantz); Barnard Hughes (Marcellus/Priest); Linda Marshall (Ophelia); Geoff Garland (Lucanius); Robert Milli (Horatio); Frederick Young (Bernardo); John Gielgud (Ghost); Hugh Alexander; John Etherington; Christopher Culkin; Richard Sterne; Alex Giannini; Carol Teitel; Claude Harz; Gerome Ragni; Linda Seff.*
b.w. 199 mins. Electronovision

The importance of this is as a record of an historic production. It was filmed over two performances – June 30 and July 1, 1964 – at the Lunt-Fontaine Theatre, New York City, U.S.A. The production was by John Gielgud who also directed the stage play with the resultant expected standard. Fifteen cameras were used in the filming which leaves something to be desired in the end result. It was apparently shown on a two-nights-only basis throughout America on a limited release concept from September 1964. It was first shown in Britain at the Shakespeare Film Festival, 1972. It has recently been restored and made available again.

"...a fascinating record of a splendid performance." – Clive Hirschhorn, 'The Warner Bros. Story'.

HAMILE
(Ghana, 1965)

p.c. *Ghana Film Industry.*
d. *Terry Bishop.*
l.p. *Kofi Middleton-Mends (Hamile-Hamlet); Joe Akonor (King-Claudius); Martin Owusu(Karim-Horatio); Ernest Abbeyquaye (Ibrahim-Polonius); Fred Akuffo-Lartey (Osuru-Osric); Gad Gadugan (Abdulai-Rosencrantz, Guildenstern); Kofi Yirenskyi (Laitu- Laertes); Jacob Gharbin (Musa-Marcellus); Franklin Akrofi (Bando-Bernardo); Kwame Adunuo (Mahama-Francisco); Frances Sey (Queen-Gertrude); Mary Yirenkyi (Habiba-Ophelia); Samuel Adumuah (Awudu-Reynaldo); Sandy Arkhurst (Ghost); Auhofe Okuampa, Shanco Bruce (Grave-diggers).*
b.w. 120 mins.

Curiosity is probably the main value of this version. The words, in original English, and actions are truly Shakespeare's but the setting and dress is of the then contemporary Ghana though Tongo instead of Denmark is used for the scene. For local understanding the character's names have been changed and certain minor references have been altered for the same reason. The final result is clearly what it is – a film record of the production by the University of Ghana. The director was imported from Britain to guide what was Ghana's first feature film.

Though the use of contemporary local dress raises the question of just where to place this version, the use of the original words and the action tips the scales in favour of this section.

Shown at the Commonwealth Film Festival, G.B., 1965.

HAMLET
(Holland, 1966)

p.c. *Theater Klank en Beeld.*
d. *Hans van den Busken.*
l.p. *Members of Nieuw Rotterdams Toneel featuring: Erik Schneider; Johan Schmitz; Luc Lutz; Lies Franken; Martine Crefcoeur.*
b.w. (?) mins.

In a translation of the text by Bert Voeten, this features four extracts from the play performed by the above under the stage direction of Richard Flink.

HAMLET
(G.B., 1969)

p.c. *Woodfall.*
d. *Tony Richardson.*
l.p. *Nicol Williamson (Hamlet); Anthony Hopkins (Claudius); Judy Parfitt (Gertrude); Ben Aris (Rosencrantz); Marianne Faithfull (Ophelia); Mark Dignam (Polonius); Michael Pennington (Laertes); Gordon Jackson (Horatio); Clive Graham (Guildenstern); Peter Gale (Osric); Roger Livesey (Lucianus/Grave-digger); John Carney (Marcellus/Player); Robin Chadwick (Francisco/Player/Courtier)); John Trenaman (Bernardo/Player/Sailor); Robin Lloyd-Pack (Reynaldo/Player/Courtier); Richard Everett (Player/Courtier); John Railton (Sailor/Courtier); Michael Elphick (Courtier/Captain); Bill Jarvis (Courtier); Ian Collier (Priest/Courtier); Jennifer Tudor (Court Lady); Anjelica Huston (Court Lady); Mark Griffith (Messenger/Courtier).*
Technicolor. 117 mins.

Considered by many as a fine, if controversial, reading, this has inevitably been subject to some cutting. As might be expected with a cast of this pedigree, there are some fine moments and some of the cast are of more than passing interest. Among the latter are Anjelica Huston in an early role and Marianne Faithfull, singer and one-time associate of the Rolling Stones.

THE TRAGICALL HIFSTORIE OF HAMLET PRINCE OF DENMARK
(Canada, 1973)

p.c. *Toronto Theatre Company/Crawley Films.*
d. *René Bonnière.*
l.p. *Rick McKenna (Hamlet 1); Caroline Johnson (Hamlet 2/Ghost); Bryan Eaton (Laertes/Player); Becke Kelle (Gertrude); Dan Hennessey (Claudius); Steven Bush (Polonius/Priest); Linda Certain (Ophelia 1/Ghost); Jan Kudelka (Ophelia 2/Player); Jim Bearden (Fortinbras/Player/Sailor/Guard/Ghost); Michael Rudder (Rosencrantz); Gary Stephens (Horatio); Bill Peden (Guildenstern/Guard); Bembo Davies (Norwegian Captain/ Grave - digger/Player); Richard Ireton (Reynaldo/Osric/ Player/Ghost); Wendy Russell (Ghost/ Player); Chris Bennett (Grave-digger/Player/Guard/ Ghost); Susan Watson (Player).*
Kodak. 170 mins.

A complete version of the play, though it is somewhat modernised.

Certain parts of the text were transformed into song by George Taros. The film was shot (on 16 mm.) using one camera during several different presentations. The film cost $250,000 to make. It does not appear to have been released commercially.

HAMLET
(G.B., 1974)

p.c. *Seabourne Enterprises.*
d. *Peter Seabourne.*
l.p. *Michael Pennington; David Suchet; William Russell; Roy Marsden.*
c. 10 mins.

In this release in the Seabourne series, the contents featured are Act I, Scene 4 and Act V, Scene 1.

HAMLET
(G.B., 1976)

p.c. *Royal College Of Art.*
d. *Celestino Coronado.*
l.p. *Anthony Meyer, David Meyer (Hamlet/ Hamlet's Father); Helen Mirren (Gertude/ Ophelia); Quintin Crisp (Polonius); Barry Stanton (Claudius); Vladek Sheybal (Player/ Player Queen/Lucianus); Valentine Moon; Sally Bentley-Leek; Marina Saura; Johnathan O'Hara; Inno Sorcy; Henry-Jean; Kazimir Janus.*
Eastman Color. 67 mins.

A somewhat experimental and abbreviated version of the play, concentration is put upon the central character as a split personality. Indeed, non-identical twins are used to play Hamlet and the duality is extended by the elision of the Gertrude and Ophelia roles. The result is theatrical, without props and with exaggerated make-up and stylised costumes, staged in lighted areas of dark space. The text stands on its own, well read, as might be expected, by Helen Mirren.

This singular version was originally shot on video over the space of one week and on a budget of £2,500!

Shown at the Berlin Film Festival, W. Germany, 1977.
Shown at the Edinburgh Film Festival, Scotland, 1977.

"In effect, Coronado offers a mosaic of excerpts from HAMLET..." – Tim Pulleine, 'Monthly Film Bulletin', February, 1978.

DOGG'S TROUPE HAMLET
(U.S.A., 1977)

p.c.
d. *Ed Berman.*
l.p. *Jane Gambia; Katina Noble; John Perry.*
c. 15 mins.

This is a record of a performance of the condensed version of HAMLET by Tom Stoppard.

HAMLET
(U.S.A., 1990)

p.c. *Carolco.*
d. *Franco Zeffirelli.*
l.p. *Mel Gibson (Hamlet); Glenn Close (Gertrude); Alan Bates (Claudius); Stephen Dillane (Horatio); Ian Holm (Polonius); Helena Bonham-Carter (Ophelia); Nathaniel Parker (Laertes); John McEnery (Osric); Paul Scofield (Ghost); Sean Murray (Guildenstern); Michael Malony (Rosencrantz); David Duffy (Francisco); Peter Posthelthwaite (Player); Trevor Peacock (Grave-digger); Vernon Bodtcheff (Reynaldo); Christopher Fairbank (Player); Richard Warwick (Bernardo); Christien Anholt (Marcellus); Justin Case; Ned Mendez; Sarah Phillips; Roy York; Marjorie Bell; Roy Evans; Roger Low; Pamela Sinclair; Baby Simon Sinclair.*
c. 134 mins. S

Much the same question was posed by this film as by the M.G.M. 1953 version of **JULIUS CAESAR**. How would an essentially non-Shakespearean actor (and, in the case, an actress as well) cope with their roles? The general opinion was that they did so with honour surrounded as they were by some quality British acting support. The presence of the two stars made it possible to get together the $15,500,000 for this. Both took relatively modest salaries to help the budget. Gibson said that at age thirty-four if he had not made the film then, he would have been too old for the role. Director Zeffirelli had already made a notable **ROMEO AND JULIET** and here again did not look too closely for deep interpretive roles though some were forthcoming from some of the supporting cast. On its own level, the film has its value and an admirable music score, released on the Virgin Movie Music label, by Ennio Morricone who is perhaps best known for his work with spaghetti westerns. HBO made a self-explanatory short called **THE MAKING OF HAMLET** which, in view of the nature of the producer, was, logically, for television.

Shown as part of the Everybody's Shakespeare International Festival, London, England, 1994.
Academy of Motion Picture Arts and Sciences, U.S.A., 1991: Nominations – Best Art Direction (Dante Ferretti, Francisco lo Schiavo), Best Costume Design (Maurizio Millenotti).
National Board of Review, U.S.A., 1990: Listed second in Ten Best Films In English list.

"A spirited and colourful version." – James Cameron-Wilson, 'Film Review 1991/2'.

"He (Zeffirelli) has modernized the dialogue to adapt it to the public of today, very different to those people of the seventeenth century, so that young people may discover this great work by means of his film." – 'Cinetotal', Year 1, Number 3.

"...vigorous, workmanlike version of Shakespeare's tragedy." – 'Film Review Special No.2', 1993.

H FOR HAMLET
(Eire, 1993)

p.c. *Murphy/Thunder Productions.*
d. *Vinny Murphy.*
l.p. *Darren Monks (Hamlet); Rachel Meehan (Gertrude); Vinny Murphy (Claudius); Gavin Kelty (Laertes); Michelle Bardon (Ophelia); Daren Kenny (Horatio); Olivia Burke (Osric); Jack Lynch (Polonius); Derek Reid (Bernardo); Gerry Lee (Marcellus); Paul Conway (Player King); Suzanne O'Neill (Player Queen); Aishling Brereton, Maureen Cleary (Grave-diggers); Louise Gaffney (Player); Jennifer O'Neill (Priest).*
c. 77 mins.

Advised as being a community project, it is also given as an adaptation of the play. This would seem logical in view of the running time which would obviously mean a shortened text and the excision of some of the characters. The film has had a number of festival showings, mainly in Eire (Dublin Film Festival, Junior Dublin Film Festival and Cork International Film Festival) and Cinemagic, all, presumably, in 1993 or 1994.

HAMLET
(U.S.A., 1996)

p.c. *Castle Rock Entertainment.*
d. *Kenneth Branagh.*
l.p. *Kenneth Branagh (Hamlet); Derek Jacobi (Claudius); Julie Christie (Gertrude); Richard Briers (Polonius); Brian Blessed (Ghost); Michael Maloney (Laertes); Nicholas Farrell (Horatio); Kate Winslet (Ophelia); Charlton Heston (Player King); Rosemary Harris (Player Queen); Rufus Sewell (Fortinbras); Robin Williams (Osric); Timothy Spall (Rosencrantz); Reece Dinsdale (Guildenstern); Jack Lemmon (Marcellus); Billy Crystal, Simon Russell Beale (Grave-diggers); Richard Attenborough (English Ambassador); Ian McElhinney (Bernardo);*

Gérard Depardieu (Reynaldo); Ray Fearon (Francisco); Ravil Isyanov (Cornelius); Don Warrington (Voltemand); John Mills (Old Norway); Michael Bryant (Priest); Ken Dodd (Yorick); Sian Radinger (Prologue); Charles Daish (Stage Manager); Rob Edwards (Lucianus); Ben Thom, Perdita Weeks (Players); Jimi Mistry, David Yip (Sailors); Andrew Schofield (Young Lord); John Gielgud (Priam); Jeffrey Kissoon (Fortinbras' Captain); Judi Dench (Hecuba); Orlando Seale (Boatman); Melanie Ramsay (Prostitute); Tom Szekeres (Young Hamlet); Yvonne Gidden (Doctor); Angela Douglas, Sarah Lam (Attendants to Gertrude); Rowena King (Attendant to Gertrude/ Messenger); Peter Bygott, Riz Abbasi (Attendants to Claudius); David Blair (Attendant to Claudius/Servant); Duke of Marlborough (Fortinbras' General).
c. 242 mins. S 70mm. Scope.

Adapted by Branagh, this is set in the much later era of the last century and is rather unconventional. The accomplished end result is still Shakespeare, is beautifully mounted and in virtually full measure, too. However, the general distribution version runs one hundred and fifty minutes. Sony Classics issued the record of the film soundtrack.

Shown at the Cannes Film Festival, France, 1997. Academy of Motion Picture Arts and Sciences, U.S.A., 1996: Nominations – Best Soundtrack (Patrick Doyle), Best Adapted Screenplay (Kenneth Branagh), Best Art/Set Direction (Tim Harvey); Best Costume Design (Alex Byrne).

"The film, like the play, will have something for everyone" says Branagh. "It's a ghost story, a thriller, an action-packed murder mystery and a great tragedy that is profoundly moving. It is also extremely witty and I hope it will be thoroughly entertaining." – Pre-completion press release from Castle Rock Pictures.

✦ ✦ ✦ ✦ ✦

ÊTRE OU ÊTRE PAS
(France, 1914)

p.c.
d. *Léonce Perret.*
l.p. *Suzanne Grandais.*
b.w. (?) mins. Sil.

Though a number of sources refer to this film, details of it have been almost impossible to trace. It is suggested that it is taken from the play albeit in parody form. This may not even be the film's correct title.

HAMLET
(G.B., 1915)

p.c. *Lion's Head/Cricks and Martin.*
d. *W. P. Kellino.*

l.p.
b.w. 882 ft. (269 m.) Sil.

One thing is certain – it would be a big mistake to expect anything serious as "Mudford Amateur Dramatic Society" stages the play. The village doctor playing Claudius is called away and changes into his normal clothes during the play; the ghost sticks to the trap door; Ophelia is revealed in her dressing gown as the scenery collapses; Hamlet fails to stab himself and is pelted with eggs by the audience.

AMLETO E IL SUO CLOWN
(Italy, 1919)

p.c. *D'Ambra.*
d. *Carmine Gallone.*
l.p. *Soave Gallone (Alexandra); Luciano Molinari.*
b.w. 6365 ft. (1940 m.) Sil.

Alexandra is horrified to find her father dead in his carriage when it returns home. Two months later her mother marries John, an old family friend. Alexandra sees a parallel to the HAMLET story and, at a garden party, she uses clowns to give a version of the play scene from HAMLET. She imagines she sees guilt in John's manner and stabs him to death. Whilst under arrest, a young farmer confesses to the murder of her father. Alexandra attempts to kill herself, recovers and joins a circus with success. Invited home by her mother, she jumps to her death.

Was Soave Gallone, the wife of the director, the first female, modern dress HAMLET? No matter for the film was well received.

A SAGEBRUSH HAMLET
(U.S.A., 1919)

p.c. *Exhibitors Mutual?*
d. *Joseph J. Franz.*
l.p. *Marguerite de la Motte; William Desmond; Florence Gibson; Edward Peel.*
b.w. 5 reels. Sil.

A young man seeks vengeance against the desperado who killed his father.

Apart from the title connotation, it is trying the imagination to include this western as Shakespearean inspired. Even the revenge theme is hardly from HAMLET.

STRANGE ILLUSION
(U.S.A., 1945)

p.c. *P.R.C.*
d. *Edgar G. Ulmer.*
l.p. *James Lydon (Paul Cartwright); Sally Eilers (His Mother); Warren William (Brett Curtis); Regis Toomey.*
b.w. 85 mins.

Paul Cartwright dreams that his father's death was no accident. Returning home from school, he finds his mother and sister both infatuated by a stranger, Brett Curtis, whom Paul mentally links with a Claude

Barrington assumed killed in a mine disaster. Paul has a breakdown and visits a doctor friend of Curtis. While out for a horse ride, Paul finds a clue that, subconsciously, leads to evidence of Curtis' guilt.

A B-movie from one of the lesser Hollywood studios, this is noted as being a modern version of HAMLET by a number of sources. Well, that may be something of an exaggeration but the film certainly has a number of plot/character similarities.

IO, AMLETO
(Italy, 1952)

p.c. *Macario Film.*
d. *Giorgio C. Simonelli.*
l.p. *Erminio Macario (Amleto); Rossana Podestà (Ofelia); Franca Marzi (Gertrud); Adriano Rimoldi (Laerte); Luigi Pavese (Claudius); Giuseppe Porelli (Polonio); Marisa Merlini; Virgilio Riento; Carlo Rizzo; Alfredo Varelli; Silvio Noto; Guido Riccoli; Giancarla Vessio; Manlio Busoni; Marisa D'Auro; Aldo Majocchi; Sergio Bergonzelli; Elena Giusti.*
b.w. 103 mins.

Hamlet meets his father's ghost and learns how his uncle killed his father. The young Prince lives in fear but is very cautious and has to take refuge until he can at last outwit his enemies and become king of Denmark.

The film is also noted in a shorter version of eighty-nine minutes.

"Shakespearean parody, rather weak and in dubious taste..." – 'Intermezzo' July/August, 1953.

AASHA
(India, 1957)

p.c. *Raman Studios.*
d. *M.V. Raman.*
l.p. *Vyjayanthumala; Kishore Kumar; Pran; Raj Mohra; Minoo Mumtaz; Randhir Naima; Shivray Patanjal; Lalita Pawar; Om Prakash.*
b.w. and c. 171 mins.

An old man's son is accused of a crime but a cousin of the boy is the real evil force. The old man, disguised as an Arab, sets up a play to reveal the truth.

This Hindi film is hardly direct from Shakespeare but it does have overtones of the HAMLET theme.

DER REST IST SCHWEIGEN
(W. Germany, 1959)

p.c. *Freie Film Production.*
d. *Helmut Käutner.*
l.p. *Hardy Krüger (John H. Claudius); Peter van Eyck (Paul Claudius); Ingrid Andree (Fee (von Pohl); Adelheid Seeck (Gertude Claudius); Rudolf Forster (Major Horace); Heinz Drache (Herbert von Pohl); Boy Gobert; Rainer Penkert; Charles Regnier; Reinhold Nietschmann; Richard Allen; Robert Meyn.*
b.w. 104 mins.

In the Ruhr industrial area of Germany, the death of one of two brothers is shrouded in mystery. The dead man's business is taken over by his brother which leads to the return from America of John, the dead man's son. John's widowed mother has also married his uncle. With help, John probes his father's death. He arranges a ballet called "The Murder Of A Brother" to help solve the mystery.

The title translates as "The rest is silence", Hamlet's last words. Of this modern-day version, Käutner said: "This is not Shakespeare in a dinner jacket but the whole story seen in modern terms."

Shown at the Berlin Film Festival, W. Germany, 1959.
Shown at the Shakespeare Film Festival, Wiesbaden, W. Germany, 1964.

"More Hitchcock, less full of itself, it would have been better." – Christa Bandmann, Joe Hembus, 'Klassiker Des Deutschen Tonfilms 1930-1960'.

aka: EL RESTO ES SILENCIO

WARUI YATSU YOKU NEMURU
(Japan, 1960)

p.c. *Kurosaw-Toho.*
d. *Akira Kurosawa.*
l.p. *Toshiro Mifune (Koichi Nishi); Masayuki Mori; Takashi Kato; Takasi Shimura; Akira Nishimura; Chishu Ryu.*
b.w. 151 mins. Tohoscope.

Based on HAMLET, this is a thriller about corruption in big business in which a rather subdued man marries in order to expose his father-in-law whom he believes is responsible for the death of his own father. The film is rather let down by its ending.

Some prints appear to have been cut to one hundred and thirty-five minutes.

Shown at the Berlin Film Festival, W. Germany, 1961.

"Kurosawa effectively captures the spirit of the 1940s Warner Bros, crime dramas..." – Leonard Maltin, 'Movie And Video Guide'.

aka: THE BAD SLEEP WELL; LES SALAUDS DORMENT EN PAIX

HAMLET ACT
(U.S.A., 1962)

p.c. *University Of Wisconsin – Milwaukee Film Group.*
d. *Robert Nelson.*

l.p. *Dick Blau; Dave Fisher; Bob Whitney; Tom Mulvey.*

b.w. 21 mins. Sil.

This experimental, avant-garde short presumably had university showings.

OPHÉLIA
(France, 1962)

p.c. *Boréal.*

d. *Claude Chabrol.*

l.p. *André Jocelyn (Yvan); Alida Valli (Claudia); Claude Cerval (Adrien); Juliette Mayniel (Lucie); Robert Bernier (André); Jean-Louis Maury (Sparkos); Pierre Vernier (Paul); Serge Bento (François); Liliane David (Ginette); Sacha Briquet (Grave-digger).*

b.w. 105 mins.

Yvan, eccentric son of a wealthy industrialist, is concerned about his father's death and his mother's marriage to his uncle, Adrien. In their heavily guarded mansion, Yvan taunts his mother and stepfather and finds solace with Lucie, daughter of an estate agent, André, who disapproves of the liaison. After seeing Olivier's **HAMLET**, Yvan senses a parallel with his own situation and makes a short film, the content of which upsets his mother and stepfather. Adrien tries to kill Yvan but, having failed, commits suicide though, before dying, he tells Yvan that neither his mother nor he himself was responsible for Yvan's father's death but he, Adrien, had been made to feel guilty. Yvan, guilt-ridden, consoles himself with Lucie who assures him of his true self.

Chabrol had a number of difficulties financing this film and asked bitterly: "What do you think of a film world where you can easily make a film about a twist or rock star in 'scope and colour, and which presents so much difficulty in making a film like my OPHÉLIA? Just think of the difficulty I've had."

INMOLACION DE HAMLET
(Colombia, 1967)

p.c.

d. *Mario Mitrotti.*

l.p.

c. Short.

This 16 mm. film was an early work by the director who went on to more substantial film making in his own country. The content of the film is not known but the title translates as "The Immolation (Sacrifice) of Hamlet".

ITHELE NA YINI VASILIAS
(Greece, 1967)

p.c.

d. *Angelos Theodoropoulos.*

l.p. *Angelos Theodoropoulos; Anna Iasonidou; Giorgos Valengas; Gikas Biniaris; Athina Michaelidou; Likourgos Kallergis; Nikos Paschalides.*

b.w. 90 mins.

A free version of the play, the action is transposed to modern Greece.

The title translates as "He Wanted to be King".

QUELLA SPORCA STORIA DEL WEST
(Italy, 1967)

p.c. *Daiano/Leone.*

d. *Enzo G. Castellani (Enzo Girolami).*

l.p. *Andrea Giordano (Johnny/Hamlet); Gilbert Roland (Horace/Horatio); Ignazio Spalla(Gil/Guildenstern): Horst Frank (Claude/Claudius); Françoise Prévost (Gertrude); Enio Girolami (Ross/Rosencrantz); Gabriela Grimaldi (Ophelia); Stefania Careddu (Player); Giorgio Sanmartin (Polonio); Franco Latini; Fabio Patella; John Bartha; Franco Leo; Manuel Serrano.*

Technicolor. 98 mins. Techniscope.

Based on the HAMLET theme (but with a happy ending), this is a typical "spaghetti western" (a prolific genre at its peak about this time) in which a Texan returns home and gets involved in murder, robbery and torture.

In the 1972 release of the film in America, Giordano took the pseudonym Chip Corman. The film had a working title of "To Kill Or Not To Kill" but the finished title translates as "That Dirty Story Of The West". Sergio Corbucci claimed authorship to the story, adapted from Shakespeare, on which the script is based. Some cutting was suffered by the film in a number of countries for it was reduced to seventy-eight minutes in Germany, to eighty-seven in Spain and ninety-one in America (the Americans also claim co-production credit in some sources).

"Just try and find some iambic pentameter in this dialog." – 'American Film Institute Catalog'.

aka: JOHNNY HAMLET; DJANGO PORT SA CROIX; JOHNNY EL VENGADOR; JOHNNY – DIE TOTENGRÄBER WARTEN SCHON

OFELIAS BLOMSTERS
(Denmark, 1968)

p.c. *Lantern Film A/S for Danish Short Film Committee.*

d. *Jøn Leth.*

l.p. *Lene Adler Petersen (Ofelia).*

c. 7 mins.

As Ophelia gathers her flowers, her shattered world assembles into a bouquet of beautiful flowers and visions. Her incurable sorrow is surrounded by the bloom of spring. The images, vividly clear in her vision, cause reality to float. She walks out into the water singing, her song fading as nature's sounds increase and she is absorbed.

The director and scriptwriters based this on Ophelia's soliloquy. The title translates as "Ophelia's Flowers".

DANS LA POUSSIÈRE DU SOLEIL
(France/Spain, 1971)

p.c. *Kerfrance Production/IMF.*

d. *Richard Balducci.*

l.p. *Maria Schell (Gertie Bradford); Bob Cunningham (Joe Bradford); Daniel Beretta (Hawk Bradford); Karin Meier (Maria); Pépé Calvo (Goldoni); Perla Cristal (Carla); Manuel Otero (Ken); Colin Drake (Edwards); Lorenzo Robledo (Swann); Jack Anton (Flint); Jérôme Jeffrys (Crack); André Thévenet (Monky); Odile Astié; Pilar Vela; Ángel Del Pozo; Santiago Ontanon; Marisa Porcel; Henry Bydon; M. Quesada; Amarilla.*

Eastman Color. 84 mins.

Hawk, considered in San Angelo to be a coward and slightly mad, is incestuously desired by his mother. He seeks revenge for his father who has been murdered by his uncle, Joe. Gertie, Hawk's widowed mother, is forced into marriage by Joe to obtain the dead man's wealth. Hawk is respected by the local drunk and loved by the sheriff's daughter, Maria, but her advances are rejected. After a raid by Joe and his gang on the Swann ranch in which Swann is killed, the bereaved family is housed by Joe and Gertie. Hawk arranges a play about his father's murder which embarrasses Joe and so his gang break up the play. Maria and Hawk escape and make love. Hawk accidentally kills the sheriff who is trying to arrest Joe. Ken, the sheriff's son joins Joe's posse to hunt down Hawk. Hawk rides into town and in a gun battle Hawk, Joe, Ken and Gertie are all killed. Maria dies in a buggy accident.

HAMLET goes West again in another "spaghetti western" with an international cast. French composer Francis Lai was responsible for the pseudo-Ennio Morricone score.

aka: LUST IN THE SUN

A HERANÇA
(Brazil, 1971)

p.c. *Long Films.*

d. *Ozualdo Candeias.*

l.p. *David Cardoso (Hamlet); Bárbara Fázio (Mother); Rosalvo Caçador (Uncle); Américo Taricano (Polonio); Maria Zuleica (Ophelia); Deodides Gouveia (Laertes); Aquado Rayol (Fortinbras); Fernando Lona.*

c.? 87 mins.

Hamlet is the son of a rich farmer and he is in love with a poor black girl, Ofelia. His father and family disapprove of the romance and use every method to thwart the romance.

Brazilian sources note that this is inspired by HAMLET. There are, of course, some similarities to that story but, equally, the film has other Shakespearean overtones from ROMEO AND JULIET.

O JOGO DA VIDA E DA MORTE
(Brazil, 1971)

p.c. *Futura Filmes.*

d. *Mario Kuperman.*

l.p. *Juca de Oliviera (Cláudio); Odete Lara (Gertudes); Walter Cruz (João/Hamlet); Flávio São Tiago (Laerte); Chocolate (Polônio); Iolanda Braga (Ofélia); Benè Silva (Rosa); Rui Rezende (Reinaldo); Flávio Portho (Tostão); Francisco Martins; Ferreira Leite; Paulo Goia; Júlio Cesar; Fernando Benicasa; Lúcia Mello; Lutero Luiz.*

b.w.? 98 mins.

In a suburb of São Paolo, Brazil, João learns through the voice of his father by a medium that Cláudio, the brother of the dead man, was responsible for his death. Full of anguish, the efforts of Ofélia, who loves João, fail to consol him and he arranges a reconstruction of the death to see the reactions of Cláudio. Though convinced of his uncle's guilt, Cláudio has João sent away after João has unfortunately killed Polônio, the father of Ofélia and Laerte. Despite plans to have João killed, Laerte seeks vengeance and this sparks off the inevitable game of life and death.

Here the story is set in modern Brazil and its millieu but remains quite faithful to the story. The film was shortened to ninety minutes for release.

THE MAROWITZ HAMLET
(Holland, 1972)

p.c. *NOS.*

d. *NOS team – Uit de kunst.*

l.p. *Members of the Open Space Theatre Company featuring: David Schofield; Petronella Ford; Kay Barton; Malcolm Storry; Walter Brown; Philip Marchant; Tony Milner; Robin Sachs; Neil Cunningham; Michael O'Donoghue.*

b.w. (?) mins.

In this filmed extract of the stage play, Hamlet is shown as a boastful youth whose deeds never live up to his words. This leads to his being despised and disliked because of his incoherence and muddled thinking.

UN AMLETO DI MENO
(Italy, 1973)

p.c. *Donatello Cinematografica wth assistance from Ministero Turismo e Spettacolo.*

d. *Carmelo Bene.*

l.p. *Carmelo Bene (Hamlet); Lydal Mancinelli (Kate); Alfieri Vincenti (Claudius); Franco Leo (Horatio); Luigi Mezzanotte (Laertes); Pippo Tuminelli (Polonius); Isabella Russo (Ophelia);*

Sergia Di Guilio (William); Luciana Cante (Gertrude).
Technicolor. 73 mins.

This controversial version takes as its source 'The Story Of Hamlet' written by Jacques Laforgue in 1877. As such, for the film is both parody and farce, Shakespeare is the butt of verbal attack. Amidst it all are to be found some excellent sets and costumes, and some nudity.

Obviously something of a personal film, Bene all but monopolised its making being responsible for the music and art direction as well. The film remains a specialist item suitable for those who enjoy satirical, mocking comment on politics, culture and the like. The title translates as ONE HAMLET LESS and may have had release in some countries under this title. Some sources give a playing time of sixty-five minutes.

Shown at the Cannes Film Festival, France, 1973.
Shown at the London Film Festival, England, 1973.

aka: UN HAMLET DE MOINS

PREDSTAVA HAMLETA U MRDUŠA DONJOJ
(Yugoslavia, 1973)

p.c. *Jadran.*
d. *Kristo Papić.*
l.p. *Rade Serbedzija (Son), Milena Dravić (Girl); Zvonko Lepetić (Father); Kreso Zidarić (Boss); Ljubisa Samardzić (Manager).*
Eastman Color. 82 mins.

A town commissar, having heard reports about the play HAMLET, insists it be performed locally despite a protest from a local teacher who says it is little known there and difficult to produce. A local war hero is framed for robbery but released through lack of evidence. His son, certain that the commissar is involved, determines to find out the truth. The boy is betrayed by the girl he loves. She is forced to do so by her father, a crony of the commissar. They all play similar characters in the play and the boy, during the play, gets a confession from the town treasurer by almost choking him. The boy's father commits suicide and the boy stabs the commissar. Later the boy demands a hero's funeral for his father and orders a dance. But the boy is bleeding badly during the festivities...

In this, the director has paralleled the situation in a small town with that of HAMLET and has taken the opportunity to strike out against corruption and the people's attitude to it. Not perhaps the easiest road to take in a country where, at the time, such themes were subject to severe censorship. The title translates as "Performance Of Hamlet in the village of Mrduša Donjoj".

Shown at the Pula Film Festival, Yugoslavia, 1973 (awarded a prize).

Shown at the Sydney Film Festival, Australia, 1975.

aka: A VILLAGE PERFORMANCE OF HAMLET

INTIKAM MELEĞI KADIN HAMLET
(Turkey, 1976)

p.c. *Ugur Film.*
d. *Metin Erksan.*
l.p. *Fatma Girik (Hamlet); Sevda Ferdağ (Gertrude); Ahmet Sezerel (Ophelia); Orçun Sonat (Laertes); Reha Yurdakul (Claudius); Yavuz Selekman (Horatio); Yüksel Gözen (Polonius); Ishan Gedik (Marcellus); Aylan Orlani (Rosencrantz); Senem Kayra (Guildenstern); Baki Tamer; Nevra Serezli; Ahmet Turgutulu; Önder Güç; Ekrem Gökkaya; Coşkun Gögen; Ali Cağaloğlu.*
c. 86 mins.

Here Hamlet is characterised as a woman and, though the basic plot is maintained, the story is transposed to Turkey of 1976 and reflects and criticizes the problems of the country at that time.

After Sarah Bernhardt and Asta Nielsen as female Hamlets comes Fatma Girik. Here the Hamlet is fully female and, of course, her "fiancée", the Ophelia character, is male. The roles, therefore, must not been seen as precise but rather as characterisations and the story as allegorical rather than as a direct adaptation. Though derivative, the work comes from the imagination of director Erksan, a graduate of Istanbul University, a former writer on the cinema and later scriptwriter. The music for the film was by Shostakovich.

aka: HAMLET FEMALE – THE REVENGING ANGEL; ANGEL OF VENGEANCE

OFELIA KOMMER TIL BYEN
(Denmark, 1985)

p.c. *Fogtdal Film and Per Holst Film for The Danish Film Institute and Danish Radio/TV*
d. *Jøn Bang Carlsen.*
l.p. *Reine Brynolfsson (John); Stine Bierlich (Molly); Flemming Jørgensen (Vagn); Ingolf David (Arne); Anna Lise Hirsch Bjerrum (Rita); Else Petersen (Theodora); Hans Chr. Ægidius (Teacher).*
Eastman Color. 97 mins.

In a small Jutland village, John, the son of the village tart, mocked by all, lives a reclusive, tortured life as a grave-digger. He meets Molly, a teenage whore from the city. She is the only one who can play Ophelia and he settles naturally into the role of Hamlet for his life is troubled and he longs for a father. Love grows between them.

Not of course a true HAMLET but certainly within the spirit of the character, this does have the background of the play.

"A small village, with one street, lined with houses is a perfect setting for a story about the tragedy and comedy of this life we are thrown into." – Jøn Bang Carlsen, director of the film.

aka: HAMLET (OPHELIA COMES TO TOWN)

BLUE CITY
(U.S.A., 1986)

p.c. *Paramount.*
d. *Michelle Manning.*
l.p. *Judd Nelson (Billy Turner); Ally Sheedy (Annie); David Caruso (Joey); Paul Winfield (Luther); Scott Wilson (Perry); Anita Morris (Malvina).*
c. 95 mins. S?

Billy returns home after five years away to learn that his father died nine months earlier. He seeks revenge, believing that his stepmother and her associate, Perry, are responsible.

Though based on a book by Ross McDonald, the story influence is clear. The film is said to be awful.

"Senseless and stupid..." – Leonard Maltin, 'Movie And Video Guide'.

aka: CIUDAD PELIGROSA

HAMLET LIIKMAAILMESSA
(Finland, 1987)

p.c. *Villealfa Filmproductions.*
d. *Aki Kaurismäki.*
l.p. *Pirkka-Pekka Petelius (Hamlet); Esko Salminen (Klaus); Kati Outinen (Ophelia); Elina Salo (Gertrud); Esko Nikkari (Polonius); Kari Väänänen (Lauri Polonius); Turo Pajala(Rosencrantz); Hannu Valtonen (Simo); Mari Rantasila (Helena); Pentti Auer (Father/ Ghost); Aake Kalliala (Guildenstern); Matti Pellonpää; Vesa Mäkelä; Maija Leino; Vesa Vierikko; Pertti Sveholm; Miita Sorvali; Sanna Fransman; Erkki Astala; Jouko Mäki; Melrose; Pentti Hirvikangas; Reino Laitinen; Anton Ortamo; Ralf Nordgren; Helmeri Pelonpää; Jarmo Anio; Jalo ja Hallu.*
b.w. 86 mins.

Through Gertrud, Klaus poisons her husband. Her son, Hamlet, wipes the incriminating evidence from the glass. Hamlet inherits 51% of his father's business making him one of the richest men in the country. Klaus becomes company chairman and plans, to Hamlet's disgust, to marry Gertrud. Ophelia, daughter of Klaus' business associate, Polonius, refuses to sleep with Hamlet. Klaus plans some changes within the company about which Hamlet learns. Hamlet sees his father's ghost who wants revenge. Then Hamlet ridicules Ophelia's brother, Lauri, by giving him a toilet as an office. Lauri warns Hamlet not to bother Ophelia who wants to marry Hamlet but whom Hamlet only wants for sex. At a board meeting, Klaus' plans are blocked by Hamlet and Hamlet starts to act strangely. He takes Gertrud and Klaus to a performance of "The Importance Of Being Earnest" which is interrupted by a poisoning scene. Gertrud begs forgiveness after Hamlet has tried to kill Klaus. He accidentally kills Polonius and plans to escape. He rejects Ophelia finally and she commits suicide. Lauri returns bent on revenge but his plan goes wrong and Gertrud is poisoned. Klaus and Lauri are both killed trying to kill Hamlet. Hamlet confesses to his chauffeur, Simo, that he was responsible for his father's death. Simo kills him and destroys his plans for the business.

Finland is not the most prolific of film making countries but, judging by critical response, then quality rather than quantity seems most apt. Not least in this, since the director has chosen the well-trodden path of adapting a Shakespearean theme to modern times. The result is even more remarkable considering that this rather experimental – and thus risky – undertaking cost some £75,000 to make.

Shown at the Barcelona Film Festival, Spain, 1988.
Shown at the Berlin Film Festival, W. Germany, 1988 (very well received).
Shown at the Théâtres Au Cinéma Second Festival, France, 1991.
Filmiaura Ry, Finland, 1987: Art Direction (Pertti Hilkamo)

aka: HAMLET GOES BUSINESS

ROSENCRANTZ AND GUILDENSTERN ARE DEAD
(U.S.A., 1990)

p.c. *Brandenberg International.*
d. *Tom Stoppard.*
l.p. *Gary Oldman (Rosencrantz); Tim Roth (Guildenstern); Richard Dreyfuss (The Player); Joanna Roth (Ophelia); Ian Glen (Hamlet); Donald Sumpter (Claudius); Joanna Miles (Gertrude); Ljubo Zecevic (Osric); Ian Richardson (Polonius); Sve Medvesck (Laertes); Vili Matula (Horatio); John Burgess; Livio Badurina; Tomislav Maretic; Mare Mlacnik; Srdjan; Mladen Vasary; Zeljko Vukmirica; Branko Zavrsan.*
Technicolor. 118 mins.

Hamlet's two friends, Rosencrantz and Guildenstern, are summoned to Elsinore Castle where Claudius has seized the throne on the death of his brother and married his widow, Gertrude. They are to find out why Hamlet, who is after Ophelia, is acting so strangely. Hamlet soon discovers what they are doing and says he acts "mad" when it suits him. A player arrives at the Castle and he and his troupe perform a play designed to trap Claudius into admitting that he murdered the late king. Rosencrantz and Guildenstern receive a warning about their possible fate and they are sent to accompany Hamlet to England. They discover the letter that condemns

Hamlet to death. Hamlet has guessed the plan and, having substituted their names, jumps ship. Guildenstern tries to stab the player but the knife turns out to be a stage prop. The two are hanged.

This is not, of course, Shakespeare's play but the characters in it. The playwright is Tom Stoppard acting for the first time as a screen director bringing to the cinema the play which made him famous in the late 1960s. The film was made in the former Yugoslavia which is reflected in the cast list.

Shown as part of the Everybody's Shakespeare International Festival, London, England, 1994.
Shown at the Muestra Cinematográfica del Atlantico, Alcances, Spain, 1992.
Shown at the Valladolid Film Festival, Spain, 1990.
Venice International Film Festival, Italy, 1990: Golden Lion for Best Film.

"...much more than a burlesque variation of the Shakespeare classic, it is a solid reflection, lucid and intricate, about Destiny and the somewhat ironic game between Reality and Probability." – Daniel Monzon, 'Fotogramas'.

"Hard-going and not for those who are into action rather than words." – 'Satellite TV Europe'.

aka: ROSENCRANTZ Y GUILDENSTERN HAN MUERTO

THE PRINCE OF JUTLAND
(Denmark/France/G.B./Germany, 1993)

p.c. *Les Films Ariane with the support of Eurimages Fund of the Council Of Europe, the Hamburg Film Fund, Danish Film Institute, The European Co-production Fund (U.K.) and the participation of Canal+.*
d. *Gabriel Axel.*
l.p. *Gabriel Byrne (Fenge); Helen Mirren (Geruth); Christian Bale (Amled); Freddie Jones (Bjorn); Steven Waddington (Ribold); Brian Cox (Aetelwine); Kate Beckinsale (Edel); Tony Haygarth (Ragnor); Saskia Wickham (Gumor); Tom Wilkinson; Brian Glover; Mark Williams; Andy Serkis and others.*
Kodak. 106 mins. S

In the realm of Jutland in the sixth century the King and one of his son's are murdered by Fenge, the King's brother. This is witnessed by the other son, Prince Amled, who feigns madness to escape death. Fenge takes the crown and his brother's widow. Unsure of Amled, a plot is laid using a girl to discover if he is mad. The girl falls in love with Amled and does not betray his secret for they become lovers. Another trap is laid for Amled but he kills the spy and tells his mother the truth. She says she will no longer sleep with Fenge and urges Amled to avenge her late husband. When the girl falls pregnant, Fenge is sure that Amled is not mad and sends him to a Scottish duke with two companions. The letter they carry condemns Amled to death but he changes the letter and it is the two men who die. He aids the duke against invaders and marries his daughter. He returns home and takes his revenge.

The story here is not from Shakespeare but it is worth including this stark, powerful drama since it is based on the Danish 'Chronicle Of Saxo Grammaticus', a probable source for Shakespeare. For sure all the elements are here – the king murdered by his brother, the feigned madness, the evil escort for the prince to foreign shores and his document-changing to thwart the plot against him. There are, of course, differences particularly in the events after his arrival in Scotland and the final outcome. Amled, too, is cunning and clear thinking; his mother an innocent dupe. No rich castles are featured here for the Jutland King is more of a feudal lord; armies are counted in tens of men rather than hundreds. The film was specially previewed at the "Shakespeare On Film" season as part of the Everybody's Shakespeare International Festival at the Barbican Centre, London, England, on November 5, 1994. The director of the film had recently enjoyed international success with his film *Babette's Feast*.

THE LION KING
(U.S.A., 1994)

p.c. *Walt Disney.*
d. *Roger Allers, Rob Minkoff.*
l.p. *Animated characters.*
c. 87 mins. S

Mufasa, the lion king, is killed by his own brother, the cunning, jealous Scar. Scar intends to install a new order among the feline animals in the jungle. Simba, the prince-cub, is bothered about the death of his father and who was responsible. He goes into exile. The cub wanders and makes many friends. However, the time comes when the young prince, suspicious about the death of his father, decides he must find the truth and assert himself to his rightful position.

The synopsis rather says it all, except perhaps that the film has the typical Disney appeal to family audiences for the inevitable success. The Spanish magazine 'Fotogramas', November, 1994, neatly described the film as "Un Hamlet con melenas" (A Hamlet with bushy hair). The enjoyment of the film was enhanced by the voices of Jeremy Irons, Whoopi Goldberg, Matthew Broderick, James Earl Jones, Cheech Martin and Rowan Atkinson and the music of singer/pianist/composer, Elton John. His music was aided by the lyrics of Tim Rice. The music track was obviously made available along with much other merchandising but falls outside the scope of music for Shakespearean films in the obvious sense.

The film was available for purchase on 8 mm. from Derann Film Services., U.K.

Shown as part of the Everybody's Shakespeare International Festival, London, England, 1994.

Academy of Motion Picture Arts and Sciences, U.S.A., 1994: Nomination – Best Song (three from the film were nominated, one won); Awards – Best Soundtrack (Hans Zimmer), Best Song (Elton John, Tim Rice).

Hollywood Foreign Press Association Golden Globe Awards, U.S.A., 1995: Best Film (Comedy or Musical), Best Original Score (Hans Zimmer).

Los Angeles Film Critics' Association Awards, U.S.A., 1994: Best Animation.

National Board of Review of Motion Pictures, New York, U.S.A., 1994: Special Award – Best Family Film.

"THE LION KING relies on some impressive technical advances, but fails in its content." – 'La Cartelera', November 25, December 1, 1994.

aka: EL REY LEON

THE LION KING – PROMO
(U.S.A., 1994)

The credits are as for the feature. This short of about five minutes in colour featured Elton John performing "Can You Feel the Love Tonight". It was probably made for video originally but was available for purchase on 8 mm. from the same source as the feature and thus qualifies for inclusion. So also, due to similar availablity, does

THE CIRCLE OF LIFE
(U.S.A., 1994)

This is the opening title sequence from the film featuring the song of the title. Especially available for the home movie market, it lasts about five minutes and is in colour. Elton John is the singer heard.

✜ ✜ ✜ ✜ ✜

"To be or not to be – that is the question..." How many times have these words from Hamlet's soliloquy from Act II been uttered by aspiring actors or spoken in mock style by the individual? The question is, of course, rhetorical but it serves to make the point that HAMLET is among the best known of Shakespeare's works to the general public but, all too often, for these words alone. Yet it is one of Shakespeare's deepest plays and the Prince of Denmark one of his most enigmatic characters. It is not proposed to attempt here any discussion about, or analysis of, the character. Such topics are best left to the academics and, after all, this book is about films. Suffice, then, to say that as shown above, Hamlet has been portrayed many times and in many guises. There are doubtless many more interpretations to come, many more characters who will be inspired by the troubled Prince.

For other films with scenes from the play see **CHAPTER XXX ALL THE WORLD'S A STAGE**: MARTIN AS HAMLET (1914); LA MASCHERA CHE SANGUINA (1914); FREDDY VERSUS HAMLET (1916); HAMLET MADE OVER (1916); OTHELLO (1916)); PIMPLE AS HAMLET (1916); TO BE OR NOT TO BE (1916); ONE NIGHT ONLY (1919); DAYDREAMS (1922); KEAN (1922); HAN, HUG OG HAMLET (1922); DAS ALTE GESETZ (1923); DIE LEIBGARDIST (1926); THE LAST MOMENT (1928); THE ROYAL BOX (1929); HAN, HUG OG HAMLET (1932); THE ARIZONIAN (1935); THE GREAT GARRICK (1937); HAMLET AND EGGS (1937); KEAN (1940); TO BE OR NOT TO BE (1942); A DIARY FOR TIMOTHY (1946); PRINCE OF PLAYERS (1954); KEAN (GENIO E SREGOLATEZZA) (1957); DANGER WITHIN (1958); THE PURE HELL OF ST. TRINIANS (1960); JAK BYĆ KOCHANA (1962); SHAKESPEARE WALLAH (1965); BEREGIS AUTOMOBILYA (1966); IL PRIMO PREMIO SI CHIAMA IRENE (1969); THE MAGIC CHRISTIAN (1969); TO BE OR NOT TO BE (1983); MAITSUN ARINA (1987); HIGHLANDER II – THE QUICKENING (1990); SWAN SONG (1993); THE LAST ACTION HERO (1993)*; NORTH (1994); THE CANTERVILLE GHOST and IN THE BLEAK MIDWINTER (1995) and **CHAPTER XXXII THE IMMORTAL BARD**: THE LIFE OF SHAKESPEARE (1914); IMMORTAL GENTLEMAN (1935); PARIS 1900 (1948)*; WILLIAM SHAKESPEARE (1955); BAYLOR'S THEATER HAMLET (1958); THE HUMANITIES SERIES (1959); PATHÉ PICTORIAL 434 (1960)*; HAMLET RAZY PIĘC (1966); OPUS (1967); EXPLORATIONS IN SHAKESPEARE (1969); MASKS AND FACES (1969)*; THE WORLD OF WILLIAM SHAKESPEARE (1978); and THEATRE IN POLAND (1981).

*Denotes film extract.

CHAPTER X

JULIUS CAESAR

Dramatis Personæ:

Julius Caesar

Octavius Caesar, Marcus Antonius, M. Aemilius
Lepidus – the second triumvirate*

Cicero, Publius, Popilius Lena – senators

*Marcus Brutus, Cassius, Casca, Trebonius, Ligarius,
Decius Brutus, Metellus Cimber, Cinna –
conspirators against Julius Caesar*

*Lucilius, Titinius, Messala, Young Cato, Volumnius
– friends of Brutus and Cassius*

*Varro, Clitus, Claudius, Strato, Lucius,
Dardanius – servants to Brutus*

Flavius, Marullus – tribunes of the people

Portia – wife of Marcus Brutus

Calpurnia – wife of Julius Caesar

Artemidorus – a teacher of rhetoric

A Soothsayer

Cinna – a poet

Another poet

Pindarus – servant to Cassius

Ghost of Caesar

*Servants, Senators, Citizens, Guards, Attendants
etc.*

* Referred to as Mark Antony

Rome B.C. 44 is full of celebrations for Julius Caesar's triumphs. Not everyone is content and some, such as Marullus and Flavius, try to spread discontent. Caesar and his wife Calpurnia arrive and meet Caesar's friend Mark Antony who expresses his loyalty to his friend. A soothsayer interrupts the party bidding Caesar beware the Ides of March. Caesar brushes aside the warning and the party moves on.

Only Cassius and Brutus do not follow. The former senses uncertainty in his friend and boldly speaks his own views about Caesar, pointing out his faults which are ignored now that he is treated like a god. Three times they hear the sound of cheering. Cassius successfully feeds the discontent in Brutus. As the party returns, Caesar looks unwell but he does, however, see Cassius and feels distrust of him which he mentions to Mark Antony.

Casca tells Brutus and Cassius of what has passed. Three times Mark Antony offered Caesar the crown and it was refused three times. Caesar had a fit which evoked pity from the crowd. Cicero had spoken but in Greek and other things had happened which he could not remember. Casca leaves, accepting Cassius' invitation to dine with him the next day. Brutus, too, leaves and Cassius resolves that messages condemning Caesar shall reach him seemingly from independent sources.

That night a storm occurs which troubles Casca who is in the street. He meets Cicero and tells him of strange things he has seen. Cicero leaves and Cassius arrives and shortly after so does Cinna. They make their way to Brutus' house.

Brutus is sorely troubled and unable to sleep. His servant boy finds a message obviously thrown through his study window. It is clearly one of those designed by Cassius. He asks his servant the date and is told that it is the Ides of March.

Cassius arrives with Casca, Cinna, Decius, Metellus and Trebonius. They shake hands on their course of action but take no oath. There is debate concerning the enlistment of Cicero and the slaying of Mark Antony. Both are rejected on Brutus' advice.

They leave and Brutus is confronted by Portia, his wife, who is concerned at his manner. She entreats him to confide in her as befits their marriage. He is inclined to confide in her but is interrupted by Caius Ligarius' arrival to accompany him to the Senate.

In Caesar's house, Calpurnia has a dream of her husband's death. All the omens are bad for him yet he is determined to go out. However, he finally succumbs to his wife's wishes when Decius arrives to accompany him to the Senate. Decius belittles Calpurnia's dreams and puts other meanings to the omens. He challenges Caesar's courage and, of course, Caesar agrees to go to the Senate.

Artemidorus, a teacher, unsuccessfully tries to deliver a warning to Caesar. Portia, concerned about Brutus, sends his servant to watch him. Portia meets the soothsayer who says he hopes Caesar will speak with him. Caesar does indeed speak with him saying that the Ides of March have come. The soothsayer replies that this may be so but they have not gone. The conspirators skilfully divert Mark Antony. Metellus begs Caesar to lift his brother's banishment and the others join in the plea. Then, as arranged, Casca strikes first with his dagger and the others follow including, finally, Brutus. The deed done, Brutus reassures the other senators of their safety and the conspirators seal their bond with the blood of Caesar.

Mark Antony sends his servant seeking parlance with the conspirators which is granted. Feigning friendship, he is granted Caesar's body and permission to speak to the people after Brutus has done so. He must acknowledge this permission and must not cast blame. He agrees but Cassius is worried. These fears Brutus allays saying that he will first win over the people.

Speaking emotionally, Brutus endeavours to justify the act to free Rome of tyranny, putting Rome above his friendship. The people are swayed. Then he leaves to allow Mark Antony to speak over Caesar's bloody body. Skilfully he points out his dead friend's good points and his rejection of the crown at the same time sarcastically referring to Brutus and his fellows as honourable men. When he reads Caesar's will from which all Rome benefits, the people cry out for revenge.

Cinna is the first to die while Octavius, Caesar's adopted son, Lepidus and Mark Antony form an alliance. While Mark Antony thinks little of Lepidus, the three draw up the names of the guilty for punishment. The other conspirators flee and Cassius and Brutus join forces.

There is, however, friction between them with Brutus accusing Cassius of involvement in some bribery affair and failing to send him money for his troops. The differences are resolved and Cassius is saddened to hear of the death of Portia. Personal problems are set aside and, with their respective chief officers, they plan their action which is to march to Philippi to meet the army of Octavius and Mark Antony. That night, Brutus has a vision of Caesar who says he will see him again at Philippi.

The two armies meet and parley between the generals fails. Cassius and Brutus embrace each other fondly in case they should not meet again. The battle goes against them and Cassius begs his Parthian slave, whom he frees, to kill him. Meanwhile Octavius thinks he has Brutus but it is only one of his officers. Brutus, too, calls upon his friends to help in his suicide but none can find it their hearts to do so. In the end, the young Strato holds his dagger while Brutus pushes himself on to it.

Octavius and Mark Antony honour Brutus for his nobility and loyalty to Rome.

Note: This play marked an approximate midway point in the career of Shakespeare with the turning from English history to tragedies of an earlier era. For his source he turned to 'Lives Of The Noble Grecians And Romans Compared' by Plutarch. It is believed that the play was first produced at the new Globe theatre, London, in the autumn of 1599.

✠ ✠ ✠ ✠ ✠

LA MORT DE JULES CÉSAR
(France, 1907)

See **CHAPTER XXXII THE IMMORTAL BARD** under title **SHAKESPEARE ÉCRIVANT "LA MORT DE JULES CÉSAR"**.

JULIUS CAESAR
(U.S.A., 1908)

p.c. *Lubin Manufacturing.*
d. *Sigmund Lubin.*
l.p.
b.w. 10 mins. Sil.

As if in competition with the Vitagraph release below, this was copyrighted just before it. Some doubt exists as to whether or not this film was based on Shakespeare's play but as the film has not come to light, it is hard to decide. Given the leaning towards the Bard's works at the time, the competition between the companies to produce such works, then the final assumption is obvious.

JULIUS CAESAR, AN HISTORICAL TRAGEDY
(U.S.A., 1908)

p.c. *Vitagraph.*
d. *James Stuart Blackton.*
l.p. *Charles Kent (Julius Caesar); Maurice Costello; Florence Lawrence (Calpurnia); Paul Panzer; William Ranous (Cassius); Earle Williams (Brutus); William Shea (Citizen).*
b.w. 980 ft. (299 m.) Sil.

This used key scenes (fifteen of them) linked together to cover the basic plot of the play. The cast list is based on visual evidence and is a composite culled from various sources.

William V. Ranous is given as director and as playing Caesar by some. A tinted print is known to have been issued.

Strangely, this ran into censorship problems in its home country. One of the matters of complaint was the length of the "skirt" worn by the actors as Romans even though they were the same as worn in stage productions; another was the murder scene which was found too violent.

Whilst it was not uncommon at this time to restyle plays to concur with existing laws of decency, to cut such a key scene from an already truncated adaption must have seemed then as it does now – illogical.

Or was it? Retrospectively, perhaps the assassination of a head of state was, even though historically true, rather too sensitive in a country which had, at the time, recently suffered such events. It must be remembered, too, that such a scene on stage reached only an audience of assumed high intelligence whereas the film was open to the public at large and that public could be influenced.

"In some respects this is the best of the Shakespearean adaptations the Vitagraph Company has yet produced...But the chief points of praise are the intelligent manner in which the adaptation is managed, and the fine scenic settings that are supplied. By selecting only the vital scenes and inserting comprehensive explanatory titles in the film the story of the play is rendered fairly free from obscurity – the greatest obstacle to overcome in doing Shakespeare in moving pictures." – 'New York Dramatic Mirror', December 12, 1908.

GIULIO CESARE
(Italy, 1909)

p.c. *Itala Film.*
d. *Giovanni Pastrone.*
l.p.
b.w. 876 ft. (267 m.) Sil.

This early Italian version is an abbreviated version of the play. It differs slightly in the plot for Caesar openly boasts to Mark Antony of his ambition which is heard by Brutus who reprimands Caesar. The conspiracy, too, is overheard by a spy who tells Calpurnia.

An Italian source notes the length as 837 ft. (255 m.) and as 853 ft. (260 m.) and as being in ten scenes for the French version. The British version is noted at 875 ft. (267 m.) and at 850 ft. (259 m.) in America.

aka: JULIUS CAESAR; BRUTUS; JULÉS CÉSAR

BRUTO
(Italy, 1910)

p.c. *Milano Film.*
d. *Giuseppe de Liguoro.*
l.p. *Amletto Novelli (Julius Caesar); Giovanna Terribili Gonzalès.*
b.w. 535 ft. (163 m.) Sil.

The French release is listed as slightly longer at 545 ft. (166 m.). A second Italian version was issued in the same year.

BRUTO
(Italy, 1911)

p.c. *Cines.*
d. *Enrico Guazzoni.*
l.p.
b.w.1187 ft. (362 m.) Sil.

This is a slightly shortened version of the play. In this version the focus is on the action between the death of Caesar and the death of Brutus.

The film is noted as having been well constructed and impressive with the emphasis on spectacle. The Spanish version is listed at 1230 ft. (375 m.).

aka: BRUTUS

JULIUS CAESAR
(G.B./France, 1911)

p.c. *Urban Trading.*
d. *Charles Urban.*
l.p. *Theo Frenkel (Julius Caesar).*
b.w. 10 mins. Sil.

No further details of this short are known.

JULIUS CAESAR
(G.B., 1911)

p.c. *Cooperative Cinematograph Co.*
d. *Frank R. Benson.*
l.p. *Frank R. Benson (Marc Antony); Guy Rathbone (Julius Caesar); Murray Carrington (Brutus); Eric Maxon (Cassius); Nora Lancaster (Calpurnia); Constance Benson (Portia).*
b.w. 990 ft. (302 m.) Sil.

Based on the Stratford upon Avon performance of the time.

GIULIO CESARE
(Italy, 1913)

p.c. *Itala Film.*
d. *Giovanni Pastrone?*
l.p.
b.w. (?) mins. Sil.

Noted as having been made, its inclusion is suspect and it may have been a reissue of the earlier film from the same company. It has not been possible to trace further details.

JULIUS CAESAR
(U.S.A., 1913)

p.c. *Edison.*
d.
l.p.
b.w. (?) mins.

The Brutus/Cassius argument scene from Act IV is featured.

This was a synchronised sound version using the unsuccessful Kinetophon system.

CAJUS JULIUS CAESAR
(Italy, 1914)

p.c. *Palatino/Cines.*
d. *Enrico Guazzoni.*
l.p. *Amleto Novelli (Julius Caesar); Giovanna Terribili Gonzalès (Tertullia); Pina Menichelli (Cleopatra); Ruffo Geri (Brutus); Ignazio Lupi (Pompey); Irene Mattadra (Servilia); Bruto Castellani (Vercingetorix); Augusto Mastripietri*

(Cato); Sigira Geri (Irmidia); Orlano Ricci (Mark Antony); Carlo Duse; Lea Orlandi.
b.w. 7329 ft. (2234 m.) Sil.

More of an Italian spectacular movie than Shakespeare, it does borrow from the play and uses direct parallels with it. In the English language version, quotes from the play were used in some scenes. The film ends with the aftermath of Mark Antony's speech over Caesar's body.

In the American release, Amleto Novelli (as Caesar) becomes Anthony Novelli. Criticism of the film is generally favourable though comment is made that the lead player does not seem to age. This suggests that it covers the whole of the life of Caesar especially since his battles with the Gauls receive favourable comment on their presentation. Though the credits for the source are noted as Shakespeare's play, by implication, Caesar's own writings were also used.

aka: JULIUS CAESAR, CAYO JULIO CÉSAR; CAIO JULIO CESARE

BRUTUS AND CASSIUS
(G.B., 1918)

p.c. *Eric Williams Speaking Pictures.*
d. *Marshall Moore.*
l.p. *Eric Williams (Brutus).*
b.w. (?) mins. Sil. (see notes)

The action on the screen supported an orator (Williams in his day) on stage.

JULIUS CAESAR
(G.B., 1926)

p.c. *De Forest Phonofilms.*
d. *George A. Cooper.*
l.p. *Basil Gill (Brutus); Malcolm Keen (Cassius).*
b.w. (?) mins.

This sound-on-film short covers the quarrel scene.

One of a number of short films made in other countries by the pioneering American company, maybe this was the first Shakespeare play (well, extract) committed to sound-on-film.

JULIUS CAESAR
(G.B., 1945)

p.c. *Theatrecraft.*
d. *Henry Cass.*
l.p. *Felix Aylmer (Brutus); Leo Genn (Mark Antony); John Slater; Frederick Cooper; Ben Williams; Emrys Jones; Grace Allardyce; Arthur Hamblyn; Sydney Monckton.*
b.w. 19 mins.

Extract featuring the forum scene following the murder of Caesar, this was made for educational purposes and was one of the two films made in a series called *Famous Scenes From Shakespeare*.

JULIUS CAESAR
(U.S.A., 1948)

p.c. *Avon/Brandon.*
d. *David Bradley.*
l.p. *Harold Tasker (Julius Caesar); Robert Holt (Octavius Caesar); Charlton Heston (Mark Antony); David Bradley (Brutus); Theodor Cloak (Aemilius Lepidus); Grosvenor Glenn (Cassius); William Russell (Casca); Frederick Roscoe (Decius); Cornelius Peeples (Popilius); John O'Leary (Marullus); Arthur Sus (Cinna); Alfred Endyvean (Flavius); Homer Dietmeier (Artemidorus); Don Walker (Soothsayer); Russell Gruebner (Cinna the Poet); George Gilbert (Strato); George Hinners (Lucius); Helen Ross (Calpurnia); Mary Darr (Portia); Sam Needham (Pindarus).*
b.w. 90 mins.

This 16 mm. semi-professional film was independently produced in and around Chicago, U.S.A., using, for example, the city's Museum Of Science steps for the funeral scene. The budget was less than $15,000. Though the film has novelty interest, it is still a competent work and was one of the two films Charlton Heston made before his official Hollywood debut film *Dark City* in 1950.

An extract for educational study purposes exists as a separate item. It runs for seventeen minutes.

Locarno Film Festival, Switzerland, 1953: Best Film.

"Viewing the film is like watching an experimental, fringe theatre performance." – Samuel Crowl, 'Shakespeare and the Moving Image'.

JULIUS CAESAR
(G.B., 1951)

p.c. *Parthian Productions.*
d.
l.p. *Robert Speaight; Cecil Trouncer.*
b.w. 33 mins.

This was probably directed by Speaight, a Shakespearean actor. It was made for educational purposes.

JULIUS CAESAR
(G.B., 1953)

p.c. *Emil Katzka Productions.*
d. *Charles Deane.*
l.p. *Young Vic Theatre Company. Narrator: Ronald Howard.*
b.w. 13 mins.

This features the tent scene from the play and was part of a programme made for television. It was introduced by Ronald Howard and called *The World's A Stage*. Charles Deane is a name that will occur a number of times so it should be noted that some sources spell Deane without the final "e".

JULIUS CAESAR
(U.S.A., 1953)

p.c. *M.G.M.*
d. *Joseph L. Mankiewicz.*
l.p. *Marlon Brando (Mark Antony); John Gielgud (Cassius); James Mason (Brutus); Louis Calhern (Julius Caesar); Edmond O'Brien (Casca); Greer Garson (Calpurnia); Deborah Kerr (Portia); George Macready (Marullus); Alan Napier (Cicero); John Hoyt (Decius Brutus); Michael Pate (Flavius); William Cottrell (Cinna); Jack Raine (Trebonius); Tom Powers (Metellus Cimber); Rhys Williams (Lucilius); Douglas Watson (Octavius Caesar); Edmund Purdom (Strato); John Hardy (Lucius); John Doucette; Ian Wolfe; Chester Stratton; Lumsden Hare; Morgan Farley; Victor Perry; Bill Phipps; Michael Tolan; Michael Ansara; Dayton Lumis; John Lupton; Preston Hanson; John Parrish; Joe Waring; Thomas Browns-Henry.*

b.w. 122 mins. S

The big question preceding the appearance of what producer John Houseman called " a political thriller" was how Marlon Brando, then steeped in Method Acting, would cope with his role. He had not been the immediate choice for the role – Paul Scofield, Leo Genn and Charlton Heston had all been considered. However, the general feeling was that he did so very well. Of course, he was apparently coached by John Gielgud! Producer John Houseman had worked with Orson Welles in 1937 for the Mercury Players production and was anxious to produce the film version. Indeed, such was his zeal, that he threatened to leave M.G.M. if he did not get the job. The studio agreed but with a small budget of $2,070,000. This led to the inevitable cost-cutting and using parts from M.G.M.'s *Quo Vadis*. The film did gain for not being in colour for which the director's reason was: "It's not in color because I've never seen a good, serious, dramatic movie except maybe *Gone With The Wind*." This was, of course, at a time when colour, CinemaScope and 3-D were being used to entice back cinemagoers.

Both Houseman and Mankiewicz wanted Bernard Hermann to write the music score but the then musical director of M.G.M. felt that, because of cost, Miklos Rozsa, who was under contract, should do it. Despite Mankiewicz's displeasure, Johnny Green won and Rozsa composed an overture to be used over the credits. This did not satisfy Green who wanted Tchaikovsky's "Capriccio Italien" as the overture. To pacify both parties neither was used. Ironically, in 1975 Bernard Hermann conducting the National Philharmonic Orchestra did record a suite of the incidental music to the film in an album dedicated to "Music From Great Shakespearean Films" (English Decca) and the rejected overture was also available at one time from another source. The original soundtrack was issued by M.G.M. on its own record label and music from the film also featured on a long playing record issued by Dot many years ago.

The film is interesting also as an early example of the use of stereophonic sound. The concept was not completely new to the cinema for there had been earlier experimentation in this field. Indeed, many of the stereoscopic films and CinemaScope (or equivalent) films of the era had stereophonic sound. Here, however, the film was made in the standard format. The opportunity was not lost on Rozsa as Roy M. Prendergast explained in 'Film Music, A Neglected Art' : "...composer Miklos Rozsa immediately recognized the artistic and dramatic possibilites open to the composer through the addition of stereo sound to the film."

Mankiewicz was not happy over the première. M.G.M. leased a class theatre for it in New York but had processed the print for widescreen presentation. This led to the inevitable cropping of the picture and a heated row between the director and Nicholas Schenck, the president of Loew's and M.G.M.'s financial chief. Despite all this and M.G.M.'s pessimism, the film made a profit.

Shown as part of the Everybody's Shakespeare International Festival, London, England, 1994.
Shown at the São Paolo Film Festival, Brazil, 1953.
Shown at the Shakespeare Film Festival, Wiesbaden, W. Germany, 1964.
Shown at the Valladolid Film Festival, Spain, 1985, as part of a Mankiewicz retrospective.
Academy of Motion Picture Arts and Sciences, U.S.A., 1953: Nominations – Best Picture, Best Actor (Marlon Brando), Best Cinematography (black and white) (Joseph Ruttenberg); Award – Best Art/Set Direction (black and white) (Cedric Gibbons, Edward Carfagno/ Edwin B. Willis, Hugh Hunt).
British Film Academy, G.B., 1953: Best British Actor (John Gielgud), Best Foreign Actor (Marlon Brando).
'Harvard Lampoon' Movie Worsts, U.S.A., 1953): Most Miscast (Louis Calhern as a doddering Caesar).
National Board Of Review, U.S.A., 1953: Best American Picture, Best American Films (head of the list), Best Actor (James Mason for his role in this film and others).
'New York Times' Annual Ten Best, U.S.A., 1953: Listed fourth.
Union of Danish Film Critics, Denmark, 1954: Best Non-European film.

"An adroit version...that falters only when budget restrictions are apparent..." – David Shipman, 'The Good Film And Video Guide'.

"...an excellent film, excellent cinema, excellent entertainment, and pretty respectable art." – 'Monthly Film Bulletin', December, 1953.

JULIUS CAESAR: AN INTRODUCTION
(G.B., 1969)

p.c. *BHE/Seabourne.*
d. *Peter Seabourne.*
l.p. *Harold Innocent (Julius Caesar); John Humphrey (Brutus); Robert Fleming (Cassius); Brian Spink (Mark Antony).*
c. 28 minutes.

This is the third in this series of abridgements.

JULIUS CAESAR
(G.B., 1970)

p.c. *Commonwealth United.*
d. *Stuart Burge.*
l.p. *Charlton Heston (Mark Anthony); Jason Robards (Brutus); John Gielgud (Julius Caesar); Richard Johnson (Cassius); Robert Vaughn (Casca); Diana Rigg (Portia); Jill Bennett (Calpurnia); Richard Chamberlain (Octavius Caesar); Peter Eyre (Cinna the Poet); Alan Browning (Marullus); Christopher Lee (Artemidorus); Norman Bowler (Titinius); Andrew Crawford (Volumnius); Edwin Finn (Publius); David Dodimead (Lepidus); Michael Gough (Metellus Cimber); Derek Godfrey (Decius Brutus); Paul Hardwick (Messala); Ewan Hooper (Strato); Laurence Harrington (Carpenter); Thomas Heathcote (Flavius); Robert Keegan (Lucilius); David Neal (Cinna the Conspirator); John Moffatt (Popilius Lena); Andre Morrell (Cicero); Steve Pacey (Lucius); Preston Lockwood (Trebonius); Ron Pember; John Tate; Damien Thomas; Ken Hutchinson; Michael Keating; Trevor Adams; Christopher Cazenove; David Leland; Roy Stewart; Robin Chadwick; Liz Geghardt; Derek Hardwicke; Michael Wynne.*
Technicolor. 116 mins. Panavision.

In this version, spectacle in the style of Cecil B. DeMille seems to dominate. It varies from the basic play in parts opening, for example, with a flashback of Caesar's war in Spain. Obviously, the aspect the director has chosen scores over any stage production in the battle sequence but at the cost of the personal drama. The film did modestly well at the box office despite some poor performances.

Academy of Motion Picture Arts and Sciences, U.S.A., 1970: Nomination – Best Original Score (Michael Lewis).
'Harvard Lampoon' Movie Worsts, U.S.A., 1970: Ten Worst Movies – ninth position.

"Elementary production with a surprising number of faults and very few merits." – Leslie Halliwell, 'Halliwell's Film Guide'.

aka: EL ASESINATO DE JULIO CÉSAR

JULIUS CAESAR
(G.B., 1974)

p.c. *Realist Film Unit.*
d. *Peter Seabourne.*
l.p. *Mark Kingston (Julius Caesar); Susan Jameson (Calpurnia); Derrick Gilbert (Brutus); David Fennell (Decius Brutus); Colin Ferrell (Cassius).*
c. 14 mins.

Act II, Scene 2 and Act IV, Scene 3 are featured as excerpts here, the fourth of this particular series.

✢ ✢ ✢ ✢ ✢

CLEOPATRA
(U.S.A., 1934)

See entry in **CHAPTER I ANTONY AND CLEOPATRA**. The film is included here as it obviously deals, in part, with Julius Caesar. The Shakespearean influence is clearly evident in the short, relative section.

William Warren played Caesar.

AN HONOURABLE MURDER
(G.B., 1959)

p.c. *The Danzigers.*
d. *Godfrey Grayson.*
l.p. *Norman Wooland (Brutus); Philip Saville (Mark Anthony); John Longden (Caesar); Margaretta Scott (Claudia); Lisa Danielly (Paula); Douglas Wilmer (Cassius); Colin Tapley (Casca); Marion Mathie (Portia); Kenneth Edwards (Trebon); Stuart Saunders (Simber); Arnold Bell (Ligar); John Brooking (Sayer); Olive Kirby (Maggie); Elizabeth Saunders (Secretary).*
b.w. 69 mins.

The chairman of Empire Petroleum, Julian Caesar, plans a merger but fellow director, Cassius, plans with others to overthrow him. Brutus is persuaded and Mark Anthony is tricked into absence during the vital board meeting. Deposed, Caesar dies of a heart attack and Mark debunks Brutus' explanation in an impressive speech to shareholders. Mark becomes chairman, sacks the directors and Brutus commits suicide.

JULIUS CAESAR transposed to modern times and a big business environment has, to quote 'Monthy Film Bulletin', " a certain novelty interest." Not that it was a new idea for the British had already paved the way with **JOE MACBETH** (q.v.). The title is an obvious parody of Mark Antony's sarcastic reference to Brutus as "an honourable man".

CARRY ON CLEO
(G.B., 1964)

See **CHAPTER I ANTONY AND CLEOPATRA** for full details. Kenneth Williams played Caesar.

✢ ✢ ✢ ✢ ✢

Whilst Julius Caesar may not have been exactly as Mark Antony eulogised him (Caesar may have refused the title "king" but, according to Suetonius – 'The Twelve Caesars' – he was happy to accept other titles and offices quite unethically), he was certainly a character of importance and, indeed, charisma. He was a notorious womaniser and may have even taken a male lover. As a brilliant soldier and lover of Queen Cleopatra, he is a natural subject for the screen.

His affaire with Cleopatra was the subject of George Bernard Shaw's play and Gabriel Pascal's lengthy and costly film version of it, *Caesar And Cleopatra* (1945) with Claude Rains and Vivien Leigh in the title roles. He is, naturally, featured in the 1963 epic *Cleopatra* which owes much to Plutarch as the basic source. Caesar was played by Rex Harrison. He was featured as an historical character along with Antony and Cleopatra in the 1957 Warner Bros. film *The Story Of Mankind*. The lucky Caesar in *Una Regina Per Cesare* (France/Italy, 1962) was Gordon Scott. Lucky? Well, he did have lovely Pascale Petit as his Cleopatra. Indeed, the film records reveal many other minor

films in which the Caesar character is featured. Among them, though of merely passing interest, are the early Italian comedy *Kri Kri Giulio Cesare*, a Cines production of 1915 featuring the comic character Kri Kri ("Bloomer" in Britain; "Patachon" in some European countries). From Italy, too, but much later came *Giulio Cesare Contro I Pirati* directed by Sergio Grieco in 1962 and *Giulio Cesare, Il Conquistatore Delle Gallie* (Italy, 1962, directed by Amerigo Anton). The title role in this latter film fell to American, Cameron Mitchell. Another American, John Gavin, played the youthful Roman in Stanley Kubrick's memorable *Spartacus* (U.S.A., 1959/60). Certainly many of the films, in addition to those mentioned, about Cleopatra could have a part for Julius Caesar!

For other films with scenes from the play see **CHAPTER XXXII THE IMMORTAL BARD**: PARIS 1900 (1948)*; JULIUS CAESAR (1954); SHAKESPEARE'S THEATER (1954) and WILLIAM SHAKESPEARE (1955).

*Denotes film extract.

CHAPTER XI

KING LEAR

Dramatis Personæ:

Lear – *King of Britain*
Goneril, Regan, Cordelia – *his daughters*
Lear's Fool

Duke of Burgundy
Duke of Cornwall
Duke of Albany
Earl of Kent
Earl of Gloucester

Edgar – *son of Gloucester*
Edmund – *Gloucester's bastard son*

Old Man – *Gloucester's tenant*

King of France
Doctor
Curan – *a courtier*
Oswald – *Goneril's steward*
Gentleman – *Cordelia's attendant*
Servants to Cornwall
Captain under Edmund's command
A herald
Lear's knights, Officers, Messengers, Soldiers,
    Attendants etc.

King Lear of Britain is more than eighty years old and ready to shed his responsibilities. He plans to divide his kingdom according to his daughters' love for him. Both Goneril, married to the Duke of Cornwall, and Regan, married to the Duke of Albany, express their love profusely with unctious words and in return each receive a third of the kingdom. The king's favourite, Cordelia , for whose hand both the King of France and the Duke of Burgundy are visiting the court, sees her sisters' words only as a means to personal rewards. She speaks truthfully saying that she loves her father to the extent of her duty.

Shocked, Lear asks her to think again but she will not stoop to what would be a mercenary tactic though she loves her father dearly.

She simply questions the truth of her sisters' words. For this, Lear, never a man of even temper, gives her share of the kingdom to her two sisters, thus they have half each. The Earl of Kent intervenes on Cordelia's behalf and is banished for so doing. The Duke of Burgundy, not wanting a bride of so little worth, is no longer interested in Cordelia but the King of France sees her worth and marries her. So she leaves for France, saddened to see her father left in the care of her cunning sisters.

Lear is supposed to spend his time at the homes of both Goneril and Regan. Slowly they begin to show their true colours doing all they can to humiliate him. Fortunately, the Earl of Kent does not go away but, disguised and under the name of Caius, enlists with Lear as a servant. In this manner, aided by the court jester who taunts Goneril in rhymes, he is able to protect his master and they become friends.

Goneril demands that Lear reduce his retinue of a hundred knights. He reprimands her and goes to

Regan but Goneril sends her a letter accusing Lear of many things. Caius thrashes the messenger for which he is put in the stocks. This shocks Lear as does the lack of reception for him for Regan lives in great pomp. Goneril has already arrived spreading more lies about Lear. Regan advises him to seek Goneril's forgiveness and return with her but he is resolved to stay with Regan.

Regan, as if wishing to out-pace her sister's evil, reduces Lear's retinue even further and he is reduced to no more than a beggar. Lear's mind begins to wander and one night he rides out into a wild storm with the jester. Caius finds them both and begs them to seek shelter in a hovel. There they find a poor demented beggar. Lear sees in him the image of himself and his plight.

Caius takes Lear to Dover Castle where he still has loyal friends and goes to Cordelia in France. Alarmed at what Caius tells her, she lands in England with her army. Her attendants find Lear wandering. In his feeble state of mind, he can hardly believe that the daughter he cast aside should now be with him to help him. He begs her forgiveness and the love between them is revived as she explains that it is her duty to help her father. So the old man is taken into the care of the doctors.

Now the two sisters have, as might be expected, tired of their husbands and are both playing with the affection of the same man. This man is Edmund, himself not so virtuous having tricked his brother out of his rightful title so that he, Edmund, might become the Earl of Gloucester.

Regan's husband dies and she declares that she will marry Gloucester. Furious and full of jealousy, Goneril poisons her but her own husband discovers her crime and, aware also of her infidelity, puts her in prison where she takes her own life. Gloucester leads the combined armies of Regan and Goneril against Cordelia and is victorious. With his eye on the throne, Gloucester wants no obstacles in his way and so imprisons Cordelia and there she dies soon after.

Death also takes Lear shortly after. In his last few moments of life, Caius tries to explain to Lear that he is really the Earl of Kent, his loyal countryman, who has been with him all the while. It is to no avail for the King's mind cannot comprehend this. The Earl of Kent, himself advanced in years, is stricken with grief and dies too.

Gloucester's plans are short lived for he is slain by the brother whom he had tricked out of his inheritance and the Duke of Albany, the husband of the deceased Goneril, ascends the throne of England.

Note: The essence of the theme here predates Shakespeare by at least four centuries with "Cordelia" or her like featuring in many folklore tales. The Lear character was carried from folklore to history by Geoffrey de Monmouth in 'Historia Regnum Britanniae' (1136) and thus Raphael Holinshed declared in his 'Chronicles' (1587) that Leir (Lear) came to the throne in the year of the World, 3105. There are other sources, both in verse and prose, that Shakespeare had available to him. Known to have been performed at court on December 26, 1606, the play may have also have been at the Globe theatre the year before. Generally, the writing of the play is thought to have been in 1605 or early 1606.

✤✤✤✤✤

KING LEAR
(Germany, 1905)
p.c.
d.
l.p.
b.w. 10 mins. Sil.

This is noted by some sources but as the film is reportedly lost, the details of it, perhaps, will never be known. It is noted as possibly being an Italian film (with Ermete Novelli) of 328 ft. (100 m.) length.

KING LEAR
(U.S.A., 1909)
p.c. *Vitagraph.*
d. *William V. Ranous? (James Stuart Blackton is quoted by some sources).*
l.p. *William V. Ranous (King Lear); possibly William Humphrey (Fool); Florence Auer (Goneril); Julia Arthur (Regan?); Mary Fuller (Cordelia?); Maurice Costello; Edith Story.*
b.w. 960 ft. (293 m.) Sil.

This was one of the many Shakespeare screen adaptations by Vitagraph at this time. That, there-

fore, implies a coherent story line using important scenes from the play though, if reports can be believed, too much of the story seems to have been crammed into too little time.

The film, completely shot in a studio, was originally copyrighted as SHAKESPEARE'S TRAGEDY, KING LEAR. Some doubt exists over the cast. Some sources note that Florence Turner may have played Goneril or Regan and Julia Swayne-Gordon played Cordelia. The title role is credited by some to Costello.

RE LEAR
(Italy, 1910)
p.c. *Film d'Arte Italiana.*
d. *Gerolamo Lo Savio.*
l.p. *Amleto Novelli (King Lear); Giannina Chiantoni (Goneril or Regan); Ermete Zacconi; Francesca Bertini (Cordelia).*
b.w. 1066 ft. (325 m.) Sil.

This is a rather simplified version of the story which omits sub-plots and is more coherent for it.

Francesca Bertini became Italy's most popular film star of the era later, in 1920, going to Hollywood with a $500,000 contract.

The British version was slightly longer at 1072 ft. (327 m) and the film was also issued in coloured version of 919 ft. (280 m.).

aka: KING LEAR; LE ROI LEAR; EL REY LEAR

RE LEAR
(Italy, 1910)
p.c. *Milano Film.*
d. *Giuseppe de Liguoro.*
l.p. *Giuseppe de Liguoro (King Lear); Arturo Padovani.*
b.w. 656 ft. (200 m.) Sil.

The British release of the film is noted at 1200 ft. (366 m.). Just what was added to increase the length is not known.

aka: KING LEAR; KÖNIG LEAR

KING LEAR
(U.S.A., 1916)
p.c. *Thanhouser Film Corp.*
d. *Ernest Warde.*
l.p. *Frederick Warde (King Lear); Ernest Warde (King's Fool); Ina Hammer (Goneril); Edith Diestel (Regan); Charles Brooks (Duke Of Cornwall); Lorraine Huling (Cordelia); Boyd Marshall (King Of France); Hector Dion (Edmund); Edwin Stanley (Edgar); J.H. Gilmour (Earl Of Kent); Robert Whittier (Oswald); Wayne Arey (Duke Of Albany).*
b.w. 5 reels. Sil.

Conventional, faithful version within its confines. Comment of the era was favourable in respect of Warde and those playing the daughters and the jester. The battle scenes were noted as being on a grand scale and the photography excellent.

The film opens with Warde, looking the epitome of the conventional Shakespearean actor of the day (which he was), in contemporary dress reading from a book which then shows the first page of the play. The scene dissolves into Warde reappearing as King Lear. A contemporary review noted: "...the Vitagraph adaptors have made the mistake of trying to adhere too closely to the book...The result is that the picture fails to hold the interest of the spectators. The costumes and scenes are faithfully represented but the photography is dim in parts."

"...has little to recommend it." – 'Motion Picture Guide'.

"...deserving of almost unlimited commendation," – 'Variety', January 5, 1917.

KING LEAR
(U.S.A., 1954)

p.c.
d.
l.p. *Monty Woolley (King Lear).*
b.w. 15 mins.

This features the scene in which Lear is rejected by both his daughters.

From a series called *On Stage*, no further details are known. It may have been a short made for television originally.

KING LEAR: AN INTRODUCTION
(G.B., 1969)

p.c. *Seabourne Enterprises.*
d. *Peter Seabourne.*
l.p.
c. 27 mins.

This is the sixth, and last, of this series of extracts prepared for educational purposes.

KING LEAR
(G.B./Denmark, 1970)

p.c. *Filmways/Athena/Laterna Films.*
d. *Peter Brook.*
l.p. *Paul Scofield (King Lear); Irene Worth (Goneril); Alan Webb (Duke of Gloucester); Tom Fleming (Earl of Kent); Susan Engel (Regan); Annelise Gabold (Cordelia); Cyril Cusack (Duke of Albany); Patrick Magee (Duke of Cornwall); Jack MacGowran (Fool); Robert Lloyd (Edgar); Ian Hogg (Edmund); Barry Stanton (Oswald).*
b.w. 137 mins.

This, with cut text, was filmed in Jutland and the cold weather was real!

Shown as part of the Everybody's Shakespeare International Festival, London, England, 1994.

"...could be heavy going for the uninitiated, but often a strong and rewarding experience." – Leonard Maltin, 'Movie And Video Guide'.

KOROL LIR
(U.S.S.R., 1970)

p.c. *Lenfilm.*
d. *Grigori Kozintsev.*
l.p. *Yuri Yarvet (King Lear); Elsa Radzinya (Goneril); Galina Volchek (Regan); Valentina Shendrikova (Cordelia); Karl Sebris (Earl of Gloucester); Leonhard Merzin (Edgar); Regimantis Adomaitis (Edmund); Vladimir Emelyanov (Earl of Kent); Oleg Dal (Fool); Alexander Vokach (Duke of Cornwall); Alexei Petrenko (Oswald); Yumas Budraitis (King of France); Donatas Banionis (Duke of Albany).*
b.w. 141 mins. Sovscope.

This Russian version, based on Boris Pasternak's translation, treats the story as a folk tale with some political overtones making a contrast to the Peter Brook version. The director penned his views on his work in the book 'King Lear: The Space of Tragedy'.

The running time quoted is the longest traced. Many versions seem to run up to five minutes less.

Shown at the Cannes Film Festival, France, 1971.
Shown at the London Film Festival, England, 1971.
Shown as part of the Everybody's Shakespeare International Festival, London, England, 1994.
Chicago Film Festival, U.S.A., 1972: Silver Prize.
Milan Film Festival, Italy, 1973: Municipality of Milan Gold Medal.
First Teheran Film Festival, Iran, 1972: Grand Prix for Best Film, Best Actor (Yuri Yarvet), Film Into Literature Prize (shared).

"Yuri Yarvet made first a believable and then a moving Lear, but to me, but not a great one." – Gordon Reid reporting on the Cannes Film Festival, 1971, in 'Continental Film Review', July, 1971.

"A classic of Russian cinema..." -. Carlos Aguilar, 'Guía Del Vídeo-Cine'.

"Kozintsev...realized the impossible task of making KING LEAR possible on screen." – Kenneth S. Rothwell, 'Shakespeare and the Moving Image'.

KING LEAR
(G.B., 1976)

p.c. *Triple Action Theatre/British Film Institute Production Board.*
d. *Steven Rumbelow.*
l.p. *Chris Auvache; Gengiz Saner; Monia Buferd; Helena Paul.*
b.w. 45 mins.

An abbreviated version of the play focusing on key moments from it. Filmed entirely on location at night with torches carried by the actors for lighting, it is based on the Triple Action Theatre Group production from1973. It was probably filmed on 16 mm.

KING LEAR
(G.B., 1983)

p.c. *Granada.*
d. *Michael Elliott.*
l.p. *Laurence Olivier (King Lear); Dorothy Tutin (Goneril); Diana Rigg (Regan); Leo McKern; Anna Calder-Marshall; Colin Blakeley; John Hurt; Jeremy Kemp; Robert Lang; Robert Lindsay; David Threlfall; Brian Cox; Edward Petherbridge; Paul Curran; Esmond Knight.*
c. 180 mins.

It was not the intention to include television films in this work. But not to break this rule would have meant the exclusion of this magnificent opus by the then seventy-five year old Olivier. Anyway, it seems that the film received showings as a film in Europe so that justifies the inclusion if such justification is needed. At a cost of over £1,000,000, the studio exteriors by Roy Stonehouse were cleverly executed and Olivier's performance demanded nothing less that a fine supporting cast and a fine one it is. Some versions quote a shorter running time.

The Amandas, Norway, 1985: Technical Achievement-Music – Arne Norheim.

"...in its own class, a convincing portrayal of the title role by Olivier." – 'Lexikon Filme Im Fernsehen'.

KING LEAR – the Wellesian dream that was not to be.

In 1985, Orson Welles announced that he intended to film KING LEAR with himself in the lead role and as director and, as he put it, "with a little help from the French Culture Ministry" (later withdrawn). 'The Movie Scene' (April, 1985), reporting this said: "Hopefully this will not finish up as another of his unfinished works...". Sadly, such hope was dashed for the November issue of the same magazine had the sadder task of paying tribute to him following his death on October 10 of that year. Though television viewers had been able to see Welles as Lear in the CBS 1953 *Omnibus* programme directed by Peter Brook, who knows what masterpiece he might have produced?

✛ ✛ ✛ ✛ ✛

LE ROI LEAR AU VILLAGE
(France, 1911)

p.c. *Gaumont.*
d. *Louis Feuillade.*
l.p. *Alice Tissot; Henri Duval; Henri Gallet; Suzanne Grandais; Renée Carl.*
b.w. 1177 ft. (360 m). Sil.

A blind father is induced to transfer his property to his two daughters who promise to look after him. He lives with the first one for a while but she soon finds him onerous and sends him to her sister. There he receives similar scant attention. Dejected, he wanders and is found by his servants who take him to his lawyer. A meeting of the parties is convened and the elder daughter, to avoid a scandal, takes her father back home. She gradually begins to show remorse and compassion.

This short was one of the series "La Vie Telle Qu'elle Est". The American release is listed at 1010 ft. (309 m.).

"...intelligently produced...doesn't seem as effective as it ought to be..." – 'Kinematograph Weekly', July 22, 1911.

THE JEWISH KING LEAR
(G.B., 1912)

Professor Ball noted a film of this title made and shown in Commercial Road, London, U.K. dating from this year. Could it, perhaps, be an early version of...

THE YIDDISH KING LEAR
(U.S.A., 1935)

p.c. *Lear Pictures.*
d. *Harry Thomashefsky.*
l.p. *Maurice Krohner (David Moshele Lear); Fannie Levenstein (Hanna Lear); Eddie Pascal (Shomoi); Jacob Bergreen (Mr. Joffe); Niriam Grossmna (Toibelle); Maurice Weisman (Abraham Chariff); Jeanette Paskewich (Estelle); Esther Adler (Gittelle); MorrisTarlofsky (Moses Chorid); Rose Schwartzenberg (Servant).*
b.w. 86 mins.

A pious Jewish father tells his daughters that he plans to leave St. Petersburg, Russia, to live out his days in Jerusalem and that he is dividing his fortune among them. He refuses to listen to the daughter who defied him and became a student in St. Petersburg. The schemes of his sons-in-law bring disgrace and poverty to the father. The moral of the story unfolds but not without pain and agony.

Based on the play by Jacob Gordin, the basis of the story is clear and is transposed to the turn of the century. The dialogue is in Yiddish.

aka: THE JEWISH KING LEAR; DER YEDISHE KENIG LEAR

MIRELE EFROS
(U.S.A., 1939)

p.c. *Credo Pictures.*
d. *Josef Berne.*
l.p. *Berta Gersten (Mirele Efros); Michael Rosenberg (Nekhumtse); Louis Brandt (Donye); Ruth Elbaum (Sheyndl); Albert Lipton*

(Yosele); Sarah Kroner (Khana-Dvoire); Paula Walter (Makhle); Moise Feder (Shalmen); Jerry Rosenberg (Shloimele); Jacob Mestel (Pogorelsky); Ella Brouner (Dine); Ruben Wendroff (Badkhn); Egene Sigaloff; Moishe Schorr; Clara Deutchman.

b.w. 80 mins.

Mirele is a pious and wealthy widow in Grodno, Poland, at the turn of the century. She is devoted to her children but finds herself virtually evicted from her home by the woman she chose for her son as his wife.

Based on a play by Jacob Gordin which is sometimes known as "The Jewish Queen Lear", the underlying influence of the plot is clear. Berta Gersten who played the principal role was one of the most prominent of Yiddish actresses and she is perhaps best remembered for her fine performance in this film, which was made with dialogue in Yiddish, being the subject of a sub-titled version of it in 1978.

GUNSUNDARI KATHA
(India, 1949)

p.c.　Vauhini.
d.　K.V. Reddy.
l.p.　Relangi Venkatramaiah; K. Sivarao; T. G. Kamala; Sriranjini Jr.; Balijepalli; Malathij Seeta; Shantakumari; Govindrajulu Subbarao; Hemalatha Jr.; Lakshmikanta Kavi; Lakshmirajyam.

b.w. 172 mins.

An old man is upset when his daughter prefers to remain loyal to her crippled (because of a curse) husband. When the old man falls ill, the three sons-in-law go to seek a magic jewel to cure him. The youngest finds it but the others steal it and turn him into a bear. All ends well with the old man being cured and the cripple has his curse lifted.

Vaguely inspired by Shakespeare, the film (in the Telegu language) was remade in 1955 with the title GUNSUNDARI with K. Kameshiran, Roa Gemin and Ganesh Savilhro in the Tamil language.

The home/family syndrome has always been popular and successful in Indian cinema even back in the days of the silent film when a version of this story also appeared.

HARRY AND TONTO
(U.S.A., 1974)

p.c.　20th. Century Fox.
d.　Paul Mazursky.
l.p.　Art Carney (Harry Coombs); Ellen Burstyn (Shirley); Chief Dan George (Sam Two Feathers); Geraldine Fitzgerald (Jessie); Larry Hagman (Eddie); Arthur Hunnicutt (Wade); Phil Burns (Burt); Joshua Mostel (Norman); Melanie Mayron (Ginger); Avon Long (Leroy); Dolly Jonah (Elaine); Herbert Berghof (Rivetowski); Barbara Rhoades (Happy Hooker); Cliff DeYoung (Burt Jr.); Lou Guss (Dominic); Mike Nussbaum (Old Age Home Clerk); René Enriquez; Michael McCleery; Rashel Novikoff; Patricia Fay; Sybil Bowan; Joe Madden; Bette Howard; Muriel Beerman; Clint Young; Michael Butler; Cliff Norton; Lititia Toole; W. Benson Terry; Greg Harris; Phil Roth; Andr Philippe; Anatol Winogradoff; Sally K. Marr.

DeLuxe Color. 115 mins.

Harry is evicted from his apartment which is in a building scheduled for demolition. With his cat, Tonto, he spends some time with his son, Burt. Then he decides to visit his daughter, Shirley, in Chicago. He goes by car after problems with air and bus transport. He picks up a runaway girl, Ginger, and they seek out an old flame of hers. Norman, Burt's son, is sent to bring Harry back but he joins the two to drive West after Harry has spent some time with Shirley. Harry gives the car to the youngster and, after some more encounters, he goes to his son, Eddie, in Hollywood. Eddie's offer of accommodation is but an excuse to ask for a loan. Harry decides to take his own flat where Tonto dies and Harry wonders if he should move in with a woman who shares his love of cats.

Though set in modern America, the Lear influence is quite clear. Indeed, a firm indication is given at the start of the film when Harry is evicted quoting from the play as he is forced out.

Certainly, Harry's relationship with his children parallels that of Lear and many see the faithfulness of Tonto, the cat, akin to the simple fidelity of Lear's Fool.

Academy of Motion Picture Arts and Sciences, U.S.A., 1974: Awards – Best Actor (Art Carney), Best Original Screenplay (Paul Mazursky, Josh Greenfeld).
Atlanta Film Festival, U.S.A., 1973: Best of Festival – Second Prize, the Silver Phoenix, Best Actor (Art Carney), Best Supporting Actor (Larry Hagman), Best Supporting Actress (Ellen Burstyn), Best Director (Paul Mazursky).
Hollywood Foreign Press Association Golden Globe Awards, U.S.A., 1974: Best Actor -Musical/Comedy (Art Carney).
National Board of Review Awards, U.S.A., 1974: Best English Language Films – Listed fifth.
'New York Times' Ten Best List, U.S.A., 1974: Listed.

KING LEAR
(U.S.A., 1987)

p.c.　Cannon Films/Cannon International.
d.　Jean-Luc Godard.
l.p.　Burgess Meredith (Don Learo); Peter Sellars (William Shakespeare V); Molly Ringwald (Cordelia); Jean-Luc Godard (Professor);

Woody Allen (Mr. Alien); Norman Mailer; Kate Mailer; Léos Carax.
c. 91 mins.

Godard is under pressure to get this film ready for the Cannes Film Festival. Norman Mailer's daughter, Kate, does not like her father's screenplay which has a Mafia setting. William Shakespeare the Fifth, a detective for Cannon Cultural Division, arrives at Nyon, Switzerland. As all art and movies have been destroyed in an accident, he wants to reconstruct his ancestor's plays. He hears an old Mafia boss, Don Learo, recounting his memoirs to his daughter, Cordelia. A phrase she uses suggests AS YOU LIKE IT. He goes for long walks, is followed and mimicked. Meanwhile Learo receives flattering telexes from his daughters, Regan and Goneril, but he is upset with Cordelia. Shakespeare seeks out the Professor who is Godard capped like a fool and speaking in riddles to a reporter. A centrally heated apartment is the scene for some strange prophecies and events. In an editing room, two pieces of film have been stitched together. Mr.Alien, owner of the editing room, soliloquises glumly.

Shown at the Barcelona Film Festival, Spain, 1989.
Shown at the London Film Festival, England, 1987.

"There's little to be said about this pretentious mess except...avoid it." – Leonard Maltin, 'Movie And Video Guide.'

"Yet another of Jean-Luc Goddard's typically shapeless celluloid creations, full of bits and pieces adding up to plenty of spice but very little substance." – F. Maurice Speed, 'Film Review 1988/9'.

"Weird!" .– 'Satellite TV Europe'.

RAN
(France/Japan, 1985)

p.c. *A Serge Silberman Production for Greenwich Film Production/Herald Ace/Nippon Herald Films.*
d. *Akira Kurosawa.*
l.p. *Tatsuya Nakadai (Hidetora Ichimonji); Akira Terao (Taro Takatora Ichimonji); Jinpachi Nezu (Jiro Masatora Ichimonji); Daisuke Ryu (Saburo Naotora Ichimonji); Kazuo Kato (Kageyu Ikoma); Mieko Harada (Lady Kaede); Yoshiko Miyazaki (Lady Sué); Hitoshi Ueki (Nobuhiro Fujimaki); Shinnosuke Ikehata (Kyoami); Jun Tazaki (Seiji Ayabe); Norio Matsui (Shumenosuke); Hisashi Igawa (Shuri Kurogane); Toshiya Ito; Takeshi Kato; Kenji Kodama; Takesi Nomura; Masayuki Yui; Heihachiro Suzuki; Reiko Nanjo; Tokie Kanda; Sawako Kochi; Haruko Togo; Kumeko Otowa.*
c. 165 mins. S

In sixteenth century Japan, feudal lord Hidetora retires naming his son Taro as heir. His two other sons, Jiro and Saburo, receive castles. Saburo derides his father over the inheritance and with his retainer, Tango, is disinherited and banished. This is witnessed by two lords, Fujimaki and Ayabe. Both seek Saburo as husband for their daughters but Fujimaki offers Saburo shelter which he accepts while Tango does not. Taro's wife, Kaede, persuades him to exert his authority and he ejects his father who with his fool Kyoami goes to Jiro's castle where he is denied admission. While the sons battle with each other, wives plot and alliances raise armies, Hidetora wanders the plains and eventually goes mad. He dies when his son Saburo is killed. Only the death of the two seems to stop the fighting.

Though not credited as such, the source of inspiration is clear. Of course, language, time, place and even, in the case of the children, sex have been changed.

Shown as part of the Everybody's Shakespeare International Festival, London, England, 1994.
Shown at the first Tokyo International Film Festival, Japan, 1985.
Shown at the New York Film Festival, U.S.A., 1985.
Academy of Motion Picture Arts and Sciences, U.S.A., 1985: Nominations – Best Director (Akira Kurosawa), Best Cinematography, Best Art Direction (Yoshiro Muraki); Award – Best Costume Design (Emi Wada).
The Amandas, Norway, 1985: Best Foreign Film.
British Academy of Film and Television Arts, G.B., 1986: Best Foreign Film.
British Film Critics Circle Awards, G.B., 1986: Best Foreign Language Film; Best Director (Akira Kurasawa).
David di Donatello Awards, Italy, 1986: Best Foreign Direction (Akira Kurosawa).
Filmiaura Ry, Finland, 1986: Listed first in Best Films list; Best Director of Foreign Films (Akira Kurosawa).
Film Critics Circle of Australia, Australia, 1986/7: Best Foreign Film.
Japanese Academy, Japan, 1985: Best Music (Toru Takemitsu); Best Art Direction (Yoshiro Muraki).
Kinema Jumpo Annual Ten Best Films, Japan, 1985: Listed second in Foreign Film list.
Los Angeles Film Critics Awards, U.S.A., 1985: Best Foreign Film (shared with *The Official Story*).
Mainichi Eiga Concourse Awards, Japan, 1985: Best Film, Best Director (Akira Kurosawa).
National Board of Review, U.S.A., 1985: Listed first in Foreign Language Films list, Best Director (Akira Kurosawa).
National Society of Film Critics Awards, U.S.A., 1985: Best Film.
New York Film Critics Awards, U.S.A., 1985: Best Foreign Film.
Tokyo Blue Ribbon Prizes, Japan, 1985: Best Film, Best Director (Akira Kurosawa).
Union of Danish Film Critics, Denmark, 1986: Best Non-American Film.

This would seem an appropriate place to note the following film:

A.K.
(France/Japan, 1985)

p.c.   *Greenwich Film Production/Herald Nippon/ Herald Ace.*
d.   *Chris Marker.*
l.p.   *Documentary. Narrator: Chris Marker.*
c. 75 mins.

This is all about Akira Kurosawa with a personal history, clips from some of his films including KUMONOSU-JO but primarily about the filming of RAN. On the slopes of Mount Fuji, Japan, the director is seen at work on exteriors and crowd scenes. There are also scenes of the costumed extras rehearsing and waiting. The film notes the delays due to the bad weather. The narration is in French.

Japanese title: KUROSAWA AKIRA.

The internally feuding family theme has been used in many films and in many guises. Two are of particular note: *House Of Strangers* (U.S.A., 1949) about a financial baron and his four sons and what was effectively a remake, *Broken Lance* (U.S.A., 1954) which transposed the same story into a western setting and was nearer Shakespeare in its inspiration. The same-based story appeared again in 1961 with a circus setting as *The Big Show*. The Taiwanese film, directed by Ang Lee in 1994, *Eat Drink Man Woman* also has overtones of the plot concerning, as it does, a man and his three daughters of conflicting ideals and standards.

For other films with scenes from the play see **CHAPTER XXX ALL THE WORLD'S A STAGE**: SUCCESS (1923); LIFE BEGINS AT 8:30 (1942); THE DRESSER (1983) and SWAN SONG (1993) and **CHAPTER XXXII THE IMMORTAL BARD**: ENGLAND'S SHAKESPEARE (1939); FAIR ADVENTURE SERIES (1964) and EXPLORATIONS IN SHAKESPEARE (1969).

CHAPTER XII

THE LIFE AND DEATH OF KING JOHN

Dramatis Personæ:

King John
Prince Henry – his son
Arthur – his nephew and Duke of Britain
Queen Elinor – his mother
Blanch of Spain – his niece
Constance – Arthur's mother

Earl of Pembroke
Earl of Salisbury
Lord Bigot
Hubert de Burgh

Robert Faulconbridge – son of Sir Robert
  Faulconbridge
Philip the Bastard – his half-brother

Lady Faulconbridge
James Gurney – servant to Lady Faulconbridge

Philip of France
Lewis – the Dauphin
Melun – a French lord
Chatillion – ambassador from France.

Lymoges – Duke of Austria.
Cardinal Pandulph – the Pope's legate.

Peter of Pomfret – a prophet.
Lords, Ladies, Citizens of Angiers, Sheriff, Heralds,
  Officers, Soldiers, Executioners, Messengers,
  Attendants etc.

King Philip of France demands the return of former lands in France and the British Isles in the name of Arthur Plantagenet, the son of King John's late elder brother, Geoffrey. King John replies with a threat of war. Then a local problem is set before him.

Robert Faulconbridge and his half-brother, Philip the Bastard, are in dispute over their father's will. Sensing that Philip was sired by Richard the Lionheart (later so confirmed by Philip's mother), King John and his mother Queen Elinor find in his favour. They welcome him into the court with the title and name Sir Richard Plantagenet (to avoid confusion his original name is retained).

In France, Philip of France awaits with the Duke of Austria, Prince Arthur and others, the return of the messenger. When he does arrive, he advises that King John is not far behind him. John has brought with him Philip the Bastard and Princess Blanch of Spain. Discussions follow in order to avert war. Though Philip the Bastard tries to stir up trouble by urging John to take Angiers, where they are encamped, as Angiers has cunningly avoided taking sides until it is established who is the true King of Britain. The people of Angiers offer the solution that Princess Blanch marry the Dauphin of France. The kings agree and she takes as her dowry five areas of France plus a large sum of gold. John makes Arthur Duke of Britain, Earl of Richmond and gives him Angiers.

The Holy Legate, Pandulph, arrives from Rome and demands that King John keeps Stephen Langton out of Canterbury Cathedral. John loses his temper with

him. Threats of excommunication are made if Philip of France does not fight against John. Philip the Bastard, who dislikes the Duke of Austria, then arrives with the Duke's head.

John now feigns friendship and wellbeing towards Arthur and leaves him in the care of Hubert. He makes it clear to Hubert that he must kill the boy if necessary. While the army remains at Angiers, John and his retinue return to England.

In Northumberland Castle, Hubert shows Arthur his orders to blind him but he cannot do it. A French army lands in England. Both Elinor and Arthur's mother die and Hubert, having previously lied to King John, now tells him that Arthur is alive. John also has problems with some of his lords who are allying with the French.

Arthur takes his own life by jumping from the castle walls. The dissenting lords find his body with Philip the Bastard whom they accuse of murdering the boy. When Hubert arrives and says that Arthur is well, suspicion switches to him but he denies it.

At court, Pandulph makes his peace with King John returning rule to him by returning the crown which he had previously been given. Urged by John to meet the French army, he agrees accepting the blame for the current crisis. Philip the Bastard arrives with news that Kent has fallen and the Dauphin has taken London.

On the battlefield at St. Edmundsbury, the Dauphin refuses to heed Pandulph's pleas. John, however, leaves the field at the request of Philip the Bastard and goes to Swinstead Abbey as he is sick with a fever. He is pleased when news comes that the French supply ships have been wrecked on the Goodwin Sands thus coaxing the defecting lords back to the side of John.

Hubert tells Philip the Bastard that the King is ill, believed poisoned by a monk. Philip then tells that he has lost nearly everything in the Wash. John is carried outside the Abbey and talks with Prince Henry, John's son, when news comes that the Dauphin is approaching. As John dies, Henry learns that the French are prepared to make peace.

Note: There is no historical evidence upon which to fix a date for the writing of this play. Some sources feel it may have been written as early as 1590, drawing upon a number of sources. More commonly accepted is that it was written between 1592 and 1596 with 1594 as the most likely. The source is considered to be an anonymous two-part play 'The Troublesome Reign Of John' printed in 1591. Shakespeare's revision of it, though following the original fairly closely, tones down the violent anti-Catholicism (including the omission of the most offensive scene) as he was seeking the patronage of the Earl of Southampton, a staunch Catholic.

✢ ✢ ✢ ✢ ✢

KING JOHN
(G.B., 1899)

p.c. *British Mutoscope and Biograph Company.*
d. *William Kennedy-Laurie Dickson.*
l.p. *Herbert Beerbohm Tree (King John); Julia Neilson (Constance); Norman McKinnel (Lymoges); Lewis Walker (Philip); Dora Senior (Prince Henry); F. M. Paget (Robert Bigot); James Fisher (Earl of Pembroke); Arthur Sefton (Arthur); Gerald Lawrence (Dauphin); Franklyn McLeay (Hubert); Louis Calvert (Pandulph); William Mollison (King of France); S. A. Cookson (Earl of Salisbury).*
b.w. See text. Sil.

This early film holds a unique position in film history being the first known film of a Shakespeare play, albeit in part. Long thought lost, some parts have been found. The original is thought to have lasted about four minutes and was of four scenes – the battlefield near Angiers, the French King's tent and two scenes in the orchard at Swinstead Abbey. These latter scenes showed the death of John and the crowning of Henry.

Claims that this was a direct filming of scenes from Her Majesty's Theatre production of the period are not true. It was filmed at the production company's open air studio on the Thames embankment using a simple backdrop as scenery. It is true that the film was based on the stage production and it is on this basis and from other clues that the cast list has been prepared. Filmed in widescreen 68 mm. in September, 1899, the film premièred on September 20 of that year at the Palace Theatre, London, and at other venues in Britain, Europe and America. It

coincided with the opening of the stage version. A set of Mutoscope cards for use in peep show machines was also made available. All that survives of the film is from the third scene.

Not too much should be read into the directorial role for it was probably little more than doing the actual filming. The results must have been quite an experience for the public. Today, 70 mm. widescreen presentation is common but a century ago the moving picture was itself a new wonder one can only imagine the impact 68 mm. must have made. Even if Tree's performance now seems somewhat risible, this little film is important in many ways.

aka: BEERBOHM TREE, THE GREAT ENGLISH ACTOR

HUBERT AND ARTHUR
(G.B., 1914)

p.c. *Eric Williams Speaking Pictures.*
d. *Eric Williams.*
l.p. *Eric Williams (Hubert).*
b.w. (?) mins. Sil. (see text)

As the action unfolded on the screen, Eric Williams recited from the stage in this extract from THE LIFE AND DEATH KING JOHN.

SAEED-E-HAVAS
(India, 1936)

p.c. *Stage Film.*
d. *Sohrab Merwanji Modi.*
l.p. *Sohrab Merwanji Modi.*
b.w. Feature.

This Urdu version used the adaptation by the then influential Indian playwright Aga Hashr Kashmiri. Modi was noted for his stage productions of classical works.

✢ ✢ ✢ ✢ ✢

England's King John (1199 to 1216) is best remembered as the king whom the barons forced to sign the Magna Carta which became the foundation of an Englishman's liberty. No film of the complete Shakespeare play appears to have been made of this king whom Sir George Bellew, K.C.V.O., describes in 'Britain's Kings And Queens' as not having a single redeeming feature. He notes: "The list of King John's malefactions and stupidities is endless...", a view endorsed by most films about the English outlaw hero Robin Hood who seems to have spent most of his celluloid life in fighting King John and his cronies. He has even been portrayed comically in the Mel Brooks 1993 *Robin Hood: Men In Tights* which contains the occasional quotation and mis-quotation from Shakespeare. More seriously, the early life of John was partly featured in the James Goldman play and 1968 film *The Lion In Winter.*

CHAPTER XIII
THE LIFE OF KING HENRY THE FIFTH

Dramatis Personæ:

King Henry V
Dukes of Gloucester and Bedford – the King's brothers
Duke of Exeter – the King's uncle
Duke of York – the King's cousin

Earls of Salisbury, Westmoreland, Warwick and Cambridge
Sir Thomas Grey
Lord Scroop
Sir Thomas Erpingham
Gower, Fluellen, Jamy, Macmorris – officers in the English army
John Bates, Alexander Court, Michael Williams – soldiers in the English army
Pistol, Nym, Bardolph
Hostess Quickly of an Eastcheap tavern and Pistol's wife
Boy

An English Herald
Archbishop of Canterbury
Bishop of Ely

King Charles VI of France
Queen Isabel of France
Katherine – daughter of Charles and Isobel
Lewis, Dauphin of France
Alice – Katherine's attendant
Dukes of Burgundy, Orleans, Bourbon and Britaine
The Constable of France
Rambures, Grandpré – French Lords
Montjoy – French herald
Governor of Harfleur
French Ambassador to England

Chorus
Lords, Ladies, Officers, Attendants, Soldiers, Citizens, Messengers

A bill is due before the King which, if approved, would mean the loss of lands to the church. While the Archbishop of Canterbury believes the King, a reformed character since his accession to the throne, is well disposed towards the church, he feels it best to distract the King away from the bill. To this end he induces the King with much rhetoric, to press the English claim for former properties in France to be returned. The King is anxious that a war with France may leave the border with Scotland open to attack. The Archbishop offers to fund the war and if the King had any doubts, these disappear when the French Ambassador arrives with an insulting gift from the Dauphin of France – tennis balls.

As the King makes ready to sail from Southampton, elsewhere three soldiers, Pistol, Nym and Bardolph are at Hostess Quickly's inn. Here, Sir John Falstaff, banished former friend and carousing companion of the King, dies.

The King has an immediate problem. Lord Scroop, the Earl of Cambridge and Sir Thomas Grey have indulged in a plot to kill the king. They are duly arrested to face the ultimate penalty and the King with his forces sail for France.

In the French court, the Dauphin makes light of the English invasion but the Constable of France warns against such levity. Lord Exeter acts as herald and delivers a stern warning to the French King to return the lands or face war. The King of France promises a reply on the next day.

Meanwhile King Henry has laid seige to Harfleur. His captains talk and jest with each other as news comes of the town's surrender which lack of support from the Dauphin has forced upon the Governor. The town taken, the King plans to march to Calais.

At the French court, Princess Katherine is trying to learn a little English from her attendant, Alice. The King, the Dauphin and advisers discuss the English advance. The King, urged on by the Dauphin's tales of mockery by the French women, at last arouses himself to action. All are aware that King Henry's advance has weakened his men both in numbers and individual strength.

Nevertheless, the tired forces of Henry advance. The King finds one of his former drinking friends, Bardolph, accused of robbing a church and must face death. Henry orders his men to treat the French civilians with respect and honesty. At that moment, a messenger to King Henry from the French arrives to tell him that he should not measure his success by the taking of Harfleur. Further, King Charles is looking for compensation for loss of life and French property. The messenger receives a tough message for his master.

Again the Dauphin makes light of the English and the Constable of France reminds him of English courage.

Indeed, there are some faint hearts in the English camp as King Henry passes among his troops incognito. He hears their views and talks with them. As dawn breaks he prays for strength for his men. With good reason, too, for the French outnumber the English by five to one.

Having ridden out to view the situation, Henry returns to give a rousing speech to his men before the battle saying that those who fight on this, Saint Crispin's day, will have a proud story to tell. This seems to stir the men's spirits and they prepare for battle while the King again rebuffs the call, delivered by the herald from the Constable of France, to surrender.

Confident, the French charge but are cut down time and time again. The battle goes well for Henry but he warns that it is not over. He comes across two of his captains viewing with sadness and outrage that the French have attacked the luggage camp and killed, against the accepted rules of war, unarmed boys. The King is very angry at this.

Then the French herald arrives to concede defeat and ask for leave to collect and bury the French dead. He learns from him that the field where the battle took place was near Agincourt and so the field is thus named.

Having forgiven a soldier who spoke out against the King not realising to whom he was speaking, Henry looks at the death toll. With ten thousand French dead and many prisoners, the King is relieved that only twenty-nine English were killed (see Footnote) and orders that the holy rites be performed.

The victorious Henry now calls upon the French King. Both factions, through the Duke of Burgundy as intermediary, talk of peace but Henry insists his demands be met. King Charles begs leave to retire to consider. Henry agrees but asks that Princess Katherine stay. Henry proceeds to woo her telling her that he is no smoothed-tongue beguiler but an honest and direct-speaking man. He proposes marriage and she accepts if it pleases her father and, as all return to witness the happy couple, it is clear that it does please King Charles. He also agrees to the demands with the hope that the union of the two will spare the two countries from agression between them forever.

Footnote: Modern estimates of the French and English killed are seven thousand and about four hundred and fifty respectively. In his film version Laurence Olivier balances the figure for the English dead in the play and modern thinking with a compromise of five and twenty score (five hundred).

Note: This rather curious mixture of dramatic epic and comic pastiche dates from 1599. There had already been an anonymous play registered in 1594 on roughly the same subject though what influence this had on Shakespeare is conjectural.

✠ ✠ ✠ ✠ ✠

HENRY V
(G.B., 1913)

p.c. *Unknown – an amateur production.*
d.
l.p. *The boys of Shakespeare's school.*
b.w. (?) mins. Sil.

Though an amateur film, this was apparently shown at The Picture House, Stratford-upon-Avon. It was the policy of this venue to show films which were of local interest and did so with success. This may have been the first amateur version of a Shakespearean play to reach the screen but who can be sure?

ENGLAND'S WARRIOR KING
(G.B., 1915)

p.c. *Eric Williams Speaking Pictures.*
d. *Eric Williams.*
l.p. *Eric Williams (Henry V); Men of the Royal Scots Greys.*
b.w. (?) mins. Sil. (see text)

An on-stage reciter is accompanied by film action on screen.

The use of the soldiers was a temporal expedient as the troops were stationed at York at the time the film was being made there.

THE CHRONICLE HISTORY OF KING HENRY FIFT WITH HIS BATTELL FOUGHT AT AGINCOURT IN FRANCE by WILL SHAKESPEARE...
(G.B., 1944)

p.c. *Two Cities.*
d. *Laurence Olivier.*
l.p. *Laurence Olivier (Henry V); Robert Newton (Ancient Pistol); Leslie Banks (Chorus); Renée Asherson (Katherine); Esmond Knight (Fluellen); Harcourt Williams (Charles VI); Leo Genn (Constable); Ralph Truman (Mountjoy); Ivy St Helier (Alice); Ernest Thesiger (Duke of Bedford); Max Adrian (Dauphin); Francis Lister (Duke of Orleans); Russell Thorndike (Duke of Bourbon); Valentine Dyall (Duke of Burgundy); Morland Graham (Sir Thomas Erpingham); Robert Hannen (Duke of Exeter); Robert Helpmann (Bishop of Ely); Felix Aylmer (Archbishop of Canterbury); George Robey (Sir John Falstaff); Freda Jackson (Mistress Quickly); George Cole; Jimmy Hanley; John Laurie; Niall McGinnis; Frederick Cooper; Roy Emerton; Griffith Jones.*
Technicolor. 137 mins.

Though commonly known as **HENRY V** (and this title for the sake of brevity will be used), the film does not have a title in the usual sense. The title as listed above appears in the form of a poster advertising that a performance "will be played by The Lord Chamberlain's Men at the Globe Playhouse This Day the First of May, 1600". On this aspect, Paul Rotha in 'The Film Till Now' comments that the film "...was probably the first instance of a legitimately photographed play, inasmuch as its structure was designed constantly to remind the spectator of the fact that it was a play and not a film. When the action moved out of the Globe Theatre, it moved into fairyland, not actuality, and thus avoided that conflict between poetic speech and three-dimensional reality that has set all previous versions of Shakespeare at nought."

Olivier had wanted Vivien Leigh for the part of Katherine but David O. Selznick refused to release her following her success in *Gone With The Wind*. He had no luck either in obtaining the services of William Wyler so he directed the film himself. He, with Alan Dent, was also responsible for the screenplay which cut the text by a quarter but added the Agincourt battle scene (filmed in Ireland) and introduces the death of Falstaff (only referred to in the play) to cover the man's disgrace.

The film was budgeted at £300,000 but actually cost £400,000. Such cost would take some time to recover but the production did give a tremendous boost to the British film industry and was seen as a great achievement especially as Britain was at war. The film was seen, too, as a warning to Germany and inspirational to the British (clearly stated by the film's opening dedication). After all, could any true Englishman fail to be stirred by:

"Follow your spirit; and upon this charge,
Cry, 'God for Harry, England, and Saint George!'"
(Act III, Scene 1)

To this must be added an impressive music score by William Walton. At the time of the film's release the British record company H.M.V. issued a set of four records (they would have been the 78 r.p.m. variety and probably the large 12 inch ones) of speeches by Olivier and, of course, the music. Walton himself conducted the Philharmonia Orchestra and the same musical combination was used for the later stereo recording in 1964 of a suite of music from the film also issued by H.M.V.. Sir Charles Groves conducted the Royal Liverpool Philharmonic Orchestra in a recording of the same suite on the H.M.V. release "Walton: Music For Shakespearean Films". The suite also appeared on "Great Film Music" on the Viva label in Britain with Stanley Black conducting the London Festival Orchestra. RCA, Epic and London are companies which have all issued the music in some form but the latest release enjoys all

the benefits of modern technology. This is by Chandos, a British company, in its series dedicated to Walton's film scores. For this Neville Marriner conducted the Academy of St. Martin-in-the-Fields.

Lone Wolf, a British company releasing 8 mm. films for the home movie collector, made the film, uncut, available in the Super 8 mm. format.

In a commemorative set of stamps issued by Sierra Leone following the death of Olivier, the actor was featured on the Le9 value stamp as he appeared in this film.

Shown as part of the Everybody's Shakespeare International Festival, London, England, 1994.
Shown at the Muestra Cinematográfica del Atlantico, Cadiz, Spain, 1988.
Shown at the Muestra Cinematográfica del Atlantico, Cadiz, Spain, 1990.
Shown at the Shakespeare Film Festival, Wiesbaden, W. Germany, 1964.
Venice Film Festival, Italy, 1946: Special Mention.
Academy of Motion Picture Arts and Sciences, U.S.A., 1946: Nominations – Best Film, Best Actor (Laurence Olivier), Best Score of a Dramatic or Comedy Picture (William Walton); Special Award – Laurence Olivier for his outstanding achievement as actor, producer and director in bringing HENRY V to the screen.
Kinema Jumpo Annual Best Ten Films, Japan, 1948: Listed first in Foreign Films list.
National Board of Review Awards, U.S.A., 1946: Best Picture, Best Actor (Laurence Olivier), Ten Best Films – first position.
New York Film Critics Awards, U.S.A., 1946: Best Actor (Laurence Olivier).
'New York Times', U.S.A., Annual Ten Best List, 1946: Listed fourth.
'Picturegoer' magazine, G.B., 1946: Annual Award.
Sindicato Nazionale Giornalisti Cinematografici Italiani, Italy, 1945/50: Best Foreign Director (Laurence Olivier).
'Time' magazine, U.S.A., Annual Ten Best List, 1946: Featured in the list.

"Every so often there comes along a film which is as much an occasion as it is a work of art. This was true of...HENRY V..." – Roger Manvell, 'The Penguin Film Review No. 8'.

"It is an amazing accomplishment, something never quite done before, in which cinematic realism and theatrical illusion are subtly mixed..." – William Bayer, 'The Great Movies'.

"...a beautiful rendering of the play from the theatrical point of view." – Roger Manvell, 'Film'.

"The principal worth of HENRY V lies in its splendid colourful treatment..." – Pere Ginferrer, 'Cine y Literatura'.

"...one is stupefied by the virtuosity of the director..."
– 'Guide Akai Vidéo-Cassettes'.

"...grand music, fine acting, many – sometimes startling – innovations, this is one of the finest and certainly most interesting examples of film art ever to come out of a studio." – F. Maurice Speed, 'Film Review 1945/6'.

STUDY EXTRACTS
A compilation of extracts from the film including the Prologue and the Agincourt scene is available for study purposes. It runs for thirty minutes.

HENRY V
(G.B., 1989)

p.c. *Renaissance Films in association with the B.B.C.*
d. *Kenneth Branagh.*
l.p. *Kenneth Branagh (Henry V); Derek Jacobi (Chorus); Simon Shepherd (Gloucester); Ian Holm (Fluellen); James Larkin (Bedford); James Simmons (York); Alec MCowen (Ely); Brian Blessed (Exeter); Paul Gregory (Westmoreland); Fabian Cartwright (Cambridge); Charles Kay (Archbishop of Canterbury); Stephen Simms (Scroop); Edward Jewesbury (Erpingham); Jay Villiers (Grey); Robbie Coltrane (Sir John Falstaff); Richard Briers (Bardolph); Emma Thompson (Katherine); Daniel Webb (Gower); Jimmy Yuill (Jamy); John Sessions (MacMorris); Shaun Prendergast (Bates); Pat Doyle (Court); Judi Dench (Mistress Quickly); Michael Williams (Williams); Geoffrey Hutchings (Nym); Robert Stevens (Pistol); Christian Bale (Boy); Paul Scofield (French King); Michael Maloney; Harold Innocent; Richard Clifford; Richard Easton; Colin Hurley; Geraldine McEwan; Christopher Ravenscroft; David Lloyd Meredith; Tom Whitehouse; David Parfitt; Nicholas Ferguson; Nigel Greaves; Mark Inman; Julian Gartside; Chris Armstrong; Calum Yuill.*
Eastman Color. 137 mins. S

Though Branagh takes a different approach to the play, he also has borrowed from HENRY IV for King Henry's personal flashbacks of Falstaff and Bardolph. Chorus takes on modern garb and incidents, minor in the original, now take on more importance and are used to emphasize the changes in both the times and the King. As Olivier's version served the needs of the day, Branagh's matches the different mood of today.

While Olivier's film reflected, as he intended, the theatrical expression and thus, in general, all is clean and colourful, Branagh's view is realistic. The inn, its owners and its patrons are low life, the royal rooms are poorly lit, and the battlefield is mud, blood, sweat and tears. Yet, surprisingly in some ways, Branagh sticks to the Shakespearean numbers of the dead at Agincourt.

Even forty and more years on, any version of the play is bound to be measured against the Olivier version. Yet, is this necessary? Any play is open to interpretation. Two actor/directors from different generations have given theirs. That does not imply that one is greater, the other lesser, simply different. More important, surely, is that both can be enjoyed for both readings of the play are equally valid.

The music for the film was composed by Patrick Doyle and played by the City of Birmingham Symphony Orchestra conducted by Simon Rattle. This fine soundtrack score, often dark and sombre, was released on disc by E.M.I. A film about the making of this film was made with the title **A LITTLE TOUCH OF HARRY** and there was also a book published with the same motive. The film proper was shown at Expo '92, Seville, Spain.

Shown as part of the Everybody's Shakespeare International Festival, London, England, 1994.
Academy of Motion Picture Arts and Sciences, U.S.A., 1989: Nominations – Best Director (Kenneth Branagh), Best Actor (Kenneth Branagh); Award – Best Costume Design (Phyllis Dalton).
British Academy of Film and Television Arts, G.B., 1990: Best Director (Kenneth Branagh).
British Film Institute Awards, G.B., 1990: Best Film, Technical Achievement.
European Film Festival Awards, G.B., 1990: Best Actor (Kenneth Branagh).
'Evening Standard' Film Awards, G.B., 1990: Best Film.
'Fotogramas' magazine Best Of 1990, Spain, 1991 – Shared seventh position in Foreign Film section.
National Board of Review, U.S.A., 1989: Listed second in Ten Best Films in English list, Best Director (Kenneth Branagh).
New York Film Critics' Circle Awards, U.S.A., 1989: Best First-Time Director (Kenneth Branagh).

"Branagh...proves he's a star of considerable talent, both behind and in front of the camera." – F. Maurice Speed, 'Film Review 1990/1'.

"A different reading from Olivier's but no less impressive." – Leonard Maltin, 'Movie And Video Guide'.

"The young actor directed and starred in this impressive film trying to maintain fidelity to the original work down to the minutest detail. The result is really masterly." – 'Tele Plus' (Spanish weekly television magazine).

"Olivier's film was bright and full of patriotic pride, made to rouse a nation at war. Branagh's film is dark, made for a generation which has seen the disasters of Vietnam and distrusts any call to arms." – J. L. G. – 'Fotogramas'.

"Here Branagh makes his own version of the original text, presenting a king of complex emotions more in accord with the man himself and thus leaving aside the war-like zest." – 'TP' (Spanish weekly television magazine).

"Filmed theatre? Certainly not. With Branagh, the spectacle is there." – G.L., 'Video 7', April, 1992.

✠ ✠ ✠ ✠ ✠

King Henry V (1413 to 1422) appears to have been quite a good king and much loved by his subjects. Not only was he an excellent soldier recapturing England's interests in France, but was also a fine diplomat and patron of the arts. It is strange that his life story has not proved more of an attraction for film makers. As it is, such is the quality of the two versions that have been made that they more than compensate for the lack of quantity. Parts of the same play are covered in Orson Welles' **CAMPANADAS A MEDIANOCHE** which deals with the story of Sir John Falstaff. The King as a youthful Price Hal was featured in Rudolph Maté's film *The Black Shield Of Falworth* (U.S.A., 1954) with Dan O'Herlihy taking on the role.

For other films with scenes from the play see **CHAPTER XXX ALL THE WORLD'S A STAGE**: ROYAL CAVALCADE (1935) and RENAISSANCE MAN (1994) and **CHAPTER XXXII THE IMMORTAL BARD**: MARCH OF THE MOVIES (1939)*; THIS THEATER AND YOU (1950?)*; THE POETS EYE – A TRIBUTE TO WILLIAM SHAKESPEARE (1964)*; FAIR ADVENTURE SERIES (1964); AUS HOLZ EIN O – DAS GLOBE-THEATER DES SAM WANAMAKER (1997) and SHAKESPEARE'S THEATRE (19??)*.

* Denotes film extract.

CHAPTER XIV
MACBETH

Dramatis Personæ:

Duncan, King of Scotland
Malcolm, Donalbain – his sons

Macbeth – a Scottish nobleman
Lady Macbeth – his wife

Banquo – a Scottish nobleman
His ghost
Fleance – his son

Macduff – a Scottish nobleman
Lady Macduff – his wife
Boy – his son

Lennox, Ross, Menteith, Angus, Caithness – Scottish
 noblemen

Siward, Earl of Northumberland
Young Siward – his son

Hecate
Three Weird Sisters
Three murderers
Seyton, – an officer to Macbeth
A Gentlewoman – attendant to Lady Macbeth
A captain
An English doctor
A Scottish doctor
A porter
An old man
Apparitions, Lords, Officers, Soldiers, Messengers,
 Attendants etc.

King Duncan of Scotland learns of the victory, led by Macbeth and Banquo, over the rebellious Thane of Cawdor who has been aided by Norsemen. Returning with his friend Banquo from this victory, Macbeth, a relative of King Duncan, encounters three weird creatures in a wild area. The first greets him by his name and rank, Thane of Glamis. He is surprised and is even more so when the second hails him as Thane of Cawdor and the third as the future king. For Banquo, they predict that his sons will inherit the throne. Within a short time, a messenger arrives to tell Macbeth that he has been made Thane of Cawdor in recognition of his deeds in the battle. Though the first part of the prophecy seems to have been fulfilled, Banquo tells Macbeth, who is well aware that the King has sons to succeed him, not to read too much into the prophecy in case ambition takes root in him. However, the seeds of such ambition that the witches have planted have found fertile soil.

Arriving at his pleasantly situated home, Macbeth tells his devious, ambitious wife of his meeting. Later, King Duncan arrives with his sons, Malcolm and Donalbain, to express his thanks to his generals and is made very welcome. Hidden by her pleasant smiles are murderous thoughts in Lady Macbeth and she instills in her husband that the way to the throne can be achieved only by the death of Duncan.

The King, tired after his journey and very content at the welcome he has received, retires early to bed. As night falls, Lady Macbeth finds herself unable to carry out the deed she has planned. She and her husband speak of the King's fine qualities, of the laws of hospitality and of Macbeth's own royal position, but in the end Macbeth, urged on by his wife, carries

out the foul murder accompanied by strange visions and hearing grim voices. He returns to his wife in a greatly disturbed state. Lady Macbeth washes the blood from him and leaves the dagger with the King's grooms, who sleep with the King, smearing them with blood.

The next morning when the murder is discovered, despite the obvious evidence pointing to the grooms who lacked any motive to commit such a crime, suspicion rests on Macbeth and both Malcolm and Donalbain flee. The natural heirs gone, the crown falls to Macbeth.

Disturbed by the prophecy concerning Banquo, Macbeth arranges a great feast at which, during the night, he has Banquo, who is returning from a journey, murdered though his son, Fleance, escapes. During the feast the Queen acts with great care for her guests but Macbeth acts strangely seeing the ghost of Banquo. He suffers fearful nightmares and determines to seek out again the three weird beings.

He finds them in a cave mixing obnoxious potions and he seeks their counsel. They warn him to beware of the Thane of Fife, Macduff, of whom Macbeth is jealous. He is also told than he cannot be killed by any man born of woman and that he should fear nothing until Birnam Wood moves to Dunsinane Hill. He is happy in this prophecy but disturbed at the visions created when he asks about Banquo's heirs.

To ensure his safety he has Macduff's family murdered which alienates the other thanes. Many flee to England where Macduff is raising an army. Macbeth's wife is now troubled in mind and dies, probably by her own hand, and Macbeth himself is deeply disturbed caring not whether he lives or dies.

Uncertain about the prophecy, he shuts himself away in his castle which he believes is impregnable to siege. When one of his men tells him that he has seen Birnam Wood moving, despair sets in. Malcolm has had his men cut branches as camouflage thus giving the appearance of such a phenomenon. Macbeth attacks and, though his men fight with little spirit for his cause, he himself fights savagely to seek out Macduff. Cursed by Macduff for his vile deeds, Macbeth taunts him that his life is charmed, repeating the prophecy. Macduff, however, reveals that he was delivered by Caesarian section.

Macduff goads him to surrender and then to battle but Macbeth, issuing a warning to those who believe in the tales of witches, attacks Macduff who, after a fierce struggle, kills Macbeth and presents his head to the rightful king, Malcolm, who is acclaimed by the people.

Note: The first mention of this, the shortest of the Tragedies, is a performance at the Globe theatre on April 20, 1611. However, the style suggests that it may have been written about 1605 or 1606. Again Holinshed's 'Chronicles' was the source material used by Shakespeare. There is one school of thought that favours the view that it was written to please James Stuart who had recently (1603) become King of England as well as Scotland. He was nominal patron of Shakespeare's company and intensely interested in witchcraft. Added to this, he was reputedly descended from Banquo. This is, however, open to debate.

✤ ✤ ✤ ✤ ✤

DUEL SCENE FROM MACBETH
(U.S.A., 1905)

p.c. *American Mutoscope and Biograph Company.*
d.
l.p.
b.w. 21 ft. (6 m.) approx. Sil.

This is noted as being photographed by Billy Bitzer and was the third part of a series called *Fights Of Nations* which was designed to show various forms of combat. In any other situation it would be hard to relate Shakespeare to this theme but, well, in the movies anything is possible! As it is, this brief – the length given is that of the copy in the American Library of Congress – film is all fast and furious action of three men fighting against a painted backdrop. One (Siward?) falls dead, the other two (Macduff and Macbeth) fight on.

The 'American Film Institute Catalog' notes the length as 53 ft. (16 m.) and by others as 72 ft. (22 m.).

MACBETH, SHAKESPEARE'S SUBLIME TRAGEDY
(U.S.A., 1908)

p.c. *Vitagraph.*
d. *James Stuart Blackton.*
l.p. *Maurice Costello (Macbeth); Florence Lawrence (Lady Macbeth); Thomas H. Ince; Florence Auer.*
b.w. 843 ft. (257 m.) Sil.

A synopsis of the play, this used dramatic, rapid action scenes to condense the story and preserve coherence. At least seventeen sequences are noted.

William V. Ranous is credited as director by some and as being in the cast (as Macbeth) along with Paul Panzer and Miss Carver (as Lady Macbeth).

MACBETH
(Italy, 1909)

p.c. *Cines.*
d. *Mario Caserini.*
l.p. *Dante Capelli (Macbeth); Maria Casperini (Lady Macbeth); Amletto Novelli (Palormi?)*
b.w. 1450 ft. (442 m.) Sil.

A colour tinted version was also issued of this version of the play which appears to have more in common with Roman peplum than bleak Scotland. It is also noted as a shorter – 919 ft. (280 m.) – release. Other releases are more-or-less in line with the original in length except the American one at 1500 ft. (457 m). The alternative title suggests that the plot may have placed more emphasis upon the lady of the story.

"...was rated very high by contemporary critics and sold well abroad." – Vernon Jarrett, 'The Italian Cinema'.

aka: LADY MACBETH

MACBETH
(France, 1910)

p.c. *Film D'Art.*
d. *Henri Andréani?*
l.p. *Edouard de Max (Macbeth); Jeanne Delvair (Lady Macbeth); Réjane; Henri Pouctal.*
b.w. 1066 ft. (325 m.) Sil.

Seventeen tableaux made up this adaptation of the play.

The credits for this film are suspect. Some sources note an earlier (1908) version crediting Albert Capellani as director with the same lead star and production credited to Pathé/ Société Cinématografique des Auteurs et Gens de Lettres. These claims are difficult to substantiate and Professor Ball and others feel that there was no such film. 'Pathé Weekly Bulletin' of May 30, 1910, notes the issue of the above with the best French actors in the leading parts. It may be that the director is as above with Ferdinand Zecca supervising. Paul Mounet is also named as playing the lead role.

MACBETH
(G.B., 1911)

p.c. *Cooperative Cinematograph Co.*
d. *Frank R. Benson.*
l.p. *Frank R. Benson (Macbeth); Constance Benson (Lady Macbeth); Murray Carrington; Guy Rathbone.*
b.w. 1360 ft. (415 m.) Sil.

This is an extract from the Stratford Memorial Theatre production of the era with two great performers of the day playing the principal roles.

MACBETH
(Germany, 1913)

p.c. *HeidelbergerFilm Industrie.*
d. *Arthur Bourchier.*
l.p. *Arthur Bourchier (Macbeth); Violet Vanbrugh (Lady Macbeth).*
b.w. 5 reels. Sil.

Said to be a lost film, it is noted as being both ambitious and unusually long for the era.

Bourchier received £4000 for this enterprise which involved filming in Heidelberg with supporting German players. It was planned to be the first of a series but, despite the pedigree of the leading players, it was none too successful and no more were made. The length of the film varies with 4200 ft. (1280 m.), 4500 ft. (1371 m.) and 4700 ft. (1433 m.) being quoted by diverse sources.

MACBETH
(France, 1916)

p.c. *Éclair.*
d.
l.p. *Georgette Leblanc Maeterlinck (Lady Macbeth); Severin Mars.*
b.w. (?) mins. Sil.

Sadly another lost film which is described as a "series of illustrative scenes". Its content is open to speculation. There may be a clue in that the leading lady was a Belgian opera diva.

MACBETH
(U.S.A., 1916)

p.c. *Reliance Motion Picture Corp.*
d. *John Emerson, David Wark Griffith.*
l.p. *Herbert Beerbohm Tree (Macbeth); Constance Collier (Lady Macbeth); Wilfred Lucas (Macduff); Spottiswoode Aitken (Duncan); Ralph Lewis (Banquo); Mary Alden (Lady Macduff); Olga Grey (Lady Agnes); L. de Nowskowski (Malcolm); Seymour Hastings (Ross); Jack Conway (Lennox); Bessie Buskirk (Donalbain); Carl Forbes Jr. (Bishop); Jack Brammel (Seyton); L.Tylden, Scott McKee, Jack Leonard (Witches); Raymond Wells (Thane Of Cawdor); Madge Dyer, Francis Carpenter, Thelma Burns (Macduff's Children); George McKenzie (Doctor); Chandler House (Fleance).*
b.w. 8 reels. Sil.

This film no longer exists but was said to be very good. "Sir Herbert insisted on spouting every word of MACBETH into the camera which was a terrible waste of film. The cameraman would pull the crank out and let Sir Herbert carry on and on until the director gave a signal that they were going to film the action. Sir Herbert never found out that he was spouting MACBETH into an empty camera.", noted Anita Loos who also recalls her own recognition in the credits as "By William Shakespeare. Titles by Anita Loos".

Tree and Collier had played the same roles on the London stage but this was Tree's first American film. It is said to be faithful to the play and realistic, particularly in the battle scenes. More recent sources suggest that Erich von Stroheim may have assisted in the film which may have, later, been reduced to seven reels.

It seems that at its first showing the film was augmented by an orchestral accompaniment and, after the first day, added a comedy to alleviate the heavy drama. The film was shown in two parts. Opinion of the day indicates excellent direction, performances and production values. The appeal of the film was, according to comment, diminished without the beauty of the dialogue and, since the film had missed the flood of Shakespearean film of a few months earlier, the main attraction would be Tree. The feeling of the public was that it was proper to see such a film because of what it was.

"Lovers of Shakespeare will find much in the photo spectacle that the spoken tragedy must miss." – 'Motion Picture Illustrated'.

MACBETH
(Germany 1920/1)

p.c. *Oswald Film.*
d. *Dmitri Buchowetzki.*
l.p.
b.w. (?) mins. Sil.

Such scant information leaves the existence of the film open to speculation. However, what little information there is has about it been culled from two reliable and very diverse sources.

MACBETH
(Germany, 1922)

p.c. *Elel Film/Filmindustrie Heidelberg.*
d. *Heinz Schall.*
l.p. *Eugen Klöpfer.*
b.w. 3005 ft. (916 m.) Sil.

Despite the information available about this film, there is still a measure of doubt over its existence.

MACBETH
(G.B., 1922)

p.c. *Master.*
d. *Harry B. Parkinson.*

l.p. *Russell Thorndyke (Macbeth); Sybil Thorndyke (Lady Macbeth).*
b.w. *1175 ft. (358 m.) Sil.*

This was the first in a series called *Tense Moments From Great Plays*. The leading players are synonymous with best of British theatre.

MACBETH
(G.B., 1945)

p.c. *Theatrecraft.*
d. *Henry Cass.*
l.p. *Wilfred Lawson (Macbeth); Cathleen Nesbitt (Lady Macbeth); Felix Aylmer (Doctor);Catherine Lacey (Gentlewoman).*
b.w. *19 mins.*

Extract featuring the murder of Duncan and sleepwalking scenes, this is one of two films made for educational purposes under the title *Famous Scenes From Shakespeare*. One English source notes the duration as sixteen or seventeen minutes.

MACBETH
(U.S.A., 1946)

p.c. *Willow Productions.*
d. *Thomas A. Blair.*
l.p. *David Bradley (Macbeth); Jain Wilimovsky (Lady Macbeth); Louis Northrop (Duncan); William Bartholomay (Macduff); Virginia Nelson (Lady Macduff); J. Norton Dunn (Seyton); J. Royal Mills (Malcolm); William Sweeney (Doctor/Porter); Ann Thompson, Irene Elster, Alexander Winter (Three Witches).*
b.w. *70 mins.*

Though an amateur production, it is hardly likely that this did not have public showings if only to the students at Northwestern University, Chicago, U.S.A. where it was made. There was a budget of $5,000 and student talent and local settings were used inventively. Among the talent in the costume department was Charlton Heston. It was made on 16 mm. film and was favourably reviewed by the press at the time.

MACBETH
(U.S.A., 1948)

p.c. *Republic. A Mercury Production.*
d. *Orson Welles.*
l.p. *Orson Welles (Macbeth); Jeanette Nolan (Lady Macbeth); Roddy McDowall (Malcolm); Dan O'Herlihy (Macduff); Edgar Barrier (Banquo); Alan Napier (A Holy Father); John Dierkes (Ross); Erskine Sandford (Duncan); Keene Curtis (Lennox); Peggy Webber (Lady Macduff); Christopher Welles; Morgan Farley; Lurene Tuttle; William Alland; Brainerd Duffield; George Chirello; Gus Shilling; Jerry Farber; Charles Lederer.*
b.w. *106 mins.*

More Welles than the Bard, this film marked Welles' end with the major Hollywood studios and his first screen affiliation with Shakespeare. Shot during the summer of 1947, it took twenty-three (or is it twenty-one?) days over four months on a low budget which shows in the sets. The running time above is that of the original – and this seems to vary by a few minutes depending upon the source – but it was cut to 89 mins. and for some countries by a few more minutes.

As a teenager, Welles began his relationship with the Bard when he co-authored 'Everybody's Shakepeare' in which three plays were adapted. At age sixteen, he learned more at the Gate Theatre in Dublin, Eire, which was his opening to the Shakespearean stage in America. He produced in 1936 a black version of **MACBETH** in Harlem, New York. This is known to exist, at least in part, on film. From this, he moved, at the instigation of John Houseman, to the Mercury Theatre and JULIUS CAESAR.

For the screen version of MACBETH, Welles took quite a few liberties with the text which he attempted to explain calling it "...a kind of violently sketched charcoal drawing of a great play". Such liberties with some attempted Scottish accents as well, leaves much to be desired. Critical opinion of the film remains sharply divided. French composer Jacques Ibert wrote the music, part of which was issued on a Marco Polo record of the composer's film music in 1991 played by the Slovak Radio Symphony Orchestra.

Though the film was hardly a box office success, strangely it did find itself released for home consumption on 8 mm. by Powell Films, U.K.

Shown as part of the Everybody's Shakespeare International Festival, London, England, 1994.
Shown at the Shakespeare Film Festival, Wiesbaden, W. Germany, 1964.

"...whizzed through in three weeks with some imaginative chunks of filming.." – Angela and Elkan Allan, 'The Sunday Times Guide To Movies On Television'.

"...an interpretation bungled at every turn..." – David Shipman, 'The Good Film And Video Guide'.

"Everything is to be admired and praised in this film..." – 'Guide Akai Vidéo-Cassettes'.

"This is not MACBETH illustrated by Welles but Orson Welles giving MACBETH different dimensions..." – Jean Mitry, 'Dictionnaire Du Cinéma'.

MACBETH
(U.S.A., 1951)

p.c. *Unusual Films/Bob Jones University.*
d. *Katherine Stenholm.*
l.p. *Barbara Hudson Sowers (Lady Macbeth); Bob Jones Jr. (Macbeth); George Galstad (Malcolm); David Yearick (Macduff); Paul Vanaman (Duncan); Robert Pratt (Ross);*

Gordon Peters (Banquo); Dale Jackson (Lennox); Kenneth Myers (Donalbain); Wayne Kelly (Seyton); Bob Jones III (Fleance); Jack Yost, John Evans (Murderers); Herbert Noe (Doctor); Geraldine Barnes (Lady-in-Waiting); Theodore Mercer, Bob Osterberg, Dwight Gustafson (Witches).

c. 80 mins.

An amateur production (logically, seen by students), the film is said to have much to recommend it with a high level of support in sets, music etc. This ambitious production has obviously been shortened and subjected to some censorship in the text (the producer comes from that strongly religious part of America known as the "bible belt").

MACBETH
(G.B., 1953)

p.c. *Emil Katzke Productions.*
d. *Charles Deane.*
l.p. *Young Vic Theatre Company. Narrator: Ronald Howard.*
b.w. 13 mins.

An extract from the play, this formed part of the series *The World's A Stage.*

MACBETH
(G.B., 1960)

p.c. *Grand Prize.*
d. *George Schaefer.*
l.p. *Maurice Evans (Macbeth); Judith Anderson (Lady Macbeth); Ian Bannen (Macduff); Michael Hordern (Banquo); Felix Aylmer (Doctor); Malcolm Keen (Duncan); Jeremy Brett (Malcolm); Megs Jenkins (Gentlewoman); Barry Warren (Donalbain); William Hutt (Ross); Charles Carson (Caithness); Trader Faulkner (Seyton); Valerie Taylor (First Witch); Anita Sharp Bolster (Second Witch); April Olrich (Third Witch); Simon Lack (Menteith); George Rose (Porter); Brewster Mason; Scot Finch; Michael Ripper; Robert Brown; Douglas Wilmer.*

Technicolor. 108 mins.

Filmed on location in Scotland, this was cut to eighty minutes for its American première which was on NBC television. It is a faithful adaptation and contains a number of stalwarts of the British cinema in the cast. As a point of interest, the late Jeremy Brett played the title role in an American version for the Shakespeare Video Society in 1981 which enjoyed television transmissions. Piper Laurie was his Lady Macbeth. He also found fame later in a British television series as Sherlock Holmes.

Shown at the Berlin Film Festival, W. Germany, 1961.
Shown at the Shakespeare Film Festival, Wiesbaden, W. Germany, 1964.

"Evans is masterful as Macbeth..." – 'Motion Picture Guide'.

"...safe, tame, respectable..." – 'Monthly Film Bulletin', June, 1961.

MACBETH: AN INTRODUCTION
(G.B., 1969)

p.c. *Seabourne Enterprises.*
d. *Peter Seabourne.*
l.p. *Richard Leech (Macbeth); Jennie Goosens (Lady Macbeth); Edward Harvey (Duncan); Brian Spink (Macduff); John Barcroft (Banquo).*
c. 26 mins.

Made for educational purposes, this short was number four in a series of these study extracts.

MACBETH
(G.B., 1971)

p.c. *Playboy Productions/Caliban Films.*
d. *Roman Polanski.*
l.p. *Jon Finch (Macbeth); Francesca Annis (Lady Macbeth); Martin Shaw (Banquo); John Stride (Ross); Nicholas Selby (Duncan); Stephan Chase (Malcolm); Andrew Laurence (Lennox); Terence Bayler (Macduff); Bruce Purchase (Caithness); Bernard Archard (Angus); Paul Shelley (Donalbain); Frank Wylie (Mentieth); Noelle Rimmington; Keith Chegwin; Noel Davis; Masie MacFarquhar; Elsie Taylor; Vic Abbott; Roy Jones; Bill Drysdale; Patricia Mason; Ian Hogg; Geoffrey Reed; Nigel Ashton; Diane Fletcher; Mark Digham; Richard Pearson; Sydney Bromley; William Hobbs; Alf Joint; Michael Balfour; Andrew McCulloch; Howard Lang; David Ellison; Terence Mountain; Maxine Skelton; Paul Hennen; Beth Owen; Janie Kells; Olga Anthony; Roy Desmond; Barbara Grimes; Pam Foster; John Gordon; Aud Johansen; Dickie Martyn; Christina Paul; Don Vernon; Ann Willoughby.*

Technicolor. 140 mins. Todd-AO 35.

If Polanski's version is violent and gory – and it is – then it well within keeping of the times. For they were hard and bloody times. The text is shortened here as seems inevitable and the film is better for it, giving improved focus upon the principals.

The film was photographed in Wales in inclement weather. Way behind schedule and thus over budget, the film is said to have lost around $3,500,000. This was bad news for Playboy Enterprises who had taken on the project, already declined by Allied Artists and Universal, as it was anxious to get into the film business. Because of the company's connotations, it was subjected to criticism for Lady Macbeth's nude sleepwalking scene. Actually, it was in the original script written by Polanski and Kenneth Tynan before the Playboy involvement but was also the reason for Tuesday Weld turning down the role.

The public may not have flocked to see it, but it has been well received, particularly of late, by critics and seems to have grown in stature since its original release. It certainly seems to have been underrated when released, perhaps because of the Playboy tag.

Shown as part of the Everybody's Shakespeare International Festival, London, England, 1994.
Shown 'hors concours' at the Cannes Film Festival, France, 1972.
British Film Academy, G.B., 1972. Award: Best Costume Design (Anthony Mendelsohn for three films including this one).
National Film Board of Review, U.S.A., 1971. Best English Language Picture, Listed first in Best English Language Films list.

"...in retrospect it comes over as one of the most successful Shakespeare films ever." – John Russell Taylor, 'The Movie'.

"...his (Polanski's) highly subjective version...contained some interesting ideas..." – Jeremy Pascal, Clyde Jeavons, 'A Pictorial History of Sex in the Movies'.

"...violent but valid adaptation of Shakespeare's play." – 'Satellite TV Europe'.

Though out of chronological order, it is appropriate to include the following item here:

SHAKESPEARE: "MACBETH – POWER AND CORRUPTION"
(G.B, 1984)

p.c.
d. *Roman Polanski (of film extracts).*
l.p. *Documentary. Narrator: Orson Welles.*
c. 33 mins.

This training film, probably made on video but available on film, is included out of interest since it is relative to the play and the director. It was from the series "See, Listen, Understand" and uses the Shakespearean view of power and compared to that of other authors. Scenes from Polanski's film are featured.

MACBETH
(G.B., 1974)

p.c. *Realist Film Unit.*
d. *Peter Seabourne.*
l.p. *Mark Kingston (Macbeth); Elizabeth Hall, Alison Key, Linda Renwick (Witches).*
c. 11 mins.

Four extracts are featured here – Act I, Scene 1; Act I, Scene 3; Act II, Scene 1; and Act IV, Scene 1 – in this fifth issue in the series.

MACBETH
(Scotland, 1997)

p.c. *Cromwell Productions in association with Lamancha Productions and Grampian Television*
d. *Jeremy Freeston.*
l.p. *Jason Connery (Macbeth); Helen Baxendale (Lady Macbeth); Kenny Bryans (Macduff); Graham McTavish (Banquo); Kern Falconer (Seyton); Hildegard Neil (First Witch); Jean Tend, Phillipa Peak (Witches); Chris Gormlie (MacDonwald); Ross Dunsmore (Malcolm); John Corvie (Duncan); Ian Stuart Robertson (Ross); Phil Wallace (Lennox); Paul MacDonald (Donalbain); Dominic Borrelli (Angus); Carl Watt (Messenger); James Tovell (Fleance); Michael Leighton, Jack Ferguson (Porters); Robert Little (Oldman); Al Anderson, Stevie Allen (Murderers); Shona Donaldson (Gentlewoman); Tess Dignan (Lady Macduff); Jamie Main (Young Macduff); Andrew Mackenzie (Watchman); Roger Webb (Servant); Rob Swinton (Seyward); Andy Goddard (Messenger); Paul Curran (Young Seyward); Brian Blessed (King Edward the Confessor).*
Colour Film Services. 129 mins.

A faithful reading of the play, albeit with some editing of the text, it benefits from authentic location filming.

Though the film was made on a large budget, this was relative to its primary destination – television – and it shows in comparison to the larger budgets of other Shakespearean films of the era in whose glory this hoped to bask. Comment has also been made that the film borrowed from other genres to include the remaking of certain scenes to add a little gore (to match the then current *Braveheart* with Mel Gibson). Certainly, the film has merit with good acting from a largely, in cinematic terms, unknown but experienced, cast. Indeed, some sources note that the supporting cast overshadow the lead players in performance. Jason Connery is, of course, the son of Sean Connery.

The appearance of Brian Blessed as King Edward the Confessor is surely based on the popularity of the actor for the character does not appear in the play. There is an allusion to him in Act IV, Scene 3, when mention is made of his powers of healing in a meeting between a doctor, Macduff and Malcolm. King Edward, founder of Westminster Abbey, London, was canonised in the twelfth century.

The production company is of interest having made a number of films related to Scottish history. Its unusual method of financing – inviting the public to invest a £1,000 in a film project as a share and also appear as an extra – drew considerable attention.

One source notes the running time as one hundred and fifty minutes but the above is in line with the given length.

"...there are only a few striking cinematic touches here." – Colin McArthur, 'Sight and Sound'.

"You see what you get – honest, faithful Shakespearean dialogue in a historically accurate setting." – 'Total Film', May, 1997.

✣ ✣ ✣ ✣ ✣

THE REAL THING AT LAST
(G.B. 1916)

p.c. *British Actors.*
d. *L.C. MacBean.*
l.p. *Edmund Gwenn (Rupert K. Thunder); Nelson Keys (Lady Macbeth); Godfrey Tearle (Macduff); Owen Nares (General Banquo); Norman Forbes (Duncan); Caleb Porter, George Kelly, Ernest Thesiger (Witches); Pauline Chase, Teddie Gerard, Gladys Cooper (American Witches); Fred Volpe (Murderer); Moya Mannering (Messsenger); A.E. Matthews, Marie Lohr, Fred Kerr (Murdered People); Irene Vanbrugh (Lady); Arthur Shirley (Courtier); Leslie Henson (Charlie Chaplin).*
b.w. 2000 ft. (610 m.) Sil.

This is a comedy in which an American producer tries to modernise MACBETH showing how it might be filmed in Britain and Hollywood. The latter had dancing girls instead of witches and an appearance by an actor as Charles Chaplin.

A film of some interest for the early roles of players later of note among whom are Edmund Gwenn, A.E. Matthews and Gladys Cooper. The parody script was penned by J. M. Barrie of "Peter Pan" fame. The film had its première at a charity show for British troops.

LADY MACBETH
(Italy, 1917)

p.c. *Palatino Film.*
d. *Enrico Guazzoni.*
l.p. *Lyda Borelli (Lady Macbeth); Amleto Novelli (Macbeth); Bruno Castellani; Elena Sangro.*
b.w. (?) mins. Sil.

Derivative, of course, it is the evil Lady Macbeth who is the subject of the film. It may have been in contemporary dress and/or perhaps influenced by Leskov's 'Lady Macbeth Of Minsk' though, obviously, not directly from it.

JWALA
(India, 1938)

p.c. *Huns Pictures.*
d. *Master Vinayak.*
l.p. *Chandramohan (Angar); Ashlata (Kuntala); Ratnaprabha (Mangala); Bulbule (King); Chandrakant (Tarang); Master Vinayak; Rajani; Dhavale; Rajani; Mandre.*
b.w. 161 mins. and 165 mins.

Angar, a good general, learns from a witch, Kuntala, that his king shall die and he will become king. Though once loyal, Angar is driven by ambition and kills the king and seizes power. His wife, Mangala, disapproves and she and his friend Taranga join forces with the people against him. As he dies, Angar reaches for the throne that is beyond his reach...

This period fantasy clearly parallels MACBETH up to a point. It has some rarity value being in both Marathi and Hindi versions (the running times noted refer to these versions respectively). Long and costly, the film was a major box-office disaster from which the production company never recovered.

JOE MACBETH
(G.B., 1955)

p.c. *Film Locations. A Frankovich Production.*
d. *Ken Hughes.*
l.p. *Paul Douglas (Joe Macbeth); Ruth Roman (Lily Macbeth); Harry Green (Big Dutch); Sidney James (Banky); Bonar Colleano (Lennie); Gregoire Aslan (Duca); Kay Callard (Ruth); Walter Crisham (Angus); Robert Arden (Ross); Minerva Pious (Rosie); George Margo (Assassin); Nicholas Stuart (Duffy).*
b.w. 90 mins.

Recently wed gangster, Joe, murders gang leader Duchy for his boss, Duca. Influenced by a fortune teller, Lily, Joe's wife, wants him to become crime lord and goads him into killing Duca. Banky, Joe's friend, remains loyal but Banky's son, Lennie, resents Joe and causes trouble. Joe hires two gunmen to kill Lennie but they kill Banky. Joe is plagued by Banky's ghost and feels his control over the gang slipping. He takes Lennie's wife and child hostage but his plan misfires and they are murdered. Joe barricades himself in. Lily goes mad and is killed accidentally by Joe who is shot down by Lennie.

Purists may raise their protests at this but the film is not without some interest. It followed a common path for the British cinema in those days by importing American stars to boost appeal and make it acceptable to the American market. It was also an early film for director Ken Hughes. Though his career may have been uneven, he directed here, according to 'The Movie', "a taught gangster thriller".

"...its gimmick quality is quickly dissipated by an indifferent production." – Leslie Halliwell, 'Halliwell's Film Guide'.

aka: CAUTIVO DE TERROR

KUMONOSU-JO
(Japan, 1957)

p.c. *Toto.*
d. *Akira Kurosawa.*
l.p. *Toshiro Mifune (Taketoki Washizu); Isuzu Yamada (Asaji, his wife); Takashi Shimura (Noriyasu Odagura); Takamaru Sasaki (Kuniharu Tsuzuki); Minoru Chiaki (Yosiaki Miki); Akira Kubo (Yoshiteru, his son); Yoichi*

Tachikaya (Kunimara); Chieko Naniwa (Weird Woman).

b.w. 110 mins.

Two Samurai, Washizu and Miki, return victorious to Inui. They pass through a wood on the way to Cobweb Castle. There they meet a weird woman who tells Washizu that he will command North mansion then Cobweb Castle but Miki's son will succeed him. The first part of the prophecy comes true and Washui's wife Asaji, wants more and induces him to kill his lord. He becomes lord of Cobweb Castle and names Miki's son as his heir. Asaji then says she is pregnant and insists on the murder of Miki and his son. Miki's son escapes the murder plot and joins the lord Inui. Now desperate, Wasizu consults the weird woman who says he will be safe unless Cobweb Forest moves. This news brings spirit to his men. The next day Inui's men cut down trees and use them for cover. As the forest appears to move Washizu is shot to death by his own men.

The names have been changed, the setting switched to mediaeval Japan and there have been minor changes to the plot but the story, in essence, remains the same.

Some prints run up to ten minutes shorter.

A ten minute study extract of the scene where Asaji tries to persuade her husband to take over Cobweb Castle exists as a separate entity.

Shown as part of the Everybody's Shakespeare International Festival, London, England, 1994.
Shown at the Venice Film Festival, Italy, 1957.
Kinema Jumpo Annual Best Ten Films, Japan, 1957: Listed fourth.
Mainichi Eiga Concourse Awards, Japan, 1957: Best Actor (Toshiro Mifune).
'Time' magazine, U.S.A., 1961, Ten Best. One of the ten for this year in the Foreign selection.

"...the film screen seems a living picture on which feudal pageantry and passions are as if brushed there." – Parker Tyler, 'Classics Of The Foreign Film'.

"...dazzlingly well done in sounds and images as haunting as any in the history of the cinema..." – David Shipman, 'The Good Film And Video Guide'.

"Banquo's unquiet ghost – and the lone witch are marvels of lazy terror." – Rose London, 'Zombie'.

"...it is the subtle, deadly performance by Isuzu Yamada as his (Macbeth's) wife that haunts the imagination." – Derek Prouse, 'The Movie'.

aka: THRONE OF BLOOD; COBWEB CASTLE; CASTLE OF THE COBWEBS; LE CHÂTEAU DE L'ARAIGNÉE; TRONO DE SANGRE; DAS SCHLOß IM SPINNWEBWALD

MACBETH
(Finland, 1987)

p.c. *Villealfa Filmproductions.*
d. *Pauli Pentti.*
l.p. *Mato Valtonen (Macbeth); Pirkko Hämäläinen (Lady); Pertti Sveholm (Bankko); Turo Pajala (Make); Antti Litja (Dunkku); Aino Seppo (Wife); Sakari Järvenpää (Napoleon); Sanna-Kaisa Palo (Saara); Esko Nikkari (Einari); Paavo Piskonen (Gatekeeper); Mari Rantasila (Singer); Sakari Kuosmanen, Vesa Vierikko (Killers).*

Eastman Color. 70 mins. WS

A professional thief is driven on by poor employment prospects and then ambition which stems as much from his social conditions as by his scheming blonde companion. Destruction inevitably is the ultimate result in a world that knows nothing of Macbeth or his underworld environment. Indeed, it is a world that does not want to know.

In a modern setting, the story is rather condensed and set in the underworld of Helsinki. It was not the first time that the play had been set in the world of gangsters (see **JOE MACBETH**) nor would it be the last (see below). The film was the second in a planned trilogy of modern adaptations of Shakespearean plays by producer Aki Kaurismäki. The third based on **KING LEAR** would have been directed by Anssi Mänttäri but never materialised. The first was **HAMLET LIIKMAAILMASSA**.

Incidentally, Giuseppe Verdi (appropriately) shares the honours for the musical score.

Shown at the Muestra Cinematográfica del Atlantico, Cadiz, Spain, 1988.

MEN OF RESPECT
(U.S.A., 1990)

p.c. *Central Film City/Arthur Goldblatt Productions.*
d. *William Reilly.*
l.p. *John Turturro (Mike Battaglia); Katherine Borowitz (Ruth Battaglia); Dennis Farina (Bankie Como); Peter Boyle (Duffy); Rod Steiger (Charlie D'Amico); Stanley Tucci (Mal D'Amico); David Thornton (Philly Como); Lilia Skala (Signora Lucia); Steven Wright (Sterling); Michael Radalucco (Sol); Carl Capotorto (Don); Robert Medici (Rossi); Julie Garfield (Irene); Michael Sercio; Tony Gigante; Dan Grimaldi; Richard Petrocelli; Jeff Mazzola; John Gallagher; Joseph Carberry; Joe Paparone; Richard Spore; Vinny Pastore; Steven Randazo; Ron Maccone; Robert Moresco; Olex Kruta; Andrei Belgrader.*

Du Art Color. 113 mins.

Mike Battaglia, his friend Bankie and their gang eliminate a troublesome Greek and his mob. On the run they seek refuge in a house inhabited by a weird family of three. The old woman there tells Mike that opportunities await him and he will be a Padrino. Bankie's future promises that his son will be Padrino also. Mike's action immediately gains respect and position from Mafia Padrino, Charlie D'Amico. When Mike tells his wife, Ruth, of the prediction she goads him into fulfilling the rest of it. The opportunity comes when Charlie visits their restaurant. Ruth drugs Charlie's guards and daubs them with blood after Mike has killed Charlie. When Duffy, an Irish ganglord, finds Charlie's body the next day, Mike shoots the dazed guards. Soon, despite suspicion, Mike becomes the next Padrino. Duffy and Charlie's sons move away. Now jealous of Bankie, Mike plots to kill him but his son, Philly, escapes. At a party, Mike is haunted by Bankie's ghost. Mike goes again to the weird family and learns that he cannot be killed by man born of woman and until the stars fall from the sky. He is warned about Duffy and an attempt to kill him results in the death of both Duffy's wife and son. Now irrational, Ruth causes him problems with sleepwalking and strange behaviour. Meanwhile previously opposing factions unite and call for Philly. Mike's gang gradually desert him. Ruth takes her own life and Mike is left to face Bankie on a night of fireworks. Duffy answers Mike's taunts by telling him that he had to be ripped from his mother's womb at birth. Mike is killed by Duffy and Philly is initiated into the Mafia brotherhood.

If this sounds familiar, then so it should. It has, in concept, been done before in **JOE MACBETH** and the Finnish film noted previously. Here the play is transposed to modern times. Instead of the cheap gangsters of **JOE MACBETH**, the more topical Mafia familes, with the obligatory violence, take the centre stage. The famous sleepwalking scene by Lady M is here staged in a courtyard with the lady carrying a flashlamp! At least the film acknowledges the inspirational source. Typical of the dialogue is: "I'm not of woman born, Mikey – I'm gonna kill ya.", a strange mixture of Shakespeare and New Yorkese.

"More bad than Bard." – 'Film Review, 1992/3'.

✢ ✢ ✢ ✢ ✢

MACBETH
(U.S.S.R., 1967)
p.c.
d.   *Kiril Monachov.*
l.p.   *Boris Efimov; Sergei Gromov; Efigenia Goremkin; Sergei Soloviev; Valerie Anisimov; Nina Timofeva; The Bolshoi Ballet. The Bolshoi Theatre Orchestra (conductor: Fuad Mansurov).*
Sovcolor. 90 mins.

A ballet, this is based on the story and may have been originally made for television.

MACBETH
(W. Germany, 1970)
p.c.   *Rosa von Praunheim Filmproduktion.*

d.   *Rosa von Praunheim (real name: Holger Mischwitzki).*
l.p.
c. (?) mins.

Noted as being an extract, logically in German, from the play. It is called "an opera by Rosa von Praunheim" and thus it is included in this section. The director was also responsible for the sound, the script, operating the camera and editing.

MACBETH
(France/W. Germany, 1987)
p.c.   *Dedalus/SFPC/TFI Films Productions/Unitel. In association with ACE (New York) and with the participation of SFP.*
d.   *Claude D'Anna.*
l.p.   *Leo Nucci (Macbeth); Shirley Verrett (Lady Macbeth); Antonio Barasorda (Malcolm); Johan Leysen (Banquo); Philippe Volter (Macduff); Nicolas Sansier (Fleance); Grégoire Baldari; Anna-Caterina Antonacci; Sergio Fontana; Alain-Pascal Housiaux; Laurence Buisson; Gigi Bereaud; Anne Bertrand; Diane Broman; Agnès David; Arlette Emmery; Catherine Dubois; Denise Gudmundseth; Marianne Gutman; Vittoria Scognamiglio; Natale de Carolis; Barbara Brisick; Marco Fanti; Giuseppe Morresi. Voices: Samuel Ramey; Veriano Luchetti; Gianfranco Casarini; Gastone Sarti. The Choirs and Orchestra of the Teatro Comunale di Bologna (conductor: Riccardo Chailly).*
c. 136 mins. S

This is a film version of Giuseppe Verdi's opera which is rarely performed because of its frequent and thus expensive scene changes.

Shown "hors concours" at the Cannes Film Festival, France, 1987.

✢ ✢ ✢ ✢ ✢

In turning to the life of this eleventh century Scottish king, Shakespeare had an opportunity to introduce a number of his common themes – the supernatural, treachery, ambition and murder. All of which must have been then, as now, good material for the box-office.

The central character is both simple yet complex. Of Macbeth's courage as a soldier there is no doubt. He is strong and not afraid of the forces he can see and understand. In dealing with the darker forces then, like most people, he is unsure and insecure. When his own wife becomes the instrument of such forces, his weakness shows, what honour he has is forgotten and he is truly lost as her drive to fulfil the prophecies leads to her madness. Such a condition in great ones must not, as Shakespeare advised in HAMLET, go unwatched. Even in his final, darkest hours, Macbeth, his wife dead, his supporters all but gone, still would have the arrogance, real or otherwise, to believe in his own invincibility. Are not all men born of women? How can a wood move? Macbeth learned the answers to his cost. To echo Shakespeare's thoughts again – such a condition should be watched and, if necessary, checked.

There is no doubt that the principal roles make interesting bases for interpretation which is probably why this story of murder, an ambitious, ruthless wife and the supernatural has, logically, all the ingredients to inspire film makers. Surprisingly, however, there is not an abundance of screen versions, certainly not after the silent era. Strangely, given the ingredients of the plot, none of the modern film versions have found the same financial success as that of other film adaptations of Shakespearean works.

Indeed, it is the female of the species that attracts almost equal attention. Russian author Nicolai Leskov found the Lady Macbeth character interesting enough to make her the focal point of his story actually titled 'Lady Macbeth'. This, in turn, was the basis of *Katherina Ismailova*, filmed in U.S.S.R. in 1926. The same source and same murderous lady was the basis of the opera by Dmitri Shostakovich. This was also filmed in Russia with the same title as the 1926 film but released also with the English title *Lady Macbeth Of Mtsensk*. *Sibiriska Ledi Magbet*, the 1961 Yugoslav film directed by Andrzej Wajda, followed virtually the same story and was released with the English title *Siberian Lady Macbeth*. The subject title apart, the film's plot contains a foundation of Shakespeare analogy, not least in the ruthless, ambitious character of the lady and her gradual and total domination over her once strong lover.

Just what this lady had in her soul is in indicated by the last chord of the "Lady Mac" movement from Duke Ellington's Shakespearean suite "Such Sweet Thunder". Duke said: "...we suspect there was a little ragtime in her soul." Typical Ducal humour, of course, for there was certainly more, something far more ominous, in her character which contrasts her so deeply with an essentially weak husband. Therein, rests the challenge for those who take on these roles.

In truth, though her part is short compared to that of her husband, Lady Macbeth with her strong yet, at times, equally unsure character, seems to rival him in

the desire by actresses to portray the role. For some, the chance is unlikely for they are too readily identified with other roles. The Dutch actress, Sylvia Kristel, bemoaning her inevitable "Emmanuelle" association, said: "...I believe it will be some time before they entrust me with the role of Lady Macbeth..." ('Ciné Revue', July 13, 1978). The same fate applies equally, of course, to many actors/ actresses who have found themselves type-cast.

As the past has provided only a modest if steady flow of film versions of MACBETH, there can surely be no doubt that the future will bring new versions of this the shortest of Shakespeare's tragedies. The substance of the play and its characters can only ensure that, in some form or other, we have not heard nor seen the last "Of this dead butcher and his fiend-like queen...".

For other films with scenes from the play see **CHAPTER XXX ALL THE WORLD'S A STAGE**: WHEN MACBETH CAME TO SNAKEVILLE (1917); THE VILLAGE SQUIRE (1935); LAXDALE HALL (1952); LE RIDEAU ROUGE (1952); LE THÉÂTRE NATIONAL POPULAIRE (1956); THE DEADLY AFFAIR (1966); MISTRZ (1966); THE CHARGE OF THE LIGHT BRIGADE (1968); THE GREAT McGONAGALL (1974); IN THE FOREST (1978); SHAKESPEARE'S MOUNTED FOOT (1979); NOBODY'S FOOL (1986) and IN THE SHADOW OF THE STARS (1991) and **CHAPTER XXXII THE IMMORTAL BARD**: THE LIFE OF SHAKESPEARE (1914); B.B.C. THE VOICE OF BRITAIN (1935); MARCH OF TIME 3rd. YEAR (BRITISH EDITION) (1937); WILLIAM SHAKESPEARE: BACKGROUND FOR HIS WORKS (1950); SHAKESPEARE'S THEATER (1954); FESTIVAL IN EDINBURGH (1955); WILLIAM SHAKESPEARE (1955); FAIR ADVENTURE SERIES (1964); THE ART OF SHAKESPEARE IN "MACBETH" SERIES (1967); EXPLORATIONS IN SHAKESPEARE (1969); SHAKESPEARE: MIRROR TO A MAN (1970?) and THE WORLD OF WILLIAM SHAKESPEARE (1978).

CHAPTER XV
MEASURE FOR MEASURE

Dramatis Personæ:

Vincentio, Duke of Vienna
Angelo – his deputy
Mariana – Angelo's betrothed
Escalus – a lord
Varrius – attendant to the Duke

Claudio – a young gentleman
Isabella – his sister
Juliet – Claudio's love

Lucio – a dandy
Two similar gentlemen
Thomas, Peter – friars

Provost
A Justice
Elbow – a simple constable
Froth – a foolish gentleman
Abhorson – an executioner
Francisca – a nun
Mistress Overdone – a procuress
Pompey – tapster to Mistress Overdone
Bernardine – a dissolute prisoner
Lords, Officers, Citizens, Boy, Attendants

Vincentio, Duke of Vienna, is a gentle man and is rather lax in implementing the law. One of the laws states that any man caught having a sexual encounter with any woman other than his wife may be put to death. Vincentio is concerned at the growth of such affaires but to implement the law rigorously would be difficult and out of character for him. He decides to go away leaving the Dukedom in the control of Angelo, a stern upholder of the law, aided by his trusted counsellor, Escalus. In fact, the Duke does not go away but hides out disguised as a friar.

As it happens, young Claudio has seduced a girl and Angelo orders his execution. Escalus intercedes on behalf of the boy but Angelo says he can make no exceptions. Lucio, Claudio's friend, visits him in prison. Claudio begs him to seek out his sister, Isabella, and ask her to plead for him.

Isabella is about to take her vows as a nun but, upon hearing of her brother's plight, from Lucio, leaves immediately. The girl Claudio has seduced is her friend Juliet and she knows that Juliet truly loves Claudio and he her.

She begs Angelo to spare Claudio but he is unmoved saying that it is not a personal matter but the law. Still she pleads and Angelo asks her to return the next day. She leaves with hope for at least she has another opportunity to plead for her brother's life. Angelo's motives are different for he is taken with Isabella and the thoughts he has about her disturb him.

Angelo receives Isabella alone the next day. He boldly proposes that if she will sleep with him he will spare her brother. Shocked, she threatens to denounce him. This he passes off with scorn as his word as a man of

acknowledged pure character would surely be taken against that of a desperate woman. Now Isabella is faced with a great dilemma. Which to save – her virtue or her brother's life?

In prison, Claudio is visited by a friar (the Duke in disguise). Isabella tells Claudio of the proposition. Claudio begs her to agree but then full of remorse, recants and prepares to meet his fate. The friar speaks to Isabella saying that he will acquaint the Duke with these events and he knows that the Duke will feel betrayed by Angelo's abuse of power.

The friar tells her about the death of Ferdinand, a great soldier, at sea. With him was lost the dowry for his sister, Mariana. This woman was betrothed to Angelo who cast her aside on some pretext of dishonour though the real reason was the loss of the dowry. Then a plan is put together by the friar. He tells Isabella to accept the offer but Mariana will go in her stead. She accordingly agrees to Angelo's proposal then meets Mariana and gives her the keys to the garden which Angelo has given her for the assignation that night.

Isabella has told Angelo that she may bring a servant and cannot stay long. The excuse for the meeting, for appearances sake, is the matter of her brother. Now Angelo proves not to be a man of his word and orders the execution of Claudio and the man's head to be brought to him at five o'clock in the morning. The disguised Duke, with good reason, doubts the integrity of Angelo, and, using his own seal, is able to persuade the prison authorities to spare Claudio and send Angelo the head of a prisoner who has died earlier.

The Duke then sends a message to Angelo that his return will be quicker than expected and that he is to meet him at the city gates in the morning to return his document of authority and to hear any complaints against him. Still disguised as the friar, he tells Isabella that Claudio is dead and not to worry if matters appear against her at the moment. He tells of the Duke's imminent return and instructs her to place her complaint. He then instructs Mariana on how to play her part.

The Duke duly arrives and the transfer of authority is correctly conveyed. Then Isabella steps forward and makes her accusations of Angelo's treachery. Angelo simply retorts that Isabella is disturbed by the death of her brother. Now Mariana steps forward and says that Isabella speaks falsely because she, his wife, was the woman he met in the garden. Isabella demands that the friar be called as her witness and Angelo demands satisfaction for the slander to which the Duke agrees.

Angelo is delighted to be effectively the judge of his own case and is happy for the friar to be called. The Duke leaves for just enough time to change into the friar's clothes. Returning as such he is accused of stirring up the women to slander. The friar reprimands the Duke for leaving his charge in the hands of Angelo and is reviled at the wicked things he has witnessed. Angelo, indeed everyone, is confused and it is then that the Duke shakes off his disguise.

The Duke, despite Isabella's apologies for daring to involve him, swears his devotion to her and regrets Claudio's death for he still keeps it secret that her brother lives. Angelo, trapped by the evidence, admits his guilt and is prepared for the penalty of death the Duke imposes and thus to free Mariana. She, however, is prepared to accept him and begs the Duke to save him and, Isabella, gracious as always, pleads for him too saying that her brother had paid the penalty justly for his crime.

The Duke then brings out Claudio and pardons him and commands him to marry Juliet. Angelo, now appreciating the beauty of mercy, is ordered to care for his loving wife. The Duke takes Isabella as his wife and by her fine example puts an end to the loose living. Duke Vincentio lives happily with his duchess, the loving Isabella.

Note: This rather outspoken (for the time) treatment of sex was probably written about the same time as OTHELLO for it was performed before King James I on December 26, 1604. Shakespeare drew upon the work by the Italian Giraldi Cinthio called 'Hecatommithi'. The same plot basis was also used in 'Promos And Cassandra', a two-part play by George Whetstone in 1578, and was used by the same author in his novel of 1582 'Heptameron Of Civil Discourses'. Both of these works were known to Shakespeare and thus embroidered a tale already known to the public.

DENTE PER DENTE
(Italy, 1913)

p.c. *Latium.*
d.
l.p. *Mignon Vassalo; Lidia Gauthier; Ubaldo Piltei.*
b.w. 2780 ft. (850 m.) Sil.

The title, which means "tooth for tooth", is the general translation of the play title in Italian and, given the proliferation of classic-based films from Italy, it most likely was a version the play.

ZWEIERLEI MASS
(W. Germany, 1963)

p.c. *Bavaria Atelier.*
d. *Paul Verhoeven.*
l.p. *Hans Caninenberg (Vincentio); Lothar Blumhagen (Angelo); Martin Berliner (Escalus); Erik Schumann (Claudio); Carl Lieffen (Lucio); Willy Berling (Thomas); Edgar Wenzel, Axel Scholz (Nobles); Günter Grävert (Jailer); Max Mairich (Pompeius); Hans-Herman Schaufuss (Elbogen); Hans Jürgen Diedrich (Grauslich); Irene Marhold (Mariane); Lisa Helwig (Francisca); Heidelinde Weis (Isabella); Herbert Bötticher (Bernardino); Karola Ebeling (Julia); Herthe Saal (Procuress).*
b.w. 141 mins.

This German version of the play was made for television but has received showings outside the confines of the home, small screen.

Shown at the Shakespeare Film Festival, Wiesbaden, W. Germany, 1964.

✛ ✛ ✛ ✛ ✛

DENTE PER DENTE
(Italy, 1943)

p.c. *Atlas.*
d. *Marco Elter.*
l.p. *Carlo Tamberlani (Angelo); Caterina Boratto (Isabella); Loredana (Giulietta); Alfredo Varelli (Vincenzo); Nelly Corradi (Marianna); Memo Benassi (Lucio); Lamberto Picasso (La Scala); Osvaldo Genazzini (Claudio); Cesco Baseggio (Schiumetta); Amelia Chellini (Madamea La Spanata); Aldo Silvani (Varrio); Claudio Ermelli; Arturo Bragaglia; Lina Marengo; Amalia Pellegrini; Frederico Collino; Tina Santi.*
b.w. 83 mins.

Duke Vincenzo is about to set out on a long journey. He entrusts the rule of his dukedom to his cousin Angelo. He appears to be a stern man and an upholder of the law. He is, however, revealed as a man with a lust for power and he blackmails the girl who loves the Duke, forcing her to obey his whims using the life of her brother (condemned to death for conspiracy) as his bargaining point. The Duke returns and restores order and, naturally, ensures that the guilty receive just punishment.

CHAPTER XV – MEASURE FOR MEASURE

The title ("Tooth For Tooth" in English) owes more to the Bible than to Shakespeare but it is clearly MEASURE FOR MEASURE with some distinct changes in the story.

"...the director, Elter, has not really demonstrated the finer points of the subject, much less the comedy..." – F. Sarazani, 'Il Giornale d'Italia' , July 6, 1943.

This is another Shakespearean work that has failed to find much support from the film world. As already noted, the theme may have been considered rather outspoken but hardly so in this so-called enlightened age. With the more liberal censorship that arrived in many countries a few decades ago, the story would seem to have been a natural companion (competitor?) to works by Chaucer and Boccaccio and thus been attractive to, say, the Italian film industry which was content not only to treat the world to faithful versions of bawdy tales by the two authors mentioned but to many derivate versions, too!

CHAPTER XVI

THE MERCHANT OF VENICE

Dramatis Personæ:

Antonio – a merchant of Venice
Bassanio – his friend and Portia's suitor
Gratiano, Salerio, Solanio – friends of Antonio and Bassanio

Portia – an heiress
Nerissa – her gentlewoman-in-waiting
Balthasar, Stephano – her servants

Prince of Morocco, Prince of Arragon – suitors to Portia
The Duke of Venice

Shylock – a Jew
Jessica – his daughter
Tubal – a Jew and his friend

Launcelot Gobbo – a clown and servant to Shylock
Old Gobbo – his father

Lorenzo – in love with Jessica
Leonardo – servant to Bassanio
Magnificoes of Venice, Court Officers, Jailer, Servants, Attendants etc.

Shylock, a Jew, is a money lender in Venice and never fails to extract full satisfaction from his debtors. On the other hand, Antonio, the merchant, is a truly honourable man. He helps those in need by lending money without interest. He despises Shylock and insults him which the Jew resents.

Antonio's best friend is Bassanio who is of limited means and always borrowing from Antonio. One day he begs a loan of three thousand ducats so that he might suitably attire himself to court a rich heiress whose father has just died.

Antonio is at the moment awaiting his ships to arrive with merchandise so offers to help by borrowing from Shylock. Now the Jew chides Antonio for his previous harsh words but pretends to be friendly. He says he will accept no interest but a jocular contract should be drawn up legally. Thus Antonio signs an agreement that he will give a pound of flesh from whichever part of the body Shylock chooses in case of default.

Bassanio is upset that Antonio is prepared to sign such a contract but Antonio says it has been signed only in sport and is confident that his vessels will arrive in good time.

So Bassanio, accompanied by Gratiano, goes and wins the hand of his lady Portia. He accepts her ring swearing to wear it for ever. She takes him as he is for he has told her of his impecunious state. At the same time Gratiano falls for Nerissa, Portia's maid.

The happiness of the two couples is short lived. A message arrives from Antonio saying that his ships were lost and so his life is forfeit. He desires to see his old friend one more time. In haste the couples are married and Bassanio sets forth with wealth to pay the debt.

Antonio is in prison since the settlement day is past and Shylock will not accept payment and demands his pound of flesh. The trial is set before the court and Portia travels to Venice to aid her husband's friend. She has a friend, Bellario, who is a counsellor. She seeks, and receives, guidance and the appropriate court dress from him.

With a letter of appointment from Bellario she enters the court as "Balthasar" and Nerissa as "his" clerk. "Balthasar" pleads for mercy but Shylock demands his pound of flesh even though three-fold the amount is offered in payment. "Balthasar" concludes that the law must be upheld.

Shylock demands his pound of flesh from nearest the heart. Antonio is entreated to prepare for death and Bassanio, declaring his love for his wife, says he would willingly sacrifice all to save him. Gratiano, copying his master, makes a similar declaration.

"Balthasar" asks if the scales are ready, much to Shylock's delight who extols the virtues of the counsellor. But the Jew's joy is short-lived for he is told that the contract is for a pound of flesh only and if he sheds a drop of blood then his own wealth will be confiscated. If he takes even a fraction more than one pound, he himself faces death.

Defeated, Shylock is now only too willing to accept the money. Then "Balthasar" accuses him of trying to murder a citizen of Venice. The presiding Duke gives him his life but divides his wealth between Antonio and the State. Thus he shows Christian charity.

Generous as ever, Antonio rejects the wealth asking that, at Shylock's death, his estate be made over to his daughter whom he has disinherited for marrying a Christian, Lorenzo, Antonio's friend.

The disgruntled Shylock agrees and the Duke instructs Antonio to reward his learned counsel. Bassanio offers the three thousand ducats but the fee is declined but his counsel asks for Bassanio's gloves and, upon seeing his ring, decides to test him by demanding it. With much reluctance he agrees as does Gratiano in a similar act.

The two disguised women return home delighted with the trick they have played and how they will conduct the meeting with their husbands. The two return with Antonio and soon Nerissa is castigating Gratiano for parting with his ring. Bassanio feels the wrath of his wife though he protests that he has not given the ring to another woman.

Antonio intervenes explaining that he is the cause of all the trouble. Portia gives him a ring to give to her husband instructing that her husband is to take better care of this one. It is, of course, the same ring which Bassanio recognises and Portia explains all. Further she tells that Antonio's ships have not been lost as supposed but have arrived safely in the harbour. With all this good news, happiness prevails.

Note: This probably dates from about 1598 or 1599 possibly being written as competition to a revival of Christopher Marlowe's 'The Jew Of Malta' of a year or so earlier. There were a number of works at the time to influence this work – 'Il Pecorone' by Ser Giovanni Fiorentino and 'Gesta Romanum' among them. Certainly the play gives an indication of the attitude of the era to Jews.

THE MERCHANT OF VENICE
(U.S.A., 1908)

p.c. *Vitagraph.*
d. *James Stuart Blackton.*
l.p. *Maurice Costello; Paul Panzer; William V. Ranous (Shylock); Julia Swayne-Gordon (Portia); Florence Turner (Jessica); Thomas H. Ince.*
b.w. 995 ft. (303 m.) Sil.

Selected dramatic scenes were used to tell the story in condensed form. Some sources give William V. Ranous as director.

IL MERCANTE DI VENEZIA
(Italy, 1910)

p.c. *Film d'Arte Italiana.*
d. *Gerolamo Lo Savio.*
l.p. *Ermete Novelli (Shylock); Francesca Bertini (Portia); Olga Giannini Novelli (Jessica or Nerissa); Ferruccio Garavaglia.*
b.w. 889 ft. (271 m.) Sil.

Most of the key scenes are retained in this abbreviated version though the emphasis is on Jessica and Lorenzo rather than the main plot.

Some sources quote 1911 as the production year for this which exists in a stencil-coloured version and which may have been issued originally as a colour film. Some sources note Amleto Novelli in the role of Shylock. The film is noted for its use of exterior shots, good editing and clear lighting. About two-thirds of the film have survived.

aka: THE MERCHANT OF VENISE; LE MARCHAND DE VENISE; SHYLOCK, O EL MERCADER DE VENECIA; DER KAUFMANN VON VENEDIG

THE MERCHANT OF VENICE
(U.S.A., 1910)

p.c. *Selig.*
d. *William Selig.*
l.p.
b.w. 11 mins. Sil.

No further details are available on this short but it probably contained key scenes coherently linked.

THE MERCHANT OF VENICE
(U.S.A., 1912)

p.c. *Thanhouser.*
d. *Theodore Marston.*
l.p. *William J. Bowman (Shylock); Florence La Badie (Portia); Harry Benham (Bassanio); William Russell (Antonio); William Garwood; Mignon Anderson (Jessica); Ethyle Cooke Benham.*
b.w. 3230 ft. (985 m.) Sil.

A condensed version of the play, some sources note Barry O'Neil as director.

SHYLOCK, OU LE MORE DE VENISE
(France, 1912)

p.c. *Éclipse.*
d. *Henri Desfontaines.*
l.p. *Harry Baur (Shylock); Romuald Joubé (Antonio); Pépa Bonafé (Portia); Jean Harvé (Bassanio); Georges Saillard; Jules Berry; Denis d'Inès; Louis Jouvet.*
b.w. 1969 ft. (600 m.) Sil.

A condensed version, this omits some sub-plots (including that of Jessica) and minor incidents. Some sources note that it was made two years earlier and even a year later. It was, however, one of the last attempts in France to move stage classics to the screen and was said, by some, to be well done, effective and with some excellent location shots. Others were not so generous in their assessment finding it lacking in imagination. However, the wealth of the film must rest in having a record of Baur as Shylock.

THE MERCHANT OF VENICE
(U.S.A., 1914)

p.c. *Universal Film Manufacturing Co./Gold Seal Brand.*
d. *Phillips Smalley, Lois Weber.*

l.p. *Lois Weber (Portia); Douglas Gerrard (Bassanio); Phillips Smalley (Shylock); Rupert Julian (Antonio); Jeannie McPherson (Nerissa); Edna Maison (Jessica); Fred Wilson.*

b.w. 4 reels. Sil.

Though the precise content is not known, contemporary writings suggest that the film followed the play faithfully within the obvious restraints.

This was produced by the Carl Laemmle company as a Universal Special Feature. Otis Turner is also credited as director by some.

VENETZIANSKY TCHOULOK
(Russia, 1915)

p.c. *Khanjokov.*
d. *Piotr Tchardynine.*
l.p. *Sergei Khoudoleev; Vera Koreneva; Vera Glinskaia; Nicolai Batchilov.*

b.w. 3937 ft. (1200 m.) Sil.

Apart from the above details, nothing further has been traced of this. The title translates as "The Merchant of Venice". It is logical to assume that this was from Shakespeare. Many countries were prolific in the production of films based on classics of literature and the brief cast list suggests the right balance of players for the principal roles of the play. Ultimately, it is hard to believe there are other plays/ books of the same title of sufficient recognition to merit a screen version. In fairness, the film may be a Shakespeare derivative and, more correctly, belong in the second section.

THE MERCHANT OF VENICE
(G.B., 1916)

p.c. *Broadwest/Flag Films.*
d. *Walter West.*
l.p. *Matheson Lang (Shylock); Nellie Hutin Britton (Portia); George Skillan (Antonio); J.R.Tozer (Bassanio); Kathleen Hazel Jones (Jessica); Ernest Caselli (Lorenzo); George Morgan (Lancelot); Marguerite Westlake (Nerissa); Terence O'Brien (Tubal); John Daly (Prince of Morocco).*

b.w. 6000 ft. (1829 m.) Sil.

At the start of this film, Matheson Lang is shown with the producers negotiating his contract. He was one of a number of stage actors who made the transition to the film world. Despite a style more suited to the stage he became quite a box-office draw and his success continued into the mid-1930s. It is noted as being a literal transcription of the St. James' Theatre production to the screen. In his book 'Mr. Wu Looks Back', Lang recalls how this happened: "When we were playing THE MERCHANT OF VENICE, the Broadwest Film Company came along with a proposal that they should film the whole production just as it stood with my company and – my stage scenery! They transported the whole of the production to their

premises in Walthamstow, set up the scenery in a glass-roofed studio and photographed most of it by daylight! Strange as it may seem, the result was not so terrible as one would imagine."

THE MERCHANT OF VENICE
(G.B., 1922)

p.c. *Master.*
d. *Challis Sanderson.*
l.p. *Sybil Thorndyke (Portia); Ivan Berlyn (Shylock); R. McLeod (Bassanio).*

b.w. 1170 ft. (357 m.) Sil.

Extract No. 6 from the play taken from the series called *Tense Moments From Great Plays* and features the trial scene.

DER KAUFMANN VON VENEDIG
(Austria, 1922)

p.c.
d. *Julius Herzka.*
l.p.
b.w. (?) mins. Sil.

The Österreichisches Filmarchiv gave notice of this film but was only able to supply one further detail – the name of the cameraman (Eduard Hoesch). Since two key production roles are named, it seems logical to assume that the film existed. It is suggested that the film received limited, if any, distribution and was, perhaps, overshadowed by the Werner Krauss film from Germany which follows.

DER KAUFMANN VON VENEDIG
(Germany, 1923)

p.c. *Fellner/Phoebus.*
d. *Peter Paul Fellner.*
l.p. *Werner Krauss (Shylock/Mordecai); Henny Porten (Portia/Beatrice); Harry Liedtke (Bassanio/Giannetto); Max Schreck (Doge of Venice); Carl Ebert (Antonio/Benito); Max Grünberg (Grazanio); Cläre Romer (Nerissa); Ferdinand von Alten (Prince of Aragon); Albert Steinrück (Tubal); Gustav May (Salario); Emil Helfer (Marco); Hans Brausewetter (Launcelot); Frieda Richard (Shylock's Wife); Friedrich Lobe (Elias); Lia Ebenschutz (Rachela); Heinz-Rolf Münz (Lorenzo); Jacob Tiedtke (Beppo); Willi Allen (Ali); Carl Geppart (Reppo); Herman Thunig.*

b.w. 9206 ft. (2806 m.) Sil.

Mordecai the Jew has betrothed his daughter Rachela but she loves Lorenzo, a Christian. Giannetto's debts are paid off by Benito and when Mordecai sends his wife to them to recover the debt to pay for the wedding, they laugh at her and she dies after she has cursed them. Benito is introduced to Beatrice by Giannetto and they are attracted to each other. Benito, his ships overdue, is forced to borrow from Mordecai who exacts a harsh bond. Benito's ships are lost and Rachela elopes with Lorenzo to become a Christian. Her fiancé commits suicide. Benito is arrested for being in debt and Rachela pleads for him in vain to her father. Mordecai demands the completion of the bond – a pound of flesh from Benito. Beatrice, disguised as a lawyer, points out that he may draw no blood and Benito is freed. She tests Benito's love and the two are married as are Rachela and Lorenzo. Mordecai is desolate.

This film has posed a number of problems. The original characters are listed with the Shakespearean equivalents placed first. The story, allegedly based on Shakespeare's source material, is more a cross between Shakespeare and the director's own invention. There is also confusion between the cast as given by English sources and German ones. The 1926 British release which was shortened bears the title THE JEW OF MESTRI. The co-cinematographer was Rudolf Maté who later became a noted cameraman and director in Hollywood. The film was also available in a tinted version.

The set designs were by Herman Warm who worked on *Das Kabinett Des Doktor Caligari* and *La Passion De Jeanne D'Arc*.

Shown at the Shakespeare Film Festival, Wiesbaden, W. Germany, 1964.

aka: SHYLOCK, DER JUDE VON VENEDIG

THE MERCHANT OF VENICE
(G.B., 1927)

p.c. *De Forest Phonofilms.*
d. *Widgey R. Newman.*
l.p. *Lewis Casson (Shylock); Joyce Lyons (Portia); Christine Murray (Nerissa).*
b.w. 934 ft. (285 m.)

This early sound-on-film short features the trial scene from the play.

ZALIM SAUDAGAR
(India, 1941)

p.c. *Radha Films.*
d. *Jeejeebhoy F. Madan.*
l.p. *Kajjan; Khalil; Rani; Premlata; Hyder Bandi.*
b.w. Feature.

Khalil was an actor from the silent era, probably the first to gain star status in India. Important, too, is Madan who was the first in India to establish some form of film industry. He was also a pioneer in the days of the sound film in his homeland, filming the stage plays by his own theatrical company. As a director, he was noted for his adaptations of historical, religious and other similarly based works.

The film was in Hindi.

aka: THE MERCHANT OF VENICE

LE MARCHAND DE VENISE
(France/Italy, 1953)

p.c. *Elysée Film/Venturini Produzione Films.*
d. *Pierre Billon.*
l.p. *Michel Simon (Shylock); Andrée Debar (Portia); Massimo Serato (Antonio); Armando Francioli (Bassanio); Giorgio Albertazzi (Lorenzo); Liliane Tellini (Jessica); Olga Solbelli; Marika Spada; Carletto Sposito; Gualtiero Tumiati; Clara Auteri Pepe; Nerio Bernardi; André Hildebrand; Franco Balduci; Renato De Carmine; Alberto Collo; Toni Di Mitri; Paolo Mori; Franco Giacobini; Pamela Palma; Candy-Well.*
b.w. 102 mins

An interesting co-production if only for the opportunity it provides to see the great French actor Michel Simon in a Shakespearean role. The Venice exteriors are generally pleasant but the whole production is rather episodic.

"...is less than mediocre and the interpretation is cold and affected." – S. Nati, 'Intermezzo', July/August, 1953.

Italian title: IL MERCANTE DI VENEZIA

DE KOOPMAN VAN VENETIË
(Holland, 1967)

p.c. *Theater Klank en Beeld.*
d. *Hans van den Busken.*
l.p. *Members of Ensemble featuring: Senne Rouffaer; Sigrid Koetse; Pleuni Touw; Herman Vinck; Jan Retèl; Roger Coorens; Cor van Rijn.*
b.w. (?) mins.

This is a filmed extract of the stage performance directed by Karl Guttmann.

THE MERCHANT OF VENICE
(Italy?, 1969)

p.c. *?*
d. *Orson Welles.*
l.p. *Orson Welles (Shylock); Charles Gray (Antonio); Irena Maleva (Jessica); Alessandro Tasca; Dorian Bond.*
c. See text.

Welles' last foray into the world of Shakespeare is the least known. The reason for this is simple. Two reels of the film plus the soundtrack were stolen from the production office in Rome. Apparently one reel, complete with sound, has since come to light. The existence of the film was revealed by Welles in 1982 in an interview with Bill Krohn. Welles had wanted the attractive Oja Kodar for the role of Portia but she declined due to her lack of knowledge of English. Welles, therefore, eliminated the role of Portia.

This rare, unfinished, work is featured in the French-German-Swiss production of **1995 ORSON WELLES: THE ONE-MAN BAND** (production by Media Res Filmproduktions/ Méditerranée Film Production/Boa Film Produktion/FilmboardBerlin-Brandenburg/MAP TV/Bayerische Film-und Fernsehförderung/Centre National de la Cinématographie/Schweizer Bundesant für Kultur etc.; directed by Oja Kodar and Vassili Silović). The extracts shown in faded colour give a tantalizing glimpse of what might have been. The whole film, which lasts eighty-five minutes, approaches Welles' work from an unusual point of view. Almost ignoring his most famous works, his ventures into his other, completed, works from Shakespeare receive only brief mention.

THE MERCHANT OF VENICE: AN INTRODUCTION
(G.B., 1971)

p.c. *Seabourne/Anvil Productions.*
d. *Peter Seabourne.*
l.p. *Not known.*
c. *21 mins.*

This is one of the series of study extracts made by Seabourne.

✛ ✛ ✛ ✛ ✛

YI PIAN JOU
(Hong Kong, 1976)

p.c. *Great Wall*
d. *Xiaofeng Hu.*
l.p. *Long Jiang; Qijing Bao.*
c. *Feature.*

The alternative title listed gives the clue to the film's source of inspiration. It was made in the Mandarin language.

aka: THE POUND OF FLESH

✛ ✛ ✛ ✛ ✛

The play offers the individual a number of interpretations. The earliest edition calls it a "comicall history" – then simply meaning a play with a happy ending. Was the play a plea for understanding or an extolling of Christian virtues over pagan ones? Was, therefore, Shylock but a tragic clown or was he the symbolic victim of Jew-baiting? With such a variety of possible (controversial?) interpretations of the character it is a little surprising that there have not more been more screen versions. Given at least one obvious interpretation, the play would seemed to have been a logical choice for the Nazi cinema.

Let there be no doubt – Shylock has made his mark, not least in the use of his name to mean a hated moneylender. Such an honour has come to only a few literary characters. Charles Dickens created the epitome of the miser (Scrooge) in 'A Christmas Carol' and Cervantes created the idealistic dreamer in 'Don Quixote' (and thus the adjective "quixotic"). So Shylock stands in élite company. Thus, again, it is strange that the screen has not seen more of him. There remains, too, the disappointments that the interpretation by Michel Simon fell short of what might have been expected and that the Orson Welles version was never completed. It is, perhaps, ironic that the best interpretations are to be found in the silent era of the cinema.

It was reported that in 1969 Carlo Ponti had plans for a version of the play. Michael Longsham was tentatively noted as possible director and Peter O'Toole as one of the cast. It was apparently being prepared but, like many other projects, it seems to have come to nought.

For other films with scenes from the play see **CHAPTER XXX ALL THE WORLD'S A STAGE**: PEG OF OLD DRURY (1935); TEDDY BERGMAN'S INTERNATIONAL BROADCAST (1934) and ELIZABETH, DE WROUW ZONDER MAN (1966/7) and **CHAPTER XXXII THE IMMORTAL BARD**: THE LIFE OF SHAKESPEARE (1914); IMMORTAL GENTLEMAN (1935); PARIS 1900 (1948)*; WILLIAM SHAKESPEARE: BACKGROUND TO HIS WORKS (1950); POUND OF FLESH (1952) THE MERCHANT OF VENICE (1958) and MASKS AND FACES (1969)*.

*Denotes film extract.

CHAPTER XVII

THE MERRY WIVES OF WINDSOR

Dramatis Personæ:

Sir John Falstaff
Robin – his page
Bardolph, Pistol, Nym – his friends

Mr. Ford – gentleman of Windsor
Mrs. Ford – his wife

Mr. Page – gentleman of Windsor
Mrs. Page – his wife
William Page – their son
Anne Page – their daughter

Dr. Caius – a French physician

Mistress Quickly – his servant
Rugby – his servant

Fenton – a young gentleman

Shallow – a country justice
Slender – his cousin
Simple – Slender's servant

Sir Hugh Evans – a Welsh parson
Host of Garter Inn
Servants to Ford and Page etc.

Windsor is full of intrigues. Miss Anne Page has just inherited £100, an attraction for all the local batchelors. Slender, a suitor, is invited to dine with her. He conveys his desires by letter through Sir Hugh Evans to Mistress Quickly, Dr. Caius' housekeeper, so that she may act as go-between. Meanwhile, Sir John Falstaff, in trouble with Justice Shallow over various admitted felonies, is interested in both Mrs. Page and Mrs. Ford and writes to them both to see if they are interested in his advances.

Dr. Caius, angry at Sir Hugh's letter, sends a challenge to duel to him and vows to have Anne himself. Mistress Quickly pretends that Anne may have feelings for him and declares she knows Anne's mind.

Now when Mrs. Page and Mrs. Ford receive their (identical) letters they decide that they will teach Falstaff a lesson and plan accordingly. When their husbands discuss Falstaff with Nym and Pistol (and all agree that Falstaff loves all women), the women listen in and talk very sweetly to their husbands. Then Mistress Quickly arrives to see Anne Page.

Host and Shallow invite Ford and Page to witness the duel not knowing that the opponents have been told different places. Page goes off while Ford remains intent on playing a joke on Falstaff.

Mistress Quickly delivers to Falstaff an invitation to visit Mrs. Ford between ten and eleven o'clock when her jealous husband is away. He agrees and, learning from Mistress Quickly that Mr. Page is rarely away, accepts the idea of using his page, Robin, whom Mr. Page likes, to act as messenger to Mrs. Page.

Falstaff has another visitor with a bag of money, a Mr. Brook (actually Mr. Ford in disguise). He tells of his love for Mrs. Ford and asks Falstaff to help him woo her. Falstaff agrees to help and takes the money. He tells of his evening assignation and invites Brook to meet him later. Of course, Ford is furious that his wife has sent such an invitation and calls Page an ass for trusting women. He also wants revenge on Falstaff.

At the site of the duel, Caius waits with his servant. He curses Evans for not appearing. Elsewhere, Evans waits equally frustrated. Eventually, the matter is resolved peacefully and Host tells Caius he will take him to Anne.

Ford, Page and Robin (who is made known to Ford as Falstaff's page) meet. Ford realises that Robin's use is as a messenger and, planning to trap Falstaff, invites some friends along. Meanwhile Slender and Shallow are set to dine with Anne who promises a decision then. Mr. Page approves of the match with Slender.

Mrs. Ford and Mrs. Page execute their plan. Their servants bring in a big laundry basket and are given strict instructions. Robin announces Falstaff's back door entrance to see Mrs. Ford. Mrs. Page hides and Falstaff flatters Mrs. Ford who says that he really loves Mrs. Page. Robin calls out that Mrs. Page is coming and Falstaff quickly hides. Mrs. Page arrives with Robin and tells Mrs. Ford that Mr. Ford and his friends are coming to search the house for her visitor. Mrs. Page, aware that Falstaff is there, has him smuggled out in the laundry basket with the dirty washing to the river. When Ford arrives, he finds no hidden guest and apologises to his wife. Then the two women send Mistress Quickly to rescue Falstaff from the river. But they have not finished their chastisement of him.

Poor Anne is surrounded by suitors – Slender who loves her and meets with her parents' approval, Dr Caius, and Fenton whom she really loves but who is snubbed by her parents. Fenton gives Mistress Quickly a ring to give to Anne.

Whilst telling Bardolph of his misadventures, Falstaff is visited by Mistress Quickly with a message from Mrs. Ford who wishes to make amends. He is asked to meet her between eight and nine o'clock that morning. Brook arrives and is told of Falstaff's escapade and his meeting fixed for this morning. Now Brook is sure that he will catch Falstaff.

Having sorted out her son's Latin lessons to Mistress Quickly's confusion, Mrs. Page aids Mrs. Ford in ensnaring Falstaff again. They trick him into making a speedy exit dressed as a woman, Mrs. Ford's aunt. Again Mr. Ford is thwarted and angry to see his wife's "aunt" whom he beats severely. The wives intend to tell all to their husbands but have one more surprise for Falstaff. They plan a fairy escapade with Falstaff as Herne the Hunter but Brook conveys some of the plan to Falstaff. Mr. Page wants Anne to marry Slender but Mrs. Page wants her to marry Dr. Caius.

Slender sends his messenger to Falstaff. The boy is confused when he sees a woman (the disguised Falstaff) enter Falstaff's room. As Mrs. Ford's aunt is thought to be a witch, Slender seeks her counsel about Anne. The messenger is told that the woman has gone.

Now chaos seems to reign. Host finds he has been robbed by some Germans; Falstaff receives news that Mrs. Ford has been beaten by her husband and gets a letter from her; Fenton gets news that Anne will be Queen of the Fairies in the forest festivities that night. Poor Anne is told by her father to marry Slender and to marry Caius by her mother. Fenton enlists Host's help to get a vicar to marry Anne himself.

Again Falstaff tells Brook of his experiences and arranges for him to meet Mrs. Ford that night. At ten o'clock in the forest, Sir Hugh, dressed as a satyr, gives the fairies their orders. Falstaff, disguised as Herne, meets Mrs. Ford and Mrs. Page but they leave when the fairies disturb them. Falstaff falls on his face to hide and he is burned with tapers by the fairies who dance and sing.

Caius looks for Anne in green for so he has been advised, Slender looks for her in white but Fenton finds her and goes off with her. The Fords and the Pages tell Falstaff he has been punished enough. Mr. Ford forgives his wife and tells Falstaff he will take him to Brook so that Falstaff can return the money. Mrs Ford says that it is not necessary to do so. They all become friends again. Both Caius and Slender appear upset that their brides have turned out to be boys. Fenton returns with Anne to profess his love for her and say that they are married. Everyone is happy and Mr. Ford tells Falstaff that his promise to Brook will be fulfilled and that Brook will lie with Mrs. Ford.

Note: This farce could date from late 1599 but more probably from 1600 or 1601 and may have been commissioned for a royal occasion. Shakespeare may have drawn upon Italian sources to build his character of the thwarted seducer.

✛ ✛ ✛ ✛ ✛

THE MERRY WIVES OF WINDSOR
(U.S.A., 1910)

p.c. *Selig Polyscope.*
d. *William Selig.*
l.p. *Mistress Page; Mistress Ford!!*
b.w. 1000 ft. (305 m.) Sil.

This is an early silent adaptation by the pioneer of the cinema, Selig. Francis Boggs is noted as being in the cast. No doubt the naming of the actresses as listed above was more by way of fun than a wish for anonymity.

FALSTAFF
(France, 1911)

For details of this short film which is based on the opera by Verdi, see **CHAPTER VI FALSTAFF**.

DIE LUSTIGEN WEIBER VON WINDSOR
(Germany, 1917)

p.c. *Beck Film.*
d. *William Wauer.*
l.p.
b.w. (?) mins. Sil.

Details of this film have proved rather elusive. However, according to the few reports traced, the base for this may have been the opera by Otto Nicolai rather than the play. Some sources note Ludwig Berger as director but he was not active in the cinema much before 1920.

FALSTAFF THE TAVERN KNIGHT
(G.B., 1923)

p.c. *British and Colonial Kinematograph Company.*
d. *Edwin Greenwood.*
l.p. *Roy Byford (Sir John Falstaff); Jack Denton (Master Ford); Margaret Yarde (Mistress Ford).*
b.w. 2943 ft. (897 m.)

This extract was No. 11 in the *Gems Of Literature* series.

✛ ✛ ✛ ✛ ✛

THE LADY KILLER
(U.S.A., 1916)

p.c. *Metro.*
d.

l.p. *Ralph Herz.*
b.w. 1 reel. Sil.

An actor in female dress is shut up in a linen basket and thrown into the river.

A little known film, reference back to the plot resumé of the play will indicate the source of inspiration for this comedy.

THE MERRY WIVES OF WINDSOR
(Germany, 1928)
p.c.
d.
l.p. *Werner Krauss (Sir John Falstaff).*
b.w. (?) mins. Sil.

This entry is both intriguing and enigmatic. It raises doubt as to the existence of the film for it is included solely because of a review by 'Variety', March 20, 1929. This reads:

"FILMS IN BERLIN. Deutsches Theatre – "The Merry Wives of Windsor" by Shakespeare. The dialog has been modernized by Hans Rothe and the whole played in costumes suggesting the bustles of 1850. An amusing idea, but why it should be better than the original is hard to see. Also the figure of Falstaff is treated with a trifle too much sentimentality – evidently for Werner Krauss, who likes to stress this angle. Otherwise a brilliant performance with Krauss at his humorous best."

So, is this a film of which all records have been lost? Is it simply a case of the film having a completely different title and thus not identified? Was it a film that had only limited local showings and then disappeared into obscurity? Did 'Variety' accidentally include a review of a stage performance?

All are of course possible. The first is certainly so bearing in mind the upheaval that was to follow in Germany but to have lost all trace of it is hard to believe. This makes the second possibility feasible for the third and fourth would seem unlikely. The style of English and its preciseness certainly suggest that it was a film.

If the film did exist, it would certainly have been of interest to see Krauss in the role of Falstaff.

✣ ✣ ✣ ✣ ✣

DIE LUSTIGEN WEIBER
(Germany, 1935)
p.c. *Cine-Allianz/T.K. Tonfilm.*
d. *Carl Hoffman.*
l.p. *Leo Slezak (Falstaff); Magda Schneider (Viola); Otto Wernicke (Herr Fluth); Helmuth Hoffmann (Fenton); Willi Schaeffers (Schaal); Helmut Weiss (Schmächtig); Wolfgang von Schwindt (Wirt); Armin Schweizer (Herr Page); Aribert Grimmer (Bardolph); Ida Wüst (Frau Fluth); Gustav Püttjer (Pistol); Ruth*

Claus (Anne Page); Erwin von Roy (Nym); Maria Krahn (Frau Hurtig); Ellen Frank (Betty); Franz Zimmerman (Valentin Fluth); Eduard Wenck (Mr. Burns); Else Reval (Mrs. Burns); Walter von Allwörden (Mr. Higgins); Claus Pohl (Guard).
b.w. 88 mins.

Magda Schneider was the mother of the late Romy Schneider and a popular star of German musical films of the era. Leo Slezak, a famous opera singer in his homeland, retired from singing to become a noted comedian. He was the father of the actor, Walter Slezak.

The music for this version was by Ernst Fischer and Granz Grothe.

DIE LUSTIGEN WEIBER VON WINDSOR
(E. Germany, 1950)
p.c. *Defa.*
d. *Georg Wildhagen.*
l.p. *Sonja Ziemann (Frau Fluth); Camilla Spira (Frau Reich); Claus Holm (Herr Fluth); Paul Esser (Sir John Falstaff); Alexander Engel (Herr Reich); Eckart Dux (Fenton); Ina Halley (Anna Reich); Joachim Teege (Herr Spärlich); Gerhard Frickhöffer (Doctor Caius); Berta Monnard; Kurt Mülhardt; Charles Hans Vogt; Fritz Melchior; Herbert Richter; Erich Gühne; Edith Hancke; Edgar Pauly; Elfie Dugal; Nico Turoff; Wladimir Marfiak; Adolf von Wyhl; Gerd Ewert; Christine Salbert; Walter Weinacht; Franziska Klossak; Will Dugal; Carlo Kluge; Horst Stoletzki; Dita Hussina; Mimi Mitell; Gisela Arnold; Hans Jöckel; Hans Sanden; Heinz Gerlach; Renate Fischer; Ludwig Sachs; Lilo Walter; Wolfgang Grützmann; Freddy Teichmann; Maria Eggert; Miriam Bathy; Kurt Fritsch; Martin Rosen. Voices: Rita Streich; Martha Mödl; Hans Krämer; Herbert Brauer; Helmut Krebs; Willi Heyer; Sonja Schöner. Orchestra: Staatskapelle Berlin (conductor: Paul Schmitz); Choir of the Deutschen Staatsoper.*
b.w. 95 mins.

Film version of the opera by Otto Nicolai based on the play THE MERRY WIVES OF WINDSOR which opens with a troupe of travelling players arriving in Windsor and prepare to perform the play (thence into the opera proper).

"With such a cast of singers the film cannot fail to be vocally interesting...Sonja Ziemann and Camilla Spira make attractive wives." – 'Continental Film Review', March, 1953.

DIE LUSTIGEN WEIBER VON WINDSOR
(Austria, 1966)
p.c. *Wien Film.*
d. *Georg Tressler.*

l.p. *Norman Foster (Sir John Falstaff); Colette Boky (Frau Fluth); Mildred Miller (Frau Reich); Igor Gorin (Herr Fluth); Edmond Hershell (Herr Reich); Lucia Popp (Anna Reich); Ernst Shutz (Fenton); John Gittings (Doctor Caius); Marshall Raynor (Herr Spärlich); Rosella Hightower (Ballerina).Zagreb Symphony Orchestra (conductor: Milan Horvath).*
Technicolor. 97 mins.

Another version of the opera by Otto Nicolai, this time in colour, with an international singing cast. There are conflicting reports on the details for this film. The production year has been put as 1964 and production country as Liechtenstein. A running time of one hundred and two minutes is given by some sources and the colour as Eastman Color. The latter is logical with Technicolor responsible for the release print.

"The tale of Falstaff is told in dazzling Technicolor...Blessed with some fine operatic voices..." – 'Motion Picture Guide'.

DIE LUSTIGEN WEIBER VON WINDSOR (W. Germany, 1977)

p.c.
d. *Franco Enriques; Gerhard Reutter.*
l.p. *Clemens Schitz (Wirt); Trudeliese Schmidt (Frau Reich); Helen Donath (Frau Fluth); Karl Ridderbusch (Sir John Falstaff); Heinz Zednik (Spärlich); Anna Sukis (Anna); Claes K. Ahnsjö (Fenton); Alfred Sramek (Doctor Caius); Wolfgang Brendel (Herr Muth);*

Nikolaus Paryla.Chorus and Sinfonica Der Radiofusion von Bavaria (conductor: Rafael Kubelik).
c. 154 mins.

This is a further version of Nicolai's opera. A well-rated recording with a similar cast, possibly made at the same time as the film or which may even be the film soundtrack, was once available through Decca records.

Note: The following are the Shakespearean names for the German ones in the opera version – Frau Fluth (Mistress Ford); Herr Fluth (Master Ford); Frau Reich (Mistress Page); Herr Reich (Master Page).

✜ ✜ ✜ ✜ ✜

Falstaff was one of Shakespeare's great comic characters and one much loved by audiences. This heavy drinking rascal had been killed off in HENRY V as was Mistress Quickly. Shakespeare revived them both in THE MERRY WIVES OF WINDSOR (written, so legend has it, at the request of Queen Elizabeth I) though the Falstaff here was a somewhat different character. For more about him, see **CHAPTER VI FALSTAFF**.

For other films with scenes from the play see **CHAPTER XXX ALL THE WORLD'S A STAGE**: FALSTAFF IN WIEN (1940) and **CHAPTER XXXII THE IMMORTAL BARD**: LES AMOURS DE LA REINE ÉLISABETH (1912); THE LIFE OF SHAKESPEARE (1914) and C.E.M.A (1942).

CHAPTER XVIII
A MIDSUMMER NIGHT'S DREAM

Dramatis Personæ:

Theseus – Duke of Athens
Hippolyta – Queen of the Amazons, betrothed to Theseus
Philostrate – Master of the Revels to Theseus
Attendants to Theseus and Hippolyta

Egeus
Hermia – his daughter, in love with Lysander
Lysander – loved by Hermia
Demetrius – suitor of Hermia with the approval of Egeus
Helena – in love with Demetrius

Oberon, King of the Fairies

Titania, Queen of the Fairies
Puck, also known as Robin Goodfellow
Peaseblossom, Cobweb, Mustardseed, Moth – fairies
Other fairies attending Oberon and Titania

Peter Quince – carpenter; Prologue in the Interlude
Nick Bottom – weaver; Pyramus in the Interlude
Francis Flute – bellows mender; Thisby in the Interlude
Tom Snout – tinker; Wall in the Interlude
Snug – joiner; Lion in the Interlude
Robin Starveling, – tailor; Moonshine in the Interlude

There is a law in Athens that citizens can order their daughters to marry whom-so-ever the parents choose. The penalty for disobedience is death. In practice, the law is never invoked except now by one old man, Egeus. His daughter, Hermia, refuses to marry Demetrius because she loves Lysander.

Theseus listens to her plea that her friend, Helena, loves Demetrius and he has previously loved her. Theseus, though not approving of the law, is forced to abide by it. He gives her four days in which to change her mind.

Lysander is upset to hear of this but has a plan. He and Hermia will run away to the woods where he has an aunt and there they will marry. It happens that this cruel law does not extend beyond the city boundaries.

Hermia tells Helena who, aware that he will follow, tells Demetrius. Now the wood in which the lovers plan to meet is the home of the Fairies. As it happens, all is not well between the King of the Fairies, Oberon, and his lady, Titania. The cause of their rift is a changeling child stolen by Titania from its nurse when its mother died. Oberon wants the boy as his page but Titania refuses.

The same night as the lovers plan to meet, Oberon and Titania meet in the woods and exchange harsh words. Oberon calls for Puck, a mischievous sprite much liked by Oberon, and asks him to fetch a magic potion to drop on Titania's eyelids so that she will fall in love with the first person she sees upon awakening.

While awaiting Puck's return, Oberon sees Demetrius and Helena and hears her pleas of love to him. Oberon orders Puck to put some of the potion on Demetrius' eyelids and he describes the youth to Puck as an Athenian by his dress. As Puck goes about his mission, Oberon places the drops on Titania's eyelids.

Hermia and Lysander meanwhile have made their way to the wood but, weary, they rest. Puck seeing Lysander and his dress, takes him to be the Athenian and applies the drops to his eyelids. Unfortunately, Helena happens to wander by just as Lysander awakens and, of course, he falls in love with her. Helena was simply trying to keep up with Demetrius when she saw Lysander and stopped.

Helena cannot believe the words of love that come from Lysander's lips and believes he is mocking her. Naturally, Hermia does not understand what has happened and is upset. Demetrius, meanwhile, has become weary of his search for Hermia and Lysander and falls asleep. Oberon sees this and, Puck having told him of his error, puts some of the potion on Demetrius' eyelids. When he awakes, he sees Helena and falls in love with her. Poor Helena now has two men professing their love for her.

The situation appears to Hermia as a plot by the three to ridicule her and repudiates Helena accordingly. The two men go off to fight over Helena. Oberon sees this and, being assured by Puck that it was a genuine mistake, commands the sprite to cause a fog to confuse the men and beguile them with mimicry so that they weary. Puck is ordered to undo the damage by placing more drops in Lysander's eyes as he sleeps.

Oberon, intent upon playing a prank upon Titania, sees a clown and fixes an ass's head on his shoulders. Of course, Titania sees the clown and falls in love with him. She calls upon her fairies to attend to him which they do. Oberon takes advantage of the situation which he has contrived and she cannot refuse to give him the boy as a page. He then relents and with another potion releases her from the spell and lets the clown sleep relieved of the ass' head.

Reconciled, Oberon and Titania go in search of the lovers. The spell lifted from Lysander, he sees Hermia, his true love, and they are puzzled by the events of the past night. Helena, too, awakes and, now more rational, listens to Demetrius' words of love and accepts them as being sincere.

Old friendships restored, Demetrius resolves to ask Egeus to relent as he does not love Hermia and will not marry her. Egeus has, in fact, come to the wood looking for Hermia. When he realises the situation he agrees to the wedding of Hermia and Lysander to be held in four days time in place of her execution. Helena and Demetrius fix their wedding for the same day.

Oberon and Titania, invisible naturally, attend the weddings and hold their own festivities in the wood.

Now if anyone is upset by this tale of fairy pranks and cannot believe it, well, just pretend it was a dream. After all, there was no intent to cause offence at what is no more than a harmless Midsummer Night's Dream.

Note: This happy comedy may well have been written for an important wedding of the time, particularly between 1591 and 1598. It may have been for the wedding of the Earl of Derby to Elizabeth Vere, daughter of the Earl of Oxford as Derby's father and brother were patrons of Shakespeare. This wedding was on January 26, 1595. Topical allusions and style enforce the argument for this period and thus 1594 or early 1595 is the most likely date. As to the source, well, it seems that Shakespeare called upon his childhood memories and the variety of books he had read including Chaucer, Ovid, Plutarch and Spenser. Certainly many of the names and legends are culled from works by these authors.

✠ ✠ ✠ ✠ ✠

SONGE D'UNE NUIT D'ÉTÉ D'APRÈS SHAKESPEARE
(France, 1908)

p.c. *Le Lion.*
d.
l.p. *"Footit" (real name – Tudor Hall); Stacia de Napierkowska.*
b.w. 17 mins. Sil.

The title may indicate a free adaptation of the play. Tudor Hall was a British comic of the era.

A MIDSUMMER NIGHT'S DREAM
(U.S.A., 1909)

p.c. *Vitagraph.*
d. *James Stuart Blackton, Charles Kent.*

l.p. *William V. Ranous (Bottom); Rose Tapley (Hermia); Gladys Hulette (Puck); Maurice Costello (Lysander); Julia Swayne-Gordon (Helena); Walter Ackerman (Demetrius); Helene Costello, Dolores Costello (Fairies); Charles Chapman (Quince);Florence Turner (Titania?); Will Shea (Mechanical).*
b.w. 993 ft. (303 m.) Sil.

A typical Vitagraph production which tends to follow the play closely but with the addition of another character, Penelope, who is conspicuous by her absence in the cast list!. It is this character who, following an argument with Titania, induces Puck to put the spell on Titania.

In its 'Vitagraph Bulletin' of December 1-15, 1909, the company proclaimed: "Students of the great dramatist's works will thoroughly enjoy the careful pictorial presentation of the many scenes, while the whole play is so clearly portrayed that it will not fail to delight the spectator who is not familiar with the works of Shakespeare." So much was put into the film that it moved at a very fast pace with resultant loss of depth in the characters.

A MIDSUMMER NIGHT'S DREAM
(Italy, 1913)

p.c. *Gloria Film.*
d. *Paulo Azzuri.*
l.p. *Socrate Tommasi (Lysander); Bianca Maria Hübner (Helena).*
b.w. 35 to 45 mins. Sil.

The original title of this Italian version is unknown. There is also some doubt about the director of this film which, for its day, used advanced techniques such as dissolves and cross-cutting. The performances, too, are said to be of merit. Its apparent qualities make it all the more regrettable that only a remnant survives.

EIN SOMMERNACHTSTRAUM
(Germany, 1924/25)

p.c. *Neumann-Produktion.*
d. *Hans Neumann.*
l.p. *Theodor Becker (Theseus); Ruth Weyher (Hippolyta); Paul Günther (Egeus); Charlotte Ander (Hermia); André Mattoni (Lysander); Hans Albers (Demetrius); Barbara von Annenkoff (Helena); Paul Biensfeldt; Bruno Ziener (Milon); Rose Veldtkirch; Adolf Klein; Hans Behrendt; Tamara (Oberon); Lori Leux (Titania); Valeska Gert (Puck); Alexander Granach (Nymph); Werner Krauss (Bottom); Fritz Rasp (Snout); Ernst Gronau (Quince); Armand Guerra (Knave); Wilhelm Bendow (Flute); Walter Brandt (Snug); Martin Jacob (Starveling).*
b.w. 8297 ft. (2529 m.) Sil.

A reasonably lengthy version of the play, noted as being a pastiche of the original, which was an artistic and financial success in Germany at the time with crowds having to be turned away from the Ufa Nopllendorfplatz Theatre in Berlin when it opened. It was not for children, however, as the Berlin censor used his authority to forbid it to them. The showings there had music composed and arranged by Hans May to accompany them. Eric Borchard's American Jazz band, augmented with some string instruments, reportedly played the music extremely well, ranging from Wagner to the latest popular tunes. According to 'Variety' : "When they got hot they just tore the roof off the joint.".

aka: WOOD LOVE; A MIDSUMMER NIGHT'S DREAM; EIN HEITERES FASTNACHTSSPIEL

A MIDSUMMER NIGHT'S DREAM
(U.S.A., 1935)

p.c. *Warner Bros.*
d. *Max Reinhardt, William Dieterle.*
l.p. *James Cagney (Bottom); Dick Powell (Lysander); Joe E. Brown (Flute); Hugh Herbert (Snout); Jean Muir (Helena); Ian Hunter (Theseus); Frank McHugh (Quince); Victor Jory (Oberon); Olivia de Havilland (Hermia); Mickey Rooney (Puck); Ross Alexander (Demetrius); Grant Mitchell (Egeus); Nini Theilade (Prima Ballerina Fairy); Verree Teasdale (Hippolyta); Anita Louise (Titania); Hobart Cavanaugh (Philostrate); Dewey Robinson (Snug); Otis Harlan (Staveling); Arthur Treacher (Ninny's Tomb); Katherine Frey (Peaseblossom); Fred Sale (Mustardseed); Billy Barty (Moth); Helen Westcott (Cobweb); Kenneth Anger.*
b.w. 140 mins.

The $1,500,000 budget for this by Warner Bros. surprised Hollywood and it is still a mystery why it was done. For sure they had the talent of the director, an acknowledged theatrical genius from the early part of this century who had emigrated to Hollywood to escape Nazi persecution. It soon became apparent that he was out of his depth. He said in his programme notes. "For the first time in my life I have realised my own dreams of doing this play with no restrictions on my imagination." He does, however, appear to have felt that the film was more Dieterle's than his. Logically so, since Dieterle was far more experienced in the film-making skills.

The making of the film was not without problems. Many of the cast were not acquainted with Shakespeare. Dick Powell was then a singer though he later turned to dramatic acting and directing. Cagney got through more with acrobatics than acting in a role he did not want. To add to the problems, Mickey Rooney broke a leg and had to be wheeled around by unseen stagehands. Photographer Ernest Haller was sacked and Hal Mohr replaced him successfully.

Ernest Korngold – he had worked with Reinhardt in Europe – was engaged to write the score based on Mendelssohn's music. Commenting on the dance of the fairies in reply to an enquiry from Cagney he said: "Ah, *wunderbar*! Terrific – tremendous – stupendous – but *bad*!". The delicate ballet sequences appear nearer Busby Berkeley than ballet! However, it was the start of a long and fruitful relationship between Korngold and Warner Bros.. Of course, Mendelssohn's original music is generally always available on disc and part of the dialogue and music was released on "The Golden Age Of The Hollywood Stars", a United Artists album, which featured music and dialogue from Warner Bros. films.

The film was among the biggest box office successes of 1935 in America which rather negates the comments that the film was not a commercial success. Maybe the audiences, having seen the film, were not pleased for the critics were certainly mixed in opinions. Purists were, naturally, upset at the mutilated text though, realistically, the film was already long enough.

The film exists in shorter versions even down to one hundred and thirteen minutes in some countries. This suggests some fairly drastic excisions. The time noted above is the longest traced.

Shown as part of the Everybody's Shakespeare International Festival, London, England, 1994.
Shown at the San Sebastian Film Festival, Spain, 1994, as part of a William Dieterle retrospective.
Shown at the Valladolid Film Festival, Spain, 1988.
Academy of Motion Picture Arts and Sciences, U.S.A., 1935: Nomination – Best Picture; Awards – Cinematography (Hal Mohr), Film Editing (Ralph Dawson).

"...the passing of time has not been generous to it, but it will remain forever as an unclassifiable curiosity." – Carlos Aguilar, 'Guía del Vídeo-Cine'.

"...the studio's burnt offering to culture in general and Shakespeare in particular." – Clive Hirschhorn, 'The Warner Bros. Story'.

"...a peculiar hybrid of a film, somehow uniting Teutonic expressionism with Hollywood casting." – Tony Thomas, 'The Films of Olivia de Havilland'.

aka: LE SONGE D'UNE NUIT D'ÉTÉ; EL SUEÑO DE UNA NOCHE DE VERANO

It is appropriate to include the following short film here:

OLIVIA DE HAVILLAND TALKS ABOUT "A MIDSUMMER NIGHT'S DREAM"
(U.S.A., 1935)

p.c. *Warner Bros.*
d.
l.p. *Olivia de Havilland.*
b.w. 4 mins.

This was Olivia de Havilland's film debut. She had, however, played in the play under Reinhardt's direction at the Hollywood Bowl the previous year. Here she talks to the viewer(s) about her role, the production and the director.

This is probably the film released by Warner Bros. with the title **A DREAM COME TRUE**. A one minute extract from the film was issued for collectors on 8 mm. by Steel Valley Film Services, U.S.A.

A MIDSUMMER NIGHT'S DREAM
(G.B., 1953)

p.c. *Emile Katzke.*
d. *Charles Deane.*
l.p. *Young Vic Theatre Company. Narrator: Ronald Howard.*
b.w. 12 mins.

This extract forms part of a series made originally for television called *The World's A Stage*.

A MIDSUMMER NIGHT'S DREAM: INTRODUCTION TO THE PLAY
(U.S.A., 1954)

p.c. *Coronet Instructional Films.*
d. *James Wood Krutch.*
l.p. *Joseph Wood Krutch.*
c. 15 mins.

Selected scenes were used as an introduction to the play and the film was meant for educational purposes.

SEN NOCI SVATOJÁNSKÉ
(Czechoslovakia, 1957-59)

p.c. *Krátký Film Prague/Studio Kresleného A Loutkového Filmu.*
d. *Jiří Trnka.*
l.p. *Puppet animation.*
Eastman Color. 80 mins. S Totalvision.

This unusual version of the play is regarded by many as the master puppeteer's greatest work. For this work he substituted the normal hands, feet and faces of the puppets with ones made of a specially compounded plastic that could be moulded and sculptured. This gave a more fluid movement. The film has its restrictions in the dialogue and, naturally, such a concept of tranformation has its disadvantages but there are many pleasures in this, not verbal, but visual. Certainly the film has many ingenuities and magical moments which keep it safely out of reach of any "oddity" category.

In 1971 an English language version was presented by American producer Howard Sackler. Shorn of six minutes, the voices to be heard are: Richard Burton (Storyteller); Tom Criddle (Lysander); Ann Bell (Hermia); Michael Meacham (Demetrius); John Warner (Egeus); Barbara Leigh-Hunt (Helena); Hugh Manning (Theseus); Joss Ackland (Peter Quince); Alec McGowen (Nick Bottom); Stephen Moore (Francis Flute); Barbara Jefford (Titania); Jack Gwillim (Oberon); Roger Shepherd (Puck);

Laura Graham (Theseus' Bride). There were criticisms of this version but at least the music played by the Czech Philharmonic Orchestra (conductor: Karel Ancerl) remained intact.

Shown as part of the Everybody's Shakespeare International Festival, London, England, 1994.
Shown at the London Film Festival, England, 1959.
Shown at the Shakespeare Film Festival, Wiesbaden, W. Germany, 1964.
Shown at the Valladolid Film Festival, Spain, 1995 as part of a retrospective on the Czech animated film.
Cannes Film Festival, France, 1959: Technical Award.
Certamen CIDALC del Cine de Danza y Música, Spain, 1961: Special Prize.
International Festival of Puppet Films, Bucharest, Roumania, 1962: First Prize.
Montevideo International Film Festival, Uruguay, 1959: Second Prize.
National Czechoslovak Prize, Czechoslovakia, 1959: Václav Trojan (Music) for the blending of Shakespearean themes with Czech culture.
Venice Film Festival, Italy, 1959: Medal of Honour "hors concours".
'Time' magazine Annual Ten Best List, U.S.A., 1961. Listed in Foreign section.
Workers' Film Festival, Czechoslovakia, 1959: Prize for Artistic and Technical Perfection.

"A great way to expose this classic play to a wider audience." – 'Motion Picture Guide'.

aka: UN SUEÑO DE UNA NOCHE DE VERANO

It seems appropriate to note the following here:
SKUTECHNOST NOCI SVATOJÁNSKÉ
(Czechoslovakia, 1969)

p.c. *Dokumentárni Film/Československý Film.*
d. *Václav Táborský.*
l.p. *Documentary.*
c. 9 mins.

This is a documentary record of the making of the above listed film.

Shown at the Shakespeare Film Festival, Wiesbaden, W. Germany, 1964.

A MIDSUMMER NIGHT'S DREAM
(G.B., 1968)

p.c. *Royal Shakespeare Enterprises. A Royal Shakespeare Company/Filmways Production.*
d. *Peter Hall.*
l.p. *Derek Godfrey (Theseus); Barbara Jefford (Hippolyta); Nicholas Selby (Egeus); Hugh Sullivan (Philostrate); David Warner (Lysander); Michael Jayston (Demetrius); Diana Rigg (Helena); Helen Mirren (Hermia); Ian Richardson (Oberon); Judi Dench (Titania); Ian Holm (Puck); Paul Rogers (Bottom); Sebastian Shaw (Quince); John Normington*

(Flute); Bill Travers (Snout); Clive Swift (Snug); Donald Eccles (Starveling).
Eastman Color. 124 mins.

A version with this pedigree should have been among the best films of Shakespearean works. The general consensus of opinion is that it is the exact opposite. Brenda Davies in 'Monthly Film Bulletin' (March, 1969) describes it as "...ugly, charmless and almost devoid of enchantment or humour." What a pity!

"...makes Shakespeare's lightest and most fanciful of plays look dull and unattractive." – George Perry, 'The Great British Picture Show'.

A MIDSUMMER NIGHT'S DREAM: AN INTRODUCTION
(G.B., 1969)

p.c. Seabourne Enterprises.
d. Peter Seabourne.
l.p. ?
b.w. 25 mins.

Details of this are not known but logically contains extracts as do the others in the series. The cast, too, was probably drawn from the small group used in the others.

SOGNO DI UNA NOTTE D'ESTATE
(Italy, 1983)

p.c. Politecne Cinematografica/RAI-Radiotelevisione Italiana (Rete 2)
d. Gabriele Salvatores.
l.p. Alberto Lionello; Erika Blanc; Gianna Nannini; Flavio Bucci; Sabrina Vannucchi; Luca Barbareschi.
c. 104 mins.

Divided into three episodes, La Notte, Il Giorno and I Comici, this was probably intended for television originally. The German release was shortened by fourteen minutes.

aka: EIN SOMMERNACHTSTRAUM

A MIDSUMMER NIGHT'S DREAM
(G.B./Spain, 1984)

p.c. Cabochon Productions/Television Española. In association with Channel 4.
d. Celestino Coronado.
l.p. Lindsay Kemp (Puck); Manuela Vargas (Hippolyta); The Incredible Orlando (Titania); Michael Matou (Oberon); François Testory (Changeling/Snout/Tree); David Meyer (Lysander); Neil Caplan (Theseus/The Beast); David Haughton (Demetrius); Atilio Lopez (Bottom/Romeo); Christian Michaelson (Flute/ Juliet); Javier Sanz (Staveling/ Moon); Cheryl Heazelwood (Helena); Annie Huckle (Hermia); Kevin L'Anglaise (Snug/ Lion); José Luis Aguirre (Quince); Carlos Miranda; Nuria Moreno; Sally Lloyd; Lola Peno; Claudia Faci;

Douglas McNicol; John Knight; Jaime Cortadellas; Pedro Ruiz.
c. 77 mins.

Based on the stage production by Lindsay Kemp and David Haughton, this strange version not only abbreviates the original but introduces ROMEO AND JULIET as a sort of play within a play. The missing text only serves to diminish the possibilities of the film though it is not without its moments of imagination and inventiveness. Though originally intended for television, the film has received theatrical showings.

Spanish title: SUEÑO DE UNA NOCHE DE VERANO

A MIDSUMMER NIGHT'S DREAM
(G.B., 1996)

p.c. Channel Four Films in association with The Arts Council of England and Capitol Films An Edenwood Production.
d. Adrian Noble.
l.p. Alex Jennings (Theseus/Oberon); Lindsay Duncan (Hippolyta/Titania); Barry Lynch (Puck/Philostrate); Desmond Barrit (Nick Bottom); Monica Dolan (Hermia); John Kane (Peter Quince); Kevin Doyle (Demetrius); Daniel Evans (Lysander), Emily Raymond .(Helena); Alfred Burke (Egeus); Howard Crossley (Tom Snout); Robin Gillespie (Robin Starveling); Mark Letheren (Francis Flute); Kenn Saberton (Snug); Ann Hasson (First Fairy); Emily Button, Jane Colenutt, Tom Griggs, Darren Roberts (Principal Fairies/ Courtiers); Gemma Ashton, John Baxter, Guy Hargreaves, Dominique Poulter, Nicola McRoy, Matt Patresi, Sara Kruger, Oscar Pierce, Michelle Jordan (Fairies/Courtiers); Osheen Jones (The Boy).
c. 103 mins.

Director Noble edited the original text himself to allow more liberty in the filming of a concept derived from a 1994 stage production by the Royal Shakespeare Company. The production found success in its homeland but failed in America. To this Noble added a new character – a boy. It is through his dream that the plot unfolds. He looks on in enchantment.

The film contains a number of contemporary jokes and references plus some anachronistic elements (an Athenian forest of hanging light bulbs, for example). A number of scenes also emphasise the sexual undercurrent of the play. All of which leads to some confusion, not least in that of the intended market/age group of the film.

"...another moment where high-culture technical laziness turns a neat idea into a momentary conceit." – Mark Sinker, 'Sight and Sound'.

aka: UN SUEÑO EN UNA NOCHE DE VERANO.

A MIDSUMMER NIGHT'S DREAM
(U.S.A., Germany, 1999)

p.c. *A Fox Searchlight Pictures and Regency Enterprises presentation in association with Taurus Films.*

d. *Michael Hoffman.*

l.p. *Kevin Kline (Nick Bottom); Michelle Pfeiffer (Titania); Rupert Everett (Oberon); Stanley Tucci (Puck); Calista Flockhart (Helena); Anna Friel (Hermia); Christian Bale (Demetrius); Dominic West (Lysander); David Strathairn (Theseus); Sophie Marceau (Hippolyta); Roger Rees (Peter Quince); Max Wright (Robin Starveling); Gregory Jbara (Snug); Bill Irwin (Tom Snout); Sam Rockwell (Francis Flute); Bernard Hill (Egeus); John Sessions (Philostrate); Deidre A. Harrison (Hard-eyed Fairy); Heather Elizabeth Parisi (Bottom's Wife); Annalisa Cordone (Cobweb); Paola Pessot (Mustardseed); Solena Nocentini (Moth); Flaminia Fegarotti (Peaseblossom); Valerio Isidori (Master Antonio); Daniele Finizio, Damiano Salvatori (Dangerous Boys); Chomoke Bhuiyan (Changeling Boy); Nathalie Van Ravenstein, Venera Torti, Luce Maioli, Xenia F. Wilson (Fairy Musicians); Veronica Del Chiappa, Monica La Vezzari, Cristina Guglielmino, Alessandra Monti, Anna Cirigliano (Fairies); Elisabetta Carnevale, Chiara Stampone, Chiara Conti, Valentina Sciarrini, Alessandra Carbone (Nymphs); Paolo Risi, Davide Marotta, Sabrina Marazzi, Elisabetta La Padula (Pantomime Dwarves); Antonia Petrucca, Vittoria Danese, Marina Ficuciello, Marina Boccini (Dwarves); Roberta Galli, Anna Burt (Furies); Luisa and Lucia Nardelli (Janus Figures); Daniele Quistelli, Emanuele Gullotto, Carlo Vitale, Marco Rossetti (Fawns); Victoria Eugenia Martinez (Female Monster); Beniamino Vitale, Gianluca Del Mastro, Stefano Cesarini, Vincenzo Dettole (Satyrs); Walter Maioli, Aldo Marinucci, Gaetano Delfini, Roberto Stanco (Satyr Musicians); Paola Murgia, Alba Tiberi (Sphinxes); Francesco Caruso, Giuseppe Gambino (Winged Men); Tommaso Accardo (Forge Man); Cristina Mantis (Medusa); Isabella Rita Gallinelli (Soprano/Aida); Filippo Fugazzotto (Goat-headed Creature); Riccardo Tesi, Luca Martini, Maarizio Geri, Daniele Mencarelli, Gabriele Mirabassi (Wedding Musicians); Mauro Marino (Pharoah); Endrius Colombaioni (Fire Eater); Giancarlo Colombaioni, Angela Bonello (Jugglers); Vincenzo Moretti (Othello); Manuela Metri (Desdemona); Laura Maltoni, Ester Salis, Donato Fierro-Perez (Troupe of Actors); Danielle Ferretti, Vito Passeri, Francesco Gabriele (Greek Tragedy); Lilliana Vitale (Storyteller).*

DeLuxe Color. 121 mins. S Scope

In this version, the text has been shortened and both the geographical setting (a fictitious Monte Athena substituting for the original Athens) and the temporal one (the time is the end of the last century) have been changed.

The makers clearly aimed at the commercial market by casting a number of popular performers. Mostly they seem to have acquitted themselves at least efficiently for the film has been initially well received. Filmed in Italy on location and in the Cinecittà studios, the strong Italian presence among the supporting cast will not have escaped notice.

The sets and costumes are said to be excellent and the music borrows heavily from the classics. In all, the lack of pretensions seems to have paid off offering the public an engaging diversion.

aka: WILLIAM SHAKESPEARE'S A MIDSUMMER NIGHT'S DREAM; EL SUEÑO DE UNA NOCHE DE VERANO; EIN SOMMERNACHTSTRAUM; SOGNO DI UNA NOTTA DI MEZZA ESTATE

✤ ✤ ✤ ✤ ✤

EIN SOMMERNACHTSTRAUM IN UNSERER ZEIT
(Germany, 1913)

p.c. *Deutsche Bioscop.*
d. *Stellan Rye.*
l.p. *Grete Berger (Puck); Carl Clewing (Lysander); Jean Ducret; Anni Mews.*
b.w. (?) mins. Sil.

An old gentleman awaits with his daughter and niece the arrival of their fiancés. When they arrive they enjoy a meal on the lawn. The old man falls asleep and dreams of characters from A MIDSUMMER NIGHT'S DREAM. He awakens and believes the dream to be real. He attempts to chase off the "intruders" but finds only the couple asleep on the grass.

A modern, as the title implies, setting – for the time – version of the play which was, according to reports, rather risqué and a not very pleasant distortion of the original.

I DUE SOGNI AD OCCHI APERTI
(Italy, 1920)

p.c. *D'Ambra Film.*
d. *Lucio D'Ambra.*
l.p.
b.w. 6259 ft. (1908 m.) Sil.

This is noted as being a parody of the play.

✤ ✤ ✤ ✤ ✤

ELFENSZENE AUS DEM SOMMERNACHTSTRAUM
(Germany, 1917)

p.c. *Harmonie Film.*
d.
l.p. *Ballet of the Deutschen Opernhauses, Berlin.*
b.w. Short.

This sound (probably a sound-on-disc system) release was a scene from the ballet with music by Mendelssohn. The choreographer was Mary Zimmerman.

A MIDSUMMER NIGHT'S DREAM
(U.S.A., 1966)

p.c. *Oberon.*
d. *George Balanchine.*
l.p. *Suzanne Farrell (Titania); Edward Villella (Oberon); Arthur Mitchell (Puck); Mimi Paul (Helena); Nicholas Magallanes (Lysander); Patrick McBride (Hermia); Roland Vazquez (Demetrius); Francisco Moncion (Theseus); Gloria Govrin (Hippolyta); Richard Rapp (Bottom); Jacques D'Amboise (Court Danseur); Allegra Kent (Court Danseuse). With Members of the New York City Ballet Company.*
Eastman Color. 93 mins. Panavision.

A straight-forward version of the ballet, the music by Felix Mendelssohn is complemented by good performances of appeal to ballet lovers. One American source notes the director as Dan Eriksen. The director quoted above may well relate to the ballet rather than the filming of it.

OBERON
(DES ELFENKÖNIGS SCHWUR)
(W. Germany, 1971)

p.c. *Z.D.F.*
d. *Herbert Junkers.*
l.p. *Hans Puts (Narrator); Netta B. Ramati; Ursula Schröder-Feinen (Rezia); Heinz Bosi; René Kollo (Hüon); Jürgen Müller; Gerhard Misske (Shield Bearer); Hanner Winkler; Donald Goobe (Oberon); Feliz Smolik (Titania); Armando Andreani; Lena von Alm; Marga Schiml (Puck); Elke Estinbaum (Fatima); Iris Wachalowsky (Roschana); Ernst Craemer (Harun al Raschid); Norbert Mas (Babekan); Mariá de Francesca (Sea Girl). Bayerischen Rundfunks Chorus. Bamberger Symphoniker (conductor: Heinz Walberg).*
c. 91 mins.

This is a film of the opera by Carl Maria von Weber which was inspired by the Shakespeare play and the poem 'Oberon' by Christoph Martin Wieland. Briefly, the story concerns Oberon's search for two true lovers to placate his own love, Titania, whom he loves dearly. Puck tells him a story of Hugo de Bordeaux who has killed Charlemagne's son. The emperor, not aware of this treachery, thinks his son was killed in a duel, forgives Hugo if he will go the court of Harun al Raschid, kill him and abduct his daughter.

SEN NOCI SVATOJÁNSKÉ
(Czechoslovakia, 1985)

p.c. *Filmové Studio Barrandov.*
d. *Vladimír Sís.*
l.p. *Jiří Kyselák (Theseus); Dagmar Maštalířová (Hippolyta); Lubomir Večeřa (Lysander); Soňa Žejdová (Hermia); Zdeněk Kárný (Demetrius); Eva Trnková (Helena); Zdeněk Hanzlovský (Oberon); Jarmila Bařinková (Titania); Antonín Michna (Puck); Stanislav Olbricht; Milan Potůček; Nikola Pecháček; Petr Přibyl.*
Eastman Color. 74 mins.

A ballet version of the play which is assumed, but not confirmed, to be that by Mendelssohn.

This, one of Shakespeare's happiest comedies, offers scope for inventiveness given its dreamy setting of fantasy and love. Though the film world has presented surprisingly few versions of it (even allowing for the two very recent films), the play has certainly spawned two characters of interest – Puck and Oberon. Not to be overlooked is Mendelssohn's delightful incidental music written for the 1827 German version in Berlin by Ludwig Tieck. The influence of the play upon Ingmar Bergman in **SOMMARNATTENS LEENDE** (see **CHAPTER XXX ALL THE WORLD'S A STAGE**) – a film which had its own derivatives – is something that cannot be overlooked. The music, mentioned above, remains a perennial favourite reflecting the popularity of the play which itself reflects the genius of its author.

For other films with scenes from the play see **CHAPTER XXX ALL THE WORLD'S A STAGE**: MISTER CINDERS (1934); A MATTER OF LIFE AND DEATH (1946); HOLLYWOOD AND THE STARS (1963)*; SCORPIO RISING (1965)*; THE PROJECTIONIST (1970)*; ZELIG (1983); MURDER PSALM (1983)* and DEAD POETS SOCIETY (1986) and **CHAPTER XXXII THE IMMORTAL BARD**: THREE SEASONS (1958); OUT OF OBERAMMERGAU – CHRISTIAN STÜCKL INSZENIERT SHAKESPEARE IN INDIEN (1993).

*Denotes film extract.

CHAPTER XIX

MUCH ADO ABOUT NOTHING

Dramatis Personæ:

Don Pedro – Prince of Arragon
Balthasar – his attendant
Don John – his bastard brother
Borachio, Conrade – followers of Don John

Claudio – a young lord of Florence
Benedick – a young lord of Padua

Leonato – Governor of Messina
Antonio – his brother
Hero – Leonato's daughter

Beatrice – Leonato's niece
Margaret, Ursula – Hero's gentlewomen attendants

Friar Francis
Dogberry – a constable
Verges – a headborough
A sexton
A Boy
Messengers, Watch, Lords, Attendants, Musicians
    etc.

Leonato, the Governor of Messina, lives in his palace with his rather serious daughter Hero and his niece, the highly spirited Beatrice. She often brightens up the life of Hero.

Some soldiers returning from a war take the chance to pass through Messina again. Among them are Don Pedro, Prince of Arragon, his half-brother, Don John, Pedro's friend Claudio, a lord of Florence and a witty lord of Padua, Benedick. All are made welcome by Leonato as old friends.

Upon entering the house, Benedick immediately engages Leonato and Pedro in conversation. Now Benedick is of similar temperament to Beatrice and she soon interrupts the party and enters into a war of words with Benedick so that it would appear that they hate each other.

Claudio meanwhile has his mind on Hero and how more beautiful she has become. Pedro has his mind on the verbal conflict and comments to Leonato that they would make a lively match. Leonato dismisses the suggestion saying that in a week of marriage they would talk themselves mad. Pedro resolves to keep this idea in mind. He notices, too, Claudio's obvious attraction to Hero and when challenged about it openly admits that he loves her upon which Pedro makes the proper overtures to Leonato and the matter is joyfully settled.

With a few days to pass before the wedding, Pedro enlists the aid of the loving couple and Leonato to try and unite Beatrice and Benedick. Walking in the garden, Pedro, Claudio and Leonato, aware that Benedick can hear them, speak of Beatrice's love for him and how stupid he would be if he does take the matter seriously. And so he does, pondering upon what he has heard. When Beatrice comes to fetch him for dinner, he is kind to her despite her barbed tongue.

With one fish in the net, Hero enlists the help of her lady attendants, Ursula and Margaret, to catch the other. Hero send Margaret to inform Beatrice discretely that Ursula and Hero are talking about her in the garden. Of course, Beatrice has to hurry to the garden to listen. She hears the two women praising Benedick as a man and saying that Benedick loves Beatrice but fears that she will make jest of him. They say they cannot understand how she could reject such a noble man.

This makes Beatrice think and resolves to change her ways. So it appears that all is well for these loving couples. However, Don John is a mischief maker and hates his half-brother and, in consequence, hates Claudio also. He sets about disrupting the plans of Hero and Claudio.

He enlists, with the promise of reward, the help of Borachio, an evil man. He woos Margaret and entices her to talk to him from her mistress's window dressed in her mistress's clothes. Don John tells Pedro and Claudio that Hero has nightly male visitors to whom she speaks from her window. Shocked and disbelieving, they go to see for themselves. Of course, from what they see, they think it is Hero talking to Borachio.

Claudio is angered and denounces Hero at the wedding. Leonato is horrified and Pedro describes what they saw the night before. Hero faints and her father is heartbroken. However, the friar at the church speaks out, having witnessed Hero's facial reactions, saying that he thinks that she is guiltless.

On hearing Hero's protestations of innocence, the friar suggests a plan to Leonato. It should be let known that Hero is dead, mourning be observed and a monument erected, the idea being to shake the emotions of Claudio. Beatrice urges Leonato to go along with this plan. Despite the sadness, Benedick swears his love for Beatrice who calls upon him to challenge Claudio, his dearest friend, for the way he has shamed Hero. With reluctance he agrees.

At the same time Leonato challenges Pedro and Claudio himself but, because of his age, they refuse to meet him but when Benedick arrives the matter becomes serious. A duel is averted by the arrival of a magistrate with Borachio in his custody. The villain has been overheard telling of the deception he engineered. Now all is clear and the conniving confirmed by the flight of Don John.

Claudio, saddened and repentant, begs Leonato's forgiveness and says he will do anything to make amends. Leonato demands that he marry a cousin of Hero, who is now his heir, on the next day. Claudio agrees.

The next day at the church Claudio finds Pedro, the friar, Leonato and his niece awaiting him. The niece is hiding her face with a mask. Claudio proposes to her and she drops her mask to reveal that she is Hero. The friar says he will explain all after the wedding which is interrupted by the arrival of Beatrice and Benedick. Though learning their love has come about by trickery and still verbally fighting, they, too, wish to be married.

There are great celebrations for the married couples and the wicked Don John, captured while trying to flee, is forced to suffer by watching the enjoyment of the happy people whose lives he has tried to destroy.

Note: This is usually considered as being written between 1598 and 1600. For sure it was in the hands of the printer on August 4, 1600. There were a number of contemporary works from which Shakespeare could have drawn his material. The story of the falsely accused maiden was even then old and had already been told by two popular writers of the time – Aristo in 'Orlando Furioso' and Bandello in his 'Novelle'. Translations of these works and retellings of the story were quite prolific in the sixteenth century.

✢ ✢ ✢ ✢ ✢

MNÓGO ŠÚMA IZ NIČEGÓ
(U.S.S.R., 1955)

p.c. Moscow Film Studios.
d. Lev Samkovoi.
l.p. N. Bubnov (Don Pedro); Alexandr Katsyinski (Don John); Julia Borisova (Hero); Yuri Liubimov (Benedick); Ludmilla Tselikorskaia (Beatrice); Nadir Malishevski (Claudio); N. Pajitnov (Leonato); W. Pokrovski (Antonio); A. Emeljanov (Balthasar); W. Osenev (Borachio); A. Bisjukov (Conrade); E. Ismaliova (Margaret); A. Danilovitch (Ursula).
b.w. 96 mins.

This Russian film is, in effect, a record of a stage performance by the Evgeni Vachtangor Theatre Company.

VIEL LÄRM UM NICHTS
(E. Germany, 1964)

p.c. Defa.
d. Martin Hellberg.
l.p. Christel Bodenstein (Beatrice); Rolf Ludwig (Benedikt); Gerhard Rachold (Don Juan); Wilfried Ortmann (Don Pedro); Martin Flörchinger (Leonaldo); Ursula Körbs (Hero); Arno Wyzniewski (Claudio); Carl Balhaus (Antonio); Heidi Ortner (Ursula); Ingrid Michalk (Margarethe); Ekkehard Hahn (Balthasar); Edwin Marian (Borachio); Gerhard Bienert (Holzapfel); Rudolf Ulrich (Schlehwein); Fred Delmare (Haberkuchen); Hanns-Jörn (Page); Eberhardt Wintzen (Seekohl); Peter Dommisch (Writer); Horst Kube (Konrad); Joe Schorn, Friedrich Teitge (Servants); Claus Schulz (Narrator); Wolf Goette (Prologue); Hans-Joachim Engelmann (Bandmaster); Willi Schwabe (Father Franciscus); Hans Feldner (Citizen).
b.w. 102 mins.

This German version of the play also features ballet by a group from the Deutschen Staatsoper, Berlin, and the Hans-Otto-Theaters, Potsdam.

MNÓGO ŠÚMA IZ NIČEGÓ
(U.S.S.R., 1973)

p.c. Mosfilm.
d. Samson Samsonov.
l.p. Galina Loginova (Beatrice); Konstantin Raikine (Benedick); Tatania Bedeneeva (Hero); Vladimir Korenev (Don John); Leonid Truschkin (Claudio).
Sovcolor. 101 mins.

The title of this is sometimes given as BEAUCOUP DE BRUIT POUR RIEN, probably the French release title. The director is noted for his adaptations of classical literature.

MUCH ADO ABOUT NOTHING
(G.B., 1974)

p.c. Realist Film Unit.
d. Peter Seabourne.
l.p. Derrick Gilbert (Benedick); Alison Key (Beatrice); Linda Renwick (Margaret); Susan Jameson (Ursula).
c. 12 mins.

Act IV, Scene 1 and Act V, Scene 2 are presented as extracts in this.

MUCH ADO ABOUT NOTHING
(G.B./U.S.A., 1993)

p.c. Renaissance in association with B.B.C. Films.
d. Kenneth Branagh.
l.p. Kenneth Branagh (Benedick); Emma Thompson (Beatrice); Kate Beckinsale (Hero); Denzel

Washington (Don Pedro); Richard Briers (Leonato); Keanu Reeves (Don John); Michael Keaton (Dogberry); Robert Sean Leonard (Claudio); Brian Blessed (Antonio);Imelda Staunton (Margaret); Phyllida Law (Ursula); Ben Elton (Verges); Jimmy Yiull (Friar Francis); Gerard Horan (Borachio); Richard Clifford (Conrade); Patrick Doyle (Balthazar); Andy Hockley; Conrad Nelson; Chris Barnes; Edward Jewesbury; Alex Scott.

c. 110 mins. S

Adapted by Branagh, he presented a faithful interpretation of the play.

Following his success with **HENRY V**, Kenneth Branagh returned to familiar territory (for him) after two quite different films. His second venture into the world of screen Shakespeare boasts a highly competent cast of British performers (not least of whom is his wife at the time, Emma Thompson) and some Americans. Of these, the highly respected black actor Denzel Washington and Michael Keaton (the latter of *Batman* and *Beetlejuice* fame) are worthy of note. The film was shot in Italy and enjoyed box-office success. A record of the soundtrack was issued by Epic records and thus Patrick Doyle's score, which includes a charming version of "Sigh no more, ladies..", joined an impressive list of other composers of Shakespearean film music committed to posterity.

Shown at the Cannes Film Festival, France, 1993.

Shown as part of the Everybody's Shakespeare International Festival, London, England, 1994.

London Film Critics' Awards, Great Britain, 1994: Best British Producer (Kenneth Branagh for this film).

"Seldom has a Shakespearean text been brought to life so vividly, clearly and wittily on screen as in this exhilarating adaptation." – James Cameron-Wilson, 'Film Review 1994/5'.

"...fulfills his* attempt to show that the Avon man...was really a man of the people and not just for the snobs." – 'Satellite TV' magazine. *Branagh's.

aka: MUCHO RUIDO Y POCAS NUECES; VIEL LÄRM UM NICHTS

✛ ✛ ✛ ✛ ✛

MUCH ADO ABOUT NOTHING
(U.S.A., 1913)

p.c. *Crystal.*
d.
l.p. *Pearl White; Chester Barnett.*
b.w. 1 reel? Sil.

Two lovers are brought together after a misunderstanding.

So many films of this era had titles (but nothing else) borrowed from Shakespeare, it is almost a relief to find one that takes, at least, some inspiration as well.

ŠATY DĚLAJÍ ČLOVĚKA
(Czechoslovakia, 1913)

p.c. *ASUM.*
d. *Jára Sedláček, Max Urban.*
l.p. *Andula Sedláčeková; Jára Sedláček; Alois Sedláček; Rudolf Matucha; Karel Váňa; Josef Rozsíval.*
b.w. 1 reel? Sil.

The prologue of the play is portrayed in a free transcription.

Sadly, copies of this short are no longer extant.

WET PAINT
(U.S.A., 1926)

p.c. *Famous Players/Lasky Corp.*
d. *Arthur Rosson.*
l.p. *Raymond Griffith; Bryant Washburn; Helene Costello.*
b.w. 5107 ft. (1561 m.) Sil.

When our hero proposes to his girl a little betting takes place. He finds out and feels humiliated. He breaks off the engagement and vows to marry the next woman he meets. She, however, is already married and a compromising situation soon occurs. All seems to resolve itself and the couple are reunited but even at the wedding there is a mix up of identities.

This farce was introduced as having something to do with the play. Quite what can only be guessed from the brief resumé which bears only a slight relationship to the original.

"...makes a noble struggle to live up to its reputation...it completely surrenders itself to slapstick..." – 'Exhibitors Daily Review', May 22, 1916.

VIEL LÄRM UM NIXI
(Germany/Italy, 1942)

p.c. *L'Amato Film.*
d. *Erich Engel, Giuseppe Amato.*
l.p. *Jenny Jugo (Nixi); Albert Matterstock/Nino Besozzi (Roland); Heinz Salfner/Giuseppe Porelli (Mäki); Hans Leibelt/Enrico Viarisio (Barkas); Otto Gebühr/Gugliemo Barnabò (Majordomo); Hans Adalbert Schlettow/Paolo Stoppa; André Mattoni.*
Note: Where two names are noted, the first refers to the German version, the second to the Italian version.
b.w. 82 mins.

An industrialist's daughter, Nixi, breaks off her engagement to an indifferent fiancé with the excuse that she has been seduced by a man and the only clue to his identity is a cigarette case. Her enraged father seeks redress and goes to the police. As it happens the prefect of police has met the girl before following a traffic accident. He fell in love with her but did not have the nerve to seduce her. When the girl obstinately refuses to talk of marriage and flees to the woods, she is found by the policeman. After many misadventures, the girl eventually accepts her boyfriend's genuine proposal of marriage.

A Spanish film magazine of the era noted that Jenny Jugo was making "Muchos Ruidos Para Nada" (a Spanish interpretation of the title of the play). As can been seen from the synopsis, it would be generous even to suggest that there was much more than the slightest hint of Shakespeare inspiration. Of course, Nixi does appear to have a similar temperament to Beatrice and there is the breaking off of the engagement. The German title translates as "Much Ado About Nixi" and "Nixi" is not only an obvious play on "Nichts", the German for "nothing", but on "Trixie", a diminutive of Beatrice.

aka: NON MI SPOSO PIÙ

✛ ✛ ✛ ✛ ✛

LJUBOVJU ZALJUBOV
(U.S.S.R., 1983)

p.c. *Mosfilm.*
d. *Tatjana Berezantzera.*
l.p. *Evgenij Nesterenko (Singer); Alla Pugatcheva (Singer); Sergei Martynov (Don Pedro); Aristaikh Livanor (Don John); Lerisa*

Udovitchenko (Beatrice); Anna Isajkina (Hero); Georij Georgiu (Leonato); Algis Arlanskas (Claudio); Leonid Jermolnik (Benedick).Ballet of the Moscow Musical Academy Theatre.Symphony Orchestra of the Bolshoi Theatre (conductor: A. Kopytov).
Sovcolor. 84 mins. Sovscope.

This is obviously a classical music style/ballet version of the play.

Gosfilmfond of Russia advised that the film is in CinemaScope but since this is a trade mark of 20th. Century Fox, it is more likely that the native anamorphic system noted above was used. The songs are noted as being adapted from sonnets by Shakespeare.

✛ ✛ ✛ ✛ ✛

Though not often filmed (one wonders what happend to the planned film by Zeffirelli with Albert Finney, Carol Burnett and Alberto Sordi as the stars), this is one of Shakespeare's most enjoyable plays. That the only feature version of it in English is such a delight is surely most welcome.

For other films with scenes from the play see **CHAPTER XXXII THE IMMORTAL BARD**: THE QUESTIONING CITY (1959) and FAIR ADVENTURE SERIES (1964).

CHAPTER XX

OTHELLO THE MOOR OF VENICE

Dramatis Personæ:

Othello – the Moor
Desdemona – his wife
Brabantio – her father, a Venetian senator
Cassio – honourable lieutenant to Othello
*Ludovico, Gratiano – kinsmen of Brabantio, and
  Venetian nobles*

Iago – a villain and once Othello's friend
Emilia – his wife

Duke of Venice
Senators of Venice
Bianca – a courtesan
Roderigo – a gulled gentleman
Montano – Governor of Cyprus
Clown
*Sailors, Messenger, Herald, Officers, Venetian
  Gentlemen, Musicians, Attendants etc.*

Desdemona, the beautiful daughter of Brabantio, a rich senator of Venice, has many suitors. However, she loves Othello, a black moor liked and respected by her father. She delights in his tales of adventure and the sights he has seen and, if called away, returns as quickly as possible to hear more. His tales are justified for he has helped Venice against the Turks and is now a general in the Venetian service.

One day she induces him to tell her his life story. She is moved by the sad parts and hints that if anyone could be trained to tell such a story, that person could win her heart. With such an invitation, Othello expresses his love for her. Now her father has hopes of her marrying some local noble man with expectation. So they marry secretly.

When notice of this, as it surely would do, reaches her father he accuses Othello of witchcraft. Then news comes that the Turks are sailing for Cyprus to take the Venetian strongholds there. Othello is much needed and so has to face a court at which the Duke of Venice presides on two accounts – to answer the charge against him and to plan action against the Turks.

He pleads his case well, aided by Desdemona, and the Duke declares that any ploys he may have used are but those of a normal suitor. Brabantio is generous in defeat, and Othello, with Desdemona's consent undertakes the war against the Turks and she goes with him.

No sooner have the couple landed in Cyprus than news comes that a storm has dispersed the Turkish fleet. Another, more serious battle is to face Othello.

Michael Cassio, a young Florentine, handsome and eloquent and thus a philanderer, is Othello's dear friend and lieutenant. He had acted as Othello's go-between in his courtship of Desdemona and was a good friend to her as well as being often in their company.

Iago, a cunning man, resents Michael's promotion and resents Othello and unjustly thinks that Othello is too fond of Emilia, his wife. The festivities surrounding the arrival of Othello and Desdemona provide him with the opportunity to employ a plot.

Othello has given orders that his men be modest in their celebrations since he wants no disturbances with the local people. Michael is instructed to enforce these orders. Iago plies Michael with drink which leads to a duel with an officer, Montano, who is wounded. Trouble, much inflamed by Iago, breaks out. The consequence of which is that the contrite Michael falls from favour and is demoted.

Foolishly Michael confides in Iago who says that Desdemona really is in control and that he should use her to plead for him. This she does earnestly and Othello agrees to re-instate Michael but in his own time.

Iago enters the room during their conversation and, when Desdemona has gone, begins to sow seeds of doubt in Othello's mind about her motives and her relationship with Michael when acting for Othello in his courtship. As he believes Iago is a decent man, these questions make him ponder but he would want proof. Iago points out that she deceived her father when she married Othello could she not also deceive her husband?

Iago cunningly apologises for disturbing Othello but he begs Iago to continue. Iago urges him to put off any decision concerning Michael Cassio but ends by craftily begging Othello not to accuse his wife without proof.

Othello is unable to sleep and his days are so full of doubts that he cannot apply himself with full heart to his work. At one stage he threatens Iago with death for slandering his wife. At this stage Iago tells Othello that he has seen Michael wipe his face with a special strawberry spotted handkerchief belonging to Desdemona, a special gift from her husband.

Iago's weak wife has, at her husband's command and under the pretence of wanting to have a copy made, stolen the handkerchief from Desdemona and it is dropped so that Michael was sure to find it. Othello, feigning a headache, asks Desdemona for the handkerchief saying that it was especially woven in Egypt and has magical powers. This greatly disturbs Desdemona since she appears to have lost it but she is also disturbed at her husband's state of mind and disposition thinking some bad news has come from Venice.

Later he openly accuses her of being unfaithful, bewailing his betrayed love for her. When he leaves, much moved as might be expected of a young girl (she is much younger than her husband), she falls into a heavy sleep. Othello returns and, finding her asleep, resolves to kill her unable in his heart to have her executed. Kissing her goodbye awakens her and she sees the rage in his eyes as he bids her prepare for death. She begs to know the reason and he tells about the handkerchief then stifles her to death.

Michael enters wounded after an attack by one of Iago's men. Michael has wounded the would-be assassin though Iago kills him to prevent discovery. However, letters are found on the dead man incriminating Iago. Michael thinks that Othello had employed Iago to kill him and wants to know what wrong he has done.

Othello, realising the wrong he has done and that he is a murderer, falls upon his own sword. The people honour him in death for his noble deeds and Iago is tortured to death. News is sent to Venice of the death of the renowned general.

Note: This was performed by the King's Men at Court on November 1, 1604, and was probably written not long before then. It is unusual for its concentration of the action into but a short time and for the fact that at least one of the three principal characters – Othello, Desdemona and Iago – is on stage in each of the fifteen scenes in the play. The excellence of this play is an odd contrast to the mediocrity of its source, an Italian tale called 'Cinthio' by Giovanni Baptista Giraldi related in a 1565 collection called 'Hecatommithi'.

✛ ✛ ✛ ✛ ✛

OTELLO
(Italy, 1908)

p.c. *Cines.*
d. *Mario Caserini.*
l.p. *Mario Caserini (Othello); Maria Adele Gasperini (Desdemona); Ubaldo Mario del Colle.*
b.w. 689 ft. (210 m.) Sil.

Both coloured and tinted versions are known to have been made. The film is said to be lost.

aka: OTHELLO; OTHELLO VON VENEDIG

OTHELLO
(U.S.A., 1908)

p.c. *Vitagraph.*
d. *William V. Ranous and/or James Stuart Blackton.*
l.p. *William V. Ranous (Othello); Julia Swayne-Gordon (Desdemona); Hector Dion (Iago); Paul Panzer (Cassio).*
b.w. 15 mins. approx. Sil.

Short scenes were linked to provide a coherent narrative in this early film now believed lost.

aka: JEALOUSY

OTELLO
(Italy, 1909)

p.c. *Cines.*
d. *Mario Caserini.*
l.p.
b.w. (?) mins. Sil.

This may well be a remake of the 1908 version utilizing some of the same cast.

OTELLO
(Italy, 1909)

p.c. *Film d'Arte Italiana.*
d. *Gerolamo Lo Savio.*
l.p. *Ferruccio Garavaglia (Othello); Vittoria Lepanto (Desdemona); Cesare Dondini (Iago); Alberto Nepoti (Cassio); A. Pezzaglia (Doge).*
b.w. 1099 ft. (335 m) Sil.

This Italian version follows the play quite faithfully within its own terms.

Though noted here as in black and white, 600 ft. (183 m.) of the film was hand-coloured. The original was slightly shortened for American release (1043 ft. – 320 m.) but the British release was slightly longer at 1105 ft. (337 m.).

aka: OTHELLO; OTELLO DE MOOR VAN VENETIË

OTELLO
(Italy, 1909)

p.c. *Società Italiana Pineschi.*
d. *Enrico Novelli.*
l.p. *Rosina Balsamo; Armando Fremo; Augusto Mastripietri; Cesare Dondini.*
b.w. 850 ft. (259 m.) Sil.

Some sources note this as a parody and thus maybe it would be more suitably placed in the second section. The director used the pseudonym "Yambo".

OTELLO
(Italy, 1914)

p.c. *Società Ambrosio/Photo-Drama Producing Co.*
d. *Luigi Maggi.*

l.p. *Paolo Colaci (Othello); Lena Lenard (Desdemona); Riccardo Tolentino (Iago); Ubaldo Stefani (Cassio).*

b.w. 4888 ft. (1491 m.) Sil.

Comment of the time suggests that this was quite well done in respect of the sets though with some reservations on the portrayal of the main character. Other comments call the film a shambles but as only about a quarter of the film remains, this may account for such comment. The film had some tinted scenes. The French release was shorter at 4757 ft. (1450 m.). Claims have been made in support of both Arturo Ambrosio and Arrigo Frusta as director and for Hamilton A. Revelle in the title role.

aka: OTHELLO; OTHELLO THE MOOR (British release at 4000 ft. – 1219 m.)

OTELLO
(Italy, 1914)

p.c. *Gloria Film.*
d. *Mario Caserini.*
l.p. *Amletto Novelli (Othello); Maria Jacobini (Desdemona).*

b.w. 5 reels. Sil.

Apparently this received poor reviews in America and this was matched by public response with people walking out before the end. This is not, surprisingly, listed by Bernardini in his 'Archivio del Cinema Italiano – Volume 1 – Il Cinema Mudo'. Indeed, the above comment may refer to the other release since reviews do not always indicate the Italian source. 'Variety' notes the Ambrosio release as four parts and the above as five reels yet the original Ambrosio production is nearer five reels but who knows what editing was done before release in any country.

OTHELLO
(Germany, 1922)

p.c. *Wörner-Film.*
d. *Dmitri Buchowetzki.*
l.p. *Emil Jannings (Othello); Ica von Lenkeffy (Desdemona); Werner Krauss (Iago); Lya de Putti (Emilia); Ferdinand von Alten (Roderigo); Theodore Loos (Michael Cassio); Friedrich Khüne (Brabantio); Magnus Stofter (Montano); Ludwig Rex.*

b.w. 7680 ft. (2341 m.) Sil.

This version is based both on Shakespeare and the original tale by Cinthio.

The first showing of this was in May, 1922, and it was a private one. Comments of the period are contradictory. Some suggest it was disappointing relying upon inter-titles to express the emotions of the characters; others praise the work of Jannings (repeating his stage role), Krauss and Lenkeffy with favourable comment on the supporting cast and the quality of the production. In contrast a report from Berlin, Germany, for 'Variety' says "The whole picture is merely a stageplay which a camera happened to attend." Present day comment is favourable with praise for both Jannings and Krauss and the vivid hints of German Expressionistic style.

The film also has a curious distinction of being one of the few (perhaps the only one) silent film versions of a Shakespearean work to be made available for purchase to the public. In the early days of the company, Kodascope issued it on 16 mm. and, decades later, the film still could be bought by the public from a number of American sources on both 16 mm. and 8 mm.

Shown as part of the Everybody's Shakespeare, International Festival, London, England, 1994.
Shown at the Shakespeare Film Festival, Wiesbaden, W. Germany, 1964.

aka: THE MOOR

OTHELLO
(G.B., 1946)

p.c. *Marylebone Productions.*
d. *David Mackane.*
l.p. *John Slater (Othello); Sebastian Cabot (Iago); Luanna Shaw (Desdemona); Sheila Raynor (Emilia).*

b.w. 46 mins.

A very much abridged version of the play which imposed obvious limitations, it is quite well done. No doubt it served to introduce people to the Bard's works or to see a full version. It may even have been made for educational purposes. The production company had planned a series of such adaptations but it never materialised.

THE TRAGEDY OF OTHELLO, THE MOOR OF VENICE
(Morocco, 1951)

p.c. *Films Marceau. A Mercury Production.*
d. *Orson Welles.*
l.p. *Orson Welles (Othello); Micheál MacLiammóir (Iago); Suzanne Cloutier (Desdemona); Fay Compton (Emilia); Robert Coote (Roderigo); Hilton Edwards (Brabantio); Nicholas Bruce (Lodovicio); Michael Lawrence (Cassio); Jean Davis (Montano); Doris Dowling (Bianca); Joseph Cotten (Senator); Joan Fontaine (Page).*

b.w. 91 mins.

Welles trimmed the play a great deal for this first feature length version of the play.

The filming of this was set out in the book "Put Money In Thy Purse" by Micheál MacLiammóir in 1952 and what a troubled filming it was! As Ronald Bergan says in 'The United Artists Story': "...the problems of the jealous Moor were nothing compared to the suffering of the producer-director in getting the picture made.". Shot partly in Morocco, Venice and other parts of Italy, production was often stopped or improvised as money ran out or became available.

This inevitably shows in the finished work which was a sort of odyssey for Welles who actually started it in 1949. Various countries including France, Italy and U.S.A. are claimed as that of production by various sources. It was, however, Morocco that officially submitted it for the Cannes Film Festival. The restored version from 1992 has a re-recorded Dolby Stereo soundtrack. The music has recently been recorded by members of the Chicago Symphony Orchestra and issued on the Varese Sarabande label.

Though commonly known as OTHELLO, the title above is that on the film itself.

Shown as part of the Everybody's Shakespeare International Festival, London, England, 1994.
Shown at the Shakespeare Film Festival, Wiesbaden, W. Germany, 1964.
Shown at the Valladolid Film Festival, Spain, 1992.
Cannes Film Festival, France, 1952: Palme d'Or for Best Film (shared with *Due Soldi Di Speranza*).

"...is an unsettled work, brilliant, violent and rich in nuances." – 'Euro-Movies International', June, 1994.

FILMING OTHELLO
(W. Germany/U.S.A., 1977)

p.c. *DeutscheFernsehen/Orson Welles.*
d. *Orson Welles.*
l.p. *Documentary. Narrator: Orson Welles. With cast from the film.*
Eastman Color. 84 mins.

This film of the making of the above film was shot on 16 mm.. In essence, it was more of an interview/lecture by Welles filled with anecdotes.

Shown at the Berlin Film Festival, W. Germany, 1978.
Shown at the London Film Festival, England, 1978.
Shown at the Venice Film Festival, Italy, 1978.

OTHELLO
(G.B., 1953)

p.c. *Emil Katzka Productions.*
d. *Charles Deane.*
l.p. *Young Vic Theatre Company. Narrator: Ronald Howard.*
b.w. 14 mins.

Another in the made-for-television series *The World's A Stage*, this features the handkerchief scene.

OTHELLO
(U.S.S.R., 1955)

p.c. *Mosfilm.*
d. *Sergei Youtkevich.*
l.p. *Sergei Bondarchuk (Othello); Irina Skobtseva (Desdemona); Andrei Popov (Iago); E. Vesnik (Roderigo); Vladimir Soshalsky (Cassio); E. Teterin (Brabantio); A. Maximova (Emilia);*
M. Troyanovsky (The Doge); A. Kelberer (Montano); P. Brilling (Lodovico).
Sovcolor. 110 mins.

With a tightly edited text, this is considered to be an excellent version of the play.

In an interview published in 'Sovietskaya Kultura' at the time, director Youtkevich declared his film to be to some extent a piece of created polemics in oppostion to Welles' version. He considered that the interpretation of Othello by Bondarchuk would cause discussion. Iago is portrayed as a man with his own tragedy rather than a villain and Desdemona as a girl with a will of her own rather than the more usual placid character. The cinematographer, Eugeniy Andrikanis, said: "In our film we tried to find distinct and intrinsically cinematographic means of expression". The score by Aram Khachaturian was noted at the time as being conventional but effective.

Both sub-titled and English dubbed versions exist of the film. For the latter version, a Technicolor print was made which lost much of the richness of the original and for the dubbing, lip-synchronisation was forsaken (it would have been impossible to match precisely Shakepeare's words to the lip movements) in favour of a narrative of the edited text by English voices in loose harmony with lip movement.

Shown as part of the Everybody's Shakespeare International Festival, London, England, 1994.
Shown at the Shakespeare Film Festival, Wiesbaden, W. Germany, 1964.
Cannes Film Festival, France; 1956: Best Director (Sergei Youtkevich).
Damascus International Film Festival, Syria, 1957: Gold Medal for Realisation and Filming Shakespeare.
Mexican International Film Week, Mexico, 1956: Grand Prize "Silver Eagle".

"Youtkevich, from the start, has an original and very different concept of the work." – Mario Rodríguez Aleman, 'Shakespeare En El Cine' (issued by La Cinemateca de Cuba in conjunction with a short season of Shakespearean films in 1962).

OTHELLO
(G.B., 1965)

p.c. *British Home Entertainments.*
d. *Stuart Burge.*
l.p. *Laurence Olivier (Othello); Maggie Smith (Desdemona); Frank Finlay (Iago); Derek Jacobi (Cassio); Joyce Redman (Emilia); Robert Lang (Roderigo); Kenneth Mackintosh (Lodovico); Anthony Nicholls (Brabantio); Sheila Reid (Bianca); Harry Lomax (Duke Of Venice); Michael Turner (Gratiano); Edward Hardwicke (Montano); Michael Terris; David Hargeaves; Roy Holder; Terence Knapp; Keith Marsh; Tom Kempinski; Trevor Martin; William Hobbs; Nicholas Edmett.*
Technicolor. 166 mins. Panavision.

There seems to be a consensus of opinion that this is not a cinematographic experience but rather an important, historic record of John Dexter's stage production for the National Theatre, England, which was first seen at The Chichester Festival, England, in 1964. A commemorative set of stamps of Olivier was issued by Sierra Leone when Olivier died. The Le70 value featured the actor in the title role of this film.

Shown at the San Sebastian Film Festival, Spain, 1966.

Academy of Motion Picture Arts and Sciences, U.S.A., 1965: Nominations – Best Actor (Laurence Olivier), Best Supporting Actor (Frank Finlay), Best Supporting Actress (Maggie Smith, Joyce Redman).

"...there is no denying the power of Olivier's extraordinary individual interpretation of the Moor." – Clive Hirschhorn, 'The Warner Bros Story'.

"Cinematically unremarkable, the film is valuable as a controversial and fascinating interpretation of Shakespeare's tragic hero." – George Perry, 'The Great British Picture Show'.

OTHELLO
(G.B., 1974)

p.c. *Realist Film Unit.*
d. *Peter Seabourne.*
l.p. *Mark Kingston; Susan Jameson; Colin Farrell.*
b.w. 9 mins.

Two extracts are featured here – Act II, Scene 1 and Act V, Scene 2.

OTHELLO
(U.S.A., 1980)

p.c. *Liz White.*
d. *Liz White.*
l.p. *Yaphet Kotto (Othello); Richard Dixon (Iago); Audrey Dixon (Desdemona); Liz White (Bianca); Lewis Chisholm Jr. (Cassio); Jim Williams (Brabantio); Benjamin Ashburn (Montano); Olive Bowles (Emilia); Douglas Gray (Roderigo).*
Eastman Color. 115 mins.

Made by some friends on 16 mm. over four summers (1962 to 1966) repeating, more-or-less, their stage performances, this was something of a personal project for Liz White who financed the venture herself. Of the all-black cast, Kotto has gained fame. The film has never had commercial distribution as Liz White declined to market the film with the commercial companies at the time of its completion due to the exploitation of blacks in the film world. Subsequently, the major distributors showed no interest in its release. It was, however, shown at...

Dorothy Arzner International Film Festival, Harvard University, Harvard, U.S.A., 1986.

"The film successfully blends amateur, part-time and fully professional talent." – Peter S. Donaldson, 'Shakespearean Film/Shakespearean Directors'.

OTHELLO
(G.B./South Africa, 1988)

p.c. *Othello Productions/Focus Films/Portobello Productions.*
d. *Janet Suzman.*
l.p. *John Kahni (Othello); Joanna Weinberg (Desdemona); Richard Haddon Haines (Iago);Dorothy Gould (Emelia); Frantz Dobrowsky (Roderigo); Stuart Brown (Brabantio); Lindsay Reardon (Duke of Venice); Neil McCarthy (Cassio); Gaynor Young (Bianca); Peter Grummeck (Lodovico); Martin Le Maitre (Montano); John Whiteley (Gratiano).*
c. 199 mins.

This is a screen adaptation of the theatre version which opened in October, 1987, at the Market Theatre, Johannesburg, South Africa.

The film is said to contain social and political overtones which caused some sensation in South Africa. Though made on tape for television, it warrants inclusion here since it has had showings outside that medium presumably having been transferred to film.

Shown as part of the Everybody's Shakespeare International Festival, London, England, 1994.

OTHELLO
(U.S.A., 1995)

p.c. *Castle Rock. A Dakota Films/Imminent Films Production.*
d. *Oliver Parker.*
l.p. *Laurence Fishburne (Othello); Irne Jacob (Desdemona); Kenneth Branagh (Iago);Nathaniel Parker (Cassio); Michael Maloney (Roderigo); Nicholas Farrell (Montano); Michael Sheen (Lodovico); Anna Patrick (Emilia); Indra Ove (Bianca); André Oumansy (Gratiano); Philip Locke, John Savident (Senators); Gabriele Ferzetti (Duke of Venice); Pierre Vaneck (Brabantio).*
Technicolor. 124 mins. S

The view of the Moor is rather a personal one of the director who sees the play as a neurotic thriller driven by passion. Branagh was given responsibility for the script with a rather surprising result – much of the original has been excised. The film differs from more conventional versions with a younger Othello, the use of flashbacks and a number of love scenes.

The film was made on location in Italy which provided a different atmosphere as Branagh explained in an on-set interview for the television show *Entertainment Tonight*: "It takes us out of a kind of a perhaps dangerously English approach to what is a very sexy, passionate, erotic thriller." Fishburne was delighted with the opportunity to play the lead role and, in the same programme expressed his feelings upon receiving a telephone call: "I heard six words which were 'Kenneth Branagh. Laurence Fishburne. OTHELLO. Shakespeare'. I said 'yes'. It's five hundred years old. It is an extreme honour to play this part."

The original soundtrack was made available through Varese Sarabande records. The music is by Charlie Mole.

✤ ✤ ✤ ✤ ✤

OTHELLO
(Denmark, 1908)

p.c. *Nordisk.*
d. *Viggo Larsen.*
l.p. *Carl Alstrup; Poul Gregaard; Jørgen Lund.*
b.w. 289 ft. (88 m.) Sil.

This is noted as being an early comedy version.

aka: OTHELLO OU JE DOIS JOUER CE SOIR OTHELLO

LO SPETTRO DI JAGO
(Italy, 1912)

p.c. *Aguila Films.*
d. *Alberto Carlo Lolli.*
l.p.
b.w. 1866 ft. (575 m.) Sil.

The story in this is about rivalry over a girl and attempted vengeance by the unsuccessful lover.

Apart from the character of the title, the Shakespearean connection appears slim. However, the setting is in Cyprus which raises the possibility of a closer link. A German source notes the length as 2625 ft. (800 m.), which is considerably longer than that noted above from Italian sources. Did the Germans, therefore, really have a longer version than the Italians? Possibly they did, for the British version is noted at 2000 ft. (610 m.). In contrast, some sources quote 1066 ft. (325 m.) as the length.

aka: THE VENGEANCE OF IAGO; LE SPECTRE DE JAGO; EL ESPECTRO DE YAGO

L'EREDE DI JAGO
(Italy, 1913)

p.c. *Savoia Film.*
d.
l.p. *Maria Jacobini.*
b.w. 2789 ft. (850 m.) Sil.

A confidential secretary steals from his employer. His boss's wife suspects him and he tries to defame the wife which almost succeeds when the husband sees his drugged wife in another's arms. He realises the secretary's duplicity and dismisses him. The secretary dies in a fire caused by lions which he has set free in the boss' grounds while seeking revenge.

The employee's treachery theme, the maligned wife and the title character all recall OTHELLO and there is even, perhaps, a suggestion of MUCH ADO ABOUT NOTHING. Some sources note the film at 2631 ft. (802 m.).

aka: IAGO'S INHERTIANCE; L'HÉRITAGE DE JAGO

OTELLO
(Italy, 1920)

p.c. *Caesar Film.*
d. *Camillo De Riso.*
l.p. *Camillo De Riso (Othello); Fernanda D'Alteno (Desdemona); Eugenio Cigoli (Iago); Leone Papa.*
b.w. 3028 ft. (923 m.) Sil.

This is noted as being a parody.

SCHATTEN EINE NÄCHTLICHE HALLUZINATION
(Germany, 1922)

p.c. *Dafu.*
d. *Arthur Robison.*
l.p. *Fritz Korner; Alexander Granach; Fritz Rasp; Ruth Weyher.*
b.w. (?) mins. Sil.

A shadow conjurer arrives at a house where a man and his wife are entertaining some male guests. After his show he uses his audience as a play to show infidelity, murder and suicide. The show over, all are seated as at the start but the message has been delivered. The guests depart; husband and wife embrace.

Not truly Shakespeare, of course, but many have seen his influence in this experimental film which had no inter-titles. J. Isaac in an article 'Shakespeare As Man of the Theatre' made the point that the film portrayed visually what Shakespeare achieved verbally.

aka: WARNING SHADOWS

OTELLO
(Italy, 1923)

p.c.
d.
l.p. *Emilio Ferrari.*
b.w. (?) mins. Sil.

Little has been traced of this film which is noted as an interpretation of the play using then contemporary dress and settings. It raises doubts in view of the later entry in the third section from 1909. The film is not listed by Aldo Bernadini in 'Archivo del Cinema Italiano – Il Cinema Mudo 1905-1931'.

OTHELLO IN HARLEM
(U.S.A., 1939)

p.c.

d. *Joseph Seiden.*

l.p. *Frankie Wilson; Edna Mae Harris, Juanita Hall Singers; "Lucky" Millinder and his Orchestra; Mamie Smith.*

b.w. 85 mins.

Details of this film have been difficult to trace other than that it is an all black production and thus aimed at that ethnic market. It is noted as being a gangster film against a setting of jazz night clubs.

Logic dictates that there is a Shakespeare relationship if only in the title character and/or the basic theme. Did it perhaps predate the jazz blend concept of the 1961 film **ALL NIGHT LONG** or did it simply use jazz since it was then in vogue?

aka: PARADISE IN HARLEM

BODAS TRÁGICAS
(Mexico, 1946)

p.c. *CLASA Films Mundiales.*

d. *Carlos L. Cabello.*

l.p. *Roberto Silva (Diego); Miroslava Stern (Amparo); Ernesto Alonso (Octavio); Stella Inda (Laura); José Morcillo (Juan Manuel); Antonio R. Fausto (Juan de Dios); Lupe Inclán (Agustina); Alberto Torres (José Luis); Carolina Barret (Pepita); Luis Beristáin (Carlos); Manuel Noriega (Padre Muñoz); José Elías Moreno (Torres).*

b.w. 77 mins.

In Mexico in the last century, the wealthy Diego secretly marries Amparo because her father, Juan Manuel, opposes the union with a former servant whom he considers a thief. Diego's servant, Octavio also resents the marriage as does his wife, Laura, who loves her master. Unaware of the marriage, Juan Manuel promises Amparo to José Luis while Diego is away on a military mission. On his return Diego is greeted with physical and verbal abuse from his father-in-law. At a party Diego gets involved in a fight engineered by Octavio, and Amparo intervenes. Diego goes away and is reconciled with Amparo upon his return though not convinced of her innocence. Octavio conspires to make Diego believe that Amparo is going to run off with José Luis. Filled with anger, it is Laura who endures his wrath. As she dies she tells Diego the truth and he kills Octavio in a swamp as he tries to escape.

The film is clearly inspired by the play though the changed ending perhaps served two purposes – a happy ending, naturally, and to avoid the obvious charge of plagiarism. The latter would be hard to refute for the forbidden love/secret marriage/bride pledged to another themes are surely ROMEO AND JULIET inspired. Some sources actually consider the film to be a derivative from that play and it is thus appropriately noted in the relative chapter.

JUBAL
(U.S.A., 1955)

p.c. *Columbia.*

d. *Delmer Daves.*

l.p. *Glenn Ford (Jubal); Ernest Borgnine (Shep Horgan); Rod Steiger (Pinky); Valerie French (Mae); Felicia Farr (Naomi); Noah Beery Jr. (Sam); Charles Bronson (Reb).*

Technicolor. 101 mins. CinemaScope.

Given a job by rancher Shep Horgan, wandering cowboy Jubal soon finds himself the object of attention by Mae, Shep's wife, who has deserted her former lover, Pinky. Pinky is jealous of Jubal and slyly suggests, without foundation, that Mae and Jubal are lovers. One night, goaded by Pinky, Shep goes after Jubal who is forced to kill him. Pinky tries to rape Mae and beats her to death but not before she has told the truth to a vengeful posse.

It is a matter of opinion as to whether this film should have been included or not. Many consider it to be influenced by OTHELLO. To be sure there are certain story and character similarities – a jealous husband, an innocent man accused of a love affaire and the mischievous Iago-like villain. There the similarities end for Desdemona/Mae is far from being innocent and the husband is killed before the end of the film.

ALL NIGHT LONG
(G.B., 1961)

p.c. *Bob Roberts.*

d. *Basil Dearden.*

l.p. *Patrick McGoohan (Johnny Cousin); Marti Stevens (Delia Lane); Betsy Blair (Emily); Keith Michell (Cass Michaels); Richard Attenborough (Rod Hamilton); Bernard Braden (Berger); Paul Harris (Aurelius Rex); Maria Velasco (Benny); Harry Towb (Phales); As themselves: Dave Brubeck, Johnny Dankworth, Charlie Mingus, Keith Christie, Tubby Hayes, Bert Courtley, Ray Dempsey, Allan Ganley, Barry Morgan, Colin Purbrook, Johnny Scott, Geoffrey Holder.*

b.w. 95 mins.

Wealthy Rodney Hamilton throws a party in his converted warehouse for famous jazzman Aurelius Rex and his wife, Delia, who has given up a singing career for marriage. She rejects the offer of drummer Johnny who, financed by Berger, wants to form a new group with her as singer. By a series of lies, Johnny attempts to break up her marriage even fabricating a tape implying an affaire between Delia and Rex's manager, Cass. In anger, Rex tries to strangle Delia but the truth is revealed and they are reconciled. Johnny is left alone to his drumming.

OTHELLO, of course, but with the ending changed and modern dialogue, this is something of a hybrid film, neither a satisfactory modern version of the play, nor a good honest jazz film. Of course, jazz lovers will be happy to see the musicians and hear the music but dissatisfied with the brevity of the pieces since only Brubeck and Dankworth enjoy much playing time.

Of the cast, Richard Attenborough needs no comment, Patrick McGoohan (who turned down the role for the first screen James Bond) found television success with "Danger Man" and "The Prisoner", which now enjoy cult status, and Keith Michell scored success with a television series (and later a film) on the life of King Henry VIII of England. Of the jazz musicians, Dave Brubeck and Charlie Mingus are in the hierarchy of modern jazz. Tubby Hayes was gaining international acclaim when death took him and Johnny Dankworth went on to international fame with his wife, Cleo Laine. He was no stranger to Shakespeare having written the music for a number of the plays and recorded, with Cleo, Shakespeare's words set to music by himself and Duke Ellington. He has also been responsible for many film and television scores.

Shown as part of the Everybody's Shakespeare International Festival, London, England, 1994.

"An interesting misfire." – Leslie Halliwell, 'Halliwell's Film Guide'.

"A ludicrous combination of OTHELLO and jazz jamboree that falls flat on both counts." – David Meeker, 'Jazz in the Movies'.

aka: NOCHE DE PESADILLA

CAPRICIO ALL'ITALIANA
(Italy, 1968)

p.c. *Dino De Laurentiis Cinematografica.*
d. *Various.*
l.p. *Various.*
c. 83 mins.

This film comprises six sketches directed by Italian directors and with a variety of players. One of the sketches – **CHE COSA SONO LE NUVOLE?** – was directed by Pier Paolo Pasolini in which marionettes interpret OTHELLO and the public intervene against Iago (played by Toto). Laura Betti plays the female lead.

The running time is, of course, for the whole film.

CATCH MY SOUL
(U.S.A., 1973)

p.c. *Metromedia Producers Corporation.*
d. *Patrick McGoohan.*
l.p. *Richie Haven (Othello); Lance LeGault (Iago); Season Hubley (Desdemona); Tony Joe White (Cassio); Susan Tyrell (Emilia); Bonnie Bramlett; Allene Lubin; The Family Lotus; Delaney Bramlett and his Band.*
De Luxe Color. 95 mins.

Othello, an evangelist, baptises his followers in the Rio Grande in Mexico. Among them is the evil Iago who insinuates about Othello's desire for Desdemona. Assuring her that Iago's demon has been cast out, Othello pledges his love to Desdemona with a handkerchief with a motif. While Iago plans to capture their souls, Othello and Desdemona marry. While on honeymoon, Iago creates friction resulting in the firing of the group's chapel for which Cassio, who has been left in charge, is blamed. Othello is forced to banish Cassio and the couple found a new chapel. Iago and his wife, Emilia, help them and gradually instil in Othello's mind that Desdemona is being unfaithful with Cassio. Emilia steals Desdemona's special handkerchief. Unable to produce this for Othello he is convinced of her guilt and, urged on by Iago, kills her. When Emilia confesses, the saddened Othello stabs Iago to death.

This is based on Jack Good's musical play which he adapted from the play by Shakespeare.

"...a sort of comic strip travesty of the play..." – Tom Milne, 'Monthly Film Bulletin', December, 1973.

OTELO (EL COMANDO NEGRO)
(Spain/France, 1982)

p.c. *MB Difusion/Eurocine.*
d. *Max H. Boulois.*
l.p. *Tony Curtis (Iago); Joanna Pettet (Desdemona); Max H. Boulois (Othello); Nadiuska (Emily); Ramiro Oliveros (Cassio); Sara Mora (Bianca); Gérard Barry (Ludovic); Fernando Sancho (Bethancourt); Andrés Resino (Broderick); Tony Fuentes (Titi); Aldo Sambrell (Matano); Mario De Barros (Sony); Tom Hernández (Fergusson); Alito (Mujahid).*
Eastman Color. 106 mins. WS

Desdemona enlists the aid of General Othello in getting help to the sick and wounded during civil strife in Africa. They fall in love and, to the anger of her father, they marry. Iago, Othello's friend, is jealous of Michael Cassio and tricks him into negligence during the President's party for the couple. Michael is arrested. Iago connives to get Desdemona to intervene and at the same time makes a tape recording of a conversation with Michael which is misconstrued. There is an attempted ambush which Othello survives but learns that he must have a traitor in his camp. Michael is promoted by international authorities and survives an attack on his life. Othello, inflamed by jealousy, kills Desdemona. Emily, her friend, denounces Iago as a the trouble maker. Iago shoots her and is himself shot by Othello. Michael, loyal to his General, tries to protect him but Othello takes his own life.

This is noted as being inspired by the play. The French title for the film, as given by the director is

OTHELLO (LE COMMANDO NOIR) and the English one is OTHELLO (THE BLACK COMMANDO). Credit for the musical themes used in the film goes to Beethoven and it dominates much of the track to the exclusion of dialogue. The German release under the title OPERATION OTHELLO – DER SCHWARZE KOMMANDO is noted as running eighty-two minutes.

LA JALOUSIE
(France, 1989)

p.c. *Les Productions Lazennec.*
d. *Christophe Loizillon.*
l.p. *Nathalie Richard; Nathalie Cerda; Aladin Riebel.*
c. 15 mins.

The life of a young couple runs into difficulties when the woman discovers that her man has taken a lover. She comes back home but he is not there. There is, however, a book – OTHELLO by Shakespeare.

Though not directly from the play, the influence is clear as can be seen from the synopsis.

Shown at the Valladolid Film Festival, Spain, 1990.

✛ ✛ ✛ ✛ ✛

DESDEMONA
(Germany, 1904)

p.c. *Oskar Messterton/Deutsche Bioscop.*
d. *Franz Porten.*
l.p. *Henny Porten (Desdemona); Franz Porten (Othello); Albert Kuntzner; Emmy Dertin; Rosa Porten (Emilia?).*
b.w. 1 reel approx.

In the early 1900s a number of opera stars of the era – Enrico Caruso among them – made a series of short films, called "tonbilder", varying from ten to twenty-five minutes long in a sound system devised by Oscar Messter, the famour German film pioneer and inventor. The sound system used synchronised discs and was called Biophon and Messter took out a patent on the system in 1905. This film is the death scene from the Verdi opera. The film may date from slightly later (1907?) and be also known as OTHELLO. Messter is also given as the director by some as is Alfred Lewandowsky.

OTHELLO
(France, 1905)

p.c. *Georges Mendel.*
d. *Georges Mendel?*
l.p. *Francesco Tamagno.*
b.w. (?) mins.

As this is also known, in translation, as OTHELLO'S DEATH, this is obviously the death scene from the opera. The sound system used is unknown but was probably a disc electronically synchronised to the film. Since the lead actor was a noted operatic singer of the era, this is assumed to be an extract from the opera by Verdi.

Tamagno was typical of the type of opera singer used in these early experimental sound films.

aka: TOD OTHELLOS

OTHELLO
(Austria, 1908)

p.c. *Pathé.*
d.
l.p. *Erik Schmedes.*
b.w. (?) mins. See notes.

Noted as being a sound film with music by Verdi, this may well have been a synchronised disc system. Schmedes was the voice that was heard.

The film is intriguing. The Folger Shakespeare Library has a copy of a film from this period noting it as being made by the Austrian subsidiary of the French company. It was equipped for some form of sound accompaniment. Reason suggests that it is the film noted here. If so, the film lasts twenty-nine minutes and the Folger copy has Russian titles though, obviously, the original titles were German. The notes from Folger imply that it was a truncated version with contrasting scenery with good exteriors marred by obviously painted back-drops for the interiors. It is noted as having superior realism for the period.

OTHELLO
(Germany, 1909)

p.c. *Deutsche Mutoscop Und Biograph.*
d.
l.p. *? Ferrari (Othello)*
b.w. (?) mins.

Believed to be the scene of the death of Othello, the voice heard was that of Francesco Tamagno. It is assumed that Verdi's music came from the disc synchronized to the film system devised by Oscar Messter. It may well be that the use of Tamagno's voice was inspired by the earlier French film which was of similar content.

aka: OTHELLOS TOD

BIANCO CONTRO NEGRO
(Italy, 1913)

p.c. *Pasquali e C.*
d. *Ubaldo Maria del Colle.*
l.p. *Alberto A. Capozzi; Mary Cleo Tarlarini.*
b.w. 4920 ft. (1500 m.)

Noted as being an experimental sound film (logically by a synchronised disc system), the music is by Verdi. Thus this may well be a condensed version of the opera.

The length of the film varies from country to country with the British version at 5000 ft. (1524 m.) and French versions at 5512 ft. (1680 m.) and 4849 ft. (1478 m.). Ernesto Maria Pasquali is also noted by some as the director.

aka: BLANC CONTRE NÈGRE; BLANC ET NÈGRE; THE IRON FIST; WHITE AGAINST BLACK; BLANCO CONTRA NEGRO

MME ALDA SINGING "AVE MARIA" BY VERDI
(U.S.A., 1930)

p.c. *Vitaphone Corporation.*
d.
l.p. *Frances Alda.*
b.w. 8 mins.

Content as implied, the piece is taken from OTELLO by Verdi. The system used was sound-on-disc.

OTELLO
(Portugal, 1932?)

p.c.
d.
l.p. *Lelane Rivera ? (Desdemona).*
b.w. 8 mins.

An opera singer (possibly the one listed above) sings an aria from OTELLO by Verdi. This does not appear in 'Prontuário Do Cinema Portugués 1896-1989' by José de Matos-Cruz under such a title. It could well be that it was an extract from a feature film or a documentary of the era.

VENETZIANSKY MAVR (OTHELLO)
(U.S.S.R., 1960)

p.c. *Gruzia Film.*
d. *Vakhtang Chabukani.*
l.p. *Vakhtang Chabukani (Othello); Vera Tsignadze (Desdemona); B. Monavardiasaschvili (Cassio); Vera Mitayshvili (Emilia); Eurab Kikaleishvili (Iago); V. Ivaschkin (Duke); R. Zulukidze (Roderigo); M. Geljus (Montano); Eteri Tschabukiani (Bianca); M. Geljus (Montano); M. Dudko (Brabantio) and with artists of the Opera Theatre and Ballet of Tbilissi.*
Sovcolor. 94 mins.

A faithful rendering of the story in ballet, the music is by Alexei Machavariani.

Shown at the Shakespeare Film Festival, Wiesbaden, W. Germany, 1964.

OTHELLO
(E. Germany, 1969)

p.c. *Deutschen FernsehenFunks.*
d. *Walter Felenstein, Georg Mielke.*
l.p. *Hanns Nocker (Othello); Christa Noack von Kamptz (Desdemona); Vladimir Bauer (Jago); Hanna Schmoock (Emilia); Hans-Otto Rogge (Cassio); Hans-Erich Blasberg (Montano); Herbert Rössler (Lodovico); Peter Seufert*
(Rodrigo); Horst-Dieter Kaschel (Herold).Orchestra (conductor: Kurt Masur), Soloists and Chorus of Komischen Oper, Berlin.
c. 105 mins.

Sung in German, this is a straight-forward version of the Verdi opera.

This is a recreation of a stage performance without an audience filmed in the DEFA studios. It has the benefits of camera flexibility with close-ups etc. and, of course, spacious sets. Though originally intended for television it clearly exists as a film in its own right. The colour system used was probably OrwoColor (favoured by DEFA at this time). Alternatively, it might be the same stock as used for the Russian Sovcolor.

OTELLO
(W. Germany, 1974)

p.c. *Unitel in collaboration with E.M.I.*
d. *Roger Benamou.*
l.p. *John Vickers (Otello); Mirella Freni (Desdemona); Peter Glossop (Iago); Aldo Bottion (Cassio); Joé van Dam (Ludovico); Sefania Malagú (Emilia); Mario Macchi (Montano); Michel Sénéchal (Roderigo). The Berlin Philharmonic Orchestra; The Chorus of the Deutsche Oper (conductor: Herbert von Karajan).*
c. 148 mins.

Basically, this is the film version of the E.M.I. recording of the time of Verdi's opera.

The film offers more freedom than the usual filming of stage productions and there is a most effective performance by Mirella Freni. The same cast also appeared in Karajan's Salzburg Festival production about the same time.

OTELLO
(Holland/Italy, 1986)

p.c. *Cannon City Produktien/Cannon Productions/ Italian International Film/RAI.*
d. *Franco Zeffirelli.*
l.p. *Placido Domingo (Otello); Katia Ricciarelli (Desdemona); Justino Diaz (Iago); Urbano Barberini (Cassio); Petra Malakova (Emilia); Edwin Francis (Montano); Sergio Nicolai (Roderigo); Massimo Foschi (Lodovico); Antonio Pierfederici (Doge); Remo Remotti (Brabanzio). With voices of: Ezio Di Cesare (Cassio); John McCurdy (Lodovico); Edwin Toumajin (Montano); Constantin Zaharia (Roderigo); Giannicola Pigliuccci (Araldo).Orchestra and Chorus of Teatro De La Scala, Milan (conductor: Lorin Maazel).*
c. by Cinecittà. 123 mins. S

Impressive, certainly in terms of the lead singers, version of the opera by Verdi.

Shown as part of the Everybody's Shakespeare International Festival, London, England, 1994.

Academy of Motion Picture Arts and Sciences, U.S.A., 1986: Nomination – Best Costume Design (Anna Anni, Maurizio Millenotti).

British Academy of Film and Television Arts, G.B., 1986: Nomination – Best Foreign Language Film.

National Board of Review, U.S.A., 1988: First in Foreign Language Films list.

The Moor has obviously tempted film makers from the earliest days of the cinema and Verdi's opera based on the play is one of the most popular in its own sphere. The play, described as Shakespeare's most intense tragedy, has a central character who has earned the adjectives "dark" and "jealous". Yet the Bard is not precise on the former point and the matter has been the subject of much scholarly debate though before and since, notably, Paul Robeson played the role, Othello has generally been portrayed as black. It is not essential to the plot. The point is that he is a Moor. So, can true love can survive ethnic, cultural and religious differences? The introduction of colour is mere emphasise of this.

Was Othello jealous? Ultimately, he was but it was not part of his general character, a character offering personality contradictions. On the one hand, he is a brave, noble and respected warrior, on the other he shows his fraility and insecurity in his wrongful mistrust of Desdemona (who cannot comprehend thoughts that her husband might be jealous) and his gullibility in believing the insinuating Iago.

It is in this acceptance of Iago and his scheming that the tragedy of Othello rests. To be generally jealous in man/woman relationships would simply be a character defect, regrettable but hardly tragic. No such defect has Othello as is clearly indicated in the play.

Othello is sure of the love of Desdemona and of his own for her. That such as Iago can infect the noble Othello with doubts that spread like a cancer within is the real tragedy.

No doubt the play, with this strong plot, has inspired a number of films apart from the more obvious ones mentioned herein. Many will, perhaps, be dubious in their inspiration relying, probably erroneously, solely upon the jealousy theme.

For other films with scenes from this play see **CHAPTER XXX ALL THE WORLD'S A STAGE**: FOR AADENT TÆPPE (1911); BUMKE AS OTHELLO (1913); OTHELLO IN JONESVILLE (1913); OTHELLO (1916); THE MAD LOVER (1917); A MODERN OTHELLO (1917); CARNIVAL (1921); KEAN (1922); OTHELLO (1922); DIE LEIBGARDIST (1926); THE DECEIVER (1931); CARNIVAL (1933); MEN ARE NOT GODS (1936); CANZONE ETERNA (1941); ROSSINI (1942/3); THE MAN IN GREY (1943); LES ENFANTS DU PARADIS (1945); A DOUBLE LIFE (1947); IL PECCATO DI ANNA (1952); GIUSEPPE VERDI (1953); CASA RICORDI (1954); C'EST ARRIVÉ À ADEN (1956); SERENADE (1956); LE THÉÂTRE NATIONAL POPULAIRE (1956); KEAN (1957); SERENADE EINER GROSSEN LIEBE (1958); LANTERNA MAGIKA (1958/61); SAPTAPADI (1961); SHAKESPEARE WALLAH (1965); EL ABOMINABLE HOMBRE DE LA COSTA DEL SOL (1969); FLESH AND BLOOD SHOW (1973); SO FINE (1981); TRUE IDENTITY (1991) and DER MUSIK SAGT ALLES – ANJA SILJA (1995) and **CHAPTER XXXII THE IMMORTAL BARD**: UPLIFT AT THE LOCAL (1947); FAIR ADVENTURE SERIES (1964); MASKS AND FACES (1969)*; EXPLORATIONS IN SHAKESPEARE (1969) and SHAKESPEARE: MIRROR TO A MAN (1970?).

* Denotes film extract.

CHAPTER XXI
ROMEO AND JULIET

Dramatis Personæ:

Montague
Lady Montague – his wife
Romeo – their son
Mercutio – Romeo's friend and kinsman to Prince Escalus
Benvolio – Romeo's friend and nephew of Montague
Balthasar – Romeo's servant
Abram – Montague's servant

Capulet
Lady Capulet
Juliet – their daughter
Tybalt – nephew of Lady Capulet
Sampson, Gregory – Capulet's servants
Nurse to Juliet
Peter – the nurse's servant

Old man of the Capulet family
Escalus, Prince of Verona
Paris – a young count and kinsman to the Prince

Friar Laurence, Friar John – Franciscan friars
Three musicians
An Apothecary
An Officer
Citizens of Verona, Ladies and Gentlemen of both families, Maskers, Torchbearers, Pages, Guards, Watchmen, Servants and Attendants
Chorus

Note: The name "Laurence" may also be spelt "Lawrence" in English. Both spellings may occur in the text depending upon the individual film credits.

The two main wealthy families in Verona, the Montagues and the Capulets, carry on an ancient feud which envelopes even the servants of the families much to the distress of the other people.

Lord Capulet holds a supper to which all, except the Montagues, are invited and many pretty girls attend. Lord Montague's son, Romeo, loves Rosaline Capulet. Romeo's friend Benvolio, aware that Romeo's love is not returned, suggests he go to the supper just to see the choice of girls available. Wearing masks, they go, with their friend Mercutio, and are made welcome as their identities are not known. There Romeo sees and falls for Juliet, a Capulet, and his praise of her is overheard by Tybalt, a Capulet. He tells Lord Capulet that he has recognised Romeo as a Montague. Lord Capulet will hear of no adverse action wishing to maintain the laws of hospitality. This upsets Tybalt.

Romeo is able to talk to Juliet and is shocked to learn that she is Lord Capulet's daughter. She, too, is attracted to him and both know their love must cast aside the enmity between the families.

Later, his friends having gone, Romeo wanders in an orchard close to the Capulet's house. He sees Juliet on a balcony and her thoughts of him are translated into words. He can hide no longer and goes to her. They both know that the affection between them is ill-advised but they cannot suppress their love. Only a call to bed from the house concludes their meeting.

It is early morning when Romeo leaves and goes to see Friar Laurence, an old friend who realises that Romeo has not been to bed. He thinks he has been with Rosaline but Romeo tells him of his new love and begs the holy man to marry them that day hoping also that the marriage will heal the breach between the families. Friar Laurence can deny Romeo nothing and consents.

Juliet receives a message from Romeo and, as he has requested, meets him and the couple are married by Friar Laurence. She returns home to await her secret husband that coming night.

As it happens, Tybalt, a youth of quick temper, sees Mercutio, also quick tempered, and Benvolio in the street and taunts Mercutio about his friendship with Romeo. Despite pleas from Benvolio, a fight ensues. Romeo sees and tries to reconcile the two calling Tybalt a friend. Passions are high and a duel ensues in which Mercutio is killed. Romeo, his anger now raised, faces Tybalt and kills him.

Both grieving families are called before the Prince of Verona who has had cause to speak harshly before about their behaviour. He listens carefully to the evidence and banishes Romeo. Juliet is saddened by the news, her anger at Romeo for killing her kinsman giving way to her feelings of love.

Romeo seeks refuge with Friar Laurence when he hears of his banishment. Friar Laurence tries to console him with reason pointing out that at least he is alive. His spirit somewhat revived he plans to go to Mantua, with a promise of letters from the good Friar, but first he goes to Juliet and passes the night with her. At dawn he leaves for Mantua.

Unaware of her marriage, her father arranges a marriage for Juliet to the personable Count Paris. Despite all her entreaties he will not be moved in his resolve. In need of counsel, she goes to Friar Laurence who suggests to her a dangerous plan. To save her from this marriage he proposed she take a drug which induces a sleep as like to death as to be undetectable and lasts forty-two hours. In the meantime, Friar Laurence will send a messenger to Romeo telling of the plan. With no other way open to her, Juliet agrees and he gives her the potion.

As she is leaving, Juliet meets Count Paris and, to avoid suspicions, concurs with the proposed marriage to the delight of her father. At night she takes the potion and when Paris calls upon her the next day he finds her dead body. Happiness is suddenly turned to sadness in the Capulet household, a marriage ceremony turns into a burial.

As often happens, bad news precedes good and Romeo hears of Juliet's apparent death before the messenger from Friar Laurence arrives. Deeply saddened, he persuades an apothecary to sell him some deadly poison as he wishes to end his life. He goes to Verona and breaks into Juliet's tomb. His work is interrupted by Count Paris who recognises Romeo. An argument follows leading to a fight in which Paris is killed by Romeo. When he realises whom he has killed, Romeo promises to bury him with Juliet. Having opened the tomb, Romeo sees his love, gives her one last kiss then takes the poison.

Realising that his message has not reached Romeo and knowing that Juliet is about to awaken, Friar Laurence goes to her tomb, to free her. He is surprised to see Romeo and Paris both dead. Juliet awakens from her sleep and sees what has happened. She takes the dagger she is wearing and stabs herself.

The alarm has been raised and all gather to hear Friar Laurence relate the sad tale and how his plan went awry. The Prince of Verona rebukes the two families and the two Lords give their hands to each other as a bond of friendship. Each erects a statue in gold for the dead of the other as a homage to show how the two lovers, by their deaths, have united the two families at last.

Note: To date this play, scholars have looked to the play itself. The mention of an earthquake could be a reference to the one of 1580 and thus, from the text, would fix the date as 1591. There were other earthquakes which could put the date as 1594, 1595 or 1596. An astronomical interpretation fixes the year as 1596. More down-to-earth, the quarto edition of 1597 notes that it was acted by "Lord Hunsdon's Servants". As this was the name of Shakespeare's company from July, 1596, to March, 1597, this gives a better guide. Finally, comparison of the printer's type suggests a printing date of February or March, 1597. Thus 1596 would seem to be the year. Shakespeare's source requires no such devious deduction for it was taken from 'The Tragicall Historye Of Romeus And Juliet, Written First In Italian By Bandell And Now In Englishe By Ar. Br.'. This 1562 work was by Arthur Broke (or Brooke) is a narrative poem from Bandello (1554) via the French version by Pierre Boaistuau (1559). Elements of the story had been used by other Italian writers prior to Bandello.

✥ ✥ ✥ ✥ ✥

GIULIETTA E ROMEO
(Italy, 1902)

p.c.
d.
l.p.
b.w. (?) mins. Sil.

No details are available of this early Italian version.

ROMEO AND JULIET
(G.B., 1908)

p.c. Gaumont.
d. William G. Barker?
l.p. Godfrey Tearle (Romeo); Mary Malone (Juliet); James Annand (Tybalt); Gordon Bailey (Mercutio).
b.w. 1240 ft. (378 m.) Sil.

Twenty-five scenes from the Lyceum Theatre, London, production which, in effect, opened the theatre doors to cinema audiences, were featured in this. There is some doubt about who took the directorial chair.

ROMEO AND JULIET, A ROMANTIC STORY OF THE ANCIENT FEUD BETWEEN THE ITALIAN HOUSES OF MONTAGUE AND CAPULET
(U.S.A., 1908)

p.c. Vitagraph.
d. James Stuart Blackton or William V. Ranous.
l.p. Paul Panzer (Romeo); Florence Lawrence (Juliet); Charles Chapman (Montague); John G. Adolfi (Tybalt); Charles Kent (Capulet); William V. Ranous (Friar Lawrence); Harry Salter; William Shea (Peter); Miss Louise(?) Carver (Nurse).
b.w. 915 ft. (279 m.) Sil.

Florence Lawrence was later lured away from her $15 Vitagraph per week contract to a $25 one with Biograph where she became the Biograph Girl. She was probably the first real star of the screen. Here she was to be seen in linked extracts from the play put together to make a coherent release.

Strangely, Vitagraph promoted the film as being in nine scenes even though there were more.

Extract shown as part of the Everybody's Shakespeare International Festival, London, England, 1994.

ROMEO E GIULIETTA
(Italy, 1908)

p.c. *Cines.*
d. *Mario Caserini.*
l.p. *Mario Caserini (Romeo); Maria Gasperini (Juliet); Fernanda Negri Pouget.*
b.w. 738 ft. (225 m.) Sil.

Francesca Bertini may have also been in the cast.

GIULIETTA E ROMEO
(Italy, 1910)

p.c.
d. *Giuseppe de Liguoro.*
l.p.
b.w. (?) mins. Sil.

Even though the director was quite prolific and there are a number of Shakespearean film adaptations by him, no further details of this have been found.

ROMÉO ET JULIETTE
(France, 1911)

p.c. *Pathé.*
d. *Gérard Bourgeois.*
l.p.
b.w. 2 reels. Sil.

Details of this early French version have not been traced.

ROMEO AND JULIET
(U.S.A., 1911)

p.c. *Thanhouser.*
d. *Theodore Marston.*
l.p. *Julia M. Taylor (Juliet); George Lessey (Romeo); Mrs. George W. Watson (Nurse);William Garwood (Friar Lawrence?).*
b.w. 2000 ft. (610 m.) Sil.

A condensed version of the play, this maintains many of the key scenes with careful use of inter-titles and some some genuine scenery to match the well photographed exteriors. Sadly, only fragments of the film remain.

The film was produced to contain two complete stories of one reel each so that distributors could show either or both. Some sources note Irma Taylor as the female lead and Barry O'Neil as director. Part one of the film is said to no longer exist and the length is approximate.

ROMEO AND JULIET
(G.B., 1912)

A French source notes this as a film of a performance of the play at London's Lyceum Theatre. However, this is not confirmed by British sources. Such film records were common at this time and it may be that French archives have information lost to the British ones or, more probably, it refers to the 1908 film listed above.

ROMEO E GIULIETTA
(Italy, 1912)

p.c. *Film d'Arte Italiana/S.A.P.F.*
d. *Ugo Falena.*
l.p. *Francesca Bertini (Juliet); Gustavo Serena (Romeo); Ferruccio Garavaglia; Giovanni Pezzinga.*
b.w. 2378 ft. (725 m.) Sil.

This early version of the story comes to the screen as a commendable attempt to move away from the fragmentary style of presentation. Apart from the exterior beauty of Verona itself, Bertini gave a feminine beauty to the role of Juliet plus a sense of understanding of silent screen acting. It may be a French co-production. A number of sources note the director as Gerolamo LoSavio. A coloured version is known to exist and the British release version was shorter at 2342 ft. (714 m.).

aka: GIULIETTA E ROMEO

ROMEO AND JULIET
(U.S.A., 1916)

p.c. *Quality Pictures Corp.*
d. *John W. Noble and Francis X. Bushman.*
l.p. *Francis X. Bushman (Romeo); Beverley Bayne (Juliet); John Davidson (Paris); Horace Vinton (Escalus); Robert Cummings (Friar Laurence); Eric Hudson (Montague); Fritz Leiber (Mercutio); Edmund Elton (Capulet); Leonard Grover (Old Man); Alexandre J. Herbert (Friar John); Olaf Skavlan (Benvolio); Edwin Boring (Balthasar); W. Lawson Butt (Tybalt); William Morris (Abraham); Joseph Dailey (Peter); Helen Dunbar (Lady Capulet); Adella Barker (Nurse to Juliet); Genevieve Reynolds (Lady Montague); Ethel Mantell (Rosaline); Barry Maxwell; William H. Burton; Leonard Grover Jr.; Alexander Loftus; A.P. Kaye; Bary Macollum Norman MacDonald; John Burke; Morgan Thorpe; Lewis Sealy; Edwin Eaton; E.P. Sullivan; Robert Vivian; Eric Hudson; Jack Blake; Ben Higgins; Charles A. Smiley; Joseph Robeson Harry Sothern; Marie Booth; Violet Hall Caine; Emma Kemble; Blanche Davenport; Dorothy Kingdon; Venie Atherton; John D. Murphy; Richard Barthelmess.*
b.w. 8 reels. Sil.

According to reports of the time, the film followed the play faithfully. It was said to have cost $250,000 with an "Italian" village being built at Brighton Beach, New York. It was one of a number of films made to celebrate the three-hundredth anniversary of

Shakespeare's death. One American source notes the length as five reels though current sources quote eighty minutes as duration. As the film is lost, the truth may never be known.

ROMEO AND JULIET
(U.S.A., 1916)

p.c. Fox Film Corp.
d. J. Gordon Edwards.
l.p. Theda Bara (Juliet); Harry Hilliard (Romeo); Walter Law (Friar Laurence); Glen White (Mercutio); Alice Gale (Nurse); Einar Linden (Paris); Elwin Eaton (Montague); John Webb Dillon (Tybalt); Edwin Holt (Capulet); Victory Bateman (Lady Montague); Helen Tracy (Lady Capulet); May De Lacey; Jane Lee; Kathleen Lee.
b.w. 7 reels. Sil.

As might be expected the emphasis – and the camera – here was on Theda Bara rather than the plot which did, apparently, follow the play quite faithfully. Like a number of other films, it was released to co-incide with the three-hundredth anniversary of the death of Shakespeare. It may not have been the equal of the contemporary M.G.M. version in artistic merit but it did have Theda Bara and that pleased the public.

ROMEO E GIULIETTA
(Italy, 1918)

p.c. Savoia Film.
d. Emilio Grazziani Walter.
l.p. Armando Falconi.
b.w. 4009 ft. (1222 m.) Sil.

A German source notes a film of similar details as having been made six years earlier.

ROMEO AND JULIET
(U.S.A., 1936)

p.c. M.G.M.
d. George Cukor.
l.p. Leslie Howard (Romeo); Norma Shearer (Juliet); John Barrymore (Mercutio); Basil Rathbone (Tybalt); Edna May Oliver (Juliet's Nurse); Andy Devine (Peter); C. Aubrey Smith (Lord Capulet); Henry Kolker (Friar Lawrence); Ralph Forbes (Paris); Violet Kemble-Cooper (Lady Capulet); Reginald Denny (Benvolio); Conway Tearle (Prince of Verona); Maurice Murphy (Balthasar); Virginia Hammond (Lady Montague); Robert Warwick (Lord Montague); Anthony Kemble-Cooper (Gregory Capulet); Ian Wolfe (Apothecary); Vernon Downing (Samson Capulet); Anthony March (Mercutio's Page);Howard Wilson (Abraham Montague); Carlyle Blackwell Jr. (Tybalt's Page); Katherine De Mille (Rosalind); John Bryan (Friar John); Wallis Clark; Dean Richmond Bentor; Lita Chevret; Jeanne Hart; Dorothy Granger; Harold Entwistle; José Rubio; Charles Bancroft.
b.w. 130 mins.

Grandiose, no-expense-spared version from Hollywood, this was producer Irving Thalberg's dream project which was at least faithful to the original.

The film has an interesting background. Thalberg had a battle to convince M.G.M. to make the film and similarly that his wife, Norma Shearer, should take the female lead. She was thirty-six years old and thus hardly the age that Shakespeare envisaged for the heroine. For the reason of age – he was forty-three – Leslie Howard turned down the male lead role. So, too, did Frederic March, the first choice, and later choices Clark Gable, Errol Flynn and Robert Donat. In the end, Howard agreed. There was no argument about accepting a role by John Barrymore whose career was well into decline. He accepted a flat fee of $20,000 which would help support his affaire with starlet Elaine Barrie and his drink habit. The latter was a constant problem during the shooting, not overcome by his being put in a sanitarium, though he did deliver a flamboyant, effective performance. The budget was planned at $1,500,000, Thalberg promised to do it at $800,000 but the final cost was over $2,000,000 and it only just managed to recoup it. It was, however, among the top money-taking films of 1936/37.

Shown at the Shakespeare Film Festival, Wiesbaden, W. Germany, 1964.
Academy of Motion Picture Arts and Sciences, U.S.A., 1936: Nominations – Best Picture, Best Actress (Norma Shearer), Best Supporting Actor (Basil Rathbone).
National Board of Review Awards, U.S.A., 1936: Listed eighth in Best American Films list.
'New York Times' Annual Ten Best List, U.S.A., 1936: Listed sixth.

ROMEO AND JULIET
(G.B./Italy, 1954)

p.c. Verona Productions/Universal Cine/United Artists (London).
d. Renato Castellani.
l.p. Laurence Harvey (Romeo); Susan Shentall (Juliet); Flora Robson (Nurse); Bill Travers (Benvolio); Mervyn Johns (Friar Laurence); Enzo Fiermonte (Tybalt); Giovanni Rota (Prince of Verona); Aldo Zollo (Mercutio); Sebastion Cabot (Capulet); Lydia Sherwood (Lady Capulet); Norman Wooland (Paris); Giulio Garbinetti (Montague); Nietta Zocchi (Lady Montague); Dagmar Josipovich (Rosaline); Luciano Bodi (Abraham); Thomas Nicholls (Friar John); John Gielgud (Chorus).
Technicolor. 138 mins.

The richness of the visual quality here may, for some, offset the excision of some scenes and cutting of the text.

Shot in various cities in Italy, often using local workers as actors, this was initially considered a disaster for most concerned. Harvey was considered a failure as the male lead and Susan Shentall, who had been discovered when she was dining in a restaurant, as unimpressive in her sole screen appearance as his co-star. She left acting to marry immediately after completion of the film. Apparently a nude bathing sequence was censored.

Despite the adverse comment that has surrounded this film from the time it arrived on the screen, it did pick up a few prizes and time seems to have mellowed, even reversed, the comments about it. It was chosen for the annual Royal Film Performance in England in 1954. The music featured in the film was available on record on the Epic label.

Shown at the Shakespeare Film Festival, Wiesbaden, W. Germany, 1964.
Shown at the Valladolid Film Festival, Spain, 1986, as part of a short selection of films related to the play.
British Cinematic Association Awards, G.B., 1954: Photography (Robert Krasher).
British Film Academy, G.B., 1954: Best costumes.
Kinema Jumpo Ten Best Films, Japan, 1954: Listed third in Foreign Language Films list
National Board of Review Awards, U.S.A., 1954: Best Foreign Picture, Best Foreign Films – First on the list, Best Director (Renato Castellani).
'New York Times' Annual Ten Best List, U.S.A., 1954: Listed tenth.
Venice Film Festival, Italy, 1954: Best Film – Lion Of St. Mark.

"Only Flora Robson brought a breath of real presence to the muted shambles." – Angela and Elkan Allan, 'The Sunday Times Guide To Movies On Television'.

"Superb and beautiful." – John Gielgud.

"...among the most beautiful works the cinema has offered us." – Noel Coward.

aka: GIULIETTA E ROMEO

GIULIETTA E ROMEO
(Italy/Spain, 1964)

p.c. *Imprecine/Hispamer.*
d. *Riccardo Freda.*
l.p. *Gerónimo Meynier (Romeo); Rosemarie Dexter (Juliet); Carlos Estrada (Mercutio); Toni Soler (Nurse); Umberto Raho (Friar Lawrence); Andrea Bosic (Capulet); José Marco (Paris); Antonella Della Porta (Lady Capulet); German Grech (Tybalt); Elsa Vazzoler (Lady Montague); Antonio Gradoli (Montague); Bruno Scipioni (Balthasar); Mario de Simone (Peter); Franco Balducci (Benvolio).*
Eastman Color. 97 mins. Cromoscope.

This much shortened version of the play is difficult to judge since it was originally made in Italian and then dubbed into English for American release.

The film was not released until 1968 in America (reduced to ninety minutes) in commercial competition with Zeffirelli's film. This led to some legal battles. The music for the film was taken from the works of Tchaikovsky and Rachmaninoff.

aka: LOS AMANTES DE VERONA; JULIETA Y ROMEO

ROMEO AND JULIET
(G.B., 1966)

p.c. *Royal Academy of Dramatic Art/Regent Polytechnic Institute.*
d. *Val Drum, Paul Lee.*
l.p. *Clive Francis (Romeo); Angela Scougar (Juliet); Hayward Morse (Mercutio); Damien Court-Thomas (Tybalt); Veronica Clifford (Nurse).*
b.w. 107 mins.

A record of a stage performance by students of the Academy, it has the advantages and disadvantages of being what it is.

ROMEO AND JULIET
(G.B./Italy, 1968)

p.c. *British Home Entertainments/Verona Productions/Dino De Laurentiis Cinematografica*
d. *Franco Zeffirelli.*
l.p. *Olivia Hussey (Juliet); Leonard Whiting (Romeo); Milo O'Shea (Father Laurence); Pat Heywood (Nurse); Murray Head (The Chorus); Michael York (Tybalt); John McEnery (Mercutio); Natasha Parry (Lady Capulet); Robert Stephens (Prince Of Verona); Keith Skinner (Balthazar); Richard Warwick (Gregory); Bruce Robinson (Benvolio); Dyson Lovell (Sampson); Paul Hardwick (Lord Capulet); Robert Bisacco (Count Paris); Aldo Miranda (Friar John); Ugo Barbone (Abraham); Antonio Pierfederici (Lord Montague); Esmerelda Ruspoli (Lady Montague); Roy Holder (Peter); Dario Tanzini; Maria Fracci; Roberto Antonelli; Carlo Palmucci. Prologue and epilogue narrator: Laurence Olivier.*
Technicolor. 150 mins.

Cuts have inevitably been made in this, one of the most successful in all respects, of Shakespeare on the screen.

Filmed in a number of towns in Italy, the lead players, both unknown, were at least about the correct ages. It was, of course, a gamble but, for the most part, one that was successful. The lack of their experience shows at times but Zeffirelli's cuts saved them long speeches. The few moments of nudity are both in keeping with the scene and in no way exploitive. The richness of the colour, the excellent sets and fine costumes gained much justified praise and box office success. 'Variety', the American magazine noted it in fifth position in its list of annual top money-taking films of 1969 in America with takings of $14,500,000. In Britain, it was chosen for the Royal Film Performance, 1968.

For the music Zeffirelli called upon Nino Rota. An excellent score (released on disc by Cloud Nine records) was the result with a particularly haunting theme. A number of labels have issued various versions of the music featured – RCA/Camden, Capitol, Columbia and United Artists. The theme plus others by Nino Rota can be found on "Nino Rota Movies" played by an orchestra conducted by Carlo Savina on the Cam label. An earlier recording was made by the famous America composer/conductor Henry Mancini. The theme formed part of a suite "Music by Nino Rota" and appeared on "Henry Mancini Conducts The London Symphony Orchestra In A Concert Of Film Music". Mancini himself played the piano on this RCA release.

Dialogue from the film was released on record by Capitol (U.S.A) and quickly sold over a million. Capitol also issued a selection on four long playing records of dialogue and music. In 1970, the same company issued a disc of the musical score without dialogue.

There is a considerable variation in the running time of the film between countries. The above is noted for the French version with the American issue at twelve minutes less and the Italian release at twenty-two minutes shorter.

Shown as part of the Everybody's Shakespeare International Festival, London, England, 1994.

Thessaloniki Film Festival, Greece, 1968: Special Prize.

Academy of Motion Picture Arts and Sciences, U.S.A., 1968: Nominations – Best Picture, Best Director (Franco Zeffirelli); Awards – Best Cinematography (Pasquale De Santis), Best Costume Design (Danilo Donati).

Hollywood Foreign Press Association Golden Globe Awards, U.S.A., 1968: Best English Language Foreign Film, Most Promising Newcomer Female (Olivia Hussey), Most Promising Newcomer Male (Leonard Whiting).

Kinema Jumpo Annual Ten Best Films, Japan, 1968: Listed second in Foreign Films list.

'Los Angeles Times' Best of the Sixties Poll, U.S.A., 1970: Readers' choice – Best Films 3 =, Best Director (Franco Zeffirelli). Industry's choice – Best Films 3 =, Best Adapted Screenplay 2 =.

National Board of Review Awards, U.S.A., 1968: Best Director (Franco Zeffirelli), Best English Language Films – Listed second.

Sindicato Nazionale Giornalisti Cinematografici Italiani, Italy, 1968: Best Director (Franco Zeffirelli), Best Music (Nino Rota), Best

Cinematography – Colour (Pasqualino De Santis), Best Art Direction (Luciano Puccini), Best Costume Design (Danilo Donati).
Society of Film and Television Arts, G.B., 1968: Best Costume Design (Danilo Donati).

A promotional short was released for the film and it is logical to include it here:

THE TEENAGE LOVERS OF VERONA (G.B./Italy, 1968)

Credits as above.
c. 7 mins.

Zefferelli is shown directing a scene with Whiting and Hussey.

ROMEO AND JULIET (G.B., 1974)

p.c. *Seabourne Enterprises.*
d. *Peter Seabourne.*
l.p. *Michael Pennington (Romeo); Natasha Pyne (Juliet); Roy Marsden; William Russell.*
c. 8 mins.

This short contains the Prologue and Act V, Scene 3.

✠ ✠ ✠ ✠ ✠

LE DIABLE ET LA STATUE (France, 1902)

p.c. *Georges Méliès.*
d. *Georges Méliès.*
l.p.
b.w. (?) mins. Sil.

An early film by the noted fantasy director loosely inspired by the story, this is listed by some sources as ROMÉO ET JULIETTE but denied as such by the Cinémathèque Méliès which should know. A German source notes **LE DIABLE GÉANT OU LE MIRACLE DE LA MADONE** (seemingly an alternative title) as being based on the play and this, about 131 ft. (40 m.), was made by Méliès. The scenes concern two statues of Venetian lovers which come to life and enact a balcony scene. It is, however, even more intriguing because of...

BURLESQUE ON ROMEO AND JULIET (U.S.A., 1902)

p.c. *Edison.*
d. *Thomas Edison.*
l.p.
b.w. 80 ft. (24 m.) Sil.

Professor Ball ('Shakespeare On Silent Film') believes this was derived from a film by Méliès or an imitator and the 'American Film Institute Catalog' suggests that the film itself was of foreign origin which leads back to the film immediately above. The Edison Catalog (No. 135) lists it as imported also. There was apparently a balcony scene in it which, if the repetition may be forgiven, leads back to the film above.

ROMÉO SE FAIT BANDIT
(France, 1910)

p.c. *Pathé.*
d.
l.p. *Max Linder.*
b.w. 541 ft. (165 m.) Sil.

Romeo climbs the enclosure wall to embrace his Juliet but her father sends him away and takes Juliet away. Romeo, disguised as a bandit and aided by three friends, kidnaps her father and ties him to a tree. Meanwhile Juliet has set out for Romeo's house. Then, the father receives a ransom note for Juliet. He makes an appeal to Romeo who has clearly found his girl and married her!

As can be realised from the above synopsis, the link with Shakespeare is, at best, thin. The credits for the film are believed lost but the film itself is regarded as being amusing and interesting even though it is hardly accurate to the original. Despite being noted in black and white, most of the film – 459 ft. (140 m.) of it – was hand-coloured. The American release is noted as 528 ft. (161 m.).

aka: ROMEO TURNS BANDIT

ROMEO AND JULIET IN OUR TOWN
(U.S.A., 1911)

p.c. *Selig Polyscope.*
d. *Otis Turner.*
l.p. *Hobart Bosworth; Betty Harte; Kathlyn Williams.*
b.w. 1000 ft. (305 m.) Sil.

The extent of the Shakespeare influence in this is limited to the enmity between two families and the love between the children of each – Romeo Smith and Juliet Brown.

aka: ROMEO AND JULIET IN TOWN; ROMEO AND JULIET

INDIAN ROMEO AND JULIET
(U.S.A., 1912)

p.c. *Vitagraph.*
d. *Lawrence Trimble.*
l.p. *Florence Turner (Juliet); William Wallace Reid (Romeo); Harry Morey (Kowa); James H. Reid (Capulet); Adelaide Ober (Neok/Nurse); Harold Wilson (Oyenkwe/Friar).*
b.w. 15 mins. approx. Sil.

One of a number of films using Shakespearean themes transposed to other settings, the publicity put out by the production company said: "It is far more Shakespearean than Shakespeare." ('Vitagraph Life Portrayals', January 17-February 1, 1912).

ROMEO AND JULIET
(U.S.A., 1913)

p.c. *Biograph.*
d. *Travers Vale.*
l.p. *Alan Hale; Louise Vale; Lionel Barrymore; Franklin Ritchie; Gretchen Hartman.*
b.w. 500 ft. (152 m.) Sil.

A feud exists between an Irish and an Italian family. Mike Montague and Pete Capulet. All ends well when Romeo and Juliet escape in a rag wagon.

Hardly true Bard, but some elements of the story remain in this modernised version. The film length is approximate.

KARLIGHEDENS FIRKLØVER
(Denmark, 1914)

p.c. *Nordisk.*
d. *Alfred Kohn.*
l.p. *Henry Seeman (Aage Krag); Johanne Fritz-Petersen (Else Juel); Oscar Stribolt (Baron Browning); Amanda Lund (Countess Toledo); Frederik Jakobsen (Dixon); C. Bruun; C. Lauritzen; A. Andersen; J. Spangsfeldt.*
b.w. (?) mins. Sil.

The Claytons and the Marshalls are friends and want their respective daughter, Else, and son, Bruce, to marry. Else is not so keen on the idea and flirts with Baron Brown. He falls for Else and confides in an old friend, Countess Toledo. The Butler, Dixon, reads ROMEO AND JULIET and sees a way to bring the young couple together. The two families pretend to feud. The young couple decide on another course and openly flirt with the Baron and the Countess. To their surprise, they marry and suggest that the Baron and the Countess do the same.

The names in the synopsis are taken from the anglicized version. The working title for the film was "Romeo Og Julie".

aka: ROMEO AND JULIET; A MODERN ROMEO AND JULIET; A DOUBLE EVENT; ROMÉO ET JULIETTE; ROMEO Y JUILETA; ROMEO UND JULIA; ROMEO E GIULIETTA; ROMEO OCH JULIA; ROMEO OG JULIE ELLER KJÆRLIGHTENS FIRKLØVER

ROMEO AND JULIET
(G.B., 1915)

p.c. *Lion's Head/Cricks and Martin.*
d. *W. P. Kellino.*
l.p. *Willy Clarkson (as himself).*
b.w. 970 ft. (296 m.) Sil.

A schoolboy sticks chocolate on the bare back of the lady in front...a footman shouts down the ear-trumpet of an old man...the stage hands and the orchestra leave as "Mudford Amateur Dramatic Society" stages the play.

Clarkson is seen at the beginning of the film preparing the cast.

ROMEO AND JULIET
(U.S.A., 1920)

p.c. *Universal/Star.*

d. *Vin Moore.*

l.p. *Walter Hiers (Romeo); Dorothea Wolbert (Juliet).*

b.w. 1694 ft. (516 m.) Sil.

This comedy version may also have the title ROMEO AND JOLLY JULIETS.

ROMEO UND JULIA IM SCHNEE
(Germany, 1920)

p.c. *Ebner/Maxim/Ufa.*

d. *Ernst Lubitsch.*

l.p. *Lotte Neumann (Julia); Gustav von Wangenheim (Romeo); Julius Falkenstein; Josefine Dora; Jacob Tiedtke; Marga Köhler; Ernst Rückert; Paul Passarghe; Hermann Picha; Paul Biensfeldt.*

b.w. 3104 ft. (946 m.). Sil.

In a Bavarian village the families Kapulethofers and the Montekugers are at war. Neither has any intention of letting their children marry each other.

This is a parody of the story with a strong bucolic flavour.

aka: ROMÉO ET JULIETTE DANS LE NEIGE

DOUBLING FOR ROMEO
(U.S.A., 1921)

p.c. *Goldwyn Productions.*

d. *Clarence Badger.*

l.p. *Will Rogers (Slim/Romeo); Sylvia Breamer (Lulu/Juliet); Raymond Hatton (Steve/Paris) Sydney Ainsworth (Pendleton/Mercutio); Al Hart (Big Alec/Tybalt);Roland Rushton (Minister/Friar Lawrence); C.E. Thurston (Duffy/Benvollo); Cordelia Callahan (Maggie/Maid); John Cossar (Foster/Capulet); William Orlamund (Movie Director); Jimmie Rogers (Jimmie Jones).*

b.w. 5297 ft. (1615 m.) Sil.

Out of work when his boss changes to rearing sheep, cowboy Slim goes into the movies where his girl wants him to be a lover like Douglas Fairbanks. He fails hopelessly and returns home to find that his girl now thinks Romeo is the greatest lover. Slim dreams the events of the play after reading it and he acts out the hero in Fairbanks style. When he awakes he rushes his girl off to the parson.

A parody, of course, 'Variety' said: "The picture is a laugh from start to finish...". The credit for the story is given to Elmer Rice and two Wills – Rogers and Shakespeare! The former takes credit for the contemporary inter-titles, the latter for the older ones. One source notes the Rogers main character role as "Sam".

JULIET AND HER ROMEO
(G.B., 1923)

p.c. *Bertram Phillips.*

d. *Bertram Phillips.*

l.p. *Queenie Thomas; Peter Upcher; Frank Stanmore; Adeline Hayden Coffin; Jeff Barlow; Fatty Phillips.*

b.w. 2000 ft. (610 m). Sil.

One in the series of *Syncopated Picture Plays* which were burlesque versions of famous plays and themes and which seemed to use, wholly or in part, the same cast. Other themes in the series were Dickens and Faust.

ROMEO AND JULIET
(U.S.A., 1924)

p.c. *Pathé Exchange.*

d. *Harry Sweet.*

l.p. *Ben Turpin (Romeo); Nathalie Kingston; Alice Day (Juliet).*

b.w. 1867 ft. (569 m.) Sil.

Yet another parody of the story with, this time, the boss-eyed comedian, Ben Turpin, and in this he is adorned with a moustache.

ACROSS THE DEADLINE
(U.S.A., 1925)

p.c. *William Steiner.*

d. *Leo Maloney.*

l.p. *Leo Maloney (Clem); Josephine Hill (Shirley); Thomas Lingham (Martin Revelle); Bud Osborne (Ben); Florence Lee (Mrs. Revelle); Rulon Slaughter (Rance Ravelle).*

b.w. 5 reels. Sil.

The son and daughter of feuding clans fall in love. When the boy saves the girl's brother from a lynch mob (he was innocent, anyway), the warring factions are reconciled.

'Motion Picture Guide' says "Romeo and Juliet transposed to the American West.". Well, that is, perhaps, a little generous though the bare essentials of the story are there. Maloney was a popular cowboy star of the era.

GUILTY GENERATION
(U.S.A., 1931)

p.c. *Columbia.*

d. *Rowland V. Lee.*

l.p. *Leo Carrillo (Mike Palmero); Boris Karloff (Tony Ricca); Robert Young (Marco); Constance Cummings (Maria); Emma Dunn; Leslie Fenton; Murray Kinnell; Elliott Rothe; Ruth Warren.*

b.w. 82 mins.

Two gangsters, Mike Palmero and Tony Ricca are fighting for control of the bootlegging business. Mike's daughter, Maria, fears her father and despises his activities. She also falls in love with Tony's son, Marco. They keep their affaire secret for fear that

Mike will kill Marco. They marry and, when he discovers the truth, Mike orders Marco's death but Mike's wife steps in and kills her husband to prevent further bloodshed.

The essence of the story is, no doubt, familiar but it is not Shakespeare but one of many films adopting the theme of the famous love story. Various Shakespearean themes were destined to be transposed to gangster land settings. Somewhat prophetically the magazine 'Time' wrote: "...A lively gang picture...Critics wondered whether HAMLET wouldn't make a better gangster plot than ROMEO AND JULIET."

"...a spirited re-working of the ROMEO AND JULIET story." – Clive Hirschhorn, 'The Columbia Story".

aka: LOS HIJOS DE LOS GANGSTERS

LACHENDE ERBEN
(Germany, 1933)

p.c. *Ufa.*
d. *Max Ophüls.*
l.p. *Heinz Rühmann; Max Adalbert; Lien Deyers; Lizzi Waldmüller; Julius Falkenstein; Ida Wüst; Walter Janssen; Friedrich Ettel.*
b.w. 76 mins.

Here the story, only loosely inspired by the source, is transposed to the famous wine growing area of the Rhineland in Germany. The transposition is to one of comedy.

"Romeo and Juliette in the guise of Rhenish buffoonery with song." – Christa Bandmann, Joe Hembus, 'Klassiker Des Deutschen Tonfilms 1930-1960'.

ESPOIR OU LE CHAMP MAUDIT
(France, 1936)

p.c. *Sport Film.*
d. *Willy Rozier.*
l.p. *Jacqueline Roman (Isabelle); Pierre Larquey (Martion); Robert Lynen (Pierre); Gaston Jacquet (Grigeu); Constant Rémy (Aubert); Sinoël; Brochard; Cècile Didier; Gildès; Victor Vina; Marfa d'Hervilly.*
b.w. 92 mins.

In the Dordogne, France, two young people, aware of each since they were young, fall in love. Unfortunately, their farming families are always feuding. But love conquers all. For a fuller outline of the general story see ROMEO UND JULIA AUF DEM DORFE listed later.

Based on the novel by Gottfried Keller 'Die Leute von Seldwyla', this has an obvious Shakespearean influence. In 1941, the French magazine 'Le Film Complet' published the story of the film with illustrations under the title 'Roméo Et Juliette Au Village'. Thus it would appear to be prophetic in appearing some months before work would begin on the Swiss version of the same story (see below).

VILLA DISCORDIA
(Argentina, 1938)

p.c.
d. *Arturo S. Mom.*
l.p. *Olinda Bozán; Paquito Bustos; Santiago Gómez Lou; Delia Garces; Gloria Fernández; Juan Carlos Thom y Rufino Córdoba; Guillermo Battaglia.*
b.w. 78 mins.

This is a modern version of the play, presumably set in the country of production.

BOSSEMANS ET COPPENOLLE
(Belgium, 1938)

p.c. *Les Films Gaston Schoukens (Brussels).*
d. *Gaston Schoukens.*
l.p. *Gustave Libeau (Bossemans); Marcel Roels (Coppenolle); Léon Carny (Bossemans' son); Charlotte Duschesne (Coppenolle's daughter); Colette Darfeuil (Violette); Mony Doll (Waitress); Adolphe Denis (Salesman); Georgette Méry (Mme.Coppenolle); Billy Pitt (Mme. Chapeau); Sinoël (Violette's friend); Aimos (Trainer); Dorian; Dumanoir.*
b.w. 84 mins.

Libeau and Coppenolle are bitter rivals in their support of opposing football teams. The daughter of Libeau is in love with the son of Coppenolle. All climaxes in a football match.

The Shakespearean rivalry theme transposed to football. What would Will have thought of this! It seems to have scored in Belgium where it was a stage success before reaching the screen.

JULIETA Y ROMEO
(Spain, 1940)

p.c. *Cinedia.*
d. *José María Catellví.*
l.p. *Marta Flores (Julieta); Enrique Guitart (Romeo); Teresa Idel; Arturo Cámara; Leonor María; Josefina Ramón; Francisco Hernández; Juan Barajas; Salvador Carrillo.*
b.w. 87 mins.

The beautiful young widow the Marquesa of Olmeda has spent many years living with her spinster sisters-in-law in a gloomy ramshackle house in the village of Villacara. Her only suitor is Romeo who robbed her of her purse when she was off-guard in church. She offers, by press advertisement, to meet the handsome thief to get the purse back. He agrees to do so to her embarrassment. Now she is set to inherit a fortune from a deceased uncle. This is disputed by a cousin and the only proof of this are some letters her late uncle sent to a dear friend. Romeo offers them to her in exchange for marriage. When she refuses, he throws the letters on the fire to prove that his love is beyond desire for wealth. The two sisters-in-law, anxious not to be deprived of a fortune, suggest to the cousin that he marries Julieta. He duly arrives at the village and installs himself in a hotel where Julieta comes to him. She is surprised to find that her cousin is none other than Romeo. They marry and live happily ever after.

A number of Spanish sources claim that this comedy, from the work by José María Penán, was inspired by Shakespeare. Title roles apart, the connection is really slim.

ROMEO UND JULIA AUF DEM DORFE
(Switzerland, 1941)

p.c. Pro Film Genossenschaft für Filmproduktion.
d. Hans Trommer, Valerien Schmidely.
l.p. Margrit Winter (Vreneli Marti); Erwin Kohlun (Sali Manz); Johannes Steiner (Albert Manz); Emil Gyr (Marti); Emil Gerber (Black Violinist); Anni Dürig (Frau Marti); Walburga Gmur (Frau Manz); Ella Kottusch (Elise); Dorli Zäch (Vreneli as a child); Richard Schuhmacher (Sali as a child); Ursula von Wiese (Emmi); Gustav Gnehm (Guest); Hans Fehrmann (District Deputy); Fred Lucca (Tramp); Jimmy Ramp (Young Man); Louis Mattlé (Lawyer); Max Röthlisberger (Sali's Friend).
b.w. 103 mins.

In a farming community near Zürich, Switzerland, Vreneli and Sali are inseparable as children. Their two families find themselves in legal conflict over a piece of land belonging to the illegitimate son of the late owner. The Manz family buys it at auction but Marti has occupied it and will not return it. This leads to protracted court action, financially crippling for both. The two children are now adults and in love, a fact soon discovered by their fathers which leads to a fight. Marti is hospitalised obviously having lost his reason and Vreneli has to sell the farm to clear debts. The two lovers realise that their situation is hopeless and plan to spend one happy day together before they part forever. However, the next day they feel they cannot part and drift away in a boat together. When the boat is found, it is empty.

Though with Shakespearean overtones, this is again based on the novel by Gottfried Keller. This rarely seen film has been described as "the most beautiful, most authentic of all Swiss films". It was made in the Swiss-German dialect and later re-release versions have a running time of ninety-four minutes (1943), eighty-four minutes (1978) and eighty two minutes when shown in London, England, in 1994. The film with French sub-titles is noted as running ninety minutes. The music by Jack Trommer was played by the Orchestre de la Suisse Romande (conductor: Dolf Zinsstag). A record of it was released by Adriano records in 1978.

Extracts from the film are featured in Peter Neuman's 1993 film for Schweizer Fernsehen, *Spuren Der Zeit-Film Helden Im Reduit*, which focuses on the Swiss cinema in relation to World War II.

Shown as part of the Everybody's Shakespeare International Festival, London, England, 1994.

aka: ROMÉO ET JULIETTE AU VILLAGE; DER SCHWARZE GEIGER; ROMEO E GIULIETTA AL VILLAGGIO

ROMEO Y JULIETA
(Mexico, 1943)

p.c. Posa Films.
d. Miguel M. Delgado.
l.p. Mario Moreno "Cantinflas" (Taxi Driver/Romeo); María Elena Marquez (Girl/Julieta); Ángel Garasa (Fray Lorenzo); Andrés Soler; José Baviera; Emma Roldan; Tito Junco; Estanislao Schellinsky; Jorge Reyes; J. Ortiz de Zarate; G. Rodríguez Familiar; María de la Paz Jarero; Conchita Gentil Arcos; Rafael Icardo.
b.w. 104 mins.

Following a disturbance, a taxi driver explains how he lost his girl because his car had broken down. He picks up a drunken actor and his friend. The actor wants to die because the father of his girl forbids the relationship. The friend, with a promise of a new car, induces the taxi driver to pose as a famous Shakespearean actor to impress the girl's father. At a dinner, the taxi driver finds himself forced to play Romeo in a performance sponsored by the father. The play is interpreted literally ending in a brawl. The police chief is sympathetic, the father relents but the taxi driver is in trouble with the theatrical authorities!

The credits clearly state that this is inspired by the Shakespearean work and it surely is. For the play within the film follows the familiar story but with a difference. Liberties are taken with the ending but, of course, this is a vehicle for the great Mexican comedian and therefore the accent is on comedy though there is an underlying plea for parental tolerance.

"Cantinflas", was Mexico's best known comedian and much loved in the world of Hispanic cinema. Outside that sphere he is best remembered for his role as Passepartout in *Around The World In Eighty Days*. This success led to the starring role in *Pepe* which was a total failure whereupon he returned to more familiar territory both geographically and artistically in Mexico.

Shown at the Valladolid Film Festival, Spain, 1986, as part of a short selection of films related to the play.

SHUHUDAE EL-GHARAM
(Egypt, 1944)

p.c. El Nile Films.

d. *Kamil Selim.*
l.p. *Ialia Mohrad; Ibrahim Hamouda; Anwar Wagdi; Bishara Warim.*
b.w. 90 mins.

This Egyptian interpretation of the theme uses tribal disputes and hatred and the intent of poisoning the son's mind as its basis. As might be expected, love conquers all in the end.

BODAS TRÁGICAS
(Mexico, 1946)

See **CHAPTER XX OTHELLO, THE MOOR OF VENICE** for full details.

ANJUMAN
(India, 1947)

p.c. *Nargis Arts Concern.*
d. *Akhtar Hussain.*
l.p. *Nargis (Juliet); Jairaj (Romeo); Durga Khote; Raj Rani; K. Sapru; Amanullah; Neelum; R. A. Khan.*
b.w. 140 mins.

Strongly influenced by the Shakespeare play, this was made in the Hindi language. Nargis was an actress of some beauty and very popular in her homeland.

Some sources note the film as having been made in 1948. Another Hindi language film of the same title was made in India in 1986. Directed by Muzzafar Ali. The title similarity is coincidental for the later film is a social melodrama though it does have a theme of a girl being forced into marriage but loving someone else.

aka: ROMEO AND JULIET

LES AMANTS DE VÉRONE
(France, 1948)

p.c. *C.I.C.C.*
d. *André Cayette.*
l.p. *Pierre Brasseur (Raffaele); Serge Reggiani (Angelo); Anouk Aimée (Georgia); Martine Carol (Bettina Verdi); Marcel Dalio (Amadeo Maglia); Louis Salou (Maglia); Marianne Oswald (Laetitia); Charles Deschamps (Sandrini); Roland Armontel (Blanchini); Philippe Lemaire; Yves Deniaud; Palmyre Levasseur.*
b.w. 110 mins.

In modern Venice a film of ROMEO AND JULIET is being made. The stars are a young glass blower and the daughter of a bitter ex-fascist official. Trouble comes from the girl's crooked fiancé who tries to have the boy murdered and when this fails he stirs up the girl's family to kill him. The two die on Juliet's tomb in the film studio.

From a script by Jacques Prévert, this is basically the story told within the filming of the story itself.

Shown at the Shakespeare Film Festival, Wiesbaden, W. Germany, 1964.

"The interpretation is one of unfortunate inequality."
– André Bazin, 'L'Écran Français'.

LA POSESIÓN
(Mexico, 1949)

p.c. *Cinematográfica Grovas.*
d. *Julio Bracho.*
l.p. *Jorge Negrete (Román); Miroslava Stern (Rosaura); Eva Martino (Lupe); Domingo Soler (Don Pedro); Julio Villarreal (Don Miguel); Isabela Corona (Roque's Wife); Luis Aceves Castañeda (Roque); Gilberto González (Pánfilo); Agustín Isunza (Jaramillo); Antonio R.Fausto (Simón); Manuel Dondé (Don Santiago); José Baviera (Judge); Adela Sequeyro; Francisco Jambrina; Diana Ochoa; Humberto Rodríguez; Félix Medel; Lupe Inclán; José Chávez; Trio Calaveras; Trio América.*
b.w. 103 mins.

A dispute between two wealthy land owners over a piece of mountain land causes trouble for their respective son and daughter who are in love. Inevitably, bitterness and tragedy follow.

The theme as briefly noted above clearly reflects the famous story and so justifies claims that it was Shakespeare inspired. The film is more directly based on the novel 'La Parcela' by José López Portillo y Rojas. The running time is also given as ninety-eight minutes. The story had been filmed twice before in Mexico:

LA PARCELA
(1921)

p.c. *Evow/Vollrath/Camus.*
d. *Ernesto Vollrath.*
l.p. *Luis Ross; Guillermo Hernández Gómez; Agustín Carrillo de Albornoz; Juan Canals de Homes; Carmen Bonifant; Enrique Cantalaúba; Elvira Ortiz; Delia Palomera; Marina Cabrera; Eduardo Sánchez; Clodomiro Morales; Isidro D'Olace.*
b.w. Feature. Sil.

and

NOBLEZA RANCHERA
(1938)

p.c. *La Mexicana.*
d. *Alfredo del Diestro*
l.p. *Alfredo del Diestro; Carmen Hermosillo; Ramón Armengod; Adria Delhort; Ricardo Mutio; Miguel Inclán; Agustín Isunza; Rafael Icardo; Pepe Martínez; Ricardo Alpuente; Rodolfo Calvo; Paco Martínez; Fortunato Gámiz; Catalina Reyes; Alfonso Parra; Paco Obregón; Clifford Carr; Gerardo del Castillo.*
b.w. 94 mins.

ROSEANNA McCOY
(U.S.A., 1949)

p.c. *A Samuel Goldwyn Production.*

d. *Irving Reis.*

l.p. *Joan Evans (Roseanna); Farley Granger (Johnse Hatfield); Raymond Massey (Randall McCoy); Charles Bickford (Devil Anse Hatfield); Richard Basehart (Mounts); Marshall Thompson (Tolbert); Aline MacMahon (Sarie); Gigi Perreau (Allifair); Hope Emerson (Levisa); Peter Miles (Little Randall); Lloyd Gough (Phamer); Elizabeth Fraser (Bess); Mabel Paige (Grandma Sykes); Almira Sessions (Zinny).*

b.w. 89 mins.

In West Virginia at the turn of the century, the Hatfields and the McCoys continue an ancient feud. At a country fair, young Johnse Hatfield falls in love with Roseanna McCoy and helps her when she is stung by a bee. One night he abducts her and, despite an initially cool reception, is accepted by the Hatfields. One of the family, Mounts, creates trouble and the fighting starts leading to the wounding of Roseanna's little brother. After the battle, Mounts is killed and Johnse and Roseanna flee. Each side holds its fire. The love of the couple ends the feud.

ROMEO AND JULIET go West again! It does not take much imagination, despite a happy ending, to note the story source even though it was based on a novel by Alberta Hannum. Even one character's name, again using a little imagination, takes on a familiar sound.

THE YOUNG LOVERS
(G.B., 1954)

p.c. *Group Film Productions.*

d. *Anthony Asquith.*

l.p. *Odile Versois (Anna); David Knight (Ted); Joseph Tomelty (Moffatt); Paul Carpenter (Gregg); Theodore Bikel (Joseph); Jill Adams (Judy); David Kossof (Szobek); Betty Marsden (Mrs. Forrester); John McClaren (Margetson); Peter Illing (Dr. Weissbrod); Peter Dyneley (Regan).*

b.w. 96 mins.

Ted, a young American working for American Intelligence in London meets, at the ballet, Anna, a girl from an Iron Curtain country and they fall in love. Realising their problems, they know they must part but already the security forces from both sides are alarmed. When Anna finds she is pregnant she arranges to meet Ted but he is arrested as a traitor. He escapes and contacts Anna who escapes from her own guard and meets him at Folkestone. They steal a fishing boat, pursued by police and officials. When wreckage is found the chase is called off and a note from Anna tells her father that they are running away not because of their guilt but because of his. The sailing boat has, however, survived.

Here the familiar theme with a guarded happy ending (at least for the lovers) was brought up to date at that time. It is not a case of feuding families but tacitly feuding countries and ideals, for the Cold War was a very hot subject then. Another twenty-five years were to pass before Anna's message would have effect.

British Film Academy Award, 1954: Best Screenplay.

aka: LOS JÓVENES AMANTES

ROMEO Y JULITA
(Argentina, 1954)

p.c. *Producciones General Belgrano.*

d. *Enrique Carreras.*

l.p. *Amelita Vargas; Alfredo Barbieri; Estaban Serrador; Tito Climent; Susana Campos.*

b.w. 74 mins.

This is believed to be a parody of the story.

UN FANTASMA LLAMADO AMOR
(Spain, 1956)

p.c. *Gonzalez-Llama.*

d. *Ramón Torrado.*

l.p. *Conchita Goyanes; Elías Rodríguez; Carlos Casaravilla; Félix Dafauce; Carlos Romero Marchent; Josefina Serratosa; Xan das Bolas; Antonio Riquelme; María Isbert.*

b.w. 83 mins.

A little boy and a little girl unwittingly recreate the story of Romeo and Juliet guided by a learned old country man.

WEST SIDE STORY
(U.S.A., 1961)

p.c. *Mirisch/Seven Arts.*

d. *Robert Wise.*

l.p. *Natalie Wood (Maria); Richard Beymer (Tony); Russ Tamblyn (Riff); George Chakiris (Bernardo); Rita Moreno (Anita); Tony Mordente (Action); Tucker Smith (Ice); Simon Oakland (Lt. Schrank); Willam Bramley (Officer Krupke); Ned Glass (Doc); José De Vega (Chino); Sue Oakes (Anybody's); John Astin (Glad Hand); Jay Norman (Pepe); Penny Stanton (Madame Lucia); Gus Trikonis (Indio); Robert Thompson (Luis); Eliot Field (Baby John); Larry Roquemore (Rocco); David Winters (A-Rab).*

Technicolor. 152 mins. Panavision 70.

On the West Side of New York City, Riff, leader of the Jets, looks to Tony for support in challenging the Puerto Rican Sharks, led by Bernardo, to a rumble (fight). At a dance held on neutral territory, Tony falls in love with Bernardo's sister, Maria, and she begs him to stop the fight. He fails and Bernardo accuses him of cowardice upon which Riff comes to his defence and is killed by Bernardo who, in turn, is killed by an incensed Tony. Maria finds she cannot be angry with Tony and when he goes into hiding she sends a message to him with Anita. Anita is mawled by the Jets and, in anger, tells him that Maria is dead. Stricken with grief, Tony is killed by one of the vengeful Sharks. Maria turns on the two gangs as they carry away Tony's body.

Bernstein's successful stage show found equal, if not more, fame on the cinema screen with slightly rearranged sequences. Of course, it is ROMEO AND JULIET in modern dress and with modern text and racial hatred instead of opposing families. There are some memorable songs that have become standards – "Maria", "Tonight" and "Somewhere" among them. To be enjoyed also is the choreography of Jerome Robbins and the superb opening panoramic shot of the area. A dance extract was included in the 1985 M.G.M. compilation film directed by Jack Haley Jr., *That's Dancing*.

Home movie collectors equipped with an anamorphic projection system can enjoy the opening shot in particular (often truncated in videogram releases) and the film in general as it should be seen – in full widescreen glory – thanks to its issue on 8 mm. by Dieter Kempski of Germany who also issued a trailer in the same format.

The film soundtrack, released in America by Columbia, headed the list of best selling record albums for fifty-four weeks there and remained in the top ten best sellers for nearly two years. This, added to a run of one hundred and fifty-three weeks in the British sales charts, ensured sales of many millions and its permanent availability. The stage cast version also sold well for Columbia and should not be ignored. Bernstein has also recorded the music as a suite and recorded the show with Kiri Te Kanawa and José Carreras as the leads.

Though not without its critics, the box office ('Variety' statistics report American receipts for 1962 as $11,000,000) and awards speak for themselves. It also spawned over the years a number of derivative films about rival gangs of different racial and social backgrounds which owed little to the original inspiration (the 1986 **FIRE WITH FIRE** and **CHINA GIRL** from the following year both fall into this category). The film – though not Shakespeare – also inspired what is considered the first Japanese musical in the Hollywood tradition – *Asphalt Girl*. Made in 1965, Seiji Hiroake and Hiroshi Sakamoto were the leading players. The Israeli *Kazablan* (1971) which Menahem Golan directed has also been noted as a derivative film. Ironically, the story concept was, more-or-less, pre-dated (other than by Shakespeare) by the 1956 French film *Pardonnez Nos Offenses* (directed by Robert Hossein).

Shown as part of the Everybody's Shakespeare International Festival, London, England, 1994.
Shown at the FilmFest München, Germany, 1996, as part of a tribute to Robert Wise, the director, who was in attendance.

Shown at the Valladolid Film Festival Spain, 1986, as part of a short selection of films related to the play.
Academy of Motion Picture Arts and Sciences, U.S.A., 1961: Nomination – Best Screenplay (Based on Material from Another Medium) (Ernest Lehman); Awards – Best Picture, Best Director (Robert Wise), Best Supporting Actor (George Chakiris), Best Supporting Actress (Rita Moreno), Best Cinematography (Color) (Daniel L. Fapp), Best Art/Set Direction (Color) (Boris Levin/Victor Gangelin), Best Sound (Todd-AO/Samuel Goldwyn Sound Dept.), Best Scoring of a Musical Picture (Saul Chaplin, Johnny Green, Sid Ramin, Irwin Kostal), Best Film Editing (Thomas Stanford), Best Costume Design (Color) (Irene Sharaff).
Directors Guild of America, U.S.A., 1961: Director Award (Robert Wise, Jerome Robbins).
'Harvard Lampoon' Movie Worsts Awards, U.S.A., 1961: Kirk Douglas Award To The Worst Actor (Richard Beymer), The Uncrossed Heart (to the least promising young actor of the year) (Richard Beymer), The Merino Award (Rita Moreno for saving WEST SIDE STORY from Natalie Wood and Richard Beymer), The Great Ceremonial Hot Dog (for the worst scenes of cinema history (Richard Beymer singing "Maria"), Worst Duos (Richard Beymer, Natalie Wood)
Hollywood Foreign Press Association Golden Globe Awards, U.S.A., 1961: Best Motion Picture-Musical, Best Supporting Actress (Rita Moreno), Best Supporting Actor (George Chakiris).
'Los Angeles Times' Best of the Sixties Poll, U.S.A., January 1970. Readers' Choice – Best Films – Listed fourth.
National Board of Review Awards, U.S.A., 1961: Listed third.
'New York Times' Ten Best List, U.S.A., 1961: Listed seventh.
New York Critics Awards, U.S.A., 1961 – Best Motion Picture.
Performing Arts Council of the University of South California Most Significant American Films, U.S.A., late 1972: Listed twelfth =.
Writers Guild of America, U.S.A., 1961: Best-Written American Musical (Ernest Lehman).

"...integration of music and story is most perfectly realised: the big solo numbers have the quality of Shakespearean soliloquies and serve the same purpose..." – Thomas Wiseman, 'Cinema'.

"The opening shots of WEST SIDE STORY are as breathtaking as anything ever put on the screen..." – John Springer, 'All Talking! All Singing! All Dancing!'.

"The perfect musical." – 'Guide Akai Vidéo-Cassettes'

LOS TARANTOS
(Spain, 1963)
p.c. *Tecisa*.

d. *Francisco Rovira Beleta.*
l.p. *Sara Lezana (Juana); Daniel Martín (Rafael); Antonio Prieto (Rosendo); Carmen Amaya (Angustias); Carlos Villafranca (Salvador); Margarita Lozano (Isabel); Antonia Singla (Sole); Aurelio Galán (Jero); José Manuel Martín (Curro); Antonio Gades (Mojigongo); Antonio Escudero (Juan); Amapola García (Antonia); Rosario Ortiz (Aurora); Antonio Lavilla (Sancho); Anselmo Batista; Andrés Batista; Antonio Guisa.*
Eastman Color. 92 mins.

Shortly after an affray between members of two rival gypsy families, the Tarantos and the Zorongos, Rafael (Taranto) meets Juana (Zorongo) at a wedding and they fall in love. When they discover their family backgrounds, they try to forget the rivalry. To cut short the relationship Juana's father announces that he has promised her to Curro, one of his deputies. Juana goes in search of Rafael so that they may run away together but Curro discovers their hideaway near the beach and brutally stabs them. Salvador, Rafael's elder brother, takes his revenge on Curro. In the blood of the dead lovers, the two families unite to put past hatred behind them.

Clearly Shakespeare inspired, though based on a play by Alfredo Mañas, this time the story is transposed to a modern gypsy setting with appropriate music and dancing.

Spanish sources list the running time as eighty-four minutes. The British release is noted at eighty-one minutes.

Shown at the Valladolid Film Festival, 1986, as part of a short selection of films related to the play.
Academy of Motion Picture Arts and Sciences, U.S.A, 1963: Nomination – Best Foreign Language Film.
Círculo de Escritores Cinematográficos, Spain, 1963: Best Film, Best Actor (Daniel Martín).
Buenos Aires Film Festival, Argentina, 1964: Prize Winner.
Sindicato Nacional del Espectáculo, Spain, 1963: Third prize for Best Film, Best Supporting Actress (Carmen Amaya).

"...an odd mixture of almost documentary realism and cloying sentimentality...Beleta's direction has some imaginative touches." – 'Monthly Film Bulletin', February, 1967.

TENI ZABYTYKH PREDKOV
(U.S.S.R., 1965)

p.c. *Studio Dovjenko.*
d. *Sergei Paradjanov.*
l.p. *Ivan Mikolajcuk (Ivan); Laria Kadocnikova (Marika); Tatiana Bestaeva (Palagna).*
Sovcolor. 95 mins.

Ivan and Marika are in love despite the hatred between their two families. She dies one day on the way to meet him as he guards his animals. After having brooded over her death, he tries to console himself by marrying Palagna. She is unfaithful with the village sorcerer. Driven on by a suicidal urge, Ivan confronts him and finds again his Marika in death.

"Romeo and Juliet in the Carpathians" is how Jean Tulard describes this in 'Guide Des Films'. Well...maybe. Certainly the beginning and end have similarities to the story.

NO SOMOS NI ROMEO NI JULIETA
(Spain, 1969)

p.c. *Copercines/Exclusivas Floralva.*
d. *Alfonso Paso.*
l.p. *Enriquetta Carballeira; Manuel Tejada; Antonio Martelo; Emilio Gutiérrez Caba; José Luis López Vázquez; Laly Soldevilla; Florinda Chico; Antonio Almoros; Carmen Luján; Emilio Rodríguez; Manuela Rodríguez; Xan das Bolas; Fernando Bilbao; Rocío Paso; Nieves Salcedo; Trinidad Rugero; Luis Rico; Jesús Enguita; José Luis Lizalde; Pedro Fenollar; José María Navarro.*
Eastman Color. 85 mins. Panoramica.

Julita and Roberto are hopelessly in love despite opposition from their families the Caporetos and the Negrescos.

This is a somewhat personal view of the story by the director.

THE SECRET SEX LIVES OF ROMEO AND JULIET
(U.S.A., 1969)

p.c. *Global?*
d. *A.P. Stootsberry.*
l.p. *Forman Shane (Romeo); Diora Carse (Juliet).*
c. Feature.

Sex version of the story and so the title probably says it all!! Surprisingly, this had a showing at the Cannes Film Festival, France, 1969. In his book 'Sex Films', Dutch author Peter Cuupers notes that the film has no compunctions in showing what he describes as "uncovered vulnerable parts". At the time the book was printed (1971) the film had run into censorship problems in Holland, and thus elsewhere probably, and he was sure it would not pass the censorship board there.

"Of the literary content of Shakespeare's famous play, nothing is left in this movie. Despite the feud between the families of Romeo and Juliet, they know enough places for love-making. Finally, they die but in their coffin they merrily continue making love." – 'Video Uit & Thuis Catalogus'.

aka: HET GEHEIME SEKSLEVEN VAN ROMEO EN JULIET

AARON LOVES ANGELA
(U.S.A., 1975)

p.c. *Columbia.*
d. *Gordon Parks Jr.*
l.p. *Kevin Hooks (Aaron); Irene Cara (Angela); Leonard Pinkey; Moses Gunn; Ernestine Jackson; Robert Hooks; José Feliciano.*

c. 99 mins.

In New York's Harlem, black boy loves Puerto Rican girl with obvious problems which include pimps, prostitutes, dope dealers and white racketeers.

The story here is transposed to modern day New York with all its implications. The story does have a happy ending. Feliciano also wrote the music for the film which was available on disc on the Private Stock label.

JAMBON D'ARDENNES
(France/Belgium, 1977)

p.c. *Reggane Films/Lamy Films.*
d. *Benoît Lamy.*
l.p. *Annie Giradot (Patronne); Ann Petersen (La Radoux); Michel Lechat (Hubert); Bonbon (Brigitte); Christian Barbier (Entrepreneur); Nathalie Van de Walle (Colette); Denise Bonmariage (Wies); Dominique Drout (Bruno); Marie-Luce Debounie (Andrée); Alain Soreil (Michel); Donat Bonmariage (Marcel).*

c. 85 mins.

Our hero is aged fifteen, the son of a high-powered mother who owns a hotel. His love works in a chip shop. There is war between the two owners of these establishments – the struggle being for the custom of the tourists. The young couple's love is the talk of the village and an explosion of temperament is inevitable but common sense finally prevails.

In this comedy inspired by the play, a few plates get broken but no blood is shed. The film was made in French.

FINYÉ
(Mali, 1982)

p.c. *Souleymane Cissé.*
d. *Souleymane Cissé.*
l.p. *Fousseyni Sissoko (Bah); Goundo Guisse (Baltrou); Ismaila Sarr (Kansaye); Ismaila Cissé (Seydou); Balla Moussa Keita (Colonel Sangaré); Oumo Diarra (Sangaré's Third Wife); Dioncounda Kone (Bah's Grandmother); Massitan Ballo (Batrou's Mother); Tata Jaye; Yacouba Samabaly; Dunanba Dani Kulibali; Karijigé Layico Tarawelé; Mamadu Tarwelé; Amara Sisé; Yusufu Sisé; Musa Sisé; Salifu Dunbiya; Fanta Kamara.*

c. 105 mins.

Bah is the son of a village elder. His girlfriend, Seydou, is the daughter of a colonel in the army. Both families oppose their relationship and the children rebel, declaring their love when they bathe together.

Seydou passes her examinations but joins a student strike. She is saved from capture by some women who are then arrested. She pleads with the authorities for them and dies in prison. Bah refuses to sign a statement prepared by the authorities and is deported. Riots flare up and the order is given for the release of the students.

Described as "an intelligent revisitation of ROMEO AND JULIET", the film relates the tale as a vigorous criticism of parental authority and political repression. All is set against the background of student unrest at the University of Bamako. The film established the director internationally.

Panafrican Festival, Ouagadougou, Burkina Faso, 1983: First Prize.

aka: THE WIND; DIE ZEIT DES WINDES

NAREKOHME GI MONTEKI I KAPULETI
(Bulgaria, 1984)

p.c. *Sophia Animation Studios.*
d. *Donyo Donev.*
l.p. *Animated characters.*

c. 90 mins.

This, Bulgaria's first feature-length animated film, takes a comic look at the famous tale and adds just a little local flavour.

FIRE WITH FIRE
(U.S.A., 1986)

p.c. *Paramount.*
d. *Duncan Gibbins.*
l.p. *Virginia Madsen (Lisa); Craig Shefter (Joe); Kate Reid (Sister Victoria); Jon Polito (William); Ann Savage (Sister Harriet); Jeffrey Jay Cohen (Mapmaker); Jean Smart (Sister Marie); Tim Russ (Jerry); David Harris (Ben); D. B. Sweeney (Baxter); Evan Mirand (Manuel); William Schilling (Watley); Penelope Sudrow (Stephanie); Franklin Johnston (Old Man); Star-Sheemah Bobatoon (Margo); Kari Wuhrer (Gloria); Smitty Smith (Keyes); Enid Saunders (Old Woman); Birde M. Hale (Arlene); Howard Storey (Police Driver); David Longsworth; Dwight McGee, Gary Chalk (Deputies); Steve J. Wright (Helicopter Pilot); Ian Tracey, Andy Gray (Panthers); Lesley McEwen; Janine Mortil, Robyn Stevan (School Gang); Ken Douglas (Davis).*

Metrocolor. 104 mins.

Joe, an inmate of a reform camp, sees Lisa, a student at a Catholic school. They fall in love. So they can meet, Lisa suggests to the school that it holds, as an act of charity, a dance for the boys at the camp. The dance is duly held and Joe and Lisa make love in the crypt of a cemetary. A guard discovers them and separates them. Joe escapes with Lisa in a stolen car.

They hide out in a log cabin but the forces of law are after them. The cabin is burned to the ground but the lovers escape. They jump from a cliff into the river below and make their getaway.

Something of an exploitation movie, the masked ball from the original is transposed to the convent; the tryst between the two lovers is transferred to a crypt. The director's infatuation with music videos influenced the dance sequence and there is plenty of music to be heard from Prince, Hewie Lewis and the News, Bryan Ferry etc. in this **WEST SIDE STORY** derivative.

"...following ROMEO AND JULIET like a drunk following memorized directions across the Bronx." – Tim Brookes (American film critic).

CHINA GIRL
(U.S.A., 1987)

p.c. *Street Lite/Great American.*
d. *Abel Ferrera.*
l.p. *James Russo (Alberto Monte); Richard Panebianco (Tony Monte); Sari Chang (Tyan-Hwa); David Caruso (Jimmy Mercury); Russell Wong (Yung-Gan); Joey Chin (Tsu- Chin); James Hong (Gung-Tu); Judith Malina (Mrs. Monte); Robert Miano (Perito); Paul Hipp (Nino); Doreen Chan; Randy Sabusawa.*
Du Art Color. 90 mins.

The resiting of a Chinese restaurant to the Italian sector of New York upsets Alberto. His brother, Tony, meets Tyan, a Chinese girl, at a disco in a neutral area. Their dance is broken up by Tyan's brother, Yung. Tony is chased back to his own territory where the Chinese are met by the Italians. The ensuing fight is stopped by the police. Both Tyan and Tony are reprimanded and confined for both sides know that war will only hurt mutual trade. Yung's cousin, the headstrong Chin, determines to exact protection money from the restaurant in the Italian zone. He blows up the restaurant damaging Monte's property and gang war erupts. The two lovers continue to meet secretly. Yung and Chin discover them but are driven off by police before they can act. Chin kills Alberto and, fearful of the results of this, Yung tries to persuade Tyan to leave with him for Hong Kong. She refuses and goes to Tony. The crazy Chin kills them both and he is killed by the Chinese.

Apart from some obvious name references in the roles, the ballroom scene is transposed to a ghetto dance hall and the balcony scene to a fire escape. Though the film is not without some good moments, the dialogue is the antithesis to that of Shakespeare.

"...a blatant mixture of *Romeo and Juliet*, *Mean Streets* and *West Side Story*." – Janet Maslin, film critic, 'New York Times'.

"A moving love story against a background of racial violence." – 'Supersonique VIDEO'.

JULIA'S GEHEIM
(Holland, 1987)

p.c. *Topaz Pictures/NOS.*
d. *Hans Hylkema.*
l.p. *Funda Müjde; Nahit Güvendi; Nigar Cankur; Vedat Gültekin; Yavuz Tuncer; MarcellaMeuleman; Andrea Vos; Casper de Boer; Bruce Gray; Lucien Spee; Winston Linger; Marten-Rijk Tousaint; Sharon Wolff; Maikel Reeder; Ozdemir Suveren; Ceylan Utlu; Mehmet Dag; Ahmet Dayan; Mustafa Lafatan; Kees Groenveld; Will Beets.*
c. 103 mins.

Arzu, daughter of an immigrant Turkish family in Holland, has integrated well into the customs and culture of Holland, so well integrated that she rebels against the marriage that her father has arranged. The conflict between father and daughter is even more emphasized when she has the role of Juliet in her high school's production of ROMEO AND JULIET for she sees the play as a reflection of her own situation.

The story, transposed to modern times, has the added themes of ethnic minorities and guest workers having to meet the different customs of their host country as well as the ever changing ways of youth.

MONTOYAS Y TARANTOS
(Spain, 1988)

p.c. *Comunicacion Visual Creativa.*
d. *Vicente Escrivá.*
l.p. *Cristina Hoyos; Juan Antonio Jiménez; Esperanza Campuzano; Mercedes Sampietro; Sancho Gracia; Queta Claver; José Sancho; Juan Paredes.*
Agfacolor. 103 mins. Panoramica.

Two Andalucian gypsy families, one rich and powerful, the other whose only wealth is in dancing, revive old, bitter hatreds and rivalries. When Manuel Taranto meets the beautiful Ana Montoya the situation becomes explosive as both families reject their pleas of love. The inevitable blood-tinged tale unfolds to its equally inevitable conclusion.

In effect, this is a remake of the 1963 Spanish film directed by Francisco Rovira Beleta though it is generally considered to be inferior to the earlier film. Again, therefore, the story is transposed to a modern Spanish gypsy environment.

Shown at the Judogestveni Festival, Moscow, Russia, 1990, as part of an anthology of Spanish film.
Shown at the Montreal Film Festival, Canada, 1989.
Shown at the Mostra de Valencia/Cinema del Mediterrani, Spain, 1995, as part of a Vicente Escrivá retrospective.
Shown at the Valladolid Film Festival, Spain, 1990.
ACACE, Spain, 1989: Best Music.

aka: LOVE, HATE AND DEATH

CHAPTER XXI – ROMEO AND JULIET

RAMI OG JULIE
(Denmark/France, 1988)

p.c. *Film Cooperativet Danmark in cooperation with C. CosmosC, K-Films Paris, Co-produktionsfonden DR/FI and the Danish Film Institute.*

d. *Erik Clausen.*

l.p. *Sofie Gråbøl (Juliet); Saleh Malek (Rami); Steen Jørgensen (Frank); Mohammad Bakri (Mawan); Kjeld Løfting (Bob); Anne Nøjgaard (Juliet's Mother); Jamal El Khatib (Mohammed); Khaled Ibrahim Alsbeihi (Rami's Brother); Paprika Steen; Peter Belli.*

c. 113 mins.

In a modern concrete suburb of Copenhagen lives a mixture of Danes, political refugees and immigrants divided into two camps. Rami, a Palestinian refugee, meets Juliet while he is trying to escape from a gang of thugs led by Frank. The couple fall in love but Rami has to go to Germany to get his cousin, who has escaped from Beirut, into Denmark. He tries to get a message to Juliet who goes to a party where Frank learns that she loves a "darkie" and he and his gang try to rape her. Meanwhile, Rami and his cousin are discovered and Rami is shot. Juliet, realising her love for Rami, goes to meet him at the airport but it is the terrorist cousin who gets off the airplane.

Racial prejudice replaces family hatred in this modern setting version. The director in his notes acknowledges his debt to "good old" William, but Ch. B. in 'Tous Les Films, 1988' thought it was a long way from Shakespeare. The music is by Tchaikovsky.

aka: RAMI AND JULIET

ROMEO EN JULIA OP DE BROMFIETS
(Holland, 1990)

p.c. *Stichting Jura Filmproducties.*
d.
l.p.
c. Feature.

No further details of this musical, believed to be a ROMEO AND JULIET derivative, are known. The title translates as "Romeo And Juliet On Motor-scooters".

ROMEO / JULIET
(Belgium, 1992)

p.c. *Blue Pearl Film Corp. A Paul Hespel Production.*
d. *Armando Acosta.*
l.p. *John Hurt (La Dame aux Chats); The Street Cats of Verona, Venice and New York. With the voices of: Robert Powell (Romeo); Francesca Annis (Juliet); Ben Kingsley (Capulet); Vanessa Redgrave (Lady Capulet); John Hurt (Mercutio); Victor Spinetti (Tybalt); Maggie Smith (Rozaline); Quentin Crisp (Benvolio); John Haggart (Prince); Theo Cowan (Father Lawrence).*

c. 123 mins. S

Described as a film-concert experience (even though the film has its own soundtrack recorded by the London Symphony Orchestra under the baton of André Previn, the film may have a live orchestra to play the music which is mainly the ballet music to ROMEO AND JULIET by Prokofiev), this is a difficult film to categorise. It is not pure Shakespeare though his words are spoken for the cats; it is not true ballet since it has a spoken text. So, it is placed here in a sort of half-way stage.

Over four hundred hours were shot on video taking more than five thousand hours of editing, selecting and recording. Ninety-nine percent of the film is in slow motion. The finished work was then transferred to film.

The world première of the film was on June 20, 1992, at the Palais des Beaux Arts, Brussels, Belgium. Since then it has been on a world tour of appropriate venues. The title of the film is shown as ROMEO (silhouette of a walking black cat facing right) JULIET.

Shown at the Venice Film Festival, Italy, 1990, where it was well received.

"I have never seen a film like this and will probably never see again. This film is about happiness, love and beauty." – John Hurt.

"It's not simply a film, it's a poem." – Oleg Prokofiev, son of the composer, Sergei Prokofiev.

"It tempts you with beautiful images that take your breath away." – 'Gazet Van Antwerpen'.

"...of indescribable beauty." – 'Kölnische Rundschau'.

THE PUNK AND THE PRINCESS
(G.B., 1993)

p.c. *Videodrome/M2-Feature Film.*
d. *Mike Sarne.*
l.p. *Charlie Creed-Miles (David); Vanessa Hadaway (Rachel); David Shawyer (David's Father); Jess Conrad (Rachel's Father); Peter Miles (Shakespeare); Yolanda Mason; Jacqueline Skarvellis; Alex Mollo; R.J. Bell; Martin Harvey; David Doyle; Helen Gill; Matthew Salkeld; William Sarne.*

c. 96 mins. S

In London's Notting Hill area, an unemployed punk, David, falls in love with the middle class Rachel who is acting in Shakespeare in a pub theatre.

This is a contemporary reworking of the tale. Its British première – a preview, in fact -was on

November 11, 1993 as part of the "Shakespeare On Film" presentation (part of the Everybody's Shakespeare International Festival) at the Barbican Centre, London.

"Mike Sarne...fails to coax convincing performances from his young cast..." – Charles Bacon, 'Film Review 1995/6'.

TROMEO AND JULIET
(U.S.A., 1996)

p.c. *A Lloyd Kaufmann/Michael Herz Production for Troma.*

d. *Lloyd Kaufmann.*

l.p. *Jane Jensen (Juliet Capulet); Will Keenan (Tromeo Que); Maximillian Shaun (Cappy Capulet); Valentine Miele (Murray Martini); Steve Gibbons (London Arbuckle); Steven Blackehart (Benny Que); Sean Gunn (Sammy Capulet); Ness (Debbie Rochon); Patrick Connor (Tyrone Capulet); Flip Brown (Father Laurence); Earl McKoy (Monty Que); Wendy Adams (Ingrid Capulet); Tamara Craig Thomas (Georgie Capulet); Stephen L. Loniewski (Harry); Antonia Lurie (Brittany); Gene Terinoni (Detective Scalus); Garon Peterson (Fu Chang); Jacqueline Tavarez (Rosy); John Fiske (Vic); Manon Kelley (C-D Rom Woman); Joe Fleishaker (Hunk); Tiffany Shepis (Peter); Caroline Smith (Pauline); Brian Fox (Bill Shakespeare); Joseph Anthony (Flavio); Peter James Kelsch (Bluto); Lemmy (Narrator) etc.*

Agfacolor. 104 mins.

The film, within its own terms, follows the story faithfully except for the ending. Tromeo and Juliet kill her father. The reason for the family feud is revealed. Cappy Capulet and Monty Que were business partners in a pornographic film deal. Mrs. Que had an affaire with Cappy and then married him, later bearing Juliet. Tromeo, the result of the affaire, was passed off as Monty Que's son and Monty signed aways his business rights to keep what he thought was his own flesh and blood. Thus Tromeo has married his sister.

The Chorus/Narrator, in a parody of Shakespearean verse, sets the scene in modern Manhattan. Anyone expecting a *WEST SIDE STORY* without music is in for a shock. Monty Que is black and a drunk; Cappy Capulet lusts after Juliet; Juliet's friend (the nurse equivalent) is a much-tattooed lesbian; Father Laurence has a penchant for little boys...to that can be added nipple piercing, decapitation, finger amputation, punks, sex, dope, obscenity and...is there anything offensive left? Well, the end credits, which now seem to last for ever, are really very funny which is more than can be said for the film which is supposedly meant to be so in a sick sort of way. Alas, poor Will!

WILLIAM SHAKESPEARE'S ROMEO AND JULIET
(U.S.A., 1996)

p.c. *Bazmark.*

d. *Baz Luhrmann.*

l.p. *Leonardo DiCaprio (Romeo); Claire Danes (Juliet); John Leguizamo (Tybalt); Brian Dennehy (Montague); Paul Sorvino (Capulet); Diane Venora (Mrs. Capulet); Pete Postlethwaite (Father Laurence); Harold Perrineau (Mercutio); Paul Rudd (Dave Paris); Jesse Bradford (Balthasar); Dash Mihok (Benvolio); Christina Pickles (Caroline); Zak Orth (Gregory); Miriam Margolyes (Nurse); Vondie Curtis-Hall (Captain Prince); Edwina Moore (Anchorwoman); M. Emmett Walsh (Apothecary); Jamie Kennedy (Sampson); Lupita Ochoa (Girl); Gloria Silva (Nun); Carlos Martin Manzo Ortalora (Petruchio); Pedro Altamirano (Peter); Michael Corbett (Rich); Harriet Harris (Susan); Margarita Wynne; Rodrigo Escandon; Carolyn Valero; Paco Morayta; Mario Cimarro; Des'ree; Ismael Iguiarte; Ricardo Barona; Cory Newman; Jorge Abraham; Farnesio de Bernal; Quindon Tarver; Catalina Botello.*

De Luxe Color. 120 mins. S Scope.

Verona Beach, close to Santa Monica, is a focal point for young people. There, Romeo and Juliet meet and fall hopelessly in love. Unfortunately, their respective families are traditional enemies and rivals for control of the area. Violence erupts.This contemporary version of the play from Australian director Luhrmann, met with much success upon initial release in America and, subsequently, elsewhere. The greatly edited dialogue is by the Bard but the setting for the familiar story is today with guns, cars and rock music. The disc of the soundtrack, released by Capitol, was very successful.

Though the film was not without its critics, the general feeling was that it broke new ground in bringing Shakespeare to a wide audience while maintaining the beauty of his words. Much credit has gone to the leading performers and to the director's innovative ideas in ignoring traditionalism yet keeping the verse as a part of the whole rather than as a dominant *raison d'être*. He clearly saw the need to identify with the present.

Academy of Motion Picture Arts and Sciences, U.S.A., 1996: Nomination – Best Art/Set Direction (Catherine Martin, Brigitte Broch).

Berlin Film Festival, Germany, 1997: Best Actor (Leonardo DiCaprio); Alfred Bauer Prize for Innovation in Direction (Baz Luhrmann); Public Prize.

British Academy of Film and Television Arts, G.B., 1997: David Lean Award for Best Direction (Baz Luhrmann); Best Adapted Screenplay (Craig Pearce,

Baz Luhrmann); Best Production Design (Catherine Martin); Anthony Asquith Award for Best Music (Nellee Hooper, Craig Armstrong, Marius de Vries). Internationaler Preis für Film-und Medienmusik, Germany, 1997 – Special Prize to The Cardigans and the song "Lovefool" as featured in and in relation to the film.
London Film Critics' Awards, G.B., 1998: Best Actress (Clare Danes).

"In its fashion...it is a faithful adaptation...the liberties taken with the text ultimately holds it nearer to the original spirit of the book." – 'Fotogramas', March, 1997.

"It's got action, spectacle and romance and it aims to entertain." – José Arroyo, 'Sight and Sound'.

✢ ✢ ✢ ✢ ✢

ROMÉO ET JULIETTE
(France, 1900)

p.c. *Phono Cinéma Théâtre.*
d. *Clément Maurice.*
l.p. *Emilio Cossira (Romeo).*
b.w. 1 reel?

Gounod's opera provided the basis for this short extract. The sound was by means of a synchronized phonographic system. The aria was probably "Ah! L'élève le Soleil".

ROMEO UND JULIA
(Germany, 1909)

p.c. *Deutsche Vitascope.*
d.
l.p. *Madame Luisa Tetrazzini (Julia).*
b.w. 203 ft. (62 m.)

Stated as being a sound film (synchronised disc system), this was an aria from the opera by Gounod performed by a diva of the era.

ROMEO E GIULIETTA
(G.B., 1927?)

p.c. *De Forest Phonofilms.*
d.
l.p. *Otakar Marak (Romeo); Mary Cavanova (Juliet).*
b.w. 543 ft. (166 m.)

This features a song from the opera ROMEO AND JULIET by Gounod.

One of a number of short sound films produced in England by this company, it is of six minutes duration. Its production date is uncertain.

ROMEO I DZULETTA
(U.S.S.R., 1954)

p.c. *Mosfilm.*
d. *Lev Arnshtam, Leonid Lavrovsky.*
l.p. *Galina Ulanova (Juliet); Yuri Zhdanov (Romeo); Sergei Koren (Mercutio); A. Lapauri*

(Paris); Alexei Yermolayev (Tybalt); A. Radunski (Capulet); V. Kidryushov (Benvolio); L. Loschilin (Friar Lawrence); S. Uvarov (Montague).Unknown orchestra (conductor: G. Rozhdestvensky).
Sovcolor. 94 mins.

Ballet version based on the Shakespearean play with the omission of one or two scenes. Prokofiev's score has been edited and paraphrased in this adaptation for the Bolshoi Ballet which was restaged for the camera.

Shown as part of the Everybody's Shakespeare International Festival, London, England, 1994.
Shown at the Shakespeare Film Festival, Wiesbaden, W. Germany, 1964.
Cannes Film Festival, France, 1955: Special Prize for the transposition of ballet to the screen and the interpretation by Ulanova.
International Film Festival of Classical, National and Modern Dance Expression, U.S.S.R., 1957: First Prize in Clasical Ballet Class.

ROMEO AND JULIET
(G.B., 1966)

p.c. *Poetic Films. A Paul Czinner Production.*
d. *Paul Czinner.*
l.p. *Margot Fonteyn (Juliet); Rudolf Nureyev (Romeo); David Blair (Mercutio); Desmond Doyle (Tybalt); Anthony Dowell (Benvolio); David Rencher (Paris); Julia Farron (Lady Capulet); Michael Soames (Lord Capulet); Georgina Parkinson (Rosaline); Gerd Larsen (Nurse); Leslie Edwards (Escalus); Betty Kavanagh (Lady Montague); Ronald Hind (Friar Lawrence); Christopher Newton (Lord Montague); Ann Jenner; Diane Horsham; Carol Hill; Ann Howard; Margaret Lyons; Jennifer Penney; Deanne Bergsma; Monica Mason; Carole Needham; Keith Rosson; Robert Mead; Lambert Cox; Kenneth Mason; Ian Hamilton; Laurence Ruffell; Artists of The Royal Ballet.Orchestra of The Royal Opera House (conductor: John Lanchberry).*
Eastman Color. 126 mins.

Prokofiev's music is the music again for this ballet version. Here a stage performance was recreated in a studio and filmed with a number of cameras and the results edited together. Ballet lovers will appreciate the performances by the leading dancers and by those of some of the supporting dancers.

Shown as part of the Everybody's Shakespeare International Festival, London, England, 1994.

ROMÉO ET JULIETTE
(France/Germany, 1992)

p.c. *Opéra de Lyon/RM Arts/Société Française de Production/La Sept/RTP/Centre Nationale de la Cinématographie/Ministère de la Culture/ Bayerisch Rundfunk.*
d. *Alexandre Tarta.*

l.p. *Pascale Doye (Juliet); Nicolaus Dufloux (Romeo); Hacene Bahiri (Mercutio); Stanislas Wiesniewski (Father Lawrence); Pierre Advokatoff (Tybalt); Kasumi Sanada, Jocelyne Mocogni (Nurses), Philippe Lormeau (Benvolio); Elizabeth Amiel; Nathalie Delassis; Christelle Dorier; Dominique Laine; Daniele Pater; Chantal Requena; Thierry Allard; Jean-Pascal Cottalorda; Boncif Hamadagini and other members of the Ballet de Opéra Lyon.Orchestre de Opéra Lyon (conductor: Kent Nagano).*
c. 85 mins. WS.

A modern (in sets, effects, settings and costume) version of the ballet by Prokofiev under the auspices of choreographer Angelin Preljocaj, this is very different from the usual concept. Set in an imaginary town, it emphasises the difficult points of the social differences between the rich and the poor.

Logic dictates that this was intended for television primarily. However, the production partnership and its format may also indicate its availability beyond the home screen.

aka: ROMEO UND JULIA

✣ ✣ ✣ ✣ ✣

Unquestionably one of the most performed and most popular of the Bard's plays, it surely ranks among the greatest love stories of all time. Certainly, as has been shown, the ill-fated lovers theme has been a popular one in the cinema. As early as 1910 Germany took the young love theme to the beach in the Messter production *Romeo und Juliet am Strand.*

Popular, too, has been the use of the names, precisely or in resemblance. Indeed the name "Romeo" is used in the English language to mean a lover, rather like "Casanova" but with less licentious connotations. Spain used the names but changed the story to one of a man accusing his wife of infidelity so that he could pursue his own in *Juliet Engaña A Romeo* (1964, directed by José M. Zabalza). Another Spanish film clearly denied by the negatives in the title (*No Somos Ni Romeo Ni Julieta* – directed by Alfonso Paso in 1970) any direct influence of the play yet still used two lovers from rival families as the plot. The couple were on screen briefly and incidentally in Blake Edwards' comedy *Skin Deep* from 1989 and that was surely but one of many similar inconsequential appearances.

As important as young love may be, what separates this love story from others is the all-important other theme of hatred which endeavours to thwart and destroy the love of the two young people. In *Two's Company* (G.B., 1936, directed by Tim Whelen) it was British aristocracy versus American wealth that provided the barrier for the lovers. The situation was more depressing in *Romeo, Julie A Tma* (Czechoslovakia, 1959, directed by Jiri Weiss with

Ivan Mistrik and Dana Smatna). Described by Ado Kyrou in 'Amour, Erotisme Et Cinema' as a "...marvelous love song in the setting of Jewish persecution.", this neatly sums up the theme of thwarted love, in this case by the Nazis, with the Juliet (a Jewish girl) making the ultimate sacrifice to save her Romeo. Indeed, this excellent film almost merits an entry of its own. The theme of opposing factions frustrating lovers was echoed in the Danish/Swedish/Icelandic co-production of 1967 Den Röde Kappel (directed by Gabriel Axel) but the action was set in Viking times. Nordic, too, but far more modern and set in the world of pop music, the Svensk production *Ola and Julia* (directed by Jan Halldoff) with Monika Ekman and Ola Hakansson claimed to be inspired by the famous tale but had only a slight resemblance to it.

With a Western setting ("Spaghetti Western", to be precise), there was more than a hint of the story in *Dove Si Spara di Pi* (Italy/Spain, 1967), with Peter Lee Lawrence and Cristina Galb as the lovers. One of the families was indicatively named Mounter and the heroine was called, as might be expected, Juliet.

Romanoff And Juliet (U.S.A., 1961) was directed by Peter Ustinov from his own play. The play on the names of the title is obvious and in this the young lovers are from Russia and America. Their love problems are resolved by the tiny country of Concordia whose vote at the United Nations both countries seek.

Twenty years later, the young lovers theme was revamped in Franco Zeffirelli's *Endless Love* made in America. The film was of the era and thus more liberated. Still, people found the film as endless as the title.

Of course, the theme has, as has already been seen, its variations. The most common is the happy ending which almost seems to destroy the meaning of the play. The moral of which must surely be obvious. Why interfere with a marvellous work that has proven its worth over the centuries? It is also rather a puzzle that there has been no true, complete version of the play on film for thirty years.

For other scenes from this play see **CHAPTER XXX ALL THE WORLD'S A STAGE:** ALGY GOES ON STAGE (1910); BUMPTIOUS AS ROMEO (1911); NICHOLAS NICKLEBY (1912); LIZA ON THE STAGE (1915); PORTRET DORIANA GREYA (1916); DAVID GARRICK (1916); A FOOTLIGHT FLAME (1917); THE SENTIMENTAL BLOKE (1919); KEAN (1922); THE TROUPER (1922); DAS ALTE GESETZ (1923); THE PERFECT FLAPPER (1924); TRIUMPH (1924); BROMO AND JULIET (1926); BLUEBEARD'S SEVEN WIVES (1926); WIE EINST IM MAI (1926); CURED HAMS (1927?); DRAMA DELUXE (1927); THE HOLLYWOOD REVUE (1929); GIVE US THIS

NIGHT (1936); IT'S LOVE I'M AFTER (1937); THE GOLDWYN FOLLIES (1938); KEAN (1940); BUCK PRIVATES COME HOME (1947); NICHOLAS NICKLEBY (1947); CARNAVAL NO FOGO (1949); THE MISADVENTURES OF BUSTER KEATON (1951); GALA FESTIVAL (1952); LAS TRES ALEGRES COMADRES (1952); PRINCE OF PLAYERS (1954); MÄDCHEN IN UNIFORM (1958); MARJORIE MORNINGSTAR (1958); SERGEI PROKOFIEV (1958); STAGE STRUCK (1958); CARRY ON TEACHER (1959); GYALOG A MENNY-ORSZÁGBA (1959); HOLLYWOOD AND THE STARS (1963)*; MAYA PLISTESKAYA (1964); PANIC BUTTON (1964); SHAKESPEARE WALLAH (1965); EL ABOMINABLE HOMBRE DE LA COSTA DEL SOL (1969); THE TURNING POINT (1977); FONTEYN AND NUREYEV – A BALLET LEGEND (1985); MISHIMA: Λ LIFE IN FOUR CHAPTERS (1985); RENDEZ-VOUS (1985); ANNA – DER FILM (1988); OGNENNYI ANGEL (1991) and SWAN SONG (1993) and **CHAPTER XXXII THE IMMORTAL BARD**: IMMORTAL GENTLEMAN (1935); SHAKESPEARE IN LOVE (1998); EVE'S FILM REVIEW (1925); ONE DAY IN SOVIET RUSSIA (1941); SOME HIGHLIGHTS OF MONTY'S MOSCOW VISIT (1947); WILLIAM SHAKESPEARE – BACKGROUND FOR HIS WORKS (1950); SHAKESPEARE'S THEATER (1954); WILLIAM SHAKESPEARE (1955); ROMEO AND JULIET (1963); FAIR ADVENTURE SERIES (1964); EXPLORATIONS IN SHAKESPEARE (1965); MASKS AND FACES (1969)*; SHAKESPEARE: MIRROR TO A MAN (1970?); THE WORLD OF WILLIAM SHAKESPEARE (1978); and ROMEO UND JULIA ODER LIEBE, MORD UND TOTSLAG (1979?)*.

*Denotes film extract.

CHAPTER XXII
THE TAMING OF THE SHREW

Dramatis Personæ:

Introduction:-
A Lord, later posing as a servant
Christopher Sly
Bartholomew – page to the Lord, posing as Sly's wife
A company of strolling players
Huntsmen and Servants to the Lord
Hostess of a tavern

Play proper:-
Baptista Minola – rich gentleman of Padua
Katharine (Kate) – his daughter, a shrew*
Bianca – his other daughter

Petruchio – suitor to Kate
Grumio – Petruchio's servant
Curtis – Petruchio's servant

Lucentio – in love with Bianca, later posing as Cambio
Vicentio – his father
Tranio – Lucentio's servant, later posing as Lucentio
Biondello – Lucentio's page

Gremio – a pantaloon, suitor to Bianca
Hortensio – a suitor to Bianca, later posing as Litio
A Pedant – later posing as Vicentio
A Tailor, a Haberdasher, a Widow Servants to Baptista, Petruchio, Lucentio

* The name has a variety of spellings in English, Katherine and Catherine being two of them.

In Padua lives Baptista, a rich gentleman who has two daughters, the fair, gentle Bianca and her elder sister, Katharine. Now Katharine is also attractive but with a foul temper. Her father will not consent to give Bianca's hand to any of her many suitors until Katharine, known as the Shrew, is married.

The boisterous, happy Petruchio comes to Padua seeking a wife. Hearing about Katharine he sets out to tame her and make her his wife. So he approaches her father for permission to woo her. Baptista has his doubts since even at that moment Katharine's music teacher is feeling the fierceness of her temper. Petruchio is blunt and asks what dowry Baptista will provide. Baptista, sensing his resolve, agrees the sum of twenty thousand crowns and half of his estate upon his death and the bargain is sealed.

Petruchio sets out on his plan countering Katharine's every angry word and obnoxious temperament with an opposite response of sweetness and peace. Though Katharine, of course, angrily denies it, Petruchio tells her father that they will wed on the next Sunday.

The wedding day arrives and bride waits angrily at the church for Petruchio who arrives late, without any of the finery promised and meanly dressed. He cannot be persuaded to change his attire saying that she is marrying the man not the clothes. As the ceremony proceeds, Petruchio acts most coarsely even hitting the priest. Even Katharine trembles in fear. After the ceremony, he calls for wine in the church and throws some at the sexton and everyone thinks it is a very mad marriage.

To the amazement of the guests, Petruchio does not go the sumptuous feast provided by Baptista but simply carries off his bride on a miserable horse. On the journey, he curses at the horse if it stumbles and displays bad temper.

After a tortuous journey, they arrive at Petruchio's home. Katharine gets nothing to eat as her husband finds fault with everything and throws the food at the servants. He even complains about the bed.

The following day, though he speaks sweetly to her, his fault-finding denies her food and her attempts to induce the servants to bring her food secretly fail as they will not disobey their master. She muses sadly over her husband's attitude and wonders if he married her to starve her. When he brings her a small portion of food, she rejects it out of anger. He signals it to be taken away but she asks that it be left. Petruchio points out that even a small service requires thanks. She complies and thus shows the first sign of mellowing. She is rewarded by being able to eat.

Petruchio declares that they will dress up and go to see her father but when the haberdasher brings in a cap, he is castigated for his work though Katharine says she will wear it. He tells her she can have one like it when she is a gentle person. Katharine, her spirit refurbished a little by the food, speaks out demanding the cap. He pretends to misunderstand and pretends that he thinks that she is asking to see the gown made for her. Again he attacks the workmanship and denies her it though he quietly rewards the makers for their trouble and his odd behaviour.

He tells Katharine that they will go to her father in the poor clothes they have and leave to be there in time for dinner. She dares to argue about the time with him but he wants her so subdued that she will not even argue about this. Only at this stage will he consent to take her to her father.

As they journey to her father, she dare not contradict her husband even when he makes the most ridiculous statements. Along the way they meet an old man whom Petruchio addresses as a fair young maid and insists that Katharine embrace him. And so she does but when she addresses him as though he were a young girl, Petruchio asks her if she is mad. She begs the man's pardon blaming the sun in her eyes for her mistake. The old man exclaims that they are a strange couple and adds that he is going to Padua to see his son. Petruchio recognises him as Vincentio, the father of Lucentio, who is to marry Katharine's sister, Bianca. He is happy that his son has made such a fortunate match. They then journey together to Padua.

At the wedding feast, which also includes another married couple, Hortensio and his bride, sly jests are made at Petruchio for his choice of bride. He bears them all well but when Baptista also joins in, it is too much for Petruchio and he suggests a wager. He says that each should call for his wife and the first one to come wins for the relevant husband. Confident, the other two agree on the wager of twenty crowns and, in fact, raise it to a hundred crowns.

Lucentio sends for Bianca but, to Petruchio's amusement, she says she is busy. Petruchio says they should entreat their wives to come which Hortensio does. But his wife declines thinking he has some prank in mind and bids him come to her. Then, to his fellows' amazement, Petruchio sends the servant to command his wife's presence. They are shocked when Katharine appears and, when, in answer to Petruchio's enquiry, she sees the other two are sitting by the fire, she meekly obeys his command to fetch them.

When the women appear, Baptista adds more money to the wager at the sight of the changed Katharine. Petruchio is not done. He makes more demands on Katharine to which she meekly complies. The other two women are not so subdued and voice their feelings where upon Petruchio commands Katharine to tell them what a wife's duties are to her lord and master. Now Katharine is again famous in Padua though not as a shrewish wife but as duteous and obedient one.

Note: The basic situation for this play seems to have been suggested by "A Merry Jest Of A Shrew And Curst Wife Lapped In Morel's Skin For Her Good Behaviour", an anonymous ballad dating from about 1550. This is not commonly thought of as the source because Shakespeare does not follow the violent path of the ballad, however, resorting to the more humanist approach as set out in 'A Merry Dialogue Declaring The Properties Of Shrewd Shrews And

Honest Wives' (Erasmus) and 'The Office And Duty Of An Husband' (Vives). In fact, there seems to be no single source but rather a number of fairly contemporary works and some from earlier times. There are those who even suggest a lost original as the source and, to complicate matters, an anonymous 'The Taming Of A Shrew' was printed in 1594 and thought to be by Shakespeare (an idea since discredited). The date of writing also is difficult to place. Various performances and publications sometimes add confusion between the work proper and the above-mentioned anonymous work but, in summary, 1593 seems the most probable date.

✤ ✤ ✤ ✤ ✤

LA BISBETICA DOMATA
(Italy, 1908)

p.c. *Società Italiana Pineschi.*
d. *Lamberto and Azeglio Pineschi.*
l.p.
b.w. *614 ft. (187 m.) Sil.*

Details of this early Italian version are unknown.

THE TAMING OF THE SHREW
(U.S.A., 1908)

p.c. *American Mutoscope and Biograph Company.*
d. *David Wark Griffith.*
l.p. *Florence Lawrence (Katherine); Arthur Johnson (Petruchio); Linda Arvidson; Charles Inslee; George Gebhardt; Harry Solter; William J. Butler; Guy Hedland; Wilfred Lucas.*
b.w. *1048 ft. (319 m.) Sil.*

An edited version in ten sequences, this maintained the essence of the full story even if there are some strange anachronisms. The film, if the surviving piece is any guide, provides an insight into the genius that was to evolve in Griffith and a delight in Miss Lawrence.

"...one of the snappiest, funniest films of the kind ever made...only the stirring, interesting portions of the play are depicted; at the same time the story is clearly, though concisely told." – promotional material from 'Biograph Bulletin', 1908.

LA MÉGÈRE APPRIVOISÉE
(France 1911)

p.c. *Éclipse.*
d. *Henri Desfontaines.*
l.p. *Cécile Didier (Katherine); Romuald Joubé (Petruchio); Trouhanova; Yvonne Barjac; Denis d'Inès; Jean Hervé.*
b.w. *1076 ft. (328 m.) Sil.*

One source notes Clément Maurice as director but Desfontaines is generally quoted. As the film is believed lost, then the matter is open to speculation. At the time it was noted as being a somewhat simplified interpretation in ten settings.

THE TAMING OF THE SHREW
(G.B., 1911)

p.c. *Cooperative Cinematograph Co.*
d. *Frank R. Benson.*
l.p. *Frank R. Benson (Petruchio); Constance Benson (Katherine).*
b.w. *1120 ft. (341 m.) Sil.*

Film record taken from the Stratford Memorial Theatre production by the F. R. Benson Company. Will Barker is noted by some sources as director.

No copies of this exist.

LA BISBETICA DOMATA
(Italy, 1913)

p.c. *Società Anonima Ambrosio.*
d. *Arrigo Frusta.*
l.p. *Gigetta Morano (Katherine); Eleuterio Rodolfi (Petruchio).*
b.w. *1982 ft. (604 m.) Sil.*

It is noted by some that Ambrosio may have supervised the directing of the film which was considered at the time to be of good quality. Some sources put the film longer at 2201 ft. (671 m.).

aka: LA REVÊCHE APPRIVOISÉE (French release at 1637 ft. – 499 m.)

THE TAMING OF THE SHREW
(G.B., 1915)

p.c. *British and Colonial Kinematograph Company – Voxograph.*
d. *Arthur Backner.*
l.p. *Arthur Backner (Petruchio); Constance Backner (Katherine).*
b.w. *2000 ft. (610 m.) Sil. (see text).*

The wooing scene is featured here.

Using the Voxograph system, the action was synchronised to off-stage reciters. Every effort was made to keep the lips in correct movement but the results were said to be disappointing. Understandably so if actors had to move quickly to the other side of the screen in scene changes.

THE TAMING OF THE SHREW
(G.B., 1923)

p.c. *British and Colonial Kinematograph Company.*
d. *Edwin J. Collins.*
l.p. *Lauderdale Maitland (Petruchio); Dacia Deane (Katherina); Cynthia Murtagh (Bianca); M. Gray Murray (Baptista); Somers Bellamy (Gremio); Roy Beard (Lucentio).*
b.w. *2022 ft. (616 m.) Sil.*

Number 2 in the series *Gems Of Literature*, this condensation fixes its attention on the wooing of Katherina by Petruchio using substantial amounts of the original text in the inter-titles. The Bianca sub-plot is all but excised.

"The action is sensibly put over...and the performances are adequate." – Luke MacKernan, Olwen Terris, 'Walking Shadows'.

THE TAMING OF THE SHREW
(U.S.A., 1929)

p.c. *Pickford Corp./ Elton Corp. for United Artists.*
d. *Sam Taylor.*
l.p. *Mary Pickford (Katherine); Douglas Fairbanks (Petruchio); Edwin Maxwell (Baptista); Joseph Cawthorn (Gremio); Clyde Cook (Grumio); Dorothy Jordan (Bianca); Geoffrey Wardwell (Hortensio).*
b.w. *73 mins.*

A very much shortened version of the play, the director suffered greatly at the time for his apparent impudence with the credit that read "additional dialogue by Sam Taylor" (apparently this was a myth which Mary Pickford later tried to dispel). He was, however, obviously aiming for a commercial audience and the early days of the talkies must have allowed some licence. This was the only film that the then Mr. and Mrs. Fairbanks made together. Personal problems were evident and the marriage was on the decline and it was not the best role for Douglas Fairbanks. He apparently was being quite cruel to his wife at the time and was less than professional by failing to learn his lines, was hypercritical and often arrived late. The film did have the benefit of William Cameron Menzies and Laurence Irving in charge of the décor. Both the critics and the public seemed to like it (though some sources say to the contrary) and it made over $1,000,000 profit.

The film was restored, new music and effects added, and prepared for widescreen presentation by Matty Kemp in 1966. This re-release was edited by seven minutes and the quality of the sound which was originally on discs was improved by modern techniques. The original was also released in silent format with inter-titles which may account for the variation in running time given by different sources.

Shown as part of the Everybody's Shakespeare International Festival, London, England, 1994.
Shown at the Shakespeare Film Festival, Wiesbaden, W. Germany, 1964.

'New York Times', U.S.A., Annual Ten Best, 1929: Listed fifth.

"It was a superb piece of showmanship. The choice of a Shakespearean play was astute, for it meant that the dialogue was free from criticism" – Paul Rotha, 'The Film Till Now'.

aka: LA FIERECILLA DOMADA; DER WILDERSPENSTIGEN ZÄHMUNG

HATHILI DULHAN
(India, 1932)

p.c. *Madan Theatre.*

d. *Jeejeebhoy F. Madan.*
l.p. *Abbas; Laxmi; Patience Cooper; Muktan Beguni; Shahia; Leela.*
b.w. Feature.

This version of the play in Hindi was another Shakespearean effort from the pioneer Madan. Anglo-Indian actress Patience Cooper was a consistent member of his company and was among the earliest of female film stars in India.

aka: THE TAMING OF THE SHREW

BAAP RE BAAP
(India, 1955)

p.c. *Kardar Productions.*
d. *Abdul Raschid Kardar.*
l.p. *Kishore Kumar; Chand Usmani; Smriti Biswas; Jayant; Ulhas Banerjee; Maruti; Leela Mishra,*
b.w. Feature.

This Hindi version of the play was from a noted Indian director The cast comprised a number of popular, reliable local thespians.

UKPOSCHENIE STROPTIVOY
(U.S.S.R., 1960)

p.c. *Mosfilm.*
d. *Sergei Kosolov.*
l.p. *Andrei Popov (Petruchio); Ludmila Kassatkina (Katherine); Olga Krassina (Bianca); Vladimir Blagoobrasov (Baptista); Mark Perzovski (Hortensio); Antoni Kleodurski; Vladimir Seldin (Lucentio).*
b.w. 92 mins.

Though listed as a television film, there is reason to believe that it was also released theatrically in its homeland. It was a record of a theatre performance directed by Alexei Popov.

THE TAMING OF THE SHREW
(U.S.A./Italy, 1966)

p.c. *Royal Films Int./F.A.I.*
d. *Franco Zeffirelli.*
l.p. *Richard Burton (Petruchio); Elizabeth Taylor (Katherina); Cyril Cusack (Grumio); Michael Hordern (Baptista); Michael York (Lucentio); Alfred Lynch (Tranio); Victor Spinetti (Hortensio); Natasha Pyne (Bianca); Alan Webb (Gremio); Giancarlo Cobelli (Priest); Mark Dignam (Vincentio); Roy Holder (Biondello); Gianni Magni (Curtis); Lino Capolicchio (Gregory); Alberto Bonucci (Nathaniel); Roberto Antonelli (Philip); Anthony Gardner; Ken Parry; Bice Valori.*
Technicolor. 126 mins. Panavision.

If the 1929 version presented the film world's couple of the era, then this version did so for the film world's couple of the 1960s. Again the play has been rather cut and mauled and even has a song borrowed from TWELFTH NIGHT though the scriptwriters do acknowledge their source "without whom they would have been lost for words". With much of the sub-plot excised and the hero portrayed as a heavy drinker, purists found much to offend. Perhaps they should have not looked so deeply but accepted the film for what it was – self indulgent fun for the Burtons. It is this that carried the film along.

Nino Rota, famous for his music for many Fellini films, was engaged for the score. One of the themes is featured on the Cam record release called "Nino Rota Movies" with Carlo Savina conducting the orchestra.

The film was chosen for the British Royal Film Performance in 1967. There are variations in running times of a few minutes between the versions shown around the world.

Piccolo Films of West Germany issued a well-packaged, edited two-reel version for collectors on 8 mm. with dialogue in, naturally, German.

Academy of Motion Picture Arts and Sciences, U.S.A., 1967: Nomination – Best Costume Design (Irene Sharaff, Danilo Donati).
Shown as part of the Everybody's Shakespeare International Festival, London, England, 1994.
Mario Gromo Trophy, Italy, 1966/7.

"...there's an engaging vitality about it all..." – Angela and Elkan Allan, 'The Sunday Times Guide To Movies On Television'.

"...definitely not for purists...it was...a good-looking, fun-filled, over-the-top romp in which its two super-stars were clearly having a great time of it." – Clive Hirschhorn, 'The Columbia Story'.

aka: LA MÉGÈRE APPRIVOISÉE; LA MUJER INDOMABLE; DER WIDERSPENSTIGEN ZÄMUNG; LA BISBETICA DOMATA; HET TEMMEN VAN DE FEEKS

The following film contains scenes from the film and it seems logical to note it here:
MAN AND WOMAN
(U.S.A., 1972)

p.c. *Learning Corporation of America (of this edited version).*
d. *Franco Zeffirelli (of the original film).*
l.p. *Elizabeth Taylor (Katherine); Richard Burton (Petruchio). Narrator: Orson Welles.*
Technicolor. 33 mins.

Using scenes from the film, this was issued as an edited version in the series *Great Themes In Literature*. The theme here was the battle of the sexes and the Shakespearean view is compared with the views of Henrik Ibsen, Edward Albee and Tennessee Williams on the subject. Educational outlets were the obvious target of this 16 mm. release.

THE TAMING OF THE SHREW
(G.B., 1974)

p.c. *Seabourne Enterprises/Anvil Films.*

136

d. *Peter Seabourne.*
l.p. *Madeline Blakeney (Kate); David Suchet (Petruchio); Roy Marsden (Hortensio); Peter Kelly (Grumio).*
c. 13 mins.

Act I, Scene 2 and Act II, Scene 1 are the extracts featured in this short which opens with a view of an Elizabethan stage.

✤ ✤ ✤ ✤ ✤

WHEN TWO HEARTS ARE ONE
(U.S.A., 1911)

p.c. *Kalem.*
d.
l.p. *Sidney Drew.*
b.w. 1 reel? Sil.

A wife insists on taking her dog on honeymoon. Her husband rebels.

Apparently the play was somewhat paralleled in this comedy which was highly praised at the time.

THE IRON STRAIN
(U.S.A., 1915)

p.c. *Triangle.*
d. *Reginald Barker.*
l.p. *Dustin Farnum; Louise Glaum; Charles K. French.*
b.w. 4 reels. Sil.

The spoilt daughter of a rich man displays her temper. On a trip to Alaska she sees an apparently wild man who falls in love with her. She is kidnapped, married forcibly and gradually tamed. When she returns home it is with her husband and child.

Apparently the taming of the heroine follows closely the method set out by Shakespeare.

aka: A MODERN TAMING OF THE SHREW

IMPOSSIBLE CATHERINE
(U.S.A., 1919)

p.c. *Virginia Pearson.*
d. *John B. O'Brien.*
l.p. *Virginia Pearson (Catherine Kimberly); J. H. Gilmour (Grant Kimberly); William B. Davidson (John Henry Jackson); Ed Roseman (Rosky); James Hill (Kewpie); John Walker (Herbert Drake); Mabel McQuade (Dorothy Kimberly); Sheldon Lewis (White Cloud).*
b.w. 5 reels. Sil.

The unruly daughter of a multimillionaire meets a rich young man who drags her off to his lumber camp. There he forces her to act like a normal woman. He is hurt in a fight when he is protecting her honour. She realises how silly she has been and falls in love with him.

'Motion Picture Guide' refers to this as a modern version with some justification according to the synopsis. The source is also recognised by the name of the principal character.

KOLTHIESELS TÖCHTER
(Germany, 1919/20)

p.c. *Messter/Ufa.*
d. *Ernst Lubitsch.*
l.p. *Henny Porten (Gretel/Liesel); Emil Jannings (Peer); Jacob Tiedtke (Mathias Kölhiesel); Gustav von Wangenheim (Paul); Willi Prager; Ernst Lubitsch.*
b.w. 3703 ft. (1129 m.) Sil.

Bucolic humour about two sisters, one sweet and charming, the other shrewish.

Taken in part from the play and set in Bavaria, Germany, the film owed much of its success to the presence of Henny Porten who played both the sisters. Since the film is not essentially Shakespearean (it is based on a farce by Hans Kräly), only brief details of the various remakes are noted:

Germany, 1930:
p.c. *Nero-Film/Henny Porten-Filmproduktion.*
d. *Hans Behrendt.*
l.p. *Henny Porten, Fritz Kampers, Leo Peukert, Heinz Leo Fischer.*
b.w. 2486 m.

Germany, 1943:
p.c. *Tobis.*
d. *Kurt Hoffmann.*
l.p. *Heli Finkenzeller, Eduard Köck, Oscar Sima, Erika von Thellmann.*
b.w. 2466 m.

W. Germany, 1955:
p.c.
d. *Géza von Bolvary.*
l.p. *Doris Kirchner. With title: Ja, Ja Die Liebe In Tirol. No further details known.*

W. Germany, 1962:
p.c.
d. *Axel von Ambesser.*
l.p. *Liselotte Pulver, Heinrich Gretler, Helmut Schmidt, Dietmar Schönherr.*
c. 93 mins.

DARING YOUTH
(U.S.A., 1923)

p.c. *Principal Pictures.*
d. *William Beaudine.*
l.p. *Bebe Daniels (Anita); Norman Kerry (John); Lee Moran (Arthur); Lillian Langdon (Mrs. Allen); George Pearce (Mr. Allen); Arthur Hoyt (Winston).*
b.w. 6 reels Sil.

Sources note this as being a modern adaptation of the play.

THE UNTAMED LADY
(U.S.A., 1926)

p.c. Paramount.
d. Frank Tuttle.
l.p. Gloria Swanson; Lawrence Gray; Joseph Smiley.
b.w. (?) mins. Sil.

In this variation on the theme, a hot tempered society girl is tamed by a yachtsman during a sea trip on his boat.

YOU MADE ME LOVE YOU
(G.B., 1933)

p.c. British International Pictures.
d. Monty Banks.
l.p. Stanley Lupino (Tom); Thelma Todd (Pamela); John Loder (Harry); James Carew (Oliver); Gerald Rawlinson (Jerry); Charles Mortimer (Mr. Daly); Arthur Rigby Jr. (Brother); Charlotte Parry (Mother); Hugh Wright (Father); Syd Crossley (Bleak); Monty Banks (Taxi Driver).
b.w. 70 mins.

Tom, a songwriter, sees a girl in a traffic jam and writes a song about her. He visits the girl, Pamela, who is spoilt and rich. Thanks to a trick by her father, they end up married and Tom then starts to tame his new wife. Her fury gradually subsides and she begins to fall in love with him but is only tamed when he promises divorce.

Typical, noisy, British musical of the era, that puts the story into a then modern setting.

SECOND BEST BED
(G.B., 1936)

p.c. Capitol Productions.
d. Tom Walls.
l.p. Tom Walls (Victor); Jane Baxter (Patricia); Greta Gynt (Yvonne); Carl Jaffe (George); Veronica Rose (Jenny); Edward Lexy (Murdoch); Tyrell Davis (Whittaker); Martita Hunt (Mrs. Mather); Mai Bacon (Mrs. Whittaker); Ethel Coleridge (Mrs. Knuckle); Davy Burnaby (Lord Kingston); Gordon James (Judge).
b.w. 83 mins.

Victor, a wealthy batchelor, marries Patricia. She, too, is rich but spoilt and with a quick temper. He tries to turn her into an obedient wife but his gallant attention to other women only succeeds in making her run off to Monte Carlo. Reconcilliation eventually comes about even if Patricia is not completely tamed.

Another attempt at up-dating the story, this comedy appears surprisingly suggestive for its time of origin.

LA BISBETICA DOMATA
(Italy, 1942)

p.c. Excelsa Film.
d. Ferdinando Maria Poggioli.
l.p. Amedeo Nazzari (Pietruccio); Lila Silvi (Catina); Laura Gazzalo (Battista, her father); Rossana Montesi (Bianca, her sister); Paolo Stoppa (Righetto); Carlo Romano (Remo); Aldo Capacci (Luciano); Elvira Marchionni (Ortensia); Checco Durante (Biondelli); Armando Migliari (Guarnacci); Giuliana Pitti (Maria); Mario Cianfanelli (Romoletto); Pina Gallini; Toto Mignone; Pepino Spadaro; Attilio Dottesi; Luciano Tajoli; Giovanni Petti; Walter Grant; Livia Minelli; Alfredo del Pelo; Ferdinando M. Poggioli.
b.w. 85 mins.

Pietruccio, having made his fortune in America, returns to wed Catina, the petulant, rebellious and uncontrollable daughter of a tailor. He pretends to please her but with seemingly heavenly patience he abuses and bullies her into becoming sweet, reasonable and submisssive.

Noted as being liberally based on the Shakespeare play and transposed to modern (well, at the time) settings. Which neatly sums it up except to add that there are a few songs for good measure.

"And, in short, there is something here to amuse one." – A. Vesce, 'Il Mattino', January 10, 1943.

MAKRANCOS HÖLGY
(Hungary, 1943)

p.c. Hunnia Studio.
d. Emil Martonffry.
l.p. Pál Jávor; Katalin Kardy.
b.w. 83 mins.

See next entry.

MAKACS KATA
(Hungary, 1943)

p.c. Mester Film.
d. Viktor Bánky.
l.p. Miklós Hajmássy; Emmi Buttykay.
b.w. 75 mins.

The two above films were both inspired by the play and are modern-day adaptations. Both take place in Budapest, Hungary, and were released at the same time in obvious competition for public appeal. It is assumed that in both cases the cast listed relates to the Petrucchio and Katherine equivalents respectively. The first title is a straight translation of the original, the second translates as "Stubborn Kata".

ENAMORADA
(Mexico, 1946)

p.c. Panamerica Films.
d. Emilio Fernández.
l.p. María Félix (Beatrix); Pedro Armendáriz (José Juan); Eugenio Rossi (Edward); José Morcillo (Don Carlos); Fernando Fernández (Father Rafael); Miguel Inclán (Joaquin); Eduardo Arozamena; Manuel Dondé; Eugenio Rossi; Norma Hill; Juan García Peña; Arturo Soto

Rangel; Enriqueta Reza; Rogelio Fernández; Trio Calaveras; Beatriz Germán Fuentes.
b.w. 99 mins.

One of Zapata's generals occupies a village and falls in love with rich young woman. She is promised to an American but when the revolutionary saves her father's life, he starts to woo her in his own rough fashion. Finally, she gives in and breaks away from everything to go as a fighter alongside her man.

The synopsis may not indicate clearly the influences upon the film but hispanic sources plainly note that one of the sources of inspiration was THE TAMING OF THE SHREW. The 1949 American/Mexican film *The Torch (Del Odio Nació El Amor)* produced by Eagle Lion, directed again by Fernández and with the same male lead was a virtual remake. Paulette Goddard and Gilbert Roland also starred as obvious attractions for American audiences supported by a mixture of Mexican and American actors.

Academia Mexicana de Ciencias y Artes Cinematográficas, Mexico, 1947: Best Film, Best Actress (María Felix), Best Incidental Actor – male (Eduardo Arozamena), Best Editing (Gloria Schoemann), Best Cinematography (Gabriel Fingueroa), Best Sound (José B. Carles), Special Prize for Best Laboratory Work (Estudios CLASA).
Asociacion de Cronista Cinematográficos de la Argentina, Argentina, 1947: Best Spanish Language Foreign Film.
Festival de Bruxelles, Belgium, 1947: First prize for photography.

CARTAS MARCADAS
(Mexico, 1947)

p.c. *Diana/Almeda.*
d. *René Cardona.*
l.p. *Pedro Infante; Marga López; René Cardona; Hermanas Julián; Alejandro Ciangherotti; Francisco Reiguera; Armando Soto La Marina; Humberto Rodríguez; René Cardone Jr.*
b.w. 92 mins.

Noted as being inspired by the play, the story here has a ranch setting and is said to be amusing with little violence or bullying.

EL CHARRO Y LA DAMA
(Mexico, 1949)

p.c. *Guillermo Alcayde.*
d. *Fernando Cortés.*
l.p. *Pedro Armendáriz (Pedro); Rosita Quintana (Patricia); Ramon Gáy (Marcellino); Miguel Ángel Ferriz (Don Guillermo); Carmen Novelty or Carmen d'Acosta (Clara); Fernando Soto Mantequilla (Constantino); Jorge Reyes (Haste); Lupe Rivas (Toribia); Francisco Reiguera (Orchestra Leader); Emilio Garibay; Gloria Oropeza; Leonor Gómez; Gloria Cansino; Alfredo Varela Sr.; Pepe Nava.*
b.w. Feature.

Patricia, the Texas-educated daughter of Don Guillermo engaged to an American, Mr. Haste, is sent to his ranch to cool her vicious temper. On the way she and her friend Clara are captured by bandits but are rescued by Constantino, the local police chief, and a cowboy, Pedro. At a party to celebrate, Pedro treats her with contempt and her temper flares. Though they kiss, Clara is tricked into identifying Pedro as the bandit who captured them. Patricia saves Pedro from hanging. He escapes and kidnaps her. Their relationship is tempestuous and they come to blows. A group of women go to rescue Patricia who, frightened by a scorpion, goes to Pedro's cabin. Pedro applies himself to taming her and frightening her with a trick crocodile. They agree to marry but she tricks him and he is arrested. A plan to steal her father's ranch is thwarted. All ends well when Pedro captures Patricia again and she reveals all. Clara finds romance and Pedro gives Patricia a good spanking.

The plot in this twists and turns but the elements are, as acknowledged by the credits, Shakespeare inspired. The film is also known as LA DAMA Y EL CHARRO.

KISS ME KATE
(U.S.A., 1953)

p.c. *M.G.M.*
d. *George Sidney.*
l.p. *Kathryn Grayson (Lilli Vanessi/Katherine); Howard Keel (Fred Graham/Petruchio); Ann Miller (Lois Lane/Bianca); Keenan Wynn (Lippy); James Whitmore (Slug); Ron Randell (Cole Porter); Bobby Van (Gremio); Tommy Rall (Bill Calhoun/Lucentio); Bob Fosse (Hortensio); Kurt Kaznar (Baptista); Willard Parker (Texan); Ann Codee; Dave O'Brien; Claude Allister.*
AnscoColor. 110 mins. S Metrovision Tri-Dee.

Singer/producer Fred Graham wants his ex-wife, Lilli Vanessi, to co-star with him in a new musical by Cole Porter based on THE TAMING OF THE SHREW. Though engaged to a Texan, Lilli agrees even though Lois, Fred's current girl friend, will play Bianca. Fred is also, unwittingly, in trouble with gangsters. His name has been used on gambling notes and two tough guys are sent to collect. They prove useful in forcing Lilli to go on for Act 2 after she and Fred have quarrelled. Lilli finally escapes with her Texan but relents and comes back for the final love scene with Fred.

The glorious years of the Hollywood musical were beginning to draw to a close when this screen adaption of the stage show was made. Fortunately there are a number of joys in this, not least, of course, the songs – fourteen of them. Both the leads could not only sing but could also act. Wynn and Whitmore may not have been able to sing but their "Brush Up Your Shakespeare" is good fun. Then, too, there are the delightful legs – that is not to say that the rest of her is not delightful also – of Ann Miller in the self-explanatory "Too Darn Hot". Other points of interest are the musical direction by Saul Chaplin and André Previn and a young Bob Fosse in the cast. A musical extract from the film was included in the M.G.M. 1976 compilation directed by Gene Kelly, *That's Entertainment Part II* and a dance extract in *That's Dancing* (1989) directed by Jack Haley Jr. also from M.G.M.

Many of the songs were available on the soundtrack recording issued originally by M.G.M. records. It seems to be in and out of the catalogue and was re-issued a few years ago by C.B.S. records.

The film has enjoyed a number of revivals of late mainly due to the sporadic bursts of interest in 3-D films. This was certainly one of the better ones of the genre and the two film system at least offered the opportunity of stereophonic sound.

Shown at the Shakespeare Film Festival, Wiesbaden, W. Germany, 1964.
Academy of Motion Picture Arts and Sciences, U.S.A., 1954: Nomination – Best Scoring of a Musical Picture (Saul Chaplin, André Previn).

"...the film has value in its spectacular attractions." – 'Ciné Revue', November 23, 1978.

aka: EMBRASSE-MOI, CHÉRIE; BESAME CATALINA; KÜß MICH KÄTCHEN

MÁS FUERTE QUE EL AMOR
(Mexico/Cuba, 1953)

p.c. *Besné (Mexicana/Cubana).*
d. *Tullio Demicheli.*
l.p. *Jorge Mistral; Miroslava Stern; Chelo Castro; Néstor de Barbose; Sergio de Valle; Carmen Guash; Maritza Rosales; Armando Alonso.*
b.w. 77 mins.

This is said to be a free, modern adaptation of the play.

LA FIERECILLA DOMADA
(Spain/France, 1955)

p.c. *Benito Perojo/Vascos-Interproduction.*
d. *Antonio Román.*
l.p. *Carmen Sevilla (Catalina); Alberto Closas (Don Beltrán); Tip y Top; Claudine Dupuis (Bianca); Raymond Cordy (Baptista); Manuel Goméz Bur (Mario); Luis Sánchez Pola (Octavio); Jacques Dynam (Grumio); Carlos Mendi (Geronimo); Gianni Glory (Lisardo); Sigfredo Burmam; Raoul Bellroy; Manuel Guitián; Manuel Requena; Manuel Alcen; María Luisa Monero; Pedro Valdivieso; Felisa Condado; María Lázaro; María del Carmen Sebastian; Josefina Serratosa; Conchita Velasco.*
Gevacolor. 95 mins. SUPER-P-VISION

In the middle ages while on his way to deliver a gem to a rich merchant in the Italian town of Gandía, the rakish Beltrán comes upon some robbers trying to steal a deer. He saves it for the owner who is revealed as a beautiful but terperamental woman. Upon arrival he is surprised to find that she is Catalina, the merchant's daughter with the reputation of being a shrew. He kisses her and she dares him to return. He does and before her father a wedding pact is made. She imprisons him but he escapes by tricking the two foppish suitors of Bianca, Catalina's sister. They take his place in prison and when the wedding day comes they are found cold and starving. Beltrán arrives for the wedding dressed in rags with riff-raff for company. After a tedious journey and a tempestuous stop at an inn, they arrive at his home where he starves her and makes her life uncomfortable. He tells her that she can go home as she is not a proper wife. Despite a wild storm they set out and Catalina is afraid which leads to love and reconciliation.

Inspired by Shakespeare's play (the credits note it as a free adaptation), the film was conceived for the bright Spanish screen idol of the day, Carmen Sevilla, and gave her an opportunity to prove her ability and her talent as a singer. Her co-star, Alberto Closas, had only just arrived from Argentina when the film was made. The story takes much from the original including the character names. Thus it could almost qualify for inclusion in the first section.

The print shown recently on Spanish television revealed that the colour (Gevacolor negative/ Agfacolor positive) has not stood the test of time well with much dilution and fading. This is a pity for the film is not without its own interest within the Spanish cinema. To be noted is an early appearance by Conchita Velasco who achieved her own fame. Among the technical credits are names that also became important – Ricardo Muñoz Suay and José Isbert.

Shown at the Shakespeare Film Festival, Wiesbaden, W. Germany, 1964.
Circulo de Escritores Cinematográficos, Spain, 1956: Best Leading Actress (Carmen Sevilla), Best Leading Actor (Alberto Closas).
Sindicato Nacional de Espectáculo, Spain, 1956: Best Leading Actress (Carmen Sevilla).
Triunfo, Spain, 1956: Best Actress (Carmen Sevilla).

aka: LA MÉGÈRE APPRIVOISÉE

IL BISBETICO DOMATO
(Italy, 1980)

p.c. *Capital Film.*
d. *Franco Castellano, Giuseppe Pipolo.*
l.p. *Adriano Celantano; Ornella Muti; Pippo Santonastasso; Edith Peters.*
c. 104 mins.

A voluptuous woman tries desperately to seduce a sullen, quarrelsome batchelor. He firmly withstands her advances with great resolve.

The synopsis of this Italian comedy raises some questions. How could any man resist Miss Muti and why should he want to do so? What has this to do with Shakespeare? The answer to the first is simply for the sake of the plot. To the second, well, the plot is really a role reversal of the TAMING OF THE SHREW. Linguists will probably have noted that the title of the film is the "male version" of the Italian name for the play.

aka: LE VIEUX GARÇON; EL SOLTERÓN DOMADO; DIE GEZÄHMTE WIDER-SPENSTIGE

10 THINGS I HATE ABOUT YOU (U.S.A., 1999)

p.c. *Mad Chance/Jaret Entertainment. A Touchstone Presentation.*
d. *Gil Junger.*
l.p. *Julia Stiles (Katarina "Kat" Stratford); Heath Ledger (Patrick Verona); Larisa Oleynik (Bianca Stratford); Joseph Gordon-Levitt (Cameron); Larry Miller (Walter Stratford); Andrew Keegan (Joey); David Krumholtz (Michael); Susan May Pratt (Mandella); Gabrielle Union (Chastity); Daryl Mitchell (Mr. Morgan); Allison Janey (Ms. Perky); David Leisure (Mr. Chopin); Kyle Cease (Bogey); Terence Heuston (Derek); Cameron Fraser (Trevor); Eric Reidman; Greg Jackson; Quinn Maixner; Demegio Kimbrough; Todd Butler; Dennis Mosley; Bianca Kajlich; Nick Vukelic; Benjamin Laurence; Aldan Kennedy; Jelani Quinn; Jesse Dyer; Aaron Therol; Carlos LaCamara; Heather Taylor; Joshua Thorpe; Travis Miller; J.R. Johnson; Wendy Gottlieb; Brian Hood; Art Karczag; Laiva Kenny; Alice Evans; Jesper Inglis; Nick Brown; Monique Powell; Brian Mashburn; Kay Hanley; Michael Eisenstein.*
c. 92 mins. S

In Padua, Seattle, Cameron falls for Bianca whose father will not allow her out on dates until her sister, "Kat" finds a boyfriend. "Kat" is a difficult girl and Cameron, funded by Joey (he also wants Bianca), induces Patrick Verona to go out with her. Aided by information from Bianca, Patrick persuades "Kat" to go with him to a party where she gets drunk and is helped by Patrick. Bianca arrives at the party with Cameron, goes with Joey but leaves with Cameron. "Kat" admits to Bianca that Joey took her virginity. Joey again funds Patrick to take "Kat" to the prom. There "Kat" learns of the whole scheme but, later, in school, reads a poem admitting her love for Patrick. Both sisters get the boy they want.

The Shakespearean references abound but often only the essence of the plot remains. Though Patrick is no Petruchio, the film is amiable with many new, young players. It appears to have enjoyed reasonable success and the soundtrack was released by Hollywood Records.

"...this bubble-gum THE TAMING OF THE SHREW is meant to be good for you..." – Peter Matthews, 'Sight and Sound', July, 1999.

aka: 10 RAZONES PARA ODIARTE

✢ ✢ ✢ ✢ ✢

As a "battle of the sexes" comedy, this play has its attractions for the film maker not interested in a direct screen version. Elements from the play occur in other films and was, in particular, the theme for **KISS ME KATE** as noted above. The idea of the shrewish wife being ultimately tamed with a spanking was in essence borrowed for the John Wayne/Maureen O'Hara 1952 film set in Ireland, *The Quiet Man*. The couple starred again in the western *McLintock!* (U.S.A., 1963) which followed to some extent the previous film but Ford was, in this, nearer to the original plot.

Back in the silent screen days, the fiery girl taming men with a whip was the subject of the Art Cinema production *Revenge* (1928 – directed by Edwin Carewe). Dolores Del Rio was the stormy maid and Leroy Mason, the bear tamer who tames her. More gentle was the story of a haughty princess wooed and humiliated into love by a prince in Carl Dreyer's *Der Var Engang* (Denmark, 1922), a film once thought lost though, even now, only fifty-four minutes of it are extant. The 1940 film from 20th. Century Fox, *Public Deb No. 1* featured a rich socialite with Communist leanings spanked by a waiter (to the delight of her uncle) and who eventually tames her. George Murphy, Brenda Joyce and Ralph Bellamy starred.

Though based on a story by Rabindranath Tagore, the second part of Satyajit Ray's *Teen Kanya* (India, 1961) with Soumitra Chatterji and Aparna Das Gupta, bore a strong resemblance to Shakespeare's plot. In this episode (called "Samapti"), a young man marries the local tomboy and, by humiliating and rejecting her, he ends up with a loving wife.

In 1968 French Director Claude Sautet was reported that he wanted to make a modern version of the play. The theme was to have been about a banker who marries a fashionable interior decorator and then discovers her temper. Lino Ventura was suggested for the Petruchio/banker role. It does not, however, appear to have been made.

For other films from this play see **CHAPTER XXX ALL THE WORLD'S A STAGE**: ENCHANTMENT (1921); ELSTREE CALLING (1930); STAR IMPERSONATIONS (1930); CASANOVA IN BURLESQUE (1944); FRAU WIRTIN HAT AUCH EINEN GRAFEN (1968) and **CHAPTER XXXII THE IMMORTAL BARD**: IMMORTAL GENTLEMAN (1935); WILLIAM SHAKESPEARE:BACKGROUND FOR HIS WORKS (1950); SHAKESPEARE: MIRROR TO A MAN (1970?).

CHAPTER XXIII
THE TEMPEST

Dramatis Personæ:

Prospero – the deposed but rightful Duke of Milan
Miranda – his daughter
Antonio – his brother and usurper

Alonso, King of Naples
Sebastian – his brother
Ferdinand – son of the King of Naples

Adrian, Francisco – lords
Gonzalo – an old, honest councillor

Caliban – a savage, deformed slave
Trinculo – a jester
Stephano – a drunken butler
Ariel – an airy spirit
Iris, Ceres, Juno, Nymphs, Reapers, spirits
Master of a ship
Boatswain
Mariners, Other spirits

Prospero and his daughter Miranda are the sole human inhabitants of an island. They live in a cave and Prospero practises magic and has released many tree spirits imprisoned by the island's previous enchantress, Sycorax. The most important of these is Ariel who is visible only to Prospero. He is in charge of Caliban, a monster, the son of Sycorax, and whom he teases and ensures that he carries out the menial tasks.

Prospero can also control the elements so when a storm occurs he assures his daughter that the occupants of a ship at sea will come to no harm. He tells her how his brother, Antonio, with the aid of the King of Naples, usurped his position as Duke of Milan and set the two of them adrift at sea. Thanks to a friend, Gonzalo, they had enough provisions to get them to the island. He tells how he has educated her and that the storm was raised to ensure that the ship's occupants landed on the island for among them are his brother and the King of Naples, as well as the King's son, Ferdinand.

Ariel explains all about the storm and that he has left the King and Antonio looking for Ferdinand. No crew member is dead but each thinks himself the sole survivor. Then Prospero asks more work of him but Ariel protests and recalls Prospero's promise of freedom. But Prospero reminds him of his previous fate under Sycorax and retains his loyalty.

Ariel goes to Ferdinand and sings a song to him saying that his father is lost. The bemused lad follows Ariel's voice to Prospero and Miranda. The girl is amazed at his beauty and her father explains that the youth has been looking for his lost companions. Ferdinand, too, is attracted to Miranda, thinking that she is a goddess – a case of love at first sight. Prospero is pleased but determines to test the youth's character and magically fixes him to the spot where he stands. When chided by Miranda, he explains that she should be careful having seen no other young men. In fact, he is testing her as well.

Ferdinand knows he is powerless to disobey Prospero and sets about the tasks set for him. Prospero, invisible, watches as Miranda tries to help her love and smiles at his daughter's disobedience of her father. On hearing Ferdinand's praise of her beauty, Prospero is happy, seeing his daughter as the future Queen of Naples. When Miranda offers herself as Ferdinand's wife, Prospero becomes visible and expresses his delight at their love and explains that he has been testing them.

He leaves them happily together and goes to Ariel who tells how he has plagued the King of Naples and Antonio with visions and reminders of their treachery. They seem to repent and are brought to Prospero. With them comes old Gonzalo who had helped Prospero many years before. Antonio and the King beg forgiveness and are impressed with Miranda's beauty.

As Ferdinand professes his new love and vitality, Prospero advocates that the past be forgotten. A grand reunion takes place, Ariel is set free and Prospero buries his books of magic. They set sail for their native land where they arrive safely.

Note: The style of writing suggests a late play and this is borne out by the record of a performance on November 1, 1611, and it also formed part of the celebration for the wedding of Elizabeth, King James' daughter, during the winter of 1612/1613. As to the source, this remains unknown though contemporary accounts of various shipwrecks could well have made their mark. There are, too, oblique references, unrelated to the setting, to the New World (as it was then) which only confuse more rather than clarify matters.

✠ ✠ ✠ ✠

THE TEMPEST
(G.B., 1905)
p.c. *Urban Trading Co.*

d. *Charles Urban.*
l.p. *J. Fisher White (Gonzalo); S. A. Cookson (Alonzo); W. A. Haines (Boatswain); Lyn Harding (Antonio).*
b.w. 150 ft. (46 m.) Sil.

Shipwreck scenes from the production at His Majesty's Theatre, London, England. Herbert Beerbohm-Tree is noted by some sources as director and leading player. Tinted and coloured prints may have existed.

THE TEMPEST
(G.B., 1908)
p.c. *Clarendon.*
d. *Percy Stow.*
l.p.
b.w. 780 ft. (238 m.) Sil.

Langford Reed provided the screenplay making it into a fantasy film following the theme of a magician regaining his dukedom by bewitching the ship-wrecked usurper.

Comment suggests that the production was well handled with clear simple inter-titles. It was filmed both in a studio and in the countryside.

Shown as part of the Everybody's Shakespeare International Festival, London, England, 1994.

THE TEMPEST
(U.S.A., 1911)
p.c. *Thanhouser.*
d. *Edwin Thanhouser.*
l.p. *George A. Lessey.*
b.w. 1 reel. Sil.

The contents and quality of this release will remain unknown as the film was one of those lost in a fire at the company's warehouse. Comment at the time said that the film added little to the company's reputation.

LA TEMPÊTE
(France, 1912)
p.c. *Éclair.*
d.
l.p. *Charles Krauss.*
b.w. 1887 ft. (575 m.) Sil.

Prospero, a student of the occult, is expelled from Milan. Set adrift in a boat, he lands on an island where live Caliban and Ariel. Sixteen years later, the galley of the King of Naples arrives and so does Ferdinand who meets and falls in love with Miranda. Prospero finds them and reveals his identity. They all return to Naples where the couple marry.

The film is believed lost but the Shakespeare base is clear.

ALOCHHAYA/AANDHI
(India, 1940)
p.c.
d. *Dinesh Ranjan Das.*

l.p.
b.w. Feature.

No further details of this Indian version of the play have been traced except that it was made in both Hindi and Bengali under the respective titles above.

aka: THE TEMPEST

THE TEMPEST
(G.B., 1969)
p.c. *A Rafters Players Production.*
d. *Nicholas Young, David Snasdell.*
l.p. *Christopher Scoular (Prospero); Michael Menaugh (Ferdinand); Vanessa Blackmore (Miranda); Richard Phethean (Ariel); Johnny Eccles (Caliban); David Alleyn (Antonio); Richard Hermitage (Stefano); Christopher Temple (Sebastian).*
b.w. 85 mins.

This is essentially an amateur film made and funded by the company as a record (probably on 16 mm.) of its own stage performance. The intention was commendable but the results show all the problems of such an effort which was shot during three weeks in Cornwall, England. Logically, nobody makes such an amateur film of this length without showing it to some members of the public and thus it warrants inclusion here.

THE TEMPEST
(G.B., 1974)
p.c. *Realist Film Unit.*
d. *Peter Seabourne.*
l.p. *Mark Kingston (Prospero); Elizabeth Hall (Miranda); Derrick Gilbert (Ferdinand).*
c. 14 mins.

This short contains Act I, Scene 2 and Act III, Scene 1 performed on a reconstruction of an Elizabethan stage.

✤ ✤ ✤ ✤ ✤

THE TEMPEST
(U.S.A., 1921)
p.c. *Pathé.*
d.
l.p. *Tom Santschi; Harry Lonsdale; Patrica Palmer; Strake Patteson; George Kunkle.*
b.w. 2000 ft. (610 m.) Sil.

A young man is shanghaied but is thrown overboard during a storm at sea. He comes to an island where he falls in love with the daughter of the lighthouse keeper. Confusion follows when a boy he tries to protect is revealed as the girl's brother.

The story is obviously vaguely inspired by the Shakespeare play. French sources note a Pathé release with the same title in translation about this time and it is probably this film suitably adapted.

LA TEMPESTAD
(Spain, 1943)

p.c. *Cepicsa.*

d. *Javier de Rivera.*

l.p. *Julia Lajos; Mariano Alcón; María Luisa Gerona; Manuel Arbó; Rufino Inglés; Pablo Alvarez Rubio; Fred Galiana; José Portes.*

b.w. 84 mins.

Though vaguely based on the Shakespearean work, this is a "zarzuela" (operetta) by Ramós Carrión and Chapí.

FORBIDDEN PLANET
(U.S.A., 1956)

p.c. *M.G.M.*

d. *Fred McLeod Wilcox.*

l.p. *Walter Pidgeon (Dr.Morbius); Anne Francis (Altaira Morbius); Warren Stevens (Lt. Ostrow); Leslie Nielsen (Commander Adams); Richard Anderson (Chief Quinn); Jack Kelly (Lt. Farman); Earl Holliman (Cook); George Wallace (Bosun).*

Eastman Color. 98 mins. CinemaScope

In 2004AD, Dr. Morbius, survivor from a lost space ship, lives on the planet Altair-4 with his daughter, Alta, and robot servant. Commander Adams and his crew visit but are coldly received. Morbius tells of the mysterious murder of his crew and shows the relics of the Krell civilisation. Following a death and an attack by a semi-invisible monster, one of the crew, at the cost of his own live, solves the mystery. The Krells had not allowed for the dangers of the "monsters from the id". Morbius dies trying to halt the monster his sub-conscious has created; Alta leaves with Adams whom she loves.

Irving Black and Allen Adler are quoted as the source story for this enjoyable science fiction opus but the influence is clearly Shakespeare's THE TEMPEST. Even Morbius' young daughter – Anne Francis looking delectable in her miniskirts – is given to paraphrasing Shakespeare.

Of the film, famous science fiction writer, Arthur C. Clarke, said in an interview with Philip Strick ('Continental Film Review', March, 1966): "Perhaps my favourite science fiction film is **FORBIDDEN PLANET** because although it has some flaws it's the only one to convey the wonder and strangeness of space and of course it had a first class story pinched straight from Shakespeare."

Derann Films Services (U.K.) made the film available for home movie enthusiasts by releasing it on 8 mm.

Shown as part of the Everybody's Shakespeare International Festival, London, England; 1994.

"Worthy and entertaining." – 'Cine Y Más'.

"...some have seen this as a space reworking of THE TEMPEST, conferring a respectability it little deserves." – David Shipman, 'The Good Film And Video Guide'.

"It's a pity they didn't lift some of Shakespeare's language." – 'The New Yorker'.

"Perhaps the most interesting of the space robot films..." – David Annan, 'Robot The Mechanical Monster'.

aka: PLANET INTÈRDITE; PLANETA PROIBIDA; ALARM IM WELTALL

AGE OF CONSENT
(Australia, 1969)

p.c. *Nautilus Productions.*

d. *Michael Powell.*

l.p. *James Mason (Bradley Morahan); Helen Mirren (Cora); Jack MacGowran (Nat Kelly); Neva Carr-Glyn (Ma Ryan); Antonia Katsaros (Isabel Marley).*

c. 104 mins.

Brad, a disenchanted artist, lives on the Great Barrier Reef where he mets the drunken Ma Ryan and her attractive daughter, Cora. Cora poses for Brad as his model which delights him and gives him enthusiasm. Cora delights in her newly found sexual desires. Nat Kelly, a rough acquaintance of Brad, arrives and spoils the situation. Cora and Ma Ryan fight over money and Ma Ryan falls to her death. An accidental death verdict is given, Kelly is arrested and Brad and Cora are left to themselves.

Like a number of directors, Powell had a dream of making his own version of THE TEMPEST with James Mason as Prospero and Mia Farrow as Ariel. Again like many directors, he could not raise the finance for it despite many years in trying to do so. So many see this film as his variation on the original. The British release version is six minutes shorter and had a replacement music track.

THE TEMPEST
(G.B., 1979)

p.c. *Boyd's Co./Berwick Street/No.8 Films.*

d. *Derek Jarman.*

l.p. *Heathcote Williams (Prospero); Karl Johnson (Ariel); Toyah Willcox (Miranda); Peter Bull (Alonso); Richard Warwick (Antonio); Elizabeth Welch (Goddess); Jack Birkett (Caliban); Peter Turner (Trinculo); Ken Campbell (Gonzalo); David Meyer (Ferdinand); Claire Davenport (Sycorax); Peter Turner (Trinculo); Christopher Biggins (Stephano); Neil Cunningham (Sebastian); Angela Whittington; Kate Temple; Helen Wellington-Lloyd.*

Eastman Color. 95 mins.

The late Derek Jarman's view of this Shakespearean play is as might be expected – unconventional, encompassing the mood of the time of production and modern dress and music. Purists may well find his controversial approach with full frontal male nudity and homosexual musical scenes not only bizarre but unacceptable.

Jarman in the film *There We Are, John* (G.B., 1993, a British Council production directed by Ken McMullen) told interviewer John Cartwright: "My idea of the film was very conventional despite the Americans not liking it."

Shown at the Edinburgh Film Festival, Scotland, 1979.
Shown as part of the Everybody's Shakespeare International Festival, London, England, 1994.

"...the most visually ravishing of Jarman's movies." – Martin Sutton, 'The Movie'.

TEMPEST
(U.S.A., 1982)

p.c. *Columbia.*
d. *Paul Mazursky.*
l.p. *John Cassavetes (Philip Dimitrious); Geena Rowlands (Antonia Dimitrious); Vittorio Gassman (Alonzo); Susan Sarandon (Aretha); Raul Julia (Kalibanos); Jerry Hardin (Harry); Anthony Holland (Sebastian); Paul Stewart (Philip's Father); Jackie Gayle (Trinc); Molly Ringwald (Miranda); Lucianne Buchanan (Dolores); Vassilis Glezakos (Greek Boat Captain); Carol Ficatier (Gabrielle); Sam Robards (Freddy); Luigi Laezza, Sergio Nicolai (Sailors); Peter Lombard (MacKenzie); Cynthia Harris (Cynthia); Betsy Mazursky; Murray Grand; Paul Mazursky; Fred Pasternack; Nadine Darling; Camille Lefka; Nina Kolment; George Moscaidis; John Marolakos; Sheila Ozden; Theodoros Kavalieros; Jerry Hewitt; Barry Mitchell; Al Cerullo; Nicos Mousoullis; Clint Chin; Evanthia Glezakou; Stella Nastou; Rudy Cherney; Thanasis Pagonis.*
Color by De Luxe. 142 mins. S

New York architect, whose wife is having an affaire, takes off with his own lover and daughter to a Greek island whose only other inhabitant is a simple minded goatherd. The relationships falter during the summer. While the wife, her lover and his son are cruising a storm brings the ship to the island. New relationships are formed, old ones repaired. All return to New York.

Allegedly, this comedy was based on Shakespeare's work but the connection is slight. The storm is supposed to have been created by the architect, leaving only some of the names in derivative form or directly as in the case of the architect's daughter – Miranda – as the connection.

In an interview in 'Fotogramas', Susan Sarandon said: "Paul Mazursky's TEMPEST was a good idea, but when I read the script, my character didn't interest me in the least." John Cassavetes told her not to worry and that it would all work out well. And it did.

Shown at the Venice Film Festival, Italy, 1982.

aka: DER STURM

RESAN TILL MELONIA
(Sweden, 1989)

p.c. *PennFilm Studio/Svenska Filminstitutet/ Sandrew Film and Theatre/Filmhuset/Svenska Ord/ Sveriges Television/TV-Skrivstugan/ Lskonsten/AB Filmteknik/Norsk Film.*
d. *Per Ahlin.*
l.p. *Animated characters. Voices: Allan Edwall (Prospero); Robin Carlsson (Miranda); Olle Sami (Ferdinand); Tomas von Brömssen (Ariel); Ingvar Kjellson (Captain), Jan-Olof Strandberg (William); Ernst Günther (Caliban); Jan Blomberg; Hans Alfredson; Eva Rydberg; Nils Eklund.*
Fujicolor. 104 mins. WS

Two sinister individuals set out for Melonia, a beautiful, tranquil island. Here, though occasionally the volcano exerts its presence to establish its authority, lives the magician Prospero with his daughter, Miranda, his apprentice, Ariel, and his gardener, Caliban. On the evil island of Plutonia lives Ferdinand who wishes to escape from it. Ferdinand must face the storm Prospero has conjured. This he does safely with the help of Ariel and so he meets Miranda...

This animated work based on THE TEMPEST involved five years work by the director whose output has mainly been for television. The title translates as "Journey to Melonia".

Shown at the Valladolid Film Festival, Spain, 1990.

PROSPERO'S BOOKS
(Netherlands/France/Italy, 1991)

p.c. *Allarts/Cinea/Camera One/Penta in association with Elsevier Vendex Film/Film Four International/VPRO Television/Canal Plus/ NHK. Financial assistance from Eurimages Fund, Stichting Produktiefonds Voor Nederlandse Films and Pierson, Heldring and Pierson.*
d. *Peter Greenaway.*
l.p. *John Gielgud (Prospero); Michael Clark (Caliban); Michael Blanc (Alonso); Erland Josephson (Gonzalo); Isabelle Pasco (Miranda); Tom Bell (Antonio); Kenneth Cranham (Sebastian); Mark Rylance (Ferdinand); Gérard Thoolen (Adrian); Jim van der Woude (Trinculo); Pierre Bokma (Francisco); Michiel Romeyn (Stephano); Paul Russell, Emil Wolk,*

Orphéo, James Thierree, (Ariel); Marie Angel (Iris); Deborah Conway (Juno); Ute Lemper (Ceres); Mirale Jusid; Hélène Zellweger; Hélène Busnel; Florence Gielen.

c. 120 mins.

On a secluded island Prospero, the deposed Duke of Milan, sits in exile surrounded by magical spirits and begins to improvise the text of THE TEMPEST...At the end Prospero orders all his books to be destroyed but two are saved – a volume of Shakespeare's plays and the small volume that completes it – the text of THE TEMPEST. Prospero begs the audience to forgive him and to be set free.

John Gielgud had long wanted to make a film of his stage performance. In seeking a director, his thoughts had turned to Akira Kurasawa and he had even written to Ingmar Bergman. In the end Peter Greenaway was the choice with superb results pictorially. All the characters are voiced by Gielgud.

Some of the music by Michael Nyman for the film has been recorded by the composer's own band bearing the film's title and issued by Argo (a part of the Decca group). An extract from this record has also been issued by Argo on a disc of Nyman's music in general, again played by the composer's band.

Shown as part of the Everybody's Shakespeare International Festival, London, England, 1994.
Shown at the Venice Film Festival, Italy, 1991.

"Intriguing and visually spectacular...Some might find it tiresomely innovative; others will just let the magic flow over them." – 'Film Monthly', April 1992.

"An intriguing, controversial, infuriating and unforgettable work from a master filmmaker..." – James Cameron-Wilson, 'Film Review 1992/3'.

"...this is only indirectly a 'version' of THE TEMPEST. It would be truer to call it a variation in the musical sense, an annotated commentary, or – quite literally – a reading of it." – Jonathan Summers, 'Sight And Sound'.

✤ ✤ ✤ ✤ ✤

In screen adaptation terms this is not one of Shakespeare's most influential works. Few other films seem to have looked to it for inspiration with the possible exception of *Yellow Sky* (U.S.A., 1948). This western could be seen to parallel the story. Here a gang of outlaws come across a ghost town inhabited by an old prospector and his unusual granddaughter. The influence of the old man soon divides the gang into a final shoot-out. Gregory Peck, Anne Baxter, Richard Widmark and James Barton were directed by William A. Wellman for 20th. Century Fox.

Thus the play is obviously seen as a challenge to film directors for many have seen it as a means of personal expression. The public, therefore, has little or nothing to turn to for a faithful presentation of it on screen.

For other films with scenes from this play see **CHAPTER XXX ALL THE WORLD'S A STAGE**: LOVE STORY (1944) and NOBODY'S FOOL (1985) and **CHAPTER XXXII THE IMMORTAL BARD**: EXPLORATIONS IN SHAKESPEARE (1969).

CHAPTER XXIV

TITUS ANDRONICUS

Dramatis Personæ:

Titus Andronicus – a noble Roman General
Marcus Andronicus – his brother and a Tribune.
Lucius, Quintus, Martius and Mutius – sons of Titus
Lavinia – daughter of Titus
Young Lucius – son of Lucius
Publius – son of Marcus
Semptronius, Caius and Valentine – kinsmen to Titus
Saturninus – son of the late Emperor of
Rome and, then, Emperor himself
Bassianus – brother of Saturninus
Aemilius – a noble Roman

Tamora – Queen of the Goths
Alarbus, Demetrius, Chiron – her sons
Aaron – a Moor loved by Tamora
A Captain
A Messenger
A Clown
A Nurse and a black child
Romans, Goths, Senators, Tribunes,
Officers, Soldiers and Attendants

Saturninus, son of the late Emperor of Rome, and his brother, Bassianus, accept the wishes of the people in the choice of the hero Titus Andronicus as the new emperor. Titus enters in triumph bringing Tamora, Queen of the Goths, and her sons, prisoners from his victory. Lucius, son of Titus, demands a sacrifice and, despite the pleas of Tamora, her eldest son, Alarbus, is so proscribed. Lucius returns from his bloody act and his father pays homage to the Roman dead. Tamora vows vengeance against Titus and his family. Then Titus is greeted by his daughter, Lavinia, and his brother, Marcus who advises him that the crown is his.

Titus, however, does not want this burden but asks that he may choose the next ruler. Both pretenders to the crown state their cases and Titus chooses Saturninus. In return, Saturninus offers the role of empress to Lavinia whom he loves. His family so honoured, Titus pledges his allegiance and Saturninus treats the captive Tamora with due regard to her rank and sets her free.

Bassianus is in love with Lavinia and snatches her away. Helped by Lucius, Marcus and Mutius, he makes his escape and Titus is forced to kill his own son, Mutius, for his part in the matter. Saturninus goes after Lavinia but Lucius returns and makes it clear that Lavinia will not be returned. Though Titus disowns Lucius, Saturninus rebukes Titus and all his family. To add further insult, he takes Tamora as his empress.

Titus is ill-disposed to listen to the pleas of his family to bury Mutius with honour but finally agrees. Meanwhile, Bassianus has married Lavinia and, despite the anger of his brother, begs the Emperor to forgive Titus who had, in fact, defended the imperial honour. Tamora advises Saturninus to comply bearing in mind the esteem in which Titus

is held by the people. Through the intervention of Tamora, friendship between all parties is restored.

Not all is calm between Chiron and Demetrius, the sons of Tamora, for they are both in love with Lavinia. Aaron the Moor intervenes in their dispute. Later, the two brothers join the imperial hunt party. Their mother meets Aaron (who, with a bag of gold, has an air of mischief about him) and professes her love for him but Bassianus and Lavinia come upon her. They say they will tell the Emperor and Tamora is found by her sons in a state of distress. Demetrius stabs Bassianus. Tamora tells them to do what they will with Lavinia. They drag her away having thrown the body of Bassianus into a pit. It is this same pit into which Quintus and Martius fall and which Aaron uses as evidence to place blame upon them.

Aaron leads the Emperor to the spot and, with the bag of gold as motive and a letter as proof, condemnation of Martius and Quintus seems inevitable. However, Titus craves leave to prove the innocence of his sons but this is denied though Tamora hints that she will intervene.

Martius and Quintius face execution. Lucius arrives intent upon violence to save his brothers as, clearly, Titus' entreatments have been to no avail. Marcus enters with Lavinia who has been ravished, her hands cut off and her tongue cut out by Demetrius and Chiron. Horrified at what they see, neither Titus, nor Marcus nor Lucius knows whether she cries for her dead husband or for the impending fate of her brothers. The same three men receive an offer from the Emperor by way of Aaron. If any one of them will cut off his hand and send it to the Emperor, the two youths will be freed.

They argue, each one, the right to sacrifice their hand but Titus tricks them and, with Aaron's help, severs his own hand. Aaron leaves with the hand and with villainy in mind. A messenger returns with the hand and the heads of his two men. Titus vows revenge and sends Lucius to the Goths to raise an army.

Some time later at a banquet, the spirits of Titus and his family are low and full of hatred for those who have wronged them. Young Lucius is rather scared by his disfigured aunt and drops his books. It is through these that Lavinia, aided by a stick in her mouth and guided by her stumps, is able to communicate the names of her husband's killer and her own abusers. Even young Lucius is enraged and agrees to help in Titus' plans.

The boy delivers gifts of weapons and a scroll to Demetrius and Chiron. Aaron realises that Titus has discovered the truth. Another truth is then revealed with the arrival of a nurse with a black child, the offspring of Aaron and Tamora. Both Demetrius and Chiron turn on Aaron and, in accordance with Tamora's wish, want to kill the child. Aaron, however, is against this but they all realise what is at stake and so connive together. They learn that only the midwife, the nurse and Tamora know of the child. Aaron kills the nurse and arranges to have the child substituted by a recently delivered white child.

Titus declines mentally, indulging in archery games of make-believe vengeance, writing to the gods and he even uses a clown as messenger to the Emperor. Saturninus is angry at the apparent libel the writings contain. He is outraged by the message from the clown whom he condemns to be hanged. His fury against Titus is interrupted by Aemilius who bring news of the arrival of Lucius with an army of Goths. Tamora suggests that she meet Titus to induce him to intervene for both are aware that Lucius has much public support. Meanwhile, Aemilius is sent as envoy to Lucius to seek a parley at the Titus' house.

In Lucius' camp, there is encouragement for all with the news of the support in Rome. Then a Goth arrives with Aaron and his child as prisoners. When Lucius threatens to hang them both, Aaron pleads for the child's life admitting that it is Tamora's child he has sired. He also tells of the crimes of Demetrius and Chiron and of his part in putting the blame on Lucius' brothers. Though Aaron is unrepentant, Lucius spares him for the moment as Aemilius arrives. A parley is arranged.

Tamora and her two sons go to Titus and, using his deranged mind to her advantage, pretends to be Revenge personified who has come to help him. She plans to lure Lucius to the house while she uses her wiles to disperse the Goths. Titus agrees to send for Lucius and some of the princes of the Goths to attend a banquet. Entrusting the task to Marcus, he then demands that Tamora leave her two "ministers" Rape and Murder (her two sons). The two men are content to stay.

However, Titus is not as mad as he seems to be and straight away Demetrius and Chiron are bound and gagged. Lavinia is brought in to see her abusers face the summary of their crimes and to catch the blood that pours from them as Titus cuts their throats.

Lucius greets his uncle and agrees to go to his father taking along Aaron and his child. The Emperor and Emperess enter the home of Titus for the banquet. Titus dresses himself as a cook while Lavinia hides behind a veil. Titus makes all welcome and bids them eat. He cleverly makes Saturninus agree that it is right to kill a deflowered, disgraced woman and then kills Lavinia. When questioned about this act, Titus tells of her ordeal at the hands of Demetrius and Chiron.

The Emperor demands their presence but Titus points out that the two made up the meal just eaten. Titus then stabs Tamora. He, in turn, is stabbed by Saturninus who meets a similar fate at the hand of Lucius.

Rome hails Lucius as Emperor following his account of the list of crimes that have been commited by the former imperial family. Lucius orders that Aaron, still unrepentant, be buried in earth up to his breast and no-one may feed him. He commands that the dead be properly interred all except Tamora whose body shall be left to the beasts of prey. The new emperor has to restore both his family and the wellbeing of Rome.

Note: This bloody play was first published in 1594 (a copy was discovered in Sweden in 1904 and it confirms the play's performances by various groups in the same year). It may well date from 1590 or even earlier but is certainly one of Shakespeare's earliest works. It may well have been influenced by the prose 'History of Titus Andronicus' and most certainly by Ovid's 'Metamorphoses' Book VI. Some critics dismiss the play and others claim it to be a reworking of a much older one.

✤ ✤ ✤ ✤ ✤

TITUS
(U.S.A., 1999)

p.c.

d. *Julie Taymor, Christopher Dunne.*

l.p. *Anthony Hopkins (Titus); Jessica Lange (Tamora); Laura Fraser; Alan Cumming; John Turturro; Jonathan Rhys Meyers; Kristin Scott Thomas; Julie Taymor.*

c.

Noted as being in production at the time of writing, the above information is, at best, provisional. It is being filmed in Croatia and at the Cinecittà studios in Rome. It is the first directorial work from Taymor who has chosen a path that is anachronistic, blending various time periods to reflect that Shakespeare is just as relevant to today as he ever was. Hopkins describes the work as "bordering on the absurd. Bizarre, brutal, entertaining."

Generally considered one of Shakespeare's least popular plays, it was not until 1954 that it saw any type of revival. Thus it is not hard to see why there have been no film versions of it before. One can only imagine what pre-1960's censorship would have thought of dismembering, disembowelling, rape, multilation, murder, adultery and unwitting cannabalism. The list reads like a resumé for one of those "video nasties" that seemed to haunt the film/video market some years ago.

The play is not without interest for it introduces certain themes that Shakespeare would use again – a scheming, enigmatic woman, feigned madness, Titus himself foreshadowing the simple soldier in Othello and Aaron projecting the devious Iago. It is, in fact, Aaron who, small though his role may be, is the strongest and most pivotal character in what is a flawed work.

A number of characters seem ill-defined. Tamora is lacking in clear, explained action that defies what is meant to be a vengeful character. Certainly, there is no reason given why the Goths should rise up against their conqueror at the whim of their conqueror's son and against their own queen. Yet, above these faults, remains Titus Andronicus, the bench mark for Shakespearean characters to come – the simple soldier who puts honour even above his family.

CHAPTER XXV
THE TRAGEDY OF KING RICHARD THE SECOND

Dramatis Personæ:

King Richard II
His Queen
Bushy, Bagot, Green – his servants
His uncles:
   John of Gaunt, Duke of Lancaster
   Edmund of Langley, Duke of York
   Henry Bolingbroke, Duke of Hereford – son of John
   of Gaunt and later King Henry IV
Duke of Aumerle – son of the Duke of York
Duchess of York
Duchess of Gloucester
Thomas Mowbray, Duke of Norfolk
Duke of Surrey
Lord Berkeley
Earl of Northumberland

Earl of Salisbury
Henry Percy (called Hotspur) – his son
Lord Ross
Lord Willoughby
Lord Fitzwater

Bishop of Carlisle
Abbot of Westminster

Lord Marshal
Sir Pierce of Exton
Sir Stephen Scroop

Welsh captain
Lady attendant to the Queen
Lords, Heralds, Officers, Soldiers, Groom,
   Gardeners, Keeper, Messenger, and Attendants

King Richard II and his uncle, John of Gaunt, discuss Gaunt's son, Henry Bolingbroke and his disagreement with Thomas Mowbray. Accused by Bolingbroke of misappropriating funds and of plotting the Duke of Gloucester's death, Mowbray says this is slander and explains the matter though he admits that once he plotted Gaunt's death. Richard remains impartial and, when the two cannot make peace, they, Bolingbroke and Mowbray, are ordered to settle the matter, as gentlemen, in the lists at Coventry.

At his palace, Gaunt discusses the tournament with his sister-in-law who hopes that Bolingbroke will be successful and so revenge her husband's death. However, on St. Lambert's Day, the day of the tournament, as the two men prepare to meet, Richard intervenes, banishing Bolingbroke for ten years (which he later reduces to six) and exiling Mowbray ordering them never to meet. An old and saddened Gaunt is relieved and tells his son to look upon the order as a long journey.

Richard hears that Gaunt is sick and he needs Gaunt's wealth to fund the Irish wars. Richard goes to him and there meets also his other uncle, the Duke of York. They talk and York leaves. When Gaunt dies, York warns against seizing the estate as Bolingbroke is still alive and such action may antagonise people. Ignoring this, Richard makes York, his trusted man, Lord Governor of England while Richard goes to fight the Irish.

A number of lords are unhappy about Richard's actions and leadership. His taxes on the ordinary people and fines on the nobles are now exceeded by

wanton theft. Northumberland, Willoughby and Ross ride to join Bolingbroke, now Duke of Lancaster, who has sailed for England with a small army. Worcester and many others defect too.

The Duke of York learns that his own son has defected. He is confused and worried because of the office he bears and the division among his kinsmen. Richard's allies, fearing the common people, desert to Ireland or Bristol. He hears, too, of the death of the Duchess of Gloucester. Nevertheless, he calls for men to fight.

In Gloucestershire, Bolingbroke and Northumberland have joined forces. Northumberland's son, Henry Percy, sent by his uncle (Worcester), offers his services advising that the Court has been disbanded and that York with some three hundred men is at Berkeley nearby. So Bolingbroke and York meet. York will not acknowledge Bolingbroke as Duke of Lancaster as he was banished and is now a traitor. Bolingbroke contends that he was banished as Duke of Hereford but as Lancaster he claims his rights. This York understands yet is faced with upholding the law or helping Bolingbroke who looks to him as if he were his father. The two pass the night at Berkeley castle where Bolingbroke wins over York. The next day they march on Bristol capturing the castle. Richard's followers there, accused of misleading the King and upsetting the Queen, are sentenced to death.

As Bolingbroke then sets off to Wales to deal with Owen Glendower, Richard arrives, glad to be back in his own kingdom in spite of the problems. He believes that, as King, right is with him but news comes of the desertion of twenty thousand Welsh troops to Bolingbroke. The loss of Bristol is another blow but more so is the defection of York.

Bolingbroke, also in Wales near Flint Castle, hears of Richard's landing and the desertion. In fact, Richard is at Flint Castle and Bolingbroke sends a message of conciliation demanding the lifting of his banishment and the restoration of his title and chattels. In return, he will humble himself before the King. Richard, at first calling Bolingbroke a traitor, concedes to receive him. The King knows not what to do or say but Bolingbroke kneels at his feet. They make a sort of peace and agree to go to London together.

The Queen leaves Langley for London after learning from the gardeners that Richard has been all but deposed. In Parliament, questions, accusations and denials are in abundance. York brings news that Richard has proclaimed Bolingbroke his heir and invites him to take the crown. Bolingbroke has all the lords in the Parliament arrested. York returns with Richard, who with ill-grace, hands over the regalia of office. Bolingbroke has Richard sent to the Tower of London and proclaims the following Wednesday as the day of coronation.

The Queen seeks out Richard on his way to the Tower. He and Northumberland entreat her to go to France as Richard is to be sent to Pomfret. Richard warns Northumberland that the day may come when he may have to turn against the king he has helped enthrone.

The Duke and Duchess of York discuss the contrasting entries into London by the former king and the new King Henry. Then their son admits that he is involved in a plot to kill the King at Oxford. The Duke rides off to warn the King while the Duchess tells her son to get to the King first and seek his pardon. This he does and is pardoned. York arrives with the evidence of the plot followed by the Duchess to plead for her son. The King keeps his word and promises action against the other eleven conspirators.

At Windsor Sir Pierce of Exton ponders on the meaning of some words the King has uttered taking them to mean that he wants Richard dead and decides to act for the King. At Pomfret Castle, Richard talks mindlessly to himself. He become wild when food is brought to him and kills one of his keepers with an axe. Exton kills Richard.

The King is brought news of the defeat and deaths of most of the conspirators by his loyal lords to whom he expresses gratitude. Exton enters with a coffin containing Richard's body. Angered, Henry says this was not his intention and Exton can expect no reward. Henry, his conscience uneasy, intends to visit the Holy Land to atone for Richard's death.

Note: A private presentation of the play in 1595 leaves scholars little choice but to place this as the year of its writing. It came at a time when Queen Elizabeth I was very conscious about the political repercussion of plays. Thus the deposing of Richard was excised for the play's 1597 printing. Written in poetry, the play reflects the character of its subject, a weak but poetic king more given to the muses than monarchy.

✤ ✤ ✤ ✤ ✤

RICHARD II
(G.B., 1974)

p.c. *Realist Film Unit.*
d. *Peter Seabourne.*
l.p. *Colin Farrell (Richard II); Mark Kingston (John of Gaunt); Paul Chapman (Duke of York).*
c. 12 mins.

The eighth in this series features Act II, Scene 1 and Act V, Scene 5.

✤ ✤ ✤ ✤ ✤

Poor Richard II hardly lived up to the standards of his illustrious father, the Black Prince. He was said to be rather effeminate and only on a few occasions rose to the heights that monarchy can demand. His second marriage to Isabella of France was frowned upon by the people and marked a decline in his judgement and deeds. His death is still open to some speculation – was he starved to death, murdered or, as legend persists, did he escape?

With such an intriguing character it is surprising that no films, other than the listed extract, have been made. The cinema has long abandoned the concept that an historical film is all love scenes, sword fights and battles and has produced a number of excellent historical/political dramas. There should surely be appeal to an English film maker if only for the nationalistic speech by John of Gaunt: "...This royal throne of kings, this scepter'd isle,...This blessed plot, this earth, this realm, this England..." (Act II, Scene 1).

For other films with scenes from the play see **CHAPTER XXX ALL THE WORLD'S A STAGE**: SHOW OF SHOWS (1929) and **CHAPTER XXXII THE IMMORTAL BARD**: FAIR ADVENTURE SERIES (1964) and EXPLORATIONS IN SHAKESPEARE (1969).

CHAPTER XXVI
THE TRAGEDY OF KING RICHARD THE THIRD

Dramatis Personæ:

Edward IV – King of England
Elizabeth – his Queen
Edward, Prince of Wales – his elder son and later
*   King Edward V*
Richard, Duke of York – his younger son
George, Duke of Clarence – brother to Edward IV
Richard, Duke of Gloucester – brother to Edward IV
*   and later King Richard III*
Duchess of York – mother of King Edward IV, the
*   Duke of Clarence and the Duke of Gloucester*
Queen Margaret – widow of King Henry VI
Lady Anne – widow of Edward, Prince of Wales, son
*   of King Henry VI. Later wife of King Richard III*
Edward Plantagenet, Margaret Plantagenet –
*   children of the Duke of Clarence*

Henry, Earl of Richmond – later King Henry VII

Cardinal Bourchier – Archbishop of Canterbury
Thomas Rotherham– Archbishop of York
John Morton – Bishop of Ely
Christopher Urswick – a priest

Anthony Woodeville, Earl Rivers – brother of Queen
*   Elizabeth*
Marquess of Dorset, Lord Grey – sons of Queen
*   Elizabeth by a previous marriage*
Duke of Buckingham

Duke of Norfolk
Earl of Surrey – son of the Duke of Norfolk
Earl of Oxford
Lord Hastings
Lord Stanley (also known as Earl of Derby)
Lord Lovel
Sir Thomas Vaughan
Sir Richard Radcliffe
Sir William Catesby
Sir James Tyrell
Sir James Blount
Sir Walter Herbert
Sir William Brandon

Sir Robert Brackenbury – Lieutenant of the Tower
Keeper in the Tower
Lord Mayor of London
Sheriff of Wiltshire
Tressel, Berkeley – gentlemen attendants to Lady
*   Anne*

Ghosts of Henry VI, Edward Prince of Wales, and
*   other victims of King Richard*
Lords, Gentlemen, Ladies, Priest, Bishops, Page,
*   Scrivener; Pursuivant, Aldermen, Messengers,*
*   Councillors, Attendants, Soldiers, Citizens,*
*   Murderers, etc.*

Richard, Duke of Gloucester, is well aware of his character and misshapened form. He learns that his brother, George, Duke of Clarence, has been imprisoned in the Tower of London based on the fears of the dying King Edward IV that someone with the initial G threatens his line of descent. There is no love for Richard from Anne, widow of the Prince of Wales, and certainly not from the Queen and Margaret, widow of Henry VI. They all think that he is guilty of a number of murders. Richard is, however, intent on wooing Anne. More, too, he plans revenge on those who are against him and loyal to the Queen.

In the Tower, Clarence is murdered at Richard's instigation despite his promise to intervene for his freedom. Clarence dies knowing that it is at his brother's command. The King is horrified at the news of Clarence's death as he had reversed the imprisonment order and was trying to make peace in the family. Shortly after, Edward dies which brings much grief to his mother, the Duchess of York, who has now lost two sons and is having to console her two grandchildren, the son and daughter of Clarence.

Prince Edward, Prince of Wales, is welcomed to London and immediately calls for his brother, Richard, Duke of York. Their uncle Richard assumes the role of Lord Protector for Edward and Richard. The latter clearly despises his uncle Richard and is not happy at having to stay in the Tower. He has heard that their uncle, Clarence, was murdered there.

The Duke of Buckingham throws in his lot with Richard. They start to murder any opposition to their plans and many nobles meet death. Richard then tries to deny Edward's right to the crown by spreading rumours that he is a bastard. The princes are denied visits by their mother and other family members and even by Anne who is now Richard's wife, though this is something she regrets. Soon, Richard is declared King. The family of the late King Edward and its supporters now live in fear of their lives conscious of the fact that many nobles have been killed.

The Queen falls ill and Richard, anxious to be rid of any doubt to his rights to the throne, engages a villain to kill the two young princes in the Tower which is duly done. Meanwhile, Buckingham senses that he may have made a mistake in supporting Richard when

Richard fails to honour his promises to him. Buckingham deserts to the camp of Henry Tudor, Earl of Richmond, who is gathering support. When Queen Anne strangely dies, Richard is intent on marrying Elizabeth, his niece, daughter of the late King, to strengthen his claim to the throne.

Both the former Queens and Richard's mother are worried and horrified at Richard's conduct. Even so, Richard boldly enlists Queen Elizabeth's help in the wooing of her daughter. News then comes of the growing support for Richmond and of the forces amassing against the King.

Not all goes well for Richmond as he encounters storms and the defeat and capture of Buckingham. Both armies assemble at Bosworth and both leaders survey the field and make their plans. Richard is confident that he outnumbers Richmond's forces. Both commanders retire to their respective tents to sleep.

Richard's sleep is a troubled one. During the night the ghosts of those he has murdered visit and taunt him. Richard awakens from the torment and expresses his fears to Sir Richard Ratcliffe.

In the opposing camp, Richmond makes a rousing speech to his men. A subdued Richard finds the spirit to rouse his men, too. The battle goes against Richard and he is slain. The crown is offered to Henry, Earl of Richmond who pardons all and, with a wish to marry Elizabeth of York, plans to unite the two contending parties for the throne thus ending the strife between them.

Note: The material sources for Shakespeare were diverse. As with other plays he relied upon Holinshed's 'Chronicles'. A work generally attributed to Sir Thomas More, 'Life Of Richard the Third' and 'Historia Anglica' by Polydore Vergil doubtless helped. He may well have been influenced also by the anonymous play 'The True Tragedie of Richard the Third' (printed 1594) and even by a three-part Latin play by Thomas Legge 'Richardus Tertius' from 1579. The play almost certainly dates from between 1591 and 1594.

✤ ✤ ✤ ✤ ✤

RICHARD III, A SHAKESPEARE TRAGEDY
(U.S.A., 1908)

p.c. *Vitagraph.*
d. *James Stuart Blackton and/or William V. Ranous.*
l.p. *Maurice Costello; Paul Panzer; Thomas Ince; Florence Lawrence; Harry Salter; Julia Swayne-Gordon; William V. Ranous; Florence Auer; Florence Turner.*
b.w. 990 ft. (302 m.) Sil.

One of the many silent adaptations by Vitagraph of Shakespearean works, this contains action and dramatic scenes which manages to convey the story in about fifteen minutes.

"A grand reproduction of Shakespeare's sublime tragedy. A magnificent subject surpassing in every detail all previous efforts. The most powerful effusion of Shakespeare's genius, elaborately staged, gorgeously costumed and superbly acted." – Poster for the film.

RICHARD III
(G.B., 1911)

p.c. *Co-operative Cinematograph Co.*
d. *Frank R. Benson.*
l.p. *Frank R. Benson (Richard III); Constance Benson (Lady Anne); Eric Maxon (Earl of Richmond); Violet Farebrother (Queen Elizabeth); Alfred Brydone (Edward IV); Harry Caine (Hastings); Murray Carrington (Clarence); Marion Rathbone (Queen Margaret); Moffat Johnston (Buckingham); James Berry (Henry VI); Kathleen Yorke (Edward,Prince of Wales); Hetty Kenyon (Richard, Duke of York); James Maclean (Norfolk); Victor McClure (Surrey); R. L. Conrick (Earl Rivers); Wilfred Caithness (Stanley); George Manship (Oxford); L. Rupert (Sir Richard Radcliff); H. James (Sir James Tyrrel); Alfred Wild (Sir William Catesby); Cecil Dighton (Sir James Blount); John Howell (Sir Robert Brackenbury); John Victor (Lord Mayor of London); Elinor Aikin (Duchess of York); H. O. Nicholson, A. Wild (Murderers).*
b.w. 1385 ft. (422 m.) Sil.

An abbreviated version, which also borrows from HENRY VI Part 3, this is what it is – a film record of the Stratford Memorial Theatre production of the period. The film was shot in the mornings of one week. It consists of mobile tableaux in a series of thirteen scenes of key moments of the stage production.

The film was the last of a series (the rest are lost) of four plays by the F.R. Benson Company to be committed to film. The cast list is based on that for the stage performance of April 21, 1911.

"Benson played Richard with his customary vigour and flamboyance." – Roger Manvell, 'The Movie'.

KING RICHARD III
(U.S.A., 1912)

p.c. *Sterling Camera And Film Co.*
d. *James Keene.*
l.p. *Frederick Warde (Richard III); Mr. Gomp (King Edward IV).*
b.w. 4400 ft. (1341 m.) Sil.

Originally copyrighted as MR. FREDERICK WARDE IN SHAKESPEARE'S MASTERPIECE

"THE LIFE AND DEATH OF KING RICHARD III", reviews of the time suggest that the film followed the play faithfully. M.B. Dudley is also given as director.

Shown at the closing of the Venice Film Festival, Italy, 1997.

RICHARD III
(France, 1912)

p.c. *Film D'Art.*
d. *André Calmettes.*
l.p. *Philippe Garnier (Richard III); Henri Krauss; Olga Demidoff.*
b.w. 988 ft. (301 m.) Sil.

This French adaptation may have had another title.

KÖNIG RICHARD III
(Germany, 1922)

p.c. *Oswald-Film/Veidt.*
d. *Max Reinhardt.*
l.p. *Conrad Veidt and the Reinhardt Company.*
b.w. (?) mins. Sil.

Some sources note this as being produced three years earlier.

RICHARD III
(G.B., 1955)

p.c. *Laurence Olivier Productions/London Films/Big Ben Films.*
d. *Laurence Olivier.*
l.p. *Laurence Olivier (Richard III); John Gielgud (Clarence); Claire Bloom (Lady Anne); Ralph Richardson (Buckingham); Alec Clunes (Hastings); Cedric Hardwicke (Edward IV) ; Stanley Baker (Henry Tudor); Laurence Naismith (Stanley); Norman Wooland (Catesby); Mary Kerridge (Queen Elizabeth); Pamela Brown; Helen Haye; John Laurie; Esmond Knight; Michael Gough; Andrew Cruickshank; Russell Thorndike; Nicholas Hannen; Clive Morton.*
Technicolor. 161 mins. VistaVision.

Adapted by Olivier and Alan Dent, with some addition to Shakespeare's play, the directorial chair was originally offered to Carol Reed who declined, so Olivier took on the task himself as well as repeating on screen one of his most successful stage roles. The film received considerable critical acclaim which was not matched by immediate financial success. An excellent music score was the result of the third teaming of Olivier with Sir William Walton. The prelude from the score was issued by the British H.M.V. company in a recording by the Philharmonia Orchestra under the baton of the composer in 1964 and an R.C.A. version was also issued. The prelude featured again on a British Decca release "Music From Great Shakespearean Films" in 1975 played by the National Philharmonic Orchestra, Bernard Hermann conducting. This latter version was re-issued as part of "Great Film Music" on the British Viva label. A further version of the same piece appeared on "Walton: Music From Shakespearean Films" on British H.M.V.. This time it was the Royal Liverpool Philharmonic Orchestra providing the music under Sir Charles Groves' baton. More recently, the music was featured on a Chandos release featuring film music by Walton played by the Academy of St. Martin-in-the-Fields conducted by Neville Marriner.

Following the death of Olivier, his career was featured on stamps by two countries. This film was represented in the set from Sierre Leone (stamp value Le200) and on the L700 value stamp from the 1990 San Marino set "I Grandi dello Spettacolo".

Shown as part of the Everybody's Shakespeare International Festival, London, England, 1994.
Shown at the Muestra Cinematográfica del Atlantico, Cadiz, Spain, 1989.
Shown at the Shakespeare Film Festival, Wiesbaden, W. Germany, 1964.
Academy of Motion Picture Arts and Sciences, U.S.A., 1956: Nomination – Best Actor (Laurence Olivier).
Berlin Film Festival, W.Germany, 1956: International Prize – Silver Bear.
British Film Academy, G.B., 1955: Best Film, Best British Film, Best British Actor (Laurence Olivier).
Hollywood Press Association, U.S.A., Golden Globe Awards, 1956: Best English-Language Foreign Film.
Kinema Jumpo Annual Ten Best Films, Japan, 1956: Listed third in Foreign Films list.
National Film Board of Review, U.S.A., Awards 1956: Included in Best Foreign Films.
'New York Times' Annual Ten Best List, U.S.A., 1956: Listed first.
'Time' magazine's Annual Ten Best List, U.S.A., 1956: One of the four films listed in the Foreign section.

"...remarkable production which remains faithful to the piece..." – Jean Tulard, 'Guide Des Films'.

"Compelling adaptation...excellent even if somewhat theatrical production, great performances by the cast." – 'Lexikon Filme Im Fernsehen'.

"Not the best of his (Olivier's) Shakespearean films, but certainly the most dynamic..." – Robin Bean in an article entitled "Thirty Years On...", 'The Movie Scene', February, 1985.

RICHARD III
(G.B., 1974)

p.c. *Realist Film Unit/Seabourne Enterprises.*
d. *Peter Seabourne.*
l.p. *Paul Chapman (Richard III); Alison Key (Lady Anne).*
c. 12 mins.

A reconstruction of an Elizabethan stage is the setting for the famous opening soliloquy (Act I, Scene 1) and Richard's wooing of Lady Anne (Act I, Scene 2).

RICHARD III
(France/Switzerland, 1984)

p.c. *Centre Dramatiques Des Alpes/Maison De La Communication Audiovisuelle/Télévision Suisse Romande. With the assistance of the Ministry Of Culture.*

d. *Raúl Ruiz.*

l.p. *Ariel García-Valdes (King Richard III); Annie Perret (Queen Elizabeth); Gilles Arbona (Buckingham); Philippe Movier-Genoud (Queen Mary); Marie-Paule Tristram (Anne); Marc Belton (Catesby/King Edward IV); Charles Schmitt (Clarence); Michel Ferber (Hastings); Louis Beyler (Stanley).*

c. 135 mins.

French language version based on Georges Lavaudant's stage adaptation.

Shown at the Cannes Film Festival, France, 1986, as part of "Perspective Du Cinéma Français".

✤ ✤ ✤ ✤ ✤

LES ENFANTS D'EDOUARD D'ANGLETERRE
(France, 1910)

p.c. *Film D'Art?*
d. *André Calmettes?*
l.p.
b.w. 1175 ft. (358 m.) Sil.

The young Edward V, King of England, enters London for his coronation. His uncle, the Duke of Gloucester, desires the throne and ponders how to rid himself of the boy king and the King's brother. Gloucester declares them bastards and incarcerates them in the Tower of London. The Duke of Buckingham helps them to escape but they are recaptured and delivered into the hands of assassins. Mortally wounded in battle, Gloucester succumbs to remorse as his conscience conjures up visions of his victims.

The credits for this film are vague and those listed in some doubt. Confusion occurs often with the later, 1914, film. Though not completely true to Shakespeare, the elements are surely there though, obviously, subject to the influence of English history.

aka: THE PRINCES IN THE TOWER

THE PRINCES IN THE TOWER
(G.B., 1913)

p.c. *Hepworth Manufacturing Co.*
d. *E. Hay Plumb.*
l.p. *Eric Desmond; Ruby Belasco.*
b.w. Short. Sil.

The precise content of this is not known though, by implication, it is obvious. It is not thought to be truly

from Shakespeare though it is not always easy to be precise when history is involved. However, the castle set used was the same one as in **HAMLET** made by the same company in the same year.

LES ENFANTS D'EDOUARD
(France, 1914)

p.c. *Cosmograph.*
d. *Henri Andréani.*
l.p. *Jean Delvair (Queen Elizabeth); Jean Toulout (Duke of Buckingham); Georges Wague (Duke of Gloucester); Miss Suterre, Marcelle Fleury (The Princes); ? Jacquinet (King Edward); Miss Maiapolska (Rachel); René Alexandre (Tyrell)?*

b.w. 3 or 4 reels. Sil.

Basically, a remake of the 1910 film, it is not, in essence, from Shakespeare but is included for completeness since the production company credits the inspiration to the Bard. Actually, even its content is not factual – the final battle occurs in the street and Richard dies in the palace. This rather destroys the English releasing company's boast that it was adapted from the works of William Shakespeare and that it was historically faithful. Still, it seems to have had some praise at the time.

aka: THE PRINCES IN THE TOWER; THE CROWN OF RICHARD III; LA MORTE DEI FIGLI DI RE EDUARDO

THE PRINCES IN THE TOWER
(G.B., 1928)

p.c. *British Filmcraft.*
d. *George Banfield, Leslie Eveleigh.*
l.p. *G.H. Mulcaster (Duke of Gloucester); Mary Clare (Queen Elizabeth); Gabrielle Morton Lady Anne); Albert Raynor (King Edward IV); Connie Harrid (Prince Edward); Bunty Fosse (Prince Richard).*

b.w. 1935 ft. (590 m.)

Taken from the *Ghosts Of Yesterday* series, this is described as an historical ghost story. It is not acknowledged as being from Shakespeare but neither is another in the series properly credited to its obvious source. From its implied content it probably was at least inspired by the play. Though the story of the princes is a matter of historical fact, the ghost aspect can hardly be so considered. The film is therefore included as a matter of completeness.

TOWER OF LONDON
(U.S.A., 1939)

p.c. *Universal.*
d. *Rowland V. Lee.*
l.p. *Basil Rathbone (Richard, Duke of Gloucester); Boris Karloff (Mord); Barbara O'Neil (Queen Elizabeth); Ian Hunter (King Edward IV); Vincent Price (Duke of Clarence); John Rodion (Lord De Vere); John Sutton (John Wyatt); Miles Mander (King Henry VI); Rose Hobart*

(Anne Neville); Ronald Sinclair (Prince Edward); Leo G. Carroll; Nan Grey; Lionel Belmore; Ralph Forbes; Frances Robinson; Donnie Dunagan; Ernest Cossart.

b.w. 92 mins.

Following the Shakespearean view of Richard III, this shows how the deformed king with the help of his executioner, Mord, kills his way to the throne. His victims include King Henry VI, the Duke of Clarence and the young King Edward and his brother. He is finally crushed at the battle of Bosworth Field.

Some good performances, notably one by Basil Rathbone in the lead, and good photography help this along. John Rodion, who plays Richard when younger, is Basil Rathbone's son.

Shown as part of the Everybody's Shakespeare International Festival, London, England, 1994.

"Rathbone provides a most vivid portrayal..." – 'Variety'.

"Shakespeare's RICHARD III, stripped of its poetry but with all the gore intact..." – Clive Hirschhorn, 'The Universal Story'.

aka: LA TOUR DE LONDRES; LA TORRE DE LONDRES

TOWER OF LONDON
(U.S.A., 1962)

p.c. AIP/Admiral.
d. Roger Corman.
l.p. Vincent Price (Richard Of Gloucester); Michael Pate (Sir Ratcliffe); Robert Brown (Sir Justin); Joan Freeman (Lady Margaret); Justice Eatson (Edward IV); Richard McCauly (Clarence); Sara Selby (Queen Elizabeth); Sandra Knight (Mistress Shore); Richard Hale (Tyrus); Eugene Martin (Prince Edward); Donald Losby (Prince Richard);Bruce Gordon (Earl of Buckingham); Joan Camden (Anne).

b.w. 79 mins.

Similar to the preceding entry minus the executioner. Vincent Price graduated from the role of Clarence to the lead in this version.

Francis Ford Coppola is credited as dialogue director.

"Screen writers...probably were more inspired by their bank managers than by Shakespeare." – Ronald Bergan, 'The United Artists Story'.

"Disappointing remake...despite the presence of...Vincent Price." – 'Satellite TV Europe' magazine.

RICHARD III
(G.B., 1995)

p.c. A Bayly/Paré Production in association with United Artists Pictures Developed for Mayfair International with the participation of British Screen and First Look Pictures
d. Richard Loncraine.
l.p. Ian McKellen (Richard III); Annette Bening (Elizabeth); Robert Downey Jr. (Rivers); Jim Broadbent (Buckingham); Nigel Hawthorne (Clarence); Maggie Smith (Duchess of York); Kristin Scott-Thomas (Anne); Dominic West (Henry Richmond); John Wood (Edward IV); Adrian Dunbar (Tyrell); Linus Roach; Christopher Bowen (Prince Edward); Edward Jewkesbury (King Henry); Bill Paterson (Radcliffe); Matthew Groon (Young Prince); Kate Steavenson-Payne (Princess Elizabeth); Tim McInnerny (Catesby); Roger Hammond (Archbishop); Dennis Lill (Lord Mayor); Edward Hardwicke (Stanley); Ryan Gillmore (George Stanley); Donald Sumpter (Brackenbury); Marco Williamson (Prince of Wales); Andy Rashleigh (Jailer); Bruce Purchase; James Dreyfus; David Antrobus.

Eastman/Kodak. 106 mins. S WS

The England of the 1930s has been plagued by a civil war resulting in the death of the King. His successor, Edward, and his American wife, Elizabeth now rule and with three children the succession seems secure. However, Edward's deformed brother, Richard, has other plans. This charismatic man is endowed with talents to compensate for his physical misfortune. He is a charming seducer of women and a leader of men. With these talents he embarks upon his ambitious dream to sit upon the throne of England.

The text is Shakespeare which makes its placing here debatable. Should it be in the first section? The temporal setting and the costumes were the decisive factors. Set in a ficticious England of the 1930s, this well-received version of the play surely illustrates the durability of the plot. In making such a time transfer, director Loncraine was conscious of the need to make the film appeal to the public. He stated (quite correctly) that Shakespeare was not an élitist writer. He wrote his plays for the people and Loncraine expressed his similar intent to make a film which everyone could understand.

The time setting, the clearly Nazi-styled uniforms and rallies, the tanks and modern warfare, all reflect events of quite recent history. These are events with which everyone can identify even if only through media retrospective coverage. This, of course, in its way, makes the film pertinent and achieves the intended aims. As Ian McKellen said: "It takes no strain in the story to set it in a modernish period, to see these people in a modern world...and see that their behaviour is echoed today and they are behaving not like characters in some far distant pageant but like characters on the world stage within living memory." (The Movie Show!).

McKellen, an actor of undoubted pedigree, not least in the works of Shakespeare, had played the role in the successful version at the National Theatre, London, England, recalled in the same programme: "There is always a point when you're in a show in the theatre when you say to the director 'Why can't we film it?'" The reply was the catalyst for this film and the encouragement for McKellen to work on the script for it.

For those wanting an audio souvenir of the film, the soundtrack album was issued by Mercury. Trevor Jones was responsible for the music.

Academy of Motion Picture Arts and Sciences, U.S.A., 1995: Nominations – Best Art/Set Direction (Tony Burrough), Best Costume Design (Shuna Harwood).
Berlin Film Festival, Germany, 1996: "Silver Bear" for Best Director (Richard Loncraine).
British Academy of Film and Television Arts, England, 1997: Best Production Design (Tony Burrough), Best Costumes (Shuna Harwood)
'Evening Standard' Film Awards, London, 1996: Best Film, Best Technical Achievement (Tony Burrough).
Hollywood Foreign Press Association Golden Globe Awards, U.S.A., 1996: Nomination – Best Actor (Ian McKellen).
London Film Critics' Awards, England, 1996: Best Actor (Ian McKellen).

aka: RICARDO III, DE WILLIAM SHAKESPEARE

✢ ✢ ✢ ✢ ✢

The death of Richard III at the Battle of Bosworth (1485) remains one of the most important events in English history. Not only was Richard the last king to be killed in battle, but his death marked the end of the feud known as the War of the Roses, so named because the opposing sides had, as emblems, roses – the Lancastrians, the red rose and the Yorkists, the white rose. But what of Richard himself?

Shakespeare follows the same line as some Tudor historians about King Richard III of England (1483 to 1485). Thus he is depicted as deformed – hence the Crouchback (Crookback) name – and evil. In consequence, any film following this view does not necessarily do justice to the man. He may well have been ambitious and unscrupulous, but later research does not always confirm that he was particularly bad or greatly deformed.

Be that as it may, the Olivier interpretation seems to have stuck in the public imagination. When the late Peter Sellers recorded, with some success, a monologue version of the Beatles' song "A Hard Day's Night" in 1965, it was very much in the Olivier style, the music being cunningly transposed to a madrigal lilt. Sellers' Olivier/Richard "chopped off the words of the lyric so that every one seemed a head falling off the block." (Alexander Walker – 'Peter Sellers') and he even appeared garbed as the King in television performances of it (*The Music Of Lennon And McCartney*) transmitted on December 16, 1965! On another point of trivia, the 1978 French film about horse racing, *Mon Royaume Pour Un Cheval*, borrowed its title, as linguists may have guessed, from King Richard's last words: "A horse!, A horse! my kingdom for a horse!."

For other films with scenes from this play see **CHAPTER XXX ALL THE WORLD'S A STAGE**: PEG OF OLD DRURY (1935); PRINCE OF PLAYERS (1954); L'IMPORTANT, C'EST D'AIMER (1975); ¡QUE NOS IMPORTA LA REVOLUCIÓN! (1972); THE GOODBYE GIRL (1977) and LOOKING FOR RICHARD (1996) and **CHAPTER XXXII THE IMMORTAL BARD**: STRATFORD ADVENTURE (1954); SHAKESPEARE'S THEATRE (1954); FAIR ADVENTURE SERIES (1964) and MASKS AND FACES (1969)*.

*Denotes film extracts.

CHAPTER XXVII
TWELFTH NIGHT or WHAT YOU WILL

Dramatis Personæ:

Orsino – Duke of Illyria
Valentino, Curio – attendants to the Duke

Sebastian – Viola's brother
Antonio – a sea captain and Sebastian's friend
Viola – Sebastian's sister
A Sea Captain – Viola's friend
Olivia, a countess

Sir Toby Belch – her uncle
Malvolio – her steward
Maria – her woman
Fabian, Feste (a clown) – her servants

Sir Andrew Aguecheek
Lords, Priest, Sailors, Officers, Musicians and
  Attendants

Sebastian and Viola are twins, born within the same hour. It is also within an hour that they suffered separation in a shipwreck. Viola is saved by the captain and a few sailors and lands on the shores of Illyria. The twins are so alike in looks and feelings that only their dress distinguishes them and so it is natural that Viola should be more than distressed at the apparent loss of her brother. She is consoled only by the news that he was seen strapped to the ship's mast.

Viola learns that Illyria is ruled by Orsino, a duke of dignity, besotted with love for the fair Olivia, a beautiful woman who lost her parents and then her brother. Since his death, she abhors the sight of men. Viola, touched by Olivia's love for her dead brother, expresses her wish to live with Olivia as her servant. Olivia, however, lives as a recluse admitting nobody to her home.

Viola decides upon a plan. Dressing as a man, she seeks to enter the service of Count Orsino as a page. With the help of the captain she is transformed into the image of her missing brother (who is, as it happens, not dead) and, again through the captain's good offices, she is accepted into Orsino's court under the name of Cesario. There Cesario quickly makes a good impression and is soon Orsino's most favoured attendant and confidant.

He tells Cesario of his love and its constant rejection leading him to a slothful life. Now the true side of Cesario begins to tell as "he" realises that "he" loves Orsino. Through debate and anecdotes she tries to imply to him that there may be another who loves him but he cannot believe that anyone has such a strong love as he has.

When a servant returns to Orsino with yet another rejection and a message that Olivia intends to remain cloistered for another seven years, Orsino prevails upon Cesario to go to Olivia and plead his case. Cesario goes with reluctance not really wishing to present Orsino's case to what is now a rival in love.

Such is Cesario's persistence that Olivia permits entry and even unveils her face to the bold visitor. Olivia, in fact, is quite taken with the handsome youth and feels a passion for him unaware, of course, of the disguise.

Cesario praises Olivia's beauty and explains what "he" would do if "he" were her suitor. Cesario does not forget to extol the virtues of Orsino which Olivia already knows but she sends Cesario away saying that "he" should tell Orsino to send no more messengers unless it is Cesario to tell how Orsino has accepted her words.

Olivia sends a servant after Cesario with the gift of a ring. Cesario now finds "himself" in a difficult position. Oblivious of apparent difference in rank, Olivia has fallen in love with "him". With difficulty, Cesario tells Orsino of Olivia's wish but he wishes Cesario to go again. For the meantime, Orsino orders the performance of a song of unrequited love which brings sadness to Cesario.

When Orsino sees the sadness of his page, he assumes that "he" is in love and asks Cesario about this. Cesario's reply leads Orsino to believe that Cesario loves an older woman though, of course, the reference is to himself.

Calling once more upon Olivia, Cesario is made readily welcome and Olivia openly declares her love. Cesario has no choice but to threaten never to come again and professes never to be able to love a woman.

Upon leaving Olivia, Cesario is challenged by one of Olivia's rejected suitors. But Cesario is saved from having to reveal all by a stranger who accepts the challenge. This is in vain for the local justice officers arrest the stranger for a crime committed some years before. He demands money from Cesario who does not know him but in gratitude does hand over some to him. The stranger accuses Cesario of ingratitude claiming to have saved "him" from death and calling him Sebastian. Before Cesario can question him, he is taken away. This does arouse Cesario's hopes that Sebastian may be alive and it transpires that the stranger, Antonio, a sea captain, had saved Sebastian's life. When Sebastian wished to visit Illyria, he had accompanied him even though he put himself at risk having wounded Orsino's nephew some years before. This is the crime for which he has now been arrested. Having given Sebastian money, it is no wonder that he was surprised when, having searched for him, he came across Cesario who did not recognise him.

Fearing another confrontation, Cesario makes for home as quickly as possible. Indeed, the adversary does return and, by chance, meets Sebastian and believes him to be Cesario. They begin to fight but this is stopped by Olivia who, thinking that Sebastian is Cesario, invites him into the house.

Sebastian is surprised at Olivia's charm and beauty and does not object to the bold advances she makes though wonders if she is a little unbalanced. She, too, finds her Cesario slightly changed. This change inspires Olivia to send for a priest and the two are married. Sebastian then leaves to find his friend Antonio to tell him the good news.

After Sebastian has left, Orsino and Cesario arrive at Olivia's home just as the prisoner is brought before the Duke. Antonio sees Cesario and thinking "he" is Sebastian accuses him of ingratitude after all Antonio had done in saving his life. Orsino says that Cesario has been his page for some three months. This Olivia confirms with much praise for Cesario and soon Orsino realises that Olivia has strong feelings for Cesario. Orsino turns on Cesario with threats of death which Cesario expresses willingness to suffer if it pleases the Duke.

Olivia, not anxious to lose what she believes is her recently acquired husband, tells of the marriage and the priest is sent for to confirm this. Despite Cesario's protest, Orsino declares that he does not want to see them again. But as he is about to leave, Sebastian arrives and greets his new wife. All are amazed at the similarity between Cesario and Sebastian. Cesario then reveals that "he" is really Viola.

Now, Olivia is not displeased at having married a handsome man so like the person with whom she had fallen in love. Orsino, his hopes for Olivia as a bride dashed, turns his thoughts to Viola. He recalls the looks of his former page and the many hints, now obvious, made of love. In the end he vows to marry Viola and Olivia offers her home and the priest to perform the ceremony.

So both Viola and Sebastian are wed on the same day and the misfortune of shipwreck has led to the good fortune of happy marriages.

Note: Though there is evidence to suggest that this may have been written in 1599 and another theory places the first performance in early 1601, it is perhaps safer to place the date as about 1600. The sources for it are plentiful with Plautus' 'Manaechmi' and the Italian 'Ignanni' as the main contenders. Latterly the Italian play 'Gl'Ingannati', Sydney's 'Arcadia', the play of 'Sir Clyomon and Clamydes' and Forde's 'Parsimus' could well have had an influence.

✠ ✠ ✠ ✠ ✠

TWELFTH NIGHT
(U.S.A., 1910)

p.c. *Vitagraph.*
d. *Charles Kent.*
l.p. *Charles Kent (Malvolio); Florence Turner (Viola); Julia Swayne-Gordon (Olivia); Tefft Johnson (Orsino); Marin Sais (Maria); Edith Storey (Sebastian); William Humphrey (Toby Belch); James Young (Andrew Aguecheek).*
b.w. 970 ft. (296 m.) Sil.

Noted at the time as being successful and well acted and marred only by attempting to put too much of the plot in a short time and unnecessary inter-titles which, though possibly complementary to the actors, is hardly complimentary to the author. Vitagraph said: "This release will attract Shakespearean students and dramatic societies" ('Vitagraph Bulletin', November 16-30, 1909). The cast list is based on information from a number of sources but is still suspect. James Stuart Blackton and/or William V. Ranous are noted by some as the director.

"It brings to many who really enjoy this drama an opportunity to see it adequately performed and at a nominal cost." – 'Moving Picture World', February 19, 1910.

TWELFTH NIGHT
(G.B., 1953)

p.c. *Charles Deane Productions.*
d. *Charles Deane.*
l.p. *Young Vic Theatre Company. Narrator: Ronald Howard.*
b.w. 12 mins.

Extract (the letter scene) which formed part of the series made for television called *The World's A Stage*.

DVENADTSATAVA NOCH
(U.S.S.R., 1955)

p.c. *Lenfilm.*
d. *Yan Fried.*
l.p. *Klara Luchko (Viola/Sebastian); Alla Larionova (Olivia); V. Melvediev (Duke Orsino); Mikhail Yanskin (Sir Toby Belch); G. Vitsin (Sir Andrew Aguecheek); B. Freindlich (Clown); V. Merkuriev (Malvolio); S. Lukyanov (Antonio); A. Lisyankaya (Maria); S. Filippov (Fabian); A. Antonov (Sea Captain).*
Agfacolor. 90 mins.

Simple telling of the tale though not without cuts and some rearrangement leading to some shifts of emphasis. American sources note the running time as fifty-six minutes and the colour as Magicolor. Though Agfacolor is the system noted by a number of sources, probably it was in Sovcolor which is very similar to it.

Shown at the Shakespeare Film Festival, Wiesbaden, W. Germany, 1964.

"It's well directed, handsomely mounted and, for the most part, excellently acted." – 'Variety'.

"...an interesting glimpse of Shakespeare as viewed through foreign eyes..." – 'Monthly Film Bulletin', June, 1956.

"...Miss K. Luchko, a spirited Viola, and Miss A. Larionova, a generous and lovely Olivia..." – 'The Times'.

"...rare collector's piece...beautiful settings, lavish costumes..." – 'Daily Film Renter'.

aka: TWELFTH NIGHT

TWELFTH NIGHT: AN INTRODUCTION
(G.B., 1970)

p.c. *BHE/Seabourne.*
d. *Peter Seabourne.*
l.p.
c. 23 mins.

The first in this series of short films intended for educational purposes contained short extracts. The cast would probably be from the small selected group Seabourne used for the others in the series.

TWELFTH NIGHT
(G.B., 1995)

p.c. *Renaissance Films. A Fineline Features, Summit Entertainment, Entertainment Film Distributors, Circus Films and B.B.C. Films presentation.*
d. *Trevor Nunn.*
l.p. *Ben Kingsley (Feste); Nigel Hawthorne (Malvolio); Mel Smith (Sir Toby Belch); Helena Bonham Carter (Olivia); Imogen Stubbs (Viola); Toby Stephens (Orsino); Richard E. Grant (Sir Andrew Aguecheek); Steven Mackintosh (Sebastian); Imelda Staunton (Maria).*
c. 130 mins. S

The story is related with a time shift to Victorian England but with a feeling for an earlier period.

Though he was head of the Royal Shakespeare company for eighteen years, Trevor Nunn had never directed this play. His opportunity came with this film which was shot in Cornwall, England, using two magnificent country houses. To this can be added the natural beauty of Cornwall in what is the most colourful of seasons – autumn ("It is the most autumnal of Shakespeare's comedies" – Trevor Nunn).

Shown at the Cannes Film Festival, France, 1996.
Shown at the San Sebastian Film Festival, Spain, 1996.

"...from what I've seen...it looks breathtaking..." – Nigel Hawthorne.

aka: NOCHE DE REYES O LO QUE QUERAIS

✤ ✤ ✤ ✤

VIOLA UND SEBASTIAN
(W. Germany, 1972)

p.c. *Guertler/Runze.*
d. *Ottokar Runze.*
l.p. *Karin Hübner (Viola); Frank Glaubrecht (Sebastian); Inken Sommar (Olivia); Michael J. Boyle (Orsino); Heinz Theo Branding; Uwe Dallmeier; Gottfried Kramer; Herbert Stass; Renate Schubert.*
c. 93 mins.

Modern version of the story complete with beat music and hippie elements and set in rural Schleswig Holstein.

"Total failure film version of TWELFTH NIGHT...recommended only as Ottokar Runze's first work." – Robert Fischer and Joe Hembus, 'Der Neue Deutsche Film 1960-1980'.

TWELFTH NIGHT
(Australia, 1986)

p.c. *Twelfth Night.*
d. *Neil Armfield.*
l.p. *Gillian Jones (Viola/Sebastian); Ivar Kants (Orsino); Peter Cummins (Malvolio); Jacqy Phillips (Olivia); Kerry Walker (The Fool); Geoffrey Rush (Sir Andrew Aguecheek); John Wood (Sir Toby Aguecheek); Tracy Harvey (Sarah); Stuart McCreery (Antonio); Odile Le Clezio (Olivia's Maid); Igor Sas; Russel Kiefel.*
Agfacolor. 120 mins.

Made on a miserly budget, this is said to be quite well played. Some may, of course, find the Australian accents a little difficult to accept or find the modern-dress concept jarring. The director has also taken substantial liberties with the text in what is the film version of a stage production which is why, plus the present day setting, it is placed here and not in the first part. Another quirk is in the casting of a woman in the role of The Fool. It would appear to have been successful in Australia for the Australian Film Institute gave its Best Supporting Actress award to Kerry Walker for her performance.

✤ ✤ ✤ ✤

NICHTS ALS SÜNDE
(E. Germany, 1965)

p.c. *Defa.*
d. *Hanus Burger.*

l.p. *Helga Čočková (Viola); Annekathrin Bürger (Olivia); Brigitte Krause (Maria); Herwart Grosse (Malvolio); Arno Wyzniewski (Orsino); Herbert Graedtke (Sebastian); Jochen Thomas (Antonio); Hans-Joachim Hegewald (Sir Toby Belch); Rolf Römer (Sir Andrew Aguecheek); Hans Lucke (Narrator); Hans-Jürgen Plust (Sea Captain); Rainer Elvers (Clown); Carlos Rom (Clown); Rolf Herricht (Television Reporter); Günter Rüger (Barber); Joachim Siebenschuh, Dieter Schaarschmidt, Werner Möhring, Joachim Fuchs (The Four Beatles); Peter Kiwitt (Majordomo); Rudi Bernburg (Page); Alfred Lux; Georg Irmer; Paul Lewitt; Sabine Thalbacher; Agnes Kraus; Vera Byl; Hannes Vohrer; Fredy Barten; Elke Rieckhoff; Hans-Eberhard Gäbel; Karin Bischof; Monika Reeh; Günter Schwarzlose; Angelika Gründel; Emil Schomburg; Thea Beyer etc.Singers: Jutta Hoffmann (Viola); Fred Frohberg (Orsino); Gerry Wollf (Malvolio); Manfred Krug (Narrator); Manfred Raasch (Sebastian) with Chorsänger des Staatlichen Rundfunkkomitees. Dancers: Das Ballett der Deutschen Staatsoper, Berlin.Orchestras: Das Tanzorchester des Berliner Rundfunks (conductor: Günter Gollasch), Das Defa-Sinfonieorchester (conductor: Lothar Seyfarth).*

c. 106 mins.

This musical adaptation of the play – the credits clearly acknowledge the source – seems to have had a very modern slant and a strange combination of music judging by the types of orchestra involved. It suggests a mixture of the play, music (credited to Günter Deicke and Klaus Fehmel) of diverse types, and of ballet.

It may well have been a work for television but it seems to have been shown outside that sphere. Its content suggests that it be more comfortably placed in an opera/ballet section.

Note: The names of the characters portrayed have been translated from the German to the more easily recognisable English originals.

aka: WAS IHR WOLLT

✤ ✤ ✤ ✤ ✤

As in THE COMEDY OF ERRORS, Shakespeare involves the audience in a complicated world of separated twins with the added complication of the female disguised as a male. To this, was added the theme of unrequited love. Judging by the number of screen adaptations of the play, it has posed something of a challenge to the film world or has it been a case of commercial viability? As it is, no complete film of the original play exists, least of all in its original language.

For other films with scenes from this play see **CHAPTER XXX ALL THE WORLD'S A STAGE**: SHAKESPEARE WALLAH (1965); VÍZKERESZT (1968) and **CHAPTER XXXII THE IMMORTAL BARD**: TWELFTH NIGHT (1916); IMMORTAL GENTLEMAN (1935); SHAKESPEARE'S THEATER (1954); FAIR ADVENTURE SERIES (1972) and THE PHOENIX AND THE TURTLE (1972).

CHAPTER XXVIII
THE TWO GENTLEMEN OF VERONA

Dramatis Personæ:

Valentine – a gentleman
Speed – his servant

Proteus – a gentleman
Antonio – his father
Launce – Proteus' servant
Panthino – Antonio's servant

Julia – beloved of Proteus
Lucetta – her waiting woman

Duke of Milan
Silvia – his daughter
Thurio – her suitor
Eglamour

Host
Outlaws
Servants, Musicians

Valentine and Proteus, two gentlemen of Verona, are close friends and are almost constantly together. However, Proteus loves Julia and talks about her constantly. This is the one thing that annoys Valentine who tells his friend of his feelings and leaves for Milan.

Proteus sends a letter to Julia by her maid. Julia pretends disinterest even to the point of destroying the letter. She quickly puts it together again when the maid has gone and sends a reply, her warmest yet, to Proteus. He is delighted to receive this and is reading it when his father enters.

He asks Proteus what he is reading and Proteus replies that it is a letter from Valentine. He says that Valentine has found favour with the Duke of Milan and would like Proteus to join him. In inventing this Proteus soon realises that he has made a big mistake. His father, feeling that his son has been at home too long, thinks that it would be good for Proteus to go to Milan. Proteus knows his father only too well and that nothing will change his mind.

What Proteus had invented about Valentine is, in fact, true. Valentine is well liked by the Duke of Milan. There is, however, a problem. He has also fallen in love with the Duke's daughter, Silvia. She is promised to Thurio whom she despises for lacking the qualities that Valentine has.

It happens that Silvia is in the company of her two suitors and Valentine is mocking Thurio, when the Duke arrives to tell Valentine that Proteus is soon to arrive. Valentine extols the virtues of his friend and the Duke is prepared to make him welcome. Indeed, Proteus arrives immediately and he is introduced to those present.

Fate now cruelly intervenes. Valentine, as soon as he is alone with his friend, tells how he has fallen in love with Silvia and how, with the aid of a rope ladder, the two lovers plan to escape to Mantua that very evening. Unfortunately, immediately he saw Silvia, Proteus also fell in love with her.

Determined to have her for himself, he goes to the Duke and cunningly presents the facts to the Duke even including the details of the proposed flight of Silvia and Valentine. He does it in such a manner, seeming to balance his loyalty to his friend with his duty to a host who has made him so welcome, that the Duke thinks highly of him.

That night the Duke waits for Valentine and stops him. Asked where he is going, Valentine says he is going to meet a messenger who will take a letter to his father. The Duke begs him stay and craftily plans to discover his secret. The Duke explains that his daughter's stubbornness over her proposed marriage to Thurio has upset him. He himself now wishes to take a wife and to turn out his daughter. He claims that he is unskilled in the current arts of courtship and seeks advice from Valentine.

Valentine gives him general advice and, learning that the woman's father prevents them meeting, suggests that he visits the lady in her chamber using a rope ladder as means of entry. At this moment, the Duke pulls off Valentine's cloak to reveal not only the rope ladder but also a letter from Silvia. He banishes Valentine from Milan.

In Verona, Julia yearns for Proteus. She decides to go to Milan. Dressed as men for safety, she and her maid set out for Milan and arrive there just after Valentine has left. They take lodgings at an inn where they indulge in conversation with the owner. He offers to take the young "gentleman" out to hear some music for a young man is set to woo his love with song.

Though unsure of what Proteus might think, she is anxious for news of him but is shocked to find the lover is her own Proteus. She admires the lady Silvia

162

who remains faithful to Valentine and chides Proteus for the wrong he has done to his friend. Even so, Julia's love for Proteus is strong and, through the inn keeper, becomes employed, in disguise, as Proteus' page with the name of Sebastian. In this role, she has to take messages to Silvia and even the very ring that she had given to Proteus.

Sebastian takes the opportunity to tell Silvia all about Julia (herself, of course) and her love for Proteus. Silvia feels compassion for Julia and, correctly, returns the ring which gives much cheer to the disguised Julia.

As for Valentine, he is unsure of what to do being unwelcome in Milan and ashamed to return home in disgrace. He wanders aimlessly and is set upon by bandits. He tells them that he has no wealth and reveals his plight. The bandits are moved by his story and say they will spare him if he becomes their leader. His life in ruins, he has little to lose and agrees providing there are no attacks upon women or the poor.

Silvia, now under pressure from her father to marry Thurio, runs away with the help of Eglamour, an old gentleman. She has heard, incorrectly, that Valentine is in Mantua and thus heads for that city. The two pass through the area where Valentine and his men operate. Though Eglamour escapes, Silvia is captured and is to be taken to the bandit leader.

Proteus has, however, followed Silvia accompanied by his Sebastian. He boldly rescues Silvia and immediately, to the distress of his Sebastian who fears Silvia's warm response in the circumstances, again declares his love. The situation is saved by Valentine who, having heard of the capture of a lady, arrives to console and reassure the prisoner.

Caught in the act of wooing Silvia, Proteus is ashamed and repentant, confessing all. The noble Valentine not only forgives his friend, but also restores their friendship and renounces Silvia in favour of Proteus. On hearing this, Sebastian faints. This emergency aborts any emotions that Silvia may have about being so traded.

Sebastian recovers and, quick of mind, hands over the ring Proteus had given to Julia saying that "his" master had instructed "him" to give it to Silvia. Proteus, recognises the ring and asks how the "boy" obtained it. "He" replies that Julia received it and Julia is returning it.

The truth then becomes apparent and Proteus has love only for Julia. Thus the two couples are happily united. Well, it is so for a few moments for the Duke of Milan and Thurio arrive in pursuit of Silvia. Thurio demands Silvia but soon retreats when

threatened by Valentine. The Duke rebukes him for such cowardice and realises the true worth of Valentine and consents to the union with his daughter.

The Duke, generous as he is noble, pardons all the bandits whose crimes have been quite petty, and, hearing Proteus' confession, forgives him too. The two couples are married in Milan.

Note: This light comedy comes from the writer's early period and was probably influenced by 'Diana', a romance in Spanish by the Portuguese Jorge de Montemayor, and one of the tales about friendship, possibly the story of Titus and Gisippus, which was then available. He may well have read the story in the version by Sir Thomas Elyot in 'The Boke Named the Governour'. The play poses a few mysteries, not least of which are the unresolved questions and peculiarities raised by the text. These are not apparent from the above synopsis but become apparent upon reading the play. The other mystery is its date of origin. Though it was mentioned in 1598, it is generally thought to have been written about 1594. Even this date is subject to debate. Was this the year of writing or the year of revision of an existing work?

✤ ✤ ✤ ✤ ✤

ZWEI HERREN AUS VERONA
(W. Germany, 1963)

p.c. *Bavaria Atelier.*
d. *Hans Dieter Schwarze.*
l.p. *Hans Karl Friedrich; Alfred Balthoff; Rolf Becker; Eugene Wallrath; Walter Falk; Karl Lieffen; Martin Lichtnfels; Katina Hoffman; Heidelinde Weiss; Monika John; Franz Schafheitlin.*
b.w. 119 mins.

This is, of course, the German version of the play and, as with others from this source, a fairly faithful adaptation.

Though made for television, it is believed that this, as with **HAMLET** from the same studio, may well have seen limited cinema and/or festival showings.

✤ ✤ ✤ ✤ ✤

YI JIAN MEI
(China, 1931)

p.c. *Lian Hua Film Company.*
d. *Bu Wancang.*
l.p. *Ruan Lingyu (Julia); Jin Yan (Valentine); Gao Zhanfei; Lin Chuchu.*
b.w. 113 mins. Sil.

A modern version of the play, it is obviously set in its country of origin.

This was an early production from this particular company and it boasted two local stars of the era.

CHAPTER XXVIII – THE TWO GENTLEMEN OF VERONA

Shown at the XIV Edizione Pordenone Cinema Verdi, Italy, 1995, as part of "Le Giornate del Cinema Muto" retrospective.

The two cast members noted are the lead actress and actor respectively. The title translates as "A Branch of Plum Blossom".

✤ ✤ ✤ ✤ ✤

Given the peculiarities and the light-weight nature of the play, it is perhaps not surprising that film versions of it are scarce. Saying that is not meant to denigrate the work for it has its value. The lack of substance only makes it more suitable for the more intimate atmosphere of the theatre or, indeed, in home comfort on television. The latter is ideally suited to a play which relies upon so many duologues. Incidentally, the play contains the well-known song "Who is Silvia?".

In his intent to tidy up the plot and conclude with a happy ending – summed up neatly by the last line of the play "One feast, one house, one mutual happiness" – Shakespeare seems to have put this together in some haste. It was, it might be said, a portent of what was to come, a style of ending to his comedies at which the writer would become adept.

SHAKESPEARE – THE SILENT VIEW

German advertisements for

ROMEO AND JULIET (G.B., 1908)
(Gaumont)

CLEOPATRA (U.S.A., 1912)
(Helen Gardner Picture Players)

CLEOPATRA (U.S.A., 1912)
(Helen Gardner Picture Players)

A WINTER'S TALE (U.S.A., 1910)
(Thanhouser)

TWELFTH NIGHT (U.S.A., 1910)
(Vitagraph)

ROMEO AND JULIET (U.S.A., 1916)
(Quality Pictures Corp.)

OTHELLO (Germany, 1922)
(Wörner Film)

ROMEO AND JULIET (U.S.A., 1916)
(Fox Film Corp.)

THE MERCHANT OF VENICE (U.S.A., 1914)
(Universal Film Manufacturing Co./Gold Seal Brand)

HAMLET (G.B., 1916)
(Hepworth Manufacturing Company)

HAMLET (Germany, 1920)
(Art Film)

offered an unusual approach (from a number of aspects) to the story

German poster for **THE TAMING OF THE SHREW** (U.S.A., 1929)
(Pickford Corp., Elton Corp. for the United Artists)

Fy og Bi

HAN HUN OG HAMLET

Palladiums
første danske
Tone- og Sangfilm

Hamlet subjected to homeland humour in 1932.
(Palladium-Lystpil)

Same theme, different treatment –

ESPOIR OU LE CHAMP MAUDIT
(France, 1936)
(under its revised title)
(Sport Film)

**ROMEO UND JULIA
AUF DEM DORFE**
(Switzerland, 1941)
(Pro Filme Genossenschaft
für Filmproduktion)

Jíří Trnka brought his own dream-like magic to this version of A MIDSUMMER NIGHTS DREAM

SEN NOCI SVATOJÁNSKÉ (Czechoslovakia, 1957-59)

(Krátký Film Prague, Studio Kresleného. A Loutlového Filmu)

LES AMANTS DE VERONE (France, 1948)
(C.I.C.C.)

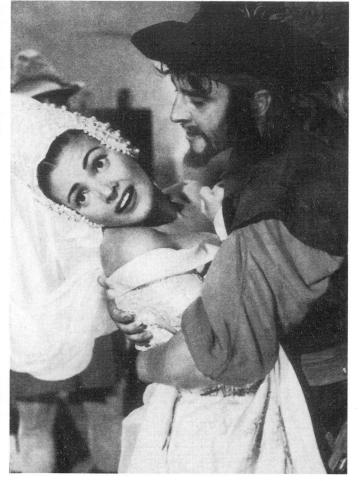

LA FIERECILLA DOMADA (Spain, France, 1955)
(Benito Perojo, Vascos-Interproduction)

OTHELLO (U.S.S.R., 1955)
(Mosfilm)

HAMLET (W. Germany, 1962)
(Bavaria Atelier)

LE MARCHAND DE VENISE
(France, Italy, 1953)
(Elysée Film/Venturini Producione Films)

DVENADTSATAVA NOCH
(U.S.S.R., 1955)
(Lenfilm)

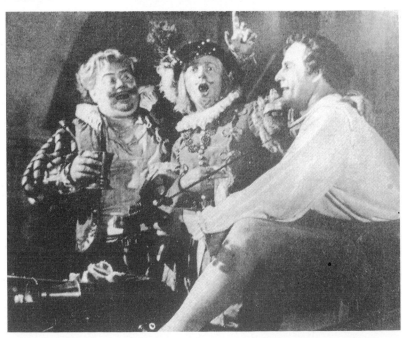

KOROL LIR (U.S.S.R., 1970)
(Lenfilm)

MACBETH (U.S.A., 1948)
(Republic. A Mercury Production)

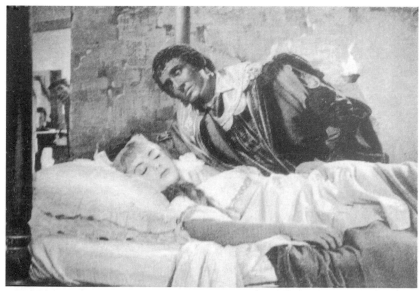

KEAN (GENIO E SREGOLATEZZA)
(Italy, 1957)
(Vides/Lux Film)

UKPOSCHENIE STROPTIVOY
(U.S.S.R., 1960)
(Mosfilm)

HAMILE (Ghana, 1965)
(Ghana Film Industry)

ROMEO I DZULETTA
(U.S.S.R., 1954)
(Mosfilm)

SHAKESPEARE, SEX AND CINEMA

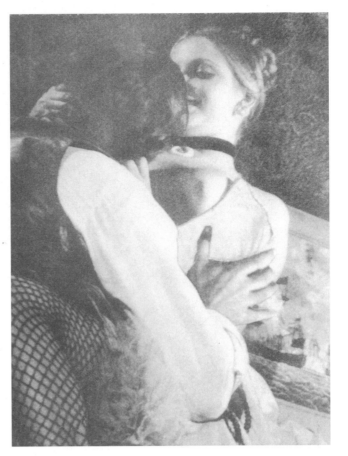

QUELLA SPORCA STORIA DEL WEST
(Italy, 1967)
(Daiano/Leone)
One of the "Spaghetti Western" versions of the story featured sex and violence.

Cleopatra had much to offer
but it was not Shakespeare in
THE NOTORIOUS CLEOPATRA

**THE SECRET SEX LIVES OF
ROMEO AND JULIET** (U.S.A., 1969)
(Global?)
Probably these were secrets the Bard did not know and perhaps that is for the best.

BEHIND THE SCENES

Louis Calhern and Marlon Brando take a break (before the Ides of March?) during the filming of **JULIUS CAESAR** (1953)

Director/star Charlton Heston keeps an eye on the filming of **ANTONY AND CLEOPATRA** (1972)

THE
ANIMATED
TALES

ROMEO AND JULIET

RICHARD III

TWELFTH NIGHT

A WINTER'S TALE

CHAPTER XXIX
THE WINTER'S TALE

Dramatis Personæ:

Leontes – *King of Sicilia*
Hermione – *his Queen*
Perdita – *their daughter*
Mamillius – *young Prince of Sicilia*

Antigonus, Camillo, Cleomenes, Dion – *lords of Sicilia*
Paulina – *wife of Antigonus*

Polixenes – *King of Bohemia*
Florizel – *Prince of Bohemia*

Archidamus – *a lord of Bohemia*
Old Shepherd – *said to be Perdita's father*
Clown – *his son*
Autolycus – *a rogue*
Emilia – *lady attendant to Hermione*
Mopsa, Dorcas – *shepherdesses*
Time (as Chorus)
A Mariner, A Gaoler, Lords, Gentlemen, Ladies, Officers, Servants, Shepherds and Shepherdesses

eontes, King of Sicily, leads a happy life with his beautiful queen, Hermione. He misses only one thing – the companionship of his old school friend with whom he corresponds, Polixenes, King of Bohemia. At last an invitation from Leontes is accepted and the two friends, to the pleasure of Hermione, enjoy themselves recounting past adventures.

When Polixenes makes ready to leave after a long stay, Leontes begs him to stay but it is Hermione's overtures that convince him to do so. This leads to suspicion by Leontes thence to jealousy and misinterpretation of every act of kindness by her to his friend. In the end he despatches Camillo, one of his lords, to kill Polixenes. Camillo knows that Hermione is faithful and helps Polixenes to return safely home where he himself stays as a good friend of Polixenes. The flight enrages Leontes so much that he imprisons his wife, taking her son, Mamillius, from her. The boy almost dies of sorrow. Leontes sends two messengers to the temple of Apollo at Delphos to enquire of his wife's fidelity.

In prison, Hermione gives birth to a daughter and her friend, Paulina, wife of the lord Antigonus, presents the child to the king hoping to stir him from his mood. It only angers the king more and he orders Antigonus to take the child and abandon her on some far island which he does.

Leontes, unable to await news from Delphos, calls his wife to trial and ignores evidence of her innocence Then news comes that Mamillius has died. Hermione faints and the remorseful king orders every help for her recovery. It is too late and she dies.

Unwittingly, Antigonus has left the little girl dressed in fine clothes and jewels, on the shores of Bohemia with a note of the name "Perdita" pinned to her. Antigonus dies in a storm at sea. While her father laments, she is found by a shepherd who, thanks to her jewels, becomes rich, and cares for her as his own daughter. She grows into a beautiful woman endowed with regal bearing.

By chance, Polixenes' son, Florizel, sees Perdita and falls in love with her. Disguised and under the name of Doricles he visits her. Polixenes is alarmed at his son's many absences and goes with Camillo, both in disguise, to the shepherd's house. As it is the feast of sheep-shearing every one is welcome to join in the fun and festivities.

"Doricles" and Perdita sit and talk, oblivious to what goes on. The disguised Polixenes approaches them and the shepherd infers that the young man will receive a good dowry (the remainder of the jewels). The boy asks that they witness the couples' betrothal. The king reveals himself, forbids the marriage and takes his son home. Despondent, Perdita resigns herself to her humble life.

Touched by her spirit and Florizel's love, Camillo, knowing that Leontes has repented, takes the couple to Sicily with the shepherd in the hope that Polixenes may calm down and Leontes be induced to mediate. Leontes greets them cordially and is taken with the beauty of Perdita and her resemblance to his own dead queen.

As Leontes explains to Florizel all that happened between him and the boy's father, the shepherd begins to assemble the facts and tells how he found the baby girl, producing the clothes and jewels to support his story. Delighted though he is to have found his daughter, he still sees in her the image of her mother.

Paulina then announces that a statue of Hermione has just been finished by an Italian master. Leontes is moved at the sight of his dead wife's statue especially as it appears to be of the correct age were she now alive. Paulina now apparently brings the statue to life.

To the amazed group, Hermione explains that she had not died but, with Paulina's help, lived on unable to forgive Leontes for the supposed death of her daughter. All are happy including Polixenes who now enters.

Having guessed that Camillo would head for Sicily, he had followed. Delighted he forgives his friend and happily consents to the union of the two young people to the delight of Hermione.

Note: May 15, 1611 is the date noted of a performance at the Globe theatre with a presentation to court some six months later. This, plus the style and tone of the play itself, suggests 1610 or early 1611 as the time of writing. In this play, Shakespeare chose to dramatize an already popular story for his source was 'Pandosto: The Triumph Of Time' written in 1588 by Robert Greene.

✢ ✢ ✢ ✢ ✢

A WINTER'S TALE
(U.S.A., 1910)

p.c. *Thanhouser.*
d. *Theodore Marston.*
l.p. *Martin Faust (Leontes); Frank Hart Crane (Polixenes); Anna Rosamond (Hermione); Mignon Anderson; Amelia Barleon (Perdita); Alfred Hanlon (Florizel); Frank Crane (Polixenes).*
b.w. 1000 ft (305 m.). Sil.

A condensed version featuring important scenes from the play, the director is noted by some as Barry O'Neil and others as Edwin Thanhouser. The film was critically well received.

RACCONTO D'INVERNO
(Italy, 1910)

p.c. *Cines.*
d.
l.p.
b.w. 948 ft. (289 m.) Sil.

No details of this early Italian version are available.

aka: A WINTER'S TALE; CONTES D'HIVER; DAS WINTERMÄRCHEN; RACCONTI D'INVERNO

RACCONTO D'INVERNO
(Italy, 1914)

p.c. *Milano Films.*
d. *Baldassare Negroni.*
l.p. *Pina Fabbri (Paulina); V. Cocchi (Leontes).*
b.w. 3360 ft. (1024 m.) Sil.

Shakespeare reads the tale to a group of friends. The plot unfolds in an abbreviated form and with some changes. At the end, his audience applauds Shakespeare.

Said to be well acted, this ambitious production was shot on location as well as in a studio and it is noted as a clear interpretation.

Its French release was shorter with a length of 3280 ft. (1000 m.). Some sources quote a year previous for production and L. Sutto as director.

aka: THE LOST PRINCESS; THE WINTER'S TALE; CONTE D' HIVER; UNA TRAGEDIA ALLA CORTE DI SICILIA; NOVELLA D' INVERNO, UNA NOVELLA DI SHAKESPEARE

DIE WINTERMÄRCHEN
(Germany, 1914)

p.c. *Belle Alliance.*
d.
l.p. *Senta Söneland; Albert Paulig; Richard Sonius.*
b.w. 30 mins. Sil.

An elusive film, at least three sources list it as being Shakespeare based.

A WINTER'S TALE
(G.B., 1953)

p.c. *Emil Katzka Productions.*
d. *Charles Deane.*
l.p. *Young Vic Theatre Company. Narrator: Ronald Howard.*
b.w. 13 mins.

This, plus others, made up a programme originally made for television with the title *The World's A Stage!*. Ronald Howard introduced each part and this one contains the final scene from the play.

THE WINTER'S TALE
(G.B., 1966)

p.c. *Cressida/Hurst Park.*
d. *Frank Dunlop.*
l.p. *Laurence Harvey (Leontes); Jane Asher (Perdita); Diana Churchill (Paulina); Jim Dale (Autolycus); Moira Redmond (Hermione); Esmond Knight (Camillo); David Weston (Florizel/Archidamas); Richard Gale (Polixenes); John Gray (Clown); Cherry Morris (Emilia); Edward Dewsbury (Old Shepherd/ Gaoler); Allan Foss (Antigonus); Michael Murray (Paulina's Steward); Monica Maughan; Joy Ring; Joanna Wake; Terry Palmer; Frank Barry; Dan Caulfield; Charmian Eyre.*
Eastman Color. 151 mins.

Film record of the "Pop Theatre" production for the Edinburgh Festival, Scotland, 1966.

The film was shown at the same festival the following year.

"...it is hard to discover any real justification for the filming of this rather uninspired production..." – 'Monthly Film Bulletin', July, 1968.

✢ ✢ ✢ ✢ ✢

A WINTER'S TALE
(U.S.A., 1909)

p.c. *Edison.*
d. *Thomas Edison.*
l.p.
b.w. 432 ft. (132 m.). Sil.

Two men carry photographs of their wives in their overcoats. In a restaurant, the overcoats accidentally get switched.

This comedy clearly acknowledges it inspirational source though the result may question the use of it.

CONTE D'HIVER
(France, 1992)

p.c. *Les Films du Losange with the participation of Soficas/Investimage/Sofiarp. With the assistance of Le Studio Canal+.*
d. *Eric Rohmer.*
l.p. *Charlotte Very (Félice); Frederic Van Den Driessche (Charles); Hervé Furic (Loïc); Michel Voletti (Maxence); Ava Loraschi (Elise); Christiane Desbois (Mother); Rosette (Sister); Jean-Luc Revol (Brother-in-Law); Haydee Caillot (Edwige); Marie Rivière (Dora); Jean-Claude Biette (Quentin). Cast of THE WINTER'S TALE: Roger Dumas (Leontes); Daniele Lebrun (Paulina); Diane Lepvrier (Hermione); François Raucher (Florizel); Edwig Navarro (Perdita); Maria Coin (Flute Player); Eric Wapler; Gaston Richard (Lords).*
c. 114 mins.

Five years after an idyllic summer affaire, Félice still hopes to see again her lover and father of her child, Elise. She has lost contact with him (Charles). Though living with Loïc, she starts an affaire with Maxence, her boss, and goes to him in Nevers to Loïc's anger. The new affaire does not go well and Félice returns to Paris and takes up again with Loïc but on a friendship basis. At a performance of THE WINTER'S TALE, Félice sees a parallel to her own situation. Whilst shopping on New Year's Eve, she sees Charles with a woman. Though initially mistaking her for his wife (she is only a friend), the couple are reunited and vow never to be separated again.

Apart from the obvious play excerpt (with which some liberties have been taken), Eric Rohmer has, in this the second of his films in his Four Seasons cycle, taken a few ideas from Shakespeare. Although mainly about relationships, there remain two basic concepts – the search for lost love and reconciliation between children and parents. Such themes are not uncommon to Shakespeare.

Shown at the Muestra Cinematográfica del Atlantico, Alcances, Spain, 1994.
Berlin Film Festival, Germany, 1992: International Critics' Award.

aka: CUENTO DE INVIERNO

✢ ✢ ✢ ✢ ✢

Not many versions of this particular play have been made in any form. Perhaps its themes of unjustified mistrust, shipwrecks and long lost offspring mingled with a touch of fantasy have already been exploited to varying degrees in other films of other plays. As it is, there appears only one full length film of this play which Esther Merle Jackson Ph. D. one time Professor of Drama at Atlanta University has described as "...a study of moral, spiritual and psychological distress.".

CHAPTER XXX

ALL THE WORLD'S A STAGE

Or should it be a screen? Certainly, the cinema is as international as any stage and in the world of cinema the influence of Shakespeare stretches, as might be expected, way beyond the direct or derivative transposition of his works to the screen. Many films – too many even to attempt a complete listing – have quoted from Shakespeare either by the spoken or written word. Many others have clearly shown him as an influence and some of those films are already noted under the individual play source. A few others, more distant in relationship, are noted below.

Equally prevalent and far easier to note, are those films which feature scenes from Shakespeare's works and actors, noted or otherwise, performing Shakespearean roles which, though forming part of the film's plot, are subordinate to the main theme. In short, what follows is a guide, certainly not complete, to the known films falling, for the most part, into this category.

ACTOR'S TROUBLES
(U.S.A., 1903)

p.c. *Selig Polyscope.*
d.
l.p.
b.w. 100 ft. (30 m.) Sil.

A Shakespearean actor whose career and finances are at a low ebb still maintains his valet. The two of them see a ghost...

A DUPED OTHELLO
(G.B., 1909)

p.c. *R.W. Paul.*
d. *Jack Smith.*
l.p.
b.w. 320 ft. (98 m.) Sil.

To take revenge on an actor, a sweep puts soot in his makeup.

There is but a slight connection with Shakespeare apart from the title character. At least the sweep used the right colour substance!

aka: THE THEATRICAL CHIMNEY SWEEP

ALGY GOES ON THE STAGE
(G.B., 1910)

p.c. *Gaumont.*
d. *Alf Collins.*
l.p.
b.w. 630 ft. (192 m.) Sil.

The Honorable Algy Slacker performs as Romeo in a cheap hall in this comedy.

BUMPTIOUS AS ROMEO
(U.S.A., 1911)

p.c. *Edison.*
d.
l.p. *John R. Climpson.*
b.w. 975 ft. (297 m.) Sil.

Bumptious organises a drama club performance of ROMEO AND JULIET with himself as the male lead. Everything goes wrong – the balcony collapses on him and there is no audience.

FOR AABENT TÆPPE
(Denmark, 1911)

p.c. *Nordisk.*
d. *August Blom.*
l.p. *Valdemar Psilander; Thyra Reimann; Nicolai Brechling; Henry Knudsen: Svend Bille; Julie Henriksen.*
b.w. 1798 ft. (548 m.) Sil.

Ejnar and Maria are the stars of OTHELLO. Maria does not love her husband but rejects Preben (Iago in the play) for the advances of Count Brisson. Preben finds a note from the Count to Maria and uses this to denounce her to Ejnar. Ejnar disguises himself and Maria's infidelity is proven. He throws her out and she arranges to see Brisson. Preben again tells Ejnar who kills her during the play accusing Brisson who withdraws.

The title translates as "Up With The Curtain". It is more widely known by the title noted below.

aka: DESDEMONA

LES AMOURS DE LA REINE ÉLISABETH
(France, 1912)

See **CHAPTER XXXII THE IMMORTAL BARD** for details.

This film opens with a performance of THE MERRY WIVES OF WINDSOR.

NICHOLAS NICKLEBY
(U.S.A., 1912)

p.c. *Thanhouser Film Corporation.*
d. *George O. Nicholls.*
l.p. *Harry Benham; Justus D. Barnes.*
b.w. 1872 ft. (571 m.) Sil.

An abbreviated version of the story by Charles Dickens, this contains the sequence where Nicholas joins the Crummles' company production of ROMEO AND JULIET and Nicholas plays Romeo.

BUMKE AS OTHELLO
(Germany, 1913)

p.c. *Continental Kunstfilm.*
d.
l.p.
b.w. 591 ft. (180 m.) Sil.

An incompetent but ambitious actor makes himself look ridiculous when he plays a Shakespearean role and has to flee from the angry spectators.

A HORSE! A HORSE!
(G.B., 1913)

p.c. *Clarendon.*
d. *Percy Stow.*
l.p.
b.w. 355 ft. (108 m.) Sil.

A cleaning lady searches for a horse for an actor playing King Richard but provides him with a donkey!

This comedy takes its title from a shortening of Richard's last words in the play – "A horse! A horse! my kingdom for a horse!".

OTHELLO IN JONESVILLE
(U.S.A., 1913)

p.c. *Edison.*
d. *Charles Brabin.*
l.p. *Herbert Prior; Mabelle Trunelle.*
b.w. 2 reels? Sil.

An out-of-work actor tries to pay for his keep by teaching a stage-struck girl and her family how to act. They attempt to stage a performance of OTHELLO at the local town hall.

MARTIN AS HAMLET
(Germany, 1914)

p.c. *Neue.*
d.
l.p. *Alberto Capozzi.*
b.w. 718 ft. (219 m.) Sil.

An actor rehearses for his role as Hamlet. His servants think he has gone mad and call for the police. At the police station his strange language ensures his detention in the cells. However, his wife arrives and saves the situation.

NINA OF THE THEATRE
(U.S.A., 1914)

p.c. *Kalem.*
d.
l.p. *Alice Joyce; Tom Moore.*
b.w. 2 reels. Sil.

An actress falls in love with an actor.

This was the first part of a serial and contains at least one scene from AS YOU LIKE IT.

HER ROMEO
(U.S.A., 1915)

p.c. *Lubin Manufacturing Corp.*
d.
l.p. *Billie Reeves.*
b.w. 1 reel. Sil.

Having read ROMEO AND JULIET, a girl induces her lover to dress as Romeo and climb a clothes line ladder to her. Chased off by her father, he is mistaken as the actor in a poor performance of the play held locally and is chased by the angry villagers.

LIZA ON THE STAGE
(G.B., 1915)

p.c. *Piccadilly.*
d. *Joe Evans.*
l.p. *Geraldine Maxwell.*
b.w. 812 ft. (247 m.) Sil.

A street-market sales girl acts in ROMEO AND JULIET in this comedy short.

MARTHA'S ROMEO
(U.S.A., 1915)

p.c. *Edison.*
d.
l.p.
b.w. Short. Sil.

In a boarding house, an actor assumes the dress of Romeo and climbs to the window to woo the cook.

Hardly perfect Shakespeare, the spirit is at least present.

PORTRET DORIANA GREYA
(Russia, 1915)

p.c. *Russian Golden Series.*
d. *Vsevolod Meyherhold, Mijail Doronin.*
l.p. *Varvara Yanova; Vsevolod Meyherhold; G. Enriton; P. Belova; I. Uvarova; Alexander Volkov; M. Doronin.*
b.w. 6969 ft. (2124 m.) Sil.

This interesting adaptation of the novel by Oscar Wilde contains a brief scene from ROMEO AND JULIET. The film is considered as one of the most important in the history of the pre-Revolution Russian cinema.

The story has, of course, been the subject of a number of screen versions.

WHEN HUNGRY HAMLET FLED
(U.S.A., 1915)

p.c. *Thanhouser.*
d.
l.p. *Harry Benham; Claude Cooper.*
b.w. See text. Sil.

An experienced actor attempts to direct an amateur troupe but his efforts are sabotaged by a young man.

Just what Shakespearean connections there may have been beyond the title and the theatrical theme is not known as only one of the two original reels survives.

DAVID GARRICK
(U.S.A., 1916)

p.c. *Pallas Pictures.*
d. *Frank Lloyd.*
l.p. *Dustin Farnum; Winifred Kingston; Herbert Standing; Frank Bonn; Lydia Yeamans Titus; Olive White; Mary Mersch.*
b.w. 5 reels Sil.

A woman falls in love with Garrick when she sees him as Romeo in ROMEO AND JULIET. Her father tries to induce him to leave the country but he promises not to marry any woman without paternal agreement. He behaves like a drunkard to try and make her forget him. His true character is later revealed and father agrees to the marriage.

This was based on the play by T. W. Robertson and contains at least one Shakespearean extract – the balcony scene from ROMEO AND JULIET.

Five other British films have been made about the life of this actor – in 1912, 1913 (two films), 1922 and 1928 – with Gerald Lawrence, Seymour Hicks, Charles Wyndham, Milton Rosmer and Gordon McLeod playing the title role respectively. **THE GREAT GARRICK** (U.S.A., 1937) was a fictionalised tale about the great actor (not based on the play as were the others). It is not known if any of the others contained scenes from Shakespearean works though, in view of the status of the character, they could well have done so.

FREDDY VERSUS HAMLET
(U.S.A., 1916)

p.c. *Vitagraph.*
d.
l.p. *William Dangman; Tod Talford; William Lytell Jr.; Daisy DeVere.*
b.w. (?) mins. Sil.

Wiggins takes Mabel to the theatre where she flirts with the actor playing Hamlet who joins her later. Freddy thwarts both Wiggins and the actor.

This one in a series of comic shorts featuring the character Wiggins.

HAMLET MADE OVER
(U.S.A., 1916)

p.c. *Lubin Manufacturing Co.*
d. *Earl Metcalf.*
l.p. *Billie Reeves; Clarence J. Elmer; William H. Turner; Carrie Williams.*
b.w. 1000 ft. (305 m.) Sil.

A bad actor appears as HAMLET. When the play flops, the manager engages a wealthy girl to play Ophelia in a revised version which contains song and dance and magic acts. The asbestos curtain falls on the actor's neck and he is tarred and feathered.

OTHELLO
(Denmark, 1916)

p.c. *Nordisk.*
d. *Martinius Nielsen.*
l.p. *Valdemar Psilander; Ebba Thomsen; Adolf Tronier Funder; Alma Hinding; Inger Nybo.*
b.w. 3911 ft. (1192 m.) Sil.

A love story about a Shakespearean actor, this contains scenes from HAMLET and OTHELLO. The working title was "En Skuespillers Krlighed" (The Love Of An Actor) with Psilander as the actor.

aka: THE ACTOR'S LOVE STORY; LES AMOURS D'UN COMÉDIEN; LOS AMORES DE UN ACTOR; DIE LIEBESGESCHICTE EINES SCHAUSPIELERS; OS AMORES DE UM COMEDIANTE; EN SKÅDESPELARES KÄRLEKSHISTORIA; EN SKUESPILLERS JÆRLIGHETSHISTORIE

PIMPLE AS HAMLET
(G.B., 1916)

p.c. *Piccadilly.*
d. *Fred Evans, Joe Evans.*
l.p. *Fred Evans.*
b.w. 2000 ft. (610 m.) Sil.

Fred Evans was a music hall comedian who went under the stage name of Pimple. His style was to parody everything and Shakespeare did not escape his attention. This particular release was described as "two reels of unmitigated humour".

TO BE OR NOT TO BE
(U.S.A., 1916)

p.c. *American Beauty.*
d. *Edward Watt.*
l.p. *Orral Humphrey; Gladys Kingsbury; Mary Talbot; Johnny Gough; Ed C. Watt.*
b.w. (?) mins. Sil.

An inept actor and his company leave one of their rural venues without paying their bills and are pursued by the police. The actor hides in a private house where he discovers some lost jewels. With the reward money he settles the bills and he and his troupe continue with their serio-comic Shakespearean performance.

Promotional material for the film notes Humphrey as "the world's greatest Shakespearean tragedian", a statement of some contention no doubt.

A FOOTLIGHT FLAME
(U.S.A., 1917)

p.c. *Fox.*
d.

l.p. *Charles Arling.*
b.w. 2 reels. Sil.

When her father opposes the romance of his daughter with an actor, the actor arranges that she seems mad after seeing him in ROMEO AND JULIET. Her father calls in a hypnotist who just happens to be Romeo. They escape in an exciting car-chase ending.

THE MAD LOVER
(U.S.A., 1917)

p.c. *Rapf-Pathé.*
d. *Léonce Perret.*
l.p. *Robert Warwick; Elaine Hammerstein; Valentin Petit; Pedro Vinzaglio; Frank McGlinn; Edward Kimball.*
b.w. 6 reels. Sil.

In this story of an American country gentleman and his wife, the husband is maddened by the passion with which the actor in a production of OTHELLO makes love to his wife playing Desdemona. He falls asleep and dreams that he is Othello and kills his wife. When he awakes he sees that not only is his wife blameless but that she has found the actor insulting.

aka: A MODERN OTHELLO; THE SHADOW OF NIGHT; THE LASH OF JEALOUSY

WHEN MACBETH CAME TO SNAKEVILLE
(U.S.A., 1917)

p.c. *Essanay.*
d.
l.p. *Victor Potel; Margaret Joslin; Harry Todd; Ben Turpin.*
b.w. Short. Sil.

Snakeville awaits with excitement the arrival of the world's greatest tragedian. The troupe duly arrives and stays at Slim's boarding house. Slim's wife is attracted to the leading actor and is overjoyed at his performance in MACBETH much to Slim's annoyance. At night, she sleepwalks thinking she is Lady Macbeth. With a knife she enters the actor's room. Fortunately, she wakes up in time but the actor leaves in a hurry and to Slim's delight.

OTHELLO
(Germany, 1918)

p.c. *Vitascope/Pagu.*
d. *Max Mack.*
l.p. *Beni Montano; Alexander Moïssi; Lya de Putti; Ellen Korth; Wilhelm Diegelmann; Rosa Valetti; Jenny Marba; Julius Falkenstein; Max Gülstorff.*
b.w. Feature. Sil.

Details of this are suspect. The content itself is unknown but it is believed to be, like many, a play within a play because a number of the cast perform dual roles (Shakespearean and others).

TUTTO IL MONDO É UN TEATRO
(Italy, 1918)

p.c. *Vay Film.*
d. *Pier Antonio Gariazzo.*
l.p.
b.w. 6371 ft. (1942 m.) Sil.

This fantasy film logically has more than just the title related to Shakespeare.

ONE NIGHT ONLY
(U.S.A., 1919)

p.c.
d. *Charles Parrot.*
l.p. *Leo White; Monte Banks; Charles Dorety.*
b.w. Feature? Sil.

A troupe of travelling actors play Shakespeare (HAMLET).

THE SENTIMENTAL BLOKE
(Australia, 1919)

p.c. *Southern Cross Feature Film Company.*
d. *Raymond Longford.*
l.p. *Arthur Tauchert; Gilbert Emery; Lottie Lydell; Stanley Robinson; Margaret Reid; Harry Young.*
b.w. 6424 ft. (1958 m.) Sil.

An idle gambler, Bill, relates the story of his courtship of and marriage to Doreen.

The film includes a visit to a theatre to see ROMEO AND JULIET the action of which Bill explains to Doreen in his own special way.

SHADES OF SHAKESPEARE
(U.S.A., 1919)

p.c. *Al Christie.*
d.
l.p.
b.w. 2 reels. Sil.

A comedy, this burlesqued amateur theatricals. It is presumed that some Shakespearean references were featured.

CARNIVAL
(G.B., 1921)

p.c. *Alliance Film Corporation.*
d. *Harley Knoles.*
l.p. *Matheson Lang; Hilda Bayley; Ivor Novello; Clifford Grey; Victor McLaglen; Florence Hunter.*
b.w. 7400 feet (2256 m.) Sil.

In Venice, a jealous actor tries to strangle his wife during a performance of OTHELLO.

An early excursion into a theme that was to become much used. There is some interest in the cast with the young Novello (noted as writer/composer of light musicals) and McLaglen (whose career seemed to consist of playing the archetypal Irishman on many occasions for John Ford).

ENCHANTMENT
(U.S.A., 1921)

p.c. *Cosmopolitan.*
d. *Robert G. Vignola.*
l.p. *Marion Davis; Forrest Stanley; Edith Shayne; Tom Lewis; Arthur Robinson; Corinne Barker; Maude Turner Gordon; Edith Lyle; Huntley Gordon.*
b.w. 6982 ft. (2128 m.) Sil.

After a performance of THE TAMING OF THE SHREW, a father decides to engage the lead actor to be a real Petruchio and tame his wild daughter. This is achieved through an amateur performance of the play in which the two take the leading roles. Of course, the couple fall in love.

DAY DREAMS
(U.S.A., 1922)

p.c. *Buster Keaton Productions for Associated Film National.*
d. *Buster Keaton.*
l.p. *Buster Keaton; Renée Adorée; Joe Roberts; Virginia Fox.*
b.w. 2476 ft. (755 m.) Sil.

A young girl receives a letter from her boy friend which induces her to day dream about him as a fabulous being. Thus Buster has the opportunity to portray some colourful characters. Among them is HAMLET.

The French actress Renée Adorée was one of the silent screen's most beautiful women. She retired from the screen in 1930 and died three years later in a sanitarium aged thirty-five.

Extant prints of the film are said to be incomplete.

Extract shown as part of the Everybody's Shakespeare International Festival, London, England, 1994.

aka: GRANDEUR ET DÉCADENCE; LOS SUEÑOS DE PAMPLINAS

KEAN
(France, 1922)

p.c. *Albatross.*
d. *Alexander Volkoff.*
l.p. *Ivan Mosjoukine; Paulina Pô; Nikolai Koline; Nathalie Lissenko; Mary Odette; Kenelm Ross; Otto Datlefsen; G. Deneubourg.*
b.w. Feature. Sil.

Based on 'Kean, ou Désordre et Génie' by Alexandre Dumas père, which was about the actor Edmund Kean, this featured a number of Shakespearen references. To those in the original (OTHELLO, HAMLET and ROMEO AND JULIET), were added further scenes from the last two named.

The work had been filmed previously in Denmark in 1910 with Martinius Nielsen and directed by Holger Rasmussen, in Italy in 1917 by Brunestelli and there was a German Ufa version of it from this same year directed by Rudolf Biebrachs. What Shakespearean content was in these is not known. The same can be said of a Portuguese one reel production from 1910 which contained a dinner scene in a tavern. There were certainly scenes in the later Italian versions made in 1940 and 1957.

HAN HUG OG HAMLET
(Denmark, 1922)

p.c. *Palladium.*
d. *Lau Lauritzen.*
l.p. *Carl Schenstrøm; Harald Madsen; Olga Svendsen; Lissen Bendix; Jørgen Lund; Oscar Stribolt; Lauritz Olsen; Christian Gottschalk; Mathilde Felum-Friis; Sigurd Langberg; Albert Kjøge; Hans W. Petersen; Alice Frederiksen; Eva Sørensen; Ingeborg Bitter; Greta Blomsterberg; Georg Busch; Karen Nielsen; Sonja Bangsaa; Sonja Mortensen; Thyra Damgaard-Nielsen; Elga Svendsen; F. Stybe.*
b.w. 5725 ft. (1745 m.) Sil.

This comedy features the Danish comic duo known as Fy and Bi (Pat and Patachon in most European countries) who were popular at the time. The film contains scenes from HAMLET.

aka: HE, SHE AND HAMLET; ER, SIE UND HAMLET; LUI, LEI, AMLETO; HIJ-ZIJ EN HAMLET; GLADE GOSSARS GÄSTPEL

THE TROUPER
(U.S.A., 1922)

p.c. *Universal.*
d. *Harry B. Harris.*
l.p. *Jack Perrin; Gladys Walter; Thomas Holding; Kathleen O'Connor.*
b.w. 5 reels. Sil.

This is a tale about a backstage girl in a travelling stock company.

The balcony scene from ROMEO AND JULIET appears in this.

DAS ALTE GESETZ
(Germany, 1923)

p.c. *Comedia-Film.*
d. *E. A. Dupont.*
l.p. *Avram Morewski; Henny Porten; Ernst Deutsch; Margarete Schlegel; Robert Garrison*
b.w.7572 ft. (2308 m.) Sil.

In nineteenth century Austria, a Jew leaves the ghetto to become an actor. From a humble production of ROMEO AND JULIET, he moves to fame and eventual reconciliation with his disapproving Rabbi father.

Scenes from HAMLET are also featured. The film was cut 6500 ft. (1981 m.) for English release and to 5500 ft. (1676 m.) for American release.

Shown at the San Sebastian Film Festival, Spain, 1990, as part of the retrospective "Volver a Nacer".

aka: THE ANCIENT LAW; BARUCH; EN JUDE

SUCCESS
(U.S.A., 1923)

p.c. *Metro.*
d. *Ralph Ince.*
l.p. *Brandon Tynan; Naomi Childers; Mary Astor; Dore Davidson; Lionel Adams; Stanley Ridges; Robert Lee Keeling; Billy Quirk; Gaylord Pendleton; John Woodford; Helen Macks.*
b.w. 7 reels. Sil.

When a drunken Shakespearean actor disappears, his wife tells their daughter that he is dead. The actor later reappears and tries to get the role of KING LEAR opposite his daughter but ends up as valet to the principal actor. His chance comes when the actor goes on a drinking spree (having learned his valet's identity) and the old man turns in a fine performance. The family is reunited.

THE PERFECT FLAPPER
(U.S.A., 1924)

p.c.
d. *John F. Dillon.*
l.p. *Sydney Chaplin; Colleen Moore; Phyllis Haver; Lydia Knott.*
b.w. 7000 ft. (2134 m.) Sil.

Flapper girls form the basic plot of this comedy.

Evidence suggests that this contained a scene from ROMEO AND JULIET.

TRIUMPH
(U.S.A., 1924)

p.c. *Paramount/Cecil B. DeMille.*
d. *Cecil B. DeMille.*
l.p. *Leatrice Joy; Rod LaRocque; Victor Carconi; Charles Ogle; Theodore Kosloff; Robert Edeson; Julia Faye; George Fawcett; Spottiswoode Aitken; ZaSu Pitts; Alma Bennett; Raymond Hatton; Jimmie Adams.*
b.w. 8 reels. Sil.

A tin magnate dies leaving all to his wastrel son providing he settles down within two years. The son, King Garnet, ends up as a tramp at the end of the two years and the business passes to William, another son by a secret marriage. Both love the factory's forewoman, Ann, who wants to be an opera singer. Smoke from a fire ruins her chances of this. When a crisis occurs in the factory, King, now an employee, and Ann work with William to restore order and King weds Ann.

This features a very brief scene from ROMEO AND JULIET (the balcony scene) with Rod LaRocque as Romeo. A running time of sixty-eight minutes is noted by a then contemporary source.

aka: TRIOMPHE

DER LEIBGARDIST
(Austria, 1925)

p.c. *Pan Film/Phoebus Film.*
d. *Robert Weine.*
l.p. *Alfred Abel; Maria Corda; Anton Edthofer; Alice Hechy; Karl Forest.*
b.w. 8267 ft. (2520 m.) Sil.

Based on a work by Franz Molnar, scenes from HAMLET and OTHELLO are featured.

BROMO AND JULIET
(U.S.A., 1926)

p.c. *Hal Roach.*
d. *Leo McCarey.*
l.p. *Charley Chase; Oliver Hardy; William Orlamond; Corliss Palmer.*
b.w. 20 mins. Sil.

A girl attempts to put on an amateur production of ROMEO AND JULIET with her boy friend as the male lead.

BLUEBEARD'S SEVEN WIVES
(U.S.A., 1926)

p.c. *First National. A Robert Kane Production.*
d. *Alfred A. Santell.*
l.p. *Ben Lyon; Lola Wilson; Blanche Sweet; Dorothy Sebastion; Diana Kane; Sam Hardy; Dick Bernard; Andrew Mack; Dan Pennell; Wilfred Lytell.*
b.w. 72 mins. Sil.

A bank clerk in love loses his cash and his job when his till is short. Taking a job as a film extra he is "discovered" and changed into a great Spanish lover by the publicity people. It brings him fame but he almost loses his girl. He sees sense in time and gives up his new career for love.

Noted at the time as being very funny, it merits inclusion because Ben Lyon and Blanche Sweet enact the balcony scene from ROMEO AND JULIET in it. The tomb scene is also featured. Lyon is credited with having discovered Marilyn Monroe. In later years – the 1950s – he and his wife, Bebe Daniels, a film star in her own right, gained local fame in Great Britain with their own radio show "Life With The Lyons" which also had its film version.

WIE EINST IM MAI
(Germany, 1926)

p.c. *Ellen Richter-Film.*
d. *Willi Wolff.*
l.p. *Karl Harbacher (Romeo); Trude Hesterberg (Julia); Ellen Richter; Adolf Klein; Walter Rilla; Paul Heidemann; Frida Richard; Alice*

Torning; Hugo Fischer-Köppe; Julius von Szöreghy.
b.w. 8711 ft. (2655 m.) Sil.

ROMEO AND JULIET scenes are featured both in theatre and film productions in this experimental film.

CURED HAMS
(U.S.A., 1927?)

p.c.
d.
l.p. *Jack Richardson.*
b.w. 1163 ft. (354 m.) Sil.

A comedy, this concerns two vaudeville actors in a small town theatre. Among their acts is a comic version of ROMEO AND JULIET (balcony scene).

Few details are known of this film and the title may not be the correct one.

DRAMA DELUXE
(U.S.A., 1927)

p.c. *Educational Pictures.*
d. *Norman Taurog.*
l.p. *Lupino Lane; Wallace Lupino; Kathryn McGuire.*
b.w. 18 mins. Sil.

A bill poster is elevated to actor when the leading man quits.

This comedy has a (comic) sequence from ROMEO AND JULIET.

THE LAST MOMENT
(U.S.A., 1928)

p.c. *Freedman-Spitz.*
d. *Paul Fejos.*
l.p. *Otto Matiesen; Lucille La Verne; Isabel Lamore; Georgia Hale; Amielka Eltar.*
b.w. 6 reels. Sil.

As an actor drowns, his past life flashes before him including his portrayal of HAMLET and the applause of the audience.

This experimental film was privately financed and was praised as a remarkable and interesting film.

THE HOLLYWOOD REVUE OF 1929
(U.S.A., 1929)

p.c. *M.G.M.*
d. *Charles F. Reisner.*
l.p. *Marie Dressler; Norma Shearer; John Gilbert; Buster Keaton; Marion Davies; Lionel Barrymore; Jack Benny; Laurel and Hardy; Nils Asther; Joan Crawford.*
b.w. and Technicolor. 116 mins.

This early sound film was typical of the assembly of artists from a studio for a revue. This had colour sequences (two-tone Technicolor). Norma Shearer and John Gilbert were featured in the balcony scene from ROMEO AND JULIET. Much of the film was shot between the hours of 7 pm. and 7 am. as the stars were working on other films during the day. As John Douglas Eames says in his book 'The M.G.M. Story', everybody except Garbo and the gateman was in it!

THE ROYAL BOX
(U.S.A., 1929)

p.c. *Warner Bros.*
d. *Bryan Foy.*
l.p. *Alexander Moïssi; Camilla Horn; Lew Hearn; Elsa Ersi; Egon Brecher; Leni Stengel; William F. Schoeller; Carlos Zizold; Greta Meyer; William Gade; Siegfried Rumann.*
b.w. 76 mins.

Based on the play by (according to German sources) Charles Coglan (or by Alexandre Dumas père, according to American sources), it is the story of British actor Edmund Kean.

Made in the German language (the first American made foreign language talkie), this contains scenes from HAMLET. It was also, technically, the first German feature-length talking picture. An English track was also made for the American release. German sources note the running time as eighty-five minutes.

aka: DIE KÖNIGSLOGE

SHOW OF SHOWS
(U.S.A., 1929)

p.c. *Warner Bros.*
d. *John G. Adolfi.*
l.p. *Winnie Lightner; John Barrymore; H.B.Warner; Monte Blue; Lupino Lane; Beatrice Lilly; Myrna Loy.*
Technicolor. 128 mins.

Crude in concept and execution, this early big musical is of great importance in cinema history. Among the pieces in this revue in two-tone Technicolor was the soliloquy from RICHARD II with John Barrymore in the role.

Extract shown as part of the Everybody's Shakespeare International Festival, London, England, 1994.

ELSTREE CALLING
(G.B., 1930)

p.c. *British International Pictures.*
d. *Adrian Brunel; Alfred Hitchcock; Jack Hulbert; André Charlot; Paul Murray.*
l.p. *Tommy Handley; Will Fyffe; Lily Morris; Anna May Wong; Gordon Harker; Cicely Courtneidge; Jack Hulbert; Donald Calthrop; John Longden; Jameson Thomas.*
b.w./c. 86 mins.

A film studio attempts to put together a television show which is an excuse for a revue compred by Tommy Handley. Anna May Wong and Donald

Calthrop perform a burlesque version of THE TAMING OF THE SHREW and Calthrop tries to recite Shakespeare between acts. Brunel's first version was rejected by the producers and so he remade it.

MADAM SATAN
(U.S.A., 1930)

p.c. *Cecil B. DeMille.*
d. *Cecil B. DeMille.*
l.p. *Kay Johnson; Reginald Denny; Lillian Roth; Roland Young; Elsa Peterson; Wallace MacDonald; Boyd Irwin; Wilfred Lucas; Tyler Brooks; Lotus Thompson; Vera Marsh; Martha Sleeper; Doris McMahon; Marie Valli; Julianne Johnston, Albert Conti etc.*
b.w. 105 mins.

A wife poses as the mysterious Madame Satan to win back the husband she fears she is losing. She holds a fancy dress party aboard a dirigible. When fire breaks out the husband saves for himself his disguised wife.

It must be admitted that the inclusion of this bizarre film is pushing the Shakespearean connection to its extreme. The reason for inclusion is that one of the guests at the party (played by Lotus Thompson) is dressed as Romeo but he has no Juliet.

STAR IMPERSONATIONS
(G.B., 1930)

p.c. *Film Weekly.*
d. *Harry Hughes.*
l.p. *Mabel Poulton (Mary Pickford); William Freshman (Ramon Novarro); Donald Calthrop (George Arliss); Mickey Brantford (Lew Ayres); Vanda Greville (Greta Garbo).*
b.w. 10 mins.

A competition with a £150 prize is arranged and several entrants impersonate Hollywood stars in famous roles. One of these is "Pickford" in THE TAMING OF THE SHREW.

THE DECEIVER
(U.S.A., 1931)

p.c. *Columbia.*
d. *Louis King.*
l.p. *Ian Keith; Lloyd Hughes; Dorothy Sebastian; Nathalie Moorhead; George Byron; DeWitt Jennings; Richard Tucker; Greta Granstedt; Murray Kinnell.*
b.w. 66 mins.

A womanising actor is murdered. But who did it?

This thriller adapted by Jo Swerling from "It Might Have Happened" by Bella Muni (wife of actor Paul Muni) had as its setting, a theatre housing a production of OTHELLO.

HAN HUN OG HAMLET
(Denmark, 1932)

p.c. *Palladium-Lystspil.*
d. *Lau Lauritzen.*
l.p. *Carl Schenstrøm; Harald Madsen; Marguerite Viby; Hans W. Petersen; Erna Schrøder; Olga Svendsen; Chr. Arhoff; Jørgen Lund; Yjnar Juhl; Arthur Jensen; Willy Bille; Chr. Schrøder; Johannes Andressen; Alex Suhr.*
b.w. Feature.

The same comedy duo starred again in this sound, musical comedy remake of their 1922 film of similar content. This was an early sound film from Denmark and the first from this particular company.

CARNIVAL
(G.B., 1933)

p.c. *British and Dominions Film Corporation.*
d. *Herbert Wilcox.*
l.p. *Matheson Lang; Joseph Schildkraut; Dorothy Bouchier; Kay Hammons; Brian Buchel; Lilian Braithwaite; Brember Wills; Alfred Rode and his Tzigane Band.*
b.w. 88 mins.

Sound remake of the 1921 film in which Lang repeats his role.

MISTER CINDERS
(G.B., 1934)

p.c. *British International Pictures.*
d. *Friedrich Zelnik.*
l.p. *Clifford Mollison; Zelma O'Neil; Renée Houston; The Western Brothers; W. H. Berry; Finlay Currie; Edmond Breon; Edward Chapman; Lorna Storm; Sybil Grove; Henry Mollison; Esme Church; Ellen Pollock; Jimmy Godden; Geraldo and his Orchestra.*
b.w. 72 mins.

A poor man, nephew of a rich man, is accused of theft but wins the heart of an American heiress who is posing as a servant.

This musical comedy features a village production (rehearsal and wild performance) of A MIDSUMMER NIGHT'S DREAM.

PEG OF OLD DRURY
(G.B., 1935)

p.c. *British and Dominions Film Corporation.*
d. *Herbert Wilcox.*
l.p. *Anna Neagle; Cedric Hardwicke; Margaretta Scott; Jack Hawkins; Hay Petrie; Marie O'Neill; Arthur Sinclair; Robert Atkins; Stuart Robertson; Dorothy Robinson; Leslie French; Tom Heslewood; Christopher Steele; Aubrey Fitzgerald; Eliot Makeham; Sara Allgood; Pollie Emery.*
b.w. 75 mins.

Peg, born in Dublin, Ireland, comes to London, England, and, under the guidance of David Garrick, becomes a celebrated actress and falls in love with him. However, she suffers from a weak heart and collapses and dies after a performance of AS YOU LIKE IT at Drury Lane.

CHAPTER XXX – ALL THE WORLD'S A STAGE

The life story of this actress, Peg Woffington, had been filmed before as *Masks And Faces* (G.B., 1917) but it had no Shakespearean play scenes. This later version also has short scenes from THE MERCHANT OF VENICE and RICHARD III.

THE ARIZONIAN
(U.S.A., 1935)

p.c. *R.K.O.*
d. *Charles Vidor.*
l.p. *Richard Dix; Margot Grahame; Preston Foster; Willie Best; Louis Calhern; J. Farrell MacDonald; James Bush; Ray Mayer; Joseph Sauers; Francis Ford.*
b.w. 76 mins.

In this Western, Marshall Tarrant has to defend and protect Silver City against outlaws. He is aided by a reformed outlaw.

The film opens with a variety show in a saloon featuring the ghost scene from HAMLET, the ghost being played by a negro under a white sheet. The scene does not get a very good reception from the saloon's boisterous clientele!

ROYAL CAVALCADE
(G.B., 1935)

p.c. *British International Pictures.*
d. *Thomas Bentley, Herbert Brenon, Norman Lee, Walter Summers, Will Kellino, Marcel Varnel.*
l.p. *Esme Percy (Lloyd George); Pearl Argyle (Anna Pavlova); Frank Vosper (Capt. Scott); Athene Seyler (Queen Elizabeth); Alice Lloyd (Marie Lloyd); C. M. Hallard (Winston Churchill); Austin Trevor (Capt. Oates); Matheson Lang (Henry V) and many more.*
b.w. 104 mins.

The events of the reign of King George V of England are seen through the travels of a penny coin. These events are portrayed through film extracts and clips and some re-enactments.

Made to celebrate the Silver Jubilee of King George V, the full cast is a line-up of the most noted stars of the British cinema of the era. Those listed above are a mere selection to indicate some of the personalities portrayed and does not represent all the main players. The interest here is in the extract from HENRY V as portrayed by Matheson Lang.

aka: REGAL CAVALCADE

THE VILLAGE SQUIRE
(G.B., 1935)

p.c. *British and Dominions Film Corporation/ Paramount British.*
d. *Reginald Denham.*
l.p. *David Horne; Leslie Perrins; Moira Lynd; Vivien Leigh; Margaret Watson; HaddonMason; Ivor Barnard.*
b.w. 66 mins.

This British comedy merits inclusion since the story revolves around a production of MACBETH by a local squire which runs into trouble. It is saved by a film star who marries the squire's daughter. The early appearance of a young Vivien Leigh is not without interest.

GIVE US THIS NIGHT
(U.S.A., 1936)

p.c. *Paramount.*
d. *Alexander Hall.*
l.p. *Jan Kiepura; Gladys Swarthout; Philip Merivale; Benny Baker; Michelle Burani; John Miltern; William Collier Sr.; Sidney Toler; Alan Mowbray; Mattie Edwards; Chloe Douglas.*
b.w. 73 mins.

A singing fisherman usurps an over-the-hill tenor in the affections of an operatic diva.

Something of a disaster at the time, its interest can only be in the score by Erich Korngold with words by Oscar Hammerstein II and, from the Shakespearean view, the ROMEO AND JULIET operatic ending.

MEN ARE NOT GODS
(G.B., 1936)

p.c. *London Films.*
d. *Walter Reisch.*
l.p. *Sebastian Shaw; Gertrude Lawrence; Miriam Hopkins; Rex Harrison; A. E. Matthews; Val Gielgud; Laura Smithson; Lawrence Grossmith; Sybil Grove; Wally Patch.*
b.w. 90 mins.

An actor's wife knows that her husband is having an affaire but with whom? She is sure it is not with her best friend. The mistress stops him murdering his pregnant wife during a performance of OTHELLO.

A somewhat dated version of the OTHELLO parallel in which a theatrical critic is persuaded to alter his review of the play. The production is a success but the actor falls for a girl and determines to kill his wife during a performance. The girl screams from the audience and the actor stops and is reunited with his wife.

Notable for the presence of Hopkins, Lawrence and an early appearance by Harrison, the music is of interest also. It is based on themes by Samuel Coleridge-Taylor's OTHELLO suite.

SHAKE, MR. SHAKESPEARE
(U.S.A., 1936)

p.c. *Vitaphone.*
d.
l.p.
b.w. (?) mins.

Little has been found about this parody.

SING, BABY, SING
(U.S.A.,1936)

p.c. *20th. Century Fox.*
d. *Sidney Lanfield.*
l.p. *Alice Faye; Adolphe Menjou; Gregory Ratoff; Patsy Kelly; Ted Healy; Dixie Dunbar; Montague Love; The Ritz Brothers; Tony Martin; Michael Whalen; Virginia Field.*
b.w. 87 mins.

A drunken Shakespearean actor chases after a night club singer who is promoted by an agent who thinks she can be a success if she can be teamed up with the actor.

This musical comedy was little more than a parody of the John Barrymore/Elaine Barrie affaire of the time. The songs included "When Did You Leave Heaven" (Oscar nominated) and "You Turned The Tables On Me".

Academy of Motion Picture Arts and Sciences, U.S.A., 1936: Nomination – Best Song (Walter Bullock, Richard Whiting).

TEDDY BERGMAN'S INTERNATIONAL BROADCAST
(U.S.A., 1936)

p.c. *Mentone.*
d. *Milton Schwarzwald.*
l.p. *Teddy Bergman; Billy Reyes; Rita Rio; Hernandez Brothers; Adrienne.*
b.w. 21 mins.

This comedy hosted by Teddy Bergman features a scene from THE MERCHANT OF VENICE. The scene is played properly then Reyes, as Antonio, challenges Bergman as Shylock to play his role in a variety of accents.

Bergman was a noted radio broadcaster of the 1930s. He later acted under the name of Alan Reed and became famous as the voice of television cartoon character Fred Flintstone.

AMBIKAPATHY
(India, 1937)

p.c. *Salem Shankar Films.*
d. *Ellis R. Duncan.*
l.p. *M.K. Thyagaraja Sivan Bhagavathar; Serukalathur Sama; N.S. Krishnan; T.S. Baliah; P.B. Rangachari; M.R. Santhanalakshmi; T.A. Mathuram.*
b.w. 210 mins. approx.

The story of the poet Kambar who wrote in Tamil, involves the son of the poet who loves a princess but fails the test required to overcome the class distinction.

It is not the fact that this is a story of love thwarted by outside factors (as in ROMEO AND JULIET) that merits the inclusion of this Tamil language film. Such class problems are an inherent and deep-rooted part of Indian culture. The film does contain a balcony love scene which, according to 'Encyclopaedia of Indian Cinema' by Ashish Rajadhyaksha and Paul Willemen, is clearly influenced by, if not borowed from, George Cukor's contemporaneous ROMEO AND JULIET.

THE GREAT GARRICK
(U.S.A., 1937)

p.c. *Warner Bros.*
d. *James Whale.*
l.p. *Brian Aherne; Olivia de Havilland; Edward Everett Horton; Melville Cooper; Lionel Atwill; Luis Alberini; Marie Wilson; Linda Perry; Lana Turner; Craig Edwards; Albert Dekker; Chester Clute; Dorothy Tree; Milton Owen; Trevor Barette; Milton Owen; E. E. Clive.*
b.w. 95 mins.

Garrick goes to France and finds himself in artistic contest with the French thespians but finds love and theatrical unity.

Hardly a biograpical film, for it does not claim to be accurate, it is a comedy. The film does open with Garrick concluding a performance of HAMLET.

HAMLET AND EGGS
(U.S.A., 1937)

p.c. *Educational Pictures.*
d. *William Watson.*
l.p. *Tim Ryan; Irene Noblette; Pat Patterson; Frank Jacquet; Douglas Leavitt; Eddie Hall; George Lessey; Cowboy Trio.*
b.w. 18 mins.

A Shakespearean actor takes a holiday in Arizona in this comedy short which contains scenes from HAMLET.

IT'S LOVE I'M AFTER
(U.S.A., 1937)

p.c. *Warner Bros./First National.*
d. *Archie Mayo.*
l.p. *Bette Davis; Leslie Howard; Olivia de Havilland; Patric Knowles; Eric Blore; Bonita Granville; Spring Byington; Vera Ann Borg; E.E. Clive; George Barbier.*
b.w. 90 mins.

The co-star fiancée of an egotistic actor (their marriage has been postponed eleven times) explodes when he becomes involved with a pretty young admirer who is infatuated with him.

The opening scene, which features a performance of ROMEO AND JULIET, establishes the relationship of the couple in this generally well-liked comedy which was originally known as "Gentlemen After Midnight". The theme of a feuding theatrical couple was repeated in **KISS ME KATE**.

THE GOLDWYN FOLLIES
(U.S.A., 1938)

p.c. *United Artists.*

d. *George Marshall, H. C. Potter.*
l.p. *Adolphe Menjou; Andrea Leeds; Kenny Baker; The Ritz Brothers; Vera Zorina; Helen Jepson; Bobby Clark; Edgar Bergen and Charlie McCarthy; Ella Logan; Phil Baker; Charles Kullman.*
Technicolor. 120 mins.

A producer hires a girl to judge his movies from the point of view of the average person.

Sam Goldwyn's first all Technicolor film cost $2,000,000 and contains a ballet sequence by George Ballanchine based on ROMEO AND JULIET. Alan Ladd has a small part as an auditioning singer. The songs, among which is "Love Walked In" (sung by Kenny Baker), are the last written by George Gershwin who died during the making of the film.

aka: ASI NACE UNA FANTASIA

FALSTAFF IN WIEN
(Germany, 1940)

p.c. *Tobis.*
d. *Leopold Hainisch.*
l.p. *Hans Nielsen; Wolf Albach-Retty; Lizzi Holzschuh; Gusti Wolf; Aribert Wäscher; Paul Hörbiger; Gustav Waldau; Bruno Hübner; Paul Otto; Senta Foltin; Hintz Fabricius; Gretl Theimer; Karl Etlinger; Karl Hellmer; Julius Brandt; Franz Heigl; Marie-Luise Schilp; Wolfgang Kieling; Helmut Bernsden; Irmgard Schmidt-Stein; Konrad Kappi; Lotte Bethke-Zitzman; Eduard Bornträger; Gaston Briese; Hugo Flink; Roselotte Kettmann; Harry Hardt; William Huch; Ottio Lange; Walter Schramm-Duncker; Max Vierlinger.*
b.w. 87 mins.

This musical is based on the life of the composer, Otto Nicolai.

As the title suggests, this work, set in the theatre world of old Vienna, contains scenes and music from his best known work – THE MERRY WIVES OF WINDSOR.

THE GREAT CONWAY
(G.B., 1940)

p.c. *S. E. Reynolds.*
d. *S. E. Reynolds.*
l.p. *Jerrold Robertshaw (Conway); Hubert Gregg; Norman Hackforth.*
b.w. 10 mins.

A Shakespearean actor becomes obsessed and murders his dresser.

The specific notation of "Shakespearean actor" in the only synopsis traced of this film indicates the presence of play extracts, quotations or use of themes.

KEAN
(Italy, 1940)

p.c. *Scalera Film.*
d. *Guido Brignone.*
l.p. *Rossano Brazzi; Germana Paolieri; Sandro Salvini; Mariella Lotti; Filippo Scelzo; Dino Di Luca; Nicola Maldacea; Orestes Fares; Dina Sassoli; Tao Ferrari; Edoardo Borelli; Renato Malavasi; Luigi Zerbinati; Liana Del Balzo; Adriano Rimoldi; Lina Marengo.*
b.w. 78 mins.

The story of Kean and his loves, his relationship with the Prince of Wales, his jealousy and his talents is revealed.

This is noted as containing scenes from HAMLET and ROMEO AND JULIET.

aka: KEAN, GENIO E SREGOLATEZZA; KEAN: GLI AMORI DI UN ARTISTA

CANZONE ETERNA
(Italy, 1941)

p.c. *Itala film.*
d. *Guido Brignone.*
l.p. *Benjamino Gigli; Emma Gramatica; Carola Holhn; Ugo Cesere.*
b.w. 74 mins.

A famous tenor finds his life interrupted by a too young wife and a too devoted mother.

A vehicle for the impressive vocal talents of Gigli, it contains a number of operatic arias including the storm and closing scene from OTELLO.

PLAYMATES
(U.S.A., 1941)

p.c. *R.K.O.*
d. *David Butler.*
l.p. *John Barrymore; Kay Kyser; Ginny Simms; Lupe Velez; May Robson; Patsy Kelly; Peter Lind Hayes; George Cleveland.*
b.w. 96 mins.

To gain a lucrative radio contract and to pay back taxes, an actor agrees to turn a band leader into a Shakespearean actor.

John Barrymore's last screen appearance was a far cry from his great days. The film's saving grace is Kay Kyser and only then if you like his style of music and foolery. One of the musical numbers is entitled "Romeo Smith And Juliet Jones".

LIFE BEGINS AT 8:30
(U.S.A., 1942)

p.c. *20th. Century Fox.*
d. *Irving Pichel.*
l.p. *Monty Woolley; Ida Lupino; Cornell Wilde; Sara Allgood; Melville Cooper; J. Edward Bromberg; William Demarest; Hal K. Dawson; Milton Parsons; William Halligan; Fay Helm;*

Milton Parsons; Inez Palange; Charles La Torre; Wheaton Chambers; James Flavin.
b.w. 85 mins.

A once-great actor turns to drink but is kept going by his crippled daughter. When a young man comes into her life, this shakes the man into reviving his career which he does in a performance of KING LEAR.

"An excellent vehicle for Woolley..." – Tony Thomas and Aubrey Solomon, 'The Films of Twentieth Century Fox'.

TO BE OR NOT TO BE
(U.S.A., 1942)

p.c. *Alexander Korda.*
d. *Ernst Lubitsch.*
l.p. *Jack Benny; Carole Lombard; Robert Stack; Stanley Ridges; Félix Bressart; Lionel Atwill; Sig Ruman; Tom Dugan; Charles Halton; Helmut Dantine; George Lynn; Miles Mander; Henry Victor; Maude Eburne; Halliwell Hobbs; Olaf Hytten; Charles Irwin; Maurice Murphy; Robert O. Davis; Leyland Hodgson; Frank Reicher; Erno Verebes; James Finlayson; Edgar Licho; Armand Wright; Peter Caldwell; Roland Varno; Alec Craig; Leslie Dennison; Wolfgang Zilzer; Otto Reichow; Gene Rizzi; Paul Barrett; John Kellog.*
b.w. 99 mins.

A famous troupe of actors is put out of business in wartime Warsaw by the Nazis. The players become involved in espionage and find their thespian skills are tested to the extreme having to impersonate Gestapo officers to prevent a traitor betraying the underground organisation.

The clue is in the title, of course, with Jack Benny playing HAMLET. This delightful black comedy and effective propaganda film in its day, was Carole Lombard's last film. It was released after her death but did not find immediate success. The topic did not amuse a country at war. Time has seen the recovery of its cost and its elevation to classic status in the film world.

Shown at the Berlin Film Festival, W. Germany, 1968, as part of a Lubitsch retrospective.
Shown at the Confrontation Cinématographique No. 28, Perpignan, France, 1992.
Shown as part of the Everybody's Shakespeare International Festival, London, England, 1994.
Shown at the Festival Internacional de Cine de Comedia, Torremolinos, Spain, 1990/1991: The film was featured along with others of Lubitsch.
Shown at the San Sebastian Film Festival, Spain, 1987, in "La Grandeza del Cine".
Academy of Motion Picture Arts and Sciences, U.S.A., 1942: Nomination – Best Score for a Dramatic or Comedy Picture (Werner Heyman).

aka: JEUX DANGEREUX; SER O NO SER; SEIN ODER NICHTSEIN

ROSSINI
(Italy, 1942/43)

p.c. *Luciano Doria for Compagnia Italiana Superfilm Nettunia.*
d. *Mario Bonnard.*
l.p. *Nino Besozzi; Paola Barbara; Camillo Pilotto; Armando Falconi; Greta Gonda; Paolo Stoppa; Memo Benassi; Cesare Fantoni; Gilda Bocci; Lamberto Picasso; Gilda Marchi; Alberto Marchiò; Massimo Pianoforini; Anna Maria Dionisi; Edoardo Toniolo.*
b.w. 112 mins.

Gioacchino Rossini enjoys some early success and goes to Naples to take charge of the San Carlo theatre. He receives acclaim and goes to Rome where his success grows even more. In his private life, he enjoys a happy marriage.

This is said to be an accurate biographical film. It contains a scene from his opera version of OTHELLO (Pietro Pauli and Gabriella Gatti are the performers for the principal roles), though, in truth, the libretto for the opera owes little to Shakespeare until the last act.

THE MAN IN GREY
(G.B., 1943)

p.c. *Gainsborough.*
d. *Leslie Arliss.*
l.p. *Margaret Lockwood; James Mason; Phyllis Calvert; Stewart Granger; Martita Hunt; Harry Scott; Helen Haye; Beatrice Varley; Raymond Lovell; Norah Swinburne; Jane Gill-Davis; Amy Veness; Stuart Lindsell; Diana King; Ann Wilton; Celia Lamb; Lupe Maguire; Drusilla Wills; Gertrude Maesmore Morris; James Carson; Roy Emmerton; Hargrave Pawson; Babs Valerie; Wally Kingston; Glynn Rowland; Patric Curwen; Lola Hunt; Mary Naylor; Ruth Woodman; A. E. Matthews; Kathleen Boutall.*
b.w. 116 mins.

Clarissa, despite a gypsy warning, forms a friendship with Hesther, her opposite in every way, while at finishing school in Regency England. They meet again later when Hesther is an actress, and Clarissa has entered a loveless marriage with Lord Rohan. Hesther and her friend, Rokeby, contrive to get themselves into Rohan's service. The inevitable conflict of emotions and eventual murder follow.

The Gainsborough Lady logo was a symbol of British cinema in the 1940s and Lockwood and Mason the top two British stars in their homeland of the era. This period melodrama (told in flash back from a then contemporary setting) features a brief scene from OTHELLO with Granger and Lockwood as the principal characters.

STAGE DOOR CANTEEN
(U.S.A., 1943)

p.c. *Sol Lesser.*
d. *Frank Borzage.*
l.p. *Cheryl Walker; William Terry; Marjorie Riordan; Lon McCallister; Margaret Early; Michael Harrison.*
b.w. 132 mins.

The slight story of romance between a soldier and a hostess at the famous Canteen served as an excuse to present a host of stars of stage and screen including Katharine Hepburn, Benny Goodman, Helen Hayes, Harpo Marx, Paul Muni and many, many more. Some of the film was shot in other cities and drama scenes, including some from Shakespeare, are featured. Some prints run ninety-three minutes. The film received Oscar nominations in the music department.

The film has been released for the home movie market by a number of companies in America and Great Britain.

aka: LE CABARET DES ÉTOILES; TRES DÍAS DE AMOR Y FE

CASANOVA IN BURLESQUE
(U.S.A., 1944)

p.c. *Republic.*
d. *Leslie Goodwins.*
l.p. *Joe E. Brown; June Havoc; Dale Evans; Majorie Gateson; Lucien Littlefield; Patricia Knox; Ian Keith; Roger Imhof; Harry Tyler; Sugar Geise; Margie Dean; Jerome Franks Jr.*
b.w. 74 mins.

A burlesque comedian in summer, a professor of Shakespeare in winter, is the way Joe passes his life until the deception is discovered by a stripper. She blackmails him into giving her the lead in THE TAMING OF THE SHREW. When the regular cast walks out on him he has to rely upon his friends from burlesque.

A surprisingly good musical comedy from one of the lesser studios, it actually has two songs with a Shakespearean theme – "Taming of the Shrew" and "Willie the Shake".

LOVE STORY
(G.B., 1944)

p.c. *Gainsborough Pictures.*
d. *Leslie Arliss.*
l.p. *Margaret Lockwood; Stewart Granger; Patricia Roc; Vincent Holman; Joan Rees; Tom Walls; Reginald Purdell; Moira Lister; Dorothy Bramhall; Vincent Holman; Joan Rees; Walter Hudd; A. E. Matthews; Beatrice Varley; Harriet Cohen.*
b.w. 113 mins.

A dying concert pianist falls in love with a half-blind pilot.

This war-time "weepie" was a big success in Britain at the time. It contains scenes throughout the film of rehearsals (with Patricia Roc) for an open air production of THE TEMPEST. Frankly, though, the film's lasting fame rests more on Hubert Bath's music for the film and, in particular, the "Cornish Rhapsody". For its British re-issue in 1948 it was cut by ten minutes.

aka: A LADY SURRENDERS

LES ENFANTS DU PARADIS
(France, 1945)

p.c. *Pathé-Cinéma.*
d. *Marcel Carn.*
l.p. *Arletty; Jean-Louis Barrault; Pierre Brasseur; Maria Casarès; Marcel Herrand; Louis Salou; Pierre Renoir; Paul Frankeur; Jane Marken; Fabien Loris; Etienne Decroux; Marcel Pêrès; Gaston Modot; Pierre Palau; Jacques Castelot; Robert Dhéry; Rognoni; Florencie; Guy Favières; Albert Remy; Auguste Bovério; John Diener; Paul Demange.*
b.w. 195 mins. (see text).

In the middle of the last century in the Parisian theatre district called the Boulevard du Crime, the enigmatic Garance, loved by many men, is saved from arrest by Baptiste, a brilliant mime artiste. He loves her and, secretly, she loves him. She, however, moves to an actor, Lemaître, and later, by way of protection, to the Comte de Montray following a crime commited by her criminal friend, Lacenaire. Years later, Baptiste, now married, and Lemaître are the foremost performers of their respective arts. Garance returns and Baptiste deserts all for her. Lemaître, knowing she cannot be his, is inspired in his performance as "Othello" and the Comte is killed by Lacenaire. Baptiste's wife confronts the lovers and Garance leaves pursued by Baptiste. In the crowds, the only woman he has ever loved is lost to him.

The running time of the original of this film is given by some sources as nearly four hours but the time quoted above is the longest officially noted by any source (most versions seem to be about 188 mins.). To make any film in an occupied country with shortages of equipment, food, secret filming because the actors are on the run, would seem an impossible task. To have made one of this quality in France under German occupation during World War II, must have been a near miracle! Made over a number of years in an atmosphere of happy co-operation, it benefits from a fine script by Jacques Prévert. Two scenes from OTHELLO are featured including the murder of Desdemona plus various quotations because the actor (Lemaître) sees Garance as his Desdemona.

Note: The title should not be translated literally. It refers to the theatre patrons who can only afford the cheapest seats in the highest balcony of a theatre called, in English, "the gods".

Shown "hors concours" at the San Sebastian Film Festival, Spain, 1992.
Academy of Motion Picture Arts and Sciences, U.S.A., 1946: Nomination – Best Writing (Original Screenplay) (Jacques Prévert).
Venice Film Festival, Italy, 1946 – Special Mention.

"...a splendid theatrical experience..." – William Bayer, 'The Great Movies'.

"This magnificent and sumptuous film, this gigantic, philisophical ballet..." – Georges Sadoul, 'French Film'.

aka: CHILDREN OF PARADISE; KINDER DES OLYMP

IT MIGHT BE YOU!
(G.B., 1945)

p.c. *Crown Film Unit.*
d. *Michael Gordon.*
l.p. *Documentary.*
b.w. 14 mins.

A doctor tells of the cases he treats. Three unconnected individuals come together in a road accident. One dies and two are seriously injured.

A propaganda film aimed at accident prevention sees dubious inclusion here. The original 'Monthly Bulletin Review' (January, 1946) suggests speeches by Brutus and Mark Antony from JULIUS CAESAR are used to indicate the public imperviousness to statistics and the dramatic course (as in the case of Antony) needed to rectify this.

A DIARY FOR TIMOTHY
(G.B., 1946)

p.c. *The Crown Film Unit for Ministry Of Information.*
d. *Humphrey Jennings.*
l.p. *Documentary. Narrator: Michael Redgrave.*
b.w. 38 mins.

Story of a young boy born during the years of World War II made to show how life went on. It includes a scene from HAMLET with John Gielgud in the Haymarket Theatre, London, production of the time.

Extract shown as part of the Everybody's Shakespeare International Festival, London, England, 1994.

A MATTER OF LIFE AND DEATH
(G.B., 1946)

p.c. *The Archers.*
d. *Michael Powell, Emric Pressburger.*
l.p. *David Niven; Kim Hunter; Roger Livesey; Robert Coote; Raymond Massey; Marius Goring; Robert Atkins.*
b.w. and Technicolor. 104 mins.

An R.A.F. pilot, Peter Carter, jumps from his aeroplane without a parachute. He is found, appar-

ently unharmed, and meets an American W. A. C., June, with whom he falls in love. He is, however, concussed and halucinates which leads to an operation on his brain. During this, he finds himself on trial before a supernatural court for his life. He wins his case as the operation is successful.

The Pyramus and Thisbe scene from A MIDSUMMER NIGHT'S DREAM is featured in rehearsal for an amateur production in this, the film chosen for the first of the British annual Royal Command Film Performances.

National Film Award, G.B., 1946: Silver Trophy – Best British Film.
'New York Times' Annual Ten Best List, U.S.A., 1946: Listed tenth.
Union of Danish Film Critics, Denmark, 1948: Best European Film.

"...a brilliant experiment which will probably be enjoyed by many and appreciated only by a few." – 'Monthly Film Bulletin', November, 1946.

aka: STAIRWAY TO HEAVEN; JOHNNY IN THE CLOUDS; UN QUESTION DE VIE OU DE MORT; A VIDA O MUERTE

BUCK PRIVATES COME HOME
(U.S.A., 1947)

p.c. *Universal.*
d. *Charles Barton.*
l.p. *Bud Abbott; Lou Costello; Tom Brown; Joan Fulton; Nat Pendleton; Don Beddoe; Beverly Simmons; Don Porter; Donald MacBride; Lane Watson; William Ching; Peter Thompson; George Beban Jr.; Jimmie Dodd; Lennie Bremen; Al Murphy; Bob Wilke.*
b.w. 77 mins.

Slicker and Herbie return from the war, smuggling into America a little French girl they have unofficially adopted. Trouble, of course, follows as they try to get her legally adopted. However, they succeed in the end.

There are no Shakespearean related scenes in this comedy but the film does have the distinction of having such a scene excised from it! This deleted scene features Costello as Romeo and Betty Alexander as Juliet in the balcony scene from a stage production of ROMEO AND JULIET.

aka: ROOKIES COME HOME; DEUX NIGAUDS DÉMOBILISÉS

A DOUBLE LIFE
(U.S.A., 1947)

p.c. *Kanin Productions for Universal-International.*
d. *George Cukor.*
l.p. *Ronald Coleman; Signe Hasso; Edmond O'Brien; Ray Collins; Shelley Winters; Millard Mitchell; Philip Loeb; Joe Sawyer; Charles la*

Torre; Whit Bissel; Elizabeth Dunne; Peter Thompson; John Drew Colt; Alan Edmiston; Art Smith; Harlan Briggs; Wilton Graff; Sid Tomak; Claire Carleton; Betsy Blair and others.
b.w. 104 mins.

A sensitive actor lives his roles to the break down of his marriage. When he plays OTHELLO with his ex-wife as Desdemona, jealousy evolves. He becomes involved with a woman of easy virtue whom he kills. He commits suicide as the police wait to arrest him.

It is a moot point as to whether this should have been placed in the chapter on OTHELLO or not. Certainly the film owes more to Shakespeare than just the scenes from the play. The film was an artistic success and was released on 8 mm. for public purchase in Great Britain.

Academy of Motion Picture Arts and Sciences, U.S.A., 1947: Nominations - Best Director (George Cukor), Writing (Original Screenplay) (Ruth Gordon, Garson Kanin): Awards – Best Actor (Ronald Coleman), Best Score for a Dramatic or Comedy Picture (Miklos Rozsa).

Hollywood Foreign Press Association Golden Globe Awards, U.S.A:, 1947: Best Actor (Ronald Coleman).

" A great film from beginning to end..." – Jay Robert Nash, Stanley Ralph Ross, 'The Motion Picture Guide'.

"George Cukor made what is basically hokum into convincing melodrama..." – Angela and Elkan Allan, 'The Sunday Times Guide to Movies on Television'.

aka: OTHELLO; DOBLE VIDA

NICHOLAS NICKLEBY
(G.B., 1947)
p.c. *Ealing Studios.*
d. *Alberto Cavalcanti.*
l.p. *Derek Bond; Cedric Hardwicke; Sally Ann Howes; Stanley Holloway; Aubrey Woods; Vera Pearce; June Elvin; Alfred Drayton; Bernard Miles; Cyril Fletcher; Cathleen Nesbitt; Mary Merrall; Sybil Thorndike; Athene Aeyler; Cecil Ramage; George Relph; Emrys Jones; Fay Compton; Jill Bacon; James Hayter; Vida Hope; Guy Rolfe; Hattie Jacques; Laurence Hanray; Roddy Hughes; Frederick Hurtwell; Drusilla Wills; Eliot Makeham; John Salew.*
b.w. 108 mins.

This version of the famous story by Charles Dickens again features a sequence from ROMEO AND JULIET performed by the Crummles' theatrical troupe.

THE PERILS OF PAULINE
(U.S.A., 1947)
p.c. *Paramount.*
d. *George Marshall.*

l.p. *Betty Hutton; John Lund; Billy de Wolfe, William Demarest; Constance Collier; Frank Faylen; William Farnum; Paul Panzer; Snub Pollard; Chester Conklin; Creighton Hale; James Finlayson; Hank Mann; Bert Roach; Francis McDonald; Chester Clute.*
Technicolor. 96 mins.

Fired from her job, Pearl White tries to become an actress. She fails but falls in love with Mike, the producer/actor of the company. By accident she become the queen of the serials in Hollywood. Temperament and World War I stop her marriage to Mike whom she has lured into films. After the war, her career declines but Mike become a stage success. In Paris, Pearl become a variety star. An accident ends her career but brings Mike to her.

An entertaining biography of Pearl White, it is an interesting insight into the early days of the movies. The Shakespearean connection is slight. Early in the film, a billboard announces a performance of ROMEO AND JULIET. All are in costume but one member of the cast is missing. Pearl arrives and is given the task of soothing a noisy audience and does so rather well.

Academy of Motion Picture Arts and Sciences, U.S.A., 1947: Nomination – Music (Best Song).

VARIETY GIRL
(U.S.A., 1947)
p.c. *Paramount.*
d. *George Marshall.*
l.p. *Mary Hatcher; Olga San Juan; DeForest Kelley; William Demarest; Frank Ferguson; Frank Faylen; Glenn Tryon; Nella Walker; Torben Meyer; Gus Taute; Jack Norton; Charles Victor; Elaine Riley; Harry Hayden; Janet Thomas; Berta Jonay etc. Plus a host of guest stars which included just about every player on the Paramount payroll at that time.*
b.w. and Technicolor. 83 mins.

Two girls go to Hollywood to seek screen careers. They become involved in many comic situations.

The slim story was based on the founding of the Variety Clubs of America and was a chance to feature the guest stars. One sequence, in colour, is a musical puppet (Puppetoon by George Pal) feline parody called "Romeow and Julicat".

aka: HOLLYWOOD EN FOLIE

CARNAVAL NO FOGO
(Brazil, 1949)
p.c. *Atlântide Cinematográfica.*
d. *Watson Macedo.*
l.p. *Anselmo Duarte; Eliana; Oscarito; Grande Otelo; Modesto de Souza; Adelaide Chiozzo; José Lewgoy; Francisco Dantes.*
b.w. Feature.

During one of the famous carnivals in Rio de Janiero, a group of friends try to organise a musical show. One of the sequences from the show is a comedy version of the balcony scene from ROMEO AND JULIET.

Two comics – Oscarito and the black Grande Otelo – play the respective roles.

TIME RUNS
(U.S.A.?, 1950)

There are reports that Orson Welles filmed some scenes from his stage revue of the above title. This is said to include a scene from HENRY VI Part 3. However, the show is noted as containing text by Milton, Dante and Marlowe. The same year he also presented "An Evening With Orson Welles" with extracts of works by Goethe, Wilde and Shakespeare (the future King Richard III killing Henry VI from HENRY VI Part 3). A part of this presentation was filmed on August 30, 1950, in Munich, Germany. The piece filmed, however, is reported as being from Oscar Wilde. The shows toured Europe with a young, unknown Eartha Kitt among the cast but the Shakespeare item remains a puzzle.

THE MISADVENTURES OF BUSTER KEATON
(U.S.A., 1951)

p.c.   *Crown Pictures and Chapman Productions.*
d.   *Arthur Hilton.*
l.p.   *Buster Keaton; Iris Adrian.*
b.w. 63 mins.

A salesman in a sports equipment shop who also owns a theatre suffers various mishaps. His production of a play is interrupted by gangsters and police and his staging of ROMEO AND JULIET is hampered by a jealous husband with a gun.

More of a series of mixed quality episodes than a coherent whole, the reason for this film's inclusion is obvious. Keaton fans will find this a poor reflection of the Keaton they know and admire and there is no point in looking for it in a Keaton filmography. This is a compilation of some of his television shows for KTTV in Hollywood repackaged for cinema release.

GALA FESTIVAL
(U.S.S.R., 1952)

p.c.   *Mosfilm.*
d.   *Vera Stoyeva.*
l.p.   *Alexander Pigorov; Galina Ulanova; Yergenia Smolemskaya; Mark Reizen; Marina Semyonova; Maxim Mikhailov; Gabovich.*
Sovcolor. 79 mins.

The story of the famous Bolshoi Theatre, Moscow, with opera and ballet extracts, features ballerina Ulanova and Gabovich in ROMEO AND JULIET. The original print was probably longer.

LAXDALE HALL
(G.B., 1952)

p.c.   *Group 3.*
d.   *John Eldridge.*
l.p.   *Ronald Squire; Kathleen Ryan; Raymond Huntley; Sebastian Shaw; Kynaston Reeves; Jameson Clark; Jean Colin; Fulton Mackay; Prunella Scales; Roddy MacMillan; Andrew Keir; Rikki Fulton; Keith Falkner.*
b.w. 77 mins.

Five car owners in the remote village of Laxdale in the Hebrides refuse to pay their road fund licences until they have a proper road. Sent to sort out the problem, a visiting parliamentary delegation is treated to an open-air performance of MACBETH during a storm. The villagers finally get their road.

aka: SCOTCH ON THE ROCKS

IL PECCATO DI ANNA
(Italy, 1952)

p.c.   *Giaguaro Film.*
d.   *Camillo Mastrocinque.*
l.p.   *Anita Vita; Ben E. Johnson; Paul Muller; Giovanna Mazzotti; Rosario Borrelli; William Demby; Pamela Winter; Gioacomo Rondinella; Roman New Orleans Jazz Band.*
b.w. 85 mins.

John, a black actor, arrives in Rome to play OTHELLO and during rehearsals his leading lady, Anna, falls in love with him. Her manager, Alberto, stops the romance when he confronts John with his past, that he was convicted of rape. Anna learns the truth from the real culprit who is killed by Alberto. John attacks Alberto and believes he has killed him. Anna goes after John and saves him from suicide.

From a story written by the lead actress, the reason for this film's inclusion is clear.

aka: THE SIN OF ANNA

LE RIDEAU ROUGE
(France, 1952)

p.c.   *Cinéphone/Gaumont.*
d.   *André Barsacq.*
l.p.   *Pierre Brasseur; Michel Simon; Monelle Valentin; Noël Roquevert; Olivier Hussenot; Jean Brochard; Geneviève Morel; Michel Etchverry; André Versini; Marcel Pêrès.*
b.w. 90 mins.

A theatre director is murdered. Suspicion falls on an old actor but is he the guilty party? The currish Ludovic, lover of Aurelia, the wife of the dead director, is revealed as the culprit. He wanted vengeance on the cynical man and to regain his own honour.

As the title is sometimes quoted as "Ce Soir On Joue Macbeth", the reference point is obvious. The script was by Jean Anouilh and some note the film as being a modern adaptation of MACBETH. Scenes from the play are featured.

"...an unjustly little known film..." – Jean Tulard, 'Guide Des Films'.

LAS TRES ALEGRES COMADRES
(Mexico, 1952)

p.c. *Mier and Brooks.*
d. *Tito Davison.*
l.p. *Amalia Aguilar; Lilia Prado; Lilia del Valle; Joaquín Cordero; Roberto Font; José Ruiz Vélez; Tito Novaro; Wolf Ruvinskis; Gloria Mestre; Diana Ochoa; Nicolás Rodríguez; Armando Arriola; Arturo Castro; Enrique Díaz Indiano; Juan García; Héctor Mateos; Juan Orraca; Manuel Trejo Morales.*
b.w. 113 mins.

Three aspiring actresses find little work as film extras and have to work as cigarette girls in a cabaret. They get involved in a number of adventures including a film test but eventually end up with their loving boy friends.

The reason for the inclusion of this musical comedy is simply the screen test scene in which each girl has to act out a role with the same actor who takes the roles of Armando Duval, Mark Antony and Romeo.

GIUSEPPE VERDI
(Italy, 1953)

p.c. *Consorzio Verdi.*
d. *Raffaelo Matarazzo.*
l.p. *Pierre Crossoy; Anna Maria Ferrero; Gaby André; Irene Genna; Tito Gobbi; Mario del Monaco; Sandro Ruffini; Laura Gore.*
Ferraniacolor. 105 mins.

As he lies on his death bed, Verdi recalls his life. He remembers his struggle for musical recognition, his successes and failures and his home life, the deaths of his wife and son and his love for the opera singer, Giuseppina Strepponi.

This Italian biopic contains extracts from OTELLO, and also briefly from FALSTAFF, and is of interest otherwise for the presence of both Gobbi and del Monaco. Though not within the scope of this book, it is of interest to note that an eight hour television series made by RAI/RTF/BBC and Swedish Radio called *The Life Of Verdi* in 1980 with Ronald Pickup and Carla Fracci featured excerpts from OTELLO and FALSTAFF. Renato Castellani directed. Other Italian films have been made of his life, both silent (*Giuseppe Verdi, Nella Vita E Nelle Gloria*, 1913, directed by Giuseppe de Liguero) and sound (*Giuseppe Verdi*, 1938, directed by Carmine Gallone), but it is not known if they contain any Shakespeare related material.

aka: VERDI; TRAGEDIA Y TRIUNFO DE VERDI

CASA RICORDI
(Italy, France, 1954)

p.c. *Documento Film/I.C.S./Cormoran Film.*
d. *Carmine Gallone.*
l.p. *Roland Alexandre; Miriam Bru; Elisa Cegani; Andrea Chechi; Danièle Delorme; Nadia Gray; Marta Toren; Gabriele Ferzetti; Marcello Mastroianni; Micheline Presle; Roldano Lupi; Fosco Giachetti; Maurice Ronet; Paolo Stoppa; Renzo Giovampietro. etc.*
Technicolor. 110 mins.

A humble music printer obtains a modest contract which blossoms to make his company famous for his future generations.

This tale of the famous music publishing house is blessed with a host of music and singers (including Mario Del Monaco, Tito Gobbi and Renata Tebaldi). Verdi was one of the clients of the publishing house and included here is the finale from OTELLO.

PRINCE OF PLAYERS
(U.S.A., 1954)

p.c. *20th. Century Fox.*
d. *Philip Dunne.*
l.p. *Richard Burton; Maggie McNamara; John Derek; Raymond Massey; Charles Bickford; Elizabeth Sellars; Eva le Gallienne; Christopher Cook; Dayton Lummis; Ian Keith; Paul Stader; Jack Raine; Stanley Hall; Sarah Padden; Eleanor Audley; Louis Alexander.*
DeLuxe Color. 102 mins. CinemaScope.

Famous actor Edwin Booth is helped by his wife, Mary, both in his career and his health. When his brother, John Wilkes, kills President Lincoln and is himself killed, Edwin faces hostility and Mary dies. He triumphs, however, in New York.

This episodic biography contains some Shakespearean scenes from ROMEO AND JULIET, RICHARD III and HAMLET.

Shown at the Shakespeare Film Festival, Wiesbaden, W. Germany, 1964.

"...a fascinating insight into the gifted but tragic family, with Burton shining in his many opportunities to perform Shakespearean passages." – Tony Thomas and Aubrey Solomon, 'The Films Of Twentieth Century Fox'.

"Curiosity value..." – Angela and Elkan Allan, 'The Sunday Times Guide to Movies on Television'.

SOMMARNATTENS LEENDE
(Sweden, 1955)

p.c. *Svensk Filmindustri.*
d. *Ingmar Bergman.*

l.p. *Ulla Jacobsson; Gunnar Bjornstrand; Eva Dahlbeck; Margit Carlquist; Jarl Kulle; Ake Fridell; Harriet Andersson; Björn Bjelvenstam; Naima Wilfstrand.*
b.w. 105 mins.

Anne, an inexperienced new wife, discovers her husband's liaison with Desirée, a former lover. Frederik, Anne's husband, is humiliated by Count Malcolm, Desirée's current lover. Desirée plans to ensnare Frederik and arranges a house party with Frederik, Anne, Count Malcolm and his wife Charlotte and Henrik, Frederik's moody son by a former marriage, as guests. During the summernight, Anne elopes with Henrik, Malcolm and Charlotte are reconciled and Desirée gets her wish. Even a maid finds romance with a bucolic groom.

Aside from the temporal connotation (see English title below), there are a number of sources that consider this Bergman film is Shakespeare influenced. Peter Harcourt in 'Six European Directors' is reminded of ROMEO AND JULIET by it. Likewise in his tome 'Amour-Erotisme Et Cinéma', Ado Kyrou notes both the influence and the references to Shakespeare (A MIDSUMMER NIGHT'S DREAM Act V Scene 1) and even likens the Harriet Andersson role to that of Puck.

The film inspired the musical show and subsequent film "A Little Night Music".

Cannes Film Festival, France, 1956: Award – Most Poetic Humour.
'New York Times' Annual Ten Best List, U.S.A., 1957: Tenth in Best Foreign Films section.
Union of Danish Film Critics, Denmark, 1957: Best European Film.

"A pensive film, full of scurrilous comic dialogue and situations..." – 'Lexikon Filme in Fernsehen'.

aka: SMILES OF A SUMMER NIGHT; SOURIRES D'UNE NUIT D'ÉTÉ; SONRISAS DE UNA NOCHE DE VERANO; DAS LÄCHELN EINER SOMMERNACHT

IKIMONO NO KIROKU
(Japan, 1955)

p.c. *Toho.*
d. *Akira Kurosawa.*
l.p. *Toshiro Mifune; Ekio Miyoshi; Yutaka Sada; Minoru Chiaki; Haruko Togo; Kiyomi Mizunoya; Kyoko Aoyama; Saoko Yonemura; Akemi Negishi; Kichijiro Ueda; Masao Shimizu; Noriko Shimura; Yoichi Tachikawa; Takashi Shimura; Kazuo Kato.*
b.w. 113 mins.

A prosperous industrialist is brought before an abitrator when he wants to move his family to Brazil to avoid a nuclear holocaust which he believes will come. His assets frozen, he cannot buy the land he wants in Brazil. Reduced to begging, he is found unstable. He commits arson and is put in an asylum. The sight of the rising sun appears to him as the holocaust.

Though not from Shakespeare and made a year before Kurosawa's first assay into that realm with KUMONOSU-JO, there are clear signs of the Bard's influence on his work. There are suggestions of HAMLET and some scenes could have been taken from KING LEAR.

C'EST ARRIVÉ À ADEN
(France, 1956)

p.c. *S.B. Films.*
d. *Michel Boisrond.*
l.p. *Dany Robin; André Luguet; Robert Manuel; Jacques Dacqmine; Elina Labourdette; Jean Bretonnière; Dominque Page; Michel Etcheverry.*
Eastman Color. 76 mins. Dyaliscope.

At the turn of the century the leading lady of a group of strolling players in Aden refuses to be part of a bargain for a peace treaty with a local prince. He abducts her and they fall in love and marry and the treaty is signed.

This contains scenes from OTHELLO.

aka: IT HAPPENED IN ADEN

SERENADE
(U.S.A., 1956)

p.c. *Warner Bros.*
d. *Anthony Mann.*
l.p. *Mario Lanza; Joan Fontaine; Sarita Montiel; Vincent Price; Vince Edwards; Joseph Calleia; Licia Albanese; Harry Bellaver; Silvio Minciotti; Frank Puglia.*
WarnerColor. 121 mins.

Operatic discovery loses the patronage and love of society woman as ambition drives him on. He seeks consolation and finds it with a Mexican girl. The society woman tries to get him back and his true love, the Mexican girl, is almost killed.

A vehicle for Mario Lanza, it features a scene from Verdi's OTELLO.

aka: DOS PASIONES Y UN AMOR

LE THÉÂTRE NATIONAL POPULAIRE
(France, 1956)

p.c. *Amor Films.*
d. *Georges Franju.*
l.p. *Documentary featuring: Maria Casarés; Jean Villar; Gérard Philippe; Georges Wilson.*
b.w. 27 mins.

About theatre production, this is said to contain scenes from OTHELLO and MACBETH.

KEAN (GENIO E SREGOLATEZZA)
(Italy, 1957)

p.c. *Vides/Lux Film.*

d. *Vittorio Gassman, Francesco Rosi.*

l.p. *Vittorio Gassman; Eleonora Rossi Drago; Anna Maria Ferrero; Helmut Dantine; Cesco Baseggio; Gérard Landry; Mario Carotenuto; Nerio Bernardi; Maria Fabbri; Amadeo Girard; Dina Sassoli; Pietro Tordi; Carlo Mazzarella; Valentina Cortese and others.*

Eastman Color. 83 mins.

This is the life story of the great Shakespearean actor of the last century, Edmund Kean. His successes and failures, his drinking, money problems and his women and his strange friendship with the Prince of Wales, all are resolved in the end when he marries the woman he loves.

Vittorio Gassman had at this time already produced the same story, based on the work by Alexandre Dumas père, for Italian television and had given stage performances of various Shakespeare plays, OTHELLO, which is featured in the film, being one of his greatest successes and it was also televised. Scenes from HAMLET are also featured in the film. Jean Paul Satre wrote the script for the film.

Kean himself was something of an institution in London in his day. His performances as RICHARD III, OTHELLO, HAMLET and KING LEAR are an indelible part of the history of the theatre.

For further references to Kean see **KEAN** (1922), **THE ROYAL BOX** (1930) and **KEAN** (1940).

Grolle D'Oro, Italy, 1956/7: Best Actor (Vittorio Gassman).

DANGER WITHIN
(G.B., 1958)

p.c. *Colin Lesslie Productions.*

d. *Don Chaffey.*

l.p. *Richard Todd; Bernard Lee; Michael Wilding; Richard Attenborough; Donald Houston; Dennis Price; Peter Arne; William Franklyn; Vincent Ball; Ronnie Stevens; Terence Alexander; Peter Jones; Andrew Faulds.*

b.w. 113 mins.

A group of officers plan an escape from an Italian prisoner of war camp during World War II by means of a tunnel. However, they find their efforts are foiled by their captors and they realise that one of them is a traitor. Only when a big escape is planned is the informant detected.

The escape is planned during a performance of HAMLET which is seen both in rehearsal and production with Dennis Price as the Prince.

aka: BREAKOUT

MÄDCHEN IN UNIFORM
(W. Germany, France, 1958)

p.c. *CCC-Films Modernes/Emile Nathan S.N.C.*

d. *Géza von Radvany.*

l.p. *Romy Schneider; Lilli Palmer; Therese Giese; Blandine Erbinger; Adelheid Seeck; Gina Albert; Sabine Sinjen; Christine Kaufmann; Margaret Jahnen; Ginette Pigeon; Paulette Dubost; Roma Bahn; Marthe Mercadier; Danik Patisson; Ulla Moritz; Tessy Aselmeier; Edith Helou; Lou Seitz; Edith Adana; Käthe Kamossa.*

Eastman Color. 95 mins.

In a German school for girls in 1910, discipline is harsh and acts of affection are few. When one is shown by Miss von Bernburg to the young Manuela, it leads to a difficult situation. The girls having given an excellent performance of ROMEO AND JULIET, Manuela continues her role of Romeo to declare her love for the teacher. Punishment leads to depression and to attempted suicide which has a strong effect upon the headmistress.

This is a remake of an earlier film with the same title. The original had a contemporary setting of the time and was directed by Leontine Sagan. It is a classic of the German cinema and was one of the films shown at the first Venice Film Festival in 1932. The remake places the story in a more historical setting at the early part of this century when such emotion between members of the same sex would have seemed truly shocking. By 1958 attitudes to such subjects were just beginning to change and the film was hardly as controversial, politically or socially, as its illustrious fore-runner in its day. It is interesting, however, to see a young Romy Schneider in a male (Shakespearean) role. She would do so again in her career.

aka: CORRUPCIÓN EN EL INTERNADO

MARJORIE MORNINGSTAR
(U.S.A., 1958)

p.c. *Beachwood Pictures/Warner Bros.*

d. *Irving Rapper.*

l.p. *Gene Kelly; Natalie Wood; Claire Trevor; Carolyn Jones; Ed Wynn; Everett Sloane; Marty Milner; George Tobias; Martin Balsam; Jesse White; Rad Fluton.*

b.w. 122 mins.

A pretty Jewish girl falls in love with the entertainment director of a holiday resort. She changes her name to help her theatrical career. He settles down to a steady job and wants to marry but when his musical show fails, he takes to drink. The girl follows him to Europe but eventually finds him, surrounded by girls, at the holiday resort. She realises that she no longer loves him and leaves unseen by him.

A college production of ROMEO AND JULIET features the tomb scene.

aka: LA FUREUR D'AIMER; MORNINGSTAR

SERENADE EINER GROSSEN LIEBE
(U.S.A./W. Germany, 1958)

p.c. *Corona-Orion.*
d. *Rudolph Maté.*
l.p. *Mario Lanza; Johann von Koczian; Zsa Zsa*
Gabor; Kurt Kasznar; Peter Capell; Hans
Söhnker.
Technicolor. 97 mins. Technirama.

A turbulent tenor falls for a deaf girl who will not marry him until she can hear him sing. He raises money for the necessary treatment. Though successful, she goes deaf again.

Highly sentimental film made to feature the temperamental singing star, this contains, among others, excerpts from Verdi's OTELLO.

aka: FOR THE FIRST TIME

STAGE STRUCK
(U.S.A., 1958)

p.c. *R.K.O.-Radio.*
d. *Sidney Lumet.*
l.p. *Henry Fonda; Susan Strasberg; Joan*
Greenwood; Christopher Plummer; Daniel Ocko;
Herbert Marshall; Pat Harrington; Frank
Campanella; John Fielder; Patricia Englund.
Technicolor. 95 mins.

An aspiring actress arrives in New York looking for stardom. Having missed an opportunity, she saves matters with an improvised scene from ROMEO AND JULIET. She is secretly coached for a new play and takes over, successfully, when its star walks out. Of course, the author of the play loves her.

Basically a remake of **MORNING GLORY**, apart from the scene mentioned above, there are brief quotations from THE MERCHANT OF VENICE and OTHELLO, references to characters from Shakespearean plays and to the man himself.

aka: EINES TAGE ÖFFNET SICH DIE TÜR

CARRY ON TEACHER
(G.B., 1959)

p.c. *Nat Cohen and Stuart Levy. A Peter Rogers*
Production.
d. *Gerald Thomas.*
l.p. *Ted Ray; Kenneth Connor; Leslie Phillips;*
Charles Hawtrey; Kenneth Williams; Joan Sims;
Hattie Jacques; Rosalind Knight; Cyril
Chamberlain; Richard O'Sullivan.
b.w. 86 mins.

When a Ministry of Education official visits their school, the pupils behave intolerably causing mayhem and sabotage. However, having heard that their headmaster planned to move to another school, their purpose is merely to get him to stay on.

The "Carry On.." series of films has already been noted under **CARRY ON CLEO** (see **CHAPTER I**

ANTONY AND CLEOPATRA). This particular one is perhaps best summed by the opening comment on the film in the book 'What A Carry On' by Sally and Nina Hibbin which is "To cane or not to cane...". It is ROMEO AND JULIET which suffers a calamitous school performance in this British comedy. Part of this scene is included in the compilation film **TO SEE SUCH FUN** (G.B., 1977).

Extract shown as part of the Everybody's Shakespeare International Festival, London, England, 1994.

aka: IST JA IRRE – LAUTER LIEBENSWERTE LEHRER

GYALOG A MENNYORSZÁGBA
(Hungary, 1959)

p.c. *Hunnia Film Studio of Hungarian Film*
Production Company.
d. *Imre Fehér.*
l.p. *Mari Törőcsik; Zoltán Latinovits; Marianne*
Krencsey; Lajos Básti; István Avar; Tibor
Benedek; József Bihary; Márta Fónay; Dezső
Garas; Dorottya Geczy; János Makláry; Sándor
Kőmíves; Mária Keresztessy; Piri Peéry; Edit
Soós; András Ambrus; Arpád Téry; Nusi
Somogyi; Emese Balogh; Gyula Bodrogi; Karola
Csűrős; István Szilágyi; Ildikó Pádua; Blanka
Péchy; József Ross; Bőske Vámosi; Gedeon
Viktor.
b.w. 96 mins.

Imre and Vera marry. Both leave their careers and move to Budapest to improve their living standard. Their marriage is empty despite their love and, made aware of this by a former boyfriend, Vera leaves to go back to acting in a travelling theatre group. Imre returns to his vocation and takes a job in a small town. By coincidence the theatre comes to the same town to play its two hundred and fiftieth performance. The play is ROMEO AND JULIET. The couple realise that they can begin again with a truer love.

aka: WALKING TO HEAVEN

KOMPOEITOR SERGEI PROKOFIEV
(U.S.S.R., 1960)

p.c. *Moscow Film Studios.*
d. *Lidia Stepanova.*
l.p. *Documentary.*
c.? (?) mins.

In this documentary about the life of the famous composer, scenes from the ballet version of ROMEO AND JULIET are featured.

LANTERNA MAGIKA
(Czechoslovakia, 1958/61)

The original edition of this film/theatre experience by Alfred Radok was made for special venues such as Expo 58 and the Brussels Exhibition where it won an award. A combination of widescreen film in colour and black and white and on-stage actors and puppets, it proved so popular that further editions were developed. The second one premièred in Moscow and included a history of Czech film. For the "sound era", the death scene of Desdemona from the opera OTHELLO was featured – and with a twist or two. The characters involved in a "silent" eternal triangle farce, hilariously find themselves in a "sound" version of OTHELLO.

Not, of course, film in the true sense and therefore not preserved, its unusual character and interest surely merits its inclusion.

THE PURE HELL OF ST. TRINIANS
(G.B., 1960)

p.c. *Vale.*
d. *Frank Launder.*
l.p. *Cecil Parker; Joyce Grenfell; George Cole; Thorley Walters; Eric Barker; Liz Frazer; Irene Handl; Dennis Price; Lloyd Lamble; Sidney James; Nicholas Phipps; Lisa Lee; Cyril Chamberlain; Raymond Huntley; Mark Dignam; George Benson; Michael Ripper; Elwyn Brook-Jones; John Le Mesurier; Wensley Pithey.*
b.w. 94 mins.

On a plea from the agent of an Emir, the girls of St. Trinians are freed after being arraigned for burning down the school. The Sixth Form is sent on a cultural tour of the Greek islands which is but an excuse to find wives from among them for the Emir's sons. The police, a school inspector and a small-time crook rescue them from a fate worse than death. The girls celebrate by setting fire to the new school.

Inspired by the comic-strip characters created by Ronald Searle, this was one of a short series of such broad comedy films. In the second in the series – *Blue Murder at St. Trinians* (1958) – there had been a very fleeting reference to HAMLET with "something rotten in the State of Denmark". This one not only has a quote from the same play but a possibly unconscious reference in the name of the judge (Slender) to a character from THE MERRY WIVES OF WINDSOR. However, it really merits inclusion because of a striptease sequence performed to Hamlet's speech "To be or not to be..". As a school inspector says in the film: "This is the final outrage, the soliloquy to striptease. What would the Bard have said." What, indeed!

Extract shown as part of the Everybody's Shakespeare International Festival, London, England, 1994.

SAPTAPADI
(India, 1961)

p.c. *Alochhaya Productions.*
d. *Ajoy Kar.*
l.p. *Uttam Kumar; Suchitra Sen; Chhabi Biswas; Tulsi Chakraborty; Taran Kumar; Chhaya Devi; Preeti Majumdar; Padmadevi; Seeta Mukhenjee; Sabita Roy Choudhury; Swagata Chakraborty.*
b.w. 163 mins.

During World War II, a Jesuit priest meets a wounded woman soldier and recognises his former love. He recalls how he won her love during a college performance of OTHELLO and how parental opposition forced them into their very differing ways of life. The woman regains consciousness and tries to commit suicide. The lovers are reunited.

In this drama in the Bengali language, the two principal stars are seen as Othello and Desdemona.

JAK BYĆ KOCHANA
(Poland, 1962)

p.c. *Film Polski.*
d. *Wojciech Has.*
l.p. *Zbigniew Cybulski; Barbara Krafftowna; Kalina Jedrusik; Tadeusz Kalinowski.*
b.w. 100 mins.

On a flight to Paris, Felicja recalls the past. Before World War II, she was going to play Ophelia opposite her lover, Wiktor, as Hamlet. To avoid acting in the Nazi theatre, she became a waitress and hid Wiktor in her flat during the occupation. Wiktor soon left and after the war she became a popular radio star. She again met Wiktor who had changed to a dissolute braggart.

Based on a short story by Kasimierz Brandys, the Shakespearean connection is obvious. The film is highly regarded and has had festival showings.

San Francisco Film Festival, U.S.A., 1963: Best Film, Best Actress (Barbara Krafftowna), Best Scenario.

aka: HOW TO BE LOVED

HOLLYWOOD AND THE STARS
(U.S.A., 1963)

p.c. *David L. Wolper.*
d.
l.p. *Documentary. Narrator: Joseph Cotten.*
b.w. 36 mins.

It must be admitted that this was one of a series made for television. However, a number of these found their way on to the sub-standard gauges and have been shown at conventions and the like. This one has had several showings in England and has been well received. Well, the topic is an attractive one for the film has the subsidiary title "Academy Awards Moments of Greatness".

Of relevance to Shakespeare is the opening of the film which is from **WEST SIDE STORY** (the marvellous opening of that film). Rita Moreno is seen receiving her Oscar in 1961 for her performance in the film. There are also scenes from **A MIDSUMMER NIGHT'S DREAM** (1935).

MAYA PLISETSKAYA
(U.S.S.R., 1964)

p.c. *Central Documentary Film Studios.*
d. *Vasily Katayan.*
l.p. *Maya Plisetskaya; Dmitri Begak; Vladimir Vasilyev; Nicholai Fadeyechev; Maris Liepa; Vladimir Tikhonov; Yuri Zhdanov.*
Sovcolor. 75 mins.

The subject matter in this documentary is, of course, the ballet dancer of the title. She is seen in ballet school and class, rehearsal and performance. Among the ballet extracts featured is one from ROMEO AND JULIET by Prokofiev. The film was made in 70mm.

Shown "hors concours" at the San Sebastian Film Festival, Spain, 1973.

PANIC BUTTON
(U.S.A., 1964)

p.c. *Yankee Productios.*
d. *George Sherman.*
l.p. *Maurice Chevallier; Eleanor Parker; Jayne Mansfield, Michael Connors; Akim Tamiroff*
b.w. 90 mins.

Faced with tax problems, a business man decides to make a bad movie to establish losses. He employs a has-been actor and a talentless, but glamorous, actress to make a pilot version of ROMEO AND JULIET. Things go wrong when the film wins a prize at the Venice Film Festival.

The film received mixed critical comment but the thought of Jayne Mansfield as Juliet is mind-boggling and perhaps even eye-boggling. A similar story was used for the later (1967) Mel Brooks film *The Producers* but without any Shakespeare connotations.

SCORPIO RISING
(U.S.A., 1965)

p.c. *Puck Film Productions.*
d. *Kenneth Anger.*
l.p. *Bruce Byron; Johnny Sapienza; Frank Carifi; Bill Dorfman; John Palone; Ernie Allo; Barry Rubin; Johnny Dodds.*
Ektachrome. 31 mins.

The myth of the American motor-cyclist, his costume, accessories, rites and self-destructive element are examined in this unusual short.

Aside from the production company name, cut-ins of Mickey Rooney as Puck in the film **A MIDSUMMER NIGHT'S DREAM** are featured.

Shown at the Film and Video Workshop Festival, Copenhagen, Denmark, 1994.
Shown at the 17th. Semana Internacional de Cine de Autor, Malaga, Spain, 1989.

SHAKESPEARE-WALLAH
(India, 1965)

p.c. *Merchant/Ivory.*
d. *James Ivory.*
l.p. *Felicity Kendall; Shashi Kapoor; Geoffrey Kendall; Laura Lidell; Madhur Jaffrey; Jim Tyler; Utpal Dutt; Parveen Paul; Prayagraj; Pincho Kapoor; Hamid Sayani; Sudershan; Partrap Sharma.*
b.w. 125 mins.

A touring troupe of Shakespearean actors enjoys varying success and fortune depending on the weather, money and the changing political climate. Love and jealousy flare between an Indian actor, the daughter of the English troupe leader and an old flame of the Indian actor. In the end the daughter is sent back to England.

The Merchant/Ivory team surely needs no introduction – it is synonymous with good cinema and the accolades that accompany it. It was the same about thirty years ago for this film received much critical acclaim. The film contains a number of extracts from plays – ANTONY AND CLEOPATRA, HAMLET, OTHELLO, ROMEO AND JULIET and TWELFTH NIGHT – and many of the actors were Shakespearean actors.

Shown as part of the Everybody's Shakespeare International Festival, London, England, 1994.
Shown at the London Film Festival, England, 1965.
Shown at the New York Film Festival, U.S.A., 1965.
Berlin Film Festival, W. Germany, 1965: Silver Bear for Best Actress (Madhur Jaffrey).
L'Académie du Cinéma, France, 1968: Prix International.
National Board of Review Awards, U.S.A., 1966: Listed tenth in Best English-Language Films list.

"The film is a rare example of genuine international synthesis." – 'Continental Film Review', January, 1966.

aka: LA COMPAÑIA SHAKESPEARE

BEREGIS AUTOMOBILYA
(U.S.S.R., 1966)

p.c. *Mosfilm.*
d. *Eldar Ryazanov.*
l.p. *Innokenti Smoktunovsky; Oleg Yefremov; Anatoli Papanov; Olga Aroseva; Andrei Mironov; Lubov Dobrzhanskaya; Tatyana Gavrilova; Georgi Zhenov; Sergei Kulagin; Evgeni Evestigneyev; Victoria Radunskaya.*
b.w. 93 mins.

A modern-day Russian Robin Hood steals cars from people who exploit others. He sells the cars and gives the money to charity. Through amateur dramatics, he becomes friendly with the policeman investigating his crimes. Though the thief attracts sympathy, he is eventually caught and sent to prison.

CHAPTER XXX – ALL THE WORLD'S A STAGE

This comedy contains a would-be amateur performance of HAMLET with Smoktunovsky parodying his own famous role.

Shown at the Edinburgh Film Festival, Scotland, 1966.

aka: AN UNCOMMON THIEF; WATCH YOUR CAR; BEWARE AUTOMOBILE

THE DEADLY AFFAIR
(G.B., 1966)

p.c. *Sidney Lumet Productions.*
d. *Sidney Lumet.*
l.p. *James Mason; Simone Signoret; Maximilian Schell; Harry Anderson; Kenneth Haig; Roy Kinnear; Max Adrian; Lynn Redgrave; Robert Flemyng; Corin Redgrave; Kenneth Ivew; Les White; June Murphy; Frank Williams; Rosemary Lord; Denis Shaw; Julian Sherrier; John Dimech; Petra Markham; Maria Charles; Amanda Walker; Judy Keirn;Sheraton Blount; Janet Hargreaves; Michael Brennan; Richard Steele; Gertan Klauber; Margaret Lacey; Members of the Royal Shakespeare Company.*
Technicolor. 107 mins.

Shocked when an official he has investigated and cleared commits suicide, agent Dobbs, aided by a semi-retired police officer, starts to investigate. He meets much opposition and has to resign to carry on the work privately. Clues lead back to the widow of the dead official and that his friend, Dieter, is not only his wife's lover but also the spy. A trap is set with the inevitable outcome.

Based on a novel by John Le Carré, this features a rehearsal in a theatre for the three witches scene ("Double, double, toil and trouble..") from MACBETH as well as excerpts from "Edward II" by Marlowe.

aka: M15 DEMANDE PROTECTION; LLAMADA PARA EL MUERTO

ELIZABETH, DE WROUW ZONDER MAN
(Holland, 1966/67)

p.c. *Theater Klank en Beeld.*
d. *Hans van den Busken.*
l.p. *Caro van Eyck; Rita Maréchal; Hans Culeman.*
b.w.? 1 reel?

This extract from a stage performance by the troupe Ensemble from the play by André Josset (here directed by Johan de Meester), itself contains an extract from another play -THE MERCHANT OF VENICE.

MISTRZ
(Poland, 1966)

p.c. *Studio Filmowe Iluzjon.*
d. *Jerzy Antczak.*

l.p. *Janusz Warnecki; Ignacy Gogolewski; Ryszardar Hanin; Henryk Borowski; Zbigniew Cybulski; Andrzej Lapicki; Igor Smialowski.*
b.w. 80 mins.

In 1944, some Polish refugees take shelter. An aspiring actor who dreams of great roles, such as HAMLET, is one of them. His talent has only been recognised in small towns and he is listed by the Germans as a book-keeper. This saves him initially from reprisal executions of educated and artistic people but when he displays his talent with a monologue from MACBETH, he, too, is shot. Years later, a young actor preparing for the MACBETH role, recalls the old master's performance.

Obviously of a patriotic nature, the film features the talented young Polish star, Zbigniew Cybulski, who died in a tragic accident the year after this was made. The title translates as "The Master".

THE CHARGE OF THE LIGHT BRIGADE
(G.B., 1968)

p.c. *Woodfall Film Productions.*
d. *Tony Richardson.*
l.p. *Trevor Howard; Vanessa Redgrave; John Gielgud; David Hemmings; Harry Andrews; Jill Bennett; Peter Bowles; Mark Burns; Howard Marion Crawford; Alan Dobie; Mark Dignam; Willoughby Goddard; T. P. McKenna; Corin Redgrave; Norman Rossington; Ben Aris; Leo Britt; Helen Cherry; Ambrose Coghill; Andrew Faulds; Ben Howard; Georges Douking; Donald Wolfit; Rachel Kempson; Roger Mutton; Valerie Newman; Peter Woodthorpe.*
De Luxe Color. 141 mins. Panavision.

Following the defeat of Napoléon, the British aristocracy is anxious for military diversion and takes on the protection of Turkey against invading Russia. The British under Lord Cardigan head for the Crimea in 1854. There is friction between the British commanders and the troops suffer poor provisions and sickness. However, a victory is obtained outside Sebastopol but this is not followed up and the Russians counter-attack. The inept British command, anxious to do something, sends the Light Brigade on a deliberate charge into the face of the Russian guns.

Donald Wolfit is seen as MACBETH at his second meeting with the witches in a scene from a London production in this version of one of the greatest military blunders in British history.

aka: LA CHARGE DE LA BRIGADE LÉGÈRE; LA ULTIMA CARGA.

FRAU WIRTIN HAT AUCH EINEN GRAFEN
(Austria/W. Germany/Italy/Hungary, 1968)

p.c. *Neue Delta-Filmproduktion/Terra Filmkunst/Aico Film/Hungaro Film.*

d. *Franz Antel.*

l.p. *Terry Torday; Jeffrey Hunter; Pascale Petit; Gustav Knuth; Jacques Herlin; Hannelore Auer; Harald Leipnitz; Heinrich Schweiger; Ralf Wolter; Edwige Fenech; Anke Syring; Erich Padalewski; Femi Benussi; Franz Muxeneder; Rosemarie Lindt; Judith Dornys.*

Eastman Color. 96 mins. Ultrascope.

A troupe of strolling players led by Susan have a performance interrupted by Napoléon's soldiers. Susan soon finds herself entrusted with secret letters, impersonating a duke and foiling a plot to kill the Emperor.

One in a series of supposedly sexy films of the era, the reason for inclusion is that the interrupted performance is of THE TAMING OF THE SHREW. Probably the Bard would have approved of Miss Torday in his play for she seems to have some sympathy with his works. In another film in the series, *Frau Wirtin Treibt Es Jetzt Noch Toller*, the lady found herself following a much-loved Shakespeare theme of dual roles, one female, the other male impersonation. Of this film Miss Torday said: "All the disguises and mix-ups are great fun – just like the Shakespeare comedies."

aka: SEXY SUSAN SINS AGAIN; OUI À L'AMOUR, NON À LA GUERRE; SUSANNA...ED I SUOI DOLCI VIZI ALLA CORTE DEL RE

VÍZKERESZT
(Hungary, 1968)

p.c. *Béla Balázs Studios.*

d. *Sándor Sára.*

l.p. *Documentary.*

b.w. 14 mins.

People who live on secluded farms come to a village to see a performance of TWELFTH NIGHT by the Universitas Ensemble. They skate home afterwards.

Included for obvious reasons, the film is said to be very beautiful. Logically so, for the director was also a leading director of photography.

Miskole, Hungary, 1968: Documentary category prize.
Oberhausen Film Festival, W. Germany, 1968: 3rd. Prize – Documentary Film Section.

aka: TWELFTH NIGHT

EL ABOMINABLE HOMBRE DE LA COSTA DEL SOL
(Spain, 1969)

p.c. *Pedro Maso Producciones Cinematográficas/ Filmayer Producción.*

d. *Pedro Lazaga.*

l.p. *Juanjo Menéndez; La Polaca; Mary Francis; Mónica Randall; Adriano Dominguez; Jorge*

Rigaud; Rafaela Aparicio; Carlos Mendy; Margot Cottens; Ricardo Merino etc.

Eastman Color. 82 mins.

The incompetent son of a rich duke is sent to work as a public relations man at a hotel He becomes a big success with the ladies to the surprise of his father and the concern of the girl who loves him.

In dream sequences, the hero appears as Mark Antony, Othello and Romeo.

IL PRIMO PREMIO SI CHIAMA IRENE (DANIMARCA – L'INCREDIBLE REALTÀ DELLA NUOVA MORALE)
(Italy, 1969)

p.c. *Dino De Laurentiis Cinematografica.*

d. *Renzo Regazzi.*

l.p. *Not known.*

Eastman Color. 103 mins. Colorscope.

Interviews, reportage, staged scenes to illustrate various sexual diversions and perversions form this typical sex report film about morality in Denmark.

Of the staged scenes, one is the "Get thee to a nunnery..." scene from HAMLET.

aka: FIRST PRIZE IRENE; PERVERSE JEUNESSE

THE MAGIC CHRISTIAN
(G.B., 1969)

p.c. *Grand Films.*

d. *Joseph McGrath.*

l.p. *Peter Sellers; Ringo Starr; Richard Attenborough; Leonard Frey; Laurence Harvey; Christopher Lee; Spike Milligan; Yul Brynner; Roman Polanski; Raquel Welch; Wilfrid Hyde White; Isabel Jeans; Caroline Blakiston; Tom Boyle; Terence Alexander; Peter Bayliss; Joan Benham; Patrick Cargill; John Cleese; Graham Chapman; Freddie Earlle; Fred Emney; Clive Dunn; Peter Graves; Hattie Jacques etc.*

Technicolor. 95 mins.

Eccentric and immensely wealthy, Sir Guy is a constant joker. He adopts a waif as his heir whom he takes on a round of destructive fun against recognised standards and institutions. Father and son purchase the "Magic Christian", a liner of unsurpassed luxury where the guests encounter chaos. Finally, they build a vat to brew a mixture of manure and animal blood and people try and grab the money strewn upon the horrible liquid.

The first lesson the young waif has to endure from his foster father is a visit to see HAMLET. For the performance, the Prince (played by Laurence Harvey) has been induced to accompany the famous soliloquy with a striptease. If that offends, then so might some of the rest of the film which does have some very funny moments.

aka: SI QUIERES SER MILLONARIO NO MALGASTES EL TIEMPO TRABAJANDO

THE PROJECTIONIST
(U.S.A., 1970)

p.c. *Maglan.*
d. *Harry Hurwitz.*
l.p. *Chuck McCann; Ina Balin; Rodney Dangerfield; Jara Kohout; Harry Hurwitz; Robert Staats; Stephen Phillips; Clara Rosenthal; Jacquelyn Glenn; Moroco; David Holiday.*
Technicolor. 88 mins.

An awkward cinema projectionist acts out the fantasies created by screen characters.

Among film extracts featured is one from **A MIDSUMMER NIGHT'S DREAM** (1935).

SUCH GOOD FRIENDS
(U.S.A., 1971)

p.c. *Sigma Productions.*
d. *Otto Preminger.*
l.p. *Dyan Cannon; James Coco; Jennifer O'Neill; Nina Foch; Burgess Meredith; Laurence Luckinbill; Ken Howard; Louise Lasser; Sam Levene; William Redfield; James Beard; Rita Gam; Nancy Guild; Elaine Joyce; Nancy R. Pollock; Lee Sabinson; Doris Roberts; Clarice Taylor; Vergina Vestoff; Joseph Papp and his Shakespeare Theater in the Park.*
Colour by Movielab.102 mins.

Apparently minor surgery on Richard Messenger reveals serious complications and sets up a chain of events. His wife attempts to find a blood donor, discovers that her husband has been having affaires and she wanders from person to person eventually ending up drunk with a photographer friend for whom she strips. He tries to seduce her but finds himself impotent. The wife returns to the hospital to learn that Richard has died.

The reason for the inclusion of this is obvious from the cast list. What the Papp troupe performed is unknown but presumably was a brief extract in New York's Central Park.

aka: DES AMIS COMME LES MIENS; EXTRAÑA AMISDAD

THE FLESH AND BLOOD SHOW
(G.B., 1972)

p.c. *Peter Walker (Heritage).*
d. *Peter Walker.*
l.p. *Jenny Hanley; Ray Brooks; Luan Peters; Judy Matheson; Candace Glendenning; Robin Askwith; Tristan Rogers; Penny Meredith; David Howey; Patrick Barr; Brian Tulley; Elizabeth Bradley; Raymond Young; Rodney Diak; Sally Lahee; Jane Cardew.*
Eastman Color. 96 mins. 3-D (part).

A company of actors take over a derelict theatre which was the scene of some strange murders during the war. The murders start again...

This exploitive horror film contains scenes from OTHELLO, the key to the original crimes. The finale of the film is in 3-D and such sensationalism was fairly typical of the producer/director.

THE MOODS OF LOVE
(G.B., 1972)

p.c. *EMI Special Films Unit.*
d. *David Wicks.*
l.p. *Narrator: Eric Porter.*
c. 21 mins.

Set in Stratford-upon-Avon, this romantic film features ten sonnets by Shakespeare.

¡QUE NOS IMPORTA LA REVOLUCIÓN!
(Spain, Italy, 1972)

p.c. *Fair Film/Midega Films.*
d. *Sergio Corbucci.*
l.p. *Vittorio Gassman; Paolo Villagio; Leo Anchóriz; Eduardo Fajardo.*
c. 105 mins. WS

An Italian priest and an Italian actor become unwilling comrades when they find themselves involved in the Mexian Revolution. Facing death from both factions, the actor finally finds his true role and rouses the people against tyranny.

A basically comic film, there are a number of references to OTHELLO and to RICHARD III including the final scene from the play which is interrupted by revolutionaries.

aka: CHE C'ENTRIAMO NOI CON LA RIVOLUZIONE; MAIS QU'EST-CE QUE JE VIENS FOUTRE AU MILIEU DE CETTE RÉVOLUTION?

THEATRE OF BLOOD
(G.B., 1973)

p.c. *Cineman.*
d. *Douglas Hickox.*
l.p. *Vincent Price; Diana Rigg; Ian Hendry; Coral Brown; Harry Andrews; Robert Coote; Jack Hawkins; Michael Horden; Arthur Lowe; Robert Morley; Joan Hickson; Dennis Price; Diana Dors; Renee Asherson; Madeline Smith; Milo O'Shea; Eric Sykes.*
DeLuxe Color. 102 mins.

A supposedly dead Shakespearean actor reappears to exact vengeance on the drama critics who have humiliated him. Each dies in the manner relative to the play they have adversely criticised which include THE MERCHANT OF VENICE, OTHELLO, CYMBELINE, ROMEO AND JULIET and KING LEAR.

This horror movie is an ideal vehicle for Vincent Price and provides him with a fine opportunity to exercise his particular style of acting. He especially rises to the moment as RICHARD III. Incidentally, the film's Spanish title is MATAR O NO MATAR...ESTE ES EL PROBLEMA which translates as "To kill or not to kill...that is the problem", a parody, of course, of an obvious Shakespearean quote.

Aside from the obvious interpretation by Price, the film is loaded with quotations and Shakespearean overtones. For students of the cinema, the opening of the film is a delight, being filled with clips from Shakespearean films of the silent era. The cast appear to have had fun making the film, too!

Shown as part of the Everybody's Shakespeare International Festival, London, England, 1994.

"...a real one-man show..." – Carlos Aguilar, 'Guía del Vídeo-Cine' .

aka: MUCH ADO ABOUT MURDER; THÉÂTRE DU SANG; THEATER DES GRAUENS

THE GREAT McGONAGALL
(G.B., 1974)
p.c. *Darlton.*
d. *Joseph McGrath.*
l.p. *Spike Milligan; Peter Sellers; Julia Foster; John Chagrin; John Bluthal; Clifton Jones; Valentine Dyall; Victor Spinetti; Charles Atom; Janet Adair.*
Eastman Color. 89 mins.

McGonagall, a Scottish weaver, falls in love with Queen Victoria and, after giving a show to the Queen, decides to devote himself to poetry. He ends up in debtors' prison. He learns to appreciate Shakespeare and, on release, gives a performance of MACBETH. He then lives in a fantasy world that he has won the admiration of the Queen, is invited to Balmoral and eventually honoured.

Sadly, not the greatest of films for two of the ex-Goons though the thought of Sellers as Queen Victoria may amuse some. Most of the actors play many parts.

L'IMPORTANT, C'EST D'AIMER
(France/Italy/W. Germany, 1975)
p.c. *Albina Productions/Rizzoli Film/T.T.T. Filmproduktion.*
d. *Andrzej Zulawski.*
l.p. *Romy Schneider; Jacques Dutronc; Fabio Testi; Claude Dauphin; Klaus Kinski.*
c. 113 mins.

A reporter-photographer attempts to seduce a declining actress. A relationship forms but she remains faithful to her amiable but weak husband. The reporter borrows money from some crooks to stage RICHARD III for her but it fails. She gives herself to him in payment for his effort. Aware of the relationship, her husband kills himself, the reporter is beaten up over the money he borrowed and the woman realises she loves him.

A film which has received mixed comment, though commercially successful, and was the first for the Polish director outside his homeland, it is of interest to see Romy Schneider as King Richard III. The version of the play as presented in the film was noted as being "unusual". The film was shortened a few months after release to one hundred and ten minutes. The Spanish lost a further five minutes.

Taormina Festival, Sicily, Italy, 1975: Best Actress (Romy Schneider).

"...the intensity of the performances of Romy Schneider and Jacques Dutronc...continue to make this an exceptional film." – 'Guide Akai Vidéo-Cassettes'.

aka: THE MAIN THING IS TO LOVE; LO IMPORTANTE ES AMAR; NACHTBLENDE; L'IMPORTANTE È AMARE

ROMEO OF THE SPIRITS
(G.B., 1976)
p.c. *Thorntip.*
d. *Nikolas L. Janis.*
l.p. *Michael Gough.*
c. 21 mins.

An alcoholic tramp, living perhaps his last day, during his search for liquor in the rubbish of London, recalls some lines of Romeo whom he played as a youth. In his sorry state, he associates a bottle with Juliet, his own desperation with that of Romeo.

This was the first part of a planned trilogy. The second part had at the time already been written and featured the character Malvolio from TWELFTH NIGHT. The third was planned to be about HAMLET. Michael Gough was to star again but it is not known if the project was ever completed.

Cork Film Festival, Eire, 1976: Fiction Short Prize.

THE GOODBYE GIRL
(U.S.A., 1977)
p.c. *Rastar for M.G.M. and Warner Bros.*
d. *Herbert Ross.*
l.p. *Richard Dreyfuss; Marsha Mason; Quinn Cummings; Paul Benedict; Barbara Rhoades; Theresa Merritt; Michael Shawn; Patricia Pearcy; Gene Castle; Daniel Levans; Marilyn Sokol; Anita Dangler; Victoria Boothby; Robert Constanzo; Nicol Williamson.*
Metrocolor. 110 mins.

Paula, a dancer, allows an actor, Elliot to move into her spare room. Paula's audition fails, Elliot's play – a homosexual version of RICHARD III – has a disastrous first night and closes. They fall in love and both get other jobs but the affaire almost ends when Elliot is spotted by a Hollywood director.

The script was written by Neil Simon and the film ranks as a very successful one commercially, taking, according to 'Variety', $41,000,000 in 1978 in America.

Academy of Motion Picture Arts and Sciences, U.S.A., 1977: Nominations – Best Picture, Best Actress (Marsha Mason), Best Supporting Actress (Quinn Cummings), Best Original Screenplay (Neil Simon); Awards – Best Actor (Richard Dreyfuss)
British Academy of Film and Television Arts, G.B., 1978: Best Actor (Richard Dreyfuss).
David di Donatello Awards, Italy, 1978: Best Direction (Herbert Ross shared with Ridley Scott for *The Duellists*), Best Actor (Richard Dreyfuss).
Hollywood Foreign Press Association, U.S.A., 1977: Best Motion Picture-Musical/ Comedy, Best Actor-Musical/Comedy (Richard Dreyfuss), Best Actress-Musical/Comedy (Marsha Mason), Best Screenplay (Neil Simon).
Los Angeles Film Critics Association, U.S.A., 1977: Best Actor (Richard Dreyfuss).

aka: LA CHICA DEL ADIOS

TO SEE SUCH FUN
(G.B., 1977)

p.c. *A Herbert Wilcox/Michael Grade Production.*
d. *John Scoffield.*
l.p. *Many and various. Narrator: Frank Muir.*
b.w. and c. 90 mins.

Music, dancing and comedy (intentional and unintentional) is the subject matter in this compilation from British films.

It had not been planned to include such films where the reference points have been noted in their own right. However, as there are a number in this one, it was felt worth including, added to which is the opening voice-over starts: "This royal throne of kings, this scepter'd isle..." from RICHARD II Act II, Scene 1. Scenes from **CARRY ON CLEO** (G.B., 1964) and **CARRY ON TEACHER** (G.B., 1959) are included as well as scenes with quotations from **LAUGHTER IN PARADISE** (G.B., 1951), **BOTTOMS UP!** (G.B., 1960) and **NEARLY A NASTY ACCIDENT** (G.B., 1961). The film may not have had circuit release in Britain and may have been sold to, or intentionally made for, television. The Shakespeare interest aside, the film is an enjoyable survey of British comedy film.

THE TURNING POINT
(U.S.A., 1977)

p.c. *Hera Productions for 20th. Century Fox.*
d. *Herbert Ross.*

l.p. *Shirley MacLaine; Anne Bancroft; Mikhail Baryshnikov; Leslie Browne; Tom Skerritt; Martha Scott; Antoinette Sibley; Alexandra Danilova; Starr Danias; James Mitchell; Marshall Thompson; Scott Douglas; Daniel Levans; Jurgen Schneider; Anthony Zerbe; Philip Saunders; Lisa Lucas; Saax Bradbury; Hilda Morales; Donald Petrie and others.*
De Luxe Color. 119 mins.

Deedee, a retired dancer, renews her acquaintance with Emma, the ageing star with the American Ballet Theatre. Deedee's daughter, Emilia, is given the chance to dance in New York and her parents go with her. However, rivalry over Emilia develops between the former friends to Emilia's confusion. A stunning performance by the girl re-unites the women.

A ballet sequence from ROMEO AND JULIET by Prokofiev is featured in this, noted as being seventeenth in the list of top money earners of 1978.

Academy of Motion Picture Arts and Sciences, U.S.A., 1977: Nominations – Best Film, Best Director (Herbert Ross), Best Actress (Anne Bancroft), Best Supporting Actor (Mikhail Baryshnikov), Best Supporting Actress (Leslie Browne), Best Original Screenplay (Arthur Laurents), Best Cinematography (Robert Surtees).
Hollywood Foreign Press Association Golden Globe Awards, U.S.A., 1977: Best Motion Picture – Drama, Best Director (Herbert Ross).
Los Angeles Film Critics Association, U.S.A., 1977: Best Director (Herbert Ross).
The Nation Board of Review Awards, U.S.A., 1977: Best English-Language Picture; Best Actress (Anne Bancroft), Best Supporting Actor (Tom Skerritt), Best English-Language Films (Listed first).
The Writers Guild of America Awards, U.S.A., 1977: Best-Written Drama Written Directly for the Screen (Avery Corman, Arthur Laurents).

aka: PASO DECISIVO; AM WENDEPUNKT

IN THE FOREST
(G.B., 1978)

p.c. *BFI Production Board.*
d. *Phil Mulloy.*
l.p. *Barrie Houghton; Anthony O'Donnell; Ellen Sheean; Joby Blanchard; Larry Dann; Nick Burton; Frank Ellis; Reginald Jessup; Nicholas McArdle; David Sinclair; Michael Mulloy; Robin Summers; Chey Walker; Robert Walker; Malcolm Coad; Ken Gregson.*
b.w. 80 mins.

Three peasants from the Middle Ages progress through various stages of English history up to the Industrial Revolution.

This contains a scene from MACBETH with the first three players noted above as Macduff, Banquo and Lady Macbeth respectively.

THE NINTH CONFIGURATION
(U.S.A., 1979)

p.c. *The Ninth Configuration Company.*
d. *William Peter Blatty.*
l.p. *Stacy Keach; Scott Wilson; Jason Miller; Ed Flanders; Neville Brand; Robert Logan; George DiCenzo; Moses Gunn; Joe Spinell; Alejandro Rey; Tom Atkins; Steve Sandor; Richard Lynch; Mark Gordon; Bill Lucking; Stephen Powers; David Healy; Tom Shaw.*
Metrocolor. 109 mins.

A clerical error puts Colonel Kane, a combat man, in charge of a special study centre for psychosis. He has to deal with many problems and when his true forté is discovered events take a strange path ending in Kane's suicide.

This contains a reference to HAMLET and a planned canine producton of JULIUS CAESAR!

SHAKESPEARE'S MOUNTED FOOT
(G.B., 1979)

p.c. *A Breck/Campbell Production for Scottish Arts Council.*
d. *Bert Eeles.*
l.p. *Alex Norton; James Copeland; Russell Hunter; Vari Sylvester; Sandy Neilson.*
c. 44 mins.

This fictional comedy is about a theatre troupe at the turn of the century touring the Scottish border area. Based on accounts of such troupes, it includes a sequence from MACBETH.

MURDER PSALM
(U.S.A., 1980)

p.c. *Stan Brakhage.*
d. *Stan Brakhage.*
l.p. *Images and extracts.*
c. (Kodak?) 18 mins.

This is a montage of hand-treated film stock, negative shots, scenes of war and violence and narrative episodes.

Though no actors as such are featured here, it is appropriate that it is included as one scene depicts a child waving sparklers while **SCORPIO RISING** is recalled and in another, in particular, a brief scene from **A MIDSUMMER NIGHT'S DREAM** (1935) is featured.

SO FINE
(U.S.A., 1981)

p.c. *Warner Bros. A Lobell-Bergman Production.*
d. *Andrew Bergman.*
l.p. *Ryan O'Neal; Jack Warden; Mariangela Melato; Fred Gwynne; David Rounds; Richard Kiel; Mike Kellin; Joel Steadman; Jessica James; Angela Pietro Pinto; Lois de Banzie; Mervin Goldsmith; Michael Lombard; Bruce Mulholland; Irving Metzman.*
Technicolor. 91 mins.

A professor whose father's clothing business is in financial difficulties is kidnapped by a gangster to save the business. While the professor is making love to the gangster's wife she splits her jeans starting a new fashion which saves the business. The gangster discovers the affaire and nearly kills his wife during her performance as Desdemona in Verdi's OTELLO.

The extract from OTELLO was performed by the Canadian Opera Company with Ennio Morricone taking credit for most of the rest of the music in this comedy. Some editing and the addition of out-takes resulted in five minutes extra for the American television.

aka: PROFESOR A MI MEDIDA; DER AUSGEFLIPPTE PROFESSOR

MEPHISTO
(Hungary, 1982)

p.c. *Mafilm (Studio Objektiv) in association with Manfred Durniok Productions.*
d. *István Szabó.*
l.p. *Klaus Maria Brandauer; Ildikó Bánásgi; Krystyna Janda; Rolfe Hoppe; Péter Andorai; György Cserhalmi; Karin Boyd; Christine Harbort; Tamás Major; Ildikó Kishonti; Sári Gencsy; Zdzislaw Mrozewski; Professor Martin Hellber; Oskár Káti; Katalyin Sólyom; Irén Bordán and many others.*
Eastman Color. 144 mins.

Hendrik Högren, an ambitious left-wing actor in Germany of the 1920s, gradually begins to rise in status. When the Nazi rise to power occurs, he impresses a Nazi general and the general's mistress helps dispel any fears about his political beliefs. To help former colleagues, he makes sacrifices in his marriage and, forced to comply with Nazi demand, he remarries. As he is about to stage a "Nazi" HAMLET, he is taken away to the Berlin Olympic Stadium to be humiliated to prove that he is only a pawn in the power game.

The reason for the inclusion of the film is obvious from the resumé of the plot. The film is German-speaking.

Academy of Motion Picture Arts and Sciences, U.S.A., 1982: Award – Best Foreign Language Film.
British Film Critics Circle Award, G.B., 1982: Best Foreign Film.
Cannes Film Festival, France, 1981: Best Script.
David di Donatello Awards, Italy, 1982: Klaus Maria Brandauer.
Hungarian National Film Festival, Hungary, 1982: Best Film.
National Board of Review, U.S.A., 1982: Listed first in Foreign Films list.

THE DRESSER
(G.B. 1983)

p.c. *Goldcrest/World Film Services for Columbia.*

d. Peter Yates.
l.p. Albert Finney; Tom Courtenay; Edward Fox; Zena Walker; Cathryn Harrison; Michael Gough; Eileen Atkins; Betty Marsden; Sheila Reid; Lockwood West; Donald Eccles; Kevin Stoney; Llewellyn Rees; Guy Manning; Anne Mannion; Ann Way.
c. 118 mins.

During World War II, a company of actors is managed by Sir, an old style actor. Past his best, he is somehow driven on by his homosexual dresser, Norman. When it is near curtain up time, Sir prepares for OTHELLO but the play is KING LEAR. He also quotes from a play that is taboo backstage – MACBETH. Despite some disasters, Sir gives a great performance and dies in his chair after the show.

Academy of Motion Picture Arts and Sciences, U.S.A., 1983: Nominations – Best Film, Best Actor (Albert Finney, Tom Courtenay), Best Director (Peter Yates), Best Screenplay Adapted from Another Medium (Ronald Harwood).
Berlin Film Festival, W. Germany, 1984: Best Actor (Albert Finney).
Hollywood Foreign Press Association Golden Globe Awards, 1984: Best Actor (Tom Courtenay shared with Robert Duvall for *Tender Mercies*).

"...very fine film.." – Jean Tulard, 'Guide Des Films'.

aka: L'HABILLEUR; LA SOMBRA DEL ACTOR; EIN UNGLEICHES PAAR

TO BE OR NOT TO BE
(U.S.A., 1983)

p.c. Brooksfilms for 20th. Century Fox.
d. Al Johnson.
p.c. Mel Brooks; Anne Bancroft; Tim Matheson; Charles Durning; José Ferrer; George Gaynes; Christopher Lloyd; George Wyner; Lewis J. Stadlen; Jack Riley; James Haake; Ronny Graham; Estelle Reiner; Earl Boen; Zale Kessler; Ivor Barry.
DeLuxe Color. 107 mins. S

Remake of the 1942 classic with Jewish overtones and Mel Brooks as HAMLET!

Academy of Motion Picture Arts and Sciences, U.S.A., 1983: Nomination – Best Supporting Actor (Charles Durning).

aka: SOY O NO SOY; SEIN ODER NICHTSEIN

ZELIG
(U.S.A., 1983)

p.c. Orion. A Jack Rollins-Charles H. Joffe Production.
d. Woody Allen.
l.p. Woody Allen; Mia Farrow; John Buckwalter; Marvin Chatinover; Stanley Swerdlow; Paul Nevens; Howard Erskine; George Hamlin; Michael Jeeter; Robert Iglesia; Ralph Bell; Eli Resnick; Gale Hansen; Edward McPhillips; Will Hussong; Richard Whiting; Peter McRobbie; Sol Lomita; Mary Louise Wilton; Erma Campbell; Robert Berger; Sharon Ferrol; Deborah Rush; Jeanine Jackson; Stephanie Farrow; Richard Litt etc.
c. and b.w. 79 mins.

At a party in 1928, Scott Fitzgerald is perplexed by an individual. An interloper posing as a baseball player is removed from a training ground in Florida. A missing clerk, Leonard Zelig, is found in Chinatown and seems to have become Chinese. He is studied by Dr. Eudora Fletcher and, after a number of trying episodes, they fall in love. But even getting married causes problems.

Not an easy film to paraphrase but, in the context of this book, all that is relevant is a scene in which Zelig's father is seen in a fleeting moment from A MIDSUMMER NIGHT'S DREAM.

Academy of Motion Picture Arts and Sciences, U.S.A., 1983: Nominations – Best Costume Design (Santo Loquasto), Best Cinematography (Gordon Williams).
Venice Film Festival, Italy, 1983: Golden Phoenix Award for Best Cinematography.

THE PASSIONATE PILGRIM
(G.B., 1984)

p.c. A Picture Company Production.
d. Charles Wallace.
l.p. Eric Morecambe; Tom Baker; Madeline Smith; Alfreda Ashworth; Tuffet the Horse. Narrator: John Le Mesurier.
Technicolor. 20 mins.

The crazy Lord Eric desires the silly Lady Madeline but has to outwit the lusty Sir Tom who is tracking down maidens using his "Good Knight Guide". Though beaten, Sir Tom returns again and again in his quest for Lady Madeline. Finally, he defeats Lord Eric only to find that the author of his guide book is E. Morecambe. Lord Eric marries Madeline while Sir Tom is entertained by two willing maidens.

Full of innuendos and music borrowed from the great composers, this will mean much to British audiences. The late Eric Morecambe formed part of a much-loved comic duo, Morecambe and Wise. Tom Baker once played Dr. Who in the cult television series of the same name. Madeline Smith's ample talents have graced many a horror film and saucy comedy. The late John Le Mesurier was a stalwart of the British cinema perhaps best remembered for his role in the television show *Dad's Army*. According to the credits, this is based on THE PASSIONATE PILGRIM XV by William Shakespeare. Even this is in a jocular vein and the Bard would surely have not been offended. A quick reference to the piece in question will reveal the joke!

THE ANGELIC CONVERSATION
(G.B., 1985)

p.c. *British Film Institute in association with Channel 4.*

d. *Derek Jarman.*

l.p. *Reader: Judi Dench. With: Paul Reynolds, Phillip Williamson.*

c. 81 mins.

Images of mainly male figures seen at windows, holding lights, on rocky coastlines and in caverns, swimming, being washed, looking and making love are counterpointed with Judi Dench reading Shakespeare's sonnets (nos. 27, 29, 30, 43, 53, 55, 56, 57, 61, 90, 94, 104, 126 and 148).

This Jarman film, mainly about homo-erotic imagery, was filmed on Super 8mm. (presumably Kodachrome) and tranferred to 35 mm. and from black and white to colour by low and high band video. Jarman described the imagery of the film as "people I like in places and spaces I like" and noted: "Whenever I show this film there is always someone in the audience who says it is the most beautiful they have ever seen."

Shown as part of the Everybody's Shakespeare International Festival, London, England, 1994.
Shown at Imagfic 86, Madrid, Spain, 1986.

FONTEYN AND NUREYEV – A BALLET LEGEND
(G.B., 1985)

p.c. *Peter Batty Productions.*

d. *Peter Batty.*

l.p. *Documentary.*

c./b.w. 90 mins.

The lives of these two famous stars of the ballet are traced individually and as a ballet partners. The stories unravel through historic film extracts and interviews.

Among the many ballet scenes are two from ROMEO AND JULIET with music by Prokofiev.

aka: FONTEYN UND NUREJEW – EINE BAL-LETTLEGENDE

MISHIMA: A LIFE IN FOUR CHAPTERS
(U.S.A./Japan, 1985)

p.c. *Zoetrope/Filmlink International/Lucas Film for The M Film Company.*

d. *Paul Schrader.*

l.p. *Ken Ogata; Masayuki Shionoya; Junkichi Orimoto; Hiroshi Mikami; Junya Fukuda; Shjigeto Tachihara; Naoko Otani; Go Riju; Masato Aizawa; Yuki Nagahara; YasosukeBando; Hisako Manda; Naomi Oki; Kenji Sawada; Sachiko Hidari; Hiroshi Katsuno; Toshiyuki Nagashima and many more.*

Technicolor/b.w. 120 mins. Panavision.

This is the biography of controversial Japanese author Yukio Mishima with sections based upon some of his novels.

A brief sequence from ROMEO AND JULIET is featured with Tsutomu Harda and Mami Okamoto in the respective roles.

Shown at the Festival Internacional de Cine, Gijon, Spain, 1995.
Shown "hors concours" at the Valladolid Film Festival, Spain, 1985.
Cannes Film Festival, France, 1985: Best Artistic Contribution (Cinematography – John Bailey, Production Design – Eiko Ishioka, Musical Score – Philip Glass).

aka: MISHIMA; MISHIMA – EIN LEBEN IN 4 KAPITELN

RENDEZ-VOUS
(France, 1985)

p.c. *T. Films/Films A2.*

d. *André Téchiné.*

l.p. *Juliette Binoche; Lambert Wilson; Jean-Louis Trintignant; Dominique Lavanant; Anne Wiazemsky; Jean-Louis Vitrac; Jacques Nolot; Arlette Gordon; Olimpia Carlisi; Serge Martina; Philippe Landoulsi; Caroline Faro; Katsumi Furukata; Madeleine Marie.*

Eastman Color. 83 mins. Scope.

Nina, an actress, after sleeping around in Paris is offered a room by Paulot but has to move when his room-mate Quentin objects. Quentin, an actor in a sex show parody of ROMEO AND JULIET, soon becomes her lover to Paulot's disgust, but commits suicide. Nina meets a theatre director who explains that Quentin was his perfect Romeo who fell in love with his daughter but survived the suicide pact in which she died. He claims to have found the perfect Juliet in Nina who now has moved in with Paulot on a platonic basis but he is unhappy with her relationship with the director. Though she forces Paulot to make love to her, the signs are all too clear.

ROMEO AND JULIET is used somewhat symbolically here though there is a brief rehearsal scene from the play.

NOBODY'S FOOL
(U.S.A., 1986)

p.c. *Island Pictures in association with Katz/Denny Productions.*

d. *Evelyn Purcell.*

l.p. *Rosanna Arquette; Eric Roberts; Mare Winningham; Jim Youngs; Louise Fletcher; Gwenn Welles; Stephen Tobolowsky; Charlie Barnett; Ronnie Claire Edwards; Belita Moreno; J.J. Hardy; William Steiss; Lewis Arquette; Cheli Chew; Sheila Paige; Scott Rosensweig; Ann Hearn; Alma Beltran; Budge Threkeld; Lisa DeBennedetti; Natalie Golden; Wylie*

Small; Kristy Kennedy; Arwen Nichols; Loraine Wallace; Rod Hart etc.
Colour by CFI. 105 mins.

Cassie, a waitress in the small American town of Buckeye Basin, is a local outcast and unmarried mother. Though she still loves Billy, the father of her child, who is now married, she becomes the lover of Riley, a stage-hand with a touring Shakespearean troupe. She joins an acting class and does well. On learning that Billy's wife is pregnant, she declines to become his mistress and accepts Riley's offer to leave with the troupe.

With scenes from THE TEMPEST and MACBETH and a soliloquy from ROMEO AND JULIET, there is good enough reason for this film's inclusion but the town itself must not be forgotten. Buckeye Basin's founder was a Shakespeare-loving frontiersman whose most famous utterance was "To be or not to be ain't much of a choice."! For the record, the Shakespearean troupe in the film comprised: Bonnie Oda Homsey; Dean Ricca; Joe Clarke; Becky Bell Maxwell; Bruce Wright; Frederick Bailey; Melissa Grier. Stephen Tobolowsky staged the sequences.

MAITASUN ARINA
(Spain, 1987)

p.c. *Juan Luis Mendiaraz.*
d. *Juan Luis Mendiaraz.*
l.p. *Santiago Ramos; Begoña Baena; Juan Luis Mendiaraz; Ramón Aguirre.*
c. 11 mins.

An escape takes place in a prison during a performance of HAMLET but only the actor in this role can escape. With the police on his trail, he hides out in a boutique called "Ofelia".

Though Spanish, this short emanates from the Basque autonomous region and was made thanks to a grant from the Department Of Culture of the local government. Miss Baena also worked with the director on the script and editing.

ANNA-DER FILM
(W. Germany, 1988)

p.c. *TV60 Filmproduktion.*
d. *Frank Strecker.*
l.p. *Silvia Seidel; Patrick Bach; Gunter Maria Halmer; Milena Vukotić; Anton Diffring; Ilse Neubauer; Ronnie Jannot; Eleanore Hirt.*
c. 90 mins. WS.

Aspiring ballerina, Anna, lives with the crippled Rainer. Their relationship is threatened when David, Anna's dancing partner, falls in love with her. Spotted by an impressario, Anna is given a new partner with great success. David is killed accidentally and Anna goes to America where she triumphs in a solo performance.

One of the many diverse dance sequences is from ROMEO AND JULIET by Prokofiev.

DEAD POETS SOCIETY
(U.S.A., 1989)

p.c. *Touchstone Pictures in association with Silver Screen Partners IV and Witt-Thomas Productions.*
d. *Peter Weir.*
l.p. *Robin Williams; Robert Sean Leonard; Ethan Hawke; Josh Charles; Dylan Kussman; Gale Hansen; Allelon Ruggiero; James Waterson; Norman Lloyd; Kurtwood Smith; Carla Belver; Leon Pownall; George Martin; Joe Aufiery; Matt Carey; Kevin Cooney.*
Metrocolor. 129 mins. S

John Keating, former pupil of Welton Academy, returns as an English teacher with some odd philosophies. His pupils find records of his secret Dead Poets Society which they revive. Following a parent's distaste at his son's appearance in A MIDSUMMERS NIGHT'S DREAM, albeit successfully, the boy commits suicide. Keating is made the scapegoat and his pupils forced to denounce him. As he leaves they show their defiance of authority and their love for him.

Apart from the obvious reference above, the film includes a number of quotations from classic literature plus the now famous impersonation by Robin Williams of John Wayne quoting Shakespeare.

Academy of Motion Picture Arts and Sciences, U.S.A., 1990: Nominations – Best Director (Peter Weir), Best Actor (Robin Williams); Award – Best Original Script (Tom Schulman).
British Academy of Film and Television, G.B,, 1990: Best Film, Best Score (Maurice Jarre).
Film Critics Circle of Australia, Australia, 1989: Best Foreign Film.
Sindicato Nazionale Giornalisti Cinematografici Italiani, Italy, 1989/90: Best Foreign Film.

aka: LE CERCLE DES POÈTES DISPARUS; EL CLUB DE LOS POETAS MUERTOS; DER CLUB DER TOTEN DICHTER

HIGHLANDER II – THE QUICKENING
(U.S.A., 1990)

p.c. *Davis-Panzer in association with Lamb Bear Entertainment.*
d. *Russell Mulcahy.*
l.p. *Christopher Lambert; Sean Connery; Virgina Madsen; Michael Ironside; Allan Rich; John C. McGinley; Phil Brock; Rusty Schwimmer; Ed Trucco; Stephen Grives; Jimmy Murray; Pete Antico; Peter Bucossi; Peter Bromilow; Jeff Altman; Diana Rossi; Max Berliner; Randall Newsome; Karin Dexler; Eduardo Sapac etc.*
Eastman Color. 100 mins. S

Connor MacLeod has built a shield over the world for protection following the break-up of the ozone layer. Twenty five years later in 2034, the need for the shield is over but it is being maintained for profit motives. MacLeod, now showing his years, meets a young woman terrorist out to discover the truth. MacLeod regains his young appearance when attacked unsuccessfully by two of Katana's winged assailants. His power regained, he summons his mentor, Ramirez, beheads Katana and destroys the shield.

In this second film in the series, Ramirez (Sean Connery) returns to aid his friend and literally drops in on a performance of HAMLET, during the grave scene, to be precise.

aka: LOS INMORTALES II

IN THE SHADOW OF THE STARS
(U.S.A., 1991)

p.c. *Allie Light and Irving Saraf with the aid of the Corporation for Public Broadcasting, National Endowment for the Arts and L. J. Skaggs and Mary C. Skaggs Foundation.*
d. *Allie Light, Irving Saraf.*
l.p. *Documentary. Members of the San Francisco Opera.*
c. 90 mins. S

This interesting insight of the world of opera and the above company in particular contains many opera sequences including a number from MACBETH by Verdi.

Academy of Motion Picture Arts and Sciences, U.S.A., 1991: Award – Best Documentary.

OGNENNYI ANGEL
(Russia, 1991)

This three part documentary was made to celebrate the centenary of the birth of the composer Sergei Prokofiev. According to the Russian film authorities, it contains Shakespearean references. Logically, it contains scenes from the ballet ROMEO AND JULIET (any biographical film about him could hardly do otherwise). It was presumably made in colour and the title translates as "Fiery Angel".

TRUE IDENTITY
(U.S.A., 1991)

p.c. *Touchstone Pictures in association with Silver Screen Partners IV/Sandollar Productions.*
d. *Charles Lane.*
l.p. *Lenny Henry; Frank Langella; Charles Lane; J. T. Walsh; Anne-Marie Johnson; Bill Raymond; Peggy Lipton; Andreas Katsulas; Michael McKean; James Earl Jones; Ruth Brown; Darnell Williams; Christopher Collins; Melvin Van Peebles; Fantasia Owens; Joe Bellan; James Landi; Beth Robbins; Jim Gavin; Shannon Holt; Judson Scott; David Martel Bryant; Lynne Griffin etc.*
Technicolor. 93 mins. S

Miles, an aspiring black actor who wishes to play OTHELLO, meets Frank Luchino, a gangster long

thought to be dead. The gangster is also backing a new production of OTHELLO. When death seems near in a pending air crash, Lucino reveals his identity to Miles. The aeroplane lands safely and a dangerous life begins for Miles because of his knowledge. After many adventures Miles reveals the truth in a performance of OTHELLO in which he has had to take the lead.

SWAN SONG
(G.B., 1993)

p.c. *Renaissance.*
d. *Kenneth Branagh.*
l.p. *John Gielgud; Richard Briers.*
c. 24 mins.

Based on a play by Chekhov, this concerns an ageing actor theorising about the nature of his profession.

This delightful short features the great Gielgud as HAMLET, KING LEAR and ROMEO.

Shown as part of the Everybody's Shakespeare International Festival, London, England, 1994.

THE LAST ACTION HERO
(U.S.A., 1993)

p.c. *Columbia.*
d. *John McTiernan.*
l.p. *Arnold Schwarzenegger; F. Murray Abraham; Art Carney; Charles Dance; Anthony Quinn; Austin O'Brien; Robert Prosky; Mercedes Ruehl; Tom Noonan; Tina Turner; Robert Prosky; Ian McKellen; Joan Plowright; Bridgette Wilson; Jason Kelly; Toru Tanaka; Noah Emmerich; Frank McRae and many others including cameo appearances by, among others, James Belushi, Chevy Chase, Sharon Stone, Little Richard, Leeza Gibbons and Jean-Claude van Damme.*
Technicolor. 130 mins. S Panavision.

A young boy is given a special ticket when he goes to see the latest movie of his hero, Jack Slater. The ticket allows him to move into the film world where he helps out his hero. But the ticket falls into the hands of a mobster who moves into the real world followed by Jack and the boy. Jack has to come to terms with the reality, so different from his screen life. He saves the life of the actor who plays him on the screen. When the mobster moves back to the movie world Jack, using a ticket stub, follows him.

$80,000,000 was the figure said by one source to be the production cost of this film (though in an interview Schwarzenegger put the figure at $65,000,000, saying that other figures were pure invention) – and part of it went on a scene from HAMLET! Arnold Schwarzenegger is not a name readily associated with classic literature on the screen but he got his chance here. Well, not quite. In school, the boy has to watch a scene from Olivier's HAMLET (presented by Joan Plowright, Olivier's third wife) but he sees his hero in the role as a far more decisive and deadly character.

"Alas, poor Yorick! I knew him...a fellow of infinite jest...". Rather, "Alas, poor Columbia" would perhaps be more appropriate for the jest has been on the company. Though the film enjoyed temporary success in Europe, the box-office takings are a long way off recouping the production costs. And this is despite the film having the "distinction" of being the first film to be advertised in space. Columbia paid $300,000 to have the name of the film painted on the side of an unmanned rocket launched in May 1993. With all the promotional stunts to support the film, it would be easy to overlook a technical development by Sony (which owns Columbia) – Sony Dynamic Digital Sound used for the first time with this film. It is also easy to be swayed by the mass of adverse comment for, although the film may not have matched its publicity claims, it does have its moments.

Extract shown as part of the Everybody's Shakespeare International Festival, London, England, 1994.

"The best sequences (such as the Schwarzenegger Hamlet) offer tantalising glimpses of the film it might have been." – review of the videogram release, 'Daily Mail', September 23, 1994.

NORTH
(U.S.A., 1994)

p.c. *New Line/Castle Rock/Columbia.*
d. *Rob Reiner.*
l.p. *Elijah Wood; Jon Lovitz; Jason Alexander; Alan Arkin; Dan Aykroyd; Kathy Bates; Faith Ford; Bruce Willis; Graham Greene; Julia Louis-Dreyfus; Reba McIntire; John Ritter; Abe Vigoda; Jussie Smollet; Andrew McCurley; Keone Young; Marc Shaiman; Robert Konstanzo etc.*
Technicolor. 87 mins. S

North, a bright young boy, goes unrecognised by his parents so he takes legal action which allows him to seek new ones. He is given a time limit in which to find them, return to his proper parents or he goes to an orphanage. Every couple he meets has some flaw and he finally realises that his true parents are the right ones for him just in time. Well, that is what he dreams. He returns home to anxious parents.

The sole reason for this film's inclusion is a brief – very brief – scene as the young boy appears as HAMLET and quoting: "To be or not to be.." and which requires prompting.

RENAISSANCE MAN
(U.S.A., 1994)

p.c. *A Cinergi-Parkway Production.*

d. *Penny Marshall.*
l.p. *Danny DeVito; Gregory Hines; Cliff Robertson; James Remar; Stacey Dash; Kadeem Hardison; Lillo Brancato Jr., Greg Sporleder; Richard T. Jones; Peter Simmons; Mark Wahlberg; Khalil Kain; Ed Begley Jr.; Ben Wright; Alanna Ubach; Isabella Hofmann; Samaria Graham; Don Reilly etc.*
Technicolor. 124 mins. S

Bill Rago, fired after fouling up an advertising presentation, finds himself in the unemployment queue. Eventually a job is found for him as a teacher at a military establishment. Here he finds that he has to educate a group of misfits. He makes no progress until, by chance, his students show interest in HAMLET. Though the path has it's set-backs, he succeeds with them with much personal involvement. The military is happy and Bill has learned something about himself.

The theme is not new. It was done at least once before, notably in *To Sir With Love* (G.B., 1967 with Sidney Poitier). This film, though, almost overflows with Shakespeare. The main structure is the use of HAMLET which is much quoted, analysed, and even receives the rap treatment. There are also quotes from ROMEO AND JULIET and HENRY V. The latter is also featured in stage performance (the rousing speech at the battle for Harfleur) with Don Reilly as Henry.

THE CANTERVILLE GHOST
(U.S.A., G.B., 1995)

p.c. *Anasazi Productions in association with Signboard Hill.*
d. *Sydney MacCartney.*
l.p. *Patrick Stewart; Neve Cambell; Cherie Lunghi; Daniel Betts; Leslie Phillips; Donald Sinden; Joan Sims; Edward Wiley; Ciaran Fitzgerald; Raymond Pickard.*
c. 88 mins. S

When an American family takes over an English haunted castle, only the father will not believe it is has no ghost and blames his daughter for the events that occur. Her love for the tortured spirit of Sir Simon de Canterville and for a young Duke finally convinces her father. She helps brings peace to the ghost who is finally reunited with his beloved wife.

This was made for television but may be shown in cinemas. If it is not shown then it should be for it is a delightful film. So, the author is breaking his own rules for a personal whim. The film is charming with many references to Shakespeare – two, verbally, to HAMLET; the playing of the ghost scene (pretty young Neve Cambell joins the short list of females playing the role of the troubled prince); Patrick Stewart, as the ghost, claiming to have known and inspired Shakespeare and the final sonnet reading is Sonnet CIX. Even the story of the ghost's situation (man induced to believe his wife is unfaithful by a trusted friend) has a familiar ring to it. Yes, there is much to enjoy including a lovely English castle and its grounds. Oscar Wilde takes credit for the short story on which this is based.

IN THE BLEAK MIDWINTER
(G.B., 1995)

p.c. *Midwinter Films.*
d. *Kenneth Branagh.*
l.p. *Richard Bryers; Michael Malone; John Sessions; Mark Hadfield; Gerard Horan; Nick Farrell; Celia Imrie; Hetta Charnley; Julia Sawalha; Joan Collins; Robert Hines; Ann Davies; Jennifer Saunders; James D. White; Edward Dewesbury.*
b.w. 98 mins. WS

Joe Harper a struggling, unemployed actor decides to stage HAMLET over Christmas with the last of his money and a loan from his agent, Margaretta who has faith in him. He signs up six actors to play twenty-four roles in the play with himself as the lead. The production takes place in a disused church which becomes home for the company for three weeks.

A comedy written by Branagh, all the typical problems occur with actors unable to remember their lines, the usual drunk, eccentrics and actors past their prime. The title is that of a Christmas carol and, appropriately, the film opened in England in time for Christmas, 1995. Made on a small budget, it is a somewhat personal film and as Branagh said of the characters portrayed: "They are all people, in various forms, that I've met or bumped into..." (Interview: *The Movie Show*, Sky Television, November 23, 1995). Many of the cast were friends of the director, some from the early years of his career, and the script was written to suit their own characters and personal improvisation was allowed to emphasise such individuality.

Shown at the Valladolid Film Festival, Spain, 1995. Venice Film Festival, Italy, 1995: Silver Lion shared with *Maborosi Hikari* and *Det Yani Dokhtar*.

"Branagh has succeeded in producing a work, at the same time modest and exhibitionist..." – Antonio Weinrichter, 'Fotogramas', February, 1996.

aka: A WINTER'S TALE; EN LO MÁS CRUDO DEL CRUDO INVIERNO; EIN WINTER-NACHTSTRAUM

DER MUSIK SAGT ALLES – ANJA SILJA
(Germany, 1995)

p.c. *Sender Fries Berlin/ARTE.*
d. *Hubert Ortkemper, Barrie Gavin.*
l.p. *Documentary featuring Anja Silja with Wieland Wagner.*
c. and b.w. 60 mins.

This documentary about the life of the operatic soprano Anja Silja contains scenes of her performance as Desdemona in the opera OTHELLO by Verdi dating from a Frankfurt production in 1965. The extracts (in black and white) are obviously on film and thus raises the question as to whether the whole performance was committed to film.

LOOKING FOR RICHARD
(U.S.A., 1996)

p.c. *Jam Productions.*
d. *Al Pacino.*
l.p. *(Of play): Al Pacino (King Richard); Harris Yullin (King Edward); Penelope (Queen Elizabeth); Alec Baldwin (Clarence); Aidan Quinn (Richmond); Vincent Angell (Gray); Estelle Parsons (Margaret); Kevin Spacey (Buckingham); Wynona Ryder (Lady Anne); Gordon MacDonald (Dorset); Madison Arnold (Rivers); Kevin Conway (Hastings); Timothy Prairie (Prince Edward); Landon Prarie (Young Prince); Bruce MacVittie, Paul Guilfoyle (Murderers); Richard Cox (Catesby); Larry Bryggman (Lord Stanley); Julie Moret (Mistress Shore); Phil Paralyze (Halberd/Messenger); Frederic Kimball (Bishop of Ely); Dan van Bargen (Ratcliffe); James Colby (Lovel); Ira Lewis (Tyrell); Andre Sogliuzzo, Neal Jones, Luke Toma (Mesengers); Marlon Pollick (Soldier).*
(Interviewees): Kevin Kline; Kenneth Branagh; John Gielgud; Vanessa Redgrave; Peter Brook; James Earl Jones; Emrys Jones; Barbara Everett; Derek Jacobi; Rosemary Harris.
(With): F. Murray Abraham; Hayley Barr; Gil Bellows; Son Berry; Nicholas Berry; Robin Berry; Kate Burton; Dominic Chianese; Johann Carlo; Joyce Ebert; Paul Gleason; Esther Gregory; Clare Holman; Linda Ianella Scott; Elaine Kory; Damien Leake; Viveca Lindfors; Judith Malina; Michael Maloney; Jaime Sanchez; David Satzman; Ed Setrakian; Kyle Smith; Heathcote Williams. Narrator: Al Pacino.
DuArt. 113 mins. S

Al Pacino decides to produce RICHARD III with himself in the leading role. He also wants to look into the problems that American actors and film-makers face in the works of Shakespeare. He is also anxious to learn what Shakespeare means in contemporary life. He spends much time discussing the parts of the play with his cast. He interviews a number of people including academics and actors. His travels take him from Central Park in New York to the Globe Theatre in London and, naturally, to Stratford-upon-Avon. He causes his producer much consternation.

Why is this unusual film not in the chapter about the play proper? A good question. Why is this not in the chapter which deals with documentaries about the works of Shakespeare? Another good question.

To both these questions, the answer is that it was an abitrary decision. Of course, the film is relative to both the catagories mentioned. Yet it is not a full version of the play or a precise extract or is it a true documentary. It is a mixture of both but at the same time is about actors. Hence this controlled the ultimate decision.

The film was made over a long period of time. Thus locations and appearances differ giving the film an improvised look (Geoffrey Macnab in 'Sight and Sound' likened it to Orson Welles' ventures into Shakespearean films). The audience is allowed behind the scenes to see how the actors develop their characters. The cast is allowed to express doubts and thoughts. Pacino even goes on to the streets of New York to ask public opinion about RICHARD III. He tries to understand, through academics, the historical setting of the play and the methods Shakepeare used.

This was the first feature film directed by Pacino who had previously directed (in 1990) a medium length film as yet unreleased. He was no stranger to the role of RICHARD III having played it twice before on stage. The film, rough though it may be at times, is an interesting mixture – fictional because its basic premise is about Pacino wanting to stage a play, actual/documentary because it explores a wide area of Shakespeareana, and the Bard on screen as it is punctuated by scenes actual and in rehearsal from the play itself. In all, a different film in many ways and an important deviation for the more obvious of not only the varied versions of the plays but of the educational-style documentary.

Shown at the Cannes Film Festival, France, 1996.
San Sebastian Film Festival, Spain, 1996: Donostia Prize.
London Film Critics' Award, G.B., 1998: Best Actor (Al Pacino for this film and *Donnie Brasco*) shared with Geoffrey Rush for *Shine*.

aka: EN BUSCA DE RICARDO III

✣ ✣ ✣ ✣ ✣

At best the foregoing is but a sample of films of this nature. Doubtless, many more exist and, no doubt,

you, the reader, can and will find them. The same may be said of the following which is a selection of amateur films that form part of archival footage and which extend beyond the limited interest usually associated with them. The reason for their inclusion will become evident:

THE YELLOW WEEKEND AT STANWAY
(G.B., 1923)

Nicholas Llewellyn-Davies, the adopted son of J. M. Barrie, played himself in this short film lasting twenty-eight minutes, produced and directed by Barrie. The boy is rejected by all the female guests. The inter-titles and imitation verses from AS YOU LIKE IT make it clear that he is seeking his "Rosalind". Cynthia Asquith and others from Barrie's circle of friends also appear in this record of a house party held at Stanway in Gloucestershire, England.

ROMEO AND JULIET
(G.B., 1956)

An amateur film, directed and filmed by John de Vere Loder (Lord Wakenhurst), it was one of many he filmed at this time. This one, lasting about two minutes, was of a production at London's Covent Garden in October 1956, by the Bolshoi Theatre Ballet. Galina Ulanova is featured in this colour, silent extract.

SHAKESPEARE AT HARROW
(G.B., 1957)

This short of twelve minutes duration shows scenes from KING LEAR performed in the Speech Room at Harrow School. Ronald Watkins supervised.

UNTITLED
(G.B., 1962-1965)

Number 13 in Lord Wakenhurst's collection of private films features three minutes in colour of a dress rehearsal for the production of ROMEO AND JULIET (Prokofiev) by the Canadian National Ballet in 1965. This silent extract features Frank Schaufuss (Romeo), Jacqueline Ivings (Juliet) and Jeremy Blanton (Paris).

CHAPTER XXXI
ANIMATED SHAKESPEARE

Cartoon versions of classic literature are not new to the cinema and, judging by the number on television, are as prolific as ever. It is, however, the short film in focus here, the feature-length ones being listed in the relative play chapter. The degree of relativity to Shakespeare may be slim in some cases but, after all, many were primarily made to entertain.

THE BARNYARD HAMLET
(U.S.A., 1916)

p.c.
d.
l.p. *Animated characters.*
b.w. 1 reel? Sil.

Of untraced content, probably the characters were of the farmyard feathered variety.

COL. HEZZA LIAR PLAYS HAMLET
(U.S.A., 1916)

p.c. *Bray.*
d. *J.R. Bray.*
l.p. *Animated characters.*
b.w. 1 reel? Sil.

The Colonel, suffering shock over an unfortunate investment, is offered a million dollars per week to play Hamlet with Charlie Chaplin as the grave-digger. The camera is wrecked when the director goes into hysterics during the graveyard scene. Kicked off the set, the Colonel awakens from his nightmare.

The "Col. Heeza Liar" character was featured in a series of short cartoons.

ROMEO AND JULIET
(U.S.A., 1917)

p.c. *S.S. Film Co.*
d. *Helena (Helene, according to some) Smith Dayton.*
l.p. *Animated characters.*
b.w. 1 reel. Sil.

The story is played out in rather comic style by clay figures made and manipulated by the director, a prominent sculptor of the era. She appears at the start of the film fashioning the figures from lumps of clay.

"...and in looking at the picture we are strangely conscious of the union of two of the greatest arts." – Margaret I. MacDonald, 'Moving Picture World', November 24, 1917.

ROMIET AND JULIO
(U.S.A., 1917)

p.c.

d.
l.p. *Animated characters.*
b.w. c500 ft. (152 m.) Sil.

The little cartoon is about two cats. Apart from the word play in the title, it does contain two balcony scenes. In one, Julio unmusically serenades his love from a fence before she is snatched away by her mistress; in the other, the ardent Julio floats up to his love with balloons which are punctured by a vengeful magpie.

OH'PHELIA
(G.B., 1919)

p.c. *Hepworth Picture Plays.*
d. *Anson Dyer.*
l.p. *Animated characters.*
b.w. 850 ft. (259 m.) Sil.

'Amlet drives Ophelia crazy by giving her vegetables instead of flowers and by cutting off her hair. Laertes complains to the King and Ophelia pelts the Court with vegetables. A remorseful 'Amlet joins the Boys Scouts where his first-aid manual helps save Ophelia when she nearly drowns. The couple embrace.

This was one of a number of cartoon burlesques of Shakespearean plays that Dyer made. This is the only complete one to survive.

'AMLET
(G.B., 1919)

p.c. *Hepworth Picture Plays.*
d. *Anson Dyer.*
l.p. *Animated characters.*
b.w. 600 ft. (183 m.) Sil.

'Amlet (who is a copy of Charlie Chaplin) recon-structs his uncle's crime of stealing butter by making a film. At the Elsinore Picture Palace the wicked uncle sees his crime on the screen watched by 'Amlet with the aid of a torch.

THE MERCHANT OF VENICE
(G.B., 1919)

p.c. *Hepworth Picture Plays.*
d. *Anson Dyer.*
l.p. *Animated characters.*
b.w. 800 ft. (244 m.) Sil.

Antonio, an ice-cream dealer, falls on hard times and has to borrow money from Shylock of Pathé Corner, Wardour Street, London. His pledge of a pound of flesh for non-payment falls due. Portia comes to the rescue and forces Shylock to produce his ration book but he has used all his meat tickets.

Another of Dyer's burlesques with a Wardour Street, London, England, where most of the major film companies sited their offices, setting.

"The artist takes some of the bard's characters and twists them to meet his own wicked purposes." – 'Kine Monthly Film Record', September, 1919.

ROMEO AND JULIET
(G.B.,1919)

p.c. *Hepworth Picture Plays.*
d. *Anson Dyer.*
l.p. *Animated characters.*
b.w. 850 ft. (259 m.) Sil.

In this cartoon burlesque of similar length to the others, the lovers are played by "Charles Chaplin" and "Mary Pickford".

THE TAMING OF THE SHREW
(G.B., 1920)

p.c. *Hepworth Pictorial Plays.*
d. *Anson Dyer.*
l.p. *Animated characters.*
b.w. (?) mins. Sil.

Details of this are unknown and it may never have been released or even completed.

OTHELLO
(G.B., 1920)

p.c. *Hepworth Picture Plays.*
d. *Anson Dyer.*
l.p. *Animated characters.*
b.w. 850 ft. (259 m.) Sil.

In this cartoon, the Moor is portrayed as a seaside "nigger minstrel" (descriptive comment of the era) and his love, Mona, the pretty daughter of a seaside bathing machine proprietor. The main parts of the original plot are carried out in humorous style.

Only a fragment of this film remains.

ROMEO AND JULIET
(Hungary, 1931)

p.c. *István Kató.*
d. *István Kató.*
l.p. *Animated characters.*
b.w. Short.

A silhouette animation version of the story.

Kató was a pioneer of animation in the Hungarian cinema, his career lasting from 1914 to 1957. He created most of his early work in a roof garden over a Budapest cinema using natural light and a metronome to judge exposure times.

"...*Janos the Knight* and a silhouette ROMEO AND JULIETTE...merit acclaim." – Giannalberto Bendazzi, 'Cartoons'

ROMEO AND JULIET
(U.S.A., 1933)

p.c. *Moser and Terry Educational Pictures.*
d. *Paul Terry, Frank Moser.*
l.p. *Animated characters.*
b.w. 6 mins.

This was an early entry by this company into the world of classic literature.

KOMPOSITION IM BLAU
(Germany, 1935)

p.c. *Oskar Fischinger.*
d. *Oskar Fischinger.*
l.p. *Animated images*
Gasparcolor. Short.

Solid objects are animated to interpret the overture to the opera THE MERRY WIVES OF WINDSOR by Nicolai.

The Shakespearean connection is admittedly stretched to the limit by the inclusion of this work by one of the most gifted of the experimental film makers in animation.

ALL'S WELL THAT ENDS WELL
(U.S.A., 1940)

p.c. *Terrytoons.*
d. *Mannie Davis.*
l.p. *Animated characters.*
b.w. 7 mins.

An animated, but brief, version of the tale

MUCH ADO ABOUT NOTHING
(U.S.A., 1940)

p.c. *Terrytoons.*
d. *Connie Raskin.*
l.p. *Animated characters – Dinky.*
b.w. 7 mins.

Cartoon version of the play which formed part of a series of adaptations of the classics.

ROMEO IN RHYTHM
(U.S.A., 1940)

p.c. *M.G.M.*
d. *Rudolf Ising.*
l.p. *Animated characters.*
Technicolor. 7 mins.

This cartoon features a musical interpretation of the balcony scene from ROMEO AND JULIET presented by the "Black Crow Light Opera Company".

Shown as part of the Everybody's Shakespeare International Festival, London, England, 1994.

SHAKESPEAREAN SPINACH
(U.S.A., 1940)

p.c. *Paramount.*
d. *Dave Fleischer,*
l.p. *Animated characters: Popeye; Olive Oyl; Bluto.*
b.w. 7 mins.

A cartoon spoof of ROMEO AND JULIET, no imagination is needed to guess who played the lovers! Of course, Bluto tries to spoil the performance by these two thespians and Popeye has to resort to spinach to save himself from his enemy.

This film featuring the popular character has been available for purchase on 8 mm.

BOOK REVIEW
(U.S.A., 1946)

p.c. *Warner Bros.*
d. *Robert Clampett.*
l.p. *Animated characters. Daffy Duck.*
Technicolor. 7 mins.

Though ostensibly featuring Daffy Duck, most of this cartoon is devoted to book covers that come alive. Among them is 'The Compleat Works of Shakespeare' which is portrayed as the insides of a clock springing out.

TWA CORBIES/SPRING AND WINTER
(G.B., 1951)

p.c. *Halas and Batchelor for British Film Institute.*
d. *John Halas.*
l.p. *Illustrations.*
b.w. 8 mins.

Two poems are illustrated by still drawings and paintings. The first, an anonymous Scottish poem, was illustrated by Michael Rothenstein and read by John Laurie; the second, a Shakespeare song, was illustrated by Mervyn Peake and sung by Peter Pears.

This was produced for the Festival of Britain, 1951.

JULIETA Y ROMEO
(Spain, 1958)

p.c.
d. *Pedro Sanz.*
l.p. *Animated characters.*
c. Short.

Said to be curious and intelligent, it is about two eggs who die of love in a pan.

ROMEO I JULIJA
(Yugoslavia, 1958)

p.c. *Zagreb Studios.*
d. *Ivo Vrbanić.*
l.p. *Animated characters.*
Eastman Color. 10 mins.

The ROMEO AND JULIET story is portrayed from the cavemen until the present.

A MIDSUMMER NIGHT'S DREAM
(U.S.A., 1962?)

p.c. *U.P.A.*
d. *Robert McKimson.*
l.p. *Animated characters – Mr. Magoo.*
c. 42 mins.

In the 1960s, U.P.A. embarked on a series of television shows featuring the myopic cartoon character, Mr. Magoo, as the star in famous classics of literature suitably adapted for the character. Its right to inclusion is doubtful for it has not been possible to confirm if any of the series received cinema release.

A MIDSUMMER NIGHT'S MARE
(G.B., 1964)

p.c. *Halas and Batchelor.*
d. *John Halas.*
l.p. *Animated characters.*
c. 10 mins.

This cartoon was obviously of a parody nature.

ENTER HAMLET
(U.S.A., 1967)

p.c. *New Janus Cinema.*
d. *Fred Mogubub.*
l.p. *Animated images. Narrator: Maurice Evans.*
c. 4 mins.

Illustrated by pop art images, this cartoon is based on the soliloquy from HAMLET.

Shown at the Edinburgh Film Festival, Scotland, 1965.

HAMLET
(Hungary, 1967)

p.c. *Pannónia Film Studio.*
d. *György Kovásznai.*
l.p. *Animated characters.*
c. 14 mins.

Without commentary, this is a modernised version of the story. It is noted as being a witty and playful analysis of Shakespeare.

OTHELLO – 67
(U.S.S.R., 1967)

p.c.
d. *Hitruck Fedor.*
l.p. *Animated characters.*
c? Short.

Of unknown content but probably the title gives a fair indication.

ROMEO AND JULIET
(Rumania, 1968)

p.c.
d. *Bob Călinescu.*
l.p. *Animated characters.*
b.w. Short.

In this version, the characters are portrayed by animated stones.

ROMEO I JULIA
(Poland, 1969)

p.c. *Studio Filmów Rysunkowych.*
d. *Jerzy Zitzman.*

l.p. *Animated characters.*
c. 10 mins.

Two opposing families fight each other with modern tanks and missiles. Reconciliation by the fathers of the young couple in love is welcomed by the couple's many children.

In this paper cut-out cartoon version, the director takes a satyrical view of the well-tried story to make a discourse on pacifism.

ROMEO I JULIJA
(Yugoslavia, 1969)

p.c. *Zagreb.*
d. *Zlatko Pavlinić.*
l.p. *Animated characters.*
Eastman Color. Short.

This is another version of the tale from the famous Zagreb studios.

MAKBET
(Poland, 1970)

p.c. *Cartoon Film Studios.*
d. *Alfred Ledwig.*
l.p. *Animated characters.*
c. Short.

This tells familiar story of a man obsessed with the desire and search for power.

ROMEO Y JULIETA
(Spain, 1971)

p.c.
d. *Miquel Esparbé.*
l.p. *Animated character.*
c. Short.

No further details have been traced of this.

THE 2000 YEAR OLD MAN
(U.S.A., 1974)

p.c. *Crossbow-Acre Productions in association with Leo Salkin Films.*
d. *Leo Salkin.*
l.p. *Animated characters with the voices of Mel Brooks (The 2000 Year Old Man) and Carl Reiner (The Interviewer).*
DeLuxe Color. 24 mins.

The Interviewer thrusts questions at the old man who has seen much history. Shakespeare's writing ability is one of the topics discussed in this comedy.

THE TEMPEST
(G.B., 1974-9)

p.c. *TV Cartoons.*
d. *George Dunning.*
l.p. *Animated characters.*
c. Unfinished short. (8 mins. survive)

This animation version of the play was shown as an unfinished project at the Cambridge Animated Film Festival, England, where some of the director's sketches were put on view. It was also featured in December 1979 at Britain's National Film Theatre, London. Intended as a feature by this visionary animator, Dunning, best known for *Yellow Submarine*, worked on it for five years until his death.

aka: SKETCHES FOR THE TEMPEST

BOTTOM'S DREAM
(U.S.A., 1983)

p.c. *John Canemaker.*
d. *John Canemaker.*
l.p. *Animated characters.*
c. Short.

This cartoon is a saraband based on and featuring characters in A MIDSUMMER NIGHT'S DREAM.

ROMEO I JULIJA VILIJA SEKSPIRA U IZVODENJU TRUPE MONSTRUMU I DRUZINA
(Yugoslavia, 1984)

p.c. *Zagreb.*
d. *Dušan Petričić.*
l.p. *Animated characters.*
Eastman Color. Short.

The amount of Shakespeare influence is debatable in this comic, intelligent version of the story in which all the characters are portrayed as horrible monsters. The Croatian Film Archives do, however, confirm the Shakespearean source.

NEXT
(G.B., 1989)

p.c. *Aardman Animations.*
d. *Barry Purves.*
l.p. *Animated characters.*
c. 5 mins.

This production company, noted for its award-winning claymation television advertisements, presents, through a puppet version of Shakespeare, the complete works. A record on film surely, excelled only by singer Cleo Laine on disc in "Shakespeare and All That Jazz" (all the titles in a minute and a half).

Shown at the 23rd. Festival de Cine, Alcalá de Henares, Spain, 1993.
Shown as part of the Everybody's Shakespeare International Festival, London, England, 1994.
Shown at the Valladolid Film Festival, Spain, 1993.

The following two series were originally produced for television but have received, or are available for, cinema presentation. Though made in different years, it seems logical to dispense with the listing by year and group them in alphabetical order -

SHAKESPEARE, THE ANIMATED TALES:
This project was financed by Fujisankei (Japan); Home Box Office (U.S.A.); Soyztmultfilm and Christmas Films (Russia); S4C, B.B.C. and Hit Entertainment (G.B.). All from Series 1 (S1) were

produced by Soyzmultfilm and Christmas Films (Russia) and David Edwards Studios (G.B.). Series 2 (S2) was produced by Christmas Films (Russia) and Right Angle (G.B.). Series 1 was produced in 1992 and Series 2 in 1994.

Officially listed as co-productions between Wales and Russia, all pre- and post-production was carried out in Britain. Kodak colour film stock was used in the making of all the films. Leon Garfield was responsible for the adaptations. Some six hundred people were involved in the twelve films and the cost was $3,000,000, though the rouble/sterling rate of exchange probably inflated that sum. The project survived the two coups in Russia of August, 1991 and October, 1993. All were animated in Russia except A MIDSUMMER NIGHT'S DREAM which was made in Armenia.

Royal support for the enterprise came from Prince Charles. Not only was he featured in a colour picture with "Caliban" from **THE TEMPEST** (listed below) on the front page of the British newspaper 'Daily Mail' on Saturday, November 12, 1994, but he also sent a supportive letter to S4C. His Royal Highness wrote: "In **THE ANIMATED TALES** the language and drama of William Shakespeare are interpreted by artists from another great cultural tradition. The result is still Shakespeare, as the characters are as universal now as they were when they were first created, but it is Shakespeare re-defined and reinterpreted.

As President of the Royal Shakespeare Company, I welcome this pioneering project which will bring Shakespeare's great wisdom, insight and all encompassing view of mankind to many millions from all parts of the globe who have never been in his company before. I am much impressed by the quality of the animation and by the fact that such wonderfully talented artists from Russia and Armenia have been involved in this project." (text quoted by kind permission of H.R.H. The Prince of Wales.).

Both series were released on videogram supported by a series of related books.

AS YOU LIKE IT
(S2)

d. *Alexei Karayev.*
l.p. *Animated characters with the voices of Sylvestra Le Touzel, John McAndrew and Garard Green.*
25 mins.

The animation in this was created by oil paint and pastel crayons directly on to cel.

Shown as part of the Everybody's Shakespeare International Festival, London, England, 1994.

HAMLET
(S1)

d. *Natalia Orlova.*

l.p. *Animated characters with the voices of Nicholas Farrell, Susan Fleetwood, Duncan Bell, Tilda Swinton, John Shrapnel, John Warner and Dorien Thomas.*
26 mins.

In this, the animation was created by painting directly on to glass.

This little gem has earned a number of awards including two Prime Time "Emmys" for Best Animation and Best Director in America (1993) and, also in America and in the same year, the New York Television Festival Gold for Best Animation. In Great Britain, it was nominated in 1993 for for Best Technique from the Royal Television Society and won the BAFTA Wales award for Best Animation.

Shown as part of the Everybody's Shakespeare International Festival, London, England, 1994.

JULIUS CAESAR
(S2)

d. *Yuri Kulakov.*
l.p. *Animated characters with the voices of Joss Ackland, Frances Tomelty and David Robb.*
25 mins.

Made using traditional cel animation.

KING RICHARD III
(S2)

d. *Natalia Orlova.*
l.p. *Animated characters with the voices of Antony Sher, Sorcha Cusak and Eleanor Bron.*
26 mins.

Painting on glass was the technique used in the animation for this release.

Shown as part of the Everybody's Shakespeare International Festival, London, England, 1994.

MACBETH
(S1)

d. *Nikolai Serebriakov.*
l.p. *Animated characters with the voices of Brian Cox, Zoë Wanamaker, Clive Merrison, Patrick Brennan, John Baddeley, Mary Wimbush, Val Lorraine and Emma Gregory.*
26 mins.

Filmed using traditional cel animation.

Shown as part of the Everybody's Shakespeare International Festival, London, England, 1994.

A MIDSUMMER NIGHT'S DREAM
(S1)

d. *Robert Saakiants.*
l.p. *Animated characters with the voices of Daniel Massey, Suzanne Bertish, Bernard Hill, Abigail McKern, Charles Millham, Kathryn Pogson,*

Kim Wall, Anthony Jackson and Peter Postlethwaite.
26 mins.

Conventional cel animation was used for the making of this release.

Shown as part of the Everybody's Shakespeare International Festival, London, England, 1994.

OTHELLO
(S2)

d.   *Nikolai Serebriakov.*
l.p.   *Animated characters with the voices of Colin McFarlane, Gerard McSorley and Sian Thomas.*
25 mins.

Conventional cel animation was used in the making of this.

ROMEO AND JULIET
(S1)

d.   *Ephim Gambourg.*
l.p.   *Animated characters with the voices of Claire Holman, Linus Roache, Brenda Bruce, Greg Hicks, Charles Kay and Garard Green.*
25 mins.

The conventional cel animation was employed in the making of this.

THE TAMING OF THE SHREW
(S2)

d.   *Aida Ziablikova.*
l.p.   *Puppet animation with the voices of Amanda Root, Nigel Le Vaillant and Malcolm Storry.*
26 mins.

Created by an all female team, the story is told in puppet animation.

THE TEMPEST
(S1)

d.   *Stanislav Sokolov.*
l.p.   *Puppet animation with the voices of Timothy West, Katy Behean, Alun Armstrong and John Moffat.*
26 mins.

Here the tale is told with the use of puppet animation.

Shown as part of the Everybody's Shakespeare International Festival, London, England, 1994.

TWELFTH NIGHT
(S1)

d.   *Maria Muat.*
l.p.   *Puppet animation with the voices of Fiona Shaw, William Rushton, Roger Allam, Alice Arnold, Stephen Tompkinson, Gerald James and Stefan Bednarczyk.*
25 mins.

The tale is told with the use of puppets.

Shown as part of the Everybody's Shakespeare International Festival, London, England, 1994.

A WINTER'S TALE
(S2)

d.   *Stanislav Sokolov.*
l.p.   *Puppet animation with the voices of Anton Lesser, Jenny Agutter and Michael Kitchen.*
26 mins.

Once again, puppets are used to relate the story.

"...The animation is brilliant and the essence of each play is retained..." – 'Daily Telegraph'.

"For anyone not in tune with Shakespeare, these abbreviated versions are a great way to understand the dramas and the comedies..." – 'New York Daily News'

"...the animation is superb...The play's the thing, but the Russian artists steal the show..." – 'Time'.

"...a co-production that stylishly makes all the Bard's world a highly accessible stage..." – 'USA Today'.

✢ ✢ ✢ ✢ ✢

In the world of the animated film, as in the world of performers proper, there are many parodies of Shakespearean titles and quotations. No imagination is necessary to guess the source of *Much Ado About Mutton* (U.S.A., 1947, directed by I. Sparber for Paramount) or for *Much Ado About Nutting*, a Charles Jones opus (Warner Bros., U.S.A.).

HAMLET came in for his share of parodies titles with *To Boo Or Not To Boo* (U.S.A., 1951, a "Casper" cartoon also directed by Sparber). The latter was correctly quoted for Pavel Hobl's *To Be Or Not To Be* (Czechoslovakia, 1965). It was again correctly quoted in the Terrytoon (U.S.A., 1963) directed by Connie Rasinski and featuring "Sidney". The same (mis)quote moved into modern technology with *T.V Or Not T.V.* (U.S.A., 1962), a Paramount/Famous Players cartoon directed by Seymour Kneitel. A further quote from the same speech came out as *Purr Chance To Dream* (U.S.A., 1967), a late "Tom and Jerry" cartoon directed by Ben Washam.

A common practice of cartoon makers was to parody famous film titles. *Kiss Me Kat* (U.S.A., 1953) directed by Charles Jones for Warner Bros. was an obvious reference to **KISS ME KATE**, itself derivative of THE TAMING OF THE SHREW.

CHAPTER XXXII

THE IMMORTAL BARD

Born at Stratford-upon-Avon in the county of Warwickshire, England, in 1564, William Shakespeare was the son of a glover and small rural landowner, John. His mother was Mary Arden who came from a socially more important class than her husband. The family later became among the most notable of that small town and John held the office of bailiff in 1568.

The third of eight children, William studied at the local school which he had to leave early probably due to his parents' financial situation. At eighteen he married Ann Hathaway, seven years his senior, and, shortly after, their daughter, Susanna, was born (doubtless the reason for the hasty marriage). In 1585 they had twins, Judith and Hamnet, of whom the latter died in 1596.

This middle period of his life is rather hazy in details. He is known to have gone alone to London where he mingled with the environment of the University Wits and during the years of the plague (1593-94) he wrote two poetical works dedicated to the Duke of Southampton. It was about this time that he started to write his sonnets.

This period was a rich one for the theatre both open-air and covered. They were quite advanced in construction, scenery and lighting. The actors, too, were organized into companies which sought the patronage of the nobility. They were often co-owners of the theatres and among them were writers who could turn out scripts rapidly.

Shakespeare was such an author and probably an actor of minor roles. Thanks to the patronage of the Duke of Southampton, he was co-proprietor of the Globe theatre and later the Blackfriars. He became very rich, bought a house in Stratford and secured a coat of arms for his father.

When Essex fell from grace in 1601, so too did Southampton but this does not seem to have affected Shakespeare. Much of his life from then on is revealed through documents such as publications of his works and legal papers.

In 1610, though continuing his association with the King's Men, his theatrical group, he had already retired to Stratford where he lived the comfortable, quiet life of a wealthy country gentleman. Documentation tells of the marriages of his daughters, acquisition of property (1613) and that he made his will in 1616. On April 23 of that year he died and

was interred in the choir of Holy Trinity church, Stratford, a privileged right afforded to him through the acquisition of local tithes. His wife and his daughter, Susanna, lie on either side of him there.

When Elizabeth, his granddaughter through Susanna's marriage to Doctor John Hall, died in 1670 without issue by her marriage to Tom Nash, the direct line of Shakespeare's descendants came to an end.

The Bard has been the subject of learned debate for many years. Did he write all the plays? Where did he spend those unrecorded years? Did he travel abroad? Did he write more, as yet undiscovered, works?

What is known is that he studied Latin at school which discipline surely helped in his rapid, self-taught, learning. Certainly, his court connections, contacts with foreign visitors and the availability of foreign language books all helped in forming his cultural character. These elements, combined with the theatre of the era, provided an admiral source of ideas and inspiration.

Considering his importance in literature and thus in history linked with the era in which he lived, it is surprising, not to say disappointing, that there have been no major films based on the life of William Shakespeare. Even the wonderful **SHAKESPEARE IN LOVE** is, in essence, fictional and supposedly deals only with a brief part of his life. There was talk in the late 1960s of a $15,000,000 musical by Warner Bros./Seven Arts to be called "The Bawdy Bard". No doubt, one of the many crises in the film industry caused its abandonment. There was also a television series of six episodes of fifty minutes each made by the British television company ATV in 1978 called *Will Shakespeare.*

Despite a good writer and cast – Tim Curry played the lead – the series failed to reach the heights it should have done. It may be that the successful musical show "Play On!" attract film producers but, in the meantime, that leaves just three films of any substance about the man's life and a few in which he is portrayed on the screen. These are included in the following:

SHAKESPEARE ÉCRIVANT "LA MORT DE JULES CÉSAR" (France, 1907)

p.c. *Star Film.*
d. *Georges Méliès.*
l.p. *Georges Méliès ?*
b.w. 344 ft. (105 m.) Sil.

The title, which translates as "Shakespeare Writing 'The Death Of Julius Caesar'", shows Shakespeare falling asleep after a number of attempts at writing. He dreams of some women of antiquity one of whom is burning incense. Then appear Brutus, Cassius, Casca and other conspirators who have a lively discussion and form their plan. They swear to kill Caesar. Caesar appears and the conspirators lodge their complaints as a cover for their true purpose. One draws a dagger but is reluctant to strike an unarmed man, another is not so hesitant and drives home his weapon. Shakespeare awakes full of excitement, ignores a servant who has arrived with food and stabs a chunk of bread with a knife. He enjoys a laugh with the servant. As he relaxes, the scene changes to a bust of Shakespeare, draped with the flags of all countries.

The length of the film is also noted as 390 ft. (119 m.).

Shown at the Shakespeare Film Festival, Wiesbaden, W. Germany, 1964.

aka: SHAKESPEARE WRITING "JULIUS CAESAR"; SHAKESPEARE

TEN MINUTES WITH SHAKESPEARE
(U.S.A., 1908)

p.c. *Lubin.*
d. *Sigmund Lubin.*
l.p.
b.w. 1 reel. Sil.

The title says everything yet tells nothing. It has not been able to trace a synopsis of the content so the film may not be directly related to an appearance of the character. It may relate to scenes or readings from his plays.

MODERNE ÉCOLE
(France, 1909)

p.c. *Gaumont.*
d. *Émile Cohl.*
l.p. *Trick film.*
b.w. 541 ft. (165 m.) Sil.

As the pages of a book turn, famous characters from history walk up the page, salute and then exit. Shakespeare shares this honour with Cervantes, Goethe and Dante from literature and Napoléon, Washington, Bolivar and Peter the Great from the military sphere.

LES AMOURS DE LA REINE ÉLISABETH
(France, 1912)

p.c. *Histrionic Film.*
d. *Henri Desfontaines, Louis Mercanton.*
l.p. *Sarah Bernhardt (Queen Elizabeth); Lou Tellegen (Earl of Essex); M. Chameroy (Lord Bacon); Mlle Romain (Countess of Nottingham); Marie-Louise Dorrel; Maxudian.*
b.w. 3140 ft. (957 m.) Sil.

This story of the love affaire between Queen Elizabeth I of England and the Earl of Essex was a big success in its day due, mainly, to its star. Shakespeare (played by an unknown actor), is congratulated by the Queen after a performance of THE MERRY WIVES OF WINDSOR which has been performed to celebrate the victory over the Spanish Armada.

The film was also released in a tinted version. The above length may not be that of the original since a length of 3609 ft. (1100 m.) is also quoted.

aka: ÉLISABETH REINE

THE LIFE OF SHAKESPEARE
(G.B., 1914)

p.c. *British and Colonial Kinematograph Company.*
d. *J. B. McDowell, Frank R. Growcott.*
l.p. *Albert Ward (William Shakespeare); Sybil Hare (Ann Hathaway); M. Murray Gray (Sir Hugh Clopton); Eva Bayley (Mrs. Shakespeare); Aimee Martinek (Queen Elizabeth); George Foley (Sir Thomas Lucy); Miss Bennett (Charlotte Clopton).*
b.w. 5 reels. Sil.

This biography of the playwright was surrounded by pre-publicity to include a number of dignitaries of the time. The exteriors were shot at Stratford; the interiors at the company's studios at Walthamstow using, so it is said, furniture from Ann Hathaway's cottage. Great stress was put upon accuracy which incurred an estimated cost of £4000.

In the finale, Shakespeare is seen dreaming of his plays and superimposed are scenes from THE MERCHANT OF VENICE, MACBETH, HAMLET and THE MERRY WIVES OF WINDSOR.

"Absolutely remarkable historic reconstruction." – Monatfilm, the French distributor of the film at the time.

aka: THE LOVES, ADVENTURES AND LIFE OF WILLIAM SHAKESPEARE; THE LIFE OF WILLIAM SHAKESPEARE: HIS INTRIGUES AND ROMANCES

RACCONTO D'INVERNO
(Italy, 1914)

See **CHAPTER XIX THE WINTER'S TALE**

MASTER SHAKESPEARE
(U.S.A., 1915)

p.c. *Thanhouser.*
d. *Edwin Thanhouser.*
l.p. *Florence La Badie (Miss Gray); Robert Vaughn (Lt. Stanton); Lawrence Swinburne (William Shakespeare); Robert Whittier (Lord Bacon).*
b.w. (?) mins. Sil.

The merits of Bacon and Shakespeare are discussed by a young army officer and his fiancée. The girl holds the view that Shakespeare could not possibly have written all the words credited to him. The couple are separated when he is posted far away and they both try to forget. The girl becomes an avid reader and, one day, falls into a stupor in which she is transported back to Elizabethan times. Bacon tries to abduct her and Shakespeare, a strolling player, saves her. Court affairs take over in which Shakespeare is brought before Queen Elizabeth and receives many honours. The girl wakes up and calls for her young man.

This strange mixture of fact and fiction switches often between the line of battle in Mexico and the past, thus leading to some confusion. Copies of the film no longer exist.

GLASTONBURY PAST AND PRESENT
(G.B., 1922)

p.c. *The Glastonbury Pageant Film Committee.*
d. *H. O. Martinek.*
l.p. *Neil Curtis (William Shakespeare); P. Mason (Sir Walter Raleigh); Ethel D. Hanson (The Widow); R. M. Stenner (Farmer Jenkins); Ada Hersey (Mrs. Jenkins); Sebastian Evans (Squire); J. F. Barker (Collin); M. Walker (Letty); Rev. L. S. Lewis (Bishop).*
b.w. 4024 ft. (1227 m.) Sil.

Based on the 1922 event, highlights from the history of this ancient area are presented in five episodes. Of interest in the context of this work, is an episode which includes an Elizabethan morality play which is watched by the Bard. The cast above is for that fourth episode.

AROUND THE TOWN No. 110 – SHAKESPEARE RE-VISITS STRATFORD-ON-AVON
(G.B., 1922)

p.c. *Gaumont Film Company.*
d.
l.p. *Members of the "Will Shakespeare" Company.*
b.w. (?) mins. Sil.

Dramatised scenes of Shakespeare's life (his wooing of Ann Hathaway, his farewell to her as he leaves for London and his departure for London with Philip Henslowe) are featured in this film magazine release which featured three topics in all. The film length is given as 318 ft. (97 m.) which may relate to the above excerpt only.

OLD BILL THROUGH THE AGES
(G.B., 1924)

p.c. *Ideal.*
d. *Thomas Bentley.*
l.p. *Syd Walker (Old Bill); Arthur Cleave (Bert); Jack Denton (Alf); Austin Leigh (William Shakespeare); Franzi Carlos (Ann Hathaway); Gladys Ffolliott (Queen Elizabeth); Cecil Morton York; William Pardue; Douglas Payne; Clive Currie; Wally Bosco; Cyril Dane; Bruce Bairnsfather.*

b.w. 7800 ft. (2377 m.) Sil.
In this fantasy, Old Bill dreams that he is William the Conqueror and that he is present at many events in British history. Of course, he encounters many historical figures among them – and thus the reason for the inclusion of the film here – Shakespeare and Ann Hathaway.

IMMORTAL GENTLEMAN
(G.B., 1935)

p.c. *Bernard Smith.*
d. *Widgey R. Newman.*
l.p. *Basil Gill (Shakespeare/Malvolio); Rosalinde Fuller (Ophelia/Juliet/Lady); Dennis Hoey (Soldier/Toby Belch); Anne Bolt (Jane/Maria); Edgar Owen (Ben Jonson/Mercutio); J. Hubert Leslie (Michael Drayton); Laidman Browne (Gambler/Petruchio/Feste); Fred Rains (Miser); Terence de Marney (Harry Morton/Hamlet/Romeo); Derrick de Marney (James Carter/Tybalt); Dennis Wyndham (Voyager); Ivan Berlyn (Father/Aguecheek); Leo Genn (Merchant/Shylock); Roy Byford (Squire).*
b.w. 61 mins.

Shakespeare meets with Ben Jonson and Michael Drayton in a Southwark tavern in London. As people pass, Shakespeare is reminded of characters in his plays. Shakespeare himself recites "The Seven Ages Of Man", Ben Jonson leads the singing of "Sigh No More, Ladies" and Jane sings "It was a lover, and his lass". Later, as Shakespeare sleeps, Jane stirs him thinking that he is dead. He reassures her saying that he will live for ever.

The roles portrayed suggest references to HAMLET, THE MERCHANT OF VENICE, ROMEO AND JULIET, THE TAMING OF THE SHREW and TWELFTH NIGHT.

MASTER WILL SHAKESPEARE
(U.S.A., 1936)

p.c. *M.G.M.*
d. *Jacques Tourneur.*
l.p. *Documentary. Narrator: Carey Wilson.*
b.w. 11 mins.

This short, one of the *M.G.M. Miniatures* series, was made in the wake of the company's successful **ROMEO AND JULIET.**

TIME FLIES
(G.B., 1944)

p.c. *Gainsborough Pictures.*
d. *Walter Forde.*
l.p. *Tommy Handley; Evelyn Dall; Moore Marriott; Graham Moffat; John Salew; Leslie Brindley; Olga Lindo.*
b.w. 88 mins.

Tommy and his friends are transported back to the times of Queen Elizabeth I of England and meet some

211

of the people of the era. One of the party meets Shakespeare (John Salew) in the Globe theatre struggling with the writing of ROMEO AND JULIET.

Tommy Handley was best known in his native land as a radio comedian and had considerable national fame with his show *ITMA*.

MEMORIES OF SHAKESPEARE
(West Germany, 1949)

p.c. *Hoffburg Productions.*
d.
l.p. *Documentary.*
b.w. 3 x 10 mins.

Logically made for educational purposes, these three films contain biographical material and the places associated with Shakespeare.

THE STORY OF MANKIND
(U.S.A., 1957)

p.c. *Warner Bros.*
d. *Irwin Allen.*
l.p. *Ronald Coleman; Hedy Lamarr; Groucho Marx; Harpo Marx; Chico Marx; Virginia Mayo; Agnes Moorehead; Vincent Price; Peter Lorre; Dennis Hopper; Charles Coburn; Cedric Hardwicke; Marie Wilson and many more.*
Technicolor. 100 mins.

The Spirit of Man appears before a high tribunal in Heaven to defend man following the invention of a super H-bomb. This he does by recalling scenes from history. The tribunal reserves judgement saying that the future of mankind depends upon mankind itself.

The cast is interesting, not to say unusual and even impressive. Unfortunately, the film, though unusual, was far from impressive though viewers may have had fun spotting the stars. Those doing so could have noticed Reginald Gardiner as William Shakespeare. This really explains the reason for the inclusion of the film here.

BAD CASE OF SHAKESPEARE
(G.B., 1968)

p.c.
d. *Levi Fox?*
l.p. *John Gielgud; Diana Rigg; Christopher Plummer.*
c. 40 mins.

The above named recreate the life and times of the Bard.

Some sources note a film bearing the Bard's name with content similar to the above. As the director for it is given as Levi Fox who directed a number of Shakespeare linked films in Britain, it is logical to assume that it is the same film as the above.

WILLIAM SHAKESPEARE
(Canada, 1974)

p.c. *Look Hear Productions/McConnell Advertising/ Shell Canada.*
d. *Arthur Voronka.*
l.p.
c. 25 mins.

This is a simulated "interview" with William Shakespeare.

O CONVENTO
(Portugal/France, 1995)

p.c. *Madragoa Films/Gemini Films.*
d. *Manoel de Oliviera.*
l.p. *John Malkovich (Michael); Catherine Deneuve (Hélène); Luis Miguel Cintra (Baltar); Leonor Silveira (Piedade).*
c. 87 mins. S WS

In his efforts to prove that Shakespeare was Spanish/ Jewish and not English, Professor Michael Padovic and his wife, Hélène, go to the convent at Arrábida to examine documents there. They are received by Baltar, the strange custodian, who is attracted to Hélène. To distract Michael, he involves the pretty librarian, Piedade, which leads to complications and an unexpected ending.

Obviously, not related to the life of Shakespeare, it seems worth noting this film if only for its premise. The dialogue is in English, French and Portuguese.

Shown at the San Sebastian Film Festival, Spain, 1995.

TROMEO AND JULIET
(U.S.A., 1996)

See **CHAPTER XXI ROMEO AND JULIET**.

SHAKESPEARE IN LOVE
(U.S.A., 1998)

p.c. *A Bedford Falls Production/Universal Pictures/ Miramax.*
d. *John Madden.*
l.p. *Joseph Fiennes (Will Shakespeare); Gwyneth Paltrow (Viola De Lesseps); Judi Dench (Queen Elizabeth I); Ben Affleck (Ned Alleyn); Colin Firth (Lord Wessex); Geoffrey Rush (Philip Henslowe); Simon Callow (Sir Edmund Tilney); Tom Wilkinson (Hugh Fennyman); Steven O'Donnell (Lambert); Tim McMullen (Frees); Patrick Barlow (Will Kempe); Anthony Sher (Doctor Moth); Steven Beard (Makepeace); Martin Clunes (Richard Burbage); Sandra Reinton (Rosaline); Bridget McConnel, Georgie Glen (Ladies in Waiting); Nicholas Boulton (Henry Condell); Imelda Staunton (Nurse); Barnaby Kay (Nol); Jim Carter (Ralph Bashford); Desmond McNamara (Crier); Paul Bigley (Peter, the Stage Manager); Jason Round (Tavern Actor); Rupert Farley (Barman); Jill Baker (Lady De Lesseps); Adam Barker, Harry*

Gostelow, Alan Cody (Auditionees); Gregor Truter (James Hemmings); Joe Roberts (John Webster); Simon Day (Boatman); David Curtiz (John Hemmings); Mark Williams (Wabash); Robin Davies (Master Plum); Mark Saban (Augustine Philips); Amber Glossop (Scullery Maid); Hywel Simons (Servant); Nicholas Le Prevost (Sir Roger De Lesseps); Tim Kightley (Edward Pope); Rebecca Charles (Chambermaid); Roger Frost (2nd. Boatman); Bob Barrett (George Bryan); Daniel Brocklebank (Sam Gosse); Roger Morlidge (James Armitage); Patricia Potter; Rachel Clarke, Lucy Speed (Whores); Richard Gold (Lord in Waiting); Martin Neeley (Paris/Lady Montague); John Ramm (Makepeace's Neighbour); Rupert Everett (Christopher Marlowe); The Choir of St. George's Chapel, Windsor.

c. 127 mins. S

In 1593, Will Shakespeare lacks inspiration to start a new play promised to London theatre owner Philip Henslowe who is dangerously in debt to the brutal loan shark, Fennyman. Henslowe is worried that Will may be lured away by rival promoter, Richard Burbage. Viola De Lesseps, daughter of a rich merchant, is betrothed to Lord Wessex but, delighted by Will's verses, joins Henslowe's troupe disguised as a man with the name Thomas Ken. She is soon having a passionate romance with Will. From this and with a little help from fellow playwright, Christopher Marlowe, ROMEO AND JULIET is born. The arrival of Ned Alleyn, a noted actor, is a boost to the company and "Kent" is cast as Romeo. Sir Richard Tilney, patron of Burbage and his theatre, learns about "Kent" and closes Henslowe's theatre because of immorality. Burbage, however, helps out and Will takes over as Romeo while Viola is forced to marry Wessex. Viola goes to the theatre and takes over the role of Juliet when the actor gets stage fright. The play is a great success but Tilney again tries to close it down. Queen Elizabeth intervenes and pretends that Viola is a man but makes it clears that she must go to Virginia with her husband. Will starts writing TWELFTH NIGHT and Viola wanders on a strange shore, the sole survivor of a shipwreck.

A great deal of the story, the gags and incidents are evidently derivative. Does it matter? With such a marvellous rapport between the two principal players and a delightful performance from Judi Dench (all of eight Oscar-winning minutes of it), the answer is decidedly "No". Though this project may have taken a while to reach the screen (it was scheduled some years ago with Daniel Day Lewis and Julia Roberts in the leading roles), it has been worth it. There is much to enjoy in this comedy which, despite some faults, incredibly comes together, helped by some fine supporting performances.

The romantic, period-style music from the film has, in part, been commited to disc. It can be found on the Sony Classics label.

Academy of Motion Picture Arts and Sciences, U.S.A., 1998: Nominations – Best Director (John Madden), Best Supporting Actor (Geoffrey Rush), Best Sound (Robin O'Donoghue), Best Editing (David Gamble), Best Make-up (Lisa Westcott, Veronica Brebner), Best Cinematography (Richard Greatrex); Awards – Best Picture, Best Actress (Gwyneth Paltrow), Best Supporting Actress (Judi Dench), Best Original Script (Tom Stoppard, Marc Norman), Best Costume Design (Sandy Powell for this film and *Velvet Goldmine*); Best Soundtrack (Comedy or Musical) (Stephen Warbeck), Best Art Direction/Set Direction (Martin Childs, Jill Quertier).
Berlin Film Festival, Germany, 1999: Silver Bear for Best Script (Tom Stoppard, Marc Norman).
Hollywood Foreign Press Association Golden Globe Awards, U.S.A., 1999: Best Film (Comedy/Musical), Best Supporting Actress (Judi Dench), Best Screenplay (Tom Stoppard, Marc Norman).
MTV Film Awards, 1999: Nominations – Best Movie, Best Breakthrough Performance – Male (Joseph Fiennes), Best Actress (Gwyneth Paltrow); Award – Best Kiss (Joseph Fiennes and Gwyneth Paltrow).

A very brief promo for the Oscars is known to exist on 8mm. and thus, logically, on standard gauge, and includes scenes from the film.

✤ ✤ ✤ ✤

The Shakespearean legacy lives on not only in his works which are performed regularly and especially at the Royal Shakespeare Theatre at Stratford-upon-Avon in England, but in the same town, or nearby, both his birth place and Ann Hathaway's cottage are to be seen. His final resting place, Holy Trinity church, is of interest extending beyond Shakespeare as, too, is Hall's Croft, the home of John Hall, his son-in-law, and the home of his granddaughter and her husband, Nash's House.

In London, the Globe theatre has been reconstructed on its original site and is the only London theatre with that name. The previous theatre of that name in London has been renamed the Gielgud in honour of that great actor Sir John Gielgud on his ninetieth birthday. Fortunately, and quite correctly, the appropriate authorities have maintained the Stratford buildings in excellent order and much as they were. For those unable to visit in person, a few documentary films exist about them and other Shakespeare related topics. The listing which follows concerns itself with such releases and other documentary films whose content is in some way related to Shakespeare. Some of the newsreels are untitled with unknown total running times and thus some of the titles may have been applied by others for topic identification.

WARWICK PAGEANT
(G.B., 1906)

p.c. *Charles Urban Trading Company.*
d.

l.p. *Documentary.*
b.w. 1526 ft. (465 m.) Sil.

This record of a pageant held in the grounds of Warwick Castle from July 2 to July 9, 1906, features excerpts from HENRY VI Part 3 plus excerpts from a play by Marlowe. The American release is noted as rather shorter at 380 ft. (116 m.).

SHAKESPEARE LAND
(G.B., 1910)

p.c. *Kineto.*
d.
l.p. *Documentary.*
b.w. 329 ft. (100 m.) Sil.

A travelogue, this contains scenes of places in the County of Warwickshire but particularly of Stratford-upon-Avon. Included are scenes of Shakespeare's birthplace, his school, Ann Hathaway's cottage and the Memorial Theatre.

TWELFTH NIGHT
(G.B., 1916)

p.c. *Gaumont.*
d.
l.p. *Documentary.*
b.w. (?) mins. Sil.

Released on July 19, 1916, this newsreel, *Gaumont Graphic 555*, contained about one minute of scenes of nurses and wounded soldiers at Bournbrook Military Hospital, Birmingham, England, watching an open air performance of TWELFTH NIGHT.

STRATFORD-ON-AVON
(G.B., 1918)

p.c. *Hepworth.*
d.
l.p. *Documentary.*
b.w. 579 ft. (176 m.) Sil.

This silent short contains scenes of the town and surrounding area.

EVE'S FILM REVIEW
(G.B., 1924)

p.c. *Pathé.*
d.
l.p. *Documentary*
b.w. (?) mins. Sil.

In this film magazine for women, John Gielgud and Gwen Ffrangcon-Davies in the balcony scene from ROMEO AND JULIET as performed at the Regent's Theatre, King's Cross, London, in May, 1924.

STRATFORD-UPON-AVON
(G.B., 1925)

p.c. *Hepworth Manufacturing Company.*
d.
l.p. *Documentary.*
b.w. 659 ft. (201 m.) Sil.

The emphasis in this travelogue is clearly upon Shakespeare with views of his birthplace, his school, Ann Hathway's cottage, a tree said to have been planted by Shakespeare, a public house called "Shakespeare's Hostelrie" and the church where he is buried. Superimposed characters from his plays conclude the film.

BEAUTY AND BRIGHTNESS No. 4
(G.B., 1925?)

p.c. *Harry B. Parkinson.*
d. *Harry B. Parkinson.*
l.p. *Documentary.*
b.w. 490 ft. (146 m.) Sil.

London is the focal spot of this travelogue which includes scenes from a performance of AS YOU LIKE IT enacted on a brewer's dray at the Old George Inn, Southwark.

SHAKESPEARE'S COUNTRY
(G.B., 1926)

p.c. *British Screen Classics.*
d.
l.p. *Documentary.*
b.w. 747 ft. (228 m.) Sil.

As might be expected, this is a travelogue, part of the *Wonderful Britain* series, about the Stratford-upon-Avon area with the obvious connotations.

SHAKESPEARE MEMORIAL THEATRE
(G.B., 1926)

p.c. *Topical Film Company.*
d.
l.p. *Documentary.*
b.w. (?) mins. Sil.

This extract of 56 ft. (17 m.) of a newsreel release (*Topical Budget 759-1*) features scenes both inside and outside of the Shakespeare Memorial Theatre at Stratford following its destruction by fire on March 6, 1926. This newsreel was released five days after the event.

This particular newsreel series relied heavily upon titles to supplement its pictorial message. The company was never to issue any sound versions for, like the Memorial Theatre, fire at its headquarters curtailed its activities before the arrival of sound.

SOVIET'S SALUTE TO SHAKESPEARE!
(G.B., 1926)

p.c. *Topical Film Company.*
d.
l.p. *Documentary.*
b.w. (?) mins. Sil.

Topical Budget 765-2 released on April 26, 1926 included 58 ft. (18 m.) of the celebration of Shakespeare's birthday at Stratford. A visit by a Soviet delegation is featured.

TO SHAKESPEARE'S MEMORY
(G.B., 1927)

p.c. *Topical Film Company.*

d.
l.p. *Documentary.*
b.w. (?) mins. Sil.

Birthday celebrations were again the feature of this 54 ft. (16 m.) April 28, 1927, release of *Topical Budget 818-1*.

SHAKESPEARE'S BIRTHDAY
(G.B., 1927)

p.c. *Gaumont Film Company.*
d.
l.p. *Documentary.*
b.w. (?) mins. Sil.

Released on April 28, 1927, this *Gaumont Graphic 1680* featured scenes (about one minute) in Stratford during the birthday celebrations of Shakespeare.

STRATFORD-UPON-AVON PAGEANT OF 1927
(G.B., 1927)

p.c. *Pathé.*
d.
l.p. *Documentary. With: Fairfax Lucy; Sybil Thorndike; Irene Vanburgh; Lewis Casson.*
b.w. 627 ft. (191 m.) Sil.

This pageant was held in aid of the rebuilding of the Shakespeare Memorial Theatre. Performers are seen in appropriate costumes and deliver speeches kneeling down before a statue of Shakespeare. The pageant was directed by Randle Ayrton and this film may have been specially commissioned.

SHAKESPEAREAN RECITAL AND PAGEANT
(G.B., 1927)

p.c. *Topical Film Company.*
d.
l.p. *Documentary.*
b.w. (?) mins. Sil.

This newsreel, *Topical Budget 838-1*, contains about one minute of dancing and Shakespearean performance at Burley pageant in Yorkshire, England.

BRITISH AND BEST
(G.B., 1928)

p.c. *Topical Film Company.*
d.
l.p. *Documentary.*
b.w. (?) mins. Sil.

Topical Budget 854-2 features about one minute devoted to the winning design by architect Elizabeth Scott for the Shakespeare Memorial Theatre.

SHAKESPEARE BIRTHDAY CELEBRATIONS AT STRATFORD
(G.B., 1928)

p.c. *British Pictorial Productions.*
d.
l.p. *Documentary.*
b.w. (?) mins. Sil.

This April 26, 1928, release featured Shakespeare's birthday celebrations in Stratford. The relative part lasts about a minute.

TO THE IMMORTAL BARD
(G.B., 1928)

p.c. *Topical Film Company.*
d.
l.p. *Documentary.*
b.w. (?) mins. Sil.

Topical Budget 870-1 released on April 26, 1928, contained about a minute of coverage of Stratford's celebrations of Shakespeare's birthday – the three hundred and sixty fourth!

THE BARD'S BIRTHDAY
(G.B., 1929?)

p.c. *British Screen Productions.*
d.
l.p. *Documentary.*
b.w. (?) mins. Sil.

Birthday celebrations at Stratford are once again the topic of coverage in a newsreel – about a minute or so – in this *British Screen News* release.

FAVOURITE AIRS
(G.B., 1929)

p.c. *British Sound Film Productions.*
d.
l.p. *Luella Paikin.*
b.w. 11 mins.

The above-named sings "Rigoletto", "Lo, Here the Gentle Lark" and "The Londonderry Air".

Just where to place this little film has been a problem for it is not a play or a performance of one within another film story. It is hardly a quotation either. So, it finds itself here because the second item is a musical adaptation of some lines from the narrative poem VENUS AND ADONIS. This attractive piece found itself on record as early as 1905 by Dame Nellie Melba. For music lovers, the much later version on disc by Cleo Laine with flautist James Galway merits attention. The film was re-released in 1932.

THE SHAKESPEARE MEMORIAL THEATRE
(G.B., 1929)

p.c. *Pathé.*
d.
l.p. *Documentary.*
b.w. 1066 ft. (325 m.) Sil.

This shows the laying on July 2, 1929, of the foundation stone of the new building by Lord Ampthill along with processions, speeches, views of the old theatre and builders at work.

Note: The following British silent newsreels of the same year contain coverage of this event:

HOME FOR SHAKESPEARE'S DRAMA
(British Screen News)
SHAKESPEARE MEMORIAL THEATRE
(Empire News Bulletin 332)
SHAKESPEARE MEMORIAL THEATRE
(Gaumont Graphic 1908)
TRIBUTE TO SHAKESPEARE
(Topical Budget 932-1)

**SHAKESPEARE BIRTHDAY
CELEBRATIONS 1930
(G.B. 1930)**

p.c. *Gaumont Film Company.*
d.
l.p. *Documentary.*
b.w. (?) mins. Sil.

This *Gaumont Graphic* contains coverage of the celebration in Stratford.

**H. R. H. ON SHAKESPEARE
(G.B., 1932)**

p.c. *British Paramount News.*
d.
l.p. *Documentary.*
b.w. (?) mins.

The official opening of the rebuilt Shakespeare Memorial Theatre at Stratford on Shakespeare's birthday in 1932 was performed by H. R. H. The Prince of Wales (later, briefly, King Edward VIII). *British Paramount News 121* covered this with about two minutes of sound in this newsreel. The same topic is also covered in two (and there may be more) silent newsreels:

**STRATFORD ON AVON – "SWEETEST
SHAKESPEARE – FANCY'S CHILD"**
(Pathé Gazette)
SHAKESPEARE MEMORIAL
(Gaumont Graphic)

**SHAKESPEARE
(G.B., 1934)**

p.c. *Gaumont.*
d. *J.B. Holmes.*
l.p. *Documentary.*
b.w. 10 mins.

Supervised by G.B. Harrison, this looked at biographical and historical background aspects of the man. It was possibly the first British documentary intended for the classroom.

**STRATFORD-ON-AVON: SHAKESPEARE'S
BIRTHDAY
(G.B., 1934)**

p.c. *British Pictorial Productions.*
d.
l.p. *Documentary.*
b.w. 10 mins.

These birthday celebrations in Stratford received a full issue coverage in this *Universal Talking News 396.*

**B.B.C. THE VOICE OF BRITAIN
(G.B., 1935)**

p.c. *G.P.O. Film Unit.*
d. *Stuart Legg.*
l.p. *Documentary*
b.w. 61 mins.

Scenes from a rehearsal for a sound broadcast of MACBETH are featured in this impressionistic film about the work of Britain's B.B.C.. Humphrey Jennings, noted documentary film maker, is seen as one of the witches.

**GAUMONT-BRITISH NEWS 243
(G.B., 1936)**

p.c. *Gaumont British.*
d.
l.p. *Documentary.*
b.w. (?) mins.

Released on April 27, 1936, this newsreel covered in about a minute the celebrations of Shakespeare's birthday for the year in Stratford in its "Roving Camera" section.

**MARCH OF TIME 3rd. YEAR (BRITISH
EDITION)
(U.S.A., 1937)**

p.c. *Time Inc.*
d. *Jimmy Shute.*
l.p. *Documentary.*
b.w. 23 mins.

This film review contains three topics: Child Labour – Uncle Sam, Impressario – D.O.R.A. – and it is the second one that is of interest. It covers the work of the Works Progress Administration and includes two brief sequences from its Negro Theatre Production of MACBETH as directed by Orson Welles. The cast featuring appears to be that of the touring production and not the one which played so successfully in Harlem, New York.

The American release noted this section as "An Uncle Sam Production" and the whole was issued as *March Of Time Vol. 3 Issue 4 (1936).*

**WHO WAS THE BARD OF AVON?
(G.B., 1938)**

p.c. *British Paramount News.*
d.
l.p. *Documentary.*
b.w. (?) mins.

British Paramount News 802 took a brief – about three minutes – look at a proposal to open the tomb of Shakespeare to search for proof of "true" authorship of his plays.

**ENGLAND'S SHAKESPEARE
(G.B., 1939)**

p.c. *Imperial Sound Studios for London, Midland and Scottish Railways.*
d.

l.p. *Documentary.*
b.w. 18 mins.

This travelogue of Stratford and the surrounding area covers most of the famous sights and includes the stage being set for a performance of KING LEAR.

MARCH OF THE MOVIES
(U.S.A., 1939/44?)

p.c. *Time-Life.*
d.
l.p. *Documentary.*
b.w. 20 mins.

Originally Volume 5, Issue 12 of this series was devoted to film clips from the collection held by the New York Museum of Modern Art. It was obviously later updated to include scenes from the Olivier version of **HENRY V.**

This was available for purchase by home movie collectors on 8 mm. from a number of sources.

ONE DAY IN SOVIET RUSSIA
(U.S.S.R., 1941)

p.c. *Central Newsreel Studios.*
d. *M. Slutski, R. Karmen.*
l.p. *Documentary. Narrator: Quentin Reynolds (English version).*
b.w. 56 mins.

August 24, 1940, is the featured day in the Soviet Union and aspects of life there are shown. This includes an excerpt from the ballet ROMEO AND JULIET by Prokofiev featuring Galina Ulanova as Juliet at the Kirov Theatre, Leningrad.

C. E. M. A.
(G.B., 1942)

p.c. *Strand Films for The Ministry of Information.*
d. *Alexander Shaw.*
l.p. *Documentary. Presenter: R. A. Butler.*
b.w. 17 mins.

In this piece of wartime propaganda for the arts featuring the work of the Council for the Encouragement of Music and the Arts, the Old Vic Company is seen in rehearsal and production of THE MERRY WIVES OF WINDSOR at a provincial theatre.

THE VOICE THAT THRILLED THE WORLD
(U.S.A., 1943)

p.c. *Warner Bros.*
d. *Jean Negulesco.*
l.p. *Documentary.*
b.w. 17 mins.

Though a history of sound films, the emphasis is, naturally, towards those from Warner Bros. Included is a speech from HENRY VI Part 3 spoken by John Barrymore as Richard, Duke of Gloucester.

OUR MR. SHAKESPEARE
(G.B., 1944)

p.c. *Harold Baim.*
d. *Harold Baim.*
l.p. *Documentary.*
b.w. 37 mins.

The emphasis in this travelogue of Stratford and its surroundings is clearly on the Shakespeare connection.

SHAKESPEARE'S COUNTRY
(G.B., 1944)

p.c. *Gainsborough Pictures.*
d. *Lister Lawrence.*
l.p. *Documentary. Narrator: John Gielgud.*
b.w. 11 mins.

Scenes of and around Stratford, including the obvious ones, are featured in this travelogue, one of the series *Gainsborough Miniatures.*

STRATFORD-ON-AVON
(G.B., 1945)

p.c. *Not stated.*
d. *Not stated.*
l.p. *Documentary.*
b.w. 16 mins.

Travelogue of the area which includes the Theatre, Ann Hathaway's cottage and Shakespeare's Hostelrie Inn. The "ghosts" of some of Shakespeare's characters are seen to pass. The film, on 16 mm., was issued as a teaching aid and had captions instead of commentary.

SHAKESPEARE'S BIRTHDAY
(G.B., 1946)

p.c. *The Newsreel Association Of Great Britain and Ireland.*
d.
l.p. *Documentary.*
b.w. 10 mins.

British News 309 devoted this full issue to the Shakespearean birthday celebrations in Stratford. The film was released on May 6, 1946.

SOME HIGHLIGHTS OF MONTY'S MOSCOW VISIT
(G.B., 1947)

p.c. *British Movietone News.*
d.
l.p. *Documentary.*
b.w. (?) mins.

Some two minutes of coverage in *British Movietone News No. 922A* were devoted to the above event which took place between January 6 and January 12, 1947. Included was a trip by Viscount Montgomery of Alamein to the Bolshoi Theatre to see a performance of the ballet ROMEO AND JULIET by Prokofiev.

UPLIFT AT THE LOCAL
(G.B., 1947)

p.c. *British Movietone.*
d.
l.p. *Documentary.*
b.w. (?) mins.

The Taverners, an amateur theatrical company, performs the final scene from OTHELLO at a public house in Carshalton.

This one minute item formed part of *British Movietone News Vol. 18 No. 927A* which was released on March 13, 1947.

PARIS 1900
(France, 1948)

p.c. *Panthéon.*
d. *Nicholas Védrès.*
l.p. *Documentary.*
b.w. 82 mins.

Paris from 1900 to 1914 is the subject of this compilation of then contemporary film and photographic sources with the objective of giving an idea of Parisian life at the time. Included are scenes from HAMLET (Mounet-Sully in the role), JULIUS CAESAR and THE MERCHANT OF VENICE (Fermin Gémier poses as Shylock). The film received the French Prix Louis Delluc in 1947 and was, in 1950, placed fifth in its list of best Foreign Language Films by the American National Board Of Review.

The excellent French company, Franfilmdis released the whole film on 8 mm. for collectors.

THE UPSTART CROW
(G.B., 1948)

p.c. *D.U.K. Films.*
d. *C. H. Williamson.*
l.p. *Documentary. Narrator: John Snagge.*
b.w. 36 mins.

This tour of Stratford-upon-Avon focuses on the Shakespeare connection with visits to his birthplace and the school in which he is said to have taken his first lessons. Later sequences show his possible initiation into the theatrical world and so into his subsequent relationships with the Blackfriars and Globe theatres. The narrator was a noted English broadcaster.

FROM LIVERPOOL TO STRATFORD-UPON-AVON
(U.S.A., 1949)

p.c. *M.G.M.*
d.
l.p. *Documentary.*
b.w.? 9 mins.

It is assumed that this short, one of a number made by M.G.M. about the British Isles (it may be a British production), would have included the obvious sights upon its filmic arrival in Stratford.

FAMILY PORTRAIT
(G.B., 1950)

p.c. *Wessex.*
d. *Humphrey Jennings.*
l.p. *Documentary. Narrator: Michael Goodliffe.*
b.w. 24 mins.

Commissioned for the Festival of Britain, this looks at the English both past and present in a way that one might look at a photograph album. It is a personal journey through history and geography with images of the past and present held in juxtaposition. In examining the achievements in all spheres, the film evokes such characters as Newton, Darwin, Shaftesbury and, of course, Shakespeare.

The director was a noted documentary film maker. Though this film is not particularly focused on the Bard, no work of this nature at such a time (the Festival of Britain was a major event of its day) could fail, at the very least, to mention him.

ROYAL VISITORS AT SHAKESPEARE'S BIRTHPLACE
(G.B., 1950)

p.c. *Gaumont-British.*
d.
l.p. *Documentary.*
b.w. (?) mins.

Released on April 24, 1950, *Gaumont-British News 1701* devoted about two minutes to King George VI, Queen Elizabeth and Princess Margaret on their first official visit to Stratford. Lord Iliffe shows them the Shakespeare Memorial Theatre.

SHAKESPEARE OG GRONBORG
(Denmark, 1950)

p.c. *Teknisk Films for Dansk Kulturfilm.*
d. *Jørgen Roos, Knut Hjortø.*
l.p. *Narrator: Karl Roos. With: Erik Mørk; Olaf Ussing; Annemette Svendsen; Jacob Nielsen; Ib Fürst; Ego Brønnum-Jacobsen; Ebba With.*
b.w. 10 mins.

This short is about the setting of HAMLET with scenes from the play presented. The film depicts Elsinore Castle as Shakespeare and the cast would have seen it. The script for the film was by Carl Dreyer. The title translates as SHAKESPEARE AT KRONBORG.

Shown as part of the Everybody's Shakespeare International Festival, London, England, 1994.
Shown at the Shakespeare Film Festival, Wiesbaden, W. Germany, 1964.

aka: HAMLET'S CASTLE

WILLIAM SHAKESPEARE: BACKGROUND FOR HIS WORKS
(U.S.A., 1950)

p.c. *Coronet Instructional Films.*
d.

l.p. *Documentary.*
c. 14 mins.

A brief look at the background (literary, geographical and social), featured are short extracts from ROMEO AND JULIET, THE TAMING OF THE SHREW, MACBETH and THE MERCHANT OF VENICE. William G. Brink was the educational adviser.

THIS THEATER AND YOU
(U.S.A., c1950)

p.c. *Warner Bros.*
d.
l.p. *Documentary.*
b.w. 9 mins.

Made at the time when television was about to surge in popularity in America, it extols the virtues of the cinema, the role of its manager and its place in the community. It includes an excerpt from **HENRY V** (the Olivier version.)

Reel Images, U.S.A., used to sell 8 mm. copies of this directly to the public.

SHAKESPEARE: ENGLAND TODAY
(U.S.A., 1951)

p.c. *Eastin Pictures.*
d. *Gardner Soule.*
l.p. *Documentary. Narrator: Gregory Abbott.*
b.w. 16 mins.

One of the Eastin School Films series, this takes a look at the usual sites associated with the Bard plus other views of England.

POUND OF FLESH
(U.S.A., 1952)

p.c. *Unusual Films.*
d. *Bob Walsh.*
l.p. *Bob Walsh; Elizabeth Edwards.*
b.w. 30 mins.

A sermon on self-righteousness is illustrated by scenes from THE MERCHANT OF VENICE.

THIS IS CHARLES LAUGHTON
(U.S.A., 1953)

p.c.
d.
l.p. *Charles Laughton.*
b.w. 15 mins.

Laughton, as Count Orsini, reads from TWELFTH NIGHT.

ET SLOT I ET SLOT
(Denmark, 1954)

p.c. *Teknisk Films for Dansk Kulturfilm.*
d. *Carl Dreyer.*
l.p. *Documentary. Narrator: Ib Koch-Olsen.*
b.w. 9 mins.

The castle in which HAMLET takes place is seen from an historical and architectural point of view. The title translates as CASTLE WITHIN A CASTLE.

THE HEART OF ENGLAND
(G.B., 1954)

p.c. *British Transport Films.*
d. *Michael Clarke.*
l.p. *Documentary. Narrator: Stephen Murray.*
Technicolor. 20 mins.

The focus of attention here is on the lovely Cotswolds in England with a look at English rural life. Naturally, Stratford-upon-Avon, its sights and Shakespeare are included.

SHAKESPEAREAN LIBRARY OF FAMOUS ROLES
(U.S.A., 1954)

p.c. *Shakespearean Film Library, Los Angeles.*
d.
l.p. *Documentary. Narrator and reciter: John Carradine.*
c. 13 x 4 mins.

A host of extracts from famous roles from Shakespearean plays are featured in these short films which were probably made on 16 mm.

SHAKESPEARE'S THEATER: THE GLOBE PLAYHOUSE
(U.S.A., 1954)

p.c. *Dept. of Theatre Arts, UCLA.*
d. *William and Mildred Jordan.*
l.p. *Documentary. Narrator: Ronald Coleman.*
b.w. 18 mins.

Using cardboard cut-outs as actors, the uses of the various facets of an Elizabethan theatre are explained. Brief scenes from TWELFTH NIGHT, ROMEO AND JULIET, JULIUS CAESAR and MACBETH are featured examples. Apparently the model used for the Olivier version of **HENRY V** of the Globe theatre was borrowed for this.

STRATFORD ADVENTURE
(Canada, 1954)

p.c. *National Film Board Of Canada.*
d. *Morten Parker.*
l.p. *Documentary.*
Eastman Color. 40 mins.

A basic record of how the 1953 Shakespeare Festival came about in Ontario, Canada. Included are rehearsals, preparations and short scenes from RICHARD III with Alec Guiness and Irene Worth. Tyrone Guthrie, director of the stage production, is effectively featured.

MR. THERM'S REVIEW No. 4
(G.B., 1955)

p.c. *Film Workshop for the Gas Council.*
d.

l.p. *Documentary.*
b.w. 10 mins.?

A typical film magazine, this contain four topics of which one is a visit to Stratford-upon-Avon and which features actors Anthony Quayle and Barbara Jefford.

SWAN OF AVON
(G.B., 1955)

p.c. *Plymouth Films.*
d. *John Dooley.*
l.p. *Documentary.*
b.w. 16 mins.

An attempt to recapture the world of Shakespeare that relies upon conventional connotations and views of Stratford and London and includes a model of the Globe theatre.

FESTIVAL IN EDINBURGH
(G.B., 1955)

p.c. *Associated British Pathé in association with the Films of Scotland Committee.*
d. *Douglas Clarke.*
l.p. *Documentary. Narrator: Alistair Sim.*
b.w. 14 mins.

The 1955 Edinburgh Festival is promoted with highlights from the 1954 Festival which includes a short scene from the Old Vic production of MACBETH.

WILLIAM SHAKESPEARE
(U.S.A., 1955)

p.c. *Encyclopaedia Britannica Educational Corporation.*
d. *Shakespeare's Birthday Trust.*
l.p. *Documentary.*
c. 25 mins.

Illustrated with scenes from ROMEO AND JULIET, HENRY V, JULIUS CAESAR, AS YOU LIKE IT, HAMLET and MACBETH, this is basically about the life of the Bard.

Shown at the Shakespeare Film Festival, Wiesbaden, W. Germany, 1964.

THE ENGLAND OF ELIZABETH
(G.B., 1956)

p.c. *British Transport Films.*
d. *John Taylor.*
l.p. *Documentary. Narrator: Alec Clunes.*
Eastman Color. 26 mins.

Stately homes, pictures, furniture, china, music, and, naturally, Shakespeare, are the basic contents of this trip through the England of Elizabeth I. Ralph Vaughan Williams wrote the musical score.

STRATFORD-ON-AVON
(G.B., 1956)

p.c.
d.

l.p. *Documentary.*
c. 14 mins.

A travelogue, this features the expected views and sights of the area.

Shown at the Shakespeare Film Festival, Wiesbaden, W. Germany, 1964.

SHAKESPEARE BREATHES AGAIN!
(G.B., 1956)

p.c. *British Paramount News.*
d.
l.p. *Documentary.*
b.w. (?) mins.

A brief – about one minute – item covered in *British Paramount News 2627* released on May 3, 1956 was the opening of the tomb of Sir Thomas Walsingham in Chislehurst, England, at the request of an American who was trying to prove that Christopher Marlowe wrote the plays attributed to Shakespeare.

INTRODUCING SHAKESPEARE
(G.B., 1957)

p.c. *Plymouth Films.*
d.
l.p. *Documentary.*
b.w. 10 mins.

The background to the life of Shakespeare in Stratford and London is the subject matter here.

BAYLOR THEATER'S HAMLET
(U.S.A., 1958)

p.c. *Baylor University.*
d. *Gene McKinney.*
l.p. *Documentary.*
c. 20 mins.

The technical problems of stage production are the subject of this short.

JULIUS CAESAR
(U.S.A., 1958)

p.c. *Madison (Wisconsin) Television Station (WHA-TV).*
d. *Eric Salmon.*
l.p.
b.w. 59 mins.

Characters in the play are discussed with scenes from the play in this which is available on 16 mm. film. It was one of the series *Great Plays in Rehearsal*.

THE MERCHANT OF VENICE
(U.S.A., 1958)

p.c. *Madison (Wisconsin) Television Station (WHA-TV).*
d. *Eric Salmon.*
l.p. *Documentary.*
b.w. 59 mins.

A 16 mm. film edition is known to exist of this documentary taken from the *Great Plays in Rehearsal* series, which comments on characters in the play and discusses the Shylock character, costumes, scenery etc.

THREE SEASONS
(G.B., 1958)

p.c. *Associated British Pathé for British Travel Association.*
d.
l.p. *Documentary.*
Eastman Color. 31 mins.

England in Autumn, Winter and Spring is the theme here. Sequences from the Old Vic production of A MIDSUMMER NIGHT'S DREAM are featured with Frankie Howerd (Bottom), Joyce Redman (Titania) and Paul Daneman (Quince).

ENGLISH LITERATURE OF THE ELIZABETHAN PERIOD
(G.B., 1959)

p.c. *Coronet Films.*
d.
l.p. *Documentary.*
b.w. 13 mins.

The precise contents of this are not known but the title probably explains all. Indeed, the film may even be American.

THE HUMANITIES SERIES: HAMLET, THE AGE OF ELIZABETH
(U.S.A., 1959)

p.c. *Encyclopaedia Britannica Education Corp.*
d. *Michael Langham, John Barnes, Floyd Rinker, Angus McDemott.*
l.p. *Peter Donat (Hamlet); Ton Van Bridge (Ghost); William Needles (Horatio); Charmian King (Gertrude); John Gardner (Laertes); Donald David; Max Helpman; Frank Peddie; Douglas Campbell.*
c. 4 x 30 mins.

Using maps, portraits and play excerpts Professor Maynard Mack attempts to link HAMLET with the Elizabethan era in these four short films entitled: **THE AGE OF ELIZABETH, WHAT HAPPENS IN HAMLET, THE POISONED KINGDOM** and **THE READINESS IS ALL**. The cast is taken from the Stratford Festival Company, Ontario, Canada.

Shown at the Shakespeare Film Festival, Wiesbaden, W. Germany, 1964.

THE QUESTIONING CITY
(G.B., 1959)

p.c. *Associated British Pathé.*
d. *Eric Fullilove.*
l.p. *Documentary. Narrator: Michael Redgrave.*
Eastman Color. 21 mins.

This is a visit to Cambridge and its University. Students are seen, in costume, rehearsing a scene from MUCH ADO ABOUT NOTHING.

PATHÉ PICTORIAL 434
(G.B., 1960)

p.c. *Associated British Pathé.*
d.
l.p. *Documentary.*
c. 9 mins.

One section is dedicated to the restoration and preservation of old film by the British Film Institute. Among the items featured is **HAMLET** with Forbes Robertson.

The film was available in Great Britain for purchase on 8 mm. from Derann Film Services, U.K.

SHAKESPEARE: SOUL OF AN AGE
(U.S.A., 1962)

p.c. *NBC News.*
d. *Howard Sackler.*
l.p. *Documentary. Narrator: Ralph Richardson. Reciter: Michael Redgrave.*
b.w. 54 mins.

Thirteen pieces from Shakespeare are featured in this study of the life and times of Shakespeare.

Shown at the Shakespeare Film Festival, Wiesbaden, W. Germany, 1964.

ROMEO AND JULIET
(Czechoslovakia, 1963)

p.c.
d. *Radúz Činčera.*
l.p. *Documentary.*
b.w. Short?

This award winning film (Karlovy Vary Festival, Czechoslovakia, 1963), is about the direction and staging by Krejča of the play in the National Theatre, Prague.

FAIR ADVENTURE SERIES
(U.S.A., 1964)

p.c. *Westinghouse Broadcast Company.*
d.
l.p. *Documentary with Dr. Frank Baxter.*
b.w. 29 mins.

This series of short films features Dr. Frank Baxter of the University of Southern California who discusses various aspects of Shakespeare and his plays and acts as narrator in the condensations. The individual films are:

HOW TO READ A SHAKESPEARE PLAY
The content is implied by the title.

KINGS AND QUEENS
Despite the title, this contains advice on how to read a Shakespeare play.

THE LIFE OF WILLIAM SHAKESPEARE
Content is as the title implies.

THE PRINTING OF THE PLAYS
The technology of printing in Elizabethan England is explained.

SHAKESPEARE'S STRATFORD
Maps, stills and shots of the environment give the background to the Bard's life which is contrasted with England of the 1960s. This particular issue was made in co-operation with the Shakespeare Birthplace Trust (U.K.) and the Folger Shakespeare Library (U.S.A.). Don Derendorf directed.

SHAKESPEARE'S THEATRE
This looks at a typical Elizabethan stage.

SHAKESPEARE'S WORLD AND SHAKESPEARE'S LONDON
Using portraits and views of the time, a background to the Shakespearean era is evoked.

The following in the series are all condensations:

HENRY V
(84 mins.)

KING LEAR
(140 mins.)

MACBETH
(140 mins.)

MUCH ADO ABOUT NOTHING
(84 mins.)

OTHELLO
(140 mins.)

RICHARD II
(112 mins.)

RICHARD III
(112 mins.)

ROMEO AND JULIET
(140 mins.)

TWELFTH NIGHT
(84 mins.)

THE HUMANITIES SERIES
(U.S.A., 1964)

p.c. *Encyclopaedia Britannica Educational Corporation.*
d. *John Barnes, Douglas Campbell.*
l.p. *Presenter: Douglas Campbell. With: William Squire (Macbeth); Gudrun Ure (Lady Macbeth); Duncan Lamont (Macduff); George Ragan (Banquo); Michael Gwynn(Duncan).*
c. *28 mins., 28 mins. and 33 mins.*

With the individual titles of **MACBETH 1: THE POLITICS OF POWER, MACBETH 2: THE THEMES OF "MACBETH"** and **MACBETH 3: THE SECRET'ST MAN**, these films investigate various aspects of the play and its characters with emphasis on the corruption of power, how appearances deceive and the inner torment of the principal pair.

The series is noted as being very well done and superbly acted.

Shown at the Shakespeare Film Festival, Wiesbaden, W. Germany, 1964.

PATHÉ PICTORIAL – SHAKESPEARE'S 400th. ANNIVERSARY
(G.B., 1964)

p.c. *Pathé.*
d.
l.p. *Documentary. Narrator: Wilfrid Thomas. Technicolor. 9 mins. Techniscope.*

Sad to say, but this and the two films that follow were the only attempts on film to celebrate the four hundredth anniversary of Shakespeare's birth by his native land. It is a pleasant enough travelogue focusing upon the expected sights. The Duke of Edinburgh and Lord and Lady Avon also make appearances in this *Pathé News 64/36*.

Some sources note the colour system as Eastman Color.

This Pathé News Special was issued by Derann Film Services, U.K., on 8 mm. for public purchase.

Shown at the Shakespeare Film Festival, Wiesbaden, W. Germany, 1964.

THE POET'S EYE – A TRIBUTE TO WILLIAM SHAKESPEARE
(G.B., 1964)

p.c. *Greenpark in association with The Film Producer's Guild for Central Office Of Inform - ation (overseas departments).*
d. *Gordon Hales.*
l.p. *Documentary. Narrator: Stephen Murray. Eastman Color. 20 mins.*

The film opens with Laurence Olivier's **HENRY V** before Harfleur sequence. Contrasts are made with modern Britain and Shakespeare's words are recited on the soundtrack. With poorly matched stock shots, the film obviously needed a bigger budget for its quality to match the subject matter.

Shown at the Shakespeare Film Festival, Wiesbaden, W. Germany, 1964.

SHAKESPEARE LAND
(G.B., 1964)

p.c. *Associated British Pathé.*
d. *Frederic Goode.*

l.p. *Documentary. Narrator: William Dexter. Eastman Color. 21 mins.*

Documentary for which the title is self-explanatory.

Shown at the Shakespeare Film Festival, Wiebaden, W. Germany, 1964.

FILMFALSTAFF
(Czechoslovakia, 1965)

p.c.
d. *Vojtech Jasny.*
l.p. *Documentary.*
c.? (?) mins.

The Falstaff character is used to illustrate the development and the role of man.

SHAKESPEARE PRIMER
(U.S.A., 1965)

p.c. *BFA.*
d.
l.p. *Hans Conreid.*
c. 28 mins.

In the Shakespeare Court at Claremont College, Hans Conreid reads extracts from RICHARD III, ROMEO AND JULIET, HAMLET, AS YOU LIKE IT, THE MERCHANT OF VENICE and KING LEAR. Comment is also made on the life of Shakespeare and the interpretation of some of the text.

HAMLET RAZY PIĘC
(Poland, 1966)

p.c. *Wytwórnia Filmów Dokumentalnych.*
d. *Ludwik Perski.*
l.p. *Adam Hanuszkiewicz; Gustaw Holoubek; Ignacy Gogolewski; Andrzej Łapicki.*
b.w. 17 mins.

The four above-named actors each give their interpretation of the "To be or not to be..." soliloquy from HAMLET and then a vision of a twentieth century Hamlet by Polish designer Leon Szajna.

These five views of the character give the film its title which, in English, means HAMLET TIMES FIVE.

VI Short Film Festival, Kraków, Poland, 1966: Brązowy Lajkonik (third prize).

NATIONAL YOUTH THEATRE
(G.B., 1966)

p.c. *Melstrum Films.*
d. *John Bloom, John Crome.*
l.p. *Documentary. Narrator: Michael Croft.*
b.w. 27 mins.

Excerpts – both in rehearsal and production – from CORIOLANUS are featured in this documentary about the work and the story of the National Youth Theatre.

THE ART OF SHAKESPEARE IN "MACBETH"
(U.S.A., 1967)

p.c. *University Of Washington?*
d.
l.p. *Narrator: Bertram Joseph. With: Elizabeth Shepherd; Ross Duncan.*
c. 15 mins., 16 mins., 20 mins., 19 mins., 14 mins. and 15 mins.

These six short films are individually titled: **MACBETH: PATTERNS OF SOUND, MACBETH; IMAGERY, MACBETH: CHARACTER, MACBETH: TURNING POINTS, MACBETH: TRAGEDY** and **MACBETH: A CREATIVE REHEARSAL**. Intended for educational study, scenes from the play are used as discussion and examination points.

OPUS
(G.B., 1967)

p.c. *James Archibald and Associates for the Central Office of Information.*
d. *Don Levy.*
l.p. *Documentary.*
Technicolor. 29 mins.

A promotional film, this was made to give an impression of art and culture in Britain at the time. It includes a soliloquy from HAMLET performed by David Warner.

PETER BROOK: THE TEMPEST
(France, 1968)

p.c. *Saga Film.*
d. *Peter Brook.*
l.p. *Players from the Royal Shakespeare Company.*
c. 27 mins.

Peter Brook explains and displays some unorthodox ways of presenting THE TEMPEST on stage.

EXPLORATIONS IN SHAKESPEARE SERIES
(Canada, 1969)

p.c. *Ontario Educational Communications Authority/ NBC Educational Enterprises.*
d.
l.p. *See individual releases.*
c. 12 x 29 mins.

Though many of these could justify placings under the play proper, the intention of the makers was to delve beyond the play as entertainment with examinations of situations and character relationships. Thus it was felt better to list them compactly together.

ANTONY AND CLEOPATRA: THE WORLD WELL LOST
The emphasis is placed on Antony's conflict between duty and love for Cleopatra.

AS YOU LIKE IT: DOING YOUR OWN THING
Here, the superficiality of trying to "drop out" of society and relationships is the topic examined.

CORIOLANUS: THE PEOPLE'S CHOICE
The need for a politician to compromise and communicate is the matter studied in this.

HAMLET: THE TROUBLE WITH HAMLET
Horatio, in contemporary dress, tells the story of HAMLET (as he promised his dying friend) while actors play the scenes on a platform. Cast: Brian Petchey (Hamlet); Hugh Webster (Horatio); Jackie Burroughs (Ophelia); Dawn Greenhalgh (Gertrude); Bernard Behrens (Claudius); Neil Dainard (Gravedigger?).

HENRY IV PARTS I AND II: THE MAKING OF AN IDEAL KING
The tranformation of Prince Hal and his coronation plus scenes with Falstaff at the Boar's Head Inn are shown.

KING LEAR: WHO CAN TELL ME WHO I AM?
This is an examination of the folly which King Lear opens up by his actions, his self-knowledge and awareness he subsequently gains.

MACBETH: NOTHING IS BUT WHAT IS NOT
Macbeth is viewed as a man without identity and with the need to perform his foul deeds to find himself and assert his identity.

OTHELLO: ANATOMY OF A MARRIAGE
Is marriage as it is known today out-moded? This is the matter examined through OTHELLO, his personal torment and tragic ending.

RICHARD II: HOW TO KILL A KING
The ever pertinent subject of the risk of assassination of people in high places is the topic here.

ROMEO AND JULIET: THE WORDS OF LOVE
The stress imposed by social barriers which have to be overcome by the young lovers and how they abandon social standards by devoting themselves to their love are the points made in this.

THE TEMPEST: O BRAVE NEW WORLD
The problem of how to exclude evil from the world is as prevalent now (illustrated by events of this century) as they were to Prospero. Cast: Jackie Burroughs (Ariel); Will Hutt (Prospero); Roscoe Lee Browne (Caliban).

TROILUS AND CRESSIDA: WAR, WAR, GLORIOUS WAR
Handled as a black comedy, this is interspersed with ironic songs.

MASKS AND FACES
(G.B., 1969)

p.c. *British Film Institute.*
d. *Colin Ford (compiler of material).*
l.p. *Documentary.*
b.w. and c. 91 mins.

Extracts from various Shakespearean films are used to show the changes in acting theatrical styles as captured on film. The extracts are taken from the following: **RICHARD III** (1911); **HAMLET** (1913); **OTHELLO** (1922); **DER KAUFMANN VON VENEDIG** (1923); **ROMEO AND JULIET** (1936) and **RICHARD III** (1955).

THE HUMANITIES SERIES: SHAW VS. SHAKESPEARE
(U.S.A., 1970)

p.c. *Encyclopaedia Britannica Education Corp.*
d.
l.p. *Donald Moffat (George Bernard Shaw).*
c. 3 x 35 mins.

The Irish playwright discusses his view of Julius Caesar in comparison to that of Shakespeare. The individual films are titled: **SHAW VS. SHAKESPEARE: THE CHARACTER OF CAESAR, SHAW VS. SHAKESPEARE: THE TRAGEDY OF JULIUS CAESAR** and **SHAW VS. SHAKESPEARE: CAESAR AND CLEOPATRA**.

SHAKESPEARE: MIRROR TO A MAN
(U.S.A., 1970?)

p.c. *Learning Corporation Of America.*
d. *Ian Brinnis.*
l.p. *Eileen Atkins; Brian Cox.*
c. 28 mins.

Scenes from THE TAMING OF THE SHREW, ROMEO AND JULIET, MACBETH and OTHELLO are illustrations for a lecture and discussion.

THE STRATFORD SHAKESPEARE KNEW
(U.S.A., 1971)

p.c.
d.
l.p. *Documentary.*
c. 20 mins.

A travelogue, this covers the familiar territory.

UNDERSTANDING SHAKESPEARE: HIS SOURCES
(G.B., 1971)

p.c. *Gateway Film Productions.*
d. *W. Hugh Baddeley, George Murcell.*
l.p. *Documentary. Narrator: Richard Bebb.*
c. 20 mins.

Intended for educational purposes in secondary schools, this covers Shakespeare's life, education and literary and acting influences. Extracts from his plays are presented in a would-be Globe theatre.

UNDERSTANDING SHAKESPEARE: HIS STAGECRAFT
(G.B., 1971)

p.c. *Gateway Film Productions.*
d. *W. Hugh Baddeley, George Murcell.*
l.p. *Documentary. Narrator: Richard Bebb.*
c. 25 mins.

This education film aimed at secondary school pupils, looks at how the restrictions of the theatre of his time affected Shakespeare not only in the physical restraints of the theatre but in conventions such as boys playing women's parts. Play extracts are used to illustrate these and to reflect the acting styles of the era.

THE PHOENIX AND THE TURTLE
(G.B., 1972)

p.c. *Milon Films.*
d. *Luigi V. R. Chiappini.*
l.p. *Documentary.*
c. 60 mins.

The work of the Century Theatre Company is featured in this as it tours north-west England with its mobile playhouse. Among the works featured in rehearsal is TWELFTH NIGHT.

THE PLAYERS
(Canada/Australia, 1974)

p.c. *National Film Board Of Canada/S. Australia Films.*
d. *Donald Brittain.*
l.p. *Documentary.*
c. 58 mins.

This is a record of the Canadian Stratford Shakespeare Festival on tour in Australia.

ELIZABETHAN LUTE SONG
(G.B., 1975)

p.c. *University Of Hull.*
d.
l.p. *R.H. Wells; Stephen Johnson.*
b.w. 47 mins.

The performance and explanation of Elizabethan lute songs are used to indicate the background music to Shakepeare's plays.

A SENSE OF THE OTHER
(U.S.A., 1977)

p.c. *Northwestern University.*
d.
l.p. *Wallace A. Bacon.*
c. 33 mins.

Professor Bacon shows the merit of teaching literature through performance.

SHAKESPEARE OF STRATFORD AND LONDON
(U.S.A., 1978)

p.c. *National Geographic Association/WQED TV/ Shakespeare Birthplace Trust.*
d. *Bob Walsh.*
l.p. *Documentary.*
c. 32 mins.

The contents of this are not know but, presumably, it is about the Bard's life and environment.

THE STAGING OF SHAKESPEARE
(U.S.A., 1977)

p.c. *Case Western University.*
d. *Robert Ornstein.*
l.p. *Kate Webster; Lizabeth MacKay; Ken Albers; Michael Champagne; Howard Renesland; Dan Desmond.*
c. 55 mins.

In this film the noted Shakespearean teacher and scholar, Dr. Robert Ornstein, shows, with the use of actors, how players in Shakespeare's time would have used the stage.

THE WORLD OF SHAKESPEARE SERIES
(U.S.A., 1978)

p.c. *Station WQED Pittsburg/Carnegie-Mellon University/Shakespeare Birthplace Trust.*
d. *See individual film.*
l.p. *See individual film.*
c. See individual film.

This is another case when the individual films could have well merited inclusion within the chapter devoted to the play. However, for compactness, it seems logical to list them together.

HAMLET
(35 mins. d. Bob Walsh, Zilla Clinton, Geoffrey Hitch)

Jeffrey Dench acts as narrator as scenes from the play are performed by Peter Kraus, Roy Cooper, Barbara Caruso and Cindy Carle.

THE TIME IS OUT OF JOINT
(20 mins. d. Bob Walsh)

A companion to the above, it explores the political setting to the problems of Hamlet.

MACBETH
(36 mins. d. Bob Walsh)

This is an abridgement of the play performed by Barry Snider, Carol Mayo Jenkins and Bingo O'Malley.

FAIR IS FOUL AND FOUL IS FAIR
(20 mins. d. Bob Walsh)

Historical notes as a background to the above form the basis of this release.

ROMEO AND JULIET
(36 mins. d. Bob Walsh)

The play is performed here as a condensed version by Lee Toombs, Julia Duffy, Helen Harrelson and George Hall.

STAR-CROSSED LOVER
(17 mins. d. Bob Walsh)

The play is used as a basis for an examination with England's fascination with Italy at the time it was written.

ROMEO UND JULIA ODER LIEBE, MORD UND TOTSLAG
(Austria/W. Germany/ Switzerland, 1979?)

p.c. *Neue Thalia Film for ORF, ZDF and SRG.*
d. *Gustav Trampitsch.*
l.p. *Documentary.*
c . 45 mins.

From the opening shots, it would be easy to think that this was going to be a travelogue. Of course there are scenes of Verona but the emphasis is clearly on the young lovers and thus the buildings and places associated with them. The film goes further, however, with scenes from the Zeffirelli film, scenes from the play and some from Gounod's opera performed in the arena in Verona. There is a visit to New York's West Side to look at the setting for **WEST SIDE STORY**, a look at the merchandizing of Romeo and Juliet in Verona and even the song "Fever" (sung by Helen Shapiro) is heard on the soundtrack as the lovers are mentioned in it!

The production year of this is not stated on the film which was probably made originally for television. The date is therefore a guess based on visual clues in the film. It appears to have been part of a series called *Schauplatze Der Weltliteratur*.

THEATRE IN POLAND
(Poland, 1981)

p.c.
d. *Stanislaw Moszczok.*
l.p. *Wroclaw Mime Theatre.*
c. 23 mins.

A scene from HAMLET is contained in this look at the theatre in Poland.

MACBETH: A TRAGEDY
(G.B., 1983)

p.c. *Anne Rees-Mogg?*
d. *Anne Rees-Mogg.*
l.p. *Documentary.*
c. 4 mins.

A piece of text from MACBETH is used for comparison with that from the 'Oxford Companion To English Literature'.

SHAKESPEARE'S COUNTRY
(G.B., 1983)

p.c. *Shakespeare Birthplace Trust.*
d. *Robin Whiteman.*
l.p. *Documentary.*
c. 27 mins.

The early life of Shakespeare is examined.

SHAKESPEARE'S HERITAGE
(G.B., 1983)

p.c. *Shakespeare Birthplace Trust.*
d. *Robin Whiteman.*
l.p. *Documentary.*
c. 27 mins.

Short film about the origins and history of Stratford-upon-Avon.

OUT OF OBERAMMERGAU – CHRISTIAN STÜCKL INSZENIERT SHAKESPEARE IN INDIEN
(Germany, 1993)

p.c. *3Sat/ZDF/Goethe-Institut.*
d. *Hanna Schön-Muanda.*
l.p. *Documentary.*
c. 30 mins.

From Oberammergau, Germany, scene of the famous Passion Plays, to Mysore, India, is quite a step for a German stage director and his crew. This is a record of that trip and his production in Hindi of A MIDSUMMER NIGHT'S DREAM. Scenes from the play are seen in rehearsal and in performance and there are interviews with Stückl and members of the cast: K.R. Nandini (Hermia), Prameela Bengre (Hippolyta), Santosh Kumar Kusnoor (Egeus), Mahadev (Puck) and Shashikala (Elf). The dialogue for the play is full of music and some surprising sexual overtones. Most of the cast interviews are in Hindi and the commentary in German with some English.

Though it is reasonable to assume that this was made with television in mind, it can also reasonably be assumed that the Goethe-Institut would have it available for group audiences for educational purposes and thus it merits inclusion.

AUS HOLZ EIN O – DAS GLOBE-THEATER DES SAM WANAMAKER
(Germany, 1997)

p.c. *WDR?*
d. *Barbara-Ann Riech.*
l.p. *Documentary.*
c. 10 mins.

Zoë Wanamaker, Sam Wanamaker's daughter, talks about her father's love of Shakespeare and his dream which motivated the rebuilding of the Globe. There are interviews, views of the new building and scenes from HENRY V including the Prologue spoken by Zoë.

No doubt this was made for television but it is clearly noted as being a film and so, logically, available as such.

ART OF PERSUASION: A DIFFERENT APPROACH TO ENGLISH LITERATURE
(G.B., 19??)

p.c.
d.

l.p. *Documentary.*
c. 37 mins.

Four actors/teachers discuss ways of reading MACBETH to children.

SHAKESPEARE'S THEATRE
(U.S.A., 19??)

p.c. *20th. Century Fox?*
d.
l.p. *Documentary.*
c. 13 mins.

Opening with the Globe scene from Olivier's **HENRY V** to show the activity in such a place, maps and construction details are added. This could be a re-editing of the film of similar title listed earlier but it certainly seems different.

SHAKESPEARE IN PALERMO
(France, Italy, 1998)

p.c. *Les Films D'Ici/GA & A in association with RAI*
Radiotelevisione Italiana/RAI Due/La Sept
Arte/The Municipality of Palermo/Centre
National de la Cinématographie with support
from Procirep.
d. *Vincenzi Cannioti.*
l.p. *Documentary*
c. 87 mins. S WS

The subject here is the background to the production of A MIDSUMMER NIGHT'S DREAM, a project by Shakespeare au Théâtre Garibaldi directed by Carlo Cecchi and featuring his players.

Naturally, there are, without doubt, many more documentaries on the Shakespearean and allied themes in the world. Too many, in fact, to even attempt a complete listing. To any such listing could be added those films which make reference to Shakespeare or quote from him in passing such as newsreels with British Prime Minister, Neville Chamberlain, quoting from the Bard upon his return from the (in)famous Munich meeting with Hitler in 1938. Over fifty years later, the documentary called *Central Park* (U.S.A., 1989) not only referred to characters from THE TEMPEST but showed a teacher explaining about Shakespeare and Joseph Papp and his productions of Shakespeare in the Park. What more remains before, between, and after those dates?

Certainly, with the emergence of new technology, there now exists a host of videograms from diverse sources available for rental and/or purchase on such topics. Whatever new forms are developed for bringing the performing arts and their backgrounds to the people, the Bard surely has, and will have, his place.

CHAPTER XXXIII

BRUSH UP YOUR SHAKESPEARE, START QUOTING HIM NOW!

Put away your Shakespeare! You will not find the chapter heading in any of his works for it is the title of a song from **KISS ME KATE**. The Bard would surely not have been offended as the words but reflect what many have done in centuries past and will, doubtless, do for many more to come.

Many actors and actresses have played Shakespearean roles, both as amateurs and professionals, and the Bard has been a useful standby at auditions, not just for English speaking members of the profession, but internationally. International star Omar Sharif recited the speech from HAMLET to Ophelia "Get thee to a nunnery..." while auditioning before the then current (1954) Egyptian leading lady of the screen – Faten Hamama. Hardly choice words, of course, since "nunnery" in Shakespearean times meant "brothel"! He got the role and, two years later, the girl.

No doubt, Omar Sharif is far from alone in using Shakespeare as a stepping stone to the world of cinema. So, too, has the cinema drawn on the words of Shakespeare in its scripts. Even in the cinema's limited (both in temporal and artistic terms) life, to ask "How many times has Shakespeare been quoted in films?" is simply a rhetorical question. One might as well ask how many lifetimes are needed to do the research. There are countless films that have used short, often one line, quotations. There are some other films which have featured substantial quotations, seriously or otherwise. What follows is but a brief list of such films. It is obviously far from complete and is not aimed to be so.

ACTION OF THE TIGER
(G.B., 1957)

Van Heflin, Martine Carol and Herbert Lom headed an international cast in this action adventure about rescuing refugees from Albania. The future screen 007, Sean Connery, had a minor role, too. The script over the final scene ("In peace there's nothing...the action of the tiger..") and the title is taken from the first speech from Act III, Scene 1 from HENRY V. The film was directed by Terence Young for Claridge.

ACTORS AND SIN
(U.S.A., 1952)

Like a number of other films, this is about a Shakespearean actor, here guiding and protecting the career of his daughter. As reviews clearly define the main role (played by Edward G. Robinson), it is reasonable to assume that there are some Shakespearean quotations at least. There may even be scenes from plays making the film eligible for inclusion elsewhere. Marsha Hunt plays the daughter and Dan O'Herlihy, Alice Kay, Rudolph Anders and Rick Rozman are also among the cast. The film was made in two parts – ACTOR'S BLOOD and WOMAN OF SIN, the latter unrelated to Shakespeare. United Artists produced and Ben Hecht directed the two parts of this black and white film.

APOCALIPSIS JOE
(Spain, Italy, 1970)

Leopoldo Savona directed this "spaghetti western" in colour. With little to commend it, the film runs true to formula. The taciturn, deadly gunman of the title (played by Anthony Steffen) is, between killings, dedicated to playing Hamlet and it is assumed that he at least quotes from the play. Eduardo Fajardo, Stelio Candelli and Mary Paz Pondal head the supporting cast list.

THE BAD AND THE BEAUTIFUL
(U.S.A., 1952)

Lana Turner starred with Kirk Douglas in this tale of an alcoholic woman haunted by memories of her father, also an alcoholic, and her past associations. Directed by Vincente Minnelli, it contains a sequence in which the star listens to a recording of her father giving the "Tomorrow and tomorrow..." speech from MACBETH.

DAS BILDNIS DES DORIAN GRAY
(W. Germany/Italy/Liechtenstein, 1970)

Oscar Wilde's novel 'The Picture Of Dorian Gray' is transposed to a swinging, modern London. In this Dorian (Helmut Berger) makes love to the actress Sybil (Marie Liljedahl) in an empty theatre against a background recording of her rehearsal for ROMEO AND JULIET. Richard Todd, Herbert Lom, Maria Rohm, Isa Miranda and Eleonora Rossi Drago were also featured in this colour film directed by Massimo Dallamano. The Italian title is IL DIO CHIAMATO DORIAN.

THE BLACKBOARD JUNGLE
(U.S.A., 1955)

Glenn Ford plays the new teacher at a slum school who has to overcome abuse and violence to gain respect. Anne Francis played the wife and Vic Morrow had an early role as the troublesome pupil. Sidney Poitier was cast as the student who eventually helps Ford. During his interview for the job, Ford quotes "Once more unto the breach..." from HENRY

V. M.G.M. produced and Richard Brooks directed. The film gained fame through a record used in it – "Rock Around the Clock" by Bill Haley and the Comets.

DER BLAUE ENGEL
(Germany, 1930)

Marlene Dietrich, Emil Jannings, Kurt Gerron and Hans Albers starred; Josef von Sternberg directed. Surely nothing further need be said of this Ufa classic except that there are references to HAMLET ("To be or not to be..." is quoted) and JULIUS CAESAR featured in a classroom scene.

BOTTOMS UP!
(G.B., 1960)

Comedian Jimmy Edwards was noted on radio and television in Britain for his role as a school headmaster. The theme was transferred to the big screen in this story about a headmaster who makes his bookmaker's son pose as a prince from the Middle East. Arthur Howard and Martita Hunt also appeared in this black and white film which Mario Zampi directed for Transocean. There is a scene when Edwards is about to cane five boys in one go and he misquotes the line from HENRY V: "Once more unto the breach...", the last word being transposed to "breeches" meaning "short trousers". The particular scene is featured in the compilation film TO SEE SUCH FUN (G.B., 1977).

BROADWAY FEVER
(U.S.A., 1928)

In this comedy about a maid who impersonates her mistress and wins the love of a show producer, the maid, played by Sally O'Neil, acts out scenes from ROMEO AND JULIET while dusting. Directed by Eddie Cline, also in the cast were Roland Drew, Corliss Palmer and Calvert Carter.

CALLING THE TUNE
(G.B., 1936)

Reginald Denham directed and Adele Dixon, Sally Gray, Donald Wolfit, Clifford Evans and Cedric Hardwicke starred in this light-weight, fictitious story of the record industry. An excuse for various recording artistes of the day to perform, Hardwicke recites the speech "How Sweet the Moonlight" from THE MERCHANT OF VENICE, Act V, Scene 1.

CHAPTER AND VERSE
(G.B., 1936)

This documentary directed by Stanley Hawes is all about printing (from the earliest times), paper and books. It ends with a recitation of Sonnet 55 "Not marble, nor the gilded monument".

THE CLAYDON TREASURE MYSTERY
(G.B., 1938)

Fox British remade its own film THE THIRD CLUE (listed later) which was based on 'The Shakespeare Murders' by Neil Gordon. The story of a novelist who solves the mystery of the death of a librarian and finds hidden treasure was directed by Manning Haynes with John Stuart, Garry Marsh and Evelyn Ankers heading the cast list.

THE COMEDY OF TERRORS
(U.S.A., 1963)

Trumbull, a drunken, penniless undertaker, hates his father-in-law whom he is trying poison, and his wife, Amaryllis. He mistreats his assistant, Felix, who loves Amaryllis. When the landlord, Black, demands his rent money, Trumbull plans to kill him. Black conveniently dies. Or does he? He seems to keep on reviving and quoting from MACBETH. This Alta Vista production, in colour, was directed by Jacques Tourneur with the accent on comedy rather than terror. Vincent Price, Boris Karloff, Peter Lorre and Basil Rathbone headed the cast supported by Joyce Jameson, Joe E. Brown and Beverly Hills. The play on words of the title is obvious.

CROWN AND GLORY
(G.B., 1937)

This story of the British Empire from 1895 to 1937 was made by Paramount British to celebrate the coronation of King George VI. It concludes with the speech from RICHARD II, Act II, Scene 1, "This royal throne of kings, this scepter'd isle..".

DARLING
(G.B., 1965)

Julie Christie's role as a commonplace woman who rises to marry an Italian noble with a number of affaires in between won her an Oscar. Starring with her in this film by John Schlesinger were Laurence Harvey and Dirk Bogarde. In the film, she reads the speech "This royal throne of kings, this scepter'd isle..." from RICHARD II, Act II, Scene 1.

DON Q – SON OF ZORRO
(U.S.A., 1925)

Donald Crisp directed this Douglas Fairbanks adventure which contains some quotes and near quotes from Shakespeare. Mary Astor also starred.

DOUBLE, DOUBLE TOIL AND TROUBLE
(U.S.A., 1993)

Mary-Kate and Ashley Olsen play the little girl twins who, to save their home, set out to deal with their Aunt Agatha, a wicked witch who has imprisoned her own twin sister in a mirror (Cloris Leachman in the dual role). The girls get help from an odd trio in this Dual Star/Green-Epstein Production directed by Stuart Margolin. The title and a brief quote of the two relevant lines from MACBETH are the only Shakespeare connotations.

EDGAR HAMLET
(U.S.A., 1935)

A typical Edgar Kennedy two-reel comedy from R.K.O., it tells how a quiet day is disrupted by arguments over Shakespearean speeches. Arthur Ripley directed and Florence Lake, Dot Farley and Jack Rice also starred.

EVERYTHING YOU ALWAYS WANTED TO KNOW ABOUT SEX, BUT WERE AFRAID TO ASK
(U.S.A., 1972)

Seven sketches about the obvious make up this comedy directed by Woody Allen in which he also stars. One sketch features Allen as a court jester delivering a parody of the soliloquy from Act III, Scene 1 from HAMLET.

FAME
(U.S.A., 1960)

The mixed fortunes of the pupils of a performing arts high school in Manhattan, New York, were the topic for this film directed by Alan Parker. Irene Cara, Gene Anthony Rae, Frank X. Vitolo, Darrell Kirkman and Isaac Mizrahi starred. It includes speeches and quotes from RICHARD III, Act I, Scene 1; AS YOU LIKE IT, Act V, Scene 4 and ROMEO AND JULIET, Act II, Scene 2.

LA FIN DU JOUR
(France, 1937)

Julien Duvivier directed this film about the disruption of the lives of retired actors in a special home by a new arrival, a man of many parts and a romancer. As might be expected there are quotes from Shakespeare and from ROMEO AND JULIET in particular. Michel Simon, Louis Jouvet, Victor Franzen, Madeleine Ozeray and Sylvie headed the cast.

THE FOUR FEATHERS
(G.B., 1939)

Probably the best version of this story, it was directed by Zoltan Korda and tells how a man, branded a coward, shows his true heroic colours. John Clements, June Duprez, C. Aubrey Smith and Ralph Richardson starred. Richardson, as a blind man, reads, from Braille, the speech which starts "Be not afeard; the isle is full of noises.." from THE TEMPEST, Act III, Scene 2.

THE FROG PRINCE
(G.B., 1984)

Young English girl (Jane Snowden) will only sleep with her French admirer (Alexandre Sterling) if he learns a passage from ROMEO AND JULIET. He does, of course, and recites it to her on the French Métro. Brian Gilbert directed.

FUCK HAMLET
(Germany, 1996)

Till (Till Sarrach), an unemployed actor, desperately seeks work while Anna (Marion Bordat), a street singer, arrives in Berlin to find him. Her search reveals his declining fortune. Though they eventually meet, their moments together are brief as Till is killed in an accident while looking at what is left of the infamous Wall. This DFFB production was directed in black and white "cinéma verité" style by Cheol-Mean Whang. The title apart, the film opens with Till quoting the soliloquy "To be or not to be.." (in German translation). Oliver Marlo, Otto Zorschitz, Hildegart Delfurst, Frank Lorenz Engel, Kathrin Kanne and Ina Fritsche are the other leading players. The film runs eight-two minutes.

FULL FATHOM FIVE
(G.B., 1934)

In this short film by experimental film maker Len Lye, John Gielgud is heard reading from THE TEMPEST. The title is taken from the opening line of Ariel's song from Act I, Scene 2 from the play.

GILBERT HARDING SPEAKING OF MURDER
(G.B., 1953)

Harding, a radio and television personality in Britain at the time, introduces three short murder tales. One, called FALSTAFF'S FUR COAT, concerns an actor who desires a fur coat but when he has one made, it causes him considerable trouble. Howard Marion Crawford played the actor supported by Wilfred Caithness and Andrea Melandrinos. As the story is about an actor and noting the character of the title, it is not unreasonable to assume that the actor at least quotes from Shakespeare or maybe even appears in a play scene. Otherwise, the title becomes nonsense. The Danzigers produced and Paul Dickson directed all three stories which may have been seen on television before cinema release.

GONE TO EARTH
(G.B., 1950)

Jennifer Jones, David Farrar and Cyril Cusack starred in this tale about a wild girl in Shropshire, married to a minister but who desires the local squire and her affection for her pet fox. Michael Powell and Emeric Pressburger directed. Jennifer sings "Sigh no more, ladies" from MUCH ADO ABOUT NOTHING, Act II, Scene 3, in it. The film is known as THE WILD HEART in America.

GREEN FOR DANGER
(G.B., 1946)

Alistair Sim, Sally Gray, Trevor Howard, Rosamund John and Leo Genn starred in this wartime comedy thriller. In a short scene Genn recites, and Sim finishes, "In such a night as this..." from THE MERCHANT OF VENICE, Act V, Scene 1. Sidney Gilliat directed the film.

GREGORY'S GIRL
(G.B., 1980)

Bill Forsyth directed this charming tale about an awkward Scottish schoolboy eventually finding love. Gordon John Sinclair, Dee Hepburn, Clare Crogan and Robert Buchanan starred. A classroom scene features Buchanan reading Puck's speech which ends ''...and straightway loved an ass'' from A MIDSUMMER NIGHT'S DREAM, Act III, Scene 2. This was featured in extract form as part of the Everybody's Shakespeare International Festival, London, England, 1994.

HOME GUARD
(G.B., 1941)

This short propaganda documentary directed by Donald Taylor and Ivan Moffat features Bernard Miles reading a quotation from THE LIFE AND DEATH OF KING JOHN in a Hertfordshire public house.

IN BLACK AND WHITE
(G.B., 1951)

A documentary about printing directed by John Rowden, this features a hesitant schoolboy rendering the soliloquy from Act III, Scene 1 from HAMLET. There are number of other quotations from Shakespeare's plays.

IN WHICH WE LIVE; BEING THE STORY OF A SUIT TOLD BY ITSELF
(G.B., 1943)

This propaganda short starred John Carol, Rosalyn Boulter, Russell Waters and Richard Massingham (he also directed). It tells how to make the best use of a suit. As it is being cut up it murmurs ''To die, to sleep...'' from HAMLET, Act III, Scene 1.

JACK OF ALL TRADES
(G.B., 1936)

Jack Hulbert and Robert Stenson directed this musical comedy about a penniless young man who bluffs his way into big business. Hulbert also starred with Gina Malo and Robertson Hare. At a board meeting he stirs everyone up with his delivery of ''Once more unto the breach, dear friends'' from HENRY V Act III, Scene 1.

A KING IN NEW YORK
(G.B., 1957)

Deposed King Shahdov flees to America only to find his minister has fled with the Treasury. Shahdov, tricked into making a television commercial, soon finds it a way to pay the bills. His meeting with a young boy whose parents are victims of the American witch-hunt for communists, changes his view of America. Charles Chaplin wrote, directed and played the lead in this Attica production in black and white. Clearly reflecting Chaplin's personal views of America, there are a few moments of genuine Chaplin comedy but, overall, the film is hardly a jewel in the crown of the King of Comedy. The British cast do, however, support him strongly with Dawn Addams as the female lead. Also featured are Oliver Johnston, Sid James, Maxine Audley, Michael Chaplin and Jerry Desmond. There is also the rare opportunity to witness Chaplin reciting an aggressive version of the famous soliloquy from HAMLET.

LAUGHTER IN PARADISE
(G.B., 1951)

A.B.P.C. produced this comedy about four people who must commit acts against their nature in order to inherit a legacy. In one of the stories, Michael Hordern (in a minor role) appears before magistrates and in his plea calls upon the "quality of mercy" speech from THE MERCHANT OF VENICE appealing to his own Portia in the court. He also, correctly, attributes the quotation to Shakespeare. Alistair Sim, George Cole, Fay Compton and Guy Middleton were the main plays in this black and white film directed by Mario Zampi. The scene noted above is featured in the compilation film TO SEE SUCH FUN (G.B., 1977).

THE MAN WITHOUT A FACE
(U.S.A., 1993)

Mel Gibson directed and starred in this story of a disfigured school teacher subjected to all sorts of rumours and derision. When a youth seeks proper tuition, the love of learning breaks down the barriers. Nick Stahl, Margaret Whitton, Gaby Hoffman, Geoffrey Lewis and Richard Masur formed the rest of the main cast. In the film Gibson (the teacher) likens his lot to that of Shylock and quotes from THE MERCHANT OF VENICE as he briefs his pupil. The scene was featured as an extract as part of the Everybody's Shakespeare International Festival, London, England, 1994.

LA MASCHERA CHE SANGUINA
(Italy, 1914)

An actor "recites" (well, the film was silent) a soliloquy from HAMLET, earns applause and the love of the daughter of a rich banker. There is opposition, of course, to their love but they finally marry. Alberto Capozzi played the actor in this Pasquali produced three-reeler.

THE MEN
(U.S.A., 1950)

United Artists released this Stanley Cramer production directed by Fred Zinnemann. The story about the plight of American paraplegics caused some excitement at the time, not least for a strong performance by a young Marlon Brando. It is said to contain some quotations from HAMLET. Teresa Wright, Everett Sloane and Jack Webb co-starred and scriptwriter Carl Foreman was nominated for an Oscar.

MORNING GLORY
(U.S.A., 1933)

A young Katharine Hepburn delivered the soliloquy from HAMLET in this story about a stage-struck girl who wants to become an actress. Adolphe Menjou and Douglas Fairbanks Jr. were her co-stars, Lowell Sherman directed and Miss H. won the Oscar for Best Actress in 1933. The film was remade in 1958 as *Stage Struck*.

MY DARLING CLEMENTINE
(U.S.A., 1946)

John Ford's classic story of Wyatt Earp, Doc Holliday and the gunfight at the O.K. Corral surely needs no introduction. Starring Henry Fonda, Linda Darnell, Walter Brennan, Alan Mowbray and Victor Mature. The last named, as the tubercular Holliday, completes the soliloquy from HAMLET Act III, Scene 1 for Alan Mowbray.

MY FAVOURITE SPY
(U.S.A., 1951)

Norman Z. McLeod directed this Bob Hope comedy which also featured Hedy Lamarr, Francis L. Sullivan and Mike Mazurki. Bob plays a second rate comic who has to impersonate a spy for the U.S. Government to get some microfilm. In a scene when Bob has been injected with a truth drug he picks up a skull and quotes the obvious lines from HAMLET before making the equally obvious comment about a famous singer with whom he often starred.

NEARLY A NASTY ACCIDENT
(G.B., 1961)

"Cry 'Havoc!' and let slip the dogs of war..." quotes Jimmy Edwards in this comedy about an accident-prone aircraftman who incurs his officer's wrath. Kenneth Connor causes the trouble, Shirley Eaton provides the romance and glamour. Marlow was the production company of this black and white film directed by Don Chaffey. The quote is from JULIUS CAESAR, Act III, Scene 1.

NO, MY DARLING DAUGHTER
(G.B., 1961)

This comedy, directed by Ralph Thomas, concerns the romance between a girl of independant character and her American boyfriend. Starring Juliet Mills and Rad Fulton, it features a scene in which Juliet demonstrates the sound characteristics of the dome of St. Paul's Cathedral, London, with the "Out, damned spot..." lines from Act V, Scene 1 from MACBETH.

THE NUTTY PROFESSOR
(U.S.A., 1953)

Generally considered as Jerry Lewis' best film (he produced it, directed it and starred in it), the story about a humiliated chemistry professor who invents a potion which changes him into a tough, handsome crooner owes much to the "Dr. Jekyll and Mr. Hyde" theme. According to reports (unconfirmed), the professor quotes from the speech "To be or not to be..." from HAMLET. Stella Stevens played the attractive love interest and Del Moore, Kathleen Freeman and Med Flory headed the supporting cast in this Paramount release.

OFFICE STEPS
(U.S.A., 1930)

This musical short, directed by George Hale, concerns a show producer, dancers and an old-style actor who delivers a speech full of Shakespearean quotations. This featured Jack Thompson, Gertrude McDonald, Harry McNaughton and the Phelps Sisters.

THE OLD ACTOR
(U.S.A., 1912)

W. Chrystie Miller, Mary Pickford, Kate Bruce and Charles West are the stars in this early David Wark Griffith one-reeler. The story is about a Shakespearean actor who thinks he is too old when he loses his job. He finds inspiration through a beggar and disguises himself as one. The inter-titles convey his readings of "All the world's a stage" from AS YOU LIKE IT and "...struts and frets his hour upon the stage/And is heard no more" from MACBETH, Act V, Scene 5.

PIMPERNEL SMITH
(G.B., 1941)

As Professor Horatio Smith, an apparently absent minded archaeologist prone to quoting from Shakespeare, Leslie Howard made a sort of reprise of his Scarlet Pimpernel role. Here the enemy was the Nazi regime and the problem was how to help those in peril to escape. Howard also directed this for British National (Anglo) and Francis L. Sullivan, Mary Morris and Hugh McDermott were also featured.

PRESENTING LILY MARS
(U.S.A., 1943)

The M.G.M. years for Judy Garland were generally associated with musicals. This one was no exception boasting a couple of famous bands (those of Bob Crosby and Tommy Dorsey) even though the story was about a stagestruck girl (she does the sleepwalking scene from MACBETH). Van Heflin, Richard Carlson and Marta Eggerth joined Judy in this film directed by Norman Taurog.

QUIZ SHOW
(U.S.A., 1994)

Robert Redford directed this Hollywood Pictures production based on an actual scandal from the 1950s. A Jewish contestant on a television quiz show is forced to lose in favour of a handsome young man from a good family because he is not good for the ratings. The former contestant demands an enquiry which is kept secret. The event attracts the attention of a federal investigator leading to some startling revelations. John Tuturro, Rob Morrow, Ralph

Fiennes and Paul Scofield are the principal players. At a birthday party, there is a brief family quiz involving short quotations from MACBETH, MEASURE FOR MEASURE, THE MERCHANT OF VENICE and MUCH ADO ABOUT NOTHING.

THE RAKE'S PROGRESS
(G.B., 1945)

Directed by Sidney Gilliat and starring Rex Harrison, Lilli Palmer, Margaret Johnston and Jean Kent concerns a 1930s playboy who is sent down from Oxford. A seduction scene set in a punt has the lines commencing "The barge she sat in..." from Act II Scene 2 from ANTHONY AND CLEOPATRA recited over the scene. The film has the title THE NOTORIOUS GENTLEMAN in America.

RETURN TO GLENNASCAUL
(Eire, 1951)

Produced by the Dublin Gate Theatre and directed by Hilton Edwards, this twenty-three minute short was made during a break in the filming of OTHELLO by Orson Welles. The story concerns a man who gives a stranger a lift and the stranger tells of his encounter with two women on the same road who turned out to be ghosts. The film opens with Welles, seen in silhouette on a film set, speaking as Othello and telling how he wooed Desdemona (Act I, Scene 3). He says that he is interrupting one film to make another. Welles wears his Othello beard in the film which also features Michael Laurence, Sheila Richards and Helena Hughes.

ROOM SERVICE
(U.S.A., 1938)

A dubious stage producer induces his brother-in-law to let him and his players use the hotel he manages. Trouble looms for the brother-in-law when a company executive arrives and finds that the producer has run up a large bill. The author of the play also arrives and so does mayhem. Enough mayhem to please Marxists (admirers of Groucho, Harpo and Chico, not Karl), though this R.K.O. production does not reach the heights of their earlier films. Lucille Ball and Ann Miller are around to provide female interest. In the cast, too, are Frank Albertson and Donald MacBride and William A. Seiter directed. It is included as there are two references to Shakespeare by name and Groucho delivers one line from HAMLET: "Goodnight, sweet prince".

ROSIE
(U.S.A., 1967)

Rich widow, Rosie, encouraged by her grand-daughter, decides to spend her money to the annoyance of her two greedy daughters who try to have her committed as mentally incompetent. Rosie outwits them with additional help from her lawyer. Starring Rosalind Russell, Sandra Dee and Brian Aherne, the debt to Shakespeare goes beyond the quotation "How sharper than a serpent's tooth..." (KING LEAR Act I, Scene 4). He was certainly unwittingly responsible for the idea, through diverse ways, of this Ross Hunter Production for Universal which Jacque Mapes directed.

THE SCARLET PIMPERNEL
(G.B., 1935)

Harold Young directed this version of the famous story of the foppish British aristocrat who rescues the French nobles from the guillotine during the French Revolution. Leslie Howard, Merle Oberon and Raymond Massey starred. Howard quotes "This royal throne of kings, this scepter'd isle.." speech from RICHARD II, Act II, Scene 1.

SCENE OF THE CRIME
(U.S.A., 1996)

Ben Gazzara plays a weary policeman under investigation whose daughter (Renée Ammann) falls for an actor murder suspect (Alex McArthur). It is he who, between quoting Shakespeare and driving his car (number: SHK SPIR) helps bring a serial killer to justice. Terry Winkless directed this Libra Pictures colour film.

THE SHAKESPEARE MURDERS
(Canada, 1974)

This low budget movie was made in fourteen days by producer/director Dennis Zahoruk. Garry Peterman, Alan Raeburn, Moira Sharp and Rita Floren starred in this thriller which uses references to Shakespearean plays as clues.

SHIVERING SHAKESPEARE
(U.S.A., 1929)

Anthony Mack directed this "Our Gang" comedy short which featured Jackie Cooper, Norman Chaney, Allen Hoskins, Mary Ann Jackson and Bobby Hutchins. The kids plan a stage version of 'Quo Vadis' which degenerates into a pie fight. The text parodies Shakespearean language and the manner of his Roman plays.

SON OF THE PINK PANTHER
(U.S.A, 1993)

Sooner or later, someone was bound to make this film. Logically, Blake Edwards would have the directorial chair and he does. Italian Robert Benigni plays Jacques Gambrelli, the gendarme off-spring of Maria Gambrelli and Clouseau. He rescues a beautiful Arab princess (Debrah Farentino) who has been captured by her uncle's men as hostage for money and her father's throne. Jacques is truly his father's son causing mayhem and destruction. Those who suffer include Herbert Lom and Anton Rodgers as his police superiors. Bert Kwouk (as Kato) helps him and Claudia Cardinale plays his mother. Our hero is a music and poetry lover and he quotes from Byron and Shakespeare (particularly from ROMEO AND

JULIET when he meets the princess) in this United Artists Filmauro production in colour.

SOUTH RIDING
(G.B., 1937)

Victor Saville directed this film starring Ralph Richardson, Ann Todd, Joan Ellum, Edna Best and John Clements. It concerns a working class girl with scholastic promise and the differences between the Tories and Socialists in Britain's Yorkshire. While washing up she quotes the famous "slings and arrows of outrageous fortune", from Henry V.

STAR TREK VI: THE UNDISCOVERED COUNTRY
(U.S.A., 1991)

All the cast favourites from the television series appear in this – William Shatner, Leonard Nimoy, DeForest Kelley, James Doohan, Walter Koenig, George Takei and Nichelle Nichols. Others include Christopher Plummer and William Marshall in this tale of the U.S.S. Enterprise on an uncomfortable mission of accompanying the Klingon leader (David Warner). Nicholas Meyer directed for Paramount-UIP. The dialogue is Shakespeare-themed and contains the amusing line from David Warner: "You've not discovered Shakespeare until you've read him in the original Klingon."

STRANDED
(U.S.A., 1916)

A Shakespearean actor is reduced to performing in vaudeville and falls in love with a trapeze artist. They pretend to be man and daughter but the actor is forced to kill when their secret is threatened. He recites the death scene from JULIUS CAESAR before dying at their wedding. De Wolf Hopper and Bessie Love were the main players in this Fine Arts Film Co. production in black and white. Lloyd Ingraham directed.

THAT CERTAIN AGE
(U.S.A., 1938)

It is open to debate as to where this particular film should be placed. It merits inclusion as it contains an aria sung by Deanna Durbin from the opera ROMEO AND JULIET by Gounod. This light romance directed by Edward Ludwig for Universal. Melvyn Douglas, Jackie Cooper, Irene Rich and John Halliday were also in the cast.

THIEVES LIKE US
(U.S.A., 1974)

The story of a youth who joins up with two others in a series of robberies and finds love with a simple girl only to be betrayed and gunned down had been filmed before as *They Live By Night* (U.S.A., 1948). Here, Keith Carradine and Shelley Duvall play the doomed lovers and Louise Fletcher, the betrayer. Robert Altman directed and included a scene in which the

couple make love accompanied by a radio broadcast of ROMEO AND JULIET.

THE THIRD CLUE
(G.B., 1934)

This Fox British production directed by Albert Parker with Basil Sydney, Molly Lamont and Robert Cochrane was a murder mystery about rival crooks seeking stolen jewels hidden in an old house. It was based on the novel by Neil Gordon called 'The Shakespeare Murders' and therein lies the clue, "third" or otherwise, to the film's inclusion here.

36 CHOWRINGHEE LANE
(India, 1981)

Jennifer Kendall plays the ageing, lonely spinster teacher of Shakespeare, Violet Stoneham, whose world is upset when she is assigned other duties. In search of friendship, she offers her heart and home to a young couple who abuse her kindness. This touching film has a number of quotes from Shakespeare and a reading in class from TWELFTH NIGHT. Aparna Sen directed this colour film for Film-Valas which also featured Geoffrey Kendall, Dhritiman Chatterjee, Debrashee Roy and Soni Razdan. One must not forget Kitty who plays the cat – Sir Toby Belch!

TOMBSTONE
(U.S.A., 1993)

The Wyatt Earp story hits the screen again with Kurt Russell in the role supported by Sam Elliott (Virgil Earp), Bill Paxton (Morgan Earp) and Val Kilmer (Doc Holliday). The bad guys were Michael Biehn, Stephen Lang and Powers Booth. Dana Delany was the attractive love interest. In between the two hours of gun battles and power struggles directed by George P. Cosmatos, is a theatre scene in which an actor recites in part from the pre-Agincourt speech from HENRY V. This film, in colour, was a Sean Daniel/James Jacks/Cinergi production.

THE UNDEAD
(U.S.A., 1956)

A prostitute patient is found to be the reincarnation of a witch burned at the stake in this first real horror film by Roger Corman. Pamela Duncan, Richard Garland, Allison Hayes and Richard Devon starred in this Balboa/AIP production. There are no Shakespearean quotations but much of the dialogue is in pseudo-Shakespeare form.

UP!
(U.S.A., 1976)

What does sex, rape and a man who thinks he is Adolf Hitler have to do with Shakespeare? Well, not much but who can tell what director Russ Meyer will introduce into a film? Only one thing for certain – a host of big-breasted women revealing their ample talents. Among them here are Raven De La Croix, Mary Gavin, Elaine Collins and Francesca "Kitten"

Natividad. It is she who acts as Chorus quoting from classic authors including the Bard. The, logically, male audience this film would attract, doubtless would have its mind on something other than literature!

UP POMPEII
(G.B., 1971)

Ludicrus, Ammonia, Bilius, Scrubba, Voluptia, Nausius, Erotica...hardly names that graced any of Shakespeare's plays. They were to be found, however, in this Associated London/Anglo-EMI production directed by Bob Kellett as a spin-off from the B.B.C. television series. Frankie Howerd repeated his role as the slave Lurcio and in this is mixed up in a plot to kill Nero (of which there is an incriminating scroll) in A.D. 79. Plenty of mild blue humour, scantily dressed girls and a lovely parody of "Friends, Romans, countrymen..." speech from JULIUS CAESAR by Michael Hordern. Patrick Cargill, Barbara Murray, Lance Percival and Julie Ege were also prominent in the cast.

VENGEANCE OF THE BARBARIANS
(U.S.A., 1977)

In the American West, a man known as "The Stranger" has to escort a Moorish princess back to Spain. This he does after numerous dangerous adventures. Tony Anthony, Lloyd Battista and Diana Lorys star in this oddity directed by Fernando Baldi. Sombra, an evil disfigured character in the film, quotes ludicrously the "winter of our discontent" speech from RICHARD III.

WALLS OF GLASS
(U.S.A., 1985)

As this is the story of a New York taxi driver who shows promise as a classical actor and goes to acting classes, it will be no surprise that there are a number of Shakespearean quotations. Philip Bosco played the problem-burdened mature student, Linda Thorson, his lover, and Olympia Dukakis, his ex-wife. Scott Goldstein directed for Tenth Muse Productions.

WILLIE AND PHIL
(U.S.A., 1980)

20th. Century Fox produced and Paul Mazursky directed this colour film which starred Michael Ontkean, Margot Kidder and Ray Sharkey who played the three friends who are admirers of François Truffaut and his film *Jules et Jim*. In fact they live out an on/off ménage-à-trois similar to that in the French film. Jan Miner, Tom Brennan and Julie Bovasso were also in the cast as was Lawrence Fishburne (later to star in **OTHELLO**) who quotes "To be or not to be..." in this comedy.

WITHNAIL AND I
(G.B., 1986)

Two unemployed actors on holiday in England's Lake District is the theme of this comedy drama directed by Bruce Robinson and starring Richard E. Grant, Paul McGann and Richard Griffiths. Various quotes are made from HAMLET including the speech starting "I have of late..." from Act II, Scene 2.

WITHOUT A CLUE
(U.S.A., 1988)

Dr. John Watson (Ben Kingsley) writes Sherlock Holmes stories as a front for his own brilliant detective work. He is forced to hire a rakish actor (Michael Caine) to play the character he has created. The time comes when they must face Moriarty (Paul Freeman) who is forging British bank notes and Watson realizes that his actor creation may, perhaps, have something to offer beyond his basic role. This spoof on the famous detective of literature contains some nods to Shakespeare as the intrepid pair stay at "The Shakespeare Arms" in the "Hamlet" and "King Lear" rooms plus a quote from HENRY V – "Once more unto the breach, dear friends..". An Eberhardt Stirdivant Production for ITC, Thom Eberhardt directed. Lysette Anthony, Jeffrey Jones and Nigel Davenport were also in the cast of this colour film.

WINNETOU UND SEIN FREUND OLD FIREHAND
(W. Germany, Yugoslavia, 1966)

Old Firehand (Rod Cameron saves the life of the Apache chief Winnetou (Pierre Brice) and they help save a Mexican village from a bandit gang. Technicolor and Ultrascope enhance the Yugoslav scenery in this one of a series of films based on the stories by Karl May. One of the men in the village is a British foppish former officer. He quotes from Shakespeare "All's well that ends well" saying it comes from HAMLET! Asked when HAMLET came East, he says that HAMLET went West (a figurative meaning of "west" – to disappear or die like the setting sun). Todd Armstrong, Marie Versini, Nadia Gray, Harald Leipnitz and Viktor de Kowa were the supporting players in this western directed by Alfred Vohrer released also with the English title THUNDER AT THE BORDER.

THE YELLOW CANARY
(G.B., 1943)

A woman, a supposed Nazi sympathiser, is really loyal to her country and helps foil the German attempt to blow up the harbour in Halifax, Nova Scotia. Anna Neagle played the woman with Richard Greene as the male lead, while Herbert Wilcox directed. At the start of the film, two air-raid wardens discuss the Shakespeare/Bacon controversy and one quotes the lines beginning "Be not afeard; the isle is full of noises.." from THE TEMPEST, Act III, Scene 2.

✣ ✣ ✣ ✣ ✣

The above, short as it is, merely serves to give an idea of how Shakespeare has been quoted in the cinema.

To it could be added such films as the 1937 **STAGE DOOR** with Katharine Hepburn and Ginger Rogers. As it is about a theatrical boarding house and its residents, Shakespeare is mentioned a number of times as are TWELFTH NIGHT and HAMLET but there are no quotations.

The Bard is also mentioned in **THE PRIVATE LIVES OF ELIZABETH AND ESSEX** (U.S.A., 1939). Directed by Michael Curtiz for Warner Bros., Bette Davis played the Queen who mentions Shakespeare by name and refers to his latest play. Errol Flynn, of course, played Essex while Olivia de Havilland and Alan Hale added support in this Technicolor slice of English history.

There almost is a quotation in **HELLER IN PINK TIGHTS** (U.S.A., 1960) which concerns a travelling theatrical troupe in the Wild West headed by Anthony Quinn and Sophia Loren. One of the actors is interrupted just as he starts the famous soliloquy from HAMLET.

BLAZING SADDLES (U.S.A., 1974) was also set in the West. Mel Brooks directed and Cleavon Little and Gene Wilder headed the cast list. Little, as the black sheriff, begs time to save the town saying "Don't you realise this is the last act of a desperate man?" To which Howard Johnson, the owner of the ice-cream parlour, replies: " I don't care if it's the first act of HENRY V."

It would be tempting to claim that the Shakespearean references in the last two films mentioned above are the shortest on film. Doubtless this would soon be negated by an as yet unrevealed quote or reference! Slightly longer, more frequent quotations came from Bellanger, one of the characters incorporated into the world of the fantasy hero called *Billy-Ze-Kick* (France, 1985) invented for a little girl (played by Cerise Bloc) by her father (Francis Perrin) to help her sleep.

Though slightly out of the context of this chapter, it is worth noting the spirits of Shakespearean characters which have appeared in films from time to time. For example, there are some who consider the 20th. Century Fox movie *A Gentleman's Agreement* (U.S.A., 1947) directed by Elia Kazan as being influenced by THE MERCHANT OF VENICE. Gregory Peck played the Gentile pretending to be Jewish to expose anti-Semitism. One of his speeches strongly echoes Shylock's speech "Hath not a Jew eyes?".

Similarly, the same character is felt to be paralleled in the figure of the Jewish theatre director played by Heinz Bennent in François Truffaud's *Le Dernier Métro* (France, 1980). This is pronounced in his comment during a visit by his wife played by Catherine Deneuve.

Oliver Stone's *JFK* (U.S.A., 1991) which has Kevin Costner as District Attorney Jim Garrison trying to unravel the assassination of American President John F. Kennedy could be said to have overtones of HAMLET. As Garrison says: "We have become Hamlets in our own country, children of a slain father-leader whose killers still possess the throne. The ghost of John Kennedy confronts us with the secret murder at the heart of the American dream." Stone had intended the ghost of Kennedy to appear to Garrison. Garry Olman, Sissy Spacek and Tommy Lee Jones headed the supporting cast list in this Warner Bros. film.

There was certainly no doubt of the source of a scene in the Italian film of 1969 *La Collina Degli Stivali* (one of the Terence Hill/Bud Spencer comedy "spaghetti westerns") directed by Giuseppi Colizzi. To expose the evil ways of the villain, circus performers copy Shakespeare's idea from HAMLET by acting out the misdeeds in front of him. The ring master, played by the late Lionel Stander, clearly announces the source idea.

All of which simply goes to demonstrate that in the plays, in quotations or in spirit, the works of the Bard remain a constant source of influence and inspiration.

CHAPTER XXXIV

TO BE OR NOT TO BE ...

◆ ◆ ◆ *I*ncluded in the filmography. That has been the very difficult question. Having set out rules, how easy it has been to stray from them! Certainly a number of entries offend the self-imposed guide lines set out at the start. It is hoped that the reader's "quality of mercy is not strained" and such transgressions will be forgiven. It is surely better to err on the side of qualified inclusion rather than exclusion.

There remains, however, a nebulous area of films arising from basically four factors -

1) Films surrounded by mystery and the mystery is twofold. Was the film ever made? If so, was it even Shakespeare related? So far, information is lacking to be able to prove or disprove the matter;

2) Films that have appeared on lists made in good faith by other compilers as relevant to a Shakespearean work but since disproved as so being or of doubtful connection;

3) Films whose titles or characters (correctly quoted or in parody) suggest a connection to a Shakespearean work or whose content may vaguely suggest such a connotation but one that is not strong enough to warrant inclusion elsewhere;

4) Films made for television which may have been shown outside that sphere.

This last area of film is truly suspect. In the days before the advent of video tape, all programmes were made on film. Many of these have subsequently become available for hire or purchase on the standard and sub-standard gauges. Thus they are accessible, within copyright law, to mass audiences and so merit inclusion in the filmography. In some cases it has not been possible to confirm or deny such availability. It is these that form the last group noted above.

Direct television transmissions which have subsequently been made available in videogram format or programmes especially made for that market are excluded. To attempt such a listing would open up a whole new area – an important and valid one, to be sure – of research. In the final assessment, film is film and tape is tape.

In summary, the following list, which is in alphabetical order within each section, contains a selection of items covered by these four categories. In essence, the purpose is to tie up the loose ends and to pre-empt the obvious question "Why is ABC or XYZ not included?".

Section 1:

CYMBELINE (Germany, 1925)

Traces of this title directed by Ludwig Berger occur from time to time. It has not been able to prove or disprove its existence. Berger was a noted stage director of Shakespearean plays for Max Reinhardt so it may be that it was a stage production that has been mistaken for a film. It is not listed in the Berger filmography in 'Germany' by Felix Bucher (one of a number of books issued in the Screen Series).

HAMLET (U.S.A., 1911?)

There are rumours of a version of the play starring the great Russian actress, Alla Nazimova. If such a film were made about this time it would have been made in America as she was then living there. However, though there is no evidence to confirm or deny its existence, the inclination is towards the negative as she did not, according to most records, make films until 1916.

HAMLET (Sweden, 1918)

Gosta Ekman is said to have played the title role in this film. If so details of it are impossible to find. When Ekman's son wrote his father's biography, no mention was made of it so maybe there was confusion over a stage performance.

HAMLET (Denmark, 192?)

Noted as being a Nordisk production directed by Viggo Larsen, it has not been able to confirm this. It is not listed by Nordisk whose record keeping seems to be of a high standard. Confusion may have occurred with other productions (direct and otherwise) of the play which emanated from Scandinavia about this time.

NINI 'TIRABUSCIO LA DAMA CHE INVENTO LA MOSSA (Italy, 1970)

This comedy starring Monica Vitti, Sylva Koscina, Claudio Rich and Pierre Clementi is about an actress who, after being released from prison following the assassination of Umberto I, takes up singing and accidentally invents a gesture which the public adopt. The actress dreams of playing Shakespearean roles and thus it may be that the film contains scenes or, at least, quotations from Shakespeare. Marcello Fondato directed.

ONE STEP UP (Italy, 1967)

There are two separate reports that American actress Carroll Baker was to make a film directed by Giancarlo Zagni to be called "Lady Macbeth" with the emphasis clearly on that character. Two months later, a second report notes the film under the title

CHAPTER XXXIV – TO BE OR NOT TO BE...

"One Step Up" was being made stating that this was Miss Baker's second film. As the report concerned the Italian cinema, it is presumed that second <u>Italian</u> film is meant. Miss Baker had made films before but at that time she was actively filming in Italy. Research has not revealed any such film as having been made either by Baker or Zagni.

OTHELLO (U.S.A., 1902)

Occasionally, the idea that Vitagraph made this film occurs. It is probably no more than wishful thinking for there is no evidence to support such a theory.

RICCARDO III (Italy, 1909)

Aldo Bernardini advised of an Itala Film possibly directed by Giovanni Pastrone described as a "fine picture version of a Shakespeare story". Was it this often-mentioned film or the also noted (erroneously as Shakespearean based) but untraced *Enrique III* by Pastrone. Did, as Bernardini suggests, the publicity people get the "Henrys" mixed up (HENRY IV or HENRY V?) or was the "king" wrong and the film was really RICHARD III?

ROMEO AND JULIET (U.S.A., 1903)

Rumours persist about this as a possible Vitagraph production. Again it would appear to be just what it is – a rumour.

ROMEO AND JULIET (G.B., 1926)

Mary Philbin and André Mattoni are said to have starred in a version of this play directed by E.A. Dupont. There is no evidence, as yet, to support this.

UNKNOWN, UNCONFIRMED AND/OR UNTRACED TITLES

The following represent the unsolved items from a list supplied by (but not compiled by) the Cinemateca do Museu de Arte Moderna, Rio de Janiero, Brazil. Though brief in individual film details, the list, which would seem to date from 1979 or slightly after, is both lengthy and laudable. There is but one slight fault. On a few occasions, it tends to list films under the play titles when the reference is solely to a scene from such a play within the film though the film is not itself related to Shakespeare. Of the others, the following remain unsolved mysteries.

HAMLET (U.S.S.R., 1928)

According to the list, this was directed by Leopold Sulerzicky but it has not been possible to trace the film.

IL RE LEAR (Italy, 1922)

Listed as being directed by Gustavo Salvini, the film is not in Italian film records.

MÉSURE POUR MÉSURE (France, 1935)

Max Reichman is credited with direction of this French version of MEASURE FOR MEASURE. It has not been able to substantiate this. Reichman was mainly active in the German cinema.

LA MÉGÈRE APPRIVOISÉE (France, 1933)

It has not been able to trace details of this alleged version of THE TAMING OF THE SHREW.

THE MERCHANT OF VENICE (U.S.A., 1924)

Stated as being a Luxor production this may have been an adaptation under another title or a film with scenes from the play.

ROMEO AND JULIET? (U.S.A., 1915)

Most likely the film has a different title. Efforts to find a film in which the play, in any form, is acted out by dwarfs have failed.

ROMEO I JULIET (U.S.S.R., 1925)

It has been unable to trace anything about this alleged version which Naib Genieff is said to have directed.

SEN NOCI SVATOJÁNSKÉ (Czechoslovakia, 1932)

Noted as being directed by Ladislaw Pešek, the title is Czechoslovakian for A MIDSUMMER NIGHT'S DREAM. It has not been able to trace the film but the director does seem to have had an affection for Shakespearean works.

UNTRACED TITLE (Russia, 1913)

Ivan Mosjoukine is noted as starring in a film which is in some way connected to THE WINTER'S TALE.

UNTRACED TITLE (Czechoslovakia, 1930)

The Czechoslovakian cinema authorities could not trace this film said to be related to THE MERCHANT OF VENICE and directed by Ladislaw Pesek. It may well relate to a scene from the play within a film.

UNTRACED TITLE (Czechoslovakia, 1958)

Jaroslav Prucha is noted as starring in this film which is said to be in some way related to KING LEAR.

THE VITAGRAPH ALTERNATIVES

As stated at the beginning (see **CURTAIN UP!**), there are a number of apparent duplications of productions (one by Blackton and one by Vitagraph). These are now listed out of interest:

ANTHONY AND CLEOPATRA – the two films made by Vitagraph are listed in the appropriate chapter/sections. Some sources credit the film in the first section of that chapter to Blackton and list a separate one by Vitagraph with Betty Kent as Cleopatra and Charles Chapman as Antony and Charles Kent as director. This may be the film listed in the second part of the chapter.

JULIUS CAESAR – two Vitagraph productions are noted by some sources, one directed by Blackton, the other by Ranous. The first, said to be tinted, has the following cast: Charles Kent (Julius Caesar); William V. Ranous (Mark Antony); Florence Lawrence; Paul Panzer and Earle Williams. The second has Ranous in the role of Caesar. Would Vitagraph really have made two versions of the same play in the same year?

KING LEAR – Again two versions are claimed from both Vitagraph and Blackton. The first gives the lead to Ranous with Thomas H. Ince also in the cast. The second has Maurice Costello as Lear as listed in the appropriate chapter.

Section 2:
ALIAS JULIUS CAESAR (U.S.A., 1922)

Suggested as being Shakespeare inspired, it stems neither from the Bard nor really from the famous Roman. Charles Ray starred in and directed this five-reel comedy about a man who, despite being framed by his friends, succeeds in taking his girl to a dance.

CLÉOPÂTRE (France, 1899)

This has been suggested by a number of listings as being Shakespearean based but, according to the synopsis, film no. 176 in Méliès catalogue of films does not have that honour. In 131 ft. (40 m.), as maidens adorn the tomb of Cleopatra, an evil old man forces open the tomb and cuts up the mummy to burn it. From the smoke comes a living Cleopatra and other sensations. Hardly Shakespeare, but an interesting item which has, sadly, been lost.

CLEOPATRA (U.S.A., 1963)

It took 20th. Century Fox two hundred and forty-three minutes and an incredible amount of money (it almost finished the company) to wander through the two main love affaires. It was, however, the off-screen love life of the principal stars, Elizabeth Taylor and Richard Burton which attracted attention. Rex Harrison played Julius Caesar and earned himself an Academy Award nomination for Supporting Actor. The colour photography in ToddAO brought the award for Cinematography-Colour to Leonard Shamroy with other awards for art direction/set decoration and special effects. Martin Landau, George Cole and Roddy McDowall headed the largely British supporting cast and Joseph Mankiewicz directed. Many suggest, and have so listed, that the film is based on Shakespeare. Of course, the same basic story as related in ANTONY AND CLEOPATRA and JULIUS CAESAR is covered in this film. It could hardly be otherwise as similar sources and history itself are used. Unlike the earlier epic from DeMille which used at least the spirit of Shakespearean dialogue in some scenes and

some of the characters, this one makes no such attempt. For the record, both the Fox files and the screen credits note that the film is based on "Plutarch, Suetonius, Appian, other ancient sources and 'The Life and Times of Cleopatra' by C. M. Franzero" which is surely sufficient proof.

UN ENREDO DE FAMILIA (Spain, 1943)

Directed by Ignacio F. Iquino, this Campa-CIFESA production is about two families, the Capitetos and the Tontescos, who are bitter enemies. A son of the first and a daughter of the second fall in love, marry and produce two sets of twins. These are separated when they are orphaned with one pair each in the care of the two families. Many years later, the two sets of twins meet again causing confusion and mistakes. Mercedes Vecino, Antonio Murillo, Francisco Martínez Soria and José Jaspe headed the cast list in this comparatively short (sixty-two minutes) film in black and white which clearly took its inspiration from ROMEO AND JULIET and THE COMEDY OF ERRORS.

JAJAUMA NARASHI (Japan, 1966)

Directed by Sugie Toshio, this is about Masao who is nagged by his wife, Sachiko, as he is not matching his friend Youichi in career progress. He arranges a meeting with a club hostess, Setsuko, while his wife is away with her neighbour, Fumie, keeping an eye on the latter's husband on a staff tour. Masao is found out but all ends well when Youichi has an accident and Masao is promoted to the New York office to his wife's delight. Well, apart from two dominant wives the film would not seem to justify the listing as Shakespearean influenced it has received though there are obviously shrews to be tamed.

JULIUS SIZZER (U.S.A., 1931)

It has been suggested that this was a parody of JULIUS CAESAR. In fact it was an animated short starring Tom and Jerry (not the famous Hanna-Barbera creations) and it was indeed intended as a parody, but of the Warner Bros. film *Little Caesar*.

KOMEDIA POMYLEK (Poland, 1968)

Sometimes listed as a Polish version of THE COMEDY OF ERRORS, it simply is not. It is a compilation for cinema release of three stories from literature – none Shakespearean – which were originally made for television.

MERA SPORED MERA (Bulgaria, 1981)

The title translates as MEASURE FOR MEASURE and has been noted by some sources as being a three-part adaptation of the play. The Bulgarska Nacionalna Filmoteka is quite clear about the matter. The title is the only allusion to Shakespeare, the topic of the film being quite different.

NOCHE DE REYES (Spain, 1947)

Listed by a number of sources as being a musical version of TWELFTH NIGHT, it is a story of love and vengeance and is based on a "zarzuela" (a form of operetta). Confusion has probably occurred as January 6, known in many countries as "Twelfth Night" (Epiphany), is called in Spain "Los Reyes" and thus that early part of the day from midnight is known as "Noche de Reyes" when the children receive their gifts. The film is of interest in its own right and starred Fernando Rey.

ROMEO I JULCIA (Poland, 1932)

The title surely needs no translation but it is, so the Polish film authorities confirm, the only connection to Shakespeare. Directed by Jan Nowina Przybylski, the title refers to the name of the matrimonial agency featured in the film.

EIN SOMMERNACHTSTRAUM (W. Germany, 1985)

Despite the title (the usual one for A MIDSUMMER NIGHT'S DREAM in German), anyone looking for a hint of Shakespeare will be disappointed and maybe even shocked. The reverse will apply to anyone looking for fifteen girls stripping. For what it is worth, Hannes Winkler directed and Birgitta Cimarolli was the leading "actress".

SAVKARI PASH (India, 1925)

Baburao Painter's silent film in Marathi also bears the title INDIAN SHYLOCK. Well, the main character is a greedy money-lender but that is far as a Shakespearean relationship goes. The film was remade in 1936 with the money-lender having the help of a sexy courtesan.

TROLD KAN TAEMMES (Denmark, 1914)

Directed by Helgar Madsen, this has been noted as being a version of THE TAMING OF THE SHREW by some but this is denied by the Danish Film Institute.

Section 3:
AJAWAT HAMLET (Algiers, 1996)

This tale of two sisters stranded in Paris who meet an old man who symbolises the father they lost when their parents divorced was directed by Abdelkrim Bahloul. The title apart (it translates as "The Hamlet Sisters"), the synopsis suggests a further relationship in the lost father syndrome. Emilie Altmayer and Bérénice Bejo starred.

ALL'S WELL THAT ENDS WELL (G.B., 1904)

Noted as being a comedy produced by Williamson, it is doubtful if this was relative to Shakespeare beyond the title.

ALL'S WELL THAT ENDS WELL (G.B., 1906)

A rejected lover catches a thief and wins the girl is the theme in this Gaumont production and it is not from Shakespeare though the title is.

ALL'S WELL THAT ENDS WELL (U.S.A., 1907)

A Selig production, this, the title apart, had nothing to do with the play.

ALL'S WELL THAT ENDS WELL (U.S.A., 1908)

Despite emanating from Vitagraph which was responsible for so many early screen adaptations of Shakespearean works, this was not one of them. The alternative title, A CASE OF SPIRITS, may well give a clue to its content.

ALAS! POOR YORICK (U.S.A., 1913)

Alas! poor Shakespeare, for he had nothing to do, apart from the quotation, with this Selig comedy release.

ALL'S WELL THAT ENDS WELL (G.B., 1904)

James Williamson directed this early comedy which took only the title from the Bard.

ALL'S WELL THAT ENDS WELL (G.B. 1906)

...and it was for a rejected lover who won his girl after catching a thief in this Gaumont comedy short which had nothing to do with Shakespeare.

ALL'S WELL THAT ENDS WELL (U.S.A., 1909)

A Pathé production, the title was the sole relationship to the Bard.

ALL'S WELL THAT ENDS WELL (U.S.A., 1910)

The title was obviously a popular one, but, again, it was the only connection to Shakespeare in this Dandy Film, The Electrograph Co. of Philadelphia production.

ALL'S WELL THAT ENDS WELL (G.B., 1913)

A Cricks and Martin Production, this comedy about a girl posing as a maid to save herself from marriage is clearly not from Shakespeare, despite the title of the film.

ALL'S WELL THAT ENDS WELL (France, 1913)

An Urban/Éclipse/Radios production, this concerned confusion over rooms at an inn. Shakespeare registered for the title only.

ALL'S WELL THAT ENDS WELL (Italy, 1913)

Cines mixed money lending and misunderstanding in this but borrowed the title, in translation, from Shakespeare.

ALL'S WELL THAT ENDS WELL (France, 1913)

This romance settled on the Middle Ages, not Shakespeare. Éclair produced.

ALL'S WELL THAT ENDS WELL (U.S.A., 1914)

As it probably did in this Princess production about the mix-up of two suitors seeking the hands of a widow and her daughter. Alas, the film knew not Shakespeare well enough!

ALL'S WELL THAT ENDS WELL (U.S.A., 1914)

This was produced by Mutual Educational. It borrowed the title from Shakespeare but does not appear to have given much of educational interest.

ALL THE WORLD'S A STAGE (G.B., 1915)

Made by Hepworth, Shakespeare provided possibly a little more than the title for this tale of a stage tragedian whose magic potion renders his pupils stage-struck. Alexander Aitchbee starred; Frank Wilson directed.

ALL THE WORLD'S A STAGE (G.B., 1917)

A Hagen-Double production, this was about an actress who shoots a producer. Maybe Shakespeare felt the same way about the producers of his plays but he was responsible for the title only here.

ALL THE WORLD'S A STOOGE (U.S.A., 1941)

Who says so? The Three Stooges do and so it would be wrong to expect any Shakespearean content beyond the allusion in the title.

ARIEL (Finland, 1988)

Despite the character title from THE TEMPEST, despite the fact that the film was made the year after **HAMLET LIIKEMAAILMASSA** by the same director, Aki Kaurismäki, he himself said: "The title has nothing to do with Shakespeare, I got the idea* when I was fixing up my British-made motor bike."

*for the title. Ariel is the trade name of a motor cycle in Britain.

BILLY MERSON SINGING "DESDEMONA" (G.B., 1926)

Despite the character in the title, the content in this was a comic song from De Forest Phonofilms and not the lady from OTHELLO. It was the first British made "sound-on-film" film.

COMEDY OF ERRORS (U.S.A., 1913)

Only the title has any relationship to Shakespeare in this Solax production.

A COMEDY OF ERRORS (G.B., 1915)

Cecil Birch directed this Bamford production but did not go much beyond the title for Shakespearean inspiration. The story was about a poet involved with two girls of different social standing but with the same names.

DIE FLIEGENTÜTEN OTHELLO (Germany, 1918)

This comedy translates as "The Fly-Killer Othello". What a surprise! Everyone thought it was just Desdemona that had suffered so...

FRATELLO HOMO SORELLA BONA-NEL BOCCACCIO SUPERPROIBITO (Italy, 1973)

As the title suggests, this has nothing to do with Shakespeare and, frankly, little to do with Boccaccio either. It was simply one of the many sex orientated films Italy produced around this time. It is noted here simply because the English release title was GET THEE TO A NUNNERY which is taken from HAMLET.

THE FURIES (U.S.A., 1930)

H. B. Warner, Jane Winton, Montagu Love and Lois Wilson were the principal players in this First National production directed by Alan Crosland. The story concerns a son who accuses his mother and her lover of his father's murder. The similarity to HAMLET ended there.

HAMLET (Brazil, 1977)

The title to this cartoon directed by Jos Rubero Sigueira is the only relationship to Shakespeare. It is about the United Nations Organisation's Declaration of Human Rights.

LÉONCE PLAYS OTHELLO (France, 1914)

One of the many comedies made by Léonce Perret for Gaumont, it did at least have a theme of jealousy in it.

MASS FÜR MASS (E. Germany, 1963)

The titled is interpreted as MEASURE FOR MEASURE but this cartoon by Günter Rätz has nothing to do with the Shakespearean play of the same name.

A MIDSUMMER NIGHT'S SEX COMEDY (U.S.A., 1982)

Woody Allen was responsible for this which has little to do with the Bard apart from the obvious allusion in the title.

LE MIROIR DE VENISE, UNE MÉSAVENTURE DE SHYLOCK (France, 1905)

The character name and personality are the only connections with Shakespeare here though some claim that there is more. Méliès uses an alchemist for his trickery. When Shylock pays, to his chagrin, a fortune to see a vision of his future wife, he does indeed see her but she changes to a toothless hag. He also sees himself on the gallows and the hangman waiting for him. He runs off leaving the alchemist to divide his fee among his cronies. On reflection, perhaps, these 213 ft. (65 m.) of film do offer a little of the Shakespearean spirit of the usurer being outwitted financially.

LOVE'S LABOR LOST (U.S.A., 1899)

The close similarity in title to the Shakespearean play, is the only connection in this early American Mutoscope production.

LOVE'S LABOUR LOST (G.B., 1904)

The Warwick Trading Co. had little thought for the play by Shakespeare as this comedy is about a well-dressed man throwing a tramp into a pond.

LOVE'S LABOUR'S LOST (U.S.A., 1912)

It may have been but the Lubin Manufacturing Co. found it to make this short which had nothing else to do with Shakespeare.

LOVE'S LABOR LOST (U.S.A., 1914)

Unable to write love letters, a man uses the telephone with satisfactory results in this cartoon which owed only the title to the Bard.

DIE LUSTIGEN WEIBER VON WIEN (Germany, 1931)

Géza von Bolvary directed Lee Parry, Willi Forst, Paul Hörbiger and Oskar Sima in this tale about a man fooled by women. The slight echo of the Shakespearean theme from THE MERRY WIVES OF WINDSOR can be caught here as can the obvious parody on the German translation of the title.

MEASURE FOR MEASURE (U.S.A., 1909)

Only the title was Shakespeare related in this release from the Lubin Manufacturing Co. Honesty demands that it should be noted that some sources claim that it is based on the Shakespearean play.

MISCHIEVOUS PUCK (G.B., 1911)

Puck plays tricks on a haymaker, a gardener and a motor car in this Natural Colour Kinematograph Co. production. The Puck character is the only connection to Shakespeare but the film is interesting because of its colour system (Kinemacolor) invented by George A. Smith. It was a colour illusion system using rotating red and green filters and was said to be effective.

A MODERN OTHELLO (U.S.A., 1914)

Marguerite Fischer and Harry Pollard played the wife and jealous husband in this comedy of modern life. The title character and jealousy is about as close as it came to the Shakespeare play.

A MODERN PORTIA (U.S.A., 1912)

In this one from the Lubin Manufacturing Co., a woman lawyer defends her own father who has lost his memory. The name and female lawyer character are the only Shakespearean connections.

A MODERN PORTIA (U.S.A., 1913)

Like the other film of the same title, it is the female lawyer and name aspects that form the loose Shakespearean link. Here, the lawyer takes legal action against her lover for stealing from another woman.

MUCH ADO ABOUT...!! (G.B., 1912)

...Nothing and certainly not about Shakespeare for this comedy was about a jealous man who hires a detective to investigate his wife's locked box. It was made by Cricks and Martin.

MUCH ADO ABOUT MOUSING (U.S.A., 1964)

Forget Shakespeare! The clue to the content of this M.G.M. colour cartoon is in the last word of the title. It concerns the efforts of a very famous screen cat to trap his equally famous rodent opponent. Chuck Jones directed.

MUCH ADO ABOUT NOTHING (U.S.A., 1909)

Edison used only the title for this short.

OIL'S WELL THAT ENDS WELL (U.S.A., 1958)

The title parody is the only (near) relationship to Shakespeare in this comedy from The Three Stooges.

PIMPLE'S MERRY WIVES (G.B., 1916)

A Piccadilly production directed by and starring Fred Evans, this tells of a law allowing a man to have six wives chosen by his first wife. Falstaff might well have approved but Shakespeare never wrote the script for this one!

PIMPLE'S MIDSUMMER NIGHT'S DREAM (G.B., 1916)

Another Piccadilly production with Fred Evans starring and directing, no fairies and romance were present in this – just a nightmare after eating lobster.

PUCK'S PRANKS ON A SUBURBANITE (G.B., 1906)

A gardener suffers the tricks of Puck. The character is again the only relationship to the Bard. Urban Trading Co. produced this.

THE QUALITY OF MERCY (G.B., 1914)

The story is about a magistrate who adopts a girl who has been caught stealing bread for her starving mother in the Hepworth production directed by Warwick Buckland. Alma Taylor and Harry Royston headed the cast list. Even with the presence of a magistrate (a lower court judge equivalent) in the plot, it would be straining more than the quality of mercy (from THE MERCHANT OF VENICE) to suggest a stronger Shakespearean connection.

QUEENIE OF THE NILE (U.S.A., 1915)

This comedy from Lubin Manufacturing Co. was actually a comedy about a man hired to help (as Antony) a woman who thinks she is Cleopatra but he falls for her maid, Charmian. A blow to the head restores the woman and all ends well. Not quite the Bard's version!

ROMEO AND JULIET AT THE END OF NOVEMBER (Czechoslovakia, 1971)

Directed by Jaroslav Balik, this feature has nothing beyond the characters of the title to connect it to Shakespeare.

ROMEO CONTRA JULIETA (Mexico, 1968)

Julián Soler directed and Angélica Maria, Alberto Vázquez, Fernando Soler and Alejandro Suárez starred in this Chapultepec production. The obvious title reference apart, there was nothing else to relate this Mexican comedy to Shakespeare.

THE SHAMING OF THE TRUE (G.B., 1930)

Walter Creighton directed this comedy about a woman in the audience who objects to the film and joins in it. The spooneristic title is the sole relationship to Shakespeare. Maisie Gay and Roy Roston starred in this British Instructional production.

SHYLOCK (India, 1940)

A film in the Tamil language directed by Sama Ramu, the title connotation is clear. It may, however, have a deeper relationship to Shakespeare. The theme of the film obviously involved a moneylender.

DER SHYLOCK VON KRAKAU (Germany, 1913)

Certainly there is a hint of Shakespearean motif in this story about the daughter of a pious Jew who steals from her father and runs off with her lover who has borrowed money from him. The father has a mental breakdown but recovers. The daughter dies. It was produced by Projection A.G.-Union.

THE SPIRIT OF THE HEATH (G.B., 1921)

This Zodiac production featured the Puck character showing the beauty of the world to a foolish young wife. The character name was as far as the Shakespeare connection went, however.

TAMING A SHREW (G.B., 1915)

Lily Ward starred in this Pyramid production about a nagging wife who tries to get rid of her husband. The character of the wife and the close similarity of the title to THE TAMING OF THE SHREW bear only a slight relationship to Shakespeare.

TAMING MRS. SHREW (U.S.A., 1913)

This Rex production was about a nagging wife. That and the play on the title are the sole connotations with the Bard.

TAMING OF THE SHREWD (U.S.A., 1913)

Knickerbocker may have taken the inspiration for the title from Will Shakespeare but the story was about a woman whose suffragette activities lead her to neglect her house work.

TRES ROMEOS Y UNA JULIETA (Mexico, 1960)

The title may suggest value for money in portrayal terms but this Mexican comedy directed by Chano Ureta had nothing to do with the Bard. For the record, Jorge Mistral, Antonio Badú, Elvira Quintana and Irma Dorantes headed the cast list.

EIN WINTERNACHTSTRAUM (Germany, 1935)

An old banker is suspected of theft when he reserves expensive rooms in a hotel. He is merely trying to help a poor employee of the bank to find a rich husband. That is the basis of this film directed by Géza von Bolvary with Wolf Albach-Retty, Hans Moser, Theo Lingen and Magda Schneider. The relationship to Shakespeare appears in the coincidental merging of two German translation of play titles – "Ein Sommernachtstraum" (A MIDSUMMER NIGHT'S DREAM) and "Ein Wintermärchen" (A WINTER'S TALE).

A WINTER'S TALE (U.S.S.R., 1945)

Ivanov-Vano directed this Russian cartoon which, title similarities apart, has nothing to do with Shakespeare which has been confirmed by the appropriate Russian authorities.

As pointed out elsewhere, characters and themes from Shakespearean works have, down through time, been applied to give a generic meaning to them. Thus, "Romeo" means "lover", "Othello" means "jealous husband", "Shylock" identifies as "avaricious and miserly". In consequence, many works of stage and screen relate to these but without further reference to the source. To list all such films would hardly be truthful within the context of this work and would be, frankly, an impossible task. To annotate the films with "Romeo" in the title would, alone, mean a minor work in itself. The foregoing, therefore, serves merely to show how such references have been used – and misused – in the film world.

Section 4:
B.B.C. Television programmes.

Other than those issued on videogram by the B.B.C. itself or by other companies under licence, the programmes by this famous British state radio and television company are not generally available to the public. Over the decades the B.B.C. has been responsible for some really outstanding

CHAPTER XXXIV – TO BE OR NOT TO BE...

Shakespearean transmissions. Some of these are known to exist on 16 mm. (logically, those made before the days of video) and a sample of them is listed out of interest.

HENRY IV (1961)
d. *Michael Hayes.*
l.p. *Frank Baxter (Narrator); Tom Fleming; George A. Cooper; Sean Connery; Robert Hardy, Frank Pentingell.*
b.w. 4 x 75 mins.

Scenes and analysis in four parts: Rebellion in the North; The Road to Shrewsbury; The New Conspiracy; Uneasy lies the Head.

HENRY V (1961)
d. *Michael Hayes.*
l.p. *Frank Baxter (Narrator); Robert Hardy; Juliet Cooke.*
b.w. 2 x 75 mins.

Scene and analysis in two parts: Signs of War; Band of Brothers.

HENRY VI (1961)
d. *Michael Hayes.*
l.p. *Frank Baxter (Narrator); Terry Scully; Julian Glover.*

A five part analysis with scenes: The Red Rose and the White; The Fall of a Proctor; The Rabble from Kent; The Morning's War; The Sun in Splendour.

RICHARD II (1961)
d. *Michael Hayes.*
l.p. *Frank Baxter (Narrator); David Williams; Tom Fleming.*
b.w. 2 x 75 mins.

Analysis, commentary and scenes in two parts: The Hollow Crown; The Deposing of a King.

RICHARD III (1961)
d. *Michael Hayes.*
l.p. *Frank Baxter (Narrator); Paul Daneman; Julian Glover.*

Scenes, analysis and commentary in two parts: The Dangerous Brother; The Boar Hunt.

✢ ✢ ✢ ✢ ✢

Hallmark Hall of Fame:
In 1951, Hallmark, an international company selling greetings cards, sponsored a weekly interview show hosted by Sarah Churchill, daughter of Sir Winston Churchill. This developed into the presentation of classic works.

The first Shakespearean work was HAMLET in 1953. Then followed the four listed below. A version of THE TEMPEST came next in 1960 and the series closed for the time being with Maurice Evans

repeating his role as MACBETH which saw cinema release and is thus listed appropriately. These that follow are known to exist in 16 mm. format and may be available to the public.

MACBETH (U.S.A., 1954)

This Hallmark Hall of Fame production was directed by Maurice Evans who also played the title role with Judith Anderson as Lady Macbeth. The original transmission for television was in colour for the privileged few who had the proper sets and were in the right area. A kinescope transfer exists but it is not known if it is publicly available. It runs for two hours.

RICHARD II (U.S.A., 1954)

Maurice Evans appeared in the title role of this production which George Schaefer directed. Sarah Churchill was his co-star and Kent Smith, Bruce Gordon and Richard Purdy were also featured. The existing kinescope version is in black and white and lasts two hours.

THE TAMING OF THE SHREW (U.S.A., 1956)

George Schaefer directed this which starred Maurice Evans, Lili Palmer, Diane Cilento and Philip Bourneuf. The ninety-minute production was broadcast in colour but the kinescope version is in black and white.

TWELFTH NIGHT (U.S.A., 1957)

Maurice Evans, Rosemary Harris, Dennis King and Denholm Elliott headed the cast in this colour broadcast which lasted eighty-nine minutes. David Greene directed. The existing kinescope record is in black and white.

✢ ✢ ✢ ✢ ✢

German and Austrian Television productions:
Some of these have already been noted in the appropriate chapter as they have received screenings outside the sphere of television. The following may also have been shown in cinemas:

AUF DEN SPUREN VON OTHELLO (Austria, 1997)

Confession time – this is truly a television programme from ORF. However, as its subject has obvious appeal and it includes film scenes, it was felt prudent to note it. A number of singers/actors portray the role – Chris Merritt (in the Rossini opera version), John Vickers with Mirella Freni as Desdemona from the film version of the Verdi opera, and Placido Domingo with Katia Ricciarelli as his Desdemona from their film version. Domingo appears in another version and Vladimir Atlantow is seen in the role also. The only non-operatic extract is from a German language version of the play featuring Wolfgang Reichman and Heidelinde Weis as the principal characters. This is obviously on film (does the whole version exist?)

and is in black and white. For those not interested in the subject, there are always the beauties of Venice and Cyprus to enjoy. Heidelinde Rudy directed this half-hour documentary.

KOMÖDIE DER IRRUNGEN (W. Germany, 1964)

One of a series from Bavaria Atelier, this version of THE COMEDY OF ERRORS was directed by Hans Dieter Schwarze in black and white. Erik Schumann, Irene Marhold, Claus Biederstaedt, Klaus Schwarzkopf, Manfred Lictenfeld, Edgar Wiesemann, Hanns Ernst Jägers, Ruth Kähler, Hans Martin, Margaret Carl and Hildegard Schmahl were among the cast of this ninety-six minute production.

SHALOM HAMLET (Germany, Israel, 1998)

Subtitled "Israelisch-deutsche Begegnungen Im Theater", the film (it is noted so) was produced by ZDF/3sat with an eye clearly on the fiftieth anniversary of the creation of Israel as a state. It deals with modern theatre in both Germany and Israel with obvious political overtones. A modern version of JULIUS CAESAR is featured in brief extract as an example of political incitement. HAMLET, apart from the titular umbrella use to mean theatre, is featured, in extract form, as "Die Hamletmaschine" a modern music-ballet by H. Müller which parodies the original text at times. Bettina Petry and Olov Schröer directed this sixty-minute documentary in colour.

SUCH SWEET THUNDER (W. Germany, Belgium, 1959)

Produced by SudwestFunk and Television Belge, this was clearly made on film. Chuck Kerremans directed this thirty-five minute ballet version of the suite by Duke Ellington whose orchestra provides the music. Maurice Béjart directed the Ballet-Théâtre de Paris. The Three Witches from MACBETH, ROMEO AND JULIET and HAMLET all have modern settings while the OTHELLO, A MIDSUMMER NIGHT'S DREAM, THE TAMING OF THE SHREW and ANTONY AND CLEOPATRA sequences are, within the terms of a modern ballet group, more conventional in setting. In all, this is an unusual little film which may have been seen other than on television. It was first transmitted in 1961.

WAS IHR WOLLT (W. Germany, 1962)

One of a number of films made for television by Bavaria Atelier in black and white, this was directed by Franz Peter Wirth with Karl Michael Volger, Karl Bockx, Ingrid Andree, Hans Cossy, Peter Lühr, Benno Sterzenbach, Fritz Wepper, Heidelinde Weiss and Hans Lothar starring. It is, of course, the German version of TWELFTH NIGHT. It runs for one hundred and sixty-four minutes. The same company and director were responsible for a television version of **HAMLET** which was shown in cinemas.

WAS IHR WOLLT (E. Germany, 1963)

Deutscher Fernsehenfunk produced this black and white version of TWELFTH NIGHT and Lothar Bellag directed. This ninety-six minute version may have been screened in cinemas or at festivals so it is worth noting the principal players: Gerry Wolf, Günther Simon, Joanna Clas and Christel Bodenstein.

✣ ✣ ✣ ✣ ✣

Russian television productions:
Like many countries, Russia has produced numerous telefilms/teleplays. Few have ever been seen outside the former Communist Bloc countries. Some have found their way to the big screen and are noted elsewhere. Sadly, the political differences which existed between the former U.S.S.R. and many parts of the world restricted access to information. The Shakespearean film output from that part of the world has been impressive and it seems worth noting, in brief, known Shakespearean telefilms. Whether or not they have been seen other than on television is not known but let that not be a deterrent to their inclusion:

ANTOINI I KLEOPATRA (1980)

p.c. *Ekran.*
d. *Evgenia Simonov, Leonid Lchelkin.*
l.p. *Mikhail Ulbanov; Julia Borisova.*

Obviously, this is ANTONY AND CLEOPATRA. It would be interesting to see a Russian Cleopatra to compare with the more familiar ones. No further details are known.

CORIOLAI (1983)

p.c. *Studia Telefilmov Erevai.*
d. *R. Kallanai, A. Airaletia.*
l.p. *Ch. Abramai; O. Galoia; M. Manukia; Ch. Haeapetia.*

Again, a little-filmed Shakespeare work – CORIOLANUS – and again, there is no further information.

DVENADTSATAVA NOCH (1978)

p.c. *Ekran.*
d. *Oleg Tabakov, B. Chamrov.*
l.p. *Marina Neelova; Anastasia Bertinskai; Yuri Bogatyurev; Konstantin Raikine; Boris Sherbakov; Oleg Tabokov.*

Not the first version of TWELFTH NIGHT to grace Russian screens (big or small), of course but, regrettably, no further details are known of this particular one.

GAMLET (1969)

p.c. *Ekran.*
d. *S. Evlachishvili.*

l.p. *Maris Liepa; Irina Kholina; M. Alfimova; Sergei Raduenko; A. Kondratov.*

This is a ballet version from the Bolshoi Theatre, in colour, with music by Dmitri Shostakovich adapting some of the music he wrote for a stage performance and that he wrote for the film **GAMLET**.

KOROL DJON
(1983)

p.c. *Tsentraloe Televidenie.*
d. *Kh. Abramyah, A. Kaebmina.*
l.p. *Sos Sarkisyan; A, Movsesyan; A. Manuyan; G. Aspanyan.*

It is a pity that no further details of this can be traced for versions of KING JOHN are not plentiful.

KOROL LIR
(1984)

p.c. *Tsentraloe Televidenie. d. L. Kheifest, V. Semakov.*
l.p. *Mikhail Tsarev; Evgenia Glushenko; Viktor Lavlov; Afanasii Kochetkov.*

No further details of this version of KING LEAR are known.

MERA ZA MERU
(1988)

p.c. *Tsentrale Televidenie.*

d. *I. Petrov.*
l.p. *V. Efremov; A. Inoeiemtsev; N. Trusov; A Agarkov.*

It is not known if this version of MEASURE FOR MEASURE was made in colour or black and white. Neither is the playing time known.

ROMEO I DJULIETA
(1978)

p.c. *Ekran.*
d. *M. Bolodarski.*
l.p. *Natalia Bessnertnova; Mikhail Lavrovski.*

No further details of this ballet film with music by Tchaikovsky are available.

Swedish television:
The following film was made for television but is on film and thus available for conventional showing:

DEN TRAGISKA HISTORIEN OM HAMLET, PRIZ AR DANMARK
(1984)

p.c. *Swedish Television.*
d. *Ragnar Lyth.*
l.p. *Stellan Skargaard; Mona Malm; Pernella Walgren; Frej Lindquist; Sven Lindberg.*

This version of HAMLET was made in colour.

FINAL CURTAIN

The raising of finance for a Shakespeare film has been far from easy for independent producers. It has also been said that the Shakespeare film is box-office poison. Yet facts concerning financial returns do often contradict this though it would be ludicrous to suggest that his name was synonymous with box-office success. Like most authors whose works have been transposed to the screen, there have been successes and failures.

The cinema has seen big-budget films fail dismally; small-budget ones pull in incredible returns. Critically acclaimed films have sunk into obscurity; others, ravaged by the critics, rebuke these writers with their popularity. The Shakespeare film is no exception.

Irrespective of critical opinion (and even that can change with the passage of time), it can be said that, with a few exceptions, the ultimately successful Shakespeare film may have taken a little longer to bring its rewards. If nothing else, this surely reflects the continuing interest in such works.

Equally, the steady flow of these films, either direct or derivative, is an indication of the same. Nor must the dedication to such films by directors and the thespians themselves be overlooked. Whilst it is easy to see, for example, why noted Shakespearean actors such as Tree, Olivier, Gielgud and Branagh should wish to convey their special talents to the screen, the desire of those not normally associated with this type of role is quite incongruous. That actors like Mel Gibson and directors like Roman Polanski do so – and in both of the cases noted, with artistic success – reflects well upon all concerned, not least, of course, upon Shakespeare.

Every lover of Shakespeare will have his/her own favourite play and, logically, film. The appreciation of the latter will be, as it should be, irrespective of the ramblings of critics or the clattering of box-office tills. Certainly over the years the public, Shakespeare devotees included or not, has shown its feelings by seeing the films, watching them on television or by buying videograms of them.

If the number of versions produced of any given play is the criteria of popularity, then ROMEO AND JULIET (most filmed in all versions of all types and thus the most popular story base) and HAMLET (most filmed in direct versions by a long way) are surely the leaders. As runners-up in the competition, if a competition it be, come OTHELLO and MACBETH. Though reflecting public choice and thus financial returns, it is regrettable that a number of Shakespeare's works remain uncommitted to film.

It is to be hoped that this situation may change. In temporal relationship to Shakespeare the cinema is still a baby, albeit one that has grown rapidly. Maybe the future will produce newer artistes, directors and producers of vision to look beyond proven popularity of title and thus fill the obvious omissions. The signs are there (if reports are true) for it is said that Kenneth Branagh has formed a new production company (The Shakespeare Film Co.) and the first film is to be a musical version of LOVE'S LABOUR'S LOST with himself and Alicia Silverstone as the leading players. A new MACBETH may also be in line from the same source if reports are correct.

The international success of **SHAKESPEARE IN LOVE** certainly bodes well for Shakespere/ Shagspere/Shaxper/Shakeser (or whatever other variation of his name may occur) who, in an extensive poll and against impressive competition, was voted by the British as the man of the millenium. Even a little national bias cannot diminish such an honour. Certainly in the mind of actress Gwyneth Paltrow, obviously happy with her Oscar, he is held in high esteem. In an interview in the Spanish magazine 'Fotogramas' (April, 1999) she was asked if she thought that, bearing in mind the success of **SHAKESPEARE IN LOVE**, it would become better known than the Bard's own works. She was of the opinion that there was no film that could stand in the shadow of Shakespeare's works reminding us that, three centuries after his demise, his works are still being performed and adapted.

How true this is for, apart from the new productions noted (albeit in brief) in their appropriate places, the following are said to be in various stages of production: a contemporary version of HAMLET with Ethan Hawke in the main role; another version of A MIDSUMMER NIGHT'S DREAM titled (provisonally?) **MIDSUMMER**; Tim Blake Nelson as a college boy OTHELLO in O; and two free versions of MACBETH – **MACBETH IN MANHATTAN** directed by Greg Lombardo and another, as yet untitled, directed by Colin Perera.

Interviewed by the the aforementioned 'Fotogramas' (October, 1996) actor Al Pacino surmised that if Shakespeare were alive now, he would be writing for the cinema. The film world, however, cannot rely upon such an interesting speculation however hypothetically rewarding it may be. It can only rely upon what exists and that is a healthy legacy indeed. The works of the Bard may not always come directly to the screen but they will continue to inspire. Shakespeare wrote: "If music be the food of love, play on..." (opening line of TWELFTH NIGHT). Perhaps he will forgive a parody of those words: "If Shakespeare be the food of scripts, film on...".

GENTLEMEN AND FRIENDS, I THANK YOU FOR YOUR PAINS...

...t o which must be added gratitude to the ladies, the corporations, the societies and many other organisations who have helped in preparing this work.

Any researcher is only as good as the help received and I am particularly grateful to the following:

Aras Scannán Na H-Éirann, Dublin, Eire

The Barbican Centre, London, U.K.

Aldo Bernadini, Monteviale, Italy

B.B.C. Television, London, U.K.

Biblioteca Nazionale Centrale Vittorio Emanuele II, Rome, Italy

Bulgarska Nacionalna Filmoteka, Sofia, Bulgaria

Bundesarchiv, Berlin, Germany

Centro Sperimentale di Cinematografia, Rome, Italy

China Film Archive, Beijing, People's Republic of China

Chinese Taipei Film Archive, Taiwan, Republic of China

Cinemateca do Museu de Arte Moderna, Rio de Janiero, Brazil

Cinémathèque Méliès, Paris, France

Cinémathèque Française, Paris, France

Det Danske Filmmuseum, Copenhagen, Denmark

Egyptian Film Centre, Guiza, Egypt

Filmoteca Española, Madrid, Spain

Filmoteca Generalitat Valencia, Valencia, Spain

Filmoteca Vaticana, The Vatican

Filmoteka Narodowa w Warszawie, Warsaw, Poland

Flickers, Bristol, U.K.

Folger Shakespeare Institute, Washington D.C., U.S.A.

Godspeak, Gent, Belgium

Gosfilmofond, Moscow, Russia

His Royal Highness The Prince of Wales, St. James's Palace, London, England.

Hong Kong Film Archive Office, Hong Kong

Hrvatski Državni Arhiv, Zagreb, Croatia

Rod Jennings, Bramley, U.K.

Jerusalem Film Centre/Israel Film Archive, Jerusalem, Israel

John Kilmister, Leicester, U.K.

Kenneth Branagh Ltd., Shepperton, U.K.

Korean Film Archive, Seoul, Republic of Korea

Magyar Filmintezet Archivuma, Budapest, Hungary

Joan Marti Gabaldon, La Drova, Spain

Vinny Murphy, Dublin, Eire

Národni Filmový Archiv, Prague, Czech Republic

National Archives of Canada, Ottawa, Canada

The National Center for Jewish Films, Waltham, Mass., U.S.A.

National Film Archive of India, Pune, India

National Film Center, Kanagawa-Ken, Japan

Nederlands Filmmuseum, Amsterdam, Holland

Mr. Nohara, Panasonic Sales, Barcelona, Spain

Det Norske Filminstituttet, Oslo, Norway

Österreichisches Filmarchiv, Vienna, Austria

Pro Helvetia Schweizer Kulturstiftung, Zurich, Switzerland

Luis Romero Quiles, Gandia, Spain

Royal Film Archive, Brussels, Belgium

S4C, Cardiff, Wales

St. Bartholomew's School, Newbury, U.K.

Sinema-TV Enstitsü, Istanbul, Turkey

Suomen Elokuva-Arkisto, Helsinki, Finland

Svenska Filminstitutet, Stockholm, Sweden

Tainiothiki Tis Ellados, Athens, Greece

Universidad Nacional Autonoma de Mexico, Mexico City, Mexico

To list all the books and magazines consulted would take another chapter in itself. Many have provided no information at all, others have provided useful data, and some have opened or closed avenues of investigation. All were in their own way important and the efforts of past writers is acknowledged and respected.

The main publications that have provided information have been noted in one form or another in the text. In respect of Shakespeare's works, I have used as reference:

'The Complete Works of William Shakespeare' as edited by W.J. Craig., M.A. and published by the Oxford University Press,

'The Complete Pelican Shakespeare' in three volumes under the general editorship of Alfred Harbage and published by Pelican Books Ltd.,

'Living Shakespeare', a selection of his works in edited form on disc with appropriate books of the edited and full texts under the supervision of Bernard Grabanier and published by Odhams Books Ltd., and

'Tales from Shakespeare' by Charles and Mary Lamb, edited by Julia Briggs and published by Everyman's Library.

One person I must not fail to thank is my wife, Christine. Not solely for the onerous task of reading the text time after time does she merit tremendous gratitude but also for her patience and encouragement.

DIRECTORS' CHECK LIST

This cross reference relates only to those films listed in the various chapters that are considered to be related to the works of Shakespeare, his life or environment. In short, those titles that are listed in **BOLD** letters. The director's name is listed first followed by the titles of the films he/she has directed in alphabetical order. The chapter and, where appropriate, the section within the chapter where the film may be found is then noted. When the § appears after a film title, this indicates that doubt exists about the directorial attribution and reference should be made to the film in question.

Director's name	Film(s) directed	Chapter	Section
Abrahams, Jim	Big Business	III	2
Acosta, Armando	Romeo/Juliet	XXI	2
Adolfi, John G.	Show of Shows	XXIX	
Ahlin, Per	Resan Till Melonia	XXIII	2
Allen, Irwin	The Story of Mankind	XXXII	
Allen, Woody	Everything You Wanted to Know about Sex, but Were Afraid to Ask	XXXIII	
	Zelig	XXX	
Allers, Roger	The Lion King	IX	2
Altman, Robert	Thieves Like Us	XXXIII	
Amato, Giuseppe	Viel Lärm um Nixi	XIX	2
Andréani, Henri	Cléopâtre	I	2
	Les Enfants d'Edouard	XXVI	2
	Macbeth §	XIVl	
Anger, Kenneth	Scorpio Rising	XXX	
Antczak, Jerzy	Mistrz	XXX	
Antel, Franz	Frau Wirtin Hat Auch Einen Grafen	XXX	
Arliss, Leslie	Love Story	XXX	
	The Man in Grey	XXX	
Armfield, Neil	Twelfth Night	XXVII	2
Arnshtam, Lev	Romeo i Dzuletta	XXI	3
Asquith, Anthony	The Young Lovers	XXI	2
Athavale, Dada	Khun-E-Nahak §	IX	1
Axel, Gabriel	The Prince of Jutland	IX	2
Azzuri, Paulo	A Midsummer Night's Dream	XVIII	1
Backner, Arthur	The Taming of the Shrew	XXII	1
Baddeley W. Hugh	Understanding Shakespeare: His Sources	XXXII	
	Understanding Shakespeare: His Stagecraft	XXXII	
Badger, Clarence	Doubling for Romeo	XXI	2
Baim, Harold	Our Mr. Shakespeare	XXXII	
Balanchine, George	A Midsummer Night's Dream	XVIII	3
Baldi, Ferdinando	Vengeance of the Barbarians	XXXIII	
Balducci, Richard	Dans la Pouissière du Soleil	IX	2
Banfield, George	The Princes in the Tower	XXVI	2
Banks, Monty	You Made Me Love You	XXII	2
Bánky, Viktor	Makacs Kata	XXII	2
Barker, Reginald	The Iron Strain	XXII	2
Barker, W.G.	Hamlet	IX	1
	Romeo and Juliet §	XXI	1
Barnes, John	The Humanities Series: Hamlet, the Age of Elizabeth	XXXII	
Barrie, J. M.	The Yellow Weekend at Stanway	XXX	
Barsacq, André	Le Rideau Rouge	XXX	
Barton, Charles	Buck Privates Come Home	XXX	

Batty, Peter	Fonteyn and Nureyev – A Ballet Legend	XXX	
Beaudine, William	Daring Youth	XXII	2
Behramshah, Taimur	Bhool Bhuyaiyan	III	1
Benamou, Roger	Otello	XX	3
Bene, Carmelo	Un Amleto di Meno	IX	2
Benson, Frank R.	Julius Caesar	X1	
	Macbeth	XIV	1
	Richard III	XXVI	1
	The Taming of the Shrew	XXII	1
Bentley, Thomas	Old Bill Through the Ages	XXXII	
	Royal Cavalcade	XXX	
Berezantzera, Tatjana	Ljubovju Zaljubov	XIX	3
Bergman, Andrew	So Fine	XXX	
Bergman, Ingmar	Sommarnattens Leende	XXX	
Berman, Ed	Dogg's Troupe Hamlet	IX	1
Berne, Josef	Mirele Efros	XI	2
Billon, Pierre	Le Marchand de Venise	XVI	1
Bishop, Terry	Hamile	IX	1
Blackton, James Stuart	Antony and Cleopatra, the Love Story of the Noblest Roman and the Most Beautiful Egyptian §	I	1
	Cardinal Wolsey §	VII	2
	A Comedy of Errors	III	1
	Hamlet	IX	1
	Julius Caesar, an Historical Tragedy §	X	1
	Macbeth	XIV	1
	The Merchant of Venice §	XVI	1
	A Midsummer Night's Dream	XVIII	1
	Othello §	XX	1
	Richard III, a Shakespeare Tragedy §	XXVI	1
	Romeo and Juliet, a Romantic Story of the Ancient Feud Between the Italian Houses of Montague and Capulet §	XXI	1
Blair, Thomas A.	Macbeth	XIV	1
Blatty, William Peter	The Ninth Configuration	XXX	
Blom, August	For Aabent Tæppe	XXX	
	Hamlet	IX	1
Bloom, John	National Youth Theatre	XXXII	
Boisrond, Michel	C'est Arrivé à Aden	XXX	
Bonnard, Mario	Rossini	XXX	
Bonnière, René	The Tragicall Hifstorie of Hamlet Prince of Denmark	IX	1
Borzage, Frank	Stage Door Canteen	XXX	
Boulois, Max H.	Otelo (Comando Negro)	XX	2
Bourchier, Arthur	Macbeth	XIV	1
Bourgeois, Grard	Hamlet	IX	1
	Roméo et Juliette	XXI	1
Brabin, Charles	Othello in Jonesville	XXX	
Bracho, Julio	La Posesión	XXI	2
Bradley, David	Julius Caesar	X	1
Brakage, Stan	Murder Psalm	XXX	
Branagh, Kenneth	Hamlet	IX	1
	Henry V	XIII	1
	In the Bleak Midwinter	XXX	
	Much Ado About Nothing	XIX	1
	Swan Song	XXX	

DIRECTORS' CHECK LIST

Bray, J. R.	Col. Hezza Liar Plays Hamlet	XXXI	
Brenon, Herbert	Royal Cavalcade	XXX	
Brignone, Guido	Canzone Eterna	XXX	
	Kean	XXX	
Brinnes, Ian	Shakespeare: Mirror of a Man	XXXII	
Brittain, Donald	The Players	XXXII	
Brook, Peter	King Lear	XI	1
	Peter Brook: The Tempest	XXXII	
Brooks, Richard	The Blackboard Jungle	XXXIII	
Brunel, Adrian	Elstree Calling	XXX	
Buchowetzki, Dmitri	Macbeth	XIV	1
	Othello	XX	1
Burge, Stuart	Julius Caesar	X	1
	Othello	XX	1
Burger, Hanus	Nichts als Sünde	XXVII	3
Bushman, Francis X.	Romeo and Juliet	XXI	1
Butler, David	Playmates	XXX	
Cabello, Carlos L.	Bodas Trágicas	XX	2
Călinescu, Bob	Romeo and Juliet	XXXI	
Calmettes, André	Les Enfants d'Edouard d'Angleterre §	XXVI	2
	Hamlet (1910)	IX	1
	Hamlet (1914)	IX	1
	Richard III	XXVI	1
Campbell, Douglas	The Humanities Series	XXXII	
Candeias, Ozualdo	A Herança	IX	2
Canemaker, John	Bottom's Dream	XXXI	
Cannioto, Vincenzo	Shakespeare in Palermo	XXXII	
Capellani, Albert	Antoine et Cléopâtre	I	1
	Hamlet	IX	1
Cardona, René	Cartas Marcadas	XII	2
Carlsen, Jøn Bang	Ofelia Kommer Til Byen	IX	2
Carné, Marcel	Les Enfants du Paradis	XXX	
Carreras, Enrique	Romeo y Julita	XXI	2
Carrington, Margaret	Hamlet	IX	1
Caserini, Mario	Amleto (1908)	IX	1
	Amleto (1910)	IX	1
	Macbeth	XIV	1
	Otello (1906)	XX	1
	Otello (1909)	XX	1
	Otello (1914)	XX	1
	Romeo e Giulietta	XXI	1
Cass, Henry	Julius Caesar	X	1
	Macbeth	XIV	1
Castellani, Enzo G.	Quella Sporca Storia del West	IX	2
Castellani, Renato	Romeo and Juliet	XXI	1
Castellano, Franco	Il Bisbetico Domato	XXII	2
Castle, William	Serpent of the Nile	I	2
Catellví, José María	Julieta y Romeo	XXI	2
Cavalcanti, Alberto	Nicholas Nickleby	XXX	
Cayette, André	Les Amants de Vérone	XXI	2
Chabrol, Claude	Ophélia	IX	2
Chabukani, Vakhtang	Venetzansky Mavr (Othello)	XX	3
Chaffey, Don	Danger Within	XXX	
	Nearly a Nasty Accident	XXXIII	
Chaplin, Charles	A King in New York	XXXIII	

Charlot, André	Elstree Calling	XXX	
Chiappini, Luigi V. R.	The Phoenix and the Turtle	XXXII	
Činčera, Radúz	Romeo and Juliet	XXXII	
Cissé, Souleymane	Finyé	XXI	2
Clampett, Robert	Book Review	XXXI	
Clarke, Douglas	Festival in Edinburgh	XXXII	
Clarke, Michael	The Heart of England	XXXII	
Clausen, Erik	Rami og Julie	XXI	2
Cline, Eddie	Broadway Fever	XXXIII	
Cohl, Émile	Moderne École	XXXII	
Colleran, Bill	Hamlet	IX	1
Collins, Alf	Algy Goes on the Stage	XXX	
Collins, Edward J.	The Taming of the Shrew	XXII	1
Comerio, Luca	Amleto	IX	1
Cooper, George A.	Julius Caesar	X	1
Corbucci, Sergio	¡Que Nos Importa la Revolución!	XXX	
Corman, Roger	Tower of London	XXVI	2
	The Undead	XXXIII	
Coronado, Celestino	Hamlet	IX	1
	A Midsummer Night's Dream	XVIII	1
Cortés, Fernando	El Charro y la Dama	XXII	2
Cosmatos, George P.	Tombstone	XXXIII	
Coutinho, Eduardo	Faustão	VIII Part 2	2
Crisp, Donald	Don Q – Son of Zorro	XXXIII	
Crome, John	National Youth Theatre	XXXII	
Cukor, George	A Double Life	XXX	
	Romeo and Juliet	XXI	1
Czinner, Paul	As You Like It	II	1
	Romeo and Juliet	XXI	3
Dallamano, Massimo	Das Bildnis des Dorian Gray	XXXIII	
D'Ambra, Lucio	I Due Sogni ad Occhi Aperti	XVIII	2
D'Anna, Claude	Macbeth	XIV	3
Das, Duresh Ranjan	Alo Chhaya/Aandhi	XXIII	1
Daves, Delmer	Jubal	XX	2
Davis, Mannie	All's Well That Ends Well	XXXI	
Davison, Tito	Las Tres Alegres Comadres	XXX	
Dayton, Helena Smith	Romeo and Juliet	XXXI	
Deane, Charles	Julius Caesar	X	1
	Macbeth	XIV	1
	A Midsummer Night's Dream	XVIII	1
	Othello	XX	1
	Twelfth Night	XXVII	1
	A Winter's Tale	XXIX	1
Dearden, Basil	All Night Long	XX	2
del Colle, Ubaldo Maria	Bianco contro Negro §	XX	3
del Diestro, Alfredo	Nobleza Ranchera	XXI	2
Delgado, Miguel M.	Romeo y Julieta	XXI	2
de Liguoro, Giuseppe	Amleto	IX	1
	Bruto	X	1
	Giulietta e Romeo	XXI	1
	Re Lear	XI	1
Demicheli, Tullio	Más Fuerte Que el Amor	XXII	2
DeMille, Cecil B.	Cleopatra	I	2
	Madame Satan	XXX	
	Triumph	XXX	

Denham, Reginald	Calling the Tune	XXXIII	
	The Village Squire	XXX	
de Oliviera, Manoel	O Convento	XXXII	
Derendorf, Don	Shakespeare's Stratford	XXXII	
De Riso, Camillo	Othello	XX	2
de Rivera, Javier	La Tempestad	XXIII	2
Desai, Jayant	Bhool Bhulaiyan	III	1
Desfontaines, Henri	Les Amours de la Reine Élisabeth	XXXII	
	Falstaff	VI	1
	Hamlet	IX	1
	La Mégère Apprivoisée	XXII	1
	Shylock, ou le More de Venise	XVI	1
Dickson, William Kennedy-Laurie	King John	XII	1
Dickson, Paul	Gilbert Harding Speaking of Murder	XXXIII	
Dieterle, William	A Midsummer Night's Dream	XVIII	1
Dillon, John F.	The Perfect Flapper	XXX	
Donev, Donyo	Narekohme gi Monteki i Kapuleti	XXI	2
Dooley, John	Swan of Avon	XXXII	
Doronin, Mijail	Portret Doriana Greya	XXX	
Dreyer, Carl	Et Slot i Slot	XXXII	
Drum, Val	Romeo and Juliet	XXI	1
Duncan, Ellis R.	Ambikapathy	XXX	
Dunlop, Frank	The Winter's Tale	XXIX	1
Dunne, Christopher	Titus	XXIV	1
Dunne, Philip	Prince of Players	XXX	
Dunning, George	The Tempest	XXXI	
Dupont E. A.	Das Alte Gesetz	XXX	
Duvivier, Julien	La Fin du Jour	XXXIII	
Dyer, Anson	'Amlet	XXXI	
	The Merchant of Venice	XXXI	
	Oh'phelia	XXXI	
	Othello	XXXI	
	Romeo and Juliet	XXXI	
	The Taming of the Shrew	XXXI	
Eberhardt, Thom	Without a Clue	XXXIII	
Edison, Thomas	Burlesque on Romeo and Juliet	XXI	2
	A Winter's Tale	XXIX	2
Edwards, Blake	Son of the Pink Panther	XXXIII	
Edwards, Hilton	Hamlet at Elsinore	IX	1
	Return to Glennascaul	XXXIII	
Edwards, J. Gordon	Cleopatra	I	2
	Romeo and Juliet	XXI	1
Edzard, Christine	As You Like It	II	2
Eeles, Bert	Shakespeare's Mounted Foot	XXX	
Eldridge, John	Laxdale Hall	XXX	
Elliott, Michael	King Lear	XI	1
Elter, Marco	Dente per Dente	XV	2
Elvey, Maurice	Love in a Wood	II	2
Emerson, John	Macbeth	XIV	1
Engel, Erich	Viel Lärm um Nixi	XIX	2
Enriques, Franco	Die Lustigen Weiber von Windsor	XVII	3
Erksan, Metin	Intikam Meleği Kadin Hamlet	IX	2
Escrivá, Vicente	Montoyas y Tarantos	XXI	2
Esparbé, Miquel	Romeo y Julieta	XXXI	

Evans, Fred	Pimple as Hamlet	XXX	
Evans, Joe	Liza on the Stage	XXX	
	Pimple as Hamlet	XXX	
Eveleigh, Leslie	The Princes in the Tower	XXVI	2
Falena, Ugo	Giulietta e Romeo	XXI	1
Fedor, Hitruck	Othello – 67	XXXI	
Fehér, Imre	Gyalog a Mennyországba	XXX	
Fejos, Paul	The Last Moment	XXX	
Felenstein, Walter	Othello	XX	3
Fellner, Peter Paul	Der Kaufmann von Venedig	XVI	1
Fernández, Emilio	Enamorada	XXII	2
Ferrera, Abel	China Girl	XXI	2
Ferroni, Giorgio	Coriolano, Eroe Senza Patria	IV	1
Feuillade, Louis	Le Roi Lear au Village	XI	2
Fischinger, Oskar	Komposition im Blau	XXXI	
Fleischer, Dave	Shakespearean Spinach	XXXI	
Ford, Colin	Masks and Faces	XXXII	
Ford, John	My Darling Clementine	XXXIII	
Forde, Walter	Time Flies	XXXII	
Forsythe, Bill	Gregory's Girl	XXXIII	
Fox, Levi	Bad Case of Shakespeare §	XXXII	
Foy, Bryan	Antony and Cleopatra	I	2
	The Royal Box	XXX	
Franju, Georges	Le Théâtre National Populaire	XXX	
Franz, Joseph J.	A Sagebrush Hamlet	IX	2
Freda, Riccardo	Giulietta e Romeo	XXI	1
Freeston, Jeremy	Macbeth	XIV	1
Fried, Yan	Dvenadtsatava Noch	XXVII	1
Frusta, Arrigo	Amleto §	IX	1
	La Bisbetica Domata	XXII	1
Fullilove, Eric	The Questioning City	XXXII	
Gade, Sven	Hamlet	IX	1
Gallone, Carmine	Amleto e il Suo Clown	IX	2
	Casa Ricordi	XXX	
Gambourg, Ephim	Romeo and Juliet	XXXI	
Gariazzo, Pier Antonio	Tutto il Mondo é un Teatro	XXX	
Gaskill, Charles L.	Cleopatra	I	2
Gassman, Vittorio	Kean (Genio e Sregolatezza)	XXX	
Gavaldón, Roberto	La Vida Intima de Marco Antonio y Cleopatra	I	2
Gavin, Barrie	Der Musik Sagt Alles – Anja Silja	XXX	
Gibbins, Duncan	Fire With Fire	XXI	2
Gibson, Mel	The Man Without a Face	XXXIII	
Gilbert, Brian	The Frog Prince	XXXIII	
Gilliat, Sidney	Green for Danger	XXXIII	
	The Rake's Progress	XXXIII	
Godard, Jean-Luc	King Lear	XI	2
Goldstein, Scott	Walls of Glass	XXXIII	
Goode, Frederic	Shakespeare Land	XXXII	
Goodwins, Leslie	Casanova in Burlesque	XXX	
Gordon, Michael	It Might Be You!	XXX	
Grayson, Godfrey	An Honourable Murder	X	2
Greenaway, Peter	Prospero's Books	XXIII	2
Greenwood, Edwin	Falstaff, the Tavern Knight	XVII	1
Griffith, David Wark	Macbeth	XIV	1
	The Old Actor	XXXIII	

	The Taming of the Shrew	XXII	1
Growcott, Frank R.	The Life of Shakespeare	XXXII	
Guazzoni, Enrico	Bruto (1911)	X	1
	Bruto (1914)	X	1
	Lady Macbeth	XIV	2
	Marcantonio e Cleopatra (1916)	I	1
	Marcantonio e Cleopatra (1913)	I	2
Hainisch, Leopold	Falstaff in Wien	XXX	
Halas, John	A Midsummer Night's Mare	XXXI	
	Twa Corbies/Spring and Winter	XXXI	
Hale, George	Office Steps	XXXIII	
Hales, Gordon	The Poet's Eye – a Tribute to		
	William Shakespeare	XXXII	
Hall, Alexander	Give Us This Night	XXX	
Hall, Peter	A Midsummer Night's Dream	XVIII	1
Harris, Harry B.	The Trouper	XIX	
Has, Wojciech	Jak Być Kochana	XXX	
Hawes, Stanley	Chapter and Verse	XXXIII	
Haynes, Manning	The Claydon Treasure Mystery	XXXIII	
Hecht, Ben	Actors and Sin	XXXIII	
Hellberg, Martin	Viel Lärm um Nichts	XIX	1
Hernández, Mario	Los Gemelos Alborotados	III	2
Herzka, Julius	Der Kaufmann von Venedig	XVI	1
Hessens, Robert	Répétition Chez Jean Louis Barrault	IX	1
Heston, Charlton	Antony and Cleopatra	I	1
Hickox, Douglas	Theatre of Blood	XXX	
Hilton, Arthur	The Misadventures of Buster Keaton	XXX	
Hitchcock, Alfred	Elstree Calling	XXX	
Hjortø, Knut	Shakespeare og Gronborg	XXXII	
Hoffman, Carl	Die Lustigen Weiber	XVII	3
Hoffman, Michael	A Midsummer Night's Dream	XVIII	1
Holmes, J. B.	Shakespeare	XXXII	
Howard, Leslie	Pimpernel Smith	XXXIII	
Hu, Xiaofeng	Yi Pian Jou	XV	2
Hughes, Harry	Star Impersonations	XXX	
Hughes, Ken	Joe Macbeth	XIV	2
Hulbert, Jack	Elstree Calling	XXX	
	Jack of All Trades	XXXIII	
Hurwitz, Harry	The Projectionist	XXX	
Hussain, Akhtar	Anjumam	XXI	2
Hussain, Mohammed	Hanste Rehna	III	1
Hylkema, Hans	Julia's Geheim	XXI	2
Ince, Ralph	Success	XXX	
Ingraham, Lloyd	Stranded	XXXIII	
Ising, Rudolph	Romeo in Rhythm	XXXI	
Ivory, James	Shakespeare-Wallah	XXX	
Janis, Nikolas L.	Romeo of the Spirits	XXX	
Jarman, Derek	The Angelic Conversation	XXX	
	The Tempest	XXIII	2
Jasney, Vojtech	FilmFalstaff	XXXII	
Jennings, Humphrey	A Diary for Timothy	XXX	
	Family Portrait	XXXII	
Johnson, Al	To Be or Not To Be	XXX	
Jones, Robert E.	Hamlet	IX	1
Jordan, William and Mildred	Shakespeare Theater: The Globe Playhouse	XXXII	

Junger, Gil	10 Things I Hate About You	XXII	2
Junkers, Herbert	Oberon (Des Elfenkönigs Schwur)	XVIII	3
Kar, Ajoy	Saptapadi	XXX	
Karayev, Alexei	As You Like It	XXXI	
Kardar, Abdul Raschid	Baap Re Baap	XXII	1
Karmen, R.	One Day in Soviet Russia	XXXII	
Katayan, Vasily	Maya Plisetskaya	XXX	
Kató, István	Romeo and Juliet	XXXI	
Kaurismäki, Aki	Hamlet Liikmaailmessa	IX	2
Kaufmann, Lloyd	Tromeo and Juliet	XXI	2
Käutner, Helmut	Der Rest Ist Schweigen	IX	2
Keaton, Buster	Day Dreams	XXX	
Keene, James	Richard III	XXVI	1
Kellett, Bob	Up Pompeii	XXXIII	
Kellino, W. P.	Hamlet	IX	2
	Romeo and Juliet	XXI	2
	Royal Cavalcade	XXX	
Kent, Charles	As You Like It §	II	1
	A Midsummer Night's Dream	XVIII	1
	Twelfth Night	XXVII	1
King, Louis	The Deceiver	XXX	
Knoles, Harley	Carnival	XXX	
Kodar, Oja	Orson Welles: The One-Man Band	XVI	1
Kohn, Alfred	Karlighedens Firkløver	XXI	2
Korda, Zoltan	The Four Feathers	XXXIII	
Kosolov, Sergei	Ukposchenie Stropivoy	XXII	1
Kovásznai, Gyorgy	Hamlet	XXXI	
Kozintsev, Grigori	Gamlet	IX	1
	Korol Lir	XI	1
Krutch, James Wood	A Midsummer Night's Dream:		
	An Introduction to the Play	XVIII	1
Kulakov, Yuri	Julius Caesar	XXXI	
Kuperman, Mario	O Jogo da Vida e da Morte	IX	2
Kurosawa, Akira	Ikimono No Kiroku	XXX	
	Kumonosu-Jo	XIV	2
	Ran	XI	2
	Warui Yatsu Yoku Nemuru	IX	2
Lachman, Harry	Our Relations	III	2
Lamy, Benot	Jambon d'Ardennes	XXI	2
Lane, Charles	True Identity	XXX	
Lanfield, Sidney	Sing, Baby, Sing	XXX	
Langham, Michael	The Humanities Series: Hamlet,		
	the Age of Elizabeth	XXXII	
Larsen, Viggo	Othello	XX	2
Launder, Frank	The Pure Hell of St. Trinians	XXX	
Lauritzen, Lau	Han Hug og Hamlet (1922)	XXX	
	Han Hug og Hamlet (1932)	XXX	
Lavrovsky, Leonid	Romeo i Dzuletta	XXI	3
Lawrence, Lister	Shakespeare's Country	XXXII	
Lazaga, Pedro	El Abominable Hombre de la Costa del Sol	XXX	
Ledwig, Alfred	Makbet	XXXI	
Lee, Norman	Royal Cavalcade	XXX	
Lee, Paul	Romeo and Juliet	XXI	1
Lee, Rowland V.	Guilty Generation	XXI	2
	Tower of London	XXVI	2

Legg, Stuart	B.B.C. the Voice of Britain	XXXII	
Leth, Jøn	Otelias Blomsters	IX	2
Levy, Don	Opus	XXXII	
Lewis, Jerry	The Nutty Professor	XXXIII	
Light, Allie	In the Shadow of the Stars	XXXIII	
Liu, Fang	Thinking the Wrong Way	III	2
Lloyd, Frank	David Garrick	XXX	
Loder, John de Vere	Romeo and Juliet	XXX	
	Untitled	XXX	
Loizillon, Christophe	La Jalousie	XX	2
Lolli, Alberto Carlo	Lo Spettro di Jago	XX	2
Loncraine, Richard	Richard III	XXVI	2
Longford, Raymond	The Sentimental Bloke	XXX	
Lo Savio, Gerolamo	Re Lear	XI	1
	Il Mercante di Venezia	XVI	1
	Otello	XX	1
Lubin, Sigmund	Julius Caesar	X	1
	Ten Minutes with Shakespeare	XXXII	
Lubitsch, Ernst	Kolthiesels Töchter	XXII	2
	Romeo und Julia im Schnee	XXI	2
	To Be or Not To Be	XXX	
Ludwig, Edward	That Certain Age	XXXIII	
Luhrmann, Baz	William Shakespeare's Romeo and Juliet	XXI	2
Lumet, Sidney	The Deadly Affair	XXX	
	Stage Struck	XXX	
Lye, Len	Full Fathom Five	XXXIII	
MacBean, L. C.	The Real Thing at Last	XIV	2
McCarey, Leo	Bromo and Juliet	XXX	
MacCartney, Sydney	The Canterville Ghost	XXX	
McDermott, Angus	The Humanities Series: Hamlet, the Age of Elizabeth	XXXII	
McDowell, J. B.	The Life of Shakespeare	XXXII	
McGoohan, Patrick	Catch My Soul	XX	2
McGrath, Joseph	The Great McGonagall	XXX	
	The Magic Christian	XXX	
McKimson, Robert	A Midsummer Night's Dream	XXXI	
McKinney, Gene	Baylor Theater's Hamlet	XXXII	
McLeod, Norman Z.	My Favourite Spy	XXXIII	
McTiernan, John	The Last Action Hero	XXX	
Macedo, Watson	Carnaval no Fogo	XXX	
Mack, Anthony	Shivering Shakespeare	XXXIII	
Mack, Max	Othello	XXX	
Mackane, David	Othello	XX	1
Madan, Jeejeebhoy F.	Hathili Dulhan	XXI	1
	Zalim Saudagar	XV	1
Madden, John	Shakespeare In Love	XXXII	
Maggi, Luigi	Otello	XX	1
Maloney, Leo	Across the Deadline	XXI	2
Mankiewicz, Joseph L.	Julius Caesar	X	1
Mann, Anthony	Serenade	XXX	
Manning, Michelle	Blue City	IX	2
Mapes, Jacque	Rosie	XXXIII	
Margolin, Stuart	Double, Double, Toil and Trouble	XXXIII	
Marker, Chris	A. K.	XI	2
Marshall, George	The Goldwyn Follies	XXX	

	The Perils of Pauline	XXX	
	Variety Girl	XXX	
Marshall, Penny	Renaissance Man	XXX	
Marston, Theodore	The Merchant of Venice §	XVI	1
	Romeo and Juliet	XXI	1
	A Winter's Tale	XXIX	1
Martinek, H. O.	Glastonbury Past and Present	XXXII	
Martonffry, Emil	Makrancos Hölgy	XXII	2
Massingham, Richard	In Which We Live: Being the Story of a Suit		
	Told by Itself	XXXIII	
Mastrocinque, CamilloIl	Pecato di Anna	XXX	
Matarazzo, Raffaelo	Giuseppe Verdi	XXX	
Maté, Rudolph	Serenade einer Grossen Liebe	XXX	
Maurice, Clment	Hamlet, Scène de Duel	IX	1
	Roméo et Juliette	XXI	3
Mayo, Archie	It's Love I'm After	XXX	
Mazursky, Paul	Harry and Tonto	XI	2
	Tempest	XXIII	2
	Willie and Phil	XXXIII	
Méliès, Georges	Le Diable et la Statue	XXI	2
	Hamlet, Prince of Denmark	IX	1
	Shakespeare Écrivant "La Mort de Jules César"	XXXII	
Mendel, Georges	Othello §	XX	3
Mendiaraz, Juan Luis	Maitasun Arina	XXX	
Mercanton, Louis	Les Amours de la Reine Élisabeth	XXXII	
Metcalf, Earl	Hamlet Made Over	XXX	
Meyer, Nicholas	Star Trek VI: The Undiscovered Country	XXXIII	
Meyer, Russ	Up!	XXXIII	
Meyerhold, Vsevolod	Portret Doriana Greya	XXX	
Miekle, Georg	Othello	XX	3
Minkoff, Rob	The Lion King	IX	2
Minnelli, Vincente	The Bad and the Beautiful	XXXIII	
Mitrotti, Mario	Inmolacion de Hamlet	IX	2
Modi, Sohrab Marwanji	Khoon Ka Khoon	IX	1
	Saeed-E-Havas	XII	1
Moffat, Ivan	Home Guard	XXXIII	
Mogubub, Fred	Enter Hamlet	XXXI	
Mom, Arturo S.	Villa Discordia	XXI	2
Monachov, Kiril	Macbeth	XIV	3
Moore, Marshall	Brutus and Cassius	X	1
Moore, Vin	Romeo and Juliet	XXI	2
Moser, Frank	Romeo and Juliet	XXXI	
Moszczok, Stanislaw	Theatre in Poland	X	
Moulton, Herbert	The Hollywood You Never See	I	2
Muat, Maria	Twelfth Night	XXXI	
Mulchay, Russell	Highlander II - The Quickening	XXX	
Mulloy, Phil	In the Forest	XXX	
Murcell, George	Understanding Shakespeare: His Sources	XXXII	
	Understanding Shakespeare: His Stagecraft	XXXII	
Murphy, Vinnie	H for Hamlet	IX	1
Murray, Paul	Elstree Calling	XXX	
Negroni, Baldassare	Racconto d'Inverno	XXIX	1
Negulesco, Jean	The Voice That Thrilled the World	XXXII	
Nelson, Robert	Hamlet Act	IX	2
Neumann, Hans	Ein Sommernachtstraum	XVIII	1

DIRECTORS' CHECK LIST

Newman, Widgey R.	Immortal Gentleman	XXXII	
	The Merchant of Venice	XVI	1
Nicholls, George O.	Nicholas Nickleby	XXX	
Nielsen, Martinius	Othello	XXX	
Noble, Adrian	A Midsummer Night's Dream	XVIII	1
Noble, John W.	Romeo and Juliet	XXI	1
NOS team	The Marowitz Hamlet	IX	2
Novelli, Enrico	Otello	XX	1
Nunn, Trevor	Twelfth Night	XXVII	1
O'Brien, John B.	Impossible Catherine	XXII	2
Olcott, Sidney	As You Like It	II	1
Olivier, Laurence	Hamlet	IX	1
	The Chronical History of King Henry Fift With His Battell Fought At Agincourt in France by Will Shakespeare	XIII	1
	Richard III	XXVI	1
	Sets and Costumes for "Hamlet"	IX	1
Ophüls, Max	Lachende Erben	XXI	2
Orlova, Natalia	Hamlet	XXXI	
	King Richard III	XXXI	
Ornstein, Robert	The Staging of Shakespeare	XXXII	
Ortkemper, Hubert	Der Musik Sagt Alles - Anja Silja	XXX	
Pacino, Al	Looking for Richard	XXX	
Papic, Kristo	Predstava Hamleta u Mrduša Donjoj	IX	2
Paradjanov, Sergei	Teni Zabytykh Predkov	XXI	2
Parker, Alan	Fame	XXXIII	
Parker, Albert	The Third Clue	XXXIII	
Parker Louis N.	Henry VIII	VII	1
Parker, Morten	Stratford Adventure	XXXII	
Parker, Oliver	Othello	XX	1
Parkinson, Harry B.	Beauty and Brightness No.4	XXXII	
	Macbeth	XIV	1
Parks Jr., Gordon	Aaron Loves Angela	XXI	2
Parrot, Charles	One Night Only	XXX	
Paso, Alfonso	No Somos ni Romeo ni Julieta	XXI	2
Pastrone, Giovanni	Giulio Cesare (1909)	X	1
	Giulio Cesare (1914) §	X	1
Pavlinić, Zlatko	Romeo i Julia	XXXI	
Pentti, Pauli	Macbeth	XIV	2
Perret, Léonce	Être ou Être Pas	IX	2
	The Mad Lover	XXX	
Perski, Ludwik	Hamlet Razy Pięc	XXXII	
Petričič, Dušan	Romeo i Julija Vilija Sekspira u Izvodenju Trupe Monstrumu i Druzina	XXXI	
Phillips, Bertram	Juliet and Her Romeo	XXI	2
Pichel, Irving	Life Begins at 8:30	XXX	
Pineschi, Azeglio	La Bisbetica Domata	XXII	1
Pineschi, Lamberto	La Bisbetica Domata	XXII	1
Pipolo, Giuseppe	Il Bisbetico Domato	XXII	2
Plumb, E. Hay	Hamlet	IX	1
	The Princes in the Tower	XXVI	2
Poggioli, Ferdinando Maria	La Bisbetica Domata	XXII	2
Polanski, Roman	Macbeth	XIV	1
	Shakespeare: "Macbeth - Power and Corruption"	XIV	1
Porten, Franz	Desdemona	XX	3

Porter, Edwin S.	The Seven Ages	II	2
Potter, H. C.	The Goldwyn Follies	XXX	
Powell, Michael	Age of Consent	XXIII	2
	Gone to Earth	XXXIII	
	A Matter of Life and Death	XXX	
Preminger, Otto	Such Good Friends	XXX	
Pressburger, Emric	Gone to Earth	XXXIII	
	A Matter of Life and Death	XXX	
Purcell, Evelyn	Nobody's Fool	XXX	
Purves, Barry	Next	XXXI	
Raman, M. V.	Aasha	IX	2
Ranous, William V.	King Lear §	XI	1
	Othello §	XX	1
	Richard III, a Shakespeare Tragedy §	XXVI	1
	Romeo and Juliet, a Romantic Story of the Ancient Feud Between the Italian Houses of Montague and Capulet §	XXI	1
Rapper, Irving	Marjorie Morningstar	XXX	
Raskin, Connie	Much Ado About Nothing	XXXI	
Reddy, K. V.	Gunsundari Katha	XI	2
Redford, Robert	Quiz Show	XXXIII	
Rees-Mogg, Anne	Macbeth: A Tragedy	XXXII	
Regazzi, Renzo	Il Primo Premio Si Chiama Irene (Danimarca – l'Incredible Realtà Della Nuova Morale)	XXX	
Reilly, William	Men of Respect	XIV	2
Reiner, Rob	North	XXX	
Reinhardt, Max	A Midsummer Night's Dream	XVIII	1
	König Richard III	XXVI	1
Reis, Irving	Roseanna McCoy	XXI	2
Reisch, Walter	Men Are not Gods	XXX	
Reisner, Charles F.	The Hollywood Revue of 1929	XXX	
Reutter, Gerhard	Die Lustigen Weiber von Windsor	XVII	3
Reynolds, S. E.	The Great Conway	XXX	
Richardson, Tony	The Charge of the Light Brigade	XXX	
	Hamlet	IX	1
Riech, Barbara-Ann	Aus Holz ein O – Das Globe-Theater des Sam Wanamaker	XXXII	
Rinker, Floyd	The Humanities Series: Hamlet, the Age of Elizabeth	XXXII	
Ripley, Arthur	Edgar Hamlet	XXXIII	
Robison, Arthur	Schatten eine Nächtliche Halluzination	XX	2
Robinson, Bruce	Withnail and I	XXXIII	
Rodolfi, Eleuterio	Amleto	IX	1
Rohmer, Eric	Conte d'Hiver	XXIX	2
Román, Antonio	La Fierecilla Domada	XXII	2
Roos, Jørgen	Shakespeare og Gronborg	XXXII	
Rosi, Francesco	Kean (Genio e Sregolatezza)	XXX	
Ross, Herbert	The Goodbye Girl	XXX	
	The Turning Point	XXX	
Rosson, Arthur	Wet Paint	XIX	2
Roudés, Gaston	Falstaff	VI	1
Rovira Beleta, Francisco	Los Tarantos	XXI	2
Rowden, John	In Black and White	XXXIII	
Rozier, Willy	Espoir ou le Camp Maudit	XXI	2
Ruiz, Raúl	Richard III	XXVI	1

DIRECTORS' CHECK LIST

Rumbelow, Steven	King Lear	XI	1
Runze, Ottokar	Viola und Sebastian	XXVII	2
Ryazanov, Eldar	Beregis Automobilya	XXX	
Rye, Stellan	Ein Sommernachtstraum in Unserer Zeit	XVIII	2
Saakiants, Robert	A Midsummer Night's Dream	XXXI	
Sackler, Howard	Shakespeare: Soul of an Age	XXXII	
Sahu, Kishore	Khoon-E-Nahag	IX	1
Salkin, Leo	The 2000 Year Old Man	XXXI	
Salmon, Eric	Julius Caesar	XXXII	
	The Merchant of Venice	XXXII	
Salvatores, Gabriele	Sogno di una Notte d'Estate	XVIII	1
Samkovoi, Lev	Mnógo Súma Iz Ničegó	XIX	1
Samsonov, Samson	Mnógo Súma Iz Ničegó	XIX	1
Sanderson, Challis	The Merchant of Venice	XVI	1
Santell, Alfred A.	Bluebeard's Seven Wives	XXX	
Sanz, Pedro	Julieta y Romeo	XXXI	
Sára, Sándor	Vízkereszt	XXX	
Saraf, Irving	In the Shadow of the Stars	XXX	
Sarne, Mike	The Punk and the Princess	XXI	2
Saville, Victor	South Riding	XXXIII	
Savona, Leopoldo	Apocalipsis Joe	XXXIII	
Schaefer, George	Macbeth	XIV	1
Schall, Heinz	Hamlet	IX	1
	Macbeth	XIV	1
Schlesinger, John	Darling	XXXIII	
Schmidely, Valerien	Romeo und Julia auf dem Dorfe	XXI	2
Schön-Muanda, Hanna	Out of Oberammergau - Christian Stückl Inszeniert Shakespeare in Indien	XXXII	
Schoukens, Gaston	Bossemans et Coppenolle	XXI	2
Schrader, Paul	Mishima: A Life in Four Chapters	XXX	
Schwarze, Hans Dieter	Zwei Herren aus Verona	XXVIII	1
Schwarzwald, Martin	Teddy Bergman's International Broadcast	XXX	
Scofield, John	To See Such Fun	XXX	
Seabourne, Peter	Antony and Cleopatra	I	1
	As You Like It: An Introduction	II	1
	Hamlet	IX	1
	Henry IV Part 1: An Introduction	VIII	1
	Henry IV Part 2	VIII Part 2	1
	Julius Caesar: An Introduction	X	1
	Julius Caesar	X	1
	King Lear: An Introduction	XI	1
	Macbeth: An Introduction	XIV	1
	Macbeth	XIV	1
	The Merchant of Venice	XVI	1
	A Midsummer Night's Dream:An Introduction	XVIII	1
	Much Ado About Nothing	XIX	1
	Othello	XX	1
	Richard II	XXV	1
	Richard III	XXVI	1
	Romeo and Juliet	XXI	1
	The Taming of the Shrew	XXII	1
	The Tempest	XXIII	1
	Twelfth Night	XXVII	1
Sedláček, Jára	Saty Dělají Člověka	XIX	2
Seiden, Joseph	Othello in Harlem	XX	2

Seiter, William A.	Room Service	XXXIII	
Selig, William	The Merchant of Venice	XVI	1
	The Merry Wives of Windsor	XVII	1
Selim, Kamil	Shuhudae El-Gharam	XXI	2
Sen, Aparna	36 Chowringhee Lane	XXXIII	
Serebriakov, Nikolai	Macbeth	XXXI	
	Othello	XXXI	
Shakespeare's Birthday Trust	William Shakespeare	XXXII	
Shanker, S.	As You Like It	II	1
Shaw, Alexander	C. E. M. A.	XXXII	
Sherman, George	Panic Button	XXX	
Sherman, Lowell	Morning Glory	XXXIII	
Shute, Jimmy	March of Time 3rd. Year (British Edition)	XXXII	
Sidney, George	Kiss Me Kate	XXII	2
Silović, Vassili	Orson Welles: The One-Man Band	XVI	1
Sís, Vladimír	Sen Noci Svatojánské	XVIII	3
Simonelli, Giorgio C.	Io, Amleto	IX	2
Slutski, M.	One Day in Soviet Russia	XXXII	
Smalley, Phillips	The Merchant of Venice	XVI	1
Smith, Jack	A Duped Othello	XXX	
Snasdell, David	The Tempest	XXIII	1
Sokolov, Stanislav	The Tempest	XXXI	
	A Winter's Tale	XXXI	
Soule, Gardner	Shakespeare: England Today	XXXII	
Stenholm, Katherine	Macbeth	XIV	1
Stenson, Robert	Jack of All Trades	XXXIII	
Stepanova, Lidia	Kompoeitor Sergei Prokofiev	XXX	
Stootsberry, A. P.	The Secret Sex Lives of Romeo and Juliet	XXI	2
Stoppard, Tom	Rosencrantz and Guildenstern Are Dead	IX	2
Stow, Percy	The Tempest	XXIII	2
	A Horse! A Horse!	XXX	
Stoyeva, Vera	Gala Festival	XXX	
Strecker, Frank	Anna - Der Film	XXX	
Sullivan, Frederick	Cymbeline	V	1
Summers, Walter	Royal Cavalcade	XXX	
Sutherland, A. Edward	The Boys From Syracuse	III	2
Suzman, Janet	Othello	XX	1
Sweet, Harry	Romeo and Juliet	XXI	2
Szabó, István	Mephisto	XXX	
Táborský, Václav	Skutechnost Noci Svatojánské	XVIII	1
Tarta, Alexandre	Roméo et Juliette	XXI	3
Taurog, Norman	Drama Deluxe	XXX	
	Presenting Lily Mars	XXXIII	
Taylor, Donald	Home Guard	XXXIII	
Taylor, John	The England of Elizabeth	XXXII	
Taylor, Sam	The Taming of the Shrew	XXII	1
Taymor, Julie	Titus	XXIV	1
Tchardynine, Piotr	Venetziansky Tchoulok	XVI	1
Téchiné, André	Rendez-vous	XXX	
Terry, Paul	Romeo and Juliet	XXXI	
Thanhouser, Edwin	Master Shakespeare	XXXII	
	The Tempest	XXIII	1
Theodoropoulos, Angelos	Ithele Na Yini Vasilias	IX	2
Thomas, Gerald	Carry on Cleo	I	2
	Carry on Teacher	XXX	

Appendix 14

Thomas, Ralph	No, My Darling Daughter	XXXIII	
Thomashefsky, Harry	The Yiddish King Lear	XI	2
Torrado, Ramón	Un Fantasma Llamado Amor	XXI	2
Tourneur, Jacques	The Comedy of Terrors	XXXIII	
	Master Will Shakespeare	XXI	
Trampitsch, Gustav	Romeo und Julia oder Liebe, Mord und Totslag	XXXII	
Tressler, Georg	Die Lustigen Weiber von Windsor	XVII	3
Trimble, Lawrence	Cardinal Wolsey §	VII	2
	Indian Romeo and Juliet	XXI	2
Trnka, Jiří	Sen Noci Svatojánské	XVIII	1
Trommer, Hans	Romeo und Julia auf dem Dorfe	XXI	2
Turner, Otis	Romeo and Juliet in Our Town	XXI	2
Tuttle, Frank	The Untamed Lady	XXII	2
Ulmer, Edgar G.	Strange Illusion	IX	2
Urban, Charles	Julius Caesar	X	1
	The Tempest	XXIII	1
Urban, Max	Šaty Ďelají Človĕka	XIX	2
Vale, Travers	Romeo and Juliet	XXI	2
van den Busken, Hans	Elizabeth, De Wrouw Zonder Man	XXX	
	Hamlet	IX	1
	De Koopman van Venetië	XVI	1
Van Sant, Gus	My Own Private Idaho	VIII Part 2	2
Varnel, Marcel	Royal Cavalcade	XXX	
Védrès, Nicholas	Paris 1900	XXXII	
Verhoeven, Paul	Zweierlei Mass	XV	1
Vernon, Charles	The Seven Ages of Man	II	2
Vidor, Charles	The Arizonian	XXX	
Vignola, Robert G.	Enchantment	XXX	
Vinayak	Jwala	XIV	2
Vohrer, Alfred	Winnetou und Sein Freund Old Firehand	XXXIII	
Volkoff, Alexander	Kean	XXX	
Vollrath, Ernesto	La Parcela	XXI	2
von Praunheim, Rosa	Macbeth	XIV	3
von Radvany, Géza	Mädchen in Uniform	XXX	
von Sternberg, Josef	Der Blaue Engel	XXXIII	
Voronka, Arthur	William Shakespeare	XXXII	
Vrbanić, Ivo	Romeo i Julija	XXXI	
Walker, Peter	The Flesh and Blood Show	XXX	
Wallace, Charles	The Passionate Pilgrim	XXX	
Walls, Tom	Second Best Bed	XXII	2
Walsh, Bob	Pound of Flesh	XXXII	
	Shakespeare of Stratford and London	XXXII	
	The World of Shakespeare Series	XXXII	
Walter, Enrico Grazziani	Romeo e Giulietta	XXI	1
Wancang, Bu	Yi Jian Mei	XXVIII	2
Warde, Ernest	King Lear	XI	1
Watson, William	Hamlet and Eggs	XXX	
Watt, Edward	To Be or Not To Be	XXX	
Wauer, William	Die Lustigen Weiber von Windsor	XVII	1
Weber, Lois	The Merchant of Venice	XV	1
Weine, Robert	Der Leibergardist	XXX	
Weir, Peter	Dead Poets Society	XXX	
Welles, Orson	Campanadas a Medianoche	VI	1
	Filming Othello	XX	1
	Macbeth	XIV	1

	The Merchant of Venice	XVI	1
	The Tragedy of Othello, the Moor of Venice	XX	1
West, Walter	The Merchant of Venice	XVI	1
Whale, James	The Great Garrick	XXX	
Whang, Cheol-Mean	Fuck Hamlet	XXXIII	
White, Liz	Othello	XX	1
Whiteman, Robin	Shakespeare's Country	XXXII	
	Shakespeare's Heritage	XXXII	
Wicks, David	The Moods of Love	XXX	
Wilcox, Fred McLeod	Forbidden Planet	XXIII	2
Wilcox, Herbert	Carnival	XXX	
	Peg of Old Drury	XXX	
	The Yellow Canary	XXXIII	
Wildhagen, Georg	Die Lustigen Weiber von Windsor	XVII	3
Williams, Eric	England's Warrior King	XIII	1
	Hamlet	IX	1
	Hubert and Arthur	X	111
Williamson, C. H.	The Upstart Crow	XXXII	
Winkless, Terry	Scene of the Crime	XXXIII	
Wirth, Franz Peter	Hamlet	IX	1
Wise, Robert	West Side Story	XXI	2
Wolff, Willi	Wie Einst im Mai	XXX	
Yates, Peter	The Dresser	XXX	
Young, Harold	The Scarlet Pimpernel	XXXIII	
Young, James	As You Like It §	II	1
Young, Nicholas	The Tempest	XXIII	1
Young, Terence	Action of the Tiger	XXXIII	
Youtkevich, Sergei	Othello	XX	1
Zampi, Mario	Bottoms Up!	XXXIII	
	Laughter in Paradise	XXXIII	
Zahoruk, Dennis	The Shakespeare Murders	XXXIII	
Zecca, Ferdinand	Cléopâtre	I	2
Zeffirelli, Franco	Hamlet	IX	1
	Man and Woman	XXII	1
	Otello	XX	3
	Romeo and Juliet	XXI	1
	The Taming of the Shrew	XXII	1
	The Teenager Lovers of Verona	XXI	1
Zelnik, Friedrich	Mister Cinders	XXX	
Ziablikova, Aida	The Taming of the Shrew	XXXI	
Zinnemann, Fred	The Men	XXXIII	
Zitzman, Jerzy	Romeo i Julia	XXXI	
Zulawski, Andrzej	L'Important, C'est d'Aimer	XXX	